PILGRIM IN THE RUINS

A Chapel Hill Book

PILGRIM
IN THE RUINS

A Life of Walker Percy

JAY TOLSON

The University of North Carolina Press

Chapel Hill & London

First published by The University of North Carolina Press in 1994

Originally published by Simon & Schuster

Manufactured in the United States of America

The paper in this book meets the guidelines for permanence and
durability of the Committee on Production Guidelines for Book
Longevity of the Council on Library Resources.

Library of Congress Cataloging-in-Publication Data
Tolson, Jay.
Pilgrim in the ruins : a life of Walker Percy / Jay Tolson.
p.   cm.
Originally published: New York : Simon & Schuster, © 1992.
"A Chapel Hill book"—Ser. t.p.
Includes bibliographical references (p.) and index.
ISBN 0-8078-4447-0 (pbk. : alk. paper)
1. Percy, Walker, 1916–   —Biography. 2. Novelists,
American—20th century—Biography. 3. Philosophers—United
States—Biography. 4. Physicians—United States—Biography.
I. Title.
[PS3566.E6912Z844   1994]
813'.54—dc20   93-36154
[B]   CIP
98   97   96   95   94   5   4   3   2   1

For Margaret Jordan Tolson
and
in memory of John J. Tolson III (1915–1991)

The Percy Family: A Selected Genealogy

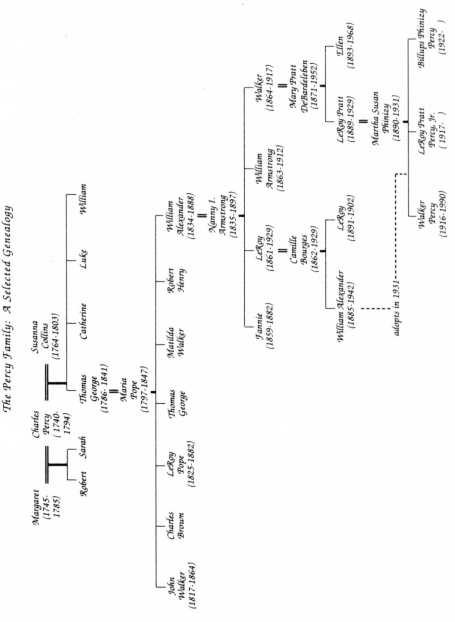

Table of Contents

Preface

When I first approached Walker Percy with the idea of writing his biography, he responded politely but firmly. "The only thing more boring than writing my own memoir," he wrote back in his cryptic doctorly scrawl, "is the prospect of collaborating with somebody on a biography." Collaboration was not what I had in mind, but I decided it was best not to press my case. That was in 1985.

Two years later, in the early spring of 1987, I wrote again. *The Thanatos Syndrome,* his sixth novel, had just come out, and Percy was in a slightly more receptive mood. "Come on down," he said to me on the phone, "and we can at least talk—just as long as we don't discuss my decrepit character."

I went to Covington and we talked, passing most of a warm May morning in the sun-flooded living room of what Percy called his "shotgun" cottage. Our conversation was loose, rambling, and frequently interrupted. There were many phone calls, and Percy's wife, Bunt, occasionally had questions about household matters. The interruptions were not unpleasant. They left me time to reflect and to observe the waterfowl as they paddled by on the tea-brown water of the Bogue Falaya, which flows only a few feet from the Percys' back door.

Assiduously avoiding the forbidden topic, I was struck, first of all, by the appearance of the man, the long, lanky frame, the weathered-looking skin, the wide forehead, the gulf-blue eyes, alternately guarded and piercing. He was dressed casually, in chinos, a plaid shirt, and jogging shoes, and he slumped deep into his chair while he carefully went about the business of determining who exactly I was and what I was up to. But Percy, I quickly saw, was anything but relaxed. In fact, though I had often heard him described as "laid-back," I saw something quite different that morning: a gracious, easy, almost avuncular manner straining against a powerful, nervous intensity, an almost furious energy. This tension occasionally manifested itself in sudden small muscular twitches or spasms, assertions of that inner energy against the composed, placid surface. Simply put, he seemed a man intensely uncomfortable in his own skin and yet, by dint of effort and will, capable of presenting a composed and rather casual persona. This self-control impressed me, though I wondered at what cost it had been won.

Our curious non-interview proceeded unpromisingly until noon, when we decided to take lunch at a place in town, a French restaurant located only a few blocks from his daughter's bookstore, the Kumquat. It turned out to be a cool, quiet place, not too crowded, and best of all, it served a good strong drink. During a long, well-lubricated meal, we both began to loosen up, and I started to see his witty, humorous side, his love of sly caricature, and his fondness for surprising turns of language. (He was still savoring some malapropisms related to him by a doctor-friend in the area: "old-timer's disease" for Alzheimer's disease, "Cadillac arrest" for cardiac arrest, and—Percy's favorite—"fireballs of the Eucharist" for fibroids of the uterus.) Still, it remained my distinct impression that this very private man would have been much happier had I suddenly announced that I had given up my plan to write about him. Near the end of our lunch, though, a bit of luck came my way. A young man seated at the table behind us—though apparently unable to see Percy—began talking to his companion, a young woman, about his favorite author.

"He lives near here," the young man explained, "and keeps an office upstairs in that bookstore down the street."

We knew, of course, whom he was talking about. Trying to maintain our desultory conversation, neither Percy nor I could resist tuning in on what his fan was saying, but soon the strain of eavesdropping and talking at the same time grew too difficult. The young man had come to a subject that Percy and I were most eager to follow in detail, an impromptu review of *The Thanatos Syndrome*.

"Maybe we should observe a moment's silence," I suggested.

"I think that might be in order," Percy replied, with a smile and soft chuckle that I feared might give our game away.

It didn't, we listened, and the experience was altogether rewarding.

In addition to its illicit pleasures, that fleeting moment confirmed my belief that complicity in vice is one of the better ways of beginning an association. It allows you to see your fellow conspirator at something close to his worst—and that is both a privilege and a revelation. "Yes," Percy as much as acknowledged, "I'm a little vain and almost as much of a snoop as you are. Which you certainly are, by the way." Which I certainly was.

To some extent, that moment in the restaurant established the key of all our further dealings. From that afternoon on, Percy generously provided me with any information I needed. He guided me to friends and relatives. He granted me access to letters, papers, personal records, and on occasion, without my asking, he would talk about his past, freely and sometimes painfully, certainly more freely than I would ever have expected. But indispensable as all this was, our most productive exchanges were those that involved a little game of mutual spying, psychological eavesdropping, in which we both attempted to listen around our conversation in order to pick up clues about what the other was really up to. Needless to say, this was a game at which Percy was a master—as anyone who has read his novels will know. Novice that I was, I felt it was a privilege to be given the chance to play—and more than a privilege. It was to discover something I had hoped but never realistically expected to find: an extraordinary continuity between the man's life and his work.

One must be careful here, of course. The temptation to read a writer's work through his life can lead to reductivism or even worse distortions. Percy's work, moreover, can be read, understood, and richly enjoyed without the least knowledge of his life story, and I would be the last to suggest otherwise. Yet knowledge of his life story reveals the remarkable extent to which Percy saw his work as a form of knowledge, an essay toward understanding what would help him live his life. Artist though he was, Percy became and remained a moralist who saw the end of art not in formal perfection but in the adequacy of its gesturing toward the truth that would make him free.

The life story of Walker Percy—physician, novelist, philosopher, moralist—is to a large extent the story of survival against great odds. It is the story of one man's attempt to overcome a fateful legacy of family and culture, place and history. But if that sounds melodramatic, let me qualify. If Walker Percy bore burdens that were heavy, they were by no means uniquely so. One could even say that some of them—including his birth into a wealthy, widely respected, and highly accomplished southern family—were indistinguishable from privileges.

So why write about this person, Walker Percy, if his plight is not remarkable? The answer is simple. His response to his fate was. It was even something of a mystery.

The outline of the mystery is this: An intelligent, attractive man in his early thirties, a man with a promising medical career ahead of him, decides not only to abandon his profession and become a writer but also to embrace a religion, Catholicism, upon which he, an ardent believer in science, had previously looked with respectful but thoroughgoing skepticism. He also decides at roughly the same time to give up the ways of a minor Lothario and marry a young woman he had met a few years before and with whom he had since conducted a fitful on-again off-again relationship.

Just the ordinary stuff of life, one might say. Perhaps. But behind these decisions there seems to have been a gamble, a wager for mortal, and even immortal, stakes. From what little direct testimony we can lay hands on, Percy was at rock bottom in his early thirties. "I'll tell you something," he told a young photographer, Mark Morrow, who came to his home in Covington, Louisiana, "the day I turned thirty was one of the worst days of my life. I just thought I was never going to amount to anything."

In despair, Percy took a gamble. He abandoned the future he had been preparing for (and which had been made somewhat problematic by a mild but persistent case of tuberculosis) and set off on a completely unanticipated course—the life of a writer.

Why should a person come to terms with a difficult fate by embracing an even more difficult solution? That, obviously, is a large question, requiring a long answer. For now, I shall say only that such a decision touches on a kind of heroism, an intellectual and spiritual bravery. And one concern of this book is how, and to what extent, Percy's life constituted a heroic, or at least an exemplary, life.

Some may object that such a concern is entirely contrary to what has become the primary object of biography in our time, which is to expose the feet of clay. Heroism, after all, is an archaic notion belonging to times irretrievably past. To be concerned with it bespeaks a mentality hopelessly unevolved. If such a preoccupation is, in fact, regressive, I freely own up to suffering from it. But I would quickly add that the examination of an exemplary life does not oblige one to ignore flaws. The interest of an exemplary person depends largely on the complexity, and sometimes the enormity, of his or her flaws. The problem with modern biography—or "pathography," as Joyce Carol Oates has aptly dubbed it—is its lack of a tragic sense, and a resulting tendency to see the subject's failings against some implied perfectibilist ideal rather than against the limitations of a human fate. The implication always seems to be that the biographer could have done better. It is little wonder that contemporary biography often seems to have no higher goal than, as Elizabeth Hardwick once said, to "diminish the celebrated object and aggrandize the biographer."

But even those who are willing to allow that the exploration of heroism is a legitimate biographical goal may rightly wonder at my choice of subject. Percy, first of all, was a writer, and except for a few notable exceptions of the Byron–Hemingway ilk, writers tend not to lead outwardly eventful lives. Percy, moreover, seems to have been intent on avoiding drama, opting instead for what appears to have been a life of subdued provincial domesticity. But this is only an appearance, for Percy's small-town withdrawal contains within its seemingly placid confines a fierce anchoritic struggle. His life was not short on its own kind of drama, a quieter, less visible sort that might properly be called, in W. B. Yeats's sense of the word, poetic: It was drama that arose out of the quarrel with himself.

There is also a Pascalian dimension to Walker Percy's life, evident in the wager that he made in his early thirties and present in almost all of his novels, in which his characters risk all in order to escape lives of quiet desperation. The source of all human misery, Pascal observed, is man's inability to remain alone and content in his room, and Percy took this formula as a personal challenge. All writers do, to an extent. But few have addressed it so directly or, in doing so, made it seem so centrally the problem of our times. Percy's probing of this question necessarily brought him to consider the core American ideal—the pursuit of happiness—and his critical reflections upon the nature of human happiness are what make him the most important American moralist since Ralph Waldo Emerson, a thinker, not incidentally, with whom Percy was profoundly at odds.

At issue in Percy's plumbing of the soul's restlessness is a large question: Is there an individual, irreducible self that is worth saving? And, if so, how best to preserve it in an age that reduces the self to a problem that is to be solved by one or another therapeutic regime or else subsumed under some progressive ideal of a larger social good? Obviously, such concerns put Percy in that long line of thinkers who have been collectively dubbed "existentialists." Not that this greatly clarifies matters. As Percy often remarked, the label has been so widely used and misused that it has become virtually meaningless. What is interesting, however, is the question of how this scion of a prominent southern family came to be concerned with ideas usually associated with an assortment of marginalized European artists and intellectuals. Existential-

ism seems more rightly the province of tormented souls like Kierkegaard
and Dostoyevsky than of affable if somewhat remote southern M.D.'s. It
would also appear to be more at home in St. Petersburg or Copenhagen,
on the Left Bank or in Greenwich Village, than in America's Deep
South.

This seeming anomaly merits an explanation, and I will begin with an
extended look at the world from which Percy came. By world I mean
both the South that Percy grew up and lived in—which is in itself a
fairly broad sweep of territory—and the South of his forefathers. As it
turns out, the Percy family has played an important part in the shaping
of this region ever since the first Percy arrived in the late eighteenth
century. Their roles at various moments of southern history have been
almost archetypal—prosperous planters, politicians, military officers,
progressive corporate lawyers, and businessmen. And just as the Percys
have had a decisive influence on the shape of their region's history, so
have the various twists and turns of southern history determined a great
deal about the Percys' lives.

Walker Percy's attitude toward this interconnected legacy of family
and regional history is itself one of the keys to the man. At times, it
involved a stance of repudiation. Like Stephen Dedalus, Walker Percy,
and his many fictional self-transformations, from Binx Bolling in *The
Moviegoer* to Dr. Tom More in *The Thanatos Syndrome*, tend to view
history as a nightmare from which they hope to awake. On numerous
occasions, Percy rejected the tag "southern writer" as both condescending and irrelevant. ("Was Cervantes labeled an Andalusian writer?" he
once asked at a writers' conference.) Sometimes he would allow that he
was a writer of the New South, quickly adding that since the salient
feature of the New South is its declining distinctiveness from the rest of
the nation, a writer of the New South should be considered as nothing
more than an American writer.

Wanting to escape from the nightmare of history and being able to do
so are two different things, and for all Percy's efforts to distance himself
from the wisteria and mint julep trappings of the Old South mystique
and even from the more serious Faulknerian concerns with the tragic
shape of southern history (and the rhetoric that inevitably accompanies
such concerns), Percy nonetheless remained mired in distinctively
southern preoccupations with religion, race, family, defeat, and honor.
Not that any of these is uniquely southern, of course. But in the South,
they all come with their own special baggage. And if Percy approached
them from a slightly different angle from that of Faulkner, Styron, Warren, Foote, or a dozen other southern tragedians, if he tried to view them
with something of a comic–satiric eye, he was still no less engaged by

them. If, to paraphrase Karl Marx, history repeats itself, first as tragedy and then as farce, Faulkner has given fine literary shape to its first repetition and Percy (among others) to its second.

The great themes of southern history have a way of not going away, and perhaps none of them returns more insistently than what Richard King, in his study of the South's cultural awakening between 1930 and 1955, A *Southern Renaissance,* calls the family romance. The preoccupation with family in southern letters stems, says King, from an enduring fact of southern life and society from antebellum times to the present—the "absence of strong extra-familial institutions." The white South, at least, has persistently functioned as a loose society of families held together by certain myths and codes. The South's defeat in the Civil War, far from destroying these myths, actually increased their ideal luster. At the center of a highly romanticized family order was the lordly figure of the father, surrounded by loyal and dependent black "retainers," a pure but largely ineffectual wife, and admiring sons and daughters. The father was the standard-bearer of a world that had died with the Civil War but whose ideals were still the only ones worth living and dying for. Evil was all that came in the wake of defeat—greedy Scalawags and Carpetbaggers who exploited the confused black populace for power and gain; Yankee industrialists and financiers who sought to exploit the riches of the South and give it nothing in return; the decline of honor and honorable behavior; uppity subordinates, particularly uppity blacks; moral looseness in all areas of life.

If the southern family romance seems so much hypocrisy and wishful thinking, it would be callow to dismiss it with a condescending sneer. For one thing, it worked, at least up to a point, by providing a certain order and direction for postwar southern society, and one would have to be very certain of one's certainties to say that it was the worst of all possible arrangements. For another, it embodied some values that are not easily dismissed, including honor, loyalty, and a sense of personal responsibility for others. The ease with which such values were corrupted or distorted for base ends—including the perpetuation of race and class distinctions—should not blind outsiders to the fact that they were not always thus corrupted.

And it is precisely amid the ambiguities of the southern family romance that the Percy family has struggled and sometimes, to use Faulkner's word, "prevailed." They have their roots in the antebellum South, a much rawer world than later myths would imply, lived and fought through the war that brought an end to the old order (at least in its purest form), fought the political wars of Reconstruction, and figured in the economic rise of the New South. But if the Percys have often prevailed, they have also fallen victim to maladies that routinely afflicted southerners of their class and station—above all, to the dark and often suicidal despair that accompanied the maintenance of a highly formalized but essentially lonely social role.

Walker Percy is heir to that tradition of accomplishment and desperation. His work is his attempt to see his way through it, to find the glimmer of comic hope behind the stern tragic mask. But his is not a parochial labor. We are all heirs to complex legacies that seem, by turns, sustaining and death-dealing. What is more, the spiritual loneliness that Percy so artfully limns seems increasingly the problem faced by all people living in a world that has become, or is becoming, modern.

Here among the graves in the twilight I see one thing only, but I see that thing clear. I see the long wall of a rampart sombre with sunset, a dusty road at its base. On the tower of the rampart stand the glorious high gods, Death and the rest, insolent and watching. Below on the road stream the tribes of men, tired, bent, hurt, and stumbling, and each man alone. As one comes beneath the tower, the High God descends and faces the wayfarer. He speaks three slow words: "Who are you?" The pilgrim I know should be able to straighten his shoulders, to stand his tallest, and to answer defiantly: "I am your son."

—WILLIAM ALEXANDER PERCY,
Lanterns on the Levee

1

Magic City

———◆———

The Vaughts lived in a castle fronting on a golf links. It was an old suburb set down in a beautiful green valley across a ridge from the city. There were other ridges, the last wrinkle of the Appalachians, which formed other valleys between them, and newer suburbs and newer country clubs.

—WALKER PERCY, *The Last Gentleman*

The nickname given to Birmingham, Alabama—the "Magic City"—may sound like the worst sort of Chamber of Commerce boosterism, but in fact there was considerable justification for the epithet. The city was conceived virtually overnight, in 1870, when a group of twelve businessmen formed a land company in north central Alabama's Jefferson County. In clumsy legalese, they set forth their goal as "the buying and selling of lots with the view to the location, laying off and effecting the building of a city." With luck and proper guidance, the founders believed, the new town might eventually develop into one of the great cities of the South, perhaps even rivaling Atlanta as the hub of southern commerce and transport. One of the twelve men, Colonel James R. Powell, suggested the name Birmingham, having recently returned from a visit to the English industrial city. The suggestion carried.

The men of Elyton Land Company were dreamers, but they had sound reasons for their optimism. Birmingham, like Atlanta, was ideally situated at a natural crossroads between the upper and lower South, and the moment was as propitious as the place. The expanding network of railroad lines throughout the South made the emergence of a major inland entrepôt not merely a possibility but a practical necessity, and Birmingham stood a good chance of becoming that city. The founders' ambition was clearly drawn into their plan for the city's layout: The tracks of two major railroad lines, the Alabama & Chattanooga and the North & South, formed the axial spine of the future metropolis.

If Birmingham lagged behind Atlanta in years, it had at least one advantage over the Georgia city. Birmingham lay at the heart of a mineral-rich region. Great deposits of coal, iron ore, and bituminum made up a vast and barely tapped subterranean treasure. In other words, Birmingham possessed what the new industrial nation needed: not only a major source of energy but essential raw materials for construction and manufacturing. The only other thing needed was people with the energy and capital to bring this great wealth out of the ground and work it.

Such people were not long in coming, and two of them, as it turned out, would have a direct influence on the fortunes of the Percys of Alabama. In the spring of 1872, Daniel Pratt, a successful cotton gin manufacturer from Montgomery, came to Birmingham with his son-in-law, Henry Fairchild DeBardeleben. Wasting no time, they soon acquired a controlling interest in the moribund Red Mountain Iron and Coal Company. The company's problem, a common one throughout the South, was undercapitalization. Dependent, like many other southern concerns, on northern investors, Red Mountain felt the cold when a chill wind blew on northern markets. And the temperature was definitely dropping. Unless the company could come up with money to rebuild its blast furnaces in nearby Oxmoor, it would face certain extinction. Pratt moved decisively, putting up the capital and placing his son-in-law in charge of operations.

Pratt and DeBardeleben were, in many respects, an odd business couple, united more by fate, marriage, and the perverse attraction of opposites than by simple compatibility. A native New Englander who migrated to the South to make his fortune, Pratt was almost too neatly a paragon of Yankee virtues—thrift, diligence, responsibility, restraint, caution. His steady application and shrewd business sense had earned him one of the largest fortunes in pre–Civil War Alabama.

DeBardeleben, by contrast, was more the reckless individualist. The son of a South Carolina planter who had moved to Alabama in the 1830s (and grandson of a Hessian mercenary who had fought for the British during the American War of Independence), DeBardeleben lost his father shortly after his birth in 1840. His mother then moved into the house of her neighbor and friend, Daniel Pratt, who took responsibility for raising and educating her three children. It was not always an easy job, as Pratt's Yankee severity and concern for self-control came up against Henry's more willful and impulsive nature.

Nevertheless, the two grew close, and when Henry married Pratt's only daughter, Ellen, in 1862, the bonds were cemented. After briefly serving in the Confederate Army during the early years of the war, Henry was given charge of several Pratt concerns. But the wild streak persisted. Unlike the circumspect Pratt, DeBardeleben was always willing to take risks. Sporting a thick mustache, the rangy six-footer even looked the part of the riverboat gambler. He was, however, a tireless, even obsessive worker. When not putting in long hours at the blast furnaces, he would be out riding through the hilly pine forests on his mule, always on the lookout for telltale outcroppings or possible sites for future works.

DeBardeleben's inexperience in the coal and iron business was more than compensated for by his zeal, but even the most vigorous leadership could not have protected the Red Mountain Company from the effects of the depression of 1873. Demand for iron in Alabama, always low, fell even lower. To make matters worse, Pratt died. DeBardeleben made no excuses for the company's poor performance. Assuming full blame, he returned his year's salary to the board and oversaw the closing of the Oxmoor furnaces before tendering his resignation.

Woes did not visit themselves only upon the houses of Pratt and DeBardeleben. The panic of '73 and a cholera epidemic nearly wiped out Birmingham. In fact, if it had not been for men like DeBardeleben, who were more challenged than defeated by a bad turn of fortune, the town might have become a footnote in southern history.

DeBardeleben, having got a whiff of the "smoke" business, couldn't stay out of it. A year and a half after Pratt's death, his widow, Esther, also died, leaving most of the Pratt estate to DeBardeleben. A good part of that fortune he promptly used to buy promising coal and ore property, drawing on the advice of an English mining engineer, Joseph Squire, whom he had hired to survey the region. Then in 1878 he took another gamble. In partnership with with Truman H. Aldrich, an engineer, and James W. Sloss, a successful railroad man, he established the Pratt Coal and Coke Company. DeBardeleben's renegade tendencies soon forced his two partners out of the company, and by 1881 he was the "sole owner of the largest and most successful coal and coke company in Alabama."

That Henry F. DeBardeleben's career and Birmingham's seemed long to run on parallel tracks should come as no surprise. Their fortunes were intimately bound up. Not only was he instrumental in building the city's industrial base. He also came close to making his own little empire—and therefore, to an extent, the wider regional economy—independent of northern capital and those fateful fluctuations of the distant market. His attempt was not altruistic. DeBardeleben could be as self-aggrandizing as any of the great robber barons. Still, his success might have given his part of the South a measure of self-sufficiency that it had never known—and in truth never has. His ultimate failure, consequently, had certain tragic ramifications for his region.

In the early 1880s, fearing tuberculosis, DeBardeleben decided to leave Birmingham. Selling the Pratt Company to a syndicate, he traveled to Mexico, seeking what people at the time thought were its salubrious airs. Despite his illness DeBardeleben was not the kind of man who could remain on the sidelines for long, particularly not when things were booming back in the town that he had helped put on the map. The big company now was Tennessee Coal, Iron and Railroad (TCI), an outside outfit that had merged with a Birmingham operation—in fact, the one that had bought the Pratt Company from DeBardeleben.

Determined to "make smoke" again, he allied himself with an Englishman, David Roberts, who had been a banker in London for much of his career. Out of this union came, in 1886, two offspring: a new company, DeBardeleben Coal and Iron, and a new town, called Bessemer. Locating the town a dozen-odd miles southwest of Birmingham, DeBardeleben counted on luring new industry to the area. And so he did. DeBardeleben now had room to play. Financing new companies, arranging mergers and acquisitions, underselling his rivals, he soon had TCI screaming foul play. His ruthlessness came out in other ways as well, notably in his iron-fisted approach to organized labor. In 1890, and later in 1894, he broke miners' strikes by hiring nonunion black workers.

Recognizing a ruthless competitor when they saw one, TCI agents invited DeBardeleben to New York City for a little talk in late 1892. Their proposal was straightforward: If he would hand over all shares of his company, he would be given eight million dollars worth of newly created TCI stock and placed on the board of directors of the company. He accepted. More TCI acquisitions followed, thus making the company the third largest coal and iron company in the United States. DeBardeleben, to his partial satisfaction, was the largest single stockholder in the mammoth corporation. Yet he still lacked a controlling majority of shares. A temporary truce had to be worked out between the Alabama man and John Inman of New York.

One can easily guess the motives behind DeBardeleben's next move —simple ambition, the gambler's itch, a southerner's resentment of Yankee intrusion. In February of 1893, DeBardeleben launched a raid on Wall Street, scheming to corner the shares of TCI stock to drive up the price and squeeze out short sellers. The effort failed disastrously, largely because he had overestimated the strength of his position, and by May he had been forced to sell most of his shares to Inman. The debacle signaled more than the collapse of a personal empire. According to business historian Justin Fuller, it "also ended southern ownership and management of the principal coal and iron company in the South. Within a few years all of the southerners would be ousted, and control of TCI would pass entirely into Northern hands."

DeBardeleben was not finished. He continued to play an active role in Birmingham's economic and civic life right up until his death in 1910. But the shadow of the failed gesture hung over the man, as it did over Birmingham. The continued dominance of northerners in the economic affairs of the city, even after Reconstruction, added further insult to the injury of defeat. It was one more instance of southern inferiority to Yankee savvy. If cities have moods—and they do—then Birmingham's, even during its flush decades, was one of tentativeness, dependency, and vague demoralization. The feeling emanated from the city's elite, or at least from a goodly part of it; for despite their role in the city's miraculous growth, the leaders, the movers and shakers like DeBardeleben and Roberts (and, later, the Percys), knew all too well that they had failed to make their city stand on its own. For all their efforts, Birmingham remained a pawn to the distant fluctuations of the national market—particularly the financial and banking markets centered in New York. Birmingham, in its failure to secure a measure of economic independence, proved to be a true prototype of what came to be called the New South. That is, it never became what urbanist Jane Jacobs calls an "import-replacing city," a fully formed urban economy with complex and sustaining ties to the surrounding regional economy. It couldn't become one because, among other reasons, the most important economic decisions shaping its destiny were made elsewhere.

Not all of Birmingham's leaders felt bad about this situation, of course. As historian C. Vann Woodward has shown, many of the Redeemers who were supposedly devoted to dismantling Reconstruction and breaking the shackles of northern domination worked hand in hand with Yankee financiers and industrialists. And the results of such cooperation were not altogether bad. Lopsided though its prosperity was, Birmingham did grow (from a population of 3,086 in 1880 to 38,415 by 1900), and it did register significant gains. By 1898, for example, it was the "biggest shipping point for pig iron in the country . . . and the third largest in the world in spite of the 200 miles that separated the city from tidewater."

But Birmingham's prosperity was always precarious and contingent. TCI—to cite a crucial example—became even less a Birmingham-oriented operation in 1907, when J. Pierpont Morgan was allowed, despite Teddy Roosevelt's antitrust regulation, to absorb the company into United States Steel. TCI had entered the steel-making business in 1897, and it kept at it after being taken over. But it was never given a fair chance to compete with the Pittsburgh steel manufacturers. Freight rates and an array of industry- and government-imposed "differentials" meant that even if Birmingham produced steel more cheaply than Pittsburgh, Birmingham's finished and delivered products ended up costing more than Pittsburgh's. According to the "Birmingham Differential," the buyer of Alabama steel had to pay Pittsburgh price plus three dollars a ton plus freight from Birmingham. Southern industry was kept on a short leash, and the effect was both economically limiting and psychologically demoralizing.

Freight rates may seem a long way from the life and work of Walker Percy, but the distance is not that great—and not only because Percy was born in Birmingham a scant forty-six years after the men of Elyton Land Company conceived the idea of a city. Place and history bear heavily upon the lives of families, and the lives of families, particularly of southern families, bear heavily upon their individual members. A legacy of defeat is an unpleasant burden for any family to carry, but it is especially burdensome to those families that feel somehow responsible for the defeat, or even for a less-than-ideal compromise. It is a blot upon their honor, and as students of the South from Frederick Law Olmsted to W. J. Cash to Bertram Wyatt-Brown have noted, there is nothing more devastating to a southerner than loss of honor.

To be sure, the Percys were no more responsible for the South's various humiliations than they were for its successes, even though they had a hand in both, and on occasion a fairly decisive hand. Since the arrival of the first Percy in this country late in the eighteenth century, the Percys have been an active force in their communities, particularly in the Mississippi Delta, where they first put down roots, but in other parts of the South as well. Name just about any prominent social role—political, civic, economic, cultural, military—and there has been a Percy who has filled it, usually with distinction and usually with beneficent consequences for the community at large. They started, as did most leaders in the South, as farmers, and some have remained successful farmers to this day. Yet virtually from the first American Percy on, they have felt obliged to do more than tend to their gardens. They have served—not without self-interest but also with a real sense of obligation to the commonweal. And if they have often interpreted the public good as what is consistent with their own personal advancement, they have seldom debased the former for the sake of the latter.

The Percy family record is such an important one, in fact, that it has acquired mythical or at least legendary dimensions, merging in many ways with those two greater regional myths—the myths of the "Old South" and the "New South." The Percys' experience in Birmingham represents, among other things, a charged symbolic encounter between an archetypal "Old South" family and a protypical "New South" city, and this encounter played a crucial role in shaping the character and imagination of the writer Walker Percy.

The decision of Walker Percy's grandfather—also named Walker—to settle in Birmingham in 1886 might look like an attempted break with the past and an already heavily freighted family history, but it was probably a much simpler matter. The twenty-two-year-old lawyer, freshly out of University of Virginia Law School, may have doubted his ability to live up to the varied accomplishments of his father, William A. Percy. After all, the "Gray Eagle of the Delta" had not only distinguished himself in the Civil War but had played a crucial role in bringing his hometown, Greenville, Mississippi, and the surrounding Washington County through the vexing period of Reconstruction. Formidable as all that might have been to a young man just starting out in the world, Walker Percy had a more immediate reason for leaving his native Greenville: economics.

Primogeniture may not have been a matter of law in the United States, but in the South among the landed gentry it was a matter of practice and necessity. Even after the Civil War and Reconstruction, and the replacement of slavery with sharecropping, a great farm had to remain intact if it was to prosper. If more than one son was born to a planter, the land would most likely (though not inevitably) pass to the eldest. Walker Percy was third in line. The farm went to his oldest brother, LeRoy, who also maintained an influential law practice in town. The other brother, William, a product, like his two brothers, of U. Va. law and the University of the South, settled 150 miles north of Greenville in Memphis, Tennessee.

Walker set his sights farther afield. Word had it that a new town called Birmingham was booming, a town still so young that an outsider could break into its highest circles. So the young man went east. Behind this perfectly rational decision, however, might have figured a more sentimental reason, one having to do with family and perhaps even the mysterious power of names. Walker's grandfather, Thomas G. Percy, had also moved from Mississippi to northern Alabama some seventy-one years before. There, in Madison County, not far from Huntsville, he had settled on a plantation next to that of a close friend and former Princeton classmate, John Walker. Even though all of Thomas G.'s surviving sons had moved back to Mississippi, there remained this lingering ancestral connection to northern Alabama, and it may have turned young Walker's head in the direction of Birmingham.

Whatever the cause, the decision proved fortunate. Going into practice by himself, Walker quickly worked his way into the establishment. Nothing signaled his arrival more dramatically than his marriage to Mary Pratt DeBardeleben, the daughter of the powerful Henry F., on April 17, 1888. A handsome woman with strong German features, she was, by all accounts, both affable and intelligent. Moreover, her bookish tendencies matched those of a husband who had excelled in classics at Sewanee and who had already earned a reputation for brilliance in law. It appeared to be an ideal match.

And of course it did nothing to hurt Walker's career. Forming a brief partnership with a fellow Sewanee graduate, James Weatherly, in 1889, Percy was soon handling a large part of his father-in-law's very substantial portfolio, including real estate, corporate acquisitions, and trial work. It was a staggering load that became even more demanding when DeBardeleben became an important player in TCI. Largely because of his ties to the hard-driving coal baron, Percy became TCI's general counsel, retaining the position even after his father-in-law failed in his raid on Wall Street. In fact, Percy represented the company during the complex merger proceedings with United States Steel in 1907, and was instrumental in convincing the Justice Department that the merger did not violate antitrust laws.

Walker's career was remarkable for its unbroken upward trajectory. Partners changed—he worked with W. I. Grubb from 1895 until 1905 and then formed a lasting relationship with Augustus Benners—but he proved an almost unbeatable champion of big business interests in Birmingham. Not surprisingly, he was much sought after, and by the turn of the century he was either the attorney for, or directing officer of, most of the key banks and corporations in the city. It seems impossible that he would have had time for anything but legal work. Yet he did.

Looking the part of the convivial Gay Nineties burgher, full-faced, mustachioed, and edging toward the portliness that his era favored, Percy was a dominant figure in Birmingham society. "There was," recalls a contemporary, Sarah Comer, "a very smart set of young married people in Birmingham like the Percys, Fulenwiders, Badhams and Crawfords. They had a dinner club which they called 'The Harveys.'. . . All my friends admired Walker Percy." In addition to dinners, the Percys' intimate circle amused themselves with the diversions of the day—Ping-Pong, duplicate whist, and lotto. During the early years, such activities were pursued in and around people's homes. The Percys' house on Arlington Avenue—a turreted Gothic monster of a place—was itself a popular gathering spot. It was located in the south Birmingham neighborhood of Five Points, a pleasant little town-within-a-town boasting a wide range of ethnic and social groups and a healthy mix of private homes and businesses, all linked by a trolley line that began and ended in the Five Points circle and followed a serpentine route up, down, and around the contoured northern slopes of Red Mountain, then the southern geographical limit of the city.

As social life became increasingly organized around clubs toward the end of the nineteenth century, the Percys found themselves—not surprisingly—a much-sought-after couple. Walker himself was a member of the Southern Club, the Roebuck Club, and a variety of athletic clubs. But perhaps the most important of the Percys' associations was with the Country Club. Founded in 1898 as a driving club, when driving meant sporting about in a highly varnished rig behind a matched pair of horses, the club moved in a new direction in 1903. Only a few blocks from the Country Club's bungalow lodge, a group of pioneering sportsmen had converted a pasture into a primitive golf course. Nine tin cups were planted in small debris-cleared areas that made putting almost possible. The untended fairways were fair in name only. Twice around the course in anything close to one hundred strokes was considered a professional perfomance. Crude as it was, however, it was still a course, and with the golf craze just aborning, it seemed only natural and desirable to effect a merger between the Country Club (which had no course) and the Golf Club (which had no clubhouse). So the two came together, grew, and prospered.

[handwritten margin note: BIRTH OF GOLF IN SOUTH]

The triumph of golf in the South is itself a curious fact of cultural history. It is, as anyone who has ever played it knows, a penitential little game, as much a trial of character and bearing as of skill. (Walker Percy, the novelist, would later explore the peculiar moral dimensions of the game in almost as much depth as his northern fellow-in-letters, John Updike.) Fittingly, golf was invented by a Scotsman, for only a Calvinist could have found pleasure in a pursuit that required so much restraint for so delayed a reward. Given its special nature, the game was ideally suited to America's commercial Northeast, particularly to its successful leaders in the commercial, industrial, and professional world. For such paragons of Calvinist virtue, golf served as an ideal recreation.

But that the upper classes of the South should have taken so eagerly to this Presbyterian ordeal of a game seems somewhat less natural. In fact, it signals a profound shift in southern life. After all, these were the people, men mainly, who had long been known for their love of rowdy, lusty, brutal pursuits—and not just of hunting but of games that ranged from horseracing to cockfighting, often involving violence and blood and, quite frequently, high-stakes gambling. The switch to the genteel, highly regulated game of golf meant something was afoot. The old planters—or, more accurately, the sons of the old planters—were becoming citified. And just as they were giving up the farms, so they were abandoning the old diversions for more couth activities.

Whether such changes are gains or losses no one can say, but it is clear that they represented a lowering of the passional pitch of life, a reining in of that raw-edged individualism that W. J. Cash claimed lay at the heart of the Old South's "savage ideal." The transition was bound to be difficult at times. The uneasiness with which some of the first Birmingham golfers adapted to their tame new world led to what was certainly one of the club's more peculiar-sounding ordinances: "Any member who displays or discharges a pistol in or about the club house or grounds may be suspended." That tentative "may" speaks volumes.

By all outward signs, though, Walker Percy seems to have adapted as easily and well to the diminished key of a country club recreational life as he did to the frenetic pace of an urban business career. He was elected president of the club in 1910, and by all accounts he enjoyed the game, as did his wife.

Walker's family life seemed to run smoothly as well. Although he and his wife suffered the loss of two children in infancy, they had reason to rejoice at the vigor of their son LeRoy Pratt, born in 1889, and their daughter Ellen, born four years later.

But all was not well; "all" never is. The problem, specifically, was depression—a wracking, disabling depression that sometimes left Walker in the deepest of sloughs. The cause was partly hereditary. Dark funks ran deep in the Percy family line. Severe depression had had dramatic consequences in the lives of Walker's two uncles as well as in that of his great-grandfather, the first American Percy. But as great a role as genes may play in the development of a depressive personality—and recent research suggests that it is considerable—cultural factors are not negligible. No one has better analyzed the connections between southern culture and its core ideal, honor, and the psychic makeup of white southerners than has historian Bertram Wyatt-Brown.

Living up to the highly individualistic notion of personal honor was, as Wyatt-Brown shows, a burden borne by all white southerners, rich or poor, a burden that both grew out of and justified the existence of a vast subservient class—the black slaves and, later, the much-hobbled and Jim Crow–restricted free blacks. Honor required a great deal of virile posturing and public posing, and it imposed a wide range of social demands on those who would claim to be honorable—demands, for instance, of hospitality and conviviality. It led to idealized, and therefore strained, relations between the sexes. And of course it engendered a great deal of self-doubt. Could one possibly live up to the beau ideal? Anxiety over this question necessitated outlets that were often violent:

gaming, gambling, hunting. It even led to such public outbursts as lynch-ings and brutal acts of tarring and feathering, all intended to correct those who violated the code but also, less consciously, to vent the collective fears of those who strove so hard to live up to it.

But even with outlets, the pressure stemming from the South's system of honor was often overwhelming, fueling an individual's sense of inad-equacy and loneliness. The upper classes, the great planters, may have felt the strain even more keenly because they were expected not only to be honorable but also to serve as exemplars of gentility, graciousness, and noblesse oblige. Well before Wyatt-Brown, W. J. Cash, in his *Mind of the South,* noted that the southern social arrangement depended cru-cially on the performance of its so-called aristocracy, though Cash was skeptical of how truly aristocratic the prosperous planters were. If there was any justification for the great social and economic inequalities of the South, it was that its leaders showed genuine concern for the well-being of others. And even if this concern was often nothing more than show, a highly mannered display of politesse toward people of all stations, it was nonetheless a vigorously maintained and highly successful perfor-mance that for a time gave to even the poorest of whites a sense of worthiness and self-esteem. Why else, Cash asks, would these poor whites have so loyally followed their "captains" into the maelstrom of the Civil War? Even when they resented them, they venerated them, more often than not harboring the secret hope that if not they at least their children would rise to be such captains. Their hopes were not altogether vain. After all, most of the captains—despite their pretense to ties with old European aristocracy—were themselves of humble ori-gin, the children often of the rednecks and peckerwoods to whom they now so artfully condescended.

The lawyer Walker Percy was, of course, a scion of one of those great planter families on whom the old order so heavily depended (and fur-thermore, one of the few families whose claim to lineage Cash allowed was legitimate). He belonged to the class of people who finally failed to hold together the old system and so were now working (often with the Yankees they had once bitterly opposed) to replace it with something else, something more closely resembling the northern model of capital and industrial relations. At best, though, because of basic geographical and social differences, the new arrangement could only resemble the northern one. So Walker Percy's class was faced with trying to arrange an honorable compromise, a difficult task since honor is always inimical to compromise.

Add to this burden the fact that Percy belonged to one of those few southern families who truly did live by the ideal of service. Like other

Percys, to be sure, he craved prosperity, success, and good standing, else he would not have pursued the career that he did. He was clearly comfortable among the elite and believed in the rightness of social hierarchy. But like other members of the Percy family, he made sure that his sense of noblesse was equaled by his sense of oblige. Politically, this orientation led him to cast his lot with the Progressives, who were known for their commitment to fair and clean government and to the improvement of society through education, health care, and a host of reform measures.

Another trait Walker shared with his fellow Percys was a profound aversion to prejudice and narrow-mindedness. In his public life, he stood up for the interests of blacks and other minorities, and he found loathesome the nationwide spirit of American nativism, spurred by the immigration of southeastern Europeans. (Walker, in fact, was close to many of Birmingham's Jews, particularly a neighbor and successful businessman, Morris Adler. This affinity for the "people of the book" prefigures his grandson and namesake's own special attraction to Jews, which readers of the grandson's novels will most certainly have noticed.)

Walker harbored no strong political ambitions, but he was drawn to politicking in 1910, when he traveled to Mississippi to help his brother LeRoy in his successful bid for a U.S. Senate seat left empty by the death of Anselm J. McLaurin. LeRoy faced a tough opponent in James K. Vardaman, a populist and racist demagogue with a strong following among the Mississippi hill farmers, but he finally won in the legislature by a narrow five-vote margin. Walker returned the next year to help his brother in the regular election, a filthy mud-slinging affair during which one of the White Chief's cronies, Theodore G. Bilbo, accused LeRoy of bribing him for his vote in the earlier election. It was a lie, of course, and proved to be so, but LeRoy and his family took it as an unpardonable attack upon his honor. Will Percy, LeRoy's son, tells the story in *Lanterns on the Levee:*

> The worst day of all, as I remember it, was at Lauderdale Springs. A few of us had gone over from home to hear the speech, armed and sick at heart. Uncle Walker came to my room after midnight to say that one of our group would have to kill the bribe taker [Bilbo] in the morning as he was to attend our meeting and was scheduled to denounce Father. At six we met in the cold dreary dining-room for breakfast, Uncle Walker, his seventeen-year-old son, Leroy, and I sitting at a table to ourselves. I had target-practiced most of the night in front of the mirror, so as not to forget to release the safety. A few yards from us at a table sat our intended victim. Uncle Walker had a voice like Polyphemus', but he couldn't hit a balloon. Suddenly he

leaned across the table, pointed to the man, and boomed out the epithet which makes an American fight if he's a man. The object of his attack did not fall for the ruse, he made no motion to his hip or elsewhere, he kept on eating oatmeal.

Vardaman ended up the victor, dealing a blow to the ideals and interests that the Percys held dear, but Walker's involvement in his brother's campaigns did not leave him completely disillusioned with the political process. In fact, after the first campaign he returned to Alabama and ran successfully for a seat in the state legislature. His reason for entering politics was as selfless as it was specific: to see through the passage of two bills that he thought were essential to Birmingham's civic health. The first was a proposal to change the city's mayor-aldermen system to a commission form. Such a change was needed because many of the unpaid aldermen, thirty-two in all, routinely bought themselves into power and, once installed, just as routinely sold favors to the highest bidders. Under Percy's plan, the three commissioners would each be paid the then-respectable annual salary of seven thousand dollars, thus making them less prone to corruption. The bill passed in 1911. Percy's second goal was to end the fee system of paying sheriffs. Under that arrangement, law enforcement officers were compensated according to the number of people they arrested. The easiest way to pad one's payroll was to arrest citizens with little political clout—blacks mostly, but indigent whites would do in a pinch. The practice obviously did little to abet genuine law enforcement, and Birmingham owed Walker Percy a real debt for bringing it to its richly deserved end and leaving a regularly salaried police force in its stead.

Percy put so much work into his legislative efforts that by the end of his first term, thoroughly exhausted, he suffered a severe nervous breakdown. Although he received the best possible medical attention, there was no simple cure for what ailed him. The bouts of melancholy came and went, even while good fortune seemed to smile consistently his way. His son, LeRoy Pratt Percy, was shaping up into a fine young man in the family tradition. Tall, handsome in a round-faced way, intelligent, and affable, LeRoy had received what was then considered a classical education. In the eighth grade, he had been sent up north to Lawrenceville School, where he had distinguished himself as an able scholar. At Princeton, where he went next, "Puss" Percy accumulated an outstanding academic record, graduating in 1910 with the degree of Bachelor of Literature in English. Expected, like all Percys, to master a profession, he went on to Harvard Law School, where he studied hard and made the Law Review. A postgraduate *Wanderjahr* in Germany completed his education. Enrolled at the University of Heidelberg, he acquired the tragic-romantic Wertherian outlook that would soon become more than a pose. Joining his father's law firm in the fall of 1914, he married, almost exactly a year later, a young Georgia woman whom he had met at White Sulphur Springs during a summer vacation a few years before.

Martha Susan Phinizy, or Mattie Sue, was the third of five daughters born to Nellie Stovall and Billups Phinizy of Athens, Georgia. If Percy was a name to be reckoned with in Alabama and Mississippi, the Phinizy name was no less distinguished in Georgia. (Billups Phinizy, an extremely successful businessman in his own right, was the grandson of one of Georgia's most powerful bankers and financiers, Ferdinand Phinizy.) Strict Presbyterians, the Phinizys raised their daughters to be models of probity and self-control. Mattie Sue, born in 1890, was the third and prettiest of the five daughters—a small, delicate brunette with soft features. She had attended Lucy Cobb School in Athens and, for her "finishing," Miss Finch's in New York City. She was known as a quiet woman, a good athlete, and a gracious hostess. In every respect, she appeared to be a perfect match for young LeRoy Percy.

On September 1, 1915, in the capacious parlor of the Phinizys' large Victorian house on Milledge Avenue (where all five daughters were married), LeRoy and Mattie Sue were joined in holy matrimony. Nine months later, on May 28, 1916, the Percys had their first son, born at St. Vincent's Hospital and named Walker. Their second son, LeRoy, was born in August of the next year. But first tragedy intervened.

Despite his recurrent bouts of depression, Walker Percy had appeared to be in good spirits in early February of 1917, tired but generally bright in outlook. On Thursday, February 8, he had lunched at home with his son and proposed a hunting trip to Greenville. They would leave that evening. LeRoy, always eager for an outing, agreed. Walker then went upstairs to tend to packing. "Shortly after three o'clock," ran the story in Friday's edition of *The Birmingham News*, "LeRoy Percy heard a faint report and thought nothing about it, but later went to his father's room, and found the body lying in a trunk room adjoining where he had been accustomed to keep his sporting implements." It was a horrifying sight. His father had shot himself in the heart with a twelve-gauge shotgun.

Perhaps in deference to the Percy family, the Friday edition of Birmingham's other paper, the *Age-Herald*, described the death as an accident, but the coroner's verdict was suicide, and the *News* reported it as such. Two days later the *Age-Herald* informed its readers that Walker Percy had held several life insurance policies amounting to $120,000 and that all were incontestable because they had been held for more than a year. The possibility that Percy had been planning to take his life seemed all the more unlikely in light of his decision the previous November to cancel a sixty-thousand-dollar accident policy—a fact also reported in the *News* account. But even if his death was not premeditated, no one seriously doubted that it had been a suicide.

Not even his children or wife sought solace in that slim hope. As friends and acquaintances noted, LeRoy seemed to live most directly under the cloud of his father's suicide. To be sure, all children, or spouses, of suicides bear a particularly painful burden. Their lives are haunted by insidious questions, none ultimately answerable: What drove the suicide to such a desperate end? Were they, the survivors, in some way responsible? And would they end up doing the same thing?

LeRoy was particularly vulnerable, and not only because he was the sole surviving son. He was in many ways his father's son, pursuing the same career (indeed, working in the same office), joining the same clubs, enjoying the same diversions. Unusually intelligent men, both were hard-working, even somewhat driven, and they were both extremely successful. At the same time, they were known for their charming manner, their ease with people, and their humor. If they were fond of their drinks—in an article he wrote for *Esquire,* Walker Percy recalls his father sipping bourbon from a curing barrel that was kept in the basement during Prohibition—they were not known as heavy drinkers. Unfortunately, though, LeRoy took after the bad as well as the good in his father. He, too, was prone to depression, a tendency that grew more pronounced with years, to the concern of friends and family.

All of these points of similarity would have been quite enough to make a son feel that his destiny was tightly entwined with his father's. If anything, the feeling grew even stronger after Walker's death. As if driven by fate or a dark inner necessity, LeRoy proceeded to duplicate the pattern of his father's life. Perhaps the most obvious sign of this was LeRoy's decision to move his family from their small bungalow on Caldwell Terrace to the paternal manse at 2217 Arlington. It was a somber house—"spooky," as the novelist Walker Percy later described it, "like the Munsters' house on TV." Made of stone, with a mansard roof and a big porch girdling the front and sides, it sat high above the street, an imposing and rather ugly edifice. The rooms inside were large and dark, the gloom augmented by the dowdy wallpaper and heavy Victorian furniture. But physical details alone did not make the house oppressive; they were, after all, quite typical of the period. What made the house truly dreadful was the presence of death, the ineradicable memory of the "faint report" and the body sprawled on the floor of the trunk room upstairs. If economic necessity had forced LeRoy to move to the house, his decision would have appeared less perverse. But money was no crushing necessity.

LeRoy succeeded his father as general counsel of TCI and in other ways took over his role at the firm of Percy, Benners, & Burr. From the professional round of duties, however, he enjoyed at least one brief and romantic respite, an idyll that would have been perfect had it not been for one thing. Shortly after the United States entered the Great War on April 6, 1917, LeRoy Percy volunteered for the Army Air Corps. He proved to be an outstanding pilot—so good, in fact, that he inadvertently cheated himself out of his one great opportunity for glory in combat. Noting his proficiency in flight school, his superiors assigned the young officer to be an instructor, first at Barron and Brooks fields in Texas and then at Ebbets Field in Arkansas, which service he performed for the remainder of his tour of duty. And that was the anti-climactic rub: LeRoy never made it across the Atlantic, never saw a day of combat. Missing the big chance was a blow to the southerner's pride, particularly since his cousin Will had served gallantly in Flanders. After the armistice in November 1918, he returned to Birmingham, put away his uniform, and returned to the practice of law.

Not that the practice of law was always such a tame affair. Even as late as the 1920s, there was still something of a raw frontier edge to Birmingham. The carrying of pistols was not unheard of. In fact, even LeRoy came close to shooting it out with another lawyer, a brilliant and intimidating man named Will Denson. Fortunately, he only came close. Denson, a union lawyer who often came up against Percy and other defenders of business interests in court, was known as both a bully and a very good shot. He practiced with his pistol every morning, squeezing off fifty rounds with each hand. He had once killed a man in a gunfight, a mysterious episode for which he had not been prosecuted. Denson used his reputation as a weapon in court, intimidating his opponents with his swaggering, threatening manner and his crude, abusive tongue. His hectoring ways sometimes backfired—he had even been disbarred for a time—but he never reformed. And he won more than his share of cases.

Intimidating as Denson was, Percy was not one to wilt before abuse or threats. After a particularly heated confrontation, the two decided to settle the matter with pistols. On the appointed morning, they drove to the country and found a secluded spot. Percy asked for a chance to practice. Denson consented. Percy lined up six pine cones and blasted away. Six hits. (In this one respect, at least, LeRoy was not like his father: He was a very good shot.) Denson then asked to take some practice shots. Percy could not very well refuse. Six hits, dead and true. Percy then destroyed six more pine cones; again, Denson followed suit. The warmup rounds apparently had a conciliatory effect. "Clearly, we're both too good with these things to be doing this," said Percy. Denson agreed, and they returned to their cars, still enemies but each now more respectful of the other.

Whether or not the details were embellished by Percy's friends, the near-duel said some fairly revealing things about the man. First, of course, it showed that the old strain of southern honor—as silly in some respects as it was noble—ran as strong in LeRoy as it had in his father. It also suggested a reckless streak in the man, not a cardinal flaw of character but one that a father of three (his third son, Billups Phinizy, was born in 1922) might have been more careful to check.

There were other indications of a problem, some subtle, some overt. One appears in a letter he wrote to his uncle LeRoy in Greenville shortly after the latter had spoken out against the Ku Klux Klan at a meeting on March 1, 1922 in the Greenville courthouse, a meeting that was well attended and widely reported. Percy delivered such an articulate and forceful denunciation of the Klan that it brought national attention both to the growing problem and to LeRoy. (Soon after the speech, the editor of *The Atlantic Monthly*, Ellery Sedgwick, asked LeRoy to write an article about the "new" Ku Klux Klan, which he did, with his son Will's assistance.)

In the nephew's congratulatory letter, written on office stationery ten days later, the nephew praises his uncle for making a "great speech." It was, he writes, "the sort of speech I have been hoping for a long time that somebody would make." He then explains that Birmingham had experienced a similar rise of activity among a group called the True Americans, or TAs. (Although he didn't mention it, the Klan, too, had made big inroads in Birmingham.) Starting the year before, the nephew relates, it had been "open season" on Catholic priests, one of whom had been killed by a "jack-legged Methodist minister." Worse yet, the minister was "very promptly and enthusiastically acquitted by the jury." In the third paragraph, LeRoy sounds a rather pathetic note of complaint:

> Every jack-legged politician that comes along has to join one of these things [such as the TAs]. I believe I am the only man in Jefferson County who does not belong to anything. Our community stands sadly in lack of such constructive leadership as was evidenced by your taking charge of this Ku Klux meeting the other night. I don't know whether our community is the sort of community that could be led, but at any rate they are not.

The pathos appears most strikingly in the second sentence, in the feebly voiced boast about not belonging to anything. For this passive gesture of resistance, this tepid act of semiheroism, LeRoy gives himself

an almost reluctant pat on the back. He wants to tell his uncle that he
has done something to oppose the growing scourge, but at the same time
he knows that it is not much, certainly not in comparison with what his
uncle did in Greenville. The rather gnarled phrasing in the next sentence—and indeed throughout the letter—testifies to a man at odds
with himself, wrestling with himself, doubting himself. The question
insinuated throughout the letter is obvious: Why hasn't he, the nephew
LeRoy, behaved as gallantly in Birmingham as his uncle LeRoy did in
Greenville?

An excuse is not really called for. After all, why should nephew LeRoy
be a crusader? But he clearly felt bad about his inaction, and in the fifth
paragraph offers a most peculiar excuse:

> My time has been largely taken up lately with raising a family,
> providing for their maintenance and keeping the wolf away from the
> door in general. The law practice is bad, and I have cut off other
> sources of revenue by reason of a foolish pledge which I made in a
> misguided moment to do no more serious gambling for five years.

Yet later in the letter he all but vitiates his plea of financial hard
times. He proposes making a hunting trip to British Columbia the following fall—a six-week affair that will cost "something less than
$1,000.00 apiece." That was no small sum in those days, and a six-week
break from work would do little to help the practice. If there was a wolf
about, he wasn't exactly pawing at the door.

In fact, by outward indicators, LeRoy Percy was prospering. Like other
successful young professionals of his day, he began in the early 1920s to
make plans to move his family from his father's house into a beautifully
wooded little valley over Red Mountain that was just beginning to be
turned into an exclusive suburban neighborhood. One of Birmingham's
most prestigious architects, Hugh Martin, was drawing up plans for the
house. It would sit beneath tall oaks and pines near the bottom of the
southern slope of the mountain and face out upon a meadow that was
soon to be turned into the golf course of the Country Club of Birmingham.

In 1922, the officers of the club, anticipating the expiration of the
lease on their Lakeview property, began to look about for a new site.
They soon settled upon a 294-acre tract in Shades Valley, a vast expanse
that would accommodate two eighteen-hole golf courses as well as a
clubhouse and pool. LeRoy had a direct hand in the negotiations and
planning for the move. In 1924 he served, like his father before him, as
club president and watched helplessly as the membership divided into

two warring camps. The issue was the clubhouse design. One side favored "English" style architecture, the other colonial. Passions ran surprisingly high. When the former camp prevailed, the defeated members broke away and started their own club, Mountain Brook, only a few miles east. Despite the schism, the members of the old club initiated construction at the new site in February of 1926, and in May of 1927 the Country Club of Birmingham moved officially into its new home.

Well before that, though, in 1924, LeRoy moved his family into their new house—the house that would one day provide the model for the Vaughts' "castle" in *The Last Gentleman*. The contrast between the new place and the old one at Five Points had to be striking to the Percy boys. Life in Five Points had been an urban life, with the sound of trolley-car bells and sputtering Model Ts a constant background noise. The street was active most of the day and a good part of the night. People were always on their way to or from the corner grocery stores or visiting friends and neighbors during the busy social round. Children rode their bikes down the sidewalks or played shinny on their roller skates, and there was always a pickup game of baseball being played in the nearby park. "For those with an appetite," writes one local historian, "a street vendor could often be found peddling hot tamales along Highland Avenue." Five Points Circle was itself a growing commercial hub, and the streets radiating from it were rapidly filling with stores, parking garages (where those without private garages stored their cars at night), and a variety of churches and temples that reflected the ethnic range of this busy little town-within-a-city. Although it was a predominantly white, middle-class, and Protestant part of Birmingham, there were black neighborhoods throughout Five Points as well as one section thickly populated by newly arrived European immigrants, Germans mostly but also Swiss, Italians, and Irish. Jews, too, found it a convivial quarter, although the Klan revival of the 1920s no doubt fanned smoldering anti-Semitic as well as anti-Catholic feelings. In short, Five Points was a place where personal connections "crossed boundaries of income, race, religion, and nationality." If this variety was not unheard of in other southern cities, Five Points was unique because it contained it all within such a relatively small eighty-block area.

This was the first world that Walker Percy encountered, and many years later, he related his clearest memories of life there: "We lived on the corner of Highland and Arlington Ave., an easy streetcar ride to Five Points. Two things I remember: the first movie I ever saw, a Krazy Kat cartoon at a movie theater at Five Points. The other: a spectacular fire at the Packard Auto Co., with great black clouds of smoke. . . . Another memory: catching the streetcar on Highland with [my] black

nurse and riding the 'loop'—for a nickel—a cheap way of baby-sitting."
The old trolley that rattled its way around the serpentine Highland
Avenue "loop" was a particularly democratic mode of transport. It was
not even segregated until 1923.

But the streetcar was the dinosaur of its day. The automobile was the
future. And it was the automobile that made such developments as the
one on the other side of Red Mountain an attractive alternative to
the well-to-do. The Percys were among the first to lead the way, pioneers
of suburban living.

But they were pioneers in regal style. The house that Hugh Martin
designed for Percy was a sprawling one-floor affair, built of antiqued brick
and roofed with tile. From a large central foyer the house radiated in two
directions. In one was a formal dining room with ceiling-high wainscot-
ting, a kitchen, a large pantry, and a small, tucked-away staircase that
led up to the attic. In the other was the library, the master bedroom,
and smaller bedrooms for the boys. Behind the foyer spread a wide living
room with large picture windows that opened onto a neatly landscaped
backyard, trimmed with boxwoods and dominated by a majestic old oak.
There were also covered porches on the back and side, and a low stone
wall circled most of the house. From the hedges surrounding the front
wall down to the road sloped a broad expanse of lawn, to one side of
which lay a rose garden where LeRoy could often be seen working on
weekends.

One detail of the house reflected LeRoy's romanticism. He insisted
that wide doors be installed from the master bedroom to the terrace so
that on warm evenings he would be able to roll his bed out under the
stars. LeRoy was an avid star-gazer and owned a telescope that his oldest
son eventually inherited.

If the new house represented a dramatic break with the past, there
were still a number of ties to the old neighborhood. One was church.
After his marriage to Mattie Sue in 1915, LeRoy had abandoned Episcopalianism and followed his wife into the Presbyterian fold. At the
time, there was only one Presbyterian church in Five Points, South
Highlands Presbyterian Church, but within a year it was riven by a major
theological controversy. The conflict was between doctrinal fundamen-
talism and liberalism. The church's pastor, Henry M. Edmonds, recently
transferred from Montgomery, was a theological liberal, skeptical of such
"supernatural" notions as virgin birth and even of such doctrinal bed-
rocks as Original Sin. He emphasized, instead, the ethical message of
Christ, the "Social Gospel," and offended church elders by ignoring
those features of Christ that marked him as divine. After being examined
by the North Alabama Presbytery, he was instructed not to teach his

deviant notions from the pulpit. Instead of complying, Edmonds resigned and started his own church. On October 24, 1915, the Independent Presbyterian Church, some five hundred members strong, held its first service in Temple Emanu-El across the street from South Highlands. The Percys were among them. LeRoy, in fact, became such a strong member of Edmonds's flock that he took on the responsibility of teaching Sunday School to adults. He also served on the Board of Deacons.

The theological liberalism of Edmonds—its broad reasonableness, its tolerance of science, its emphasis on ethics and behavior rather than on mystery and belief—had little direct effect on the Percy children. The two boys attended some of the church-sponsored camps and were members of its Boy Scout Troop 28, but not even the church-led scouting activities much interested Walker. He rose perfunctorily to the rank of Second Class. As for the intensity of his beliefs, all we know is that he eventually abandoned the diluted religiosity of Edmonds, remaining an agnostic until his conversion to Catholicism at age thirty-one. But the lessons of liberal Presbyterianism were not completely lost on him. It is certainly possible to hear Percy tweaking the religion of his parents in his third novel, Love in the Ruins, when he describes Ellen Oglethorpe, the nurse whom Tom More eventually marries: "Ellen, though she is a strict churchgoer and a moral girl, does not believe in God. Rather does she believe in the Golden Rule and in doing right. On the whole she is embarrassed by the God business. But she does right."

The Percy boys, Walker and LeRoy, had another strong bond with the old neighborhood—their school. Birmingham University School, located at Twenty-eighth and Highland, was a small, select academy founded in 1922 by a retired Army officer, Captain Basil Parks. It had a small but able staff, including a colorful Latin instructor named Dr. Robert A. Mickle, who had a fierce way of staring down at a boy and telling him that he was an "infernal scoundrel." Once Dr. Mickle was invited to the Percys' for dinner, and the boys were in such awe of the man that they implored their father not to indulge in his usual preprandial cocktail. Mr. Percy informed his sons that he would not tailor his ways for any guest. The boys passed a few days in dread anticipation of Dr. Mickle's disapproving look—all for nought, of course. Dr. Mickle was more than delighted when Mr. Percy offered him a drink.

The boys' friends and classmates at BUS were the sons of Birmingham's elite—boys with last names like Roberts (DeBardeleben's old partner), Shook, and DeBardeleben. A number of his schoolmates recall Walker as the quiet brother, studious, serious, and somewhat sickly. He never ate much, and he suffered from terrible hay fever that kept his eyes itching and nose running during the fall and spring. According to one schoolmate, Paschal Shook, Jr., he was slight and frail seeming, and had almost comic difficulties keeping his knickerbockers up. From his first school years on, Walker was a good student, an avid reader, and unusually quick in mastering difficult subjects such as Latin and math. He wasn't stuffy, though. Other boys liked him. He had a sly sense of humor. Nevertheless, most of his peers agreed, there was something remote about him, a certain distance that made most boys more inclined to seek out the company of Roy. As well as being the more gregarious one, Roy seemed to be the brother who took charge. Even though he was a year younger than Walker, he seemed to have a firmer grip on the world.

Though physically coordinated, Walker, unlike Roy, was never very enthusiastic about sports. He played competently at golf and tennis, but without much zeal. After the family moved over the mountain, he and Roy would on better days ride their bikes—their Ibor-Johnson 28s—to and from school, each trying to outdo the other by never resting during the steep mountain climbs. For the most part, though, Walker preferred more sedentary pursuits. He liked to make things, particularly model airplanes, and enjoyed listening to music and reading Tom Swift novels. Without being odd, he cultivated some of the curious pursuits of the withdrawn, sending off for things in the mail and even cultivating a small literary ambition. At age ten, for example, he sent a story to *Liberty* magazine, but the magazine never replied.

Friends and relatives often came to visit the Percy boys. Henry F. DeBardeleben's grandchildren, Donie and Newton DeBardeleben, though a little older than Walker or Roy, befriended their cousins back in the Five Points days. Donie, a fetching redhead, was in many ways the older sister that the Percys never had—and sometimes the older brother as well. A scrappy tomboy, she joined the boys in baseball and other games and was quick with her fists if any outsider ever dared to hurt her brother or cousins. When the boys moved over the mountain, Donie and Newt would come from their Shades Mountain home to explore the woods with them, soon dubbing favorite spots with names like "Fat Man Squeeze" and the "Rock House."

Another set of cousins from the mother's side, the Spaldings, visited often from Atlanta, Georgia, usually around Thanksgiving. One of the Spalding boys, Jack (who later became editor of the *Atlanta Constitution*) recalls that the Georgia-Alabama football game inspired just enough partisan rivalry to give the occasion a pleasing frisson. Three years older than Walker, Jack also remembers his cousin's fondness for a Paul Whiteman record, "The Birth of the Blues," which he played over and over on a windup portable victrola.

For Walker's mother, the Spalding visits were always particularly happy occasions. She had four sisters, but Bolling was the closest to her, and the visit gave her a chance to catch up on her Georgia kin. Mattie Sue's affection was warmly reciprocated. "She was mother's favorite," Jack Spalding observed.

Mattie Sue was hard not to like. Her beauty had not spoiled her. She was smart and a good athlete, particularly strong at tennis. Yet as much as she had going for her, most people detected a certain vulnerability and frailty. She was almost too delicate, verging on the otherworldly, and being married to a depressive could not have been very reassuring. While she did her best to help her husband with his problem, she was as frightened as her sons were by his roller-coaster moods, his deepening depressions, and his occasional furious outbursts of temper. The stress within the family was high, and it had the effect of making her somewhat remote. Not that her sons remembered her with anything but fondness and devotion, but even their affection had an abstract quality to it, as though they never knew her that well. Even though their relationship with their father was often painful, it was by far the more intimate.

During the years after the move over the mountain, the adult most constantly present in the boys' lives was neither their mother nor their father but a black man named Elijah Collier, or "Lije." A former railroad employee, Collier had worked as the night watchman on the construction site of the Percys' new home, so impressing Lawyer Percy that he offered Collier a job as a general man-about-house and chauffeur. But his main responsibility, Collier quickly learned, was taking care of the boys—no easy task when it came to young Phin, who was so unruly that his father dubbed him Nicodemus, or Nick. A short, wiry man, Collier was adequate to the task. Indeed, he was a force to be reckoned with. Friends of Walker and Roy still remember Lije standing behind Walker's chair in the dining room, staring down at his charge and ordering him to finish his meal. Walker was always a skimpy eater, but Lije would not let him get away with pushing his food around the plate. Lije could be companionable as well as firm, and he and the boys, particularly Phin, played hours of cards together.

Of course, Lije-like figures were common in wealthy white southern families, but Lije was something more than the beloved retainer. He was a buffer between the boys and the gathering gloom. But not even Lije could keep the boys from noticing that something was terribly amiss in the family, or from being hurt and frightened by it. Their father's moods were wildly erratic. He could be warm and upbeat one moment, angry and depressed the next. At his best, he could be the most doting and loving of fathers. But if he happened to be in one of his bad states, he cast a pall over the household. Dinners became ordeals, particularly during the Shades Valley years, when the depressions came more often and lasted longer. Drinks before dinner might have exacerbated his bad moods. Alcohol tended to make him testy and short—"stern," as another of Percy's Georgia cousins, Nell Johnson, recalled. But he also had a furious temper and a short fuse even without drinks. Coming home from work one day, he saw Walker chasing Roy with a rope. It wasn't a rough game. Walker was only lightly hitting his brother. But Mr. Percy exploded. Grabbing Walker roughly by the arms, he ordered Roy to hit his brother in the head with the knotted end of the rope. Roy didn't want to, but his father insisted. As Roy Percy recalled many years later, "It just wasn't a happy family."

Sometimes the atmosphere was frightening. When he was about ten and his brother eleven, Roy Percy remembers, their father took them both on a hunting trip to Thomasville, Georgia. Hunting, along with gambling and golf, was one of their father's great passions, and he would go just about anywhere to hunt fowl or larger game. He particularly liked to meet his uncle LeRoy down in New Orleans to hunt ducks at the Lake Arthur Duck Club and afterward play a round of poker at the Boston Club. There was a fair amount of drinking on these occasions, and also a good bit of the playful ribbing southerners enjoy while coolly blasting birds out of the sky.

The trip to Thomasville was not the first hunting trip the boys had gone on with their father, but it was the most memorable. Something seemed off from the beginning. Their father was drinking too much. He seemed a little out of control, unhappy, strangely "weird." For some reason, he was determined to create a rivalry between the boys, urging Walker and LeRoy to outshoot each other. The boys disliked being pitted against each other, and they also disliked the undertones of their father's goading. It was aggressive, of course, but something else.

The trip left a lasting impression on the boys, particularly Walker. It later served as the inspiration for a central episode in his fifth novel, *The Second Coming*. Protagonist Will Barrett's memory of a doom-haunted hunting trip to Thomasville, on which his father shoots and very nearly kills him, is the focal point of his prolonged meditations on the pointlessness of life and the allure of suicide. "Only one event had ever happened to him in his life. Everything else that had happened afterwards was a non-event."

These meditations, in other words, were Walker Percy's way of fathoming the message behind his father's inchoate but troubling behavior on that fateful hunting trip. Will Barrett says early in the novel, "Nothing is really forgotten," and this is only slightly hyperbolic. Nothing significant—no memory that goes into making up the puzzle of identity—can be forgotten, unless one chooses to lose oneself completely, or to obliterate one's self. Will Barrett realizes that; so, like his creator, he must revisit the memory in order to break its cryptic hold. Not surprisingly, the message is horrible when finally deciphered: "He was trying to warn me. He was trying to tell me that one day it would happen to me too, that I would come to the same place he came to, and I have, I have. . . ." The place is utter despair—the sickness unto death.

> But you, old mole, you knew otherwise, didn't you? You knew the secret. I could see it in your eyes, open and clear and brown, when you were run to ground in a Georgia swamp and looking up at me. You knew the secret. But how can that be? How can it be with death and dying does the sharp quick sense of life return? For that was your secret, wasn't it? That it was death you loved most of all and loved so surely that you wanted to share the secret with me because you loved me too.

It took a long time for Percy to arrive at this degree of clarity about an experience that was immediately perceived only as confusion and menace. Certain things had to happen first, and then would come the long period of sorting out and thinking through.

LeRoy's depressions worsened. At night he would suffer from maddening insomnia, which alcohol only made worse. Losing a case or performing poorly in court would send him into a spiral of despondency. He had a brilliant mind, a scholar's mind (as the exhaustive annotations in his *Century Bibles* make clear), and he found solace in his books, particularly his beloved Conrad. But even he could see that he needed help. In 1925, Lawyer Percy made a trip up to Johns Hopkins to seek the help of some of the nation's foremost specialists on depression. One of the doctors who saw Percy found him well-adjusted and happy in his life but prey to uncontrollable depressive moods. These being the years before the breakthroughs in psychopharmacology, there was little that the psychiatrists at Hopkins could do.

Of course, life went on for the Percys, indeed rather grandly. As prominent members of the city's elite, they were always on hand for the big occasions. When Charles Lindbergh came to Birmingham on May 5, 1927, Lawyer Percy and his family were among those to greet him. (Shaking the transatlantic aviator's hand at the Tutwiler Hotel, Walker decided then and there that his goal in life was to make the first solo flight across the Pacific.) When Bill Tilden came to play tennis, the Percy boys had tickets and good seats. LeRoy Percy was thought of as a charming, witty man, even as something of a jokester. And even his jokes were on a grand scale. Not long after the golf course at Birmingham Country Club was finished, for example, LeRoy Percy challenged one of his fellow club members to a high-stakes golf match. Percy's friend was allowed to find any partner he wanted. Not being overly sporting, his friend chose the club pro. Percy kept his own partner a secret. All he said was that he would be coming from out of town. The mystery partner arrived the night before the match, but no one was allowed to meet him. The next day, while his opponents waited anxiously at the first tee, Percy and his partner arrived in a chauffeured car with window curtains drawn. Out stepped Percy first. A small crowd waited eagerly to see who would follow. They were not disappointed. It was none other than Bobby Jones, who by then had already won more U.S. Amateur and U.S. Open crowns than any other golfer in the game (and who would go on to win the "Grand Slam"—the U.S. Open, the U.S. Amateur, the British Open, and the British Amateur—in 1930). The famed golfer-attorney from Atlanta was a friend of Percy's and quite willing to help him pull off the prank. It was all in good fun, of course. Yet, in a way, it was almost too grand a gesture.

During the spring of 1928 things took a sharp turn for the worse. Robert McDavid Smith, a Birmingham attorney, lived about two blocks from the Percy house when he was a boy. While his family was out for one of their Sunday drives, they passed by the Percy house and saw LeRoy working in the yard, stooped down among the rose bushes. The Smiths slowed to wave hello, and Percy stood to wave back. His shirt-sleeves were rolled up, Smith remembers, but another detail was more striking: Both of Percy's wrists were wrapped in white bandages. After his father drove on, the eight-year-old boy asked his parents what the bandages were for. They told him that Mr. Percy had had an accident in his bathroom. Later Smith learned the truth. It had been Mr. Percy's first attempt at suicide.

The year 1929 proved to be a bleak one, and not only for the Percy family. It was the year of the great crash. The resounding crescendo came in October, as thousands of bankers and brokers were ruined, but tremors had disturbed the country during the summer months before. In Birmingham alone, five banks closed and two high-ranking bank officials shot themselves. But financial concerns did not seem foremost on the mind of LeRoy Percy that summer. As planned, he sent his two older sons off to Camp Winnippee in Eagle River, Wisconsin, where many of the boys' Birmingham friends went. Fighting another bout of melancholia, Percy himself traveled to French Lick, Indiana, for rest and recuperation. It did not seem to help. Mattie Sue got in touch with

Uncle LeRoy in Greenville, knowing that he was the person with the
greatest influence on her husband. The timing couldn't have been worse
for Uncle LeRoy. His wife, Camille, was having serious heart troubles,
and he hated being away from her. Nevertheless, he came to Birmingham, perhaps sensing that things were very desperate this time. His visit
appeared to do some good. In a letter dated simply "Thursday night"
Mattie Sue wrote to thank him for coming:

> Dear Uncle LeRoy—
>   I wish I could half-way thank you enough for coming over. It helped
> us all *so much*. Today is the best day Roy has had. He has had no
> tenseness at all, in spite of "The Crouching Beast"—
>   I do feel so much better about him in every way—I will try so hard
> to get him to do what we agreed on was the best—

It would be interesting to know what they "agreed on was the best."
Positive thinking, most likely. Perhaps temporary abstention from alcohol. A few days off from work. In any case, on Tuesday, July 9, LeRoy
Percy did not go to the office. He remained at home in bed while Mattie
Sue went over the mountain to shop. According to the July 10 story in
The Birmingham News, the maid was looking for Mr. Percy shortly after
11:00 A.M. when she heard the sound of a gun in the attic. She went up
the small stairs next to the pantry and found the underwear-clad body
on the floor. There was a "gaping wound through the chin," said the
paper, and later the coroner found that the charge from the twenty-
gauge gun "came out through the top of his head."
    The story got out quickly. Indeed, Mattie Sue was still downtown
when she heard newsboys shouting out the breaking news. "Prominent
Birmingham lawyer takes his life!" They didn't give the lawyer's name.
They didn't have to. Mattie Sue turned to her shopping companion and
said, "It's LeRoy."

2

From New South
to Old

———•———

If it hadn't been for Uncle Will, Walker Percy once said, he probably would have ended up a car dealer in Athens, Georgia. Percy was not being snide. He thought ill neither of the car trade nor of Athens. One of his best friends later in life was a car dealer; and Athens is a town to which he had strong family ties. It was to Athens that his family moved after his father died, and had it not been for a surprising turn of events, he might well have gone on living there for the rest of his life.

Mattie Sue's father, Billups Phinizy, had been a very successful businessman in Athens, indeed one of the more successful in Georgia. Her grandfather, Ferdinand Phinizy II, was reputed to be the richest man in Georgia in his day—and also one of the more scrupulous. Even though it left him temporarily broke, Ferdinand Phinizy at the end of the Civil War made good on all Confederate currency that his banks issued.

Billups Phinizy, like his father, prospered in a number of pursuits, in farming, banking, and insurance. Amassing a comfortable fortune, he built a beautiful Queen Anne style mansion on Milledge Avenue, one of Athens's two main streets. Unfortunately, Billups suffered a turn of fortune. Near the end of his life he saw most of his wealth eaten up by the boll weevil invasion. His plight was not unique. During the 1920s, cotton farmers throughout the South lost their crops to the voracious little gray weevil. Some were hit so hard that they dropped cotton forever and turned to other crops, including peanuts. But the weevil dealt Billups Phinizy a double blow. In addition to losing his crops, he had to underwrite huge bank losses, subject as he was, as all bank stock-holders then were, to "double liability" on every dollar invested. By the time he died in 1927, Billups Phinizy was living in considerably strait-ened circumstances.

But neither hard times nor the loss of her husband broke Nellie Stovall Phinizy. She came of hardy stock. Her grandmother, Mary Jane Wilson, the wife of a Presbyterian missionary, had been the first white woman to die north of the Vaal River in South Africa, and there was something of the missionary toughness and determination in her granddaughter. Her own grandchildren recall her as one of the last great Victorians, a loving woman but fiercely self-controlled. Stiff upper lip was the code she lived by, and the code she imposed on her five daughters. In the Phinizy household, one simply did not complain.

But if she was firm, Nellie Stovall was not cold. She was devoted to the well-being of her five daughters. There was no question of not invit-ing Mattie Sue to come live with her when tragedy struck. Mattie Sue accepted the offer, understandably eager to put the recent past behind her. (Some Birmingham friends thought her too eager: They were shocked when she wore a red dress at the reception after LeRoy's fu-neral.) Quickly wrapping up business in Birmingham (with the help of LeRoy's law partner, D. K. McKamy, and her Atlanta brother-in-law Hughes Spalding), she sold the house to a colorful Auntie Mame–like character named Margaret Busch, who later claimed to have communion with the ghost of LeRoy. Mattie Sue moved to Athens in time for her sons to enroll in the local public schools, and while the boys adjusted to the new town and made new friends, she kept busy planning and laying out an elaborate garden in her mother's yard and playing the occasional game of tennis. To all of her kin, though, it was obvious that her husband's death had taken an enormous toll on her spirits. "She always looked sad," one of her Athens nieces remembered.

The Percy family, by all accounts, passed a tranquil year in their grandmother's house at 324 Milledge Avenue. It was a large, comfortable place, with great sweeping porches and elaborate gingerbread trim. In-side were plenty of rooms for the boys to roam through—thirty-three in all—most rather grandly appointed. Indeed, the chandeliered elegance would seem to have been somewhat at odds with the rather severe character of Nellie Stovall. Her strictness was hard to ignore; it left a lasting impression on her grandsons.

The youngest, Phin, who was eight during the year in Athens, re-

membered that she had inflexible rules about certain things. Some bore
a clear Presbyterian mark. On Sundays, for example, work was absolutely
forbidden. Even cutting out pictures with scissors, he discovered, was
unacceptable. But perhaps his most vivid memory of his grandmother
was that of her sitting at her large mahogany roll-top secretary, going
over the family accounts with an almost terrible intensity. She seemed,
to the young boy, forever at that desk, and it is easy to understand why
she was. The Wall Street crash of October and the ensuing Depression
had put an even larger dent in the family's diminished resources. She
was, as she once explained to Thomas Tillman, the husband of her
youngest daughter, trying to make a living out of a dwindling income.

Not that the boys felt any pinch. They lived well in the big house.
There were plenty of servants, including a white chauffeur named
Haines. John Horton, a black man, oversaw all domestic operations.
The boys went to the YMCA, played golf and tennis and swam at the
Club, and were quickly accepted by their classmates at school. "They
stood out for two reasons," recalled Nell Johnson, who was only a year
and a half older than her thirteen-year-old cousin Walker. "First of all,
we had never known a family to move in with grandparents. And second, the two older boys wore corduroy knickers." Walker's academic
prowess impressed his teachers, particularly his English teacher, Miss
Ruby Anderson. Outside the classroom, he mastered two important
skills: He learned to drive a car and to play the guitar. (For the rest of
his life, Percy would be a competent guitarist, fond of folk and Western
songs.)

As in Birmingham, Walker remained somewhat to himself, absorbed
in his hobbies. Flying a model airplane in Sanford Stadium, he had
perhaps his most memorable Athens experience. The plane went down
in the middle of the varsity football team's scrimmage and was returned
to him by Georgia's famed All-American end, "Catfish" Smith.

The Athens experience lasted only a year, but it left a deep impression
on the future novelist. Like his brother Phin, Walker never forgot his
grandmother or her stern notions of probity and self-discipline. Nana, as
she was called by most of her grandchildren, remained for him something
like the embodiment of the Protestant work ethic, a model for which he
remained everlastingly grateful.

After a year of relative calm, Mattie Sue must have had mixed feelings
when William Alexander Percy, LeRoy's cousin, came to visit in the
spring of 1930. There was no denying the man's charm, and Mattie Sue
was certainly not immune to it. At the same time, though, Will Percy
lived life in that higher Percy key. It is hard to imagine a more vivid

embodiment of the Percy obsessions with high honor and duty. Her boys, she knew, were in awe of him and of his storied reputation.

"We had heard of him, of course," Walker Percy later wrote. "He was the fabled relative, the one you like to speculate about. His father was a United States senator and he had been a decorated infantry officer in World War I. Besides that, he was a poet. The fact that he was also a lawyer and a planter didn't cut much ice—after all the South was full of lawyer-planters. But how many people did you know who were war heroes and wrote books of poetry? One had heard of Rupert Brooke and Joyce Kilmer, but they were dead."

Uncle Will—for that is what the boys called their cousin—was forty-five at the time of the visit, a trim and fit-looking man who, despite his gray hair, impressed Walker most of all with a "youthfulness—and an exoticness." A seasoned traveler, Uncle Will had just returned from a trip to the South Seas, where he had lived on the beach at Bora Bora. But beneath his cousin's worldliness and his infectious charm, Walker detected an undercurrent of sadness, most visible in Will's deeply set gray-blue eyes. "They were beautiful and terrible eyes, eyes to be careful around. Yet now, when I try to remember them, I cannot see them otherwise than as shadowed by sadness."

Will's dark underside was, if anything, even darker that year. He had lived through a particularly bleak patch that included not only the suicide of his cousin but his mother's death in October and his father's on Christmas Eve. (After his father's death, Will commissioned a statue of a medieval knight leaning upon his sword and had it installed in the Percy family lot at the cemetery. It is called *The Patriot.*) The South Seas trip had been Will Percy's attempt to put some of the pain behind him, and no doubt had helped, but there was no simple anodyne for what he was suffering from. Still grieving, he invited Mattie Sue and the boys to come spend the summer with him in Greenville.

If Mattie Sue had fears of upsetting the tranquil life she had created in Athens, she overcame them. When the school year finished, she and the boys took Uncle Will up on his invitation. The trip from the hills of north Georgia to the fertile lowlands of the Mississippi Delta was more than a physical journey. It was a passage through time and cultures. The real starting point of this second journey was the boys' native town of Birmingham. From that "New South" city, with its industry and bright new suburbs, and a brief interlude in college-town Athens, the family was heading backward to an older South, a world redolent, in Walker Percy's words, of "ancient hatreds and allegiances, allegiances unto death and love of war and rumors of war and under it all death." They were heading to the ancestral grounds.

The story of the Percys of Mississippi is a long and rich one, a tale of high deeds and low, many of which have been obscured by legendary overlays or fanciful retellings. In *The Percys of Mississippi*, historian Lewis Baker has done a fine job of separating facts from legend, but Will Percy's memoir, *Lanterns on the Levee*, remains the indispensable starting point. Despite errors of fact (many of which are caught by Baker) and a distinct partisan bias, the book captures something no objective history could— the spirit of the family. So important is the Percy family romance to the future novelist that its broad outlines will be given here.

Will Percy paints a colorful picture of the arrival of the first Percy, his great-great-grandfather Charles, in what was then known as West Florida. He came with a shipload of slaves and a Spanish grant to lands near Natchez. According to a family genealogy compiled by Robert Hereford Percy, the exact year of arrival was 1776, which pokes one hole in Will Percy's account: The land grant couldn't have been from the Spanish government, because from 1763 to 1780 that stretch of territory was controlled by the English. The land patent, therefore, would have been granted by King George III. In any case, Charles did settle there, and when the Spanish regained control of the region they thought so highly of him that they made him an alcalde, or magistrate, in the local government.

Charles's main interest, however, was farming, and he set about transforming some six thousand acres of wilderness into arable fields. The staple crop from the time of his arrival right up to his death was indigo, and Charles made a very good living from it. After building the plantation, which he dubbed Northumberland Place, Charles began casting about for a mate. Will Percy claims that he finally settled upon "an intelligent French lady from the other side of the river," but again the genealogical record causes us to doubt him. It identifies Charles's bride as Susanna Collins—not a name that one would immediately think of as French. By wife Susanna, Charles had six children, two of whom died in infancy, but apart from those painful but quite common losses life seemed to be going smoothly.

Then calamity struck. The exact date is unknown, but sometime in the early 1780s, a woman named Margaret Percy appeared on the scene and declared that she was Don Carlos's long-abandoned wife. As proof she presented their son, Robert, born in Kilkenny, Ireland, in 1762, and now an officer in the British Navy. It was a painful moment for Charles, the respected and prosperous alcalde, but he managed to work out a peaceful resolution and Margaret settled nearby. Even Robert seemed to come to terms with the arrangement. After his mother's death in 1785, he graciously accepted Susanna as his stepmother.

But Charles Percy was not a man at peace with himself. His friends noted that he was prone to bouts of melancholy, and that these bouts worsened during 1793, leading to paranoid delusions. Certain that his neighbors were out to get him, he finally snapped, and on January 30, 1794, in the dark of night, Charles walked to a nearby stream (henceforth called Percy Creek), tied a sugar kettle to his neck, and jumped in. As Will Percy concluded, "He was not exactly a credit to anybody, but, as ancestors go, he had his points."

One of those points was his usefulness to the Percy family legend. As the first in a line of colorful personages, Charles provided Will Percy with a dramatic opening for a spirited family chronicle. (The story would also find its way into Walker Percy's sixth novel, The Thanatos Syndrome.)

Melancholia and suicide have a prominent place in the Percy family saga, as we have already seen in the Birmingham chapters of the tale. Believers in a strict higher justice will be pleased to learn that the illegitimate line seems to have been more decisively cursed by Don Carlos's condition than the legitimate one, although even in the bastard line there have been exceptions. The first was Thomas G. Percy, the only son of Charles and Susanna to survive childhood. After his mother's death in 1803, he inherited most of his father's wealth, and, after attending the College of New Jersey (later renamed Princeton College), became one of the luminaries of Wilkinson County, Mississippi.

In 1815, however, Thomas went through a more difficult test. The trouble began when a prominent local lawyer named George Poindexter, a man who would one day play an important role in Mississippi politics, became convinced that Percy, his friend and neighbor, was having an affair with his wife. The truth of the matter is impossible to establish, but likely as a result of the controversy, Percy moved first to Kentucky and then to northern Alabama. There he settled on a plantation in Madison County next to the estate of a college friend, John W. Walker, the first U.S. senator from Alabama. In 1816, Percy married Maria Pope, the sister of Walker's wife and the daughter of a prominent Huntsville citizen, LeRoy Pope. Percy lived the life of the leisurely planter, apparently content with a large library, a house full of children, and the occasional trip to New York City. Considering his rocky start, he had a good life. Five of his eight children survived the various afflictions of childhood, and four of them—the male progeny—received good undergraduate and professional training. While footing the considerable expenses of farm and family, Thomas also managed, in 1831, to buy a sizable piece of land in Washington County, Mississippi, one of the ten counties located in the rich Mississippi Delta. It was a fortunate purchase both for the Percys and for Mississippi.

Seven years after Thomas Percy's death in 1841, his widow and three of his sons—John Walker, LeRoy, and William Alexander—decided to forsake their professional careers (medicine in Walker and LeRoy's cases, law in William's) and set out for the land their father had purchased on Deer Creek. This was not a light-hearted decision. The Mississippi Delta, roughly 150 miles long and 50 miles wide, was definitely pioneer country in the 1840s, a rough and rugged place that killed many who tried to wrest a living from it.

Rich soil drew pioneers to the Delta—farmers, mostly, from other parts of the South where the land had played out and the plantation system had turned unproductive. From Kentucky, the Carolinas, and Virginia, they came with their slaves, armies of black men and women, to transform the thickly forested terrain into workable farmland. Hence from the beginning of its settlement in the second decade of the nineteenth century, the Delta had nearly three times as many blacks as whites—a demographic fact that would be of central importance to the region's politics and culture.

One geographical peculiarity of this riparian land is that it does not drain directly into the Mississippi but, as Will Percy noted, "tilts back from it towards the hills of the south and east," where the waters are gathered by the small rivers and ultimately the Yazoo and returned to the Mississippi just above Vicksburg. For this reason, the first settlers settled on the banks of the Mississippi, where the ground was highest, and gradually fanned out to the banks of the lesser Delta rivers—the Sunflower and Bogue Falaya, among others. Wherever they settled, though, the planters and their slaves faced mighty odds. First they had to clear the thick vine-tangled forests of cypress, water-oak, and sweet-gum. Then, once they had drained the ubiquitous swamps of their ankle-high waters, they had to contrive ways of protecting the land from the periodic floods. The sweltering summer heat was not the only factor complicating these labors; the swamps were ideal breeding grounds for snakes, yellow fever, and malaria-carrying mosquitoes.

Into this world unfit for man, woman, or beast—or most beasts, anyway—came the three Percy sons in 1848, two of them with wives, and they quickly built a large log cabin on Deer Creek. Will Percy's memories of his great-aunt and grandmother show two rather contrasting personalities. Aunt Fannie, John Walker's wife, was a creature of exquisite delicacy, a slender woman who smelled "faintly of orris-root." Prone to sudden naps and inexplicable sobbing, she suffered, Will learned, from a genteel and quite common addiction to morphine. "Being the only wicked thing she ever did, it must have been doubly consoling." Her little vice did not prevent her from having strict notions of propriety, and her judgments carried weight. One local grandee who committed the indiscretion of living with a black concubine was so decisively cut by her that he decided to leave the region. For all her strangeness, Aunt Fannie survived the war and Reconstruction, outliving both her husband and her daughter.

More typical of the frontier type, Will thought, was his paternal grandmother, Nanny Armstrong, or Mur, as he called her. "Left on the plantation during the war, alone with her three babies, while my grand-father [William Alexander], an opponent of secession and a lukewarm slave-owner, was away fighting to destroy the Union and preserve the institution of slavery, she not only raised her little brood single-handed and under the handicap of increasing poverty, but managed the thou-sand-acre place." Managing the farm was no small matter, particularly as the war drew to its end. After word of Lincoln's Emancipation Proc-lamation trickled down to Mississippi, many blacks left the farm. Others simply refused to work anymore. How Mur managed to convince the few remaining blacks on Deer Creek to put in the cotton crop is difficult to imagine, but she did—and did so without the help of the two brothers who had stayed behind on the farm with her. By the end of 1864, John Walker was dead and LeRoy was paralyzed. Yet when the war finally ended and William returned to the farm, the family, according to Will, "managed to live for a year or more on the proceeds from the sale of that cotton crop."

If Mur was a remarkable person, her husband, William Alexander, was no less so. By the end of his life, in fact, he had become one of the legendary figures of the Delta. The legend begins with the war he had campaigned so hard to prevent. His efforts focused specifically, and suc-cessfully, on sending one of the new antisecession delegates to the state-wide secession convention called shortly after Lincoln's election. His was a quixotic campaign, of course. The voices of conciliation were easily drowned out, and Mississippi became the second state to quit the Union.

Once defeated, William Percy did not stay home and lick his wounds. Like so many other southern gentlemen opposed to secession, he never thought for a moment of abandoning his beloved state or his equally beloved South, however wrong they happened to be. Honor required loyalty, and it was unthinkable for a man such as Percy to ignore the claims of honor.

Percy served in his home state until the fall of Vicksburg in 1863 and then was sent to Virginia to participate in some of the most devastating battles of the war. One of the worst was at Cold Harbor, where, writes Lewis Baker, he "saw seven thousand Union troops killed in half an hour, a mechanical slaughter that mocked the notion of war as a gallant fray." Percy returned to Mississippi before Lee's surrender at Appomattox only to witness a less dramatic but probably more demoralizing winding-down of the war. As an assistant adjutant general on General H. B. Hodges's staff, he was assigned the hopeless task of stemming desertion in face of imminent defeat. As if that were not enough, conditions in Mississippi were bleak, particularly in the Delta, where the few remaining levees not destroyed by Grant were washed away by high waters during the last year of the war. When finally demobilized, Percy returned home to a bog.

The recognition accorded Percy for his war record was great—among Delta folk he was known by his unofficial rank, Colonel Percy, or alternatively, by his sobriquet "Gray Eagle." But his stature did not rest solely upon his martial gallantry. Just as important was his role in rebuilding the Delta, a role that called on his considerable organizational and political skills.

Historians have closely scrutinized the interests and behavior of men like Percy during the Reconstruction and Redemption eras. They have noted in particular that Percy's sort, known as "Bourbons" or "Old Captains," pursued their own interests under the noble guise of "redeeming" the southern states from the corrupt Radical Republican governments imposed upon them by the vengeful Yankee victors. While publicly denouncing corrupt officeholders, Carpetbaggers, Scalawags, and all other agents of northern interference in southern affairs, these very same Redeemers were often busy cutting private deals with northern financiers and railroad men and indeed with leaders of the despised Republican party itself. There were even some scions of the old Confederacy who allowed their names to be attached to Carpetbag projects. According to C. Vann Woodward, it "was a poor subsidiary of an Eastern railroad that could not find some impoverished brigadier general to lend his name to a letterhead."

The ranks of the Redeemers were filled not only by the old planters. In fact, the Bourbons were a distinct minority among the Redeemers, far outnumbered by a powerful new congeries of entrepreneurs, merchants, and professionals. Percy himself belonged to that minority of the old order which managed, beginning in 1865, to move successfully to the forefront of the new elite. He was able to not only because he was shrewdly alert to the needs of his community but also because he was a professional man, a lawyer, as well as a landowner.

After returning from the war, Colonel Percy decided to put his legal training to use, opening a practice in nearby Greenville and aligning himself with forward-thinking "conservative" Democrats in the area. The first item facing responsible citizens of the Delta was rebuilding the levees, a political feat as much as an engineering one. Percy helped organize a three-county levee board and convinced planters to accept bonds as payment for labor. Rebuilding the levees was not an isolated problem, and Percy knew it. "He realized," Lewis Baker writes, "that the levee district's tax base needed to be expanded: Delta planters would have to reestablish their operations, and new settlers would have to be brought in."

To achieve these broader goals, Percy became active in efforts to bring railroads to Washington County, a campaign not unanimously popular with local citizens. Nevertheless, beginning in the 1870s, new rail lines began to run throughout the Delta, strengthening Greenville's position as a cotton market and luring new settlers to the region. As the tax base grew, however, so did the tax burden. Republicans in charge of local and state governments imposed heavy property taxes on landowners. They claimed that such revenues were needed to improve public services, and they were, but the white planters believed that their tax money was being used only to further Republican graft and corruption. The Board of Levee Commissioners saw the problem clearly: If they were to raise money for levee construction, they would first have to get rid of property taxes.

Thus Percy and his cohorts joined forces with other Mississippi "conservatives" in order to fight the Republicans on the tax front. Beginning in 1873, the Gray Eagle organized a series of taxpayers' conventions, meeting first in Greenville and then in Jackson. At these gatherings, conservatives devised strategies for retaking the legislature—plans that had little chance of succeeding as long as the opposition was unified. Fortunately for the conservatives, rivalries among Republican politicians were erupting throughout the state, leaving black voters confused about whom to back. Many were convinced to throw their support behind white Democratic candidates who claimed to represent their best interests. In the fall of 1874, Percy played shrewdly on one such local Republican rivalry and got himself elected to the state legislature. When the legislature convened in January of 1876, Percy was appointed to a committee to investigate corruption in Governor Adelbert Ames's administration. Soon thereafter the legislature presented a lengthy bill of impeachment to the Senate, but rather than undergo a trial, Ames retired and a Delta planter was appointed temporary governor.

The conservative victory in Mississippi was repeated throughout the South, and while it wiped out established networks of political corruption it inevitably introduced new ones. Redemption, as the triumph over Reconstruction was called, also spelled calamity for the newly freed blacks, whose political position steadily eroded. In 1890, for instance, a new Mississippi state constitution instituted poll taxes and citizenship tests that virtually stripped blacks (and many poor whites) of their voting right. Similar constitutional measures followed in other southern states.

It would, however, be a mistake to say that Percy entered politics to disenfranchise blacks—although he cannot be completely exonerated of this unintended consequence. His controlling motive was to rebuild the Delta and to rid it of obviously corrupt officeholders. His two terms in the state legislature accomplished those goals, at least to his satisfaction, and even though he was elected speaker of the house during his second term and was urged to run for the U.S. Congress, he saw fit to return to his Greenville practice and to local affairs.

Percy was not without ego or ambition, but his actions attested to an almost classical conception of the political life. According to this ideal, one served in the public realm only to achieve a very specific end, the health and prosperity of the community, as well as the advancement of one's own interests. Percy believed that his interests—political, economic, cultural—were in harmony with the best interests of Greenville, Washington County, and the Delta, and to a remarkable degree they were. Farmers and merchants and professionals found in Percy an articulate champion of their dreams: improved opportunities for business, good schools for their children (and Greenville, as we shall see, soon acquired one of the best school systems in the state, if not in the South), and protection from the Mississippi River. Largely because of the influence of men like Percy, Greenville became a pocket of enlightenment. One striking instance of this was the remarkable tolerance of minorities, particularly of Jews, a tolerance that extended into all spheres of life. In fact, Greenville's first mayor after Reconstruction was a Jew, Jacob Alexander, and Jews continued to play prominent roles in Greenville civic life.

But the community that Percy loved and idealized, like the polis of antiquity, depended in great measure on profound inequalities. The base of the local economy was still agricultural, and in order for the big farms to survive during those decades before mechanization, the planters had to come up with a new labor arrangement to replace slavery. The solution was sharecropping. It was in many ways an institution as "peculiar" as slavery, from which, according to its strongest critics, it was not far removed. Ideally, of course, the arrangement promised a degree of independence and prosperity to the hard-working (and lucky) cropper, but the majority found themselves caught up in an endless cycle of debt that kept them and their families in hand-to-mouth misery. In most cases, the well-being of the cropper, white or black, depended on the largesse of the planter, which was not dependably large. Those planters who treated their croppers fairly, and Colonel Percy was among them, became perhaps the system's most forceful advocates. It was hard for them to imagine why sharecropping shouldn't benefit all parties involved.

For all its flaws, the system endured through the 1930s and even beyond. Mechanization did not completely kill it. The arrival of tractors, harvesters, and other machinery simply made it possible for the planters to get along with fewer laborers. In a much diminished, vestigial form, sharecropping survives to this day. But certainly from the 1870s to the 1930s, sharecropping flourished. It was a prominent fact of economic life throughout the rural South. And nowhere was it more prominent than in the Delta. Not surprisingly, this fact had consequences in other realms, notably the social and political. And the Gray Eagle's son, LeRoy, found himself in the middle of the battles that erupted there.

The enemies in this struggle were, quite simply, the haves and the have-littles. It was a war between the rich planter gentry and the poor yeoman farmers, and the fact that both sides were white accounts for the long period of coexistence that preceded the outbreak of hostilities. Fear and contempt of the black man had long kept whites together, muting if not completely dissolving class resentments. Even the poorest white man felt that there was always somebody who was worse off than he was; and because he was white he felt there was a chance (however slim in reality) of improving his station in life.

But it did not take long for the poorer whites to realize whom the post-Reconstruction arrangement favored. As C. Vann Woodward explains, the "white leaders of the Black Belt found themselves in somewhat the position their predecessors the Carpetbaggers had enjoyed. They became heirs to the control of more-or-less submissive or intimidated Negro voters, plus whatever constitutional devices had been erected (and not forthwith destroyed) for the control of the white counties."

In Mississippi, the situation had clear-cut geographical dimensions. The ten counties of the Delta, by far the richest part of the state, had disproportionate power in state politics. This was so because the great planters, the Bourbons, had a paternalistic hold over the black voters of the Delta, and with that hold they could dominate elections. Shrewd Delta politicians, such as John Sharp Williams, would arrange for minor offices to be given to black supporters. This naturally outraged poor white Mississippians, who were told that any disloyalty to the party would allow Carpetbaggers and blacks to regain influence in the state. The dominance of the Delta politicians led to regional inequities. For even though they were wealthier than the rest of the state, the Delta counties did not bear their fair share of the state's tax burden. At the same time, Delta counties benefited more from tax dollars. Schools and public services were better in the Delta than in the hills or the pine barrens. Quite rightly, the poor white farmers who barely eked a living out of the deficient red clay soil of Mississippi's higher counties felt shortchanged.

What Mississippi clearly had was the makings of a revolt—a "revolt of the rednecks," Robert D. Kirwan called it in his history of Mississippi's fifty-year populist revolution. The years of this long political upheaval— 1876 to 1925—roughly coincided with LeRoy Percy's career.

Born in 1861, the second of five children, LeRoy attended local public schools and then went on to the University of the South in Sewanee, Tennessee. His two brothers, William and Walker, two and three years his junior, respectively, followed him there, thus for a time constituting a minor Percy dynasty at that academic bastion of southern gentility. At Sewanee LeRoy made a small name for himself by successfully opposing the establishment of Greek fraternities on the grounds that they were undemocratic. His father's republican idealism had not been lost on LeRoy.

Returning to Greenville after college, Percy read the law in the office of his father's friend, Judge Shall Yerger, and soon fell in love with a local belle, Camille Bourges. As the name suggests, Camille was of French descent. Her mother, Marie Camille Generelly, and her father, Ernest, had both been born in New Orleans, but they were, in their grandson's words, "just as French as if they had landed day before yesterday from Lyon or Tours." Ernest had come to the Delta when cotton was booming, bringing his aristocratic wife and their four daughters. After an unsuccessful go at farming and several abortive business ventures in Greenville, Ernest became what he was best suited to be: a colorful local character. Gallically self-assured, content in his garden, he was "bon bourgeois" to the core. His ineptness at business never seemed to weaken Ernest's self-esteem, nor for that matter his wife's. "Their trouble, and their strength," wrote Will Percy, "was that they recognized no betters. Not that they minded Anglo-Saxons or took their own religion hard, but they regarded their poverty as an incident and their position as an immutability."

Marie Camille was less than delighted when LeRoy Percy began courting her daughter. Unlike most mothers in Greenville, she was unimpressed by the Percy name. That LeRoy was an Episcopalian was a definite strike against him. And if that was not bad enough, he was known, this dashing young Sewanee graduate, as "something of a gay blade." An indefatigable chaperone, Mme. Bourges became even more attentive when young Percy was about; yet somehow he managed to press his suit.

Before marrying, LeRoy decided to study for a law degree at the University of Virginia, but this was to be no leisurely undertaking, no casual three-year perusal of tomes punctuated by bouts of student frivolity. The thought of Camille waiting back in the Delta proved to be a sharp spur to his concentration. Finishing his degree in only one year, he returned to Greenville, joined Judge Yerger's practice, and in December of 1884, married the beautiful Camille. For the sake of appearances, the ceremony might have come a little earlier. LeRoy and Camille's first son, William, was born just six months after the taking of vows. Mme. Bourges's worst suspicions about her son-in-law had been confirmed.

Did LeRoy represent a falling-off from the high standards established by his father? Probably not. The distant always seem less peccable; the warts of the proximate always show more clearly. It is a matter of simple optics. Nevertheless, the historical imagination seems to feed on this illusion of generational decline, and chroniclers of the Percy story, including the Percys themselves, are a forceful case in point. Both Will Percy in *Lanterns on the Levee* and Walker Percy in his various novels use family decline as a recurrent theme. Neither treats the problem as being merely a simple deterioration of character, with each successive generation descending further from glory. They conceive of it, rather, as a gradual lowering of the tenor of the times, a lowering which in turn reduces the heroic possibilities of life.

Will Barrett in *The Last Gentleman*, for example, reflects upon the "family pattern":

> It was an honorable and violent family, but gradually the violence had been deflected and turned inward. The great grandfather knew what was what and said so and acted accordingly and did not care what anyone thought. He even wore a pistol in a holster like a Western hero and once met the Grand Wizard of the Ku Klux Klan in a barbershop and invited him then and there to shoot it out in the street. The next generation, the grandfather, seemed to know what was what but he was really not so sure. He was brave but he gave too much thought to the business of being brave. He too would have shot it out with the Grand Wizard if only he could have made certain it was the right thing to do.

As tempting as it is to identify the "great grandfather" and the "grandfather," it would be wrong to conclude that the former was the Gray Eagle or that the latter was LeRoy. Indeed, the great-grandfather seems more like a composite of the Gray Eagle and LeRoy, while the "grandfather" appears to be an even more complicated composite of the Birmingham Percys—both grandfather Walker and his son LeRoy Pratt—

and Will Percy. But if there are no exact biographical pegs for this tale of gradual decline, there is at least some sense of when things began to go decidedly wrong. The outer struggle began to turn into an inner one during LeRoy's lifetime, and did so because standards—right and wrong, good and bad—began then to lose their clarity.

They did so, of course, because the men who upheld those standards, the Delta Bourbons in particular, began to lose their assured place of control and dominance. Ironically, many of the Bourbons helped bring about their own decline. The most obvious instance of this was the support that several members of Percy's circle, including Greenville's newspaper editor, Captain J. S. McNeilly, and the local congressman, General T. C. Catchings, gave to the new Mississippi constitution. By effectively disenfranchising blacks and giving more representation to the predominantly white counties, the constitution of 1890 weakened the political base of the Delta captains and made it possible for a new breed of populist leader to come to the fore. Of course, the more astute members of Percy's set had realized what was at stake; Percy's partner Judge Shall Yerger had fought disenfranchisement. But they were too small a minority at the state convention to protect their interests.

Colonel Percy did not live to see the onset of the "redneck revolt" or even the constitutional alteration that made it possible. He died in 1888. But LeRoy promptly took up the causes that his father had championed, particularly that of strong levees. The importance of a reliable defense against the Mississippi had been forcefully brought home by a great flood in 1890. LeRoy not only served on the levee board but also became an officer in the newly established Levee Guard, an armed force charged with preventing sabotage during high-water periods. (It was not uncommon for unscrupulous Arkansans to breach Mississippi levees in order to ease pressure on their own, or for equally self-interested Mississippians to do the same to Arkansas levees.)

LeRoy also saw the same value in railroad construction as his uncle did, and when the Illinois Central came to the Delta proposing to do what it had done in the Midwest—that is, help farmers develop land adjacent to their tracks—he became their legal representative.

But while LeRoy and the Delta prospered, new powers in the state were beginning to exercise their will. The Mississippi governor from 1894 to 1899, Anselm J. McLaurin, "Old Anse," was just one of the rising political stars who did not see eye to eye with Percy and his ilk. "Old Anse" directly provoked LeRoy when he began to load the levee board with his political hacks. But when Percy protested, McLaurin pointed his finger at an earlier embarrassing episode when one of Percy's friends, General S. W. Ferguson, had mishandled levee funds and then fled the country to escape the mounting scandal. McLaurin had his full revenge when the newly staffed levee board dismissed Percy and Yerger as their legal counsel.

The war did not end there, of course, but continued through successive electoral battles between Percy's friends and McLaurin's. Each side scored victories. Perhaps one of the more peculiar developments in the conflict was that it led Percy to back James K. Vardaman in the gubernatorial election of 1903. Vardaman, a Greenwood newpaper editor, was one of the first populist leaders to exploit the rich possibilities of poor-white resentment. The strategy was simple: exploit crude racism by approving lynching and opposing public schooling for blacks. And just to convince the white fundamentalists that you were one of them, speak out for prohibition and denounce the high living of the wealthy plutocrats.

It was a winning formula, aimed in large part at people just like Percy, and one day it would put the two at odds. But in 1903, Percy considered only two things: Vardaman, a Delta man, appreciated the importance of strong levees, and his opponent, Judge Frank Critz, was McLaurin's choice.

The election of 1903 was a decisive one for the development of Mississippi politics. It was the first election in which the party hierarchy did not determine the winner of the primary. Because it was a truly "open" primary, a persuasive orator like Vardaman was able to build a solid base of popular support and win. Once in power, Vardaman began to make good on his promises diverting money (except for what was needed to maintain the levees) and public services away from the Delta and toward the "hill" counties.

Even more disturbing to Delta planters was the demagogue's racist rhetoric. Labor shortages on the farms, always a problem, were becoming even more acute. Blacks, quite simply, saw no future in a state like Mississippi and were beginning their exodus northward. It was not a sudden movement, of course, and in fact many blacks left the hill counties for the Delta, where they knew they would receive better treatment. Still, prospects looked bad, and planters like Percy had to consider alternatives.

One such alternative was foreign labor. It was not a completely new idea. Since 1876, Chinese had been imported to work as sharecroppers; during the 1880s, Italians were brought in. In 1897, LeRoy Percy got directly involved in an experiment in Arkansas—a farm employing Italian farmers exclusively. After a shaky start, the Sunnyside farm took off, and soon Percy was touting its success to convince Italian officials to send more migrant workers to the Delta. He also began spending more time in Washington, working to change immigration policies and laws. But his efforts were largely fruitless on both fronts, and indeed they ended by backfiring. The Italian consul in New Orleans encouraged Italian laborers to go farther west, to Texas, and in 1907 the Justice Department investigated Percy and his Sunnyside partners on charges of peonage. They were found innocent, but the damage was done. It would be increasingly difficult to recruit foreigners to the Delta.

Given this turn of events (and the further menace of an impending boll weevil invasion), the last thing Percy wanted in 1908 was for Vardaman to win his bid for the U.S. Senate seat. Vardaman's racist polemics had, if anything, grown more vicious during his term as governor, and they were producing the expected result. Blacks were leaving the state and the Delta. Furthermore, Vardaman's attacks on big business and his promise to regulate the trusts ran directly contrary to the efforts of men like Percy to bring business to the state. And finally, Vardaman was running against one of Percy's best friends, a fellow Sewanee graduate and U.S. congressman, John Sharp Williams. Percy's man won the election, but with such a narrow margin that it boded ill for the future.

Sensing the shape of things to come, Percy began to paper over differences with old enemies, notably McLaurin, who as the other U.S. senator from the state would inevitably face Vardaman in the 1911 election. As it turned out, Percy's timing could not have been better, for in December of 1908, "Old Anse" died, leaving the seat open for a legislative election. Percy decided to run against the "White Chief," Vardaman, confident not only of his own allies but also of most of McLaurin's. Largely because it was a restricted election, he won. It was not a resounding victory, though, and Percy knew that he would have a slim chance of beating the White Chief in the popular election of 1911. He did not, however, anticipate the scurrilous tactics his foe would use (particularly the trumped-up bribe charge brought by Bilbo, "the self-accused bribe-taker") nor the extent of outright loathing he would encounter on the campaign trail.

However inevitable the outcome of the 1911 race had been—Vardaman received seventy-nine thousand votes to Percy's twenty-one thousand—LeRoy and, even more strongly, his son Will saw the election as the tragic turning point not only in the family's fortunes but in the course of southern history. It was dramatic proof of bottom rail on top. All that remained for the old Bourbons were honorable holding measures, the maintenance of a certain style while all about them went to spoil under the misrule of the demos. Of the defeated senator, Will wrote: "Father did not like to lose at poker or golf or politics; in fact, he couldn't be called a good loser, if by that is meant one who loses without visible irascibility. But in this, the great defeat of his life, he was tranquil and found smiles and little spurts of merriment for his broken-hearted supporters. The only effect on him I could detect was an inner sadness, beyond reach, the kind of look I suppose Lazarus never outgrew after he had once died."

This is not to say that LeRoy Percy immediately wilted. He went on to have many fine hours, notably during his stand against the renascent Ku Klux Klan in 1922. His speeches and his article in *The Atlantic Monthly* brought him national attention, and letters of support and congratulation poured in. But there was no question in the Percy household that a great war had been lost. "Thus at twenty-seven," wrote Will, the perpetual epigone, "I became inured to defeat: I have never since expected victory."

3

Uncle Will

———◆———

*And about him I will say no more than that he was the most extraordinary man I
have ever known and that I owe him a debt which cannot be paid.*

—WALKER PERCY

At some point during the summer of 1930, Will Percy invited Mattie
Sue and her sons to stay on in Greenville. The boys were polled, and
though they all liked their grandmother and life in Athens, they concluded that it would be more fun to stay on with Uncle Will. "It was the
difference," Walker Percy said, "between a fairly strait-laced Georgia
Presbyterian household and a sort of lapsed-Catholic Episcopalian looseness, very sociable, with people always drifting in and out of the house."

Casual as it all seems, the decision could not have been an easy one
for Uncle Will. As well as forcing him to give up some of his privacy
and freedom, the added responsibility would take a toll on the activity
that he valued most—the writing of poetry. Will Percy had few delusions
about his greatness as a poet. He knew full well that he was out of step
with the poets who were busy "making it new," Pound, Eliot, Stevens,
and others. Nevertheless, this knowledge did not prevent him from
taking his poetry seriously. It was his means of holding chaos and despair
at bay. Put another way, it was the solution to the central problem of
his life, the problem of his difference. To jeopardize this sanctuary was

not only spirit-threatening but life-threatening. Will's bravery in this instance, as in so many others, should not be underestimated.

William Alexander Percy had always been "different," and different in the way "normal" folk, particularly normal twentieth-century Americans, find most troubling. A precocious child, delicate in manner and mien, he had early on developed an interest in music and, stranger yet, religion. Even his father didn't know what to make of him, describing him as "the queerest chicken ever hatched in a Percy brood." Will's brother LeRoy, Jr., born in 1881, a lover of horseriding, rough play, and guns, conformed much more closely to their father's ideal of hardy boyhood.

But Will was neither lonely nor spurned in the bosom of his family. The women—his grandmothers and aunts—doted on him, as did his black nurse, Nain, who was probably his most constant companion during the earliest years of his life. Will's earliest memory was of a song that Nain used to sing while holding him in her arms, rocking him. "I would try not to cry, but it made me feel so lost and lonely that tears would seep between my lids and at last I would sob until I shook against her breast. 'What's de madder, peeps?' she would say. 'What you cryin' fur?' But I was learning not so much how lonely I could be as how lonely everybody could be, and I could not explain." This account may seem like a late Romantic's overripe fancy, but Will credits Nain's song as being his first introduction to the tragic view of life—a sense of the "tears of things . . . something hard to live with, but impossible to live, as I would live, without." His fond memories of Nain also introduce two of the dominant themes of his memoir and therefore, since the book is a philosophical testimony, two of the central tenets of his philosophy of life.

The first is Will's belief in the solitary character of human existence. Despite the supports of a warm family and friends, despite the respect and admiration that he would win in his little corner of the South, Will came to accept the view that every creature was alone, and that the hope for self-transcendence (such as the one promised by the Catholic faith he embraced for so many years) was no more than sweet illusion, desirable but, to him, forever lost. His notion of human solitude could almost be described as a dulcet anticipation of the core idea of existentialism, but in fact Will's views hark back to an ancient philosophical creed, the Stoicism of Marcus Aurelius. They do so because they also embrace a special notion of virtue: virtue as the obligation to serve others no matter how profoundly separate each individual is from every other. European existentialists would have to find other ethical strategies to cope with the fact of human solitude, some turning to Marxism and others turning to a rigorously philosophical version of Christianity, but to Will the answer lay in Aurelius' *Meditations*.

The other theme introduced in the Nain story is Will's idealization of blacks. Here, as elsewhere, he credits them with being more attuned to spiritual reality, more closely connected with the natural poetry of the world. There is more than a touch of Rousseau's "noble savage" in this notion, and Will would have been the last to deny it. He often alluded to his conviction that Western civilization has robbed man of his capacity for spontaneity and joy. Blacks—as well as other noble savages Will encountered on his travels—still had that capacity. But as we shall see, this notion also had its obverse side: a belief that blacks, lacking discipline, were wholly incapable of self-governance. This defect, as Will understood it, was not endemically racial but the consequence of age-old cultural habits, and it doomed blacks to perpetual childhood and a life of dependency. To be sure, there is an unresolved ambivalence in Will's view. If blacks are trapped in childhood, but the adult world of whites is hollow and soulless (if adequately governed), then how can blacks take control of their own destinies without losing their souls? Indeed, Will's confusion about this seeming dilemma added to his sense of a tragic pattern to history.

As a small child, however, Will could only count himself lucky for his proximity to the society of black southerners—and not just to Nain. His first childhood companion, a boy named Skillet, he celebrates as a consummate conversationalist who "outdistanced any white child in inventiveness, absurdity, and geniality." As a storyteller and word-conjurer, Skillet was so compelling that he convinced Will one day that if a group of buzzards circling above them "was to ever light, the world would burn up." It is easy to see why Skillet remained all that Will could recall "of what must have been long months of my childhood."

But Will was fortunate as well in having aunts and grandmothers who relished his differences and, in many ways, encouraged them. They applauded his early efforts at the piano, they read romances to him, and they thrilled, at least at first, at his unusual piety. Enrolled at seven in the local convent school, Will soon carried his religiosity beyond acceptable bounds. He declared that he wanted to become a priest. Even his Catholic mother thought that too much and withdrew him from the care of the Sisters of Mercy. Turned over to a local eccentric named Judge Griffin, a mad inventor and tinkerer who had very eighteenth-century ideas about the Supreme Being and a broad love of literary classics, Will still managed to preserve his treacly piety. "I must have been an unbearable prig," he records, and indeed on one occasion he told his tutor that they should desist from reading *Othello*. It was, he declared, "immoral." Griffin made no defense. Instead, they moved on to one of the Bard's tamer plays, *The Merchant of Venice*.

Will's parents soon concluded that the judge's wandering curriculum might not be the best thing for bringing their otherworldly son back to earth. But apparently they thought him still too tender for the rough and tumble of the public school, however excellent Greenville's public schools were. So they hit upon a compromise: Mornings he would spend on Latin and French with Father Koestenbrock, the parish priest, and afternoons would be devoted "to whatever else immature minds require" with E. E. Bass, the superintendent of city schools.

Bass, in fact, was almost solely responsible for the excellence of Greenville's schools. Fresh out of the University of Missouri, he had come down the river in 1884 and stopped off in Greenville for what he thought would be a brief teaching stint before heading on to greater things. The public schools were in a wretched state, attended only by the sons of parents too poor to provide tutors or to pay for private school, but within a few years, Bass had turned things around. He cleaned up the schools, made them coeducational, instituted grade levels, and re-organized courses. The private schools and tutors began to suffer by comparison. Bass's efforts produced a string of Mississippi education firsts: "the first science laboratory, the first music department, the first kindergarten, and in 1890, the first high school graduation." Green-ville's emergence as the Delta's—and to some extent, Mississippi's—cultural Mecca stems in large measure from the excellence of its public schools, and for that E. E. Bass deserves most of the credit.

Bass was himself an inspired and highly unorthodox teacher who was only occasionally faithful to the syllabus of whatever course he was teaching. As Will Percy later recounted, "He'd come storming into the classroom with a cocoon when I'd prepared with boundless boredom the lesson on Burke's *Speech on Conciliation,* and the hour would trip by gaily while he explained that the cocoon's poor inmate never got to be a person but was always a transition. Always a becoming, never a being—a sort of Bergson bug." (Will's experience of E. E. Bass's peculiarly effective pedagogy eventually trickled down to his adopted son, Walker. In the latter's essay "The Loss of the Creature," first published in 1968, we find a recommendation highly reminiscent of the Bassian approach to teaching: "I propose," wrote Percy, "that English poetry and biology should be taught as usual, but that at irregular intervals, poetry students should find dogfishes on their desks and biology students should find Shakespeare sonnets on their dissecting boards.")

At fifteen, Will was sent to Sewanee, to follow the higher educational

path blazed by his father and uncles. In fact, he was sent under instruction to enroll in the local military academy to prepare for the university,
but after taking one look at the students parading about the grounds in
uniform, Will rebelled. He went directly to the university, took the
entrance exam, and passed.

The University of the South, Episcopal in religion, shabby-genteel in
style, was strong on humanities and weak, Will approvingly observed,
on sociology and science. It was referred to only as Sewanee, the name
of the small Tennessee mountain town in which it was located, and its
three-hundred-odd students lived in boardinghouses and dormitories
"presided over by widows of bishops and Confederate generals." Despite
his relative youth, Will worked hard and excelled, particularly in English
—no surprise, considering the literary preferences of his early tutors.
Raised somewhat apart from children his own age, Will now found
himself amidst a crowd of peers, or near-peers. Younger than most classmates, and certainly smaller, he was adopted into their larger social
world. With men like Paul Ellerbe, Harold Abrams, and Sinkler Man-
ning he formed fast friendships, usually based on shared literary and
intellectual interests. One of the Sewanee friends, Huger Jervey, "brilliant and bumptious then," not only remained close to Will throughout
his life but also later, while a professor at Columbia Law School, befriended Walker Percy while he studied at Columbia's College of Physicians and Surgeons.

Will's Arcadian idyll, as he was wont to describe it, was marred by
only two experiences. The first was the loss of his faith. It did not happen
suddenly or immediately. For a while, indeed, he made a monthly ten-
mile trip down a treacherous mountain road to the town of Winchester.
There, in the local Catholic church, he made his confession, heard
mass, and took communion. If Will's drift into lifelong apostasy was
almost imperceptible, it culminated decisively on the day he realized
that "no priest could absolve me, no church could direct my life or my
judgement." From then on, he wrote, "I would be living with my own
self."

Will did not give the date of this significant moment, but one might
conjecture that a family tragedy during the summer of 1902 played some
part in his religious crisis. In August of that summer, while the family
was vacationing in Hot Springs, Arkansas, Will's brother LeRoy had
accidentally shot himself in the stomach while showing a friend how to
use a .22. He walked back to the hotel under his own steam and bravely
boasted to his father that he was all right. He wasn't. It was a nasty gut
wound, and these were the days before antibiotics. He died within a
week. His parents were devastated, as was Will. The death was not only

grievous to the surviving son. It posed a special burden. Now he would have to be the man his father had expected LeRoy to be—the sort of man, in other words, who Will feared he could never be.

Since he was only nineteen when he graduated from college, Will's parents decided it wouldn't be bad for him to go abroad before preparing for a profession. So he journeyed to Paris, found an eight-dollar-a-month room in a dank-smelling boardinghouse, and spent a year haunting the museums, attending the occasional Sorbonne lecture, and perfecting his sense of solitude and loneliness. "I was sick for a home I had never seen and lonely for a hand I had never touched. So for a year I ate and walked and lived and slept with loneliness, until she was so familiar I came not to hate her but to know whatever happened in however many after years she alone would be faithful to me."

To this point, at least, Will's passage through life so closely resembles that of other sensitive, intelligent men of his class and generation that it could be called a typical fin-de-siècle experience, complete with spiritual crisis. The delicate child in a can-do society, overly self-conscious, comes slowly to manhood in a world shaped by a generation of aggressive, confident captains of business and industry. What can he, the pale epigone, do in this world that will possibly live up to what his father (or grandfather, or great-grandfather) did? Faced by such a challenge, many such youths found themselves at least temporarily becalmed, in the horse latitudes of career crisis, uncertain what to do next with their lives.

Will's own career uncertainties never got out of hand, thanks to a long-established family tradition. He would, quite simply, become a lawyer. Did he resist this foregone conclusion? His memoir suggests that he did not, even though he privately entertained literary ambitions. "All along of course I had a sneaking persistent desire to write, but I realized I had nothing to write about, being ignorant of man and of his home, this dark sphere, and even of that palpitating speck, myself." The excuse, while eloquent, seems somewhat disingenuous. After all, every apprentice writer must struggle with the problem of finding his subject, and the problem continues well beyond apprenticeship. Behind Will's decision lurks what one suspects was a larger doubt: his fear that a literary career was not really a respectable pursuit, at least not in the eyes of his father.

And his father's approval mattered terribly. Even though everything in his own nature militated against his becoming a man like LeRoy, Will, no rebel, tried desperately to live up to his father's expectations. Not in all ways, though. He found outlets for his differences. He made compromises between what he could be and what he thought he should be. And these compromises were not all bad.

In choosing a law school, for example, he shrewdly reconciled paternal expectations with his own interests. Rather than attending the University of Virginia, where his father and uncles had gone, Will headed off to Harvard, though not, as he freely admitted, for academic reasons. He knew that Boston offered a cultural life—particularly symphonies and operas—that he would not find in Charlottesville. He never regretted the choice. "I have enjoyed spells of more intense happiness," he wrote, "but never three years of as uninterrupted happiness as I did at the Harvard Law School."

At Harvard, too, Will made his first, unsuccessful attempts at romantic love. He dated several women during his years at Cambridge but grew particularly close to a Radcliffe student named Elsie Singer. But even with Elsie he came up against an impossible barrier—the inability to combine physical longings with his idealized notions of womanhood. Lewis Baker, referring to one of Will's Cambridge-era poems ("To Lucrezia"), interprets his plight in terms that Will himself would have approved. The problem, quite simply, was that Will invested his ideal woman with a purity that was beyond all human possibility. And according to an impossible logic, he believed that if a woman was attractive enough to excite him she could not be "pure." "Will's young lady friends could match this idealized version of pure Southern Womanhood only by being completely unattractive to him," Baker concludes. "Unable to find a middle ground between homely ladies and beautiful whores, Will remained alone."

This extreme idealization of women was not really so unusual among late-Victorian gentlemen. What makes it distinctive, however, is Will's solution. Instead of resolving the dilemma in the more usual way, marrying a virtuous maiden and rutting with "whores," Will chose to remain alone. He did carry on long platonic relationships with a number of women, including his cousin Janet Dana, but a certain remoteness was required in keeping them going.

Considering his inclinations and interests, it was remarkable how well Will fit in when he returned to Greenville. Actually, to say "fit in" diminishes his accomplishment, for he did not simply become the odd, marginal "bachelor" that every town tolerates. He became a leader, a widely respected voice, and even something of a local hero—no mean accomplishment for a man who was also, at least during his private time, a poet.

The poet in Will had even met with some success. During his last year at Harvard, McClure's magazine had accepted his poem "Winter's Night." Even though the poem did not appear until three years later, its acceptance was enough to convince him that he might have talent. Yet he was ambivalent about literary success; he insisted that the poem be published anonymously. Another chance development gave further encouragement to Will's literary side. The autumn after his graduation from Harvard, Sewanee lost its professor of English, John Bell Henneman, and asked Will to fill in for a semester. He accepted and, despite great self-doubt, proved to be successful and popular. His students, in fact, went to the unusual length of writing him a letter of appreciation at the end of the semester. Will could have stayed on, but reluctantly he decided that academia was not the life for him. His Greenville friend and mentor, the poet and teacher Carrie Stern, warned him that the pedagogical life would leave him little time or energy for writing. So he descended from the mountain, uncertain what life in Greenville would demand of him but ready to give it a try.

As it turned out, life in his Delta home demanded a great deal. As well as work in his father's law office, he was soon involved in his father's senatorial campaigns and then, in 1912, with flood relief efforts. He was quickly learning the Percy role, defending railroad and business interests, standing up for progressive measures, leading the perennial campaign for strong levees, helping out whenever his services were needed. He even felt closer to his father and savored their daily strolls to and from the office. Despite his many commitments, though, Will wrote and published more during this time than he would during the rest of his life. In addition to magazine acceptances, a volume of his poems, *Sappho in Levkas and Other Poems,* was published by Yale University Press in 1915. Thematically, these poems were the first articulation of his most cherished notions: the tragic incompatibility of spiritual and physical love, the inevitability of solitude, the nobility of defeat ("Glimpsing our kinship with the farther stars;/ Defeated always—but how splendidly!")

As successful as Will was in so many areas, he was not content. A mounting uneasiness, compounded by suspicions of his parents' disapproval of his literary ways, prompted him to spend part of 1916 in New York. But again, escape proved to be no solution. The big city swirl and rush were finally not for him. That left him facing a terrible uncertainty: What next? The question might have paralyzed him had the war in Europe not provided a temporary answer.

The Great War, as Paul Fussell and others have pointed out, was a shattering experience for the generation that lived through it. To them, and indeed to the generations that came after, Western culture would never be the same. Honor, glory, chivalry, the big abstractions, the noble causes—these would all henceforth be viewed with irony and suspicion by most postwar artists and intellectuals on both sides of the Atlantic. Not all of them, of course. There were bound to be exceptions, and Will Percy was one. For him the war had the ironic effect of confirming his deepest beliefs. Will was spared disenchantment because he entered the war believing that defeat and disillusionment were man's fate. This was partly his own personal credo and partly the legacy of southern history. Southerners, unlike other Americans, were well acquainted with the lessons of defeat.

At the same time, Will clung to the notion that the war was just. There was, in his eyes, a good side and a bad side, and the fate of civilization depended on the outcome of their struggle. Far more than many Americans, Will saw the Germans as the culpable party and the French and English as virtuous crusaders. But if Will embraced this rather Manichean conception of the war, there was one person very close to him who did not: his father. LeRoy Percy made it no secret that he thought the war was a tragic muddle, with all sides bearing part of the blame. Furthermore, he worried that Woodrow Wilson's naive idealism would eventually pull America into the war, despite the president's pledge to keep the country neutral.

It seems odd that Will, who normally thought his father so wise in the ways of the world, would in this instance have disagreed with him. Was it Will's one gesture of rebellion? It seems unlikely. Rather, one suspects, Will needed to believe the war was just in order to ennoble, or at least to justify, his more selfish motives for entering the fray. For what Will most deeply craved was a chance to live fully and dangerously, fighting for a noble cause. And if the cause was not all that noble, then he would at least make it seem so.

The situation became all but unbearable for Will when Janet Dana became a nurse and went to France in 1916. He had to do something. So he joined the Commission for Belgian Relief under Herbert Hoover. That proved unsatisfying, of course: all paperwork and no action. (Worse yet, it forced him to see that German "atrocities" in Belgium were trumped-up fictions.) Salvation loomed only when America entered the war in 1917.

He promptly returned home and enlisted. Underweight and frail, Will barely made it into officer training camp. Once in, he barely made it through. Sent to France, he served as an instructor in the Ninety-second Division (a division of black enlisted men commanded by white officers) before finally making it to the front as a staff officer in the Thirty-seventh Division. Though bitterly disappointed that he was not made a platoon leader, Will soon enough saw action. In the Battle of the Argonne and in various battles in Belgium, Will found himself on dangerous night rounds or bravely carrying messages between isolated units. Walking down shell-torn roads under intermittent enemy artillery fire, carnage all around him, Will overcame his terror with a grim fatalism. Even when shells rained down most heavily, he refused to duck, refused to break into a run. If it was his time, Will forced himself to think, it was his time. For his almost suicidal valor, he was awarded the Croix de Guerre. But the medal mattered far less than the experience, which he described as the "only great thing" he had ever been part of:

> That short period of my life spent in battle is the only one I remember step by step—as if it moved sub specie aeternitatis. Not that I enjoyed it; I hated it. Not that I was fitted for it by temperament or ability, I was desperately unfitted; but it, somehow, had meaning, and daily life hasn't: it was part of a common endeavor, and daily life is isolated and lonely.

The sentiments summed up in this confession came to constitute the core of Will's ethos, and echoes of it resound throughout Walker Percy's novels and philosophical writings. The horror of "dailiness" is in fact the starting point for many of Walker Percy's works, and if it is not the central problem it is always at least one of the problems. Similarly, the search for something equaling the intensity and purpose of war provides the direction of his narratives and of his philosophical arguments.

Why Will's ethos appealed to Walker is, of course, an important question. Quite obviously, Walker must have sensed that Will's profound dissatisfaction with everydayness was not altogether unlike his own father's. But while such discontent had led LeRoy Percy to an even more crippling despair and ultimately to suicide, it had not destroyed Will. Will had been able to live with it. He had overcome it, even mastered it. But how? The question was in no sense academic. For even at age fourteen, and probably from the moment he learned of his father's suicide in the summer of 1929, Walker had embarked on a search. "I didn't feel guilty or responsible the way some children of suicides do—I didn't feel that way at all," Percy once explained. "I was angry. And I was determined not only to find out why he did it but also to make damn sure that it didn't happen to me." Will, quite simply, was the first and most important part of Walker's education. The novelist would, in fact, never cease pondering Uncle Will's lessons—not simply his values but the example of his valiantly lived life.

Enduring existence on a diminished scale was perhaps the most urgent lesson. Will's solution, Walker and his brothers quickly saw, was a fierce commitment to the well-being of his little world, the town of Greenville and its inhabitants. War had been his moment on life's larger stage. As for big city life, he had sampled that before the war and found it wanting. Greenville, for all its limitations, became Will's best hope for involving himself in something larger than himself. An individual could make some difference in such a community. As proof, Will had the example of his own ancestors.

Ironically, though, the qualities that most distinguished Greenville, its tight sense of community, the supportiveness and tolerance among all its citizens, faced a severe threat during the postwar years. The demographic changes that were prelude to this challenge began even before World War I. Thanks to expanding economic opportunities in the Delta, poor whites from the hill counties had begun to come down and settle in places like Washington County. Baptists and Methodists, by and large, they took a dim view of the looser ways of river-town life, the gambling and whoring, to be sure, and even the drinking that most Greenvillians had long viewed as an established element of the good life.

The fundamentalists also reacted uneasily to the Greenville tradition of religious tolerance. The town's Jews, Protestants, and Catholics not only worked and played together—it was not considered remarkable, for instance, that one of LeRoy Percy's partners was a Jew—they also married each other. To the white fundamentalist set, this was wicked stuff. In the realm of race relations, however, the poor whites' reactions were conditioned less by moral than by economic and political considerations. They saw Greenville's large black population as a vast pool of cheap labor, exploited by rich planters and townsmen to keep the system tilted in their favor. They understood why the rich white folk treated the blacks so solicitously. To rise in the Delta, the poor whites realized, they would first have to push the black folk out. To that end, a little intimidation was viewed as desirable.

Given these potential conflicts, it was only a matter of time before some catalyst set them in motion. The agent proved to be the Ku Klux Klan. Reborn in 1916 thanks largely to the success of D. W. Griffith's racist extravaganza, *The Birth of a Nation,* the white (and Protestant) supremacist group swelled to a four million national membership by 1924. Nor did the membership consist strictly of marginal figures. In 1921, President Warren G. Harding had allowed himself to be sworn in as a Klansman.

Almost inevitably, the Klan arrived in Greenville, although at first it didn't pose much of a threat to the town's tranquility. The local klavern was small and secretive; it wielded little influence. In fact, few citizens paid the Klan much mind until early in 1922, when a successful circuit speaker named Joseph G. Camp secured permission to deliver a Klan lecture at the Greenville courthouse. A public address struck Greenville's "Old Guard" as too bold a bid for recognition. LeRoy Percy prepared a counteraddress and urged all his friends to be present for the March 1 meeting.

They needed little encouragement. By 7:30 that evening the courthouse was packed, and the atmosphere was charged. Camp stood up and delivered the standard attack against Catholics and Jews. But religion was not the main issue. Camp went on to say that loose morals were also a concern of the Klan. Henceforth, he warned, the klavern would be keeping a close eye on people's behavior. It was not a shrewd tack. The crowd began calling for Percy even before Camp had finished. When Percy stood up, he proceeded to give the finest speech of his life. Ridiculing Camp's ethnic tirades, Percy turned grave on the subject of spying. Nothing, he promised, would more quickly destroy the fabric of community trust and tolerance. The crowd was so worked up by Percy's impassioned peroration that Camp asked a deputy sheriff to escort him to his hotel. The deputy who ceremoniously obliged was, as Will Percy noted, "an Irish Catholic and the kindliest of men."

Percy's speech was such a triumph that word of it spread quickly throughout the South. Ministers and journalists commented on it; editors asked for copies of it. Even Boston got wind of it. The Atlantic Monthly's Ellery Sedgwick asked LeRoy to expand the speech into an article, and, with Will's unacknowledged assistance, he did so. "The Modern Ku Klux Klan" appeared in the July issue of the magazine.

If LeRoy's speech brought him national recognition, it could not stop the growth of the Klan. Nor could it calm all fears. In 1922 more blacks left the Delta than ever had before. Following his own advice, LeRoy organized a local Protestant anti-Klan committee, but tensions mounted even in Greenville, where Catholics were singled out as the special target. The reason, most likely, was that Greenville's klavern had originated in the local Masonic Temple, and the Masons, at least at that time, harbored strong anti-Catholic sentiments. A number of local Catholics suddenly found themselves fired from jobs or saw their businesses boycotted.

It was an ugly time, and even though violence never broke out, there was always the threat of its doing so. For two years, LeRoy and Will carried pistols, and on one occasion a few thugs made a clumsy attempt to abduct the senator. Will was so incensed that he paid a visit to the local Cyclops and made perfectly clear what would happen if any harm was ever done to his father. "I want to let you know one thing: if anything happens to my Father or to any of our friends you will be killed. We won't hunt for the guilty party. So far as we are concerned the guilty party will be you."

Ominous as the atmosphere was, it is clear from the tone of his memoir that Will cherished the struggle of these years. The campaign to defeat the Klan's candidate for sheriff verged on the intensity of war. "The whole town was involved," he wrote, "and the excitement was at a fever heat. You never knew if the man you were talking to was a Klansman and a spy. Like German parachute jumpers they appeared disguised as friends." As it turned out, the anti-Klan forces elected their man, George B. Alexander, a hunting friend of LeRoy's. The ensuing celebration, during which the victorious revelers consumed four kegs of whiskey and nearly destroyed the Percys' house, no doubt convinced the local Klansmen of their righteousness, but from then on their power in Greenville waned. If the conflict subsided, though, it was not easily forgotten. Resentment and hostility lingered. Even Will, normally magnanimous, found it hard to put it all behind him. "An old Klansman, one who, being educated, had no excuse for being one, asked me the other day why I'd never forgiven him," Will confessed, some eighteen years after the Klan struggle. "I had to answer: 'Forgiveness is easy. I really like you. The trouble is I've got your number and people's numbers don't change.' "

As Will became an increasingly responsible town elder, his standing as a poet grew, particularly in the South. With such postwar volumes as *In April Once* and *Enzio's Kingdom* as well as his appearances in a number of new southern literary journals (*The Double-Dealer, The Lyric, The Fugitive*), Will found a respectable following. It consisted partly of genteel readers who found Percy's formal and philosophical traditionalism sympathetic, and partly of other southern writers. Many of the latter, particularly "fugitives" like John Crowe Ransom and Allen Tate, were closer to the Modernists than to Percy in their literary strategies, but they found Percy a kindred spirit in his efforts to spark a literary renascence in the region that many Americans, notably H. L. Mencken, had dismissed as a cultural desert. Likewise, Percy could not always appreciate their experimentalism, but he believed they stood for what he stood for—the traditional agrarian values. Percy's recognition was not only regional. In 1925, Yale University Press invited him to become the editor of the Yale Series of Younger Poets, a position that he held until 1930.

Though Percy may not have enjoyed the reputation of other figures in what has come to be known as the Southern Renaissance, he was definitely part of what critic Richard H. King calls an "emerging self-consciousness in Southern culture." This awakening would ultimately issue in disillusionment during the 1930s, when writers like Percy realized that the old order was gone for good and that the code of honor could apply to personal conduct alone. This sense of disenchantment would in turn lead to some of the great works of southern literature, including Will's own memoirs. But during the 1920s there was still optimism that the best values of the old order might be preserved in the South, thereby sparing it the emptiness of modernity.

Of course, even in the 1920s, some southern writers were realistic enough to see that there was no turning back. Reviewing *In April Once* in the *Mississippian*, a young William Faulkner charged that Percy was "like a little boy closing his eyes against the dark modernity which threatens the bright simplicity and colorful romantic pageantry of the middle ages with which his eyes are full." The criticism is searingly apt, all the more so because it touches on the greatest weakness of Will's character—a willed blindness to certain realities. This blindness was nowhere more dramatically or consistently evident than in his relations with his father, the man who, in Will's opinion, could do no wrong. The psychological explanation for Will's adulation is perhaps too easy to adduce. After all, LeRoy was the idol before whom Will sacrificed almost everything that was vital to his own life. It would have been very hard indeed to scrutinize this idol too closely, and Will didn't, not even during what must have been the most painful test of filial piety in his life.

It came during the flood of 1927, the last of the truly great floods to inundate the entire Delta plain. It was, in fact, such a devastating flood that the federal government, through the agency of the Corps of Engineers, finally took upon itself the burden of building and maintaining the levees.

The pre-1927 levee system had actually been quite sturdy—stronger than it had ever been, to be sure. Residents of the Delta knew, however, that the heavy snows and rains of winter and early spring would put the earthen barriers to a severe test. For weeks before the break, Greenvillians patrolled the levees, on the lookout for telltale sand boils that indicated subterranean erosion. In April things began to get out of control about fifteen miles north of town, particularly at a place called Mounds Landing. A heroic sandbagging effort could not stop the torrent when the levee finally collapsed there on April 21. Within a day the entire Delta was covered with water ranging in depth from three to twelve feet.

Greenville's mayor appointed Will Percy chairman of the flood relief committee, and Will promptly set about requisitioning supplies and erecting a temporary camptown on the levees for folks fleeing from higher waters. Despite Will's best efforts, supplies soon began to run short. The only solution, he resolved with his committee's backing, was to evacuate people to Vicksburg, including some seventy-five hundred blacks camped on the levees. After arranging for two ships to come up the river to carry the black refugees, Will received a disturbing visit from his father. LeRoy announced that most planters were opposed to the idea of evacuating the black croppers from the county. Once out of the county, he explained, they might decide never to come back. Furthermore, the blacks themselves didn't want to leave. Will, for once, resisted his father. "I insisted that I would not be bullied by a few blockhead planters into doing something I knew to be wrong—they were thinking of their pocketbooks; I of the Negroes' welfare." Furthermore, Will concluded, the relief committee was behind his plan.

LeRoy asked Will to canvass the committee one more time. Will reluctantly agreed, although he thought it pointless. The members wouldn't have had any reason to change their minds. So while the boat captains waited angrily at the levee, Will convened another meeting. This time, he was "astounded and horrified" to learn, every committee member was against shipping the blacks downriver. Only after his father's death did Will learn what happened. Between his talk with Will and the committee meeting, LeRoy had gone to every member and talked them out of voting for Will's plan. He made them all promise, moreover, not to tell Will that he had approached them. Of this duplicity and Will's reaction, Richard King offers a shrewd assessment:

> Will's authentic paternalism, uncomfortable as it may make us feel, had proved powerless before the commercial considerations of his father's kind of people. Even more startling—and telling—is that Will Percy could not bring himself to register the hurt and sense of betrayal he must have felt at the contempt his father had shown.

It is telling that Will's recorded response to the discovery of his father's betrayal was little more than the bland observation that LeRoy was a "natural gambler" whose hunch was that things would work out better if the blacks remained. But perhaps it would have been more surprising if Will had evinced anger or bitterness. So much depended, finally, on a grand illusion. Will's father had to be the perfectly honorable gentleman.

4

Greenville Days

———◆———

The Greenville of that day was an old Southern town in one way, a pioneer town and river metropolis in another; there were Yankees and Italians coming and settling with families from Kentucky, the Old Dominion, imperial China; and there was the blues singing deep ground of the blacks. It was a melting pot, that Greenville. If only it could stay that way: Aware of itself, under the flow in and out, as the most visionary town of the South, a pole and axis of the soul's America.

——CHARLES BELL

The Greenville that Walker Percy came to in 1930 would have been a sight to please his great-grandfather's eyes. With over fourteen thousand inhabitants—and 108 Chinese grocery stores—it had become the prosperous commercial center the "Gray Eagle" had dreamed of. The two principal downtown streets, Washington and Main, were filled with one- and two-story shops and businesses as well as churches and a variety of municipal buildings. On work days, when trade was likely to be most brisk down near the levees where the cotton factors were, both sides of the downtown streets would be lined with automobiles—Packards, Hudsons, and Model Ts. Those who couldn't afford a car came to town on one of the eighteen passenger buses that daily traversed the county. Connections with the outside world were good, too—a fact that would have brought further cheer to old Colonel Percy. Nine passenger lines as well as several freight trains served the town each day, while steamboats belonging to the Vicksburg Packet Company stopped regularly at the waterfront. There was even a small local airfield for those daring enough to travel by plane.

The visible signs of Greenville's progress were impressive, but the town could boast of something more distinctive than its commercial activity: civic energy and cohesion, a distinct pride of place and community, and a remarkably vigorous cultural life. For these, Greenville could in part thank its colorful past, a history that included war and recovery, great floods, devastating epidemics (especially the yellow fever epidemic in 1878), booms and busts, and occasional civil strife. All of these trials had been faced by a citizenry who, despite differences of background and race (the town's 8,370 blacks still constituted the majority of the population), had managed to pull together and overcome them.

There were many other towns in the South that could claim similar histories, but few turned out to be quite as remarkable as Greenville. Anybody traveling through Mississippi during the twenties and thirties would have quickly noticed that Greenville was worlds apart from other towns in the Delta. The difference, quite simply, was that Greenville was more alive, more open to possibilities, and certainly more tolerant of differences than most small southern towns.

But why was this so? For one thing, Greenville had an unusually enlightened leadership, an assortment of businessmen, professionals, and planters who valued ideas, art, education. The Percys figured in the vanguard of this leadership, but they were not alone. Josephine Haxton, a novelist (known by her pen name Ellen Douglas) and former resident of the town, attributes much of Greenville's cultural vitality to the vigor and influence of its Jewish community. In formal and informal ways—as teachers in the public schools, as organizers of literary salons, as patrons of theater and music—the Jews of Greenville not only kept their fellow townsmen abreast of what was going on outside Mississippi and the South but they also made things happen locally. During the thirties and forties, Will Percy's house served as a gathering place for locals and out-of-town visitors who were interested in art and ideas, but to some extent Percy merely followed the example of his former mentor, Carrie Stern, whose informal salon had meant so much to an earlier generation of aspiring artists and intellectuals.

Another factor behind the town's specialness was the simple fact of geography. For all its expanding commercial vitality, it was still a rural town, a farming community, and its connection to the soil kept it close to its past. At the same time, its place on the river kept it attuned to movement, both the literal and figurative currents of change. If Greenville had not been where it was, after all, it would never have drawn the unusual mix of people that it drew. Its location made it a cultural crossroads, where a certain measure of cosmopolitan sophistication blended with more characteristic small-town southern manners and mores.

It has often been said, with some justice, that southern manners, the elaborate demonstrations of neighborliness, politeness, grace, are nothing more than an elaborate front, a charade of sociability masking an intense uneasiness about the uncomfortable reality of other people. Such manners were essential to the southerner's sense of honor; they were outward signs of an inner condition. Yet southern graciousness, as seen by Cash or Wyatt-Brown, often did nothing more than heighten the southerner's loneliness and his psychic distance from his fellows. Manners and mannerliness did not necessarily reduce all social exchange to empty ritual and even emptier chatter, but they threatened to—and they often did. Part of Walker Percy's fate, both a curse and blessing, was that he witnessed very early on the destructive consequences of the southerner's social predicament. An early product of the suburban New South, Walker Percy had seen southern manners acted out in their most baroque form. In the country club subdivision of Birmingham, he got his first intimations of alienation and rootlessness, the conditions that would later engage his philosophical and literary interest. As an impressionable boy, Percy had seen a world where politeness and façade could quite literally drive a person to despair and suicide, even as that person maintained the pretense of happiness and fulfillment. The lesson could not have been learned in a harder way.

Coming to Will Percy's house, and to Greenville, must have been something of a puzzle to the fourteen-year-old boy. Here he saw something that resembled the social style he had observed in Birmingham—the same mannerliness, the same politeness, the same busy social whirl —yet behind the familiar forms lay something different, something more substantial. The town was reminiscent of Five Points, the neighborhood his family had lived in before moving over Red Mountain. Like Greenville, Five Points had the same busy street life and a similar variety of people, but Will Percy's household was something altogether new and different. Walker couldn't put his finger on it at first. "What with a youth's way of taking life as it comes," he later wrote, "it didn't seem so extraordinary to be living with a bachelor-poet-lawyer-planter" through whose house regularly trooped "other poets, politicians, psychiatrists, sociologists, black preachers, folk singers, itinerant harmonica players."

The site of these goings-on was a large house on the corner of Percy and Broadway, two blocks south of Main Street and about five blocks from the river. At first the house itself seemed stranger to the boy than what went on inside it. Architecturally undistinguished, it had once been, as Percy recalled, "the sort of bastard Greek Revival popular in the late 1800s, a tall, frame, gabled pile with a portico and two-story Ionic columns." Apparently it had begun to show signs of wear in the twenties, because LeRoy and Camille had hired a contractor to spruce it up while they went off on a European vacation. Upon their return, says Walker, "they found it as I first saw it in 1930: stuccoed (!), the portico and columns knocked off, a large bungalow-shaped porte cochere stuck on one side, and a sun parlor, as it was then called, stuck on the other." The hybrid curiosities of the house's exterior were muted somewhat by the trees that surrounded it, oaks, sycamores, chinaberries, and dogwoods, and also by the gardens that Will so meticulously tended.

The inside of the house held surprises as well. There were dozens of odd "angled-off" rooms that seemed to Walker to serve "no known purpose," and there was a vast and dusty attic housing an impressive assortment of World War I memorabilia, helmets, rifles, and puttees. Perhaps strangest of all, the house had its own elevator, installed by Will's father, LeRoy, for his ailing wife, Camille.

The social heart of the house was the large living room that spanned the front of the ground floor. There Will kept his huge Capehart phonograph and an equally imposing record cabinet, filled with 78 rpm recordings that ranged from Bach to Stravinski. Behind the living room on one side stood the dining room, and between it and the kitchen was the pantry, always an interesting spot for the stray visitor or house guest. (The psychiatrist Harry Stack Sullivan, for example, a guest in Will's house while touring the South to study race relations, stationed himself in the pantry, sipping vodka martinis and eavesdropping on the whites in the front rooms and the blacks in the kitchen.) The other important room in the house was Uncle Will's book-lined study, where each day after work Will would meet the various supplicants who had come to ask for advice or money.

As Walker and his brothers slowly grew accustomed to the new setting, to the easy social ambience, so markedly different from the stiffness of their grandmother's world, they began to realize that by far the most remarkable thing about the house was the man who inhabited it. He was not simply the source of the best education the boys would ever receive; he would become the fixed point, the pole star, by which they would navigate their lives.

He was, the boys quickly saw, a man of strong judgments. Although generous to a fault in dealing with others, including many people he was not fond of, he seldom revised a low opinion of a person once he formed it. Bad character was bad character as far as Will was concerned, and nothing—neither the limitations of background nor the peculiarities of genius—forgave it. And there were no exceptions. When William Faulkner came to play tennis on the Percys' concrete court, he committed the unpardonable sin of arriving drunk for the game. Will held him in low regard ever after.

But there was something even more remarkable about Will than his strictness, and that was his solitary nature. As gracious and interested a host as Will was, he never seemed more himself than when by himself. Many was the time that Walker came across Will sitting alone in his study, pensively staring off into middle space, his index finger poised above his upper lip. The look on Will's face, Walker thought, was one of profound, inexplicable sadness. The fourteen-year-old boy felt a pang of kindred sympathy.

Always something of a loner himself, even back in Birmingham, Walker now carried the weight of a terrible memory that pushed him even deeper into his own solitude. And others in Greenville saw this in young Percy. "In repose," said one of his friends, "his face took on a certain sadness." The friend was Shelby Foote, a boy of thirteen when he first met Walker Percy. Although neither boy could have known it at the time, theirs was the beginning of a life-long friendship, the most important that either man would form. The fact that both men became writers and, in a sense, rivals makes all the more remarkable the resiliency of their bond.

Foote doesn't remember the moment he met Walker, but he recalls the day Uncle Will approached him at the country club swimming pool in the late spring of 1930. "He'd been playing golf—he was a dreadful golfer, but he liked to play occasionally in those days—[and] he came over and said, 'Some kinsmen of mine are coming here to spend the summer with me. There are three boys in the group and the two older boys are about your age. I hope you'll come over to the house often and help them enjoy themselves while they're here.' " Shelby eagerly obliged. Like most people in Greenville, he knew that Uncle Will's house was a special place, and the prospect of spending time there—whoever these kinsmen turned out to be—was exciting.

Uncle Will's intuition about human chemistry was, as usual, canny. Shelby would not have been the first choice of many Greenvillians. He put off many people with his manner—brash, cocky, sometimes rude. The consensus in town was that his mother and aunt had spoiled him, and there was doubtless some truth to the charge. An only child, he was strikingly handsome, with a shock of dark hair and deeply set eyes, and his easy self-assurance must have struck many adults as insufferable vanity. But Will had good reasons to think that Shelby would make a good companion for his cousins. He was an intelligent boy, for one thing, quick and clever. Though not prematurely bookish, he was certainly alive to the possibilities of good literature. Will was drawn to a boy with such a fine and promising mind, and apparently he thought that his cousins would be too.

There was something else about Shelby that made him seem a likely mate for the Percy boys, and especially for the oldest one. Shelby was a loner, quite content spending time by himself. Never athletic, he enjoyed some of the same solitary activities that Walker favored, particularly model airplane building and reading. A similarity of natures may have owed something to a similarity of backgrounds, for Shelby, too, had experienced the loss of a parent. In 1922, when Shelby was just two months shy of six, his father died of septicemia. The family was then living in Mobile, Alabama, and the boy could hardly have known his father that well. Yet, in some ways, the fiction that Shelby would one day write would be as much a pondering of his father's fate as Percy's would be of his. The story of Foote's father was somewhat different, though: a turn-about success story cut short by death.

Shelby Foote, Sr., had been a no-count rich man's son, a gambler and a boozer right up to the day he married Shelby's mother, Lillian Rosenstock. (Her father, Morris Rosenstock, a Viennese Jew and an accountant by trade, had made his way from the Old World to the Mississippi Delta in the 1890s, soon thereafter marrying the daughter of a prominent planter.) Lillian must have had a miraculous effect on Shelby's father. Shortly after they married in 1915, he suddenly turned serious and in seven years worked his way up from shipping clerk to general manager of the Armour and Company meat-packing firm. But as fate would have it, he had little time to savor his worldly success. The responsibilities of his new position took him to the coastal town of Mobile, Alabama, and shortly thereafter he succumbed to a bacterial infection that twenty-five years later would have been cured by a few doses of penicillin.

Shelby and his mother returned to Greenville, and there Lillian Foote and one of the boy's aunts, Maud Moyse, did everything in their power to shield the young boy from the loss—too much, most townsfolk thought. But Shelby still had to come to terms with the death on his own. He did so largely by withdrawing into himself and becoming strongly self-sufficient. No doubt, many adults interpreted his precocious self-possession as arrogance, and to some extent it was, but it was also an effective means of self-protection. Shelby also acquired a preference —invaluable to the future writer—for inhabiting his own self-created worlds, realms less subject than chaotic reality to the uncontrollable turns of fate.

Shelby was not the only Greenville youth to take up with the Percy boys. There were many others, most of them children of Greenville's upper crust. In addition to the Branton boys, Buddy and John, sons of a prominent planter, other regulars at Uncle Will's house included Harvey Kerr, Bob Quina, and Raymond Kimble. Donald Wetherbee, a bright, athletic boy whose father owned Greenville's biggest hardware store, came over often to play tennis and grew particularly close to Roy. A less frequent visitor was Charles Bell, whom Walker came to know well only in his last year of high school. Charles, the son of Judge Percy Bell, was an avid stargazer, a hobby that he shared with Walker. Like Walker and Shelby, Charles would go on to have a successful literary career, building through his poetry, fiction, and cultural histories a symbolic system as ambitious as that of the poet W. B. Yeats. As Bell later explained, it was in Greenville that he first acquired a sense of the "antinomies" that animated and drove human history. But back when that system was at most a dim intimation, he and Walker would repair to one of the upstairs rooms and peer at the distant heavens through the telescope that LeRoy Percy had once kept on his Birmingham porch.

The Percy boys quickly got involved in the routines of small-town life: days at the country club or other friends' houses, the occasional evening parties or dances, movies at the Paramount. But Walker proved quickly to be more of the housebody. He was quite happy sitting in the living room listening to recordings on Uncle Will's Capeheart or, on Sunday afternoons, listening to Toscanini conducting the New York Philharmonic on the radio. If Shelby came over they might listen to music together or retreat to one of the odd "angled-off" rooms upstairs to build model airplanes. Walker preferred to build planes that actually flew— ROGs they were called (for "rises off the ground")—while Shelby liked putting together the kind that were only to be looked at, objects, one might say, of aesthetic contemplation. Slight though this difference may seem, it prefigures the contrasting views of art that the two novelists later came to. Shelby would embrace formalism, art for art's sake, while Walker would arrive at a more utilitarian position, a belief that art must serve some higher end. If nothing is more serious than the games or hobbies we pursue as children, perhaps nothing more accurately reveals what we will become than the little details of our childhood pursuits.

By far, Walker's favorite activity was observing others, as almost everybody who has known him at any point in his life attests. Even Walker's Birmingham friends remember his way of hanging back in social situations, and this reticence became more noticeable in the close, gregarious society of Greenville. Quiet, self-conscious, he was always on the fringe, following what others were saying or doing, occasionally offering some wry comment on what was going on, a witty phrase or a name summing up a person. His friends thought Walker a shrewd judge of character, incisive, funny, and sometimes painfully accurate. But some people, and on occasion his friends, felt uneasy around him. What was going on in his head, they wondered, and why didn't he say more?

One person Percy did open up with was Uncle Will. Again, the connection probably grew out of a shared sense of solitude, but there were other reasons. For one, Will was interesting, full of strong opinions about art, people, the events of the day. After listening to the news in the evening, Walker would turn to his cousin and say, "Well, what do you think, Uncle Will?" And Uncle Will would invariably have an answer.

Will also treated Walker and his brothers to something that they had not experienced since the days back in Birmingham, when their father would read aloud to them from books like *Treasure Island* or *The Jungle Book* or even his favorite Conrad novel, *Lord Jim*. Like their father, and perhaps even more enthusiastically, Uncle Will treated his young cousins to spirited readings of his favorite poets, the Romantics in particular, and of course Shakespeare. Will had a way, Walker recalled, of pointing out the good parts. "Now listen to this," he would urge, his voice growing animated as he read on. Shelby Foote, who was often included in these sessions, remembers that they were the kind of readings that made you want to go home and read the poem or play yourself.

Percy was fortunate to be raised among people who valued reading aloud—people, indeed, for whom such readings were a vital part of daily life. The practice had a lasting effect, with consequences for both Percy's fiction and his philosophical and linguistic essays. Percy's attentiveness to the spoken word, to the spin that a voice gives to an utterance, to the ironies and other undertones that are detectable only in actual speech, has become a hallmark of his fiction, and it finds its philosophical analogue in Percy's probing of the uniqueness of the act of speech and the mystery of verbal communication.

As a boy, though, Walker simply took Will's reading and his wide love of literature as an encouragement to his own green interest in writing, an interest that had first shown itself when he sent off a story to *Liberty* magazine at age ten. Although Percy consistently disavowed any literary precocity, it would have been impossible for him to deny that, beginning in his teens, he inhabited a world in which literature shaped life, giving it, according to Will's taste, a romantic and tragic shading. Uncle Will, moreover, was not merely a lover of literature; he was a figure out of it. Many figures, in fact. Part solitary *penseroso*, part Romantic artist, part chivalric knight, he was a magnificent composite of types. Not that there was anything fraudulent or even artificial about these aspects of Will's personality. Will was no poseur. And as literary as he was, he was a man of great practical and common sense, an excellent lawyer, a man who could organize and execute, a leader.

To be sure, there were those who thought Will Percy a bit much. In Charles Bell's roman à clef, *The Half Gods* (1968), a number of Delta

Landing (Greenville) citizens view Uncle Hazlewood (Will Percy) as an overly precious, sissified aesthete, and they make liberal fun of his pretentious literary gatherings where he forces his guests to listen to his lugubrious verse. This, no doubt, was one opinion among certain Greenvillians, probably those who were excluded from Will's circle. The element of resentment is obvious. Others with less obviously spiteful motives registered similar reservations about Will's otherworldly aestheticism. Will Percy did so idealize the past, particularly the times and accomplishments of his forefathers, that he was bound to find the present unacceptable; and an element of escapism does figure into the pathos that he cultivated. But the young Percy cousins saw none of this. They felt only the highest regard for Uncle Will. His tragic view was certainly consistent with their own brief experience of life, and his Stoic commitment to duty and self-control in the face of inevitable defeat was a model they hoped to live up to.

Some might say that it was too hard and demanding a model, particularly for three young and highly impressionable boys. Their mother, Mattie Sue, might have sensed that Will's example, however admirable, offered no surcease from the sort of tensions that had made life back in Birmingham so difficult, indeed so lethal. Her husband LeRoy's determination to live up to his family's high standards of achievement contributed to the brutal bouts of anxiety and self-doubt that preceded his days in court. Whenever he lost a case, as Walker later recalled, the atmosphere at home was one of absolute gloom. His father's despair filled the house. In a profoundly self-destructive way, LeRoy felt that he could never do enough to be a Percy, a true Percy. We need only recall his profound disappointment at not being given the chance to fly in combat during World War I. Will, for his part, had an impressive war record, but he still felt that he was no less a failure as a Percy. Fortunately for him, he possessed greater resources for dealing with these self-doubts. For one, he had the ability to transform them into components of his Stoic outlook. Out of self-doubt and sadness, he shaped his twilight philosophy. But Mattie Sue must have feared that this world view, so beautifully articulated by Will in his work and personal example, might come to tyrannize her sons. Besides, as anyone could see, Will was not what one would call a relaxed man, and there were already great demands placed on his life. The boys would impose an added financial burden (one that would grow even larger), forcing him to work more at his law practice than he would have chosen to. More immediately, the presence of unruly boys jeopardized what little peace and solitude Will had. Tensions were bound to run high on occasion.

Mrs. Percy was herself in a delicate position, not quite the mistress of the household but in some ways the reigning female figure. Her sons all retained a memory of her discomfort. She never seemed to know what her role was in relation to the large and boisterous staff of servants or to the aunts who lived just across the street or to the constant flow of visitors and guests, some of whom stayed for months or even for years.

The servants themselves were an eccentric crew, whose oddness Uncle Will seemed not only to countenance but to cherish. Louisa Atkins, a three-hundred-pound cook, ruled the kitchen, growing more irascible as she drank her way through the day. When her muttering grew loud, others knew to avoid her, for her temper was fierce. Arcile Ross was the more equable housekeeper, but she was not opposed to a nip herself. Ernest Jones drove the car, a skill that Uncle Will never acquired. (Most machines, including typewriters, left Uncle Will in utter bafflement.) And then there was Ford Atkins, Louisa's son, an almost mythical figure to whom Will devoted a full chapter of his memoir. "In the South," Will wrote, "every white man worth calling white or a man is owned by some Negro, whom he thinks he owns, his weakness and solace and incubus. Ford is mine." Ford—or "Fode," as he pronounced his name—had worked successively as Will's golf caddy, chauffeur, houseboy, and then general factotum. But his true role was far more complicated than any job description suggests. He was fool, jester, and licensed truth-teller. He infuriated Will with his impertinence, but he also charmed and comforted him in ways no other person could. Will Percy tells the story of how, when he was showering one evening, Ford strolled into the bathroom, leaned against the door "in the relaxed attitude of the Marble Faun, and observed dreamily: 'You ain't nothing but a little old fat man.' " It was a truth so poignantly observed that Will could only sputter, "You damn fool." Will eventually paid Ford's way through mechanics' school in Chicago, and Ford ended up in Detroit, sporadically employed by various auto companies. Yet until Will's death, Ford would call when he was in trouble or out of money, and Will would immediately oblige. The link between the two men could never be fully broken. They knew each other too well—their strengths and weaknesses—and cared for each other too much.

As if there weren't servants enough in the Percy household, yet another one came onto the scene in the fall of 1930, shortly after Martha Susan and her three sons settled permanently into Uncle Will's house. Elijah Collier, who had worked for the Percys in Birmingham and who had stayed on at the house for a year after LeRoy's suicide working for the eccentric Margaret Busch, suddenly appeared at Uncle Will's door and asked for a position. Uncle Will said that he couldn't possibly hire another person. Lije volunteered that he would work for free. Will said that such an arrangement wouldn't work either, but he was incapable of turning down a heartfelt request: Lije became the gardener and took up residence in the garage apartment behind the house. For some reason, Will never warmed to Lije, perhaps because he was a poor gardener but more likely because he lacked the charm or wild eccentricity that he favored in his staff. The boys, however, were delighted to have the diminutive, rough-hewn Lije back in their midst. He had been the one rock of steadiness in Birmingham. Phin was particularly close to Lije, and the two resumed the games of cards they had played in Alabama. Many years later, in *The Last Gentleman,* Walker conjured the figure of Lije in the character of the Vaughts' servant, John Houghton, a portrait that captures the original's rough gentleness through his style of card playing:

> An ancient little Negro with dim muddy eyes and a face screwed up like a prune around a patch of bristling somewhere near the middle of which was his mustache, he was at least sixty-five and slim and quick as a boy. He had come from the deep country of south Georgia and worked on the railroad and once as a hod carrier. He had been night watchman for the construction company when Mr. Vaught built his castle. Mr. Vaught liked him and hired him. But he was still a country Negro and had country ways. Sometimes Jamie and David would get him in a card game just to see him play. The only game he knew was a strange south Georgia game called pitty-pat. You played your cards in turn and took tricks but there was not much rhyme or reason to it. When John Houghton's turn came, he always stood up, drew back and slapped the card down with a tremendous *ha-a-a-umph!,* just as if he were swinging a sledge hammer, but pulling up at the last second and setting the card down soft as a feather.

Walker clearly paid as close attention to the ways of the black servants as Uncle Will had, and in transforming them into fictional characters often borrowed some of Will's affectionate, though undeniably paternalistic, irony. Walker's fictional portrait of Lije did not fail to note that Lije was a lady's man from whose room at night would emanate the raucous shrieks and laughter of lovers at play.

In addition to the servants, who seemed at times to run the Percy house, there were, of course, the guests, Will's friends from Sewanee, New Orleans, New York, and other far-flung spots, as well as the endless string of celebrities, writers, poets, and sociologists. Many of those guests could more properly be described as nonpaying boarders. One semiresident was Bob Horton, a former University of Tennessee football star and an amiable, handsome man. A salesman of "Staff of Life" chicken feed, he was on the road much of the time, but the Percy house was where he hung his hat. An excellent golfer, he played with the boys, and during the summers he was often charged with taking them up to Will's house in Sewanee, Tennessee. He apparently had a strong crush on Mattie Sue, but Mattie Sue gave him no encouragement. He was quite a bit younger than she, for one thing, and besides, Mattie Sue was still too submerged in her grief to take much notice of anyone.

Not that Mattie Sue made much show of her suffering or confusion. Phinizy girls were raised in the Victorian ways of the stiff upper lip. One did not talk about one's feelings, or wear one's heart on one's sleeve. But the boys could see the pain. "My poor mother," Percy would always say whenever he mentioned her in later years, and he did not mean it in any formulaic way. Phin, who recalls very little about that first year in Greenville, does remember that his brothers fought a great deal—so much, it seems, that their mother could no longer stand it. "If you don't stop your fighting," she warned, "you will kill me!" To the boys, the threat did not sound rhetorical: That Phin remembered it, and remembered too that it brought his brothers' quarreling to an end, gives some indication of how literally they took her.

However tense things might have occasionally been, and whatever misgivings Mattie Sue might have had about coming to the heart of Percy country, the family seems to have adjusted. In the fall, the two older brothers were enrolled in the ninth and tenth grades of Greenville High School, while Phin entered fourth grade at the city's elementary school. Walker quickly discovered that the schools that Superintendent E. E. Bass had dedicated his life to building were a bit more challenging than Athens High or even Birmingham University School. Back in Athens, Walker had received 90s in all of his courses except Latin, in which he earned a very respectable 88. Similarly, the year before at B.U.S., he had received 90s in all his courses. But the going at Greenville High proved immediately tougher: In the first marking period of the first term he received Cs in all of his courses—plane geometry, English, physics, and Latin. The teachers were rigorous and demanding. One of them, Miss Mary Moss, the Latin teacher, awarded the former reigning Latin scholar of Birmingham University School a string of Cs (and one D) during his first year at G.H.S.

Even though he suffered a sharp drop in grades his first year at Greenville, Walker harbored no grudges against the teachers. To the contrary, he had only praise for them, especially for his plane geometry teacher, Miss Leila Mae Shell. It was she, he claims, who gave him an appreciation of the elegance of a geometric proof. To the teenaged boy who had vowed to figure out the world—and his place in it—the order and logic of geometry were a model of how the mind might proceed. This first initiation into what Pascal called the "geometric spirit" pushed Walker toward a search for other methods that promised a similar elegance and order.

But despite Walker's romance with geometry—in which he received a final grade of B—his first year fell far short of academic distinction. Socially Walker fared little better. He was, again, the invisible man, no easy accomplishment in a school of about 250 students and fifteen teachers. As was so often the case, Roy cut the wider swath. Walker's closest friend was Shelby, who was a year behind. "We just didn't take much notice of Walker that first year," said Camille Sarason Cohan, who was a class ahead of Walker.

Camille Sarason, one of the more gifted, attractive, and popular girls in the school, would play a decisive part in bringing Walker out of his shell the next year. Even more fatefully, she would linger in Walker's memory as an ideal of unrealized love. Camille came from one of Greenville's more prosperous Jewish families—her maternal grandparents had settled in the town in the 1890s—and she seems to have excelled in all she did. A good student, editor of the newspaper, a cheerleader, she was also strikingly pretty. Not surprisingly, she was one of the more sought-after girls in her class. (In fact, she usually kept at least two boyfriends on her string, one Jewish, to satisfy her mother, and one Gentile.) But while Camille enjoyed her popularity, she was in many ways a more substantial person than most Greenville belles. There seemed to be more to her—the quick flash of intelligence and a nimble mind—and Walker was as secretly drawn to this difference as he was to her more obvious appeals.

So powerful was this attraction, in fact, that it surfaced many years later, in his fifth novel, *The Second Coming*. Will Barrett, the bewildered seeker of *The Last Gentleman*, is here brought back to life, a successful retired lawyer but still unsuccessful in making sense out his existence and still haunted by buzzing memories from his distant Mississippi childhood. One such memory, breaking forth unbidden as Barrett stumbles around a golf course on a burnished autumn day in the North Carolina highlands, concerns a girl named Ethel Rosenblum:

> Instead of the brilliant autumn-postcard Carolina mountains, he seemed to see a weedy stretch of railroad right-of way in a small Mississippi town. It wasn't even part of the right-of-way, but no more than a wedge-shaped salient of weeds angling off between the railroad tracks and the back yards of Negro cabins. It was shaped like a bent triangle, the bend formed by the curve of tracks.

Only once in his life had he ever set foot on this nondescript sec-
tor of earth. It was shortly after he had seen Ethel Rosenblum. As he
took the shortcut home after school, walking the railroad tracks which
ran behind the football field, he saw Ethel Rosenblum practicing her
cheerleading. She was in uniform, brief blue skirt flared to show gold
panties. She was short, her hair was kinky, her face a bit pocked. But
as if to make up for these defects, nature had endowed her with such
beauty and grace of body, a dark satinity of skin, a sweet firm curve
and compaction of limb as not easily to be believed. She was smart in
algebra and history and English. They competed for four years. . . .

And while they competed, Barrett goes on to explain, he secretly longed
to tell her what he felt about her. But he could never bring himself to
do so. "Not twenty words had passed between them," Barrett laments.

Reticence, shyness, reluctance to act, fear of acting wrongly if one
does act—these feelings clearly tormented the young Percy as much as
they did Barrett. They also came to assume thematic significance in his
work. The theme of failed connections among people runs consistently
through Percy's novels, although he assumes varying stances toward this
problem. At most times, he seems to suggest that it is simply part of the
human predicament, part and parcel of man's fallen estate. At others,
he seems moved toward romantic utopian defiance (most blatantly in
The Second Coming, but in other novels as well). But this movement
remains largely in the character's own imagination, a wish unfulfilled,
and therefore a prod to further pain.

For her part, Camille Sarasson Cohan admits that briefly during her
senior year she had been quietly interested in Walker: "It seemed as
though he had shot up three feet that year." But he was a year behind
her, there were other boys pursuing her, and it would have been against
the rules of the game for her to take the first step. Although the romance
never happened, Camille did do one thing that slightly altered the
trajectory of Walker's high school career. As one of the editors of the
school newspaper, *The Pica*, she appointed Walker in the autumn of
1931 to write the gossip column, "The Man in the Moon Looks Down
and Says" (eventually shortened to "The Man in the Moon"). The
appointment was shrewd. Camille had recognized Walker's observant
eye. The choice had an obvious effect on Walker. It drew him out of
himself and into the social world of his peers, providing him with a kind
of footing, a role, even a curious sort of authority. In his first column,
which opens with a tidbit about Shelby Foote, the writer seems to enjoy
his elevated perspective, though with the appropriate measure of irony:
"These youngsters! What's the world coming to? G.H.S.'s own playboy,

Shelby Foote, is having a desperate affair with Miss Virginia Gibbons. She seems to be returning his love with infinite sincerity. They will soon learn not to take a thing like that so seriously."

Walker took such things very seriously himself, but seriously in a way that might to some seem rather perverse. From the time he began dating in high school up through his first years in college, Walker focused his amorous intentions, and attentions, on one girl. Her name was Margaret Kirk, and she was a belle's belle, "a very good looking girl," Shelby Foote observed, "and cold as an icicle." Between Walker and Margaret there seems to have been little spiritual sympathy, and even less physical intimacy. "Walker says he remembers all those damn corsages and he never got so much as a peck," Foote recalled. And it was not only corsages. The hapless suitor—who was known among his classmates as something of a one-man sonnet factory—dutifully wrote his girlfriend's poems for Miss L. E. Hawkins's English classes. All for little reward.

Why Walker pursued this unpromising relationship one can only conjecture. Dating her was, of course, something of a status-booster. Margaret Kirk was desired by many, and she knew it. It is obvious, too, that she conformed to a feminine ideal that Walker largely subscribed to. Her prim good looks and *noli me tangere* manner virtually defined her as a proper young lady. Her unattainability, according to the oldest of romantic formulas, heightened her desirability. Margaret Kirk, in short, fulfilled notions of femininity that were common throughout the genteel South as well as other parts of the country that were still shaped by lingering Victorian mores. Such notions certainly shaped Will Percy's idea of womanhood, and that of other Percys as well. Walker was heir to these notions, through both precept and example. His mother, as far as we can tell, was somewhat distant herself. Walker's pursuit of Margaret Kirk, then, while certainly not the stuff of tragedy, does point to a problem that he would have with women, both in his fiction and in his life, a problem in seeing the person behind the ideal. And though it can be argued that Percy was less slave to this ideal than some critics insist, he was at least partly enchanted by it. But enchantments have their uses in literature; they may even be essential to it.

This rather strained relationship aside, Walker flourished during his junior year. His grades improved, and he took on more assignments for the newspaper—feature articles, book reviews, and poetry in addition to his gossip column. The poems were highly formal exercises, ploddingly metrical and rigorously rhymed quatrains or sonnets, treating conventional subjects ("The Rainbow") or classical themes ("A Statue of Venus Speaks"). Echoes of Will Percy's influence sound throughout his young cousin's verse, not only in the formal qualities of the poems but also in the subject matter and themes. Will's passionate defense of the planters' way of life and the benefits of enlightened paternalism (first under slavery and now under sharecropping) comes through in Walker's cheerful depiction of blacks working in a cotton field:

> By plough-shares rude your fields were tilled
> 'Neath azure summer skies
> When happy slaves the warm air filled
> With drowsy lullabies.
>
> I like to watch the workers now,
> Or hear them singing low
> Behind the steel-lipped delving plow,
> Turning back the row.

In what might seem an act of blatant nepotism, but was almost certainly not, Will Percy, appointed judge of the high school literary contest, picked his own cousin as the winner. Will was clearly embarrassed by the coincidence, because he promptly told Walker that they were the "sorriest batch of poems" he had ever seen. The embarrassment, one may fairly surmise, did not come from dishonest behavior; Will would never have knowingly picked his own kinsman. The awkwardness more likely came from the belated recognition that he had chosen Walker's poem because it distantly resembled his own.

As well as reporting on the romantic vicissitudes of his schoolmates, Walker occasionally took on subjects of greater weight. One was a look at the local effects of the Depression, now well into its third year and showing no signs of abating. The piece was a feature article about a soup kitchen established on Main Street to provide for those citizens, mainly black, who could no longer put food on their tables. The jaunty tone of the piece is inappropriate; perhaps the Talk-of-the-Town manner was Walker's way of distancing himself from what was clearly a depressing fact of everyday life. At one point, Walker remarks upon the contrasting demeanors of the whites and blacks at the segregated soup kitchen: "Perhaps on glancing through a slot in the wall into the adjoining compartment, one may see one or two white customers, silently eating their share—silently and sullenly, in direct contrast to the cheerful manner of the happy-minded negro. None seem downcast or woe-begone, but rather cheerfully optimistic, as though their sole aim is to provide for the present day." Once again, Will Percy's influence is clear: the view of the black man as a creature of the moment was a fundamental tenet of his romanticism. As Will later wrote in his memoir, "The American Negro is interested neither in the past nor in the future, this side of heaven. He neither remembers nor plans."

It is not surprising that Walker acquired Uncle Will's paternalistic attitude toward blacks. Widely shared among prosperous white southerners, it would have been part of Walker's cultural heritage, even if he had not lived in Will's house. But the example of Will made the case for enlightened paternalism seem powerfully compelling. With Will, for one thing, it was not simply talk. On his Trail Lake plantation, about twenty miles from Greenville, he put his principles of moral management to practice. Of the some 150 black families on the farm, most were sharecroppers who received half the earnings of the cotton they raised. A small number were share tenants who received about three-fourths of what their cotton brought in. The gross average income per family during the mid-1930s, according to a University of North Carolina sociologist's study, was $491.90. "In addition," writes historian Jack Kirby, the sharecroppers "received 'free' housing, water, fuel, pasturage (for those owning animals), and a garden plot." The gardens were particularly unusual in the Delta, allowing the croppers to grow much of their own food. Most planters preferred to keep their croppers dependent on the plantation store for all the necessities of life, thus adding to the workers' indebtedness. Will, by contrast, was determined to keep his farm laborers free from the vicious cycle of debt that made sharecropping little better than outright slavery.

And because he was so determined, Will felt justified in waxing lyrical over the condition of his sharecroppers, comparing it very favorably with the plight of most modern workers: "Our plantation system seems to me to offer as humane, just, self-respecting, and cheerful a method of earning a living as human beings are likely to devise. I watch the limberjointed, oily-black, well-fed, decently clothed peasants on Trail Lake and feel sorry for the telephone girls, the clerks in chain stores, the office help, the unskilled laborers everywhere—not only for their poor and fixed wage but for their slave routine, their joyless habits of work, and their insecurity." It is not hard to imagine where Walker's jocund farm workers "singing low" came from.

At the same time, even Will realized that there might be flaws in his arcadian vision. Otherwise, he would not have made what is surely one of the most painful confessions of his memoir. It concerns a visit he made to the plantation on settlement day in late autumn, the day on which the croppers were paid for their work. As Will and his driver, Ford, drove up to the plantation store, they overheard one of the croppers say, "Whose car is dat?" Another offered an answer: "Dat's *us* car." Will mistook the remark for a statement of proud corporate identity—

what was his was also theirs—but on the way home Ford set him straight: "He meant that's the car *you* has bought with *us* money. They all knew what he meant, but you didn't and they knew you didn't. They wuz laughing to theyselves." Will Percy's willingness to report such episodes, even when they challenged his most fiercely held beliefs, is precisely what gives his memoir such force. His concern for truth was at least as powerful as his convictions, and indeed the tension between the two provides his book both with one of its more winning tones (lightly self-mocking) and with much of its drama. Will's ability to contain within himself such contrary impulses is also one of the things that made him an interesting man. Internal contradictions deepened him. And that depth is what made him such a powerful influence over people. Everything that he said seemed hard-earned. It is obvious, too, why such complexity was Will's greatest bequest to the writer that Walker would become.

However, during his high school years, Walker seemed more concerned with establishing absolute truths than with delving into complexities. He was looking for certainties, and though he attended Greenville's Presbyterian church along with his brothers, he did not find them in religion or even in the Stoicism of Uncle Will. He found his answers, increasingly, in science—or, more accurately, in that exaggerated faith in science that is called scientism.

The eventual shattering of Percy's faith in the scientistic dogma is an important story, but the question is how Percy came to the creed in the first place. These are hazy matters, never easy to pinpoint, but certainly some credit goes to sheer adolescent arrogance. We are all familiar with the world-weary teenager who has seen it all already. Walker was a variation on the type, a quiet, generally polite variation who only occasionally revealed his cynical omniscience. Will Percy probably deserves some credit for Walker's relative restraint. Will certainly would not have countenanced too flagrant a display of callowness, and he was too intelligent and witty to be the butt of even the brightest teenager's condescension. Walker and Will might differ on matters. In fact they disagreed strongly over Franklin Delano Roosevelt. (Will, from the earliest days of FDR's campaign, saw him as a champion of hope and believed that his leadership might deliver the nation from the Depression. Walker didn't. He took the bleak view that no man or program could help.) But such disagreements never diminished Walker's profound regard for the man. As a result, Walker's cynicism never assumed an obvious Oedipal character. Walker's main conflict, at least in his youth, was not with his surrogate father. The father Walker was struggling against was already a ghost.

Consequently, Walker's cynicism was less a social performance than an internal, intellectual struggle: His was a mind in quest of a mechanism not only to explain life but to free him from its fatal grip. Deeply troubled, even depressed, by the mess that life had already revealed itself to be, he was eager, as he later confessed, to figure out the mess in order to avoid being sucked down into it himself. His cynicism, then, was something more than a teenager's pose, another reason, perhaps, why it seldom became a performance. His cynicism came of real desperation and urgency, and it spurred him on to a search for knowledge that would free him from what he perceived as a dreadful fate.

The knowledge that first presented itself as a possible solution was science as a model of certainty. Geometry may have been the first step toward his conversion. But it is hard to imagine that his schoolwork was what pushed him decisively in the direction of his adopted creed. He took physics in the tenth grade (receiving a final grade of B), no science in his junior year, and chemistry in his senior year (receiving a C): far from a heavy dose, and far from a distinctive performance. The teacher of those courses was E. J. Lueckenbach, a rather stern, humorless man not noted for his inspirational qualities. Walker's catechism was less a matter of courses and teachers than of solitary casting about. And an important part of this hunt was his encounter with a book, a *Summa*-like tome whose heft was matched only by its authors' ambition. Entitled *The Science of Life*, it was written by H. G. Wells and Julian S. Huxley and first published in 1929. Wells was known for his science fiction, but he was also an ardent champion of progress. He believed, that is, in its inevitability, as long as men got their minds in order, behaved rationally, and accepted their place in the natural order of things. Explaining that place was precisely what he, and the biologist Julian Huxley, had in mind when they set out to write their book.

Wells had already proved himself as something of a world-class village explainer. In fact, the new book was conceived as a sequel to his earlier, highly successful *Outline of History*, written, the author explained in the preface to *The Science of Life*, to show "all history as one process." Wells's aim had been to supplant earlier conceptions of history, such as those based on religious texts, classical literature, and tendentious national records, with the cold, hard facts. His touching faith in historical objectivity was fully in keeping with the positivist tenor of his time. Now, Wells and Huxley proclaimed, "ordinary man seems to need the same clearing up and simplifying of the science of life that the *Outline of History* and its associates and successors have given to the story of the past." Accordingly, in 1,514 pages, the authors' "precis of biological knowledge" covered everything from the structure and behavior of the lowliest single-cell organisms to the complexities of human mental function.

Walker emerged from *The Science of Life* a true believer. Life, he thought, was explicable. All one had to do was master the methods of science, become an authority. Immunity from life's buffetings was then almost assured. Although this was not the Aurelian Stoicism of Uncle Will, Walker's scientism produced a similar result: internal resilience, an ability to bend without breaking before fate's hardest blows.

Fate took a very hard turn in the spring of 1932.

On the morning of April 2, Mattie Sue decided that she needed to escape from the house for a while. She had good reason for wanting a little break. Her mother, Mrs. Billups Phinizy, had been in town for several days; the tempo of social life, always high at the Percy house, had been even higher. So around noon, she grabbed her ten-year-old son, Phin, and set out for a little spin in her Buick coupe. Away they whirled, in the direction of Metcalfe, to the northeast of Greenville. Phin recalled that the atmosphere in the car was somewhat tense. His mother said nothing and seemed at once distant, preoccupied, and upset. He didn't know what, if anything, was bothering her. Nor could he understand why, sometime around 12:30, she decided to turn off the main road onto a dirt lane that led to the house of a family named the Metcalfes. Although the Metcalfes were friends, Phin's mother had said nothing about paying them a visit. Nor did she now. Phin wondered whether she was using their road to turn around. It seemed not, because she continued at least two hundred yards down the road and started over a wooden bridge that spanned Deer Creek.

Then came the worst surprise: The left wheels of the Buick went over the side of the bridge, and before Phin realized what had happened, the car had plummeted about twenty feet into the water of the bayou. Phin screamed, but his mother seemed not to move. The car quickly filled with water, and Phin took hold of his mother's hand. Mattie Sue squeezed her son's hand in response, but she didn't speak, didn't move. Though hysterical, Phin saw that the only way out was through the right rear window. He tried to pull his mother with him as he crawled over the seat but he lacked the strength. Was she trapped behind the wheel? Why wasn't she coming? He didn't want to let go of her hand—and in fact he couldn't, because her grip was as tight as his own. Crying, he pulled in vain, now certain that both of them would drown. Then her hand went slack. He didn't want to leave his mother, but he had no choice. Crawling through the window, he paddled to the shore and ran back to the main road, uncertain of what he was doing, delirious really, sobbing as he ran down the road. Presently—Phin could not recall how long it was—a pickup truck came along and stopped. Phin climbed in and managed to make clear to the driver, an elderly man named Eddie Lafoe, what had happened. They drove back to the bridge, but by then other people were on the scene. They had pulled Mattie Sue from the car and were trying to revive her. An ambulance came next, and its crew tried its pulmoter resuscitator. Nothing worked. By then, too, Uncle Will had arrived and arranged for someone to take Phin back to the house.

And then a horrible coincidence occurred. Walker and Phin's brother Roy Percy was driving along the same road with his friend John Branton. They saw the crowd, stopped, got out, and started toward the bayou. Will saw the boy and tried to cut him off before he could get too close: "You boys shouldn't be here," he said firmly. "Get on home, now. I'll talk to you soon." But it was too late. As he staggered back to the car, tears streaming from his eyes, he muttered in stunned disbelief, "It's my mother, my mother . . ."

Will did talk to all the boys as soon as he got back home. He told them that their mother was dead. He told them, too, that he would take care of them, that he would adopt them as their legal guardian. He also made them understand things that he could not put easily in words: that he was with them in their loss, that he loved them, that he would do all that he could for them. "Uncle Will couldn't walk away from anything that looked even remotely like a responsibility," Roy Percy later remarked. The boys were a responsibility, and a big one at that. But Will made it clear that they meant much more to him than that.

Martha Susan Phinizy Percy was buried the next day. Services were held at the Percy house, conducted by the pastor of the First Presbyterian Church. The whole town grieved at the loss of a lovely, quiet woman. But grief is not incompatible with gossip, and soon rumors were flying. Perhaps the strangest one to surface was recorded in the diary of George Waring Ball, a rather eccentric man who moved in the Percy circle. "When taken from the car," he wrote in his April 3 entry, "she was dead, but it is conjectured that she may have died of heart failure. She was a very sweet young woman, and we were fond of her. We had hoped that she and Will might marry. Tragedy pursues the Percy family like Nemesis." Ball's "we" must have been a very small group. Most people who remember Will and Mattie Sue saw no signs of a romantic attraction.

Questions about the circumstances of the accident remain less well resolved. The conjecture that Mattie Sue died of heart failure appears to be no more than conjecture. But another theory, as dark in its implications as it is groundless in fact, still animates discussion. The "dark" view—which no Greenvillians from the era openly ascribe to but which all feel compelled to relate—is that Martha Susan committed suicide and that she intended to take her youngest son with her. Anything is possible, of course, and Mattie Sue had been behaving strangely that morning. But car accidents, as she well must have known, are a poor means of suicide. More significantly, before the accident, no one saw signs of heightened stress or depression in Mattie Sue. And even if she had been in private despair, it is highly unlikely that she would have endangered her own child. Only in the depths of sentimental delusion could she have imagined her youngest son better off dead with her than alive without a parent, and again, there is no record of such self-deluding behavior. To the contrary, she was known as a sensible Phinizy.

The most interesting thing about the implausible "dark" view is that it arose at all. Its creation seems to have satisfied a communal need for myth, hinted at in one of the lines from Ball's diary: "Tragedy pursues the Percy family like Nemesis." The Percys—like the Kennedys of more recent times—were the kind of people to whom tragic things happened, almost had to happen. The catastrophes in a way confirmed their standing as figures of distinction. That Mattie Sue was a Percy by marriage seemed not to matter. She still had to bear the fate of the House of Percy —or so the suicide rumor would suggest.

The rumor-charged atmosphere of Greenville did not make Will's task of comforting the boys any easier. Phin, understandably, had the roughest time. At night he would often wake up screaming and crying, terrified by strange, almost metaphysical dreams about the nature of time: When did it end, when did it begin? Will, who had moved Phin into his suite of rooms on the first floor, would get up and read to Phin, usually from the Greek myths, including the myth about Chronos and the beginning of time. When school was over he took Phin north to Johns Hopkins to be treated by a psychiatrist, a treatment that apparently was successful. As for the other two boys, Will decided to send them off on a trip, a grand tour of the West, with his secretary, Mitchell Finch, in charge. A Greenville schoolmate, Billy Francis, also went along. The travelers followed an ambitious itinerary, touring several of the large western parks before making their way to San Francisco, a city that Walker was immediately dazzled by. He was struck by the usual sights, the plunging streets, the charming Victorian houses, the crispness of the colors in the clear Pacific light. But by far the most exotic thing about the city was Chinatown. It left such a strong impression that he wrote an article about it for The Pica the next fall. He described its maze of alleys and small shops, its self-government, and even its telephone exchange.

("Twenty-four girls are employed who remember every subscriber's name," the observant reporter recalled.) Not content with surface description, he also attempted to define the "three branches of Chinese religion" and to explain why younger Chinese were abandoning the faith of their fathers for Christianity. Walker's early ventures into popular sociology were, to say the least, ambitious, a blend of colorful detail and romantic idealization.

Beyond the San Francisco experience and other specific memories, Walker took from his trip an abiding fascination with the West. Its sheer physical vastness and open space inspired a heady feeling of freedom, a sentiment that he would later, under the influence of Kierkegaard, label as one of the causes of despair, the despair of pure possibility. To the sixteen-year-old boy, however, the West felt like a pure, exhilarating release from the entanglements of the past. It was a zone of timelessness, outside history, where life could be invented, or reinvented.

The Walker who came out of this experience, while still somewhat quiet and stand-offish, cut a more commanding figure. Even before the summer trip, his peers had begun to pay attention to him, their interest piqued as much by the family tragedy as by Walker's brave manner of bearing up under it. "It was as though he'd suddenly grown three feet," said Camille Sarason Cohan. "We really began to notice him then." The lanky six-footer with curly brown hair, wide forehead, and clear blue eyes already seemed launched on some sort of journey. He still sported around with his friend Shelby, going to the Paramount Theater on Main Street after school or to the Fountain Terrace for a soda or simply driving around the Delta in Uncle Will's Model T. He still went, with his usual reluctance, to dances at the American Legion and other halls about town. And he still spent long hours around the house, listening to Uncle Will or observing the endless parade of visitors.

But in certain small ways, Walker was beginning to be his own person. One indication of this growing independence was the onset of a long disagreement with Uncle Will over a matter of national politics—specifically, Franklin Delano Roosevelt and the election of 1932. Uncle Will, not surprisingly, saw much to admire in the candidacy and person of FDR. Here, after all, was a patrician-politician, much in the mold of the late Senator Percy and indeed, of several other distinguished Percys in the ancestral line. As well as embodying the spirit of noblesse oblige, FDR had ideas that advanced the responsible-government spirit of the old Progressives in ways that a Percy would predictably find admirable. Most Percys, that is. Walker's dissent may have been a token gesture of rebellion, but more likely it issued from those deeper psychic dispositions that ultimately shape all political creeds. Whatever the case, he took sharp issue with Uncle Will's optimistic view that FDR would bring about a change for the better. With a vehemence that Walker himself would later wonder at, he insisted that no person could change things, that events would run their course regardless of personalities, and that all would be better off if they accepted the fact. Walker seemed to view Roosevelt as something of a scoundrel simply because he gave people hope.

Walker's stance is striking not least because it made him seem even more the Stoic than Will himself. It was the boy who was asserting that "a tide in the affairs of men" made individual efforts all but fruitless. Beneath this fatalism, one senses something else, a disenchantment with mankind itself. Walker, at a relatively early age, had looked at his fellow creatures and found them sorely wanting. Given the circumstances of his life, the verdict is not so surprising. But such hard judgments are always deceptive matters, sometimes masking feelings that run in contrary directions. At the very least, they reveal a strong preoccupation, if not obsession, with the very thing they seem to condemn.

In fact, it might have been more surprising if Walker had not developed an ambivalent attitude toward exceptional people. A preoccupation with heroic achievement was part of the Percy family atmosphere, and it had to be clear even to the teenaged Walker that it was something of a curse. If a Percy did not accomplish something heroic in his lifetime, as we have already seen in the examples of Walker's father, grandfather, and Uncle Will, he began to feel like an abject failure. And even before arriving at the dread certainty of such failure, a Percy had to wrestle with vexing questions: What constituted a heroic life or even a heroic act? What were the possibilities of heroism given the decreasingly heroic tenor of the world (except, of course, for the occasional interludes of war)? The question of heroism confronted Walker and his brothers not only in the example of their forefathers—Civil War officers, Klan-defying politicians, and World War I medal-winners, among others—but also in the literature they were fed. It was a literature almost tailor-made to induce hero-anxiety. In addition to Uncle Will's favorite Romantic poems and Shakespearean plays, the boys had got a strong dose of Joseph Conrad from their father, and particularly of his favorite Conrad, *Lord Jim,* a work that dealt directly with doubts about heroism, bravery, and the heroic life.

It is little wonder, then, that Walker, at this difficult time in his life, so thoroughly repudiated a man whom most Americans already regarded as a potential savior and national hero (and who won by a landslide in the November 1932 election, receiving 22,821,857 popular votes compared to Herbert Hoover's 15,761,841). Walker needed very strongly to believe that such white knights did not exist, that the age of high honor and great deeds was over. It took the pressure off him to think so. But what is denied or repressed has a way of returning. Walker's antiheroic fatalism was only a temporary release from the pressure that the sixteen-year-boy was already beginning to feel.

Returned from the trip West, Walker had a good autumn at Greenville High School, although, like everyone in town, he was saddened by the death of E. E. Bass on November 12. As superintendent of the schools for forty-nine years, Bass was the person most responsible for the excellence of education in the Delta town. Even more, he was a powerful example of the kind of person Uncle Will most valued: a man who was devoted to his community. "He learned to love life," Will said in the eulogy he delivered at the high school. "He gave as much warmth and radiance as anyone I know. His was the near perfect life."

Despite all the recent sadness, the tempo of life remained high. Greenville's troubled and down-and-out continued to troop through the house during Will's late afternoon receiving hour. They would come to his study on the first floor, spill out their hearts, and Will would give them advice or money, and often both. Friends and visitors always seemed to be dropping by or staying over, and a new long-term boarder joined the ménage, an aspiring writer named David Cohn. Cohn was an unusual man. A Greenville native who had gone off to Yale, entered business, and by the age of thirty-two, become president of Sears Roebuck-Feiblemann in New Orleans, he had decided to shuck it all for writing. In 1932, he came to Uncle Will and asked if he could stay for the weekend. He ended up staying for two years, hammering away at his typewriter until he completed his first book, a Delta memoir entitled *God Shakes Creation* (1935). Cohn had a lively mind, was interested in everything, and cultivated an extensive network of friends throughout the South and the Northeast. Among those friends was Ellery Sedgwick, the editor of *The Atlantic*. In the early 1920s, Sedgwick had remarked to Cohn that Greenville had produced more writers for a town its size than any other town in the world—an evaluation that, if anything, became truer during the next three decades. Cohn, it seems, was bitten by the desire to make his own contribution to Greenville's literary flowering, and once he set his mind to writing he produced not only books but a stream of articles on subjects ranging from race relations to the tariff for magazines that included Sedgwick's own *Atlantic*. Apart from its intrinsic worth, Cohn's first book may have had some influence on Will's decision to write his own "recollections of a planter's son."

The importance of a community of writers to the individual writer was something that Walker may have begun dimly to discern in that most literary of households in that most literary of towns. Many years later, in an essay on Melville, he would articulate what the youth only intuited: that as "lonely as is the craft of writing, it is the most social of vocations. No matter what the writer may say, the work is always written to someone, for someone, against someone." One boon to the northeastern writers of the nineteenth century, Percy explained, was their intensely shared "community of discourse," something that southern writers did not begin to acquire until the twenties and thirties of the twentieth century. Walker could write those words with authority, having spent his adolescence in one of the places where the southern literary community took shape.

During the early 1930s, Walker's contribution to the southern literary community was restricted to the pages of *The Pica*. Thanks partly to his efforts as one of the feature editors, the paper took first place in the Mississippi High School Press Association contest, a competition judged by the staff of the journalism school at the University of Missouri. Walker took the laurels for poetry, having shown himself to be an able versifier who set his fledgling enthusiasms to meter and rhyme: "Past moons, past suns,/ Past infinity/ He plunges deep and shuns/ The false reality," ran the opening lines of his ode to Einstein.

Some lines Walker came to wish he had never penned. His friend Shelby would rib him almost to the day of his death for winding up one poem with an image of the Mississippi River winding serenely southward under the sun, "Sweeping to the south in a coat of many colors." Walker contributed more than his share of articles, too. "The Man in the Moon" continued to report on various puppy loves, including that between his brother and Sarah Farish. In a less frivolous vein Walker wrote about soup kitchens, race relations in South Africa, and even his English teacher, Miss L. E. Hawkins.

As they did in his junior year, Walker's grades in his senior year reflected a decisive improvement over his sophomore performance. At the end of the first term, he received four As and one B in his academic courses, grades that really meant something back in the days when a high mark was as hard to earn as a dollar. Roy's school performance, by contrast, proved to be less than satisfactory in Uncle Will's eyes. In fact, Uncle Will had tried to enroll him in Episcopal High School in Alexandria, Virginia, at the beginning of Roy's junior year, but there had been no openings. After the first term, however, a place became available, and Roy headed off to Virginia after Christmas vacation, leaving behind a broken-hearted Sarah Farish, the girl who not many years hence would become his wife. For the first time Walker was separated not only from a close companion but also from his oldest rival. Like most brothers, Walker and Roy were competitive, and while Walker could best Roy in most academic areas, Roy held sway in all sports except tennis. (Walker, like his mother, had a powerful stroke, and his game steadily improved on Uncle Will's court.) In another area, too, Roy outshone his brother: He was always the more popular of the two.

Walker's ease with books was a cause both of astonishment and envy to his brother. On one hand, Walker never seemed to study; he breezed through his schoolwork. Yet he was always reading something, and whenever he picked up a book or a magazine, he was lost to the rest of the world. As his youngest brother, Phin, once remarked, Walker's powers of concentration were total. It hardly mattered whether he was in Will's noisy living room or on the crowded porch up at the Sewanee house, nothing could break the bubble of his concentration. And Walker read just about anything. When he wasn't taking in some book about science or scientific heroes, he was reading one or another book that Will had recommended, a literary classic or the current middlebrow best-seller. Books were a solace and refuge—and clearly a strong compensation for his limited tolerance of society.

As the school year wound down, the question of college arose. For some reason, the halls of higher learning most favored by earlier Percys —Princeton, Sewanee, and the University of Virginia—were ruled out. According to Shelby Foote, Uncle Will at that time considered the two most promising schools in the South to be Rollins College in Florida and the University of North Carolina. Walker applied to and was accepted by both, but he decided upon Carolina, probably because of Uncle Will's admiration of its progressive president, Frank Graham. Walker, as things turned out, would not be heading to Chapel Hill alone. His friend and classmate Don Wetherbee had been toying with the idea of enrolling in Duke, but when he heard that Walker was going to Chapel Hill, he decided that he might as well go there too. Different though they were in many ways, the two boys agreed that they would be roommates.

After the fifty-seven members of the Greenville senior class graduated on June 1, Walker and his brothers settled in for a summer of indolence. The Greenville routine of country club swimming and golf, dances, parties, and general "helling about the Delta," as Shelby called it, was broken only by a chaperoned house party up at Uncle Will's Sewanee house. Actually, the house was owned by Will and his college classmate, Huger Jervey, a successful New York City lawyer and a professor at Columbia Law School. Both Will and Huger had retained such fond memories of their college days and were so attached to many of the people who lived or vacationed up on the "Mountain" that they decided to buy a stucco cottage about three miles from the campus of the University of the South. It was a comfortable-sized house with a big living room and dining room on the ground floor and about six bedrooms upstairs. In addition, there was a large porch off the front and the side of the house, a perfect place for lounging in hammocks and rocking chairs. The house was named "Brinkwood" because it sat only about fifty yards from the precipitous edge of a large cove that ran like a gaping seam through several miles of the Cumberland Plateau. Called Lost Cove, it was densely wooded and full of caves and crevices, a wild stretch of territory fit only for four-legged creatures and the occasional mountain hermit. Transposed to North Carolina, it would serve Walker as the setting for the amnesiac wanderings and nearly suicidal spelunking of Will Barrett in *The Second Coming.*

The idea of the house party was an attractive one. Accompanied by Mrs. Farish, the wife of Will's law partner, Roy, Walker, Shelby, and their respective "dates," Sarah Farish, Margaret Kirk, and Mary Elizabeth Yates, would spend three cool, fun-filled weeks at Brinkwood. There was plenty to do. They could go on hikes, have picnics down by the "Natural Bridge," the cove's biggest tourist attraction, or have a refreshing swim in a nearby pond. In the evening, they could entertain themselves with cards and other games. And through it all they would barely have to lift a finger. A couple named the Harrisons took care of the grounds and did all of the cooking and cleaning. It should have been idyllic, but things quickly went awry. Everybody began to grow a little stir-crazy, and Shelby turned devilish. At one point, he began swinging Mary Elizabeth in one of the hammocks and refused to stop when she asked him to. Finally, in a towering rage, she screamed for someone to come pull Shelby away. Everybody then turned on Shelby, who seemed to grow only worse. Things went downhill after that. Sarah returned from a grocery trip only to find the boys throwing grapes at a photograph that they had stuck on the wall: The photograph was of her. That Roy and Sarah's romance survived this disastrous vacation was probably the first harbinger of their eventual and successful marriage. Walker, for his part, took from the experience a valuable personal lesson: Henceforth, he would avoid as much as possible all social entrapments, particularly those from which it was impossible to escape.

If Walker left that particular Sewanee trip with a bad taste, he did not lose his affection for Brinkwood. It was a place that he would come to often in the years ahead. Not only did he love the setting—it was a bird-watcher's paradise, for one thing—but he formed fast friendships with many of the part- and full-time residents. One of them was Robert Daniel, the adopted son of Charlotte Gailor, Will's close friend and the daughter of Bishop Thomas Frank Gailor. With Robert, a literary man who later taught at Kenyon and other universities, Walker knew he could always find a good intelligent discussion. It was in Sewanee, too, that Walker first met Allen Tate, Caroline Gordon, Andrew Lytle, and the various writers who would drift in and out of—or sometimes just around—the Agrarian movement. Apart from literati, there was a host of "Mountain" characters, including Abbo Martin, a kind of uncredentialed professor at the university. Martin lived in the SAE house in the summer and was always glad to entertain Walker and Shelby when they came by the campus. All in all, Sewanee was a place that interested Walker. It had a character, a thickly Episcopalian, upper-class southern character mixed with a little mountain madness and abandon. An unresolved character, in other words, of the sort that Walker took pleasure in trying to read.

As summer drew to a close back in Greenville, Walker had good reason to feel some uneasiness about what was to come. Having had life pull the rug from under him twice, he knew how lucky he was to be in the house of a man like Uncle Will. But he knew he couldn't lean on Will forever; in fact, he was already moving away from Will, and not only in his political views. Now, however, Walker was going to have to set his own path, and the stakes were high. The challenge was to avoid the dismal end that both his father and grandfather had come to, despite their worldly success. The challenge was to achieve success *and* happiness, or at least success and equanimity.

To that end, Walker had already made some decisions about where he was heading. Since science would eventually explain everything, including the unhappiness of man, the best way to proceed in life, he believed, was to be in the vanguard of science. As a convinced convert to this secular gospel, Walker knew that the core of his undergraduate studies would be a scientific discipline. And since one of the careers that issued most logically from such studies was medicine, he decided that he would become a doctor. In later years, Walker used to suggest that Will more or less determined the careers of his charges: Roy was assigned farming, Phin a military career, and Walker medicine. But no such assigning of roles was necessary. Walker and his brothers knew which professions were open to people of their station, including, notably, the law, the military, gentlemanly farming, the ministry, and medicine. Walker feared getting anywhere close to the law, seeing it as one of the main causes of his father's unhappiness (as well as Will's). He knew that he was not fit for the military, and he had no interest in running a huge farming operation. That left the ministry—the main qualification for which he, an agnostic, lacked—and medicine. But clearly the choice of medicine was more than a matter of elimination. It was a career that Walker believed in.

And what about literature, the world of novels and poetry and essays that Walker had been introduced to by both Will and his father? By the time Walker left Uncle Will's house he had already read—and read carefully—books that most boys his age had never heard of. Conrad's *Lord Jim,* Romain Rolland's *Jean-Christophe,* great chunks of Shakespeare, and the Romantic poets formed just part of his literary diet. Shelby recalls Walker being tremendously impressed by George Santayana's novel, *The Last Puritan,* and though Walker's favorite Russian was at first Tolstoy, he also read Shelby's favorite, Dostoyevsky. In his choice of a scientific career, Walker even fancied himself as a kind of Ivan out of *The Brothers Karamazov.*

Walker's great literary discovery during the summer of 1933 was *The Sound and the Fury,* and though his infatuation with Faulkner was far less acute than Shelby's, it would be strong enough to have a disastrous effect upon the English placement essay that Walker would have to write during his first week at Chapel Hill.

Another novel that Walker devoured, Sinclair Lewis's *Arrowsmith,* further confirmed his ideas about his future profession. Lewis's novel of 1925, as well as satirizing the philistine values of middle-class America, celebrates the new field of scientific medical research. The embodiment of this brave new world of scientific medicine is the character Max Gottlieb, patterned closely after the famous Jacques Loeb of the Rockefeller Institute. The figure of Gottlieb inspired Walker to pursue a similar career, and may have had an influence on his eventual choice of medical school and even his medical specialty. (As a kind of tribute to Lewis's character, Percy would later name one of the physicians in *Love in the Ruins* and *The Thanatos Syndrome* Max Gottlieb; in both novels, he is a good scientist and ethical man.)

So Walker already possessed a strong literary education before he headed off to college. In fact, it would be fair to say that he approached the study of science and medicine with a decidedly literary and philosophical attitude.

5

Chapel Hill

———◆———

I didn't have a very distinguished career in college and the only picture of me besides the regular class picture was a candid shot of students queued up at the local movie house (the armpit).

—"Confessions of a Movie-goer
(from the Diary of the Last
Romantic)," *a short story,*
c. 1957

The self-portrait that emerges from Walker Percy's recollections of his years at the University of North Carolina is that of a very average sort of undergraduate. Genial, bemused, only slightly out of it, Percy, according to his own accounts, pursued his studies with no more than gentlemanly application, spending most of his time "rocking on the front porch of the SAE house and going to the movies in the afternoon." A picture of Percy standing in line for the 3:30 show at the Carolina Theater does in fact appear in the 1934 college yearbook, seemingly to confirm Percy's memory of an undistinguished undergraduate career. But the picture tells only part of the story. Pressed by more persistent interviewers, Percy would admit that he devoted a goodly number of hours to work in the chemistry and biology labs. And, yes, he might add, there were some small contributions to the school magazine—only the slightest flickerings of a literary ambition.

Like most Carolina alumni of his era, Percy retained fond memories of his Chapel Hill days. To him they represented four years of a first-class education passed in an atmosphere of leafy, small-town ease in the company of the nicest assortment of fellows one could ever hope to pass time with. He particularly liked the fact that there was nothing pretentious about Chapel Hill. Memories of his father—Princeton, 1910, and Harvard Law, 1913—made him both wary and disdainful of stuffier schools and their puffed-up graduates.

Typically, too, Percy retained a high opinion of President Frank Porter Graham, the man largely responsible for the university's ascent toward academic excellence during the 1930s. Forty years old when Percy entered the university, Graham was, as one historian described him, "a compact bundle of energy and enthusiasm who believed profoundly, albeit simply, in the Presbyterian church and in liberalism." Graham's great accomplishment, according to the same historian, was to "preserve the Chapel Hill campus as an enclave of Western rational inquiry" at a time when North Carolina "was filled with vehement antiintellectualism accompanied by powerful racism in the east and a milder but pernicious racism everywhere else." That may be slightly overstating the breadth and depth of Yahooism in the Tarheel state, but North Carolina was certainly no outpost of enlightenment. And that fact made Graham's achievement all the more remarkable. Despite being repeatedly called on the carpet by state legislators for such sins as inviting "Reds" and union organizers to speak on campus, Graham overcame by dint of his forceful and undeniably impeccable character. His policies may have struck reactionaries as ultraliberal, or even "Red," but he presented them with such powerful Christian conviction that even his bitterest adversaries were confounded. "He's a sweet son of a bitch, ain't he?" declared one of his flummoxed opponents. Then, too, many of the same legislators who hotly denounced him in Raleigh had sons who were receiving an excellent undergraduate education in Chapel Hill, and most of those sons were appreciative of their president. Times being hard, even the wealthier students were impressed by Graham's efforts to accommodate the needs of the more financially strapped students, allowing them, for example, to pay for their meals with chits and not caring a great deal whether they ever made good on them. It was clear, too, that Graham had assembled a faculty of distinction, despite being able to pay salaries that ranked among the lowest offered by top American universities. Good scholars came to Chapel Hill because Graham was there. He guaranteed academic freedom and fellowship with other outstanding scholars, as well as a good library and a reputable university press.

In addition to boasting solid humanities and natural science departments, the university was gaining renown because of an impressive, and controversial, brace of social scientists, known collectively as the "Regionalists." Howard Odum, founder of the Institute for Research in Social Sciences and the journal Social Forces, enraged conservatives with

his investigations of southern economic realities, but his presence attracted other outstanding researchers, including Rupert Vance, author
of *Human Geography of the South.* The Chapel Hill Regionalists' unsentimental investigation of the varieties of southern social experience
could not have been more different from the romantic evocations of the
South put forward by the Agrarians and Fugitives in Nashville—or for
that matter by Percy's own adoptive father. (Yet it was a product of the
Chapel Hill school, Dr. Raymond Clinton, who studied Will Percy's
Trail Lake farm in 1936 and found it to be remarkably fair in its treatment of sharecroppers.)

It is hard to say how much the undergraduate Walker Percy was
affected by the Regionalists and their concerns. Superficially, it would
seem very little. In a letter that he wrote to a former classmate in 1973,
Percy confessed to how little attention he had paid to political and social
issues back in his college days: "You remember that year I knew you—
'33–'34? I've often thought what a dream world I lived in—totally unaware of what was going on—Cash's world of near revolution in Charlotte, Spindale & even Carrboro—I couldn't have cared less. Maybe we
were better off that way. (I don't remember you being political either.)"
At the same time, Percy could not have been completely ignorant of
what the Regionalists were saying, even if his knowledge of them was
restricted to what he read in the school newspaper, where their work
was frequently discussed. The stamp of their thinking can be seen in his
later writings about the South, particularly in his criticism of the failings
of the southern leadership. Furthermore, his eventual dismissal of the
Agrarian stand as well-intentioned but "feckless" would have accorded
well with the Regionalists' view. Percy always absorbed a great deal by
osmosis.

Unquestionably, though, others matters dominated Percy's attention
during his first semester at Chapel Hill. After a hard two-day drive in
the Wetherbees' Reno, Percy and his roommate were dropped off at the
university on Sunday, September 17. They unpacked their bags in their
spartan room in Manley Hall and then went for a walk around the
campus, locating the Old Well and other university landmarks before
continuing up to Franklin Street and taking a short pass through the
village of Chapel Hill. Freshman orientation began the next day, and in
addition to sitting through the usual talks by the deans, all seven
hundred entering students were required to take the English placement
test at 3:30 in the afternoon. Percy sat down at his desk and quickly
dashed off a convoluted, Faulkner-inspired description of the Mississippi
River, a misbegotten effort that promptly earned him a place in one of
the three sections of "A" English, the remedial sections that carried no

college credits. Humiliating though it was at the time, particularly since Wetherbee had placed into one of the advanced "flying squadrons" taught by Harry Russell, Percy later said that it was the best thing that could have happened to him. The instructor of the remedial class, a graduate assistant named George Sensabaugh, proved to be an excellent teacher who quickly drilled Percy out of his worst habits. Percy came out of Sensabaugh's courses with lasting regard for the clear declarative sentence.

Apart from the humiliation of the placement test, orientation week passed pleasantly enough. The Carolina Theater on Franklin Street offered free shows to all freshmen on Tuesday night, and Walker indulged his addiction. Films, like books, were a balm, providing the most reliable release from the uneasiness that would come over him whenever he was around other people for too long. Percy would go to almost any kind of movie, and the Carolina Theater—which he soon named the "armpit"—satified his appetite with its frequently rotating fare.

When classes started, Percy was enrolled in four courses, Foundations of Modern History, Elementary German, Introductory Mathematics, and "A" English. The only subject that reflected his career ambitions was the foreign language, German then being considered the obligatory language of the international scientific community. The choice could not have pleased Uncle Will, a devout Francophile and an equally avid despiser of all things Teutonic. Try as he would to get his adopted son interested in French language and literature, he would have little success, at least not while he was alive.

Percy had no trouble adapting to the social scene. He mixed easily with his classmates and during the preliminary rush week in October discovered that he particularly liked the fellows at Sigma Alpha Epsilon. Just as important, they liked him. Almost from the beginning of the term, however, Walker found that he and and his roommate were an uncomfortable match. Being from the same town might have contributed to the tension; familiarity can easily breed impatience. But there were also striking differences of character and temperament. The tall, athletic Wetherbee was a dynamo who hit the books hard and spent all of his free time at *The Daily Tarheel,* apprenticing for one of the staff positions. Percy, by contrast, was languid, doing what was necessary to get his course work done but not a lot more. Wetherbee's recollection was that Percy spent an inordinate amount of time in his bed and that he was often depressed and out of sorts. Such indolence and moodiness clearly irritated the go-getter Wetherbee, and it did not help that he found Percy distant and somewhat aloof. "We never had the typical bull sessions that college roommates have. He seemed to be too caught up with questions for which there weren't any answers." To get back at his moody roommate, Wetherbee would occasionally pick up his Bible and, in a mock-pious tone, read at random. Religion, Wetherbee knew, exasperated Percy. While there was no cataclysmic break between the two Greenville boys—Percy in fact never lost his fondness for his more energetic peer—it was clear to both of them that close quarters put a strain on their friendship. They roomed together throughout their freshman year, moving from Manley to better quarters in Old East after the winter quarter, but each went his own way the next year.

Indolent Percy might have been, but he did well in his courses, garnering two As (in English and math) and two Bs at the end of the fall quarter. The winter results were even better: straight As, all achieved with little effort, thanks largely to the preparation Percy had received at Greenville High School. Percy's academic accomplishments made him even more attractive to the upperclassmen of SAE, who considered themselves not only a fun-loving crowd but serious and hard-working as well, a self-image borne out by their consistently high academic performance. Charles Poe, the son of the editor and publisher of *Progressive Farmer* magazine, was one of the SAEs who was struck by Percy's quiet self-possession and intelligence. Ansley Cope, a senior, took an immediate liking to the young pledge, although he was surprised at his thoroughgoing cynicism and skepticism. "I remember," Cope recalled, "that he was fond of Schopenhauer and Nietzsche." Other SAEs were impressed by Percy's dry wit. He quickly became known for his knack for the devastating nickname, a talent greatly prized by undergraduates, although not by the unfortunate pledges whom Percy dubbed "Jughead" and "the Embryo." (In *The Moviegoer* it is skill in this art that earns Binx Bolling the regard of his prospective fraternity brothers at Tulane.) Considering his many assets, it came as no surprise when Percy received a bid from SAE. He quickly fell in with the young men who would be his closest friends during the next three and a half years.

Of his fellow pledges, a Wilmington boy named Jimmy Carr became particularly close to Percy. Like Percy, Carr was a lawyer's son, quiet, smart, and self-contained. The two were comfortable together, whether taking in a movie, playing the occasional game of golf, or lounging about the fraternity house. Yet close as the two SAEs grew—and they would room together all three years after the first—theirs was never an intellectual friendship. Percy, in fact, was always something of a "closet intellectual," wary of revealing his interest in ideas, books, or serious questions. In truth, he was a little embarrassed by what he perceived as an excessive preoccupation with troubling questions about life's meaning. He saw this, with some reason, as morbid and cheerless. At the same time, like many southern men, he was repelled by any immodest affectation of culture and sophistication. Consequently, to most friends he presented only a social version of himself: polite, clever, concerned, occasionally remote, but always a gentleman. And he preferred that most of his friends be like this as well. He had a horror of "artsy" types and of most intellectuals, and he insisted rather rigorously upon a clear separation of his intellectual friendships and his more social ones. Just about the only friend who saw both sides of Percy was Shelby Foote, but theirs was a special friendship, fueled as much by competition as by affection. With his SAE brothers, Percy seldom showed his other side.

In fact, the only intellectual companion Percy had until Foote arrived in Chapel Hill two years later was a young man from Lumberton, North Carolina, named Ned Boone. Boone was bookish—he later went into the publishing business in Philadelphia—and after the two met in the early autumn they would go on long walks in fields around the university, talking about their favorite books and authors. Percy was spared the need to juggle categories of friendship with Boone, because Boone ended up in a different fraternity, St. Anthony's Hall, the same one that Don Wetherbee joined. Percy and Boone saw less of each other after the first year, but a correspondence that continued until 1983 testifies to their mutual affection.

As unconcerned as Percy was with the world of politics, he, like most undergraduates, was very curious about developments in Germany. Almost every issue of the student newspaper ran stories or editorials about Hitler's rise to power and his program to build the Third Reich. The implications of "Hitlerism" were the subject of a stream of lectures. Even in 1933, the possibility of a war was a real one to student activists, many of whom were already calling for neutrality and peace at any cost.

Studying German under Dr. E. C. Metzenthin only added to Percy's curiosity about what was going on in Hitler's Germany. Metzenthin had relatives there and kept his class abreast of the latest developments. To Percy, Germany sounded both terrible and fascinating, and in the spring quarter, when Metzenthin announced that he was planning to take a group of students to Austria and Germany, Percy asked Uncle Will if he could go. This time Uncle Will did not conceal his prejudice; he urged his adopted son to go to France instead. But when Percy persisted, his guardian reluctantly gave in.

The first year at Chapel Hill, like the three that were to follow, was altogether pleasant for Percy. His grades had been good, although, to his surprise, he received a C in the only science course he took that year, a quarter-long class in botany. The mediocre performance seems not to have shaken Percy's resolve to study science, but it attests to something that would become more apparent with time: Percy was attracted more to the idea of science than to its practice.

If there was anything troubling about the first year at Chapel Hill, it was the odd coincidence that occurred at the commencement exercises on June 9. The baccalaureate sermon was delivered by Reverend Henry Edmonds of the Independent Presbyterian Church of Birmingham, the pastor of the church Percy had attended as a boy. In later years, Percy would somewhat ashamedly admit that Birmingham continued to upset him—the city as well as people from it. Only a strong sense of obligation to his aunt, who suffered from severe mental problems, brought him back to the city, and the trips always took a toll. The surprising appearance of his former minister that first year at Chapel Hill was an abrupt reminder that the past was not easy to put behind.

"Walker always had a thing about authority," Shelby Foote once observed. "It came out after that trip to Germany in 1934. He was tremendously impressed by what he saw. Tremendously impressed."

Foote came to view it as one of the paradoxes of his best friend's character that Percy could be, on one hand, a rebel and a skeptic, and on the other, a person in quest of absolutes, certainty, authority. Foote himself was a thoroughly unregenerate rebel, one whose defiance drew him into repeated scrapes with figures of authority. He found it difficult to understand how someone so like himself in so many ways, someone who scoffed at so many of the false idols of the world, could also be so vulnerable to the need for authority. By the time Percy headed off to Germany in 1934, Foote had already seen the rebellious and skeptical side of his friend's character. He had heard him deride those people who believed that FDR—or anybody, for that matter—could cure the nation's ills. Foote knew of Percy's distaste for religion and his contempt for any "truths" that could not stand up to the scrutiny of science. And he had also seen how closely Percy's cynicism could verge on nihilism. There was an icy, cold side to Percy that frightened Foote. All the more astonishing, then, was what he heard from his friend when he returned from his seven weeks abroad. For if Percy was not quite a true believer in the new Hitlerian order, he was at least profoundly impressed by what he had seen during his days in Germany.

Metzenthin's small group had boarded the SS *Black Hawk*, a two-hundred-foot freight steamer owned by the Black Diamond Line, at the port of Norfolk, Virginia, on the sixteenth of June. The group included four official enrollees—Percy, two classmates named John Kendrick and Harry McMullen, and a high school junior from New York named Fred Hammond. Tagging along was another Chapel Hill student, Walter

Graham, who had not paid Metzenthin's twenty-five-dollar enrollment fee and so was promptly dubbed the "snake in the grass." The main shipboard activities during the ten-day passage were daily German lessons, card playing, lounging on the deck, and meals. The portions at meals were skimpy, and the boys found that they were famished by bedtime. It was not a luxury cruise.

Putting in at Antwerp on the twenty-sixth, the group split up, McMullen and Hammond journeying to Paris, while the others made their way to Bonn by way of Brussels and Cologne. Kendrick recalls a short stop at the cathedral in Cologne, a strange experience, as it turned out, because of the peculiar way in which Percy behaved. Percy at the time was smoking a large cigar, and when he started to stroll into the cathedral with the lit stogie in his mouth, Kendrick advised him to put it out. "Nah," Percy waved him off. "They don't worry about things like that." As he made his way down the center aisle, a furious priest came running toward him, waving his arms and shouting, *"Nicht rauchen, nicht rauchen!"* Percy superciliously complied. Kendrick had no idea what this show of arrogance had been about, but he was struck by the brashness and flamboyance of his travel companion, and not only on that occasion. "He seemed much more worldly and confident than I, more irreverent and profane," Kendrick said. "I even seem to recall his telling me that he liked to make up outlandish tales about himself to see how other people reacted. I liked him, but he was very different from me."

In Bonn the group stayed at Schumanstrasse 56, a boardinghouse owned by the Langnickel family. After several days of exploring the town and the surrounding countryside, the professor and his two charges boarded a steamer on July sixth and slowly made their way up the Rhine, stopping at various points along the way for trips to nearby towns and for long hikes, including several days in the Black Forest. ("We met many children," Kendrick noted in his diary, "Nazi jugend, with their 'Rucksacks' marching merrily through the woods, enjoying the great world of nature.") The group finally arrived in Zurich, Switzerland, on July 23. Staying, as usual, in a pension, Percy and Kendrick roamed through the city, hiked around Lake Zurich, and took an overnight trip to the monastery of St. Gallen. Before leaving Switzerland, Percy spent a considerable part of his remaining cash on a pair of Zeiss binoculars, an extravagance that he came to regret near the end of his European wanderings. At the end of the month, the three travelers split up, Percy heading on to Vienna, Berlin, and a few other German towns before reuniting with the group in Rotterdam on August 15 for the return voyage.

The timing of Percy's visit to Vienna could not have been more fateful. Arriving the day after the Nazis assassinated the Austrian chancellor, Engelbert Dollfuss, he found the city unnaturally quiet, its streets almost empty. Percy described his reaction to this ghostly scene in a letter to Shelby Foote (which Foote quoted in an article in an autumn 1934 issue of the high school newspaper): "The disaster was far too sad and important to be acknowledged in the usual manner. The people realized that the slightest demonstration might bring on war with Germany, a most formidable enemy."

To Percy, the more memorable parts of the tour through Germany were the early days in Bonn and the hike through the Black Forest, the *Schwarzwald.* One surviving photograph captures him setting off on that hike, a small village maybe a hundred yards behind him, a fenced-off field to his left. He is striding confidently forward on a broad dirt path, walking cane in hand and looking for all the world as happy as a young American abroad could look.

The ten days in Bonn made an even more lasting impression on Percy. Herr Langnickel was himself a great Hitler enthusiast who spent hours extolling the virtues of the Führer, but Percy was particularly struck by Langnickel's teenaged son, Willy, an active and enthusiastic member of the Hitler Youth: "I had been an ordinary Boy Scout," Percy recalled, "not very good, a second-class Scout—I could never make first class on account of the knots—but he was not like an American Boy Scout. He was dead serious, with this impressive uniform, and he was graduating from the Hitler Jugend and going into the Schutzstaffel. I remember he talked about the Teutonic knights, and taking the oath at Marienburg, the ancient castle. There was a tremendous mystique there." With some revising of details—he locates the family in Tübingen—Percy later re-created this family in *The Thanatos Syndrome.* The character Father Smith recounts his visit to Germany in the 1930s and describes his German cousin's two sons:

One, Helmut, at eighteen, was older than I but became my friend. The other, Lothar, was a good deal older. I didn't like him. He was some sort of minor civil servant, perhaps a postal clerk, and also a member of the Sturmabteilung, the SA, the brownshirts. Not even his own family had much use for him. . . . Helmut was something else. He had finished the Hitler Jugend and had just been admitted to the Junkerschule, the officer-training school for the Schutzstaffel, the SS. The one great thing he looked forward to was taking his oath at Marienburg, the ancient castle of the Teutonic knights. He already had his field cap with the death's-head and his lightning-bolt shoulder patch. What he hoped to do was to become not a military policeman like many of the SS but a member of an SS division and incorporated into the Wehrmacht, the German army.

What struck Father Smith—and Walker Percy—about this young man was the fact "that he meant it. He was ready to die." Helmut takes Smith to his last Hitler Jugend exercise, a test of courage, or *Mutprobe*, in which the whole troop jumps from a twenty-foot scaffold in full battle gear. Then the troop marches and sings, hymning their devotion to flag and death. After the exercise, Father Smith continues:

> [Helmut] took me aside and told me with that special gravity of his, "You are leaving tomorrow. I wish you well. I think I know you. We are comrades. I wish to give you something." He gave me his bayonet! It was the same as a Wehrmacht bayonet but smaller, small enough to be worn on the belt in a scabbard. He withdrew the bayonet from its sheath and handed it to me in a kind of ceremony, with both hands. On the shining blade was etched *Blut und Ehre*. I took it in silence. We shook hands. I left.

Percy, like Father Smith, returned from Germany with just such a bayonet—and with an admiration for the German people that astonished his friend Shelby Foote. Percy had not been blind to the frightening aspects of the Nazis. He told Foote he had been bullied into giving the Nazi salute when Hitler passed in a parade in Berlin. Yet the truly terrifying anti-Semitic campaign he had barely, if at all, noticed. What he did notice was the sense of purpose of the true-believing Nazi. Again, in the words of Father Smith:

> What can I compare him to? An American Eagle Scout? No, because even a serious Eagle Scout is doing scouting on the side, planning a career in law, insurance, whatever. Certainly death is the farthest thing from his mind. I can only think—and this may seem strange— of the young Jesuits of the seventeenth century who were also soldiers knowing they were probably going to die some place like India, England, Japan, Canada. Or perhaps a young English Crusader signing up with Richard to rescue the holy places from the infidel.

Percy the skeptic had been shaken to the core of his skepticism by a movement that was not only defiant of death but in love with it. For it was this above all that impressed young Percy: not National Socialism, not racial purity, not industrial recovery or territorial expansion, but the oldest strain of Teutonic romanticism, the *Lebenstod* that runs from the oldest German sagas, through the romances, Wagnerian opera, and Weimar culture before erupting with terrifying vividness in the mythology and symbolism of Nazism, particularly the early and strongly cultural phase of Nazism.

It is easy to hear echoes of Uncle Will's chivalric idealism in Percy's reaction to the young Nazi zealots. These were young men who seemed as heedless before death as Will Percy had been when he walked through round after round of German artillery fire in Belgium in 1918. The terrible truths that Will had learned during the Great War he had passed on to his adopted son long before he committed them to print in his memoir. Above all, Will had communicated to Walker his conviction that life had never had more meaning than it had during the war. Daily life, by comparison, was "isolated and lonely." As heir to such notions, Walker found in the Hitler Jugend ideal objects of devotion. In admiring them, he both took after Will and rejected him. He emulated Will's nostalgia for the chivalric ideal, but he repudiated his influence by admiring the people Will most despised. It must be recalled, too, that though they were both Percys, Will was partly descended from the French Bourges, while Walker had the German DeBardelebens in his background. Ancestry may not be fate, but it counts for something.

Percy's second year at Chapel Hill was by far the most literary of his undergraduate years, and was so for two reasons. First, Percy took a heavy dose of literature, enrolling in the standard English survey during the first two quarters, a Shakespeare course in the third, and in three full quarters of German literature. The Shakespeare course was demanding in itself. It was taught by a popular professor, Dr. George Coffin Taylor, and students were expected to read all twenty plays by quarter's end. That would have been chore enough, but while Percy read his way toward *The Tempest* he was also making his way through Goethe's *Faust;* at the same time, he was coping with his assignments in chemistry and economics. With such demands, Percy would have found it difficult to attend the afternoon features at the Carolina Theater, but by all accounts his attendance at the 3:30 shows remained faithful.

Percy did not merely read literature this year. In the winter term, he contributed four pieces to *The Carolina Magazine*, two reviews and two longish articles. Why Percy ventured forth as an undergraduate writer on only these four occasions is something of a mystery. His usual response to those who asked why he didn't write more was a casual shrug of the shoulders. "Too lazy," he might add. But one reason he *did* write is clear. The magazine's editor that year, Joseph J. Sugarman, had made *The Carolina Magazine* into an excellent publication, so good, in fact, that the education editor of *The New York Times* had singled it out for praise.

Sugarman, a Phi Beta Kappa from Newark, New Jersey, came to the

editorship with a plan remarkably clear in principle. He would take what
had been primarily a "literary" magazine and turn it into a "magazine
topical and journalistic in character." He would do this by "shifting the
emphasis in material from poetry and fiction to articles and essays" and
above all by avoiding "vague sketches and aimless experimental narration," the wearisome staple of so many undergraduate magazines.

Sugarman fulfilled his promise. The articles in his magazine were
timely, crisply written, lively. They touched on matters of interest to
undergraduates but on larger issues as well. The magazine was smart, in
both the general and the 1920s Menckenesque senses of the word—
intelligent and "with it." Percy, himself an avid reader of the smart
magazines of his day, including *The Smart Set*, *Scribner's*, *Harper's*, and
The American Mercury, knew a good magazine when he saw one.

Percy's first contribution demonstrated just how savvy he was about
contemporary culture, high and low. Published in the January 1935 issue
of the magazine, the piece was entitled "The Willard Huntington
Wright Murder Case" and dealt with the mysterious intellectual "suicide" of the formerly high-brow American author, Willard Wright, and
his reincarnation in the early 1920s as the creator of the popular Philo
Vance detective stories, S. S. Van Dine. What is most striking about
the essay, apart from the confident prose, is Percy's authority in evalu-
ating the career of a complex character. A rebel from youth—he was
booted out of seven colleges before taking a degree at Harvard—Wright
had worked as a culture critic for several big newspapers and national
magazines. Like Mencken (whom he preceded as editor of *The Smart
Set*), Wright delighted in championing unfashionable, not to say reactionary, causes. A Nietzschean, he defended Germany during the Great
War and ridiculed the women's suffrage movement. In addition to books
on modern art, aesthetics, and sundry high-brow subjects, Wright wrote
a novel, *The Man of Promise* (1916), which Percy in his essay astutely
read as a fictional self-prophecy, an uncanny foretelling of "his future
condescension to popular fiction."

As Percy explains it, Wright's "suicide" began in 1923, when he
suffered a nervous breakdown and his physician prescribed "light reading" as an aid to recovery. Wright obliged, reading virtually every detective story in the language. From this successful dose of bibliotherapy, he
emerged a new man, one who busily set about penning, under the name
of S. S. Van Dine, a highly successful series of mystery stories that ran
first in *Scribner's Magazine*. As Percy described the transformation, the
"former courageous herald of the new *aesthetique* became suddenly the
casual dilettante who employed his erudition in padding murder plots, a
literary da Vinci resting prematurely on the fruits of his labor." To be

sure, Percy acknowledged, Wright raised considerably the tone and the furnishings of detective fiction: "Vance's suave discourses on Chinese ceramics or Egyptology were found to be as informative as they were amusing." But did Wright do himself grave damage by entering the lists of best-sellerdom?

Percy's weighing of that question is perhaps the most interesting aspect of his essay. On one hand, he lauded Wright's willingness to bring his intelligence and learning to bear upon a popular form, thereby not only meeting "the demands of the twentieth-century reader" but also improving him. Yet while Percy was reluctant to go along with the charges that Wright had sold out, he closed his essay with what is at least faint damnation: "However, his repeated and unavailing vows to return to more serious literature and the deprecatory attitude that he assumed toward his former work, which he brands as 'highbrow,' indicates the decadent artist, destined to grind out detective novels at regular intervals indefinitely."

That may sound more than faintly damning, and it would be—in isolation. But the rest of the essay reveals Percy's fascination with the "decadent artist" as the man who engages thoughtfully, even daringly, with popular culture. There is more than ambiguity in Percy's attitude toward this engagement. There is sympathy. The idea of the intellectual who masters a popular form in order to beguile a wide readership clearly fascinated the precocious sophomore. How could it fail to? This, after all, was a person who, between Schiller and Shakespeare, eagerly submerged himself in Hollywood's latest fare.

Percy's contribution to the February edition of the magazine was a short book review of Claude Houghton's *This Was Ivor Trent*. Competently turned, the review praised Houghton's "cheerful post-war disillusionment" and "his ability to create pulse-quickening moments of suspense without murdering one of his characters." This slight but professional job understandably grabbed far less attention than Percy's earlier article—or the one that appeared in the next issue: "The Movie Magazine: A Low 'Slick.' " Here Percy was at his playful best, skewering the trite conventions of the movie magazine in the spirit of (mostly) high fun. Percy analyzes the lockstep formulas of the slick: "Every movie interview and feature embodies one or all of three motives: to reconcile the peculiarities and weaknesses of a movie star to the ideal held by the fans, to trace the star from his honky-tonk days to his Hollywood pinnacle, and to give the world the star's philosophy of life." He delights in such absurdities as that of "stars" dispensing wisdom to the benighted fans—"Strangely enough, many articles give a star's advice for a successful married life, the premise supposedly being that practice makes perfect"—and the obligatory features that show the screen villain to be "in real life a generous and sweet person."

Apart from being a romp through one of the trashier quarters of popular culture—and a revealingly well-informed romp at that—Percy's essay shows him grappling with an issue that would one day engage him in his mature work: the power of the popular culture to certify life and experience. While this power obtains in all transactions with works of art, the highest as well as the lowest, Percy was on to a peculiarly American cultural phenomenon: the process by which even the most blatant and crude artifice is made to seem more real than reality itself. This process involves the mediation of such things as the film pulps, which exist not only to demonstrate that the "star" is real (in a fantastical sort of way) but to confer a kind of authority upon the star. Percy notes that "The *raison d'etre* of the movie magazine is the abnormal curiosity of its readers about the private life of the movie stars," a teasingly provocative observation. But Percy went nowhere with it. In fact, rather tellingly, he fails to tie it up with what he observed earlier in the essay: that the reader wants only a formulaic version of the star's "private life," a version that will heighten, or at least not destroy, the magical authority of the screen idol. Being a moviegoer himself, Percy was perhaps reluctant to investigate too closely the needs of the movie enthusiast. That would have entailed more self-scrutiny than he was then ready for. But the subject had at least been raised.

After that performance, the modest book review that appeared in the April issue of the magazine seems like a disappointing swan song to an undergraduate's promising literary career. Perhaps the only thing noteworthy about Percy's review of Francis Hacket's historical biography, *Francis the First,* is his prudish objection to Hacket's frank treatment of his subject's sex life. Percy failed to see how "such frequent descriptions of bed room episodes reveal a significant phase of Francis' character."

On this somewhat puritanical note, Percy turned away from literary endeavors and devoted himself more exclusively to science, although it was not as complete a farewell as Percy tended to suggest in later interviews. For one thing, he continued to read widely. Nevertheless, as a declared chemistry major, he would have to spend fewer hours on his back with a book and more in the labs of Venable Hall. It was something of an irony that Percy did less well in the sciences than he did in the humanities (receiving a C in chemistry in the spring quarter, for example), but he took very seriously his immersion in the world of the scientist.

Percy did not turn into a drudge, not even during his busy second year. In addition to his regular moviegoing (one cannot imagine his missing the October 7 showing of *The Last Gentleman*, starring George Arliss and Edna May Oliver), Percy drank and played with his friends at the SAE house, a group that this year also included his brother Roy. On the brisk Carolina autumn weekends, he cheered for the Tarheel football team, captained that year by George Barclay, an All-American guard. Percy even followed the team up to New York City for its game with NYU—a lackluster game, as it turned out, but it allowed him to visit the Cotton Club in Harlem. Percy invited his high school sweetheart Margaret Kirk, now attending Sweetbriar, to some of the major Carolina dances, Grail and Germans in the fall as well as the Midwinter and the Spring dances. Percy's steadfast devotion to Margaret Kirk through his undergraduate years was, to say the least, remarkable. Its most immediate consequence was to leave unchallenged Percy's notion of women being either untouchable madonnas or compliant whores. Percy never gave Kirk cause to worry about her virtue; just as remarkably, they never had a conversation that ventured beyond cautious pleasantries. Percy took none of this as strange or disagreeable. It was the way of the world. As for carnal appetites, those were satisfied—in the time-honored Chapel Hill undergraduate fashion—by the occasional visit to the red-light district in nearby Durham, a merry-grim rite of passage usually accomplished only after a great deal of alcoholic fortification.

During Percy's second year at Chapel Hill, the campus was, if anything, even more abuzz with talks and lectures about national and global problems than it had been the year before. Germany's annexation of the Saarland after a plebiscite in early 1935 was proof that the international order established by the Treaty of Versailles was on the way out, even before Germany officially repudiated the treaty later in the year. Such doings brought on a string of campus lectures. Early exiles from Germany spoke of the rising menace of Nazism, while Norman Thomas, the gentlemanly leader of the Socialist party, warned undergraduates that the only alternative to fascism in this country was socialism. The students' general reaction to all of these ominous noises was cautious and conservative. Perhaps the strongest sentiments were antiwar and isolationist, expressed in a growing number of student demonstrations. For his part, Percy remained steadfast in his opposition to FDR and New Dealism, even while he somewhat inconsistently supported the "ultra-liberal" Frank Graham. With his roommate Jimmy Carr, Percy attended the occasional open house at Graham's home, and these personal encounters with the president made Percy even more respectful of the man.

Summer vacations during Walker's undergraduate and graduate school years were, for the most part, times when Walker could do blissfully what he pleased. For this, he—and his brothers—could thank Uncle Will. Will Percy always believed in giving the boys leeway so they could come to terms with the world on their own. He did not overbear. He did not overprotect. It was clear what he thought about things and people, and the boys always knew that they could come to him for advice, sympathy, and simple human affection. Although taking on the boys had been a considerable responsibility and expense, he delighted in them, as he made repeatedly clear in letters to his closest friends. The nights that he stayed up with Phin after Mattie Sue's death were only the most dramatic proof of his devotion. In thousands of smaller ways, he showed love and concern. Yet—and this was the marvel of Will's guardianship—he also knew when to let the boys take care of themselves. In fact, he encouraged them to be independent and brave, and at no time was this more obvious than during the boys' summer vacations.

The western trip that Walker and Roy took during the summer after their mother's death was typical of the sort of freedom that Will encouraged. But at least that journey had been supervised by an adult. In the summer of 1933, before Walker went off to college and Roy went off to his last year at Episcopal High School, Will decided that the two older boys were ready to take care of themselves and sent them off to Mexico on their own. It was an odd journey. The boys—then seventeen and sixteen, respectively—traveled from New Orleans to the port of Tampico, then by train to Mexico City, where they stayed for a few days before visiting some Aztec sites near the city. Then they flew a Mexican Airline plane back to Tampico and returned to New Orleans by sea. The main thing Roy remembered about the trip was his and Walker's bafflement: They had no idea of what to do with themselves beyond Baedekerish sightseeing. "We were too young to drink or chase women," Roy Percy recalled. Surviving seemed to be their main preoccupation. When they got back to Greenville they were both mildly surprised that Will had let them go, and even more surprised that they had made it back home alive.

Each summer after that, the boys were left largely on their own. Roy began to spend more and more time out at Trail Lake, learning the details of farm management. Phin, who was sent off to McCallie School in Chattanooga, Tennessee, in the fall of 1935, would usually spend a large part of the summer at Chimney Rock Camp near Asheville. And Walker would "drift," as Uncle Will put it. Drifting consisted of reading (the "big book" of the summer of 1935 would be Mann's Magic Mountain), listening to music, driving around with Shelby, or maybe spending a few days up at Brinkwood. Will felt free to travel during the summers. If he went up to New York or out West or even to Samoa (as he did in the summer of 1936), he would leave one of the Bourges aunts—Nana Pearce or Lelia Warren—officially in charge. But since the aunts were far more trouble than any of the boys, the household would by and large run itself, with a little help from the servants. As far as the boys were concerned, this was a perfectly acceptable arrangement. With all the books and music he could want at his disposal, and with a good friend whom he could always count on for companionship, Percy could not have been happier.

If Percy experienced any disappointments during the summer of 1935, one was learning that his best friend would not be going up to Chapel Hill with him that fall. A year behind Percy to begin with, Shelby Foote had decided to take an extra year of high school, thus falling another year behind his friend. It had been Foote's plan to get up to Chapel Hill in the fall of 1935 so that he could spend at least two college years with his friend, but his plan seemed to go awry in the spring before high school graduation. Foote's rebellious streak had momentarily gotten the better of him.

During his last two years at Greenville High, Foote had served as one of the editors of the school newspaper, and for the most part had done a creditable job. On occasion, though, his irreverence had brought him into conflict with one of the faculty advisers of the paper, the starchy E. J. Lueckenbach, who happened also to be the school principal. Foote had an instinct for getting under the skin of this humorless administrator. Lueckenbach had kicked him out of study hall one day for reading "obscene" material—James Joyce's *Ulysses*. But Foote's stock fell to its lowest point in the spring of 1935 when one of his teachers, a somewhat troubled woman, went to Lueckenbach and reported that Foote had made several "improper" advances. Lueckenbach, the target of several of Foote's recent editorials, never gave the accused a chance to defend himself. He told Foote that he was expelled and that there would be no chance of appeal. Stunned, Foote went to the person he could most rely on, Will Percy. As usual, Will took matters in hand. He went down to the Weinberg Building on Washington Avenue where Foote's mother worked as a secretary and gently broke the news to her. "Lillian," he assured her, "I don't know what the trouble is, but I'll find out. Phin is at the house all by himself these days, and he would like company. Let Shelby come stay with us while I get to the bottom of this." She agreed—Lillian Foote was a long-suffering woman who never said a harsh word to her son—and Foote settled in for what he later admitted was one of the more pleasant weeks of his life. "I was a colt in clover among all those books." Meanwhile, Uncle

Will got to the bottom of the matter, and Foote was reinstated after what was, in effect, a week's vacation. Shortly thereafter, the teacher who had accused Foote quietly retired.

Foote's absolution was only partial. Mr. Lueckenbach still disliked him, perhaps even more so now that this unpleasant episode had called his judgment into question. If Foote had made no improper advances, he was still trouble in Lueckenbach's eyes. And the editorials didn't help matters at all. Lueckenbach soon got his chance for revenge. When the University of North Carolina asked for the principal's evaluation of Shelby Foote, it received an unequivocal answer: Accept under no circumstances. Not surprisingly, Foote was rejected.

But Foote was never a person easy to defeat. As September approached, Foote decided that he would go up to Chapel Hill and get himself enrolled. He knew he had at least one ace up his sleeve: the Depression. Hitching a ride with Don Wetherbee, he appeared at the registrar's office on opening day. When his turn at the desk came, Foote was immediately exposed: "We rejected you," the official said sternly.

"I know," said Foote, "but I also know that you have classes that you can't fill. Besides, I came up here all the way from Mississippi. Give me a chance."

Foote's brashness paid off. After consultation, the registrar's office reluctantly agreed to enroll him.

The rest of Foote's career at the University of North Carolina proved to be as unorthodox as the manner in which he enrolled. Early on, he decided that he really wasn't very interested in earning a degree; nor, for that matter, in attending all of his required courses. So he more or less picked and chose his way through the next two years, attending those classes, mostly literature, that he found interesting and skipping those that he thought dull. To Foote, the greatest delight was the stacks and stacks of books in the back of Wilson Library, "where I prowled in disguise as a precocious graduate student." His other main preoccupation during his two Chapel Hill years was writing. Charles Poe, Percy's SAE brother, was editor of The Carolina Magazine in 1935–36, and he was determined to preserve the high standards established by his predecessor. Foote's steady stream of contributions helped Poe achieve that goal. They were surprisingly good stories, full of southern grit and already betraying the influence of the Mississippian whom Foote idolized, William Faulkner. One of the stories had a little more reality than the editor would tolerate: It concluded with an interracial love tryst. Shelby was told to excise it, and for perhaps the only time in his literary career, he consented. But by and large, the magazine gave the aspiring writer plenty of room to cut his teeth.

Percy and Foote had good times together during the next two years, but they were not inseparable. During 1935–36, Percy roomed with three Wilmington men—Harry Stovall, Jimmy Sprunt, and Jimmy Carr—on the third floor of the SAE house. Jimmy Sprunt's father had been a friend and classmate of Percy's father at Princeton. More remarkable than the coincidence was the fact that Sprunt never mentioned their fathers' connection. Having heard about LeRoy Percy's suicide from his father, Sprunt was afraid to bring up a potentially painful subject—a delicacy that points up the profound change in manners that has occurred between that time and our own.

The four roommates were a happy group, although Stovall received more than his share of good-natured ribbing for his Catholicism. "Must you always inflict your religion on us?" Percy would chide when Stovall rose for mass early on Sunday mornings. Once the roommates went too far with Stovall, though. Every Saturday night, he would put up a sign on the door asking the janitor to wake him so he could make it to church on time. One of the roommates decided to play a joke and removed the sign. Stovall did not wake up in time and missed church. He was not amused: "Your religions may not mean anything to you," Stovall fumed, "but you sure as hell better not trifle with mine." The roommates were thoroughly chastened and apologetic. Percy never forgot Stovall's admonition—or the conviction behind it.

Foote did not become one of Percy's fraternity brothers. He was blackballed by the SAEs because of his partly Jewish background. How this unacceptable taint in Foote's bloodline became known is anybody's guess, but neither Walker nor Roy resigned to protest the blackballing. Foote, who ended up in ATO, appeared not to hold it against them. He and Walker continued to be as close as they had ever been, even making the ritual trips to Durham together—with results, on one occasion, that were stranger than usual.

On that ill-starred journey, Foote, Percy, and two other friends decided to stop at a roadhouse between Chapel Hill and Durham, a place called Pappa Rogge's, then famous for its beer and barbecue sandwiches. Sitting not far from the college boys' table was a party that already seemed fairly well into their cups—two men and their dates. One of the women began to cast flirtatious looks the way of the Chapel Hill boys, or so her boyfriend thought. The aggrieved man, deciding that the Chapel Hill group was encouraging the flirtation, came weaving over to the table and tried to start a fight. Foote stood up and hit the man with just enough force to stun him into momentary inaction. The Chapel Hill boys knew that it was time to cut a hasty retreat, but one of the women from the group caught up with them outside and headed directly for Percy, apparently mistaking him for Foote—a logical mistake, since both were wearing the same light linen jackets. What happened next Percy seemed unable to believe: The woman hauled off and punched him squarely on the nose. "You're a woman," Percy wailed, "you're a woman!" Bedlam then broke loose, as other members of the drunken party came streaming outdoors. One of them, a big lumbering bear of a man, jumped on Percy from behind, knocked him to the ground, and lay on top of him. Foote had to pry him off Percy, while the two other Chapel Hill boys held the other drunks at bay. It was a chaotic scene for a few minutes, but finally the undergraduates made it to their car and away, bruised but otherwise not badly damaged.

Percy had to put up with more than a little ribbing for the inglorious sock to the nose, but even humiliation has its uses. Many years later he created a raucous suburban brawl in *The Last Gentleman.* In that scene, an irate Levittown housewife mistakes Will Barrett, who is traveling with the "pseudo-Negro," for a real estate agent who specializes in selling houses to black buyers. Will has no idea what her agitation is all about: "But in that instant, even as he was passing the woman, whom he had forgotten, she drew back her fist clear to her earlobe and, unleashing a straight whistling blow, struck the engineer on the fleshy part of his nose, which was already swollen and tender from hay fever." The reaction to this painful sucker punch seems too painfully felt to have been manufactured out of whole cloth. "Oh, hideous exploding humiliating goddamnable nose pain, the thump-thud of woe itself. Oh, ye bastards all together."

Considering the mischief they usually got up to when they were to-gether, it was probably all to the good that Percy and Foote were sepa-rable. The aspiring doctor was carrying a heavy load of science in his junior year—several courses of chemistry as well as physics and zoology —and the going had to be rough, even for somebody who was renowned among his fraternity brothers for his remarkable powers of concentration. ("He could sit right in the middle of a crowded room in the SAE house and read a novel or a chemistry book and never miss a beat," Roy Percy once marveled.) Demanding as the work load was, Percy did well enough in his courses to be elected to Phi Beta Kappa in May, a signal accom-plishment for a junior.

Total immersion in the sciences, besides keeping Percy busy, had at least one other result: It brought his faith in the behaviorist model, then firmly entrenched in the Carolina science departments, to its highest pitch. Percy's education during these years strengthened his belief that science would eventually explain everything. The world might be head-ing to hell and war, economists might be predicting nothing but greater

woes to come, theologians might be lamenting spiritual decline (as Reinhold Niebuhr did on the Chapel Hill campus in the fall of 1935), but
young man Percy believed that science would somehow bring mankind
through. A man of science could survive even in a world without honor.
(And if Percy needed any further proof of the decline of honor, he could
have found it right on campus: In the winter of 1936, a large cheating
ring was exposed, and fifty students, including the president of the student body, were expelled.)

Percy's rather hard-nosed scientism encouraged his cynical tendencies. If man can be reduced to the sum of his chemical and biological
properties, he reasoned, why worry about his ideals, or lack thereof? But
a cynic, particularly a skeptical, scientific cynic, is not always what he
seems. Percy's scientific armor was surprisingly strong, but it had chinks.

During the summer of 1936, for example, Uncle Will gave him a copy
of a novel that he said was at least as good as his beloved *Jean-Christophe*,
a first novel written by an Atlanta journalist named Margaret Mitchell.
The romance of the Old South had never been more slickly packaged,
but Walker fell for *Gone with the Wind* at least as hard as Uncle Will did.
Not that they were alone. As well as winning the Pulitzer Prize for fiction
in 1936, the novel sold 1.5 million copies in its first year. Not surprisingly, it was the campus best-seller during Percy's senior year.

Apart from its anecdotal interest, Percy's enthusiasm for *Gone with the
Wind* sheds some light on what he then thought about southern society
and history. It suggests that for all his wariness about the southern
romance—the idealized picture of the southern gentry, the happy sub-
missiveness of blacks, the codes of honor and chivalric heroism—he was
still very much under its sway. The Chapel Hill Regionalists might have
been working hard to expose a less idyllic reality, but Percy still clung to
a version of southern society that was not so different from Uncle Will's.
Percy certainly continued to share Uncle Will's paternalistic attitude
toward blacks, and like most southerners of his class he was a staunch
segregationist. (During spring break in 1936, Percy and Foote took a bus
trip to New York City. While traveling Foote voiced his opinion that
integration would "probably not be a bad thing." Shocked, Percy replied, "I cannot believe that you, a southerner, would say that.")

The persistence of this attitude came out in Percy's relationship with
a young black man who started working for Uncle Will in early 1936,
although in many ways this friendship marked the beginning of a change.
Sixteen years old when he was taken on as a part-time butler and chauffeur, David Scott was a Greenville native who lived only a few blocks
from the Percys' house. Educated in the the local black parochial school
(and a convert to Catholicism at age thirteen), Scott had attracted

Will's attention while working as a delivery boy for the local pharmacist. Noticing, as he would, that Scott was bright, ambitious, and capable, Will told him that he should come to see him if he ever needed work. After a falling out with the pharmacist, David Scott took Will on his word, and Will promptly hired him. What was immediately remarkable about Scott was his ambition. He wanted to become a pilot, a career that would have been unthinkable to most black Delta children of that era. More important, he was determined to act on his desire. With money that he earned from work at Will's, David went out to the Greenville airfield and asked the flight instructor, a Norwegian named Sidney A. Munson, if he could take lessons. Munson agreed and lessons commenced. When Will learned what his employee was doing, he was so impressed that he insisted on paying for the flight lessons himself. Scott proved to be a natural aviator, and before turning seventeen he made his first solo flight. "The Negro Birdman of the Delta," as the Greenville paper declared him, was soon so skillful a pilot that several white farmers offered him a job as a crop-duster, a job he would have taken had it not been for the intervention of his mother and Will Percy. Crop-dusting was not a safe career, even for pilots with much more experience than the sixteen-year-old Scott had.

Walker met this unusual young man when he came home for summer vacation after his junior year, and the two quickly struck up a friendship, something that was not so unusual in the Percy household. Walker had always been close to the servants, and the servants, Scott recalled, always had a special fondness for him. With Scott, Percy shared two old interests: aviation and music. Ever since meeting Lindbergh in 1927, Percy had fantasized about soloing across the Pacific, but the fantasy had largely played itself out in the building of model airplanes. Now, however, he knew someone who had acted upon a similar fantasy, and most astonishing, that person was black. In addition to talking about aviation, Walker and David would spend hours together in the living room listening to jazz and classical music on the Capeheart, Scott going through the motions of working while Percy lay sprawled on the floor.

Intrigued as Walker clearly was by David Scott, he couldn't help thinking that something was amiss. "Walker always thought that David would end up sadly," Shelby Foote recalled, "because he was too naively trusting and optimistic." Something of Percy's feeling about David Scott is reflected in *The Last Gentleman*, in Will Barrett's thoughts about a servant who works in the Vaught household, a servant who is tellingly named David Ross. "David Ross," Will Barrett reflects, "was different from the other Negroes. It was as if he had not caught onto either the Negro way or the white way. A good-humored seventeen-year-old, he had grown too fast and was as raw as any raw youth. . . . Something about him irritated the engineer [Barrett], though. He was not cunning enough. . . . For example, he was always answering advertisements in magazines, such as *Learn Electronics! Alert Young Men Needed! Earn Fifty Dollars a Day! Send for Selling Kit!* . . . Damnation, why didn't he have better sense? He should either be cunning with a white man's cunning or cunning with a black man's cunning. As it was, he had somehow managed to get the worst of each; he had both white sappiness and Negro sappiness." What most irritates Barrett about Ross is that his vulnerability will invite abuse at the hands of whites: "But Oh Christ, David, this goddam innocence, it's going to ruin us all. You think they're going to treat you well, you act like you're baby brother at home. Christ, they're not going to treat you well. They're going to violate you and it's going to ruin us all, you, them, us."

Again, it is particularly dangerous here to identify life too closely with its literary transformation. Percy had other fish to fry in writing this scene, and David Scott is broadly caricatured. Even so, the scene reflects attitudes that Percy once felt and never completely abandoned. (One sees signs of them in his depiction of the black MIT student who renders crucial mechanical assistance to Lance Lamar in *Lancelot.*) At the center of those attitudes is a certain historical fatalism: Blacks, having suffered at the hands of whites, have acquired a certain dignity and wisdom, but any effort to lift themselves out of their less-than-desirable station in life involves a compromise of their best "black" qualities. By struggling to escape their historical fate, Percy seemed to believe, blacks could only bring greater woe upon themselves—and lose their souls in the process.

Another aspect of Percy's historical romanticism received reinforcement during his last year at Chapel Hill. While taking a heavy load of sciences, Percy signed up for a course on the history of the Napoleonic period. Taught by Professor Mitchell Bennett Garrett, the course emphasized the role of great men and great deeds—of heroism, in short. While it would be foolish to read too much into the selection of this course, it does say something about Percy's persistent ambivalence toward heroic accomplishment. On one hand, he rejected it as part of the fatal romanticism that had driven his father and his grandfather to self-destruction. On the other, Percy was fascinated by heroism and greatness, and wanted both for himself. Yet he had a horror of failing or of making a fool of himself. Above all, he did not want to appear to be ambitious, for fear of adding to his ignominy if he failed to achieve distinction. Only in little ways—as in the choice of the history elective, for example—did Percy reveal how much he was his father's son.

Percy's last year at Chapel Hill went well but not altogether triumphantly. There were some disappointments. Perhaps the worst was his rejection by Harvard Medical School. Percy not only never admitted to being turned down by the some university that his father and Uncle Will had attended; he never admitted that he had applied to it. Yet the evidence that he did so is scrawled in the corner of his college transcript: "Tr. 1/16/36 to Harvard Med. Sch." The sting of rejection was sharper than Percy ever allowed. He harbored a grudge against Harvard for the rest of his life, often caricaturing it as a center of spiritless intellectualism.

Although Percy tended to cast himself as something of a social boob, he was, in fact, anything but. One sign of his popularity was his election to several prestigious secret societies, the "13" club and the Order of Gimghoul in his junior year and Amphote Rothen in his senior. In his senior year as well, he became one of the five "rulers" of Gimghoul and was elected vice-president of Alpha Epsilon Delta, the honorary premedical fraternity. But the top social honor eluded Percy. He was not tapped by the most prestigious secret society, the Golden Fleece.

Percy had little reason to be ashamed of his performance either in or out of the classroom. While rejected by Harvard Medical School, he was accepted by Columbia's College of Physicians and Surgeons, an outstanding medical school and a leading center of "scientific" medicine. For a student who never studied that hard, he had done more than creditably in his course work. And clearly he was no social failure. Nevertheless, the little defeats weighed in Percy's memory. Election to the Golden Fleece may amount to very little in the grand scheme of things, but one of Percy's closer readers has noticed that Percy bestowed that honor "upon Kate Cutrer's shallow fiance, Walter Wade, in *The Moviegoer.*" For the writer, literature is always the best revenge.

6

The Healer's Art

———◆———

Doctors are a good lot. One cannot help thinking of them organized in a sort of medieval guild where their good qualities, the latent Christianity, might be fostered.

—WALKER PERCY, Notebook—
1951

Like all the student rooms in Bard Hall, room 1001 was claustrophobically snug, but the view from its windows offered some compensation. Looking out the western window of the tenth-floor corner room that he would occupy all four of his years at Columbia, Percy could see the Hudson River, the abrupt banks of the New Jersey shore, and the towers and suspension cables of the George Washington Bridge. Since its completion in 1931, the bridge had been widely hailed as a technological marvel, the architect Le Corbusier declaring it "the most beautiful bridge in the world" and "the only seat of grace in the disordered city." If Percy drew closer to the window and looked straight down, he could see cars beetling their way up and down Riverside Drive. Turning left and looking out his southern window he could see a sliver of Manhattan around the edge of the Neurology Institute, which stood next to Bard Hall. It was an electrical city that Percy had at his back, bristling with more activity and life than even the most tranquil of souls could at all times feel comfortable with.

New York in 1937 was nearing the end of its remarkable between-wars building spree, a construction extravaganza that transformed a city of humanly scaled brownstone neighborhoods into something a little closer to the skyscraper metropolis that it is today. Among the soaring towers put up during this era were the Empire State, the Chrysler, the McGraw-Hill, and the RCA, as well as countless hotels, hospitals, and apartment buildings. The campus on which Percy would spend most of his next four years was itself a part of that boom. In 1929, the scattered facilities of the College of Physicians and Surgeons and Presbyterian Hospital were relocated on twenty-two acres of land that stretched from 165th to 168th streets, and from the Hudson River to Broadway. The new buildings embodied the austere functionalist aesthetic that was then all but obligatory. One contemporary critic described the complex as "modern, not *moderne*—a stately pile that carries the construction of its functional honesty."

Columbia's College of Physicians and Surgeons—P&S—was one of the three top medical schools in the nation, ranking right along with Harvard and Johns Hopkins. Like the other two schools, P&S was at the forefront of investigative medicine, a strongly scientific, research-oriented approach that came from Germany and, to a lesser extent, England by way of New York's Rockefeller Institute. By the 1920s, P&S had adopted what was called "full-time medicine," the practice of providing salaries for all professors in the clinical departments so they could devote all of their time to teaching and research. While P&S did not neglect patient care or clinical work, it gave its students a heavy dose of advanced science, more, some students thought, than the average physician would ever need. Nonetheless, aspiring physicians considered it one of the more desirable schools in the nation. Some twelve to fifteen undergraduates applied for each place, drawn both by the school's excellence and by its location in New York.

Once settled in at Bard Hall, Percy paid the ritual visits to Radio City and Carnegie Hall, gawked at the towers of central Manhattan, and marveled at the park that Frederick Law Olmsted had designed at the very heart of the urban colossus (a park that Percy would put to good use in the opening scene of his second published novel, *The Last Gentleman*). But as soon as classes started, he found that he had to restrict most of his urban wanderings to his own neighborhood, the "Fourth Reich," as it was then dubbed because of its heavy concentration of German—and mostly Jewish—refugees. "To get away from the grind," Percy later related, "I'd go to the Loew's State on 181st Street and the RKO Coliseum on 183 Street."

And a grind it was. Even though medical students carried fewer courses in the first year than in any other, these six courses, particularly the three in anatomy, required extensive memorization. Most of the students' daytime hours were spent in the dissecting labs, four students to one cadaver. (Will Percy, in a letter to Charlotte Gailor, reported that Walker had "a very scrawny negro stiff to work on.") The anatomy work was not wasted on the future novelist. Percy's precision in the naming of human parts, a minor but nevertheless pleasing adornment of his mature fiction, owes much to his diligence during that first-year grind.

As a southerner, Percy was something of an outsider at Columbia. Of the 113 entering students in the class of 1941, only two others came from the South. This seemed not to trouble Percy. As he later joked, some of his best friends were Yankees. One of them, Frank Hardart, roomed directly across the hall from him in room 1002. Hardart, a native of Forest Hills, New York, was practically a hometown boy. His father was the vice-president of the Horn and Hardart restaurant chain, and he had planned to go into business himself until a college classmate at Notre Dame, Bob Gehres, talked him into taking some pre-med courses. Hardart, discovering that he was good at sciences, decided to take a stab at medicine and ended up—as did Bob Gehres, who also befriended Percy —at the College of Physicians and Surgeons. Both Gehres and Hardart enjoyed hazing Percy, calling him the "Dirty Reb" and mocking his Mississippi accent. But Percy gave back as well as he received. Gehres and Hardart were not only "damn Yankees" but "damn Papists" as well. In short, the men enjoyed their differences.

Another medical student who became part of their group was a small-town Indianan named Fred Dieterle. He made it through only the first year, but during that time he was as close to Percy—or "Rollo," as the two mysteriously called each other—as Hardart or Gehres. Like other members of their class, the four played basketball or paired up for the occasional game of squash. Percy was particularly good at the latter—a carry-over from his skill at tennis—but one match with Dieterle proved costly. Swinging his racket with more force than finesse, Dieterle unintentionally hit his opponent in the mouth, leaving dead two of Percy's upper front teeth.

Given the grave character of medical-school studies, the constant exposure, even from the first year, to illness and death, it is not surprising that the medical students went at their recreation with something close to childlike abandon. Working over human cadavers has a way of bringing home the shocking reality of the profession, and the student must begin that process of distancing himself from the immediately overpowering reality of death. He must, in a sense, lose touch with his feelings, objectifying not only the body he works on but also himself. Among the more effective releases from the pressure were humor and play, and Percy and his friends indulged in both. In addition to sharing the usual morgue humor—"What you up to, Percy?" "I'm working in dead Ernest"—they would repair to the nearby Armory Bar and Grill on Broadway for drinks. Sometimes their forms of escape were more obviously infantile. On warm evenings, the men would drop water bombs from Hardart's tenth-floor window, hoping to hit unwary pedestrians as they walked by on Haven Avenue. Clearly, Percy had found friends he could be at ease with.

To those friends, Percy seemed a surprisingly sophisticated young man. Shortly after arriving in the city, he appeared to be completely at home, comfortable and confident in navigating his way around. They were impressed, too, by his intelligence and quick grasp of difficult scientific subjects. "He never studied," Dieterle recalled. "He just seemed to be able to do whatever he wanted to do and still get great grades." Percy's Chapel Hill background stood him in good stead, but he was also a naturally quick study. Hardart recalled rarely seeing Percy at work over his medical texts; instead, he would find him on his bed reading novels or magazines, anything, really, except medicine or science. Percy was generous in helping his friends with their work. Dieterle would go to him often when he had trouble understanding something, and Percy would patiently pull things together. He was a good teacher and explainer, and he knew how to encourage somebody who was struggling: "You were slow at first, Rollo," Percy would say, "but you're like a wheel when you get rolling." Dieterle was grateful for Percy's help. Not only did the course work come hard to him, but he was a scholarship student and had to work three hours a day in the laundry—a considerable bite out of the medical student's time. Percy was well off, and though he seemed not to agonize over his advantages, he had absorbed enough of Uncle Will's outlook to know that advantages entailed responsibilities. He was generous with time and money.

"He had all the Boy Scout virtues," Dieterle recalled, "except reverence." His friends all knew where Percy stood on matters of religion. He was, as one of them said, "devoutly agnostic." In other ways as well Percy showed himself to be an ignorer, if not outright mocker, of pieties and tight-laced morality. "Tell me, Freddy, did you get any?" Percy would ask whenever Dieterle returned from a date.

Percy, his friends saw, was popular with women. No doubt because of Will Percy's extensive connections in New York, he was put on Miss Cutting's social roster beginning his first year in medical school, and was invited to many of the big debutante parties in and around the city. In addition, whenever he and Hardart were feeling flush they would plan an evening at the Stork Club or the St. Regis or the Roosevelt: "You get the table, and I'll get the dates," the Mississippi boy would tell the New York. Percy apparently had no trouble coming up with the dates. He went out with many women during his medical school years, particularly with young nurses and medical technicians, and several developed strong crushes on him. His appeal is not hard to understand. He was tall, curly-haired, blue-eyed, and handsome. As well as being courtly and charming, he was witty and a good listener. Yet Percy never gave any sign of being smitten by the women who fell for him. Charming and amorous as he could often be on a date, he always retained a distance.

That distance was obvious not only in his relationships with women. Even during the first year, Hardart noticed that Percy had a quiet, unapproachable, and even somewhat sullen side. He never knew when Percy would be in one of his "moods," since they never seemed to be caused by anything in particular. But when Percy was low, Hardart learned, it was best to stay away. Percy, it soon became clear, needed a great deal of time alone, even when he wasn't low. Hardart might occasionally accompany him to a movie, but it was obvious that Percy preferred to go by himself. Films, as Percy later explained to Robert Coles, were not just an escape. "I think at the movies I was getting to know how people looked at the world, what they thought—just as a doctor does." But Percy also enjoyed the solitude.

Solitary moviegoing was not the only activity that kept Percy distant from his peers. Starting in the fall of his first year, he would routinely disappear in the middle of the afternoon, heading up Haven Avenue to Broadway and 165th Street, where he would catch a subway downtown. Hardart and his other friends assumed that Percy was either going to see a movie or meeting a friend. They knew about Huger Jervey, Will's old college mate, who was on the faculty of Columbia Law School. Walker often met Jervey for dinner, symphonies, or the opera. But as his classmates would learn many years later, those mysterious afternoon disappearances had nothing to do with Mr. Jervey or with the movies.

Percy's journey downtown on the subway took him a little over one hundred blocks. Surfacing at Fifty-ninth and Broadway, he would walk three blocks east and four blocks downtown to an apartment on the north side of Fifty-fourth Street, between Fifth and Sixth avenues. There, at number 17, he would go to the ground-floor office of Dr. Janet Rioch. It was a sparely decorated office, maybe one picture on the wall, a few pieces of furniture, a desk, chairs, and a sofa. The decor disclosed very little about the woman who worked there, beyond suggesting that she had only the slightest interest in appearances. Her clothes—practical, straightforward, unfashionable—gave away little more. She was not a woman who spent a great deal of time on her looks. But, then, she didn't have to. A former student and colleague described her as the most beautiful analyst he had ever seen.

Percy had come to Rioch by way of Uncle Will's friend Harry Stack Sullivan. Will had called on Sullivan for help with Phin shortly after Mattie Sue's death, and apparently Sullivan had made a couple of surreptitious visits to Greenville, never letting on to the boy that he was a doctor or that he was treating him. Seeing the man in action, Percy had been impressed. Sullivan was undogmatic and practical, the sort of psychiatrist who refused to put theory before common sense. He was concerned with the whole life of a person—not just private fantasies but the person's relationships with other people, his beliefs, his values, and the quality of his life. Sometimes, Sullivan realized, a person simply needed someone to talk to, a friend. Sullivan knew whereof he spoke. He had never been a happy man himself. He lived with a number of private torments, including, many people thought, repressed homosexuality, and he drank too much. But Sullivan's flaws only increased Percy's respect for the man. When Percy began to cast about for a psychiatrist for himself, he asked Sullivan for advice. "He wasn't sure what ailed me, and I wasn't either," Percy later explained. Sullivan recommended one of the abler people he knew.

Sullivan advised well. Janet Rioch was well suited to a person like Percy. She had been born in Damoh, India, in 1905, four years after her brother, David, her only sibling. Their parents were missionaries, members of the Campbellite Christian sect, and both had been educated at a sectarian school, Butler University, in Indiana. Minnie Henly Rioch, English by birth, had become a physician before she and her husband, a Canadian, went to India to found and run a mission orphanage, and it was there that their two children were born and raised.

Like her parents and her brother, Janet went to Butler University, graduating in 1926. Four years later, she received her M.D. from Rochester University, then did internships in medicine and surgery before accepting a research grant from the Department of Psychology at Harvard Medical School. From 1933 to 1935, she served a psychiatric residency at the Shephard and Enoch Pratt Hospital in Towson, Maryland, and during that time was analyzed by Sullivan. In addition to forming a lasting professional connection with Sullivan, she also began to work with a number of his associates, including Karen Horney, Erich Fromm, and Clara Thompson. (When the Sullivanians split with the strictly Freudian analytic association in 1941, Rioch went with the former and helped found the neo-Freudian William Alanson White Institute in New York City.) Rioch had come to New York in 1935 and worked for two years at Presbyterian before accepting posts at the Vanderbilt Clinic and Roosevelt Hospital. When Percy first started seeing Rioch in the fall of 1937, she was thirty-two and single, having not long before come out of an ill-fated love affair with a Johns Hopkins physician whom she had met while working in Maryland. The tallish, dark-haired woman bore her sadness quietly, but her colleagues and friends knew that she was unhappy—and not only because she had been jilted by the man she loved (and much later married). Her sister-in-law Margaret Rioch thought that Janet never got over the fact that her mother had preferred her brother, David, giving him most of her attention and affection. Successful as she was in her professional life, self-doubts continued to trouble her. To escape, Rioch drank, sometimes heavily. But neither her drinking nor her unhappiness seemed to interfere with her performance as a physician.

Rioch, as one colleague said, was "preeminently a clinician." Not a prolific author, she published only one professional paper, and though it was respected by her peers, she had only a minor interest in theory. Her foremost concern was the patient. Following the approach of Sullivan, she proceeded by developing a strong personal relationship with her patient. Her manner was crisp and clear, but it was neither cold nor overly distant. Wary of dogma and open to individual differences, she helped to bring about individual cures.

It was her attitude and her approach, one suspects, that kept Percy coming to Rioch's office. His intellectual debt to her was considerable. His later writings on psychology and psychiatry reflect her emphasis on dealing with the individual patient rather than generic patients. But Percy owed her more than an intellectual debt. Though he would later complain that he never determined exactly what "ailed him," Rioch moved him closer to an understanding of those nagging concerns that brought him to her office in the first place: his father, depression, despair, suicide, and grave doubts about his own fate. Not only did he want to understand why his father came to the end that he came to but, as he had resolved shortly after the suicide in 1929, he wanted to make "damn sure" that he didn't come to the same end himself. Percy's fiction is in itself the strongest proof of how well she taught her patient to explore his predicament, both his past and his present.

And what does that fiction tell us about his predicament? It could easily be said that Percy's fiction, particularly the early novels, *The Moviegoer* and *The Last Gentleman*, but also *The Second Coming,* and to a lesser degree, *Lancelot,* involves a "search for the father." While this may suggest, in a general way, what much of Percy's fiction is about, it needlessly obscures the specific problems of Percy's "case": namely, the need to *escape* the father and the accursed patrimony. To escape the father, however, it was first necessary to understand him, and in undertaking this ordeal, Percy was fortunate to have come across Rioch. Both because of her own background in a foreign culture and because of her training at the feet of Sullivan, Rioch was strongly attuned to the cultural and social influences on an individual's psychic makeup.

Sullivan's early and important work in social psychology, and his close ties with anthropologists like Abraham Maslow, left him and his followers with an unmistakable legacy: an awareness of how individual psychological dysfunctions are often the result of unsuccessful accommodations to the dominant values of a given culture. This may seem obvious to us now, but we forget that it was precisely thinkers such as Sullivan who made such notions commonplace. It was also Sullivan and like-minded thinkers who began to show that certain cultures frequently function in ways that almost guarantee psychological "problems"—and, futhermore, that the problems are often healthy reactions to unhealthy social expectations and values.

In Percy's case, of course, the culture in question was that of the South. As a Sullivanian, Rioch would have set Percy thinking about what the culture of the South was really about, and specifically, what there was about it that could drive a person to madness or despair. Not that this led Percy to a rejection of the South or of his own southernness. But it helped him to see that there were aspects of this heritage that could be quite lethal, including its obsession with honor.

There was also a more purely psychological side of Percy's problem. How was he to get out from under the shadow of a father who was deeply unhappy, mercurial, occasionally cruel, yet also well meaning, loving, engaging, and highly moral? On one hand, the son naturally wanted to pattern himself after the best aspects of his father. But how could he untangle them from the worst? For the power of the good is often invested with the energy—one might even say the demonic energy—of the bad. In LeRoy Percy's specific case, feelings of unworthiness drove him to excel, in his work, in his recreation, in his family life, and even in his Sunday School teaching. Yet he still felt that he had fallen short of the Percy standard, a feeling heightened by a hereditary depressive tendency. So on came despair, abjection, too much drinking, and explosions of cruelty toward the people he most loved. A son is blown back and forth by the emotional buffetings of such a father. How can he step forward as a man himself, if being a man involves coming to such a terrible pass? Yet to remain a son forever is no solution.

How Percy dealt with such conflicts with Rioch is, again, impossible to say with certainty. But there are grounds on which to hazard a guess.

First, by choosing a woman as his analyst Percy gave a hint about what he was seeking. Rioch belonged to that half of humanity that Percy knew least: the female half. Consider the women with whom he had had relationships up to this point in his life: his mother (beautiful, well meaning, but remote), assorted maids and cooks (none of whom in his books figure as largely as male servants), his teachers (many of whom he fondly remembered, but with none of whom did he sustain a lasting relationship), Margaret Kirk (beautiful, but at least as remote as his mother), and a succession of women with whom he went on inconsequential dates. Rioch was the first woman with whom Percy had a serious, extended discussion. And this in itself is a clue to what Percy needed in order to begin to move away from his father's shadow.

Percy's choice of analyst was not merely the product of curiosity, however. It sprang from deeper sources, namely the anger that he felt toward the woman who he believed should have mediated between him and his difficult father: his mother. There is evidence to support this conjecture. It appears in the only paper Janet Rioch published. Delivered in March 1943 before the Association for the Advancement of Psychoanalysis and published shortly thereafter, the paper elaborates on the Freudian concept of transference, the crucial process in psychoanalysis through which the analysand "transfers" to his analyst feelings and fantasies acquired in the primordial relationships with parents or parent-surrogates.

In the middle of this paper, Rioch comes to the question of transference distortions, explaining how it is "just in the safest situation, where the spontaneous feeling might come out of hiding, that the patient develops intense feelings, sometimes of an hallucinatory character, that relate to the most dreaded experiences of the past. It is at this point that the nature and the use by the patient of the transference distortions have to be understood and correctly interpreted by the analyst." Rioch goes on to explain that this is a particularly tricky moment, because the patient must feel close to the analyst in order to be able to reveal the "full intensity" of his or her illusions. Then follows an example whose details put one immediately in mind of the case that Doctor Rioch had concluded only three years before delivering the paper:

> The complexity of the process, whereby the transference can be used as a therapeutic instrument and, at the same time, as a resistance may be illustrated by the following example: a patient had developed intense feelings of attachment to a father surrogate in his every day life. The transference feelings toward this man were of great value in elucidating his original problems with his real father. As the patient

became more and more aware of his own personal validity, he found this masochistic attachment to be weakening. This occasioned acute feelings of anxiety, since his sense of independence was not yet fully established. At that point, he developed very disturbing feelings regarding the analyst, believing that she was untrustworthy and hostile, although prior to this, he had succeeded in establishing a realistically positive relationship to her. The feelings of untrustworthiness precisely reproduced an ancient pattern with his mother. He experienced them at this particular point in the analysis in order to retain and to justify his attachment to the father figure, the weakening of which had threatened him so profoundly. The entire pattern was elucidated when it was seen that he was reexperiencing an ancient triangle, in which he was continuously driven to a submissive attachment to a dominating father, due to the utter untrustworthiness of his weak mother. If the transference character of this sudden feeling of untrustworthiness of the analyst had not been clarified, he would have turned again submissively to his father surrogate, which would have further postponed his development of independence. Nevertheless, the development of this tranference to the analyst brought to light a new insight.

Untrustworthy may seem too strong a word to apply to Percy's mother, but one need only consider the ways in which Mattie Sue had been, for her sons, an unreliable figure. At the very least, she had failed to provide a buffer between the boys and their father. She had barely been a presence at all. The circumstances of her death, moreover, were bound to have created further doubts in the boys' minds. If Percy believed that she committed suicide, as many people did, he would have had very good reason for thinking his mother untrustworthy. The other elements of the family drama described by Rioch seem sufficiently close to Percy's family situation to merit no special pleading.

What is most interesting about the case is that it touches upon a subject that he consistently skirted in his writing: the subject of mothers. Where, his reader may rightly ask, are the mothers among all those chaotically brooding father figures who dominate the memories of Percy's fictional heroes? Their absence—or at least their rather strangely marginal presence (as in *The Moviegoer*)—in novels so strongly concerned with families may suggest that Rioch's analysis of Percy remained ultimately incomplete, at least in one respect. To escape from the father Percy first had to find the mother. But perhaps not even the best analyst could have taken him far along in that quest. And that may explain why, at the end of three years with Rioch, Percy still believed that he had not completely figured out what ailed him.

. . .

As demanding as analysis might have been, it seems not to have taken any toll on Percy's academic performance. Fred Dieterle was in fact amazed that Percy spent every night during exam week going to the opera with Huger Jervey, the very nights when most students in Bard Hall stayed up late memorizing anatomical structure, embryology, biochemistry, and physiology. Yet Percy still received As and Bs in most of his subjects. After exams, Percy, Hardart, and Dieterle threw a party in Bard Hall, an overly bibulous evening that ended with Hardart driving his classmates and their dates around Central Park. "We were very happy that night," Dieterle recalled, "and we drove Hardart crazy by carrying on with our dates in the back seat of his car."

Back in Greenville during the summer of 1938, Percy was troubled to learn that Uncle Will was in poor health. Never a physically robust man, he was now beset by chronic hypertension. In those days, there was none of the medicine that today effectively controls high blood pressure. Will had no choice but to slow down, at least in his working life. He had already taken steps in that direction, having turned over most of his legal practice to his partner Hazlewood Farish in late 1937. This was not an altogether disagreeable necessity for Will. Even though he had been good at the law, he had always detested it, practicing it more out of a sense of family obligation than anything else. In more recent times, too, he had been bothered by what he perceived as a decline in the ethical standards of the profession. When Walker's brother Roy asked him whether he should pursue a legal career himself, Will discouraged him with the strongest possible words. "You don't need to go to law school. You can hire a lawyer like you hire a whore."

Of course, part of Will's reason for discouraging Roy from pursuing a legal career was that he had other plans for him. Roy graduated from Chapel Hill in the spring of 1938 with a degree in economics and was considering applying to Harvard Business School. But when he got home from a postgraduation tour through Europe, he discovered that Will had other ideas. In fact, the minute Roy stepped into the house, Will told him "to go upstairs and freshen up and be in my office at 11 o'clock." When he got to the office, all the managers from Trail Lake were present. Will came directly to the point: "As of noon today, I no longer have any business connection with Trailake Planting Company or Klondike Planting Company or anything else to do with this business. My son LeRoy is boss and you are going to have to deal with him, and that's the end of that."

Though Roy was surprised, he wasn't terribly upset. The business school idea hadn't been that important to him, and he knew from experience that he liked working at the farm. But he was amazed that Will had given so much responsibility to so young a man—and particularly at a time when the farm was not doing very well. It was a little like Will's decision to send him and Walker to Mexico on their own. Later, Roy told Uncle Will that he'd taken a big chance. "Well, that's right," Will replied, "but that's the only way you are going to find out. Not only that, you don't remember it, but the average age of a field-grade officer in the Confederate Army in the Civil War was in the middle twenties."

Will's decision to shed more of his responsibilities did not mean that he became idle. He still had plenty of business to tend to, his and other people's. The procession of help-seekers continued, as did the flow of friends and other visitors. And he was still tinkering with essays that he'd been writing for a number of years, mostly unfinished pieces that he'd scrawled out on legal paper and left scattered throughout the house, sometimes, as Walker discovered, wedged between the cushions of chairs or sofas. One essay, about his years at Sewanee, he'd written and published in 1927; another one, "The White Plague," dealing with the failings of the white race, he had finished in 1936. During the summer of 1938, he seemed to grow more interested in reflecting on his own life, perhaps because he felt that it was now drawing rapidly to a close. Another spur to such reflection was a letter that Walker had written in the spring. In it, Walker had discussed his belief—or was it his fear?—that being anything less than the best in one's chosen career was failure. Will had written back saying, among other things, that "My whole theory about life is that glory and accomplishment are of far less importance than the creation of character and the individual good life." Clearly, though, the letter did not strike its writer as a sufficient *apologia*. Will had much more to say, and when he and the boys headed to Sewanee for the hottest weeks of the summer, he took plenty of legal pads with him.

That summer on the mountain proved to be fairly eventful. Even getting there had a moment of drama, although one would have to call it anticlimactic. Shelby Foote and Percy had decided to drive up together, and on the way Foote proposed stopping at Faulkner's house, Rowan Oak, in Oxford, Mississippi. Foote had cooked up an excuse for intruding on the writer: He would ask him where he could get a copy of *The Marble Faun*, the collection of poems that was the first book Faulkner published. When they reached Rowan Oak and parked on the long driveway, Percy rather sullenly refused to get out and accompany Foote to the house. "I don't know that man and he doesn't know me and I'm not going to bother him," Percy announced. Foote went on by himself and had a pleasant chat with Faulkner, the first of several. At the end of the conversation, Foote mentioned that he had a relative of Will Percy's

in the car with him, an announcement that must have stirred ambivalent feelings in the writer.

During the late twenties, Faulkner had made a disastrous visit to the
house of Will Percy. Faulkner had been in Greenville with his friend
Ben Wasson, and they had been invited over to the Percys' to play
tennis. Wasson, a Greenville native, knew things were off to a bad start
when his friend, being in one of his bohemian phases, refused to wear
shoes. To make matters worse, he had been sipping on corn whiskey and
was quite drunk by the time they pulled up to the house. When the
doubles match started, Faulkner—paired with Percy—had trouble staying on his feet. At one point, he fell down while lunging for a ball. Will
called to Wasson: "I don't believe your friend feels very well. Maybe
you'd better take him for a drive." Faulkner was relieved to depart; Will's
sharp disapproval was palpable. And Faulkner was not so drunk that he
had forgotten the condescending review he had written of Will Percy's
book In April Once.

Apparently the memory of this encounter did not discourage Faulkner
from walking to Foote's car to meet Will Percy's kinsman, but Walker's
prediction proved true. Neither man had much to say to the other,
beyond pleasantries. Back on the road, Foote was ecstatic. Since leaving
Chapel Hill in 1937, he had been working at assorted odd jobs in order
to devote most of his energy to writing, and Faulkner was his idol. In
fact, when the novel that Foote was then working on was published
many years later, under the title Tournament, it was faulted as being
written too much under the shadow of Faulkner. Even Faulkner himself
said so to his friend Wasson: "If Shelby ever gets over my influence on
him as a writer, he'll be just fine." Percy's feelings about the conjurer of
Yoknapatawpha were much cooler, though not as frigid as Uncle Will's.
And although Percy was not then contemplating a writing career, he
had learned the perils of writing under Faulkner's influence.

During the few July days that Foote was at the "Brink," he and Walker
occupied themselves with building a stone "tea house" a few hundred
yards from the main house on a little trail that ran along the rim of Lost
Cove. Between bouts of physical labor, Foote noticed that Walker had
acquired some strange reading materials from medical school, perhaps
the most peculiar being a weighty tome entitled Body Water. If Walker
was having doubts about his ability to excel in his chosen profession, he
was at least going through the motions of taking it seriously. For his
part, Foote could not understand how a person who could tolerate reading Body Water couldn't stick it out through at least one volume of
Proust. But try as Foote did, he could never coax Percy through Swann's
Way. Percy found Proust to be a precious little "snob."

Shelby could stay only for a short visit; he had jobs in Greenville to return to. One was a proofreading position at the Greenville paper, the *Delta Star*, a newspaper that was already acquiring a national reputation because of the forceful and progressive leadership of its editor, Hodding Carter. After years of waging a campaign against Governor Huey Long in Louisiana, Carter and his wife, Betty, had been lured to Greenville by Will Percy, David Cohn, and other community leaders eager for a strong paper in their own town. In early 1936, the *Delta Star* began publishing, and its bold editorial policy soon made its only competitor, the *Democratic-Times*, look pallid. (Eventually, it acquired its competitor and emerged with the name *Delta Democrat-Times*.) Carter made enemies, of course, and not only by attacking Mississippi demagogues and bigots. He broke with local journalistic practice by publishing the names of whites who committed misdemeanors (a practice previously restricted to black citizens) and by giving blacks honorific titles. As well as Foote, Don Wetherbee was another young Greenvillian who came back home to work at the paper, rising eventually to managing editor before deciding to go to medical school. Wetherbee took journalism a little more seriously than Foote, who was not above allowing some of the more amusing mistakes to pass by uncorrected. ("Partly cloudy with shitty winds," read one particularly ominous weather forecast published under Foote's guard.) Still, Foote's days at the paper provided good material for the fiction he had already begun writing.

After Foote left the "Mountain," something happened that shook up the Brinkwood household, something that reminded Percy of an aspect of the South that he would have preferred to ignore. As was the custom, David Scott had not only driven Uncle Will's car to Sewanee but stayed on to help with chores around the house. Shortly after arriving, Scott met a bright and pretty young black woman who worked for a family that lived not far from Brinkwood. Striking up a summertime romance with the young woman, Scott asked Mr. Percy if he could borrow the car one evening. It was not an unusual request, and it met with the usual answer: of course. But what started out as a pleasant date quickly turned sour. As David and his date were driving down the winding mountain road, they were spotted by a couple of local policemen who tailed them and then pulled them over. The police were not content to ask for a driver's license and registration. They were bent on humiliating Scott: "What's a nigger doing driving this kind of car?" one asked. Scott was ordered out from behind the wheel, and the two policemen began to shove him around. Scott told the men that they could follow him to Mr. Percy's house if they doubted he had permission to drive the car, but they appeared not to listen. Their main concern was to break Scott down, to reduce him to tears with their threats and abuse. When they felt they had succeeded, they got back in their car and drove away. Scott took his date back to her house and returned to Brinkwood. Seeing Mr. Percy and Walker, he blurted out the whole story, eyes welling with tears as he talked. Uncle Will was furious. It confirmed everything he had always thought about the "peckerwoods," and he immediately sat down and wrote a blistering letter to the local sheriff's office. Walker stayed up late that night talking to David, trying to comfort him, but he was clearly every bit as rattled as the young man he was trying to reassure. Walker was still no progressive on the race issue, but the incident forced him to see how the system he tacitly embraced could strip a man of all dignity—and just as bad, leave him with no hope for recourse.

Another issue Walker was given cause to think about that summer was the progress of fascism in Europe. Germany's annexation of Austria on April 10 had confirmed Will's suspicions of the Germans in general and of Hitler in particular. Listening to the Fuhrer's speeches on the radio convinced him the only way to stop the megalomaniac was to fight him. Czechoslovakia would be the next target, Will knew, but things wouldn't stop there. Walker, for his part, had still not gotten over his own experience in Germany, and particularly his awe at the devotion of the young Nazis that he had seen. Even though events forced him to acknowledge the ugly side of the new Reich, he was still, relatively speaking, a Germanophile and a resolute anti-interventionist. When the Munich Pact was signed on September 29, granting Germany the Sudetenland (and, in effect, Czechoslovakia), Percy believed, along with most other Americans, that the measure would appease Hitler.

Percy's second year at medical school started with a bang. On September 21, the northeast coast of the United States was battered by one of the worst hurricanes that it had ever experienced. It came as something of a surprise, the approaching storm having been badly underestimated by meteorologists. When the first wave driven in by its winds crashed on Long Island's shoreline, the shock was registered on a seismograph in Alaska. Barometers fell to the lowest point ever recorded on land in the Northeast, and winds that blew through New York City reached 120 miles per hour. One of Percy's classmates remembers foolishly attempting to leave Bard Hall and being blown backward when he got out on the sidewalk. Percy, a connoisseur of catastrophes, savored the big blow. He was always one of those people whose spirits soared when the barometer plunged. Percy's taste for apocalyptic portents was further whetted by Orson Welles's radio dramatization of War of the Worlds, which sent panic-stricken New Yorkers screaming into the streets one Sunday evening near the end of October.

The second year offered more enduring, if milder, excitements. During the winter break, Percy stood as an usher in his brother's wedding. Roy Percy and his high-school sweetheart Sarah Farish were married in the Presbyterian church on January 3, 1939, a wedding that seemed to solidify Roy's role as the designated *paterfamilias*.

The occasion cheered Walker, who had always been fond of Sarah, but perhaps the greatest satisfaction of that year was discovering pathology. In later years, Percy would say that he had been torn between two specialties, pathology and psychiatry, but his first and strongest love was for the former. His attraction to this specialty may seem somewhat ghoulish, but working among the dead was not what appealed to Percy. What appealed to him was the purely scientific quality of pathology, its neatness and precision, its intellectuality. This should come as little surprise, considering what attracted Percy to medicine in the first place: the promise of scientific elegance and certainty. In its instruction, P&S emphasized the "mechanism of the disease" in all areas of teaching. Dr. Charles Flood, assistant dean of the medical school during Percy's years at Columbia, explained the "mechanism of the disease" as a "term coined to describe a sequence of clinical, biochemical or other events that characterize a particular disorder and its altered physiology." Within this pedagogical orientation, the specialty of pathology assumed particular salience. It was, as Percy related, where "medicine came closest to being the science it should be and farthest from the arts and crafts of the bedside manner. Under the microscope, in the test tube, in the colorimeter, one could actually see the beautiful theater of disease and even measure the effect of treatment on the disease process."

As scientific as Columbia's training was, Percy found himself increasingly dissatisfied with what he called the "sloppiness" of medicine. He learned, in other words, that medicine was an impure science—and was so, in large measure, because it involved an extremely difficult variable, the individual patient. The attraction of pathology for Percy therefore becomes more obvious: As well as being the least impure of the specialties, it freed him of the necessity of trafficking with patients.

There was also a more personal reason for Percy's drift toward pathology. The professor of the two pathology courses he took in his second year was a particularly effective teacher named Dr. William Carson von Glahn. A bachelor in his late forties, an elegant dresser with a somewhat effeminate manner, von Glahn was a man of culture as well as science. A southerner, he had graduated from Davidson and Johns Hopkins before coming to Columbia in 1920. By those students whom he befriended and invited to his Haven Avenue digs von Glahn was called—eerily to Percy, who was one of them—"Uncle Willie." Von Glahn had a way of

the appointment, though, Phin was not sure he wanted to take it. The education Phin had received during his four years at McCallie had been excellent, but he had had more than his fill of military life. In his heart of hearts, he would have preferred going to Chapel Hill or the University of Virginia, but the honor of getting the appointment—and the added bonus of being able to skip final examinations if he accepted it—overwhelmed his reservations. Shortly into plebe summer he knew he had made a mistake. By the time classes started in the fall he was making regular calls to his brother in New York, telling him that he was planning to quit. Walker had always been Phin's closest counselor; he was the one who told Phin "the facts of life," standing in the middle of Percy Street, shuffling his feet and nervously flicking his nose. When Phin had troubles he would always come to Percy, and now his troubles were great. "I told him I was going to resign, and he said, 'I don't blame you. It sounds terrible. But why don't you wait a month.' A month would go by and I'd call back and complain about the hazing in the dining room, how I couldn't stand it anymore, and instead of saying that I just had to put up with it, he would come up with small, practical ways of coping with the situation: 'Just hold out till tennis season and see if things get better when you eat at the training table. And if they don't, then leave.' " That was how Walker coaxed his brother through Annapolis the first year: by increments. "He was just the best listener I ever knew," Phin recalled. "He could get to the bottom of what was troubling people. He would have been a great psychiatrist, I'm sure."

He might have been, too, although his performance in psychiatry that year rated nothing more than a mediocre grade. It was a subject in which Percy received one of his few medical-school Cs, surprising for someone who always said that it was one of the two specialties he considered going into. Of course, psychiatry as it was taught at Columbia probably had very little to do with what he found interesting in his sessions with Janet Rioch or with what he was now beginning to read about on his own. In 1939, he bought copies of Freud's *General Introduction to Psychoanalysis* and *The Basic Works of Sigmund Freud*, and heavy annotations in both suggest that he read them carefully. Percy's reading of Freud during 1939–40 might have whetted his curiosity about strict Freudian analysis. Whether that was the cause, he decided the next year to change analysts, this time choosing a man, and a Freudian, named Goddard Booth. Walker found his year with Booth interesting enough, but, as he once tersely remarked to his friend Shelby Foote, "I could never effect a transference."

During the third year, Percy and his classmates spent more time in the wards, assuming limited responsibility for the care of patients. From

Dr. Dana Atchley, the director of the teaching program in the Department of Medicine, and his staff, the students learned to do a full patient workup, including a careful history, a physical examination, and lab work. To Percy, it seemed very sloppy science indeed. Nor was he pleased to be spending more time with patients. As he coaxed Phin through his year at Annapolis, Percy began to have grave doubts about what he was doing at P&S. He stayed, as he later admitted to Robert Coles, only because he had no idea what he would do if he left.

When Percy heard from Foote in late 1939, he learned two surprising things. First, Foote—like all good southerners, eager for a war—had joined the Mississippi National Guard shortly after Hitler invaded Poland. And second, between shifts at U.S. Gypsum, where he "pushed wallboard through a micrometer," Foote had finished his first novel. Not only that, he had sent it to Harold Strauss at Knopf, the same editor who was handling Uncle Will's memoir. Strauss and other editors there liked the manuscript but thought that it wouldn't sell. They urged him to put it "in cold storage" for a while and work on another novel, advice that Foote somewhat disappointedly took. Foote of course had no way of knowing that cold storage would run the full course of the impending war, but when his division, the Thirty-first "Dixie" Division, was mobilized into federal service the following fall, he knew that it would be a while before he got back to the book.

Percy's last year at P&S was marked by a sort of manic preapocalyptic gaiety. Now it was no longer the imagined threat of Martians marching across the George Washington Bridge that excited New York but the very real possibility of entering a brutal modern war. The bombing campaign that Hitler had waged against Britain during the summer of 1940 showed to the rest of the world that such a war respected no limits. Despite America's proclamations of neutrality, the adoption of the first peacetime draft in September made neutrality seem an increasingly vain hope. Roosevelt's reelection to an unprecedented third term in November was one way the nation expressed its nervousness about the uncertainty of the times. Despite the popularity of the Republican Wendell Willkie, voters stayed with the man they knew best, hoping that he would somehow steer the nation clear of war.

For the student–doctors at P&S, pursuing courses in twelve areas that year, the academic grind remained constant, but there was a confidence that came with being in the last year, a sense that they were going to make it through. Percy emerged from his usual ruts and took the odd outing, including a trip to Princeton for a football game with a number of Princeton graduates. It was a strange occasion for a man who always looked mockingly on "Princeton men," finding their prep-school manners and collegial chumminess both droll and pretentious. But he might have made the trip to satisfy an old curiosity. His father had gone to Princeton and liked it, and Percy was keenly interested—pathologically interested, one could say—in the things his father had done as well as in the places he had been. Places leave an imprint, and by getting to know a place, Percy knew, he might learn something significant about the person who lived in it. The fascination with the effect of place upon character would become one of the strengths of Percy's fiction, and his decision in *The Last Gentleman* to make Will Barrett a Princetonian, albeit an out-of-place one, is a clear instance of Percy's practice of locational pathology. Will Barrett's uneasiness in this most "southern" of northern colleges is a sign, among other things, of his troubled relationship with the old southern patrician society from which he comes. And the fact that Will fails to fit in may be one reason why, for all his confusion, he appears to avoid LeRoy Percy's ultimate fate.

If there was anything else remarkable about Percy's social life during his last year at Columbia, it was his ability, perfected by his four years in New York, to blend in with a variety of people and groups. A Bryn Mawr woman named Eleanor MacKenzie, who became engaged to Percy's friend Gilbert Mudge, remembered Percy at a number of parties thrown by married classmates. At all of them, he seemed natural and at ease, at once friendly and distant. Other acquaintances and classmates saw this, too. And some, such as Hardart, marveled at the way he could turn on and off his southern accent and manners. He had acquired, this longtime observer, a chameleon's gift of being able to adapt himself to the people he was with.

Yet this was not something about which Percy was particularly proud. It heightened his confusion about who, essentially, he was. In *The Last Gentleman,* Will Barrett reflects on what was clearly Percy's own accursed skill: "When with Ohioans, he found himself talking like an Ohioan and moving his shoulders around under his coat. When he was with Princetonians, he settled his chin in his throat and stuck his hands in his pockets in a certain way. Sometimes, too, he fell in with fellow Southerners and in an instant took on the amiable and slightly ironic air which Southerners find natural away from home."

The fear of the person who easily becomes like anyone else is that he may be no one. Will Barrett talks about the problem with his psychiatrist, Dr. Gamow: "This was a serious business. His doctor spoke a great deal about the group: what is your role in the group? He either disappeared into the group or turned his back on it." One can easily imagine Percy talking about similiar matters with Dr. Goddard Booth. When

Percy was not busy being a brilliant medical research scientist or losing himself in a movie, he was preoccupied by thoughts about the insubstantiality of his character, thoughts that added to his low self-esteem.

A person in Percy's predicament, plagued by self-doubts that seem hopelessly entwined with large metaphysical questions, usually finds that getting on with the business of living and working is the best way of avoiding psychological debilitation. And that is precisely what Percy intended to do—to get on with it. Whatever thoughts he had given to practicing psychiatry, he put them firmly to the side during the spring semester. He decided, instead, that he would do his internship in pathology at Bellevue Hospital in New York the next year. Whether von Glahn had much to do with this decision is hard to say, but it seems more than coincidental that he, after twenty years at Columbia, was planning to move to Bellevue the following year to become professor of pathology at New York University and Director of Laboratories at the hospital—the laboratories in which Percy would work.

Uncle Will's influence was as palpable as Uncle Willie's during the spring of 1941. *Lanterns on the Levee*, which Will had finished the previous autumn in Grand Canyon, Arizona, came out in the spring and met with immediate and largely favorable reviews as well as unexpectedly large sales. There were of course attacks from certain corners. *The Nation*, for example, faulted Percy for his old-fashioned paternalism and condescending views toward blacks. Percy took the criticism in stride, although he was somewhat annoyed that his editor had toned down sections of the book that had been most critical of white Western culture. By and large, though, Will was pleased that a book he had several times considered abandoning found such a large and avid readership. Walker also had good reason to take pride in what Uncle Will had wrought.

Medical school ended on a somewhat raucous note. In keeping with tradition, the graduating class invited the faculty to the dining room of Bard Hall for dinner and the class skit, the latter reaching new depths of offensiveness, according to all present. But alcohol flowed freely and kept things on a merry note—perhaps too merry. When the faculty started to leave, some of the student revelers decided to drop water bombs from the upper floors. The noise this occasioned on the street drew neighbors out of their apartments, angrily calling for peace and quiet. This unfortunately invited only more volleys from on high, some striking the irate neighbors. The police arrived next, just a squad car at first but soon a whole riot detachment. Before things quieted down, several young M.D.'s were hauled off in a paddy wagon, and though some uncertainty shrouds this point, one of them, it seems, was Percy.

According to his brother Roy, Percy told one of the policemen where to go—a suggestion that was not taken lightly. Percy's time in jail was short. Huger Jervey came to the precinct office to smooth things over and make Percy's bail. Percy was somewhat abashed. It was not the first time he had let his temper get out of control; nor would it be the last. For all his mildness, he had a volcanic temper that surprised no one more than himself when it erupted.

After graduation, Percy had more time on his hands than he knew what to do with. His internship at Bellevue did not begin until January 1942 —more than six months away. To while away some of that time, he and Frank Hardart decided to take a trip out West. Hardart drove down to Greenville in early July and stayed for about six days in the Percy house, an experience that he never forgot. In addition to meeting Uncle Will, itself a rare experience, Hardart was struck by the wide-open hotel atmosphere of the Percy place. By then, the daily responsibility for running the house had been turned over to Roy and Sarah, who already had a one-and-a-half-year-old son (William Alexander Percy II) and a second child on the way, but the tenor of the place was still very much the one that Will had created.

After a week of parties and golf, Percy and his friend set out in Hardart's new Buick convertible, driving first to New Orleans, then heading west through Texas to New Mexico, Arizona, Utah, and Wyoming. They visited Carlsbad Caverns and from their car watched amazed as millions of bats flew out of the caves at dusk, creating an eerie velvet cloud. They toured Bryce Canyon, slept out in their car in Jackson Hole, wandered through Yellowstone Park, visited the Navajo tribal headquarters in Gallup (witnessing one of the wildest Saturday nights either had ever seen), and spent the last three weeks of August on Eaton's Ranch in Wolf, Wyoming. What Hardart remembers most about Percy on that trip was his consistently cheerful mood. There were none of the dark spells that he had seen come over his friend in New York. The West seemed to be a tonic to him. Driving through miles of stunningly open and beautiful land, often to the accompaniment of classical music on the car radio, the two men felt completely at ease. Their sense of freedom was heightened by the knowledge of what was soon to come—not only the busyness of their professional lives (Hardart was to pursue his internship at St. Vincent's Hospital in New York) but also the mayhem of war. On that trip West, they found a kind of still point, a moment of balance and poise before the world went mad.

Percy's friendship with Hardart was curious, and yet not so unlike the ones he had cultivated at Chapel Hill: It was close, affectionate, full of good humor, but clearly circumscribed. Twenty years later, when he read *The Moviegoer*, Hardart marveled at what he called the "learned" quality of the book. "I never saw any of that in Walker. It took me completely by surprise." Hardart, of course, knew that his friend read constantly, but he never heard him talk about ideas, never heard him discourse on serious subjects. Then, as later in his life, Percy was truly an intellectual in hiding.

Percy liked Hardart as a good friend, but there was something else that drew him to the man. Percy was intrigued by Hardart's Catholicism, the quiet spiritual confidence that translated into a kind of tranquil modesty. In random notes jotted down ten years after the trip, Percy explained part of his fascination with Hardart: "An untouched field: The Catholicism of an American businessman. A good man. The faint anti-clericalism, the Protestant veneer, the stoic embarrassed tightlipped quality. F.H. and C.B." (C.B. was a friend in Covington, Chink Baldwin; F. H., clearly, was Frank Hardart.) In another note, Percy reflected further on the demeanor of the American Catholic: "Religion is embarrassing to an American—at least any show of it. A Catholic is especially sensitive to any admission of 'difference' which might set him apart, of something explicit and potentially troublesome and alienating from his fellow Americans. His love for solidarity. The deep and unfeigned Americanism of Catholics. He yearns to be the same as they and not be caught in any difference. Hence his unconscious imitation of the Protestant's interior religion."

To be sure, there were many intellectual steps between 1941 and this dissection of the American Catholic in 1951. But even in 1941, and for that matter well before, Percy had developed an oblique interest in Catholics. Their air of certainty, however muted in their "American" desire to be like other Americans, troubled him, for reasons he could not explain. That Uncle Will had been a Catholic might account for some of Walker's curiosity. But there had also been Harry Stovall at Chapel Hill, David Scott in his own household, Frank Hardart and Bob Gehres at Columbia. In just about any direction Percy looked from the house in Greenville, he faced Catholic neighbors. One day in the early 1940s, while looking at the house of one of those neighbors, the Kimbles, Percy muttered to his sister-in-law Sarah, "Why are they so sure of themselves?"

Percy parted ways with Hardart in Indiana and traveled on by himself to Chicago—a city he had not been through since the summer his father committed suicide. From the Windy City he took a train back down to Greenville, where a job was waiting for him in the laboratory of the

Gamble Brothers and Archer Clinic. But before he settled into work, he made a trip up to the "Mountain" to meet Uncle Will, who had recently returned from New York. The mountain interlude started pleasantly. Walker's medical-school classmate Gilbert Mudge and his new wife Eleanor stopped by Sewanee and came over to Brinkwood for lunch and a walk through the woods. Like most of Walker's friends they were impressed by Will. A few days after the Mudges left, Walker and Uncle Will dropped by Charlotte Gailor's house. There were three or four students visiting at the time, and all of them wanted to talk to Will Percy. Will was most obliging, but in the middle of the conversation his words suddenly started coming out garbled. Walker knew that it was an aphasic response to a stroke, and Will seemed to know it as well. Grabbing Walker by the arm, he said, as best as he could, "Let's get out of here." Walker had no medical equipment, but the next day a doctor with blood-pressure apparatus came to the house and took a reading. "It was some ungodly reading," Percy remembered, "like 280 over 150 or something like that." When Will recovered most of his speech, Walker took him up to Johns Hopkins, but Warfield Longcope, the director of the medical division and the husband of Will's oldest friend, knew that little could be done. So Walker and Will returned to Greenville.

Back in Greenville, Percy began working with the chief pathologist at the clinic, Dr. E. T. White. Percy viewed the job as something between a time-filler and a way of keeping his hand in. He had no way of knowing that it would be the most important job he would hold in his life, though not because of what he learned in the laboratory.

One of the technicians in the clinic was an attractive, confident young woman from the Delta town of Doddsville. She had come to Greenville only recently, following two years of training in medical technology at Sunflower Junior College, but she already seemed completely in control of things in the laboratory. Twenty years old, she had a head for science, knew what she was doing, and had an air of quiet confidence. The young intern noticed her long brownish-blond hair, her lively features, her guileless good looks. He was smitten. But there was something else about her that Percy could not put his finger on: She had nothing of the wilting magnolia about her, nothing of the "belle," and yet she was clearly not one of those "other" women whom one casually used and discarded. She was direct, businesslike, even blunt—so much so that her nickname, Bunt, seemed a teasingly close mnemonic of her character.

Mary Bernice Townsend—for that, Percy learned, was her real name —didn't let on what she felt any more than he did, even though she had been immediately attracted to the tall, curly-haired doctor. What she noticed about him first was his white jacket and his hands—"the gentlest looking hands," she recalled. She knew about his family, particularly about Uncle Will, as just about anybody from the Delta would. It pleased her that Percy seemed unaffected by his family's prominence. He seemed, in fact, almost painfully modest. It pleased her, too, that they seemed to hit it off. Before too long, the diffident intern asked Bunt if she would go to the movies with him, and soon the two were dating regularly.

Percy quickly learned more about Bunt. She had an older brother, Pascol Judson Townsend, and an older sister, Willie Ruth. Her mother was Nanny Laura Boyd, and her father, also Pascol Judson, had been, at least until the Depression, a successful planter and Coca-Cola distributor. The Depression had wiped him out, but he struggled on, even while serving as the mayor of Doddsville. Despite the hard times, Bunt had happy memories of her childhood. Doddsville was a tightly knit, easygoing town where children ran free and wild through the neighborhood. Bunt had been a good student both in elementary school in Doddsville and in high school in nearby Ruleville. At Sunflower Junior College she did so well in her science courses that she was elected to the college Hall of Fame. At that point, though, Bunt's schooling had to come to a temporary halt. Her parents could not pay for her to continue.

Saddened but not embittered, Bunt Townsend found the job at Gamble Brothers and started taking science courses by correspondence in order to earn her American Society of Clinical Pathology rating. Bunt learned so well and so quickly that she was soon made Dr. White's chief assistant. Even in those days, she gave the impression of being able to do anything she put her mind to.

To Percy, Bunt was the cause of a mild astonishment: He was not only attracted to her romantically. He liked her. He felt comfortable with her. He could talk with her or be quiet with her. It was something he had never experienced before, this easiness with a woman, an easiness that he had experienced previously only with male friends. Many years later, Percy told a fellow novelist that Bunt was the first woman he could be friends with, and that she became, and remained, his closest friend.

Bunt soon met Percy's second-closest friend, Shelby Foote. Now a sergeant stationed with his artillery unit in Camp Blanding, Florida, he occasionally came home on weekends. On one, Bunt fixed up Shelby with one of her friends, Liber Wood, from nearby Indianola, and the four of them went fishing on Lake Ferguson. Actually, the men did very little fishing. To Liber Wood's silent disapproval, Percy and Foote sat in the boat drinking vodka and orange sodas while the two women fished.

Bunt also met Will Percy. She came to his house on a medical call, to draw blood for an examination. When she and the attending physician entered the bedroom, Will was sitting up in bed in his black Japanese kimono, alert and cheerful. Huger Jervey was also in the room, visiting his friend for the last time. Nervously going about her work, Bunt wondered whether Will knew that she was the woman who was dating Walker. If he did, he never let on. Walker later told her that after she left Jervey sang the song "Bye Bye Baby Bunting, Daddy's Gone a Hunting" to let Uncle Will know that *he* knew who the attractive doctor's assistant was.

In Greenville that fall, Walker was granted a vision of what the future held in store if he returned home and became a small-town physician, married a woman like Bunt, played the occasional game of golf or tennis, drank with his friend Shelby, read books, and went to the movies. Not a grand life, perhaps, but a perfectly pleasant one. But even before he left for New York, he saw that prospects for such a future were anything but assured. On Sunday, December 7, Walker and Bunt made plans to drive out to the levees to shoot at turtles with Percy's .22. Percy pulled up in front of her apartment promptly at two o'clock. He was in the new green Packard convertible that he would soon drive to New York. To Bunt's puzzlement, Percy did not get out of the car. Instead, he remained seated behind the wheel, head bent slightly forward. When he finally pulled himself from the car and started toward the apartment building, Bunt could see that he looked worried. At the door, he broke the news: The Japanese had bombed Pearl Harbor. To both of them, it seemed unreal—too large an occurrence to make sense of. "Well," said Bunt, "let's go shooting."

The next day the reality came home. Bunt learned that the husband of one of the three women she worked with at the clinic had been killed during the surprise attack. Finally, the war that so many Americans had hoped to avoid was thrust upon them. When the twenty-five-year-old intern left town after Christmas, he knew that it might be some time before he saw Bunt again. With a doctor's unblinking realism, he had to wonder, too, whether he would ever again see Uncle Will, the man who had been like a father, and more than a father, for over a decade. It was not easy leaving Greenville on the eve of 1942.

7

The Shadow
of Death

———◆———

*He [Chekhov] was a doctor—and illness for a doctor is always harder to bear than
for a patient; the patient only feels, while the doctor, in addition to feeling, knows
the processes by which his organism is destroyed. In such cases we may consider
knowledge as causing the approach of death.*

—MAXIM GORKY, *Fragments from
My Diary*

Arriving in New York in the last week of December, Percy joined
some two hundred other young doctors who lived in Bellevue's intern
quarters. Percy's room was even more cramped than 1001 Bard Hall, but
he barely had time to notice. Working with eleven fellow interns in the
pathology lab, Percy quickly discovered that the pace was relentless,
numbingly so. As well as coping with the daily hospital deaths, the
Bellevue morgue took more than its share of street bums and "floaters,"
as the dead who were pulled out of the East River were called. Percy
recalled working on well over 125 cadavers during his first months of
internship, and while autopsies alone would have kept an intern busy,
they constituted only one part of the work. There were, in addition, the
endless laboratory workups, the part of pathology that Percy liked best.
Examining tissue specimens or blood under a microscope at least bore a
close resemblance to the "pure" sciences that he loved. That the intellectually demanding Dr. von Glahn ran these laboratories made the work
a little more appealing. "I am learning to do blood sugars," Percy boasted
in one of his first letters to Bunt Townsend.

But despite the small gratifications of his work, Percy's doubts about his career continued to grow. The work did not engage him in the way he believed that it should, that is, in the way it seemed to engage his fellow interns. Tired as he was at the end of the day, he still craved the diversion of movies. "I wish I was home with you tonight," he wrote Bunt, "so I could go to the movies with you." He had been to a movie by himself the night before, *The Maltese Falcon*.

Self-doubts were not the only thing that distracted Percy from his work. Uncle Will's condition, he learned, was rapidly worsening. During the third week of January, in fact, Will entered Kings' Daughters Hospital with intestinal hemorrhaging, and though he remained lucid and continued to see visitors, everybody could tell that death was close. It was remarkable, in fact, that he had survived so long. Earlier in the year, at Johns Hopkins, doctors had told Will that he had the oldest-looking body for a man his age that they had ever seen. In spirit, however, he remained a youthful man until the very end. On January 21, 1942, Will Percy died peacefully. He never complained or showed fear.

Roy immediately called Percy, but terrible as the news was, he had been fully prepared for it. Percy knew, however, that Phin wouldn't be. Phin had never realized how ill Will had been, even though, during Christmas vacation, he had thought it strange that Will remained in his kimono the whole time. As expected, the news came as a shock. "I felt cut adrift. The anchor was gone," Phin recalled. Percy told Phin that he would meet him in Washington that evening and that the two of them would take a night flight to Mississippi. They would have to get to Greenville as fast as possible. Services were to be held the next day.

Despite the short notice, the funeral was packed. The crowd spilled from inside the Percy house into the yard and out onto Percy and Broadway streets. It seemed that all of Greenville's citizens—and a great number of out-of-towners—had packed themselves into one square block, a quiet, pensive throng. Father Igoe, a Catholic priest and friend of Will's, conducted the service in the living room, but he seemed out of sorts the whole time. Some thought that he was still upset about not being allowed to administer last rites to Will Percy. (Roy Percy had turned him away at the hospital, saying that it had not been Will's wish.) Whatever the cause, Father Igoe never removed his overcoat and seemed hurried and distracted. But nothing would have broken the hushed concentration of the assembled crowd. Perhaps only the more prescient among them could imagine how thoroughly the war would change the character of Greenville, but everyone knew that Will Percy's death marked the end of an era.

. . .

Walker had little time to contemplate the meaning of Uncle Will's death, even though he received scores of condolence letters when he got back to New York. With the Japanese pushing General MacArthur's forces out of the Philippines, the country now seemed to be running on double-time, and doctors were much in demand. Medical internships were accelerated. Percy in a letter to Bunt said that he thought it wouldn't be long before he went into the Navy. It obviously pleased him to think that he might be joining the same service as Phin, who, like the rest of his classmates at Annapolis, would be commissioned in June after only three years at the Academy. Percy also discussed the grueling pace of work at the hospital. In a letter written in the middle of March, he referred to his fatigue: "This pathology is getting me down, and it's about three times easier than surgery." Each successive letter contained remarks about his growing exhaustion. He felt, he said in one, as though he were "dying."

Tiring as the work was, Percy did find some time for a restricted social life. Marcelle Dunning, who was in the same pathology rotation as Percy, recalled that he would sometimes go to the movies or go roller skating with her and other interns. It was clear to all in the pathology unit that Percy was Uncle Willie's favorite, a status that caused Percy some uneasiness, in part because von Glahn's manner was so prissy and effeminate. Apart from group outings, Percy also seems to have had a brief flirtation with a head floor nurse, "a nice upstate girl . . . brisk, swift, good-looking," recalled Percy, "one of the best of Bellevue, at least the best-looking." On one ill-starred date Percy took this nurse to the Boo Snooker Bar at the New Yorker Hotel, where they drank mint juleps, the first juleps the good southern boy had ever sipped in his life. But an evening that promised sweet romance quickly went awry. The trouble began when the bartender, who claimed to be from New Orleans, convinced Percy and his date to try his gin fizzes. Percy did and found that they were delicious. He tried a couple, not knowing that they were made of raw egg albumen, to which he was allergic (an allergy that he would one day bestow upon Tom More, the protagonist of *Love in the Ruins*). Driving his date back to her apartment in Brooklyn, where she promised to fix him dinner, Percy began to feel peculiar. In the middle of the Brooklyn Bridge, in fact, his upper lip began to swell and little sparks of light flew by the corner of his eye "like St. Elmo's fire." His condition quickly deteriorated: "In the space of thirty seconds my lip stuck out a full three-quarter inch, like a shelf, like Mortimer Snerd." To make matters worse, his eyes swelled shut. Making it to the end of the bridge, he pulled over to the side and fainted. His upstate nurse, unflappable, drove the car back to Bellevue, gave Percy a shot, and put him to bed. So much, Percy learned, for gin fizzes.

In early June Percy found that it was not just the the intern's schedule that was wearing him down. A routine chest X-ray revealed a spot—a small, quarter-sized shadow—at the apex of his right lung. It was immediately diagnosed as tuberculosis. The source was not hard to guess. Many of the derelicts who had been brought to the morgue were TB cases, and Percy, like his fellow interns, had been careless about protecting himself, sometimes performing autopsies without wearing his mask or gloves. Nor was Percy the only intern to pay for such carelessness: Four of the twelve in his group contracted TB. Dr. von Glahn was shattered by the number of interns who came down with the disease. He prided himself on running a clean operation and insisted on constant washing during all procedures. Pathology internships were notoriously dangerous, but four out of twelve was twice the usual incidence.

From the morgue Percy moved upstairs, to the TB service of Dr. J. Burns Amberson, one of the foremost "chest men" in America. Occupying a room with a view of the East River, Percy now found himself a patient. He had little to do but wait and think while doctors and nurses monitored the progress of his disease. Percy knew very well that a case such as his could heal quickly on its own. Then again, because there were no miracle drugs to attack the bacillus itself, the disease could drag on for years and possibly grow worse. The routine of rest, thermometers, and X-rays had begun.

Looking back on this time many years later, Percy described the onset of his disease as a stroke of good fortune. "I was the happiest man ever to contract tuberculosis, because it enabled me to get out of Bellevue and quit medicine." Those are the words of hindsight, of course. At the time, the doctor's spirits were anything but high. In his letters to Bunt, he gave voice to his fear that he would never recover. "I bet I'll be in a sanatorium for the rest of my life," he said in one.

But it was not only the possibility of death or long-term debilitation that troubled Percy in the early stages of his disease. There was also the war. Phin was going into active service and soon so would Roy, as indeed would most of Percy's friends and former classmates. (Shelby was already a lieutenant in the artillery.) The thought of all that was depressing: His two brothers, one with a wife and two sons, were preparing to put their lives on the line, while he lay abed in a hospital with a small lesion on his lung. It was not the same as being a shirker—far from it—but he knew he was missing the experience that Uncle Will had described as the most important that a man could face. It was hard for Percy not to feel that life had cheated him yet again. But the sentiment took the form of self-disgust rather than self-pity.

Then, finally, there was something about the disease itself that bothered Percy, as it bothered so many generations of TB sufferers: The taint of moral weakness. The persistence of this prejudice was remarkable. Ever since 1882, when Dr. Robert Koch presented a startling discovery to the Physiological Society of Berlin, the educated public had known that tuberculosis was a contagious disease caused by a bacillus. Yet an older view of tuberculosis—based partly on outmoded medicine and partly on cultural myths—persisted. According to this view, the disease was "a non-contagious, generally incurable and inherited disease, due to inherited consitutional peculiarities, perverted humors and various types of inflammations." The patient himself was largely responsible both for the onset and the persistence of the disease.

To be sure, very few illnesses remain strictly within the realm of the medical. They often take on psychological or cultural meaning, and some diseases are routinely pressed into service as metaphors. Susan Sontag has discussed this tendency in relation to cancer in *Illness as Metaphor*. But there is an even richer tradition of associations with tuberculosis, not all of them completely negative. The Romantics idealized the disease as the physical expression of soulfulness and sensitivity, and they celebrated its deathly pallor as a mark of beauty. The "White Plague," to them, was fashionable. To the Victorians (and to many of their modern heirs), consumption signaled a corrupt character, moral weakness, or lack of will. Whether the age deemed it fashionable or degenerate, turberculosis was consistently thought of as a disease bound up with the character of the sufferer. Literature preserved and reinforced the stereotypes. In Thomas Mann's *Magic Mountain*, for example, the rich array of associations with the disease are brought into play, including some new ones culled from Freudian theory, and the disease is linked, at least implicitly, to the death wish (though Mann does have the more skeptical characters in the novel express doubts about such overly "philosophical" notions). Writing well after Koch's discovery, Mann demonstrated the enduring power of the myths surrounding the disease.

Remarkably enough, such attitudes still had weight in 1942. By then, people believed that attitude and morale were the crucial factors in the recovery from, if not in the cause of, the disease. Theirs was not a silly notion. For all the exaggerations, the psychological condition of the TB sufferer was an important factor in the illness, and perhaps the most important factor in the recovery in the days before streptomycin (1946) and isoniazid (1953) were developed. Rest and an optimistic attitude were thought to be the best cure.

Unfortunately, optimism was not Percy's strongest suit. Given his own rather bleak outlook on life, he had to wonder whether his attitude would pull him through or pull him down. Based on the observations of others, there was reason to believe the latter. When Phin Percy visited his brother in Bellevue that summer, he did not see a happy or optimistic man. He saw someone who look shattered and uncertain. Having just finished PT-boat training in Melville, Rhode Island, Phin was assigned to a squadron whose boats were docked on the East River. Percy could see the boats from his hospital bed. It was a strange pass to come to.

The one immediate consolation of illness was books, a great consolation in Percy's case. Having all the time in the world to read, he decided to take up at the same point that he had earlier left off—with Dostoyevsky, his friend Foote's favorite Russian. He also turned to another writer that Foote had earlier lured him toward: Thomas Mann. During the summer after Percy's sophomore year at Chapel Hill, Foote had given him a German-language copy of *Buddenbrooks* and Percy had read it avidly. Now he turned to *The Magic Mountain* with equally keen interest. This was his story, he realized, and years later Percy would almost resent the fact that Mann had beat him to the subject. Indeed, one of Percy's two unpublished novels, *The Gramercy Winner,* would be a failed attempt to better Mann at his own game.

By August it was clear to Dr. Amberson and the other physicians on his staff that Percy's case, however mild, was not going to heal swiftly. The only course was for Percy to find a sanatorium and settle in for a long cure. The question was where. A belief current for many years was that high altitudes and cool, clear air were salubrious. The doctor who had done the most in America to foster that belief was Dr. Edward Livingston Trudeau, a graduate, like Percy, of Columbia's College of Physicians and Surgeons. Not long after losing his brother to the disease in 1865, Trudeau himself had succumbed to the "White Plague." Several attempts at cures failed, and in 1873 he went to a lodge in the Adirondack Mountains near Saranac Lake in a last-ditch effort to save his life. Miraculously, he got better, but when he returned to New York his health again began to fail. Trudeau decided to move permanently to the Adirondacks, bringing his family with him. The miracle worked again, and soon he was writing papers for medical journals "touting the Adirondacks as a health resort for the consumptive." The village of Saranac Lake grew rapidly, and in 1883, Trudeau opened the first two-patient cottage of his proposed sanatorium.

Largely because of the reputation of its founder, Trudeau Sanatorium was probably the best known in America, as famous in its way as any of the great Swiss *Kurhäuser* in Europe. When Percy began to consider possible places, it was high on the list. Bellevue always had a number of places reserved at Trudeau for its staff, and the state of New York paid for physicians who were stricken by the disease at public hospitals. Percy

could have afforded Trudeau even without state assistance. He had been
well provided for by Uncle Will. (While Roy inherited Will's portion of
Trail Lake, Walker and Phin divided the $244,000 that Will had re-
ceived for the 1940 sale of his portion of another plantation; in addition,
the three boys received equal divisions of Will's other personal and real
estate and of his extensive portfolio of stocks and bonds.)

Because of its reputation, Trudeau was crowded. Unlike other sanatoria around Saranac Lake, which like the town itself had suffered a loss
of business during the 1930s, Trudeau still had more applicants than it
could handle. The usual course for those on the sanatorium's waiting list
was to come to the town and find temporary lodging in one of Saranac
Lake's 150 registered "cure cottages," private homes, mostly, with large
sleeping porches for the invalid guests. In time, a place would come open
at one or another of the town's sanatoria.

That was the course that Percy followed. Toward the end of August,
he was taken to Grand Central Station and put on an overnight train to
Saranac Lake. Arriving early in the morning, Percy took a room in the
Riverside Inn, where he rested while he examined the list of prospective
cottages. He decided on a place at 60 Park Avenue, a large residence
with four private suites and several smaller private rooms. Considered to
be one of the best in town, it was run by a widow, a Mrs. Smithwick,
and was famous for the food prepared by her cook, Nora Harmon. Percy
took one of the attic rooms and settled in. The northern air was bracing,
even in late August. (According to a local joke, there were only two
seasons in Saranac: July and winter.) Percy wrote to Bunt on the last
day of the month: "I have left Bellevue and am up here in upper New
York. I sleep under three blankets. Shelby writes me that Greenville has
gone to hell. I hope you think about me sometimes when you're out with
your soldiers."

The brisk climate was not the only remarkable thing about the place
he had come to. Saranac Lake was an unusual town, a community given
over wholly to one enterprise: the curing of the sick. Its permanent
population down by about a thousand from its 1930 peak of eight thousand, it was a compact, densely built town with a clearly defined center
—Berkeley Square, "from which," as one writer described it, "you can
look down to the river, across to the leading hotel and Edward Livingston Trudeau's old home, or southward to a park on the shore of Lake
Flower." From the town's center radiated dozens of leafy neighborhoods,
and beyond them, on the outskirts of the town, stood most of the six
local sanatoria, Trudeau on the northern edge.

Given the presence of so many sick and suffering, Saranac Lake could
have been a very gloomy place. It wasn't. Death was a daily fact, to be

sure, and a coffin or two could usually be seen on the platform at the train station, but the atmosphere of the town was surprisingly upbeat. It was as though Trudeau's therapeutic ideal of perpetual optimism shaped the civic spirit. The townspeople, many of whom were former patients, were unintimidated by the disease. They knew how to protect themselves. Even though most of the town's full-time residents were involved in the business of caring for tuberculars, Saranac Lake had a TB infection rate that was lower than the national average.

But if Percy was caught up in the optimistic "can-cure" spirit of the the town, he did not show it. Two Trudeau patients—Marcelle Dunning, Percy's fellow intern at Bellevue, and a medical student named Barbara O'Neil—were among the few people to visit Percy at Smithwick's. The man they found when they came by in late November was not in good shape. He was, for one thing, extremely hoarse, a sleeping pill having become lodged in his throat the night before. (The twenty-six-year-old Percy had begun to suffer from insomnia, a condition that would plague him for the rest of his life.) In other ways, too, he seemed gloomy and out of sorts. Trying her best to cheer Percy up, Dunning went away from Smithwick's hoping that a place would soon come open at the "San."

The only other person to visit Percy that fall, Shelby Foote, was just as troubled by what he saw. Having recently finished Officer Candidate School in Fort Sill, Oklahoma, Lieutenant Foote was now stationed in Camp Shelby, Mississippi, and would soon be sent to Texas and then on to Europe. Concerned about his best friend, he made the long trek up to Lake Saranac and was immediately struck by Percy's utter isolation. The only people that his friend routinely saw, Foote learned, were his doctor (who came once a week), the woman who brought him his meals, and another woman who bathed him. Besides reading and listening to the radio (there was a good classical station in Montreal), Percy's only other occupation was teaching himself to play the piano on a wooden keyboard. "It was odd seeing him do those silent finger exercises," Foote recalled. He also remembered that Percy opened the drawer of his bedside to show him a pile of uncashed workmen's compensation checks. "Why haven't you cashed these?" an astonished Foote asked. "I can't, " said Percy, "It would be wrong to. I don't need them."

Describing this time as the "eeriest time of my life," Percy later recalled that he was "lonely and very depressed." No doubt he was. Yet Foote also detected an odd sort of contentment in his friend, an almost Buddhist calm, as though Percy had been given leave to enjoy what part of him had long craved: absolute solitude. Such isolation may not have made him happy, exactly, but it suited him. Moreover, it was during this period of absolute isolation and low-grade depression that Percy discovered something valuable about the kind of literature that he liked. Rather than novels brimming with society, Percy found consolation in fiction that featured lonely, cut-off, even somewhat aberrant types. He would later give precise formulation to the paradoxically cheering effect of gloomy literature, but at Saranac Lake all he knew was that he found himself reading Kafka's bleak parables and Dostoyevsky's novels of tormented spiritual seekers with something close to joy—as well as kindred sympathy. There was also a teasing simultaneity about reading *these* books at *this* time, a time when confidence in Western culture and civilization was being most darkly challenged. (On his radio Percy followed the Nazis' advance on Stalingrad and the string of alarming Japanese victories in the Philippines.)

What, the doctor wondered, was the relation of the outcast figure to the world that now seemed to be falling apart? He was either a deranged misfit, and therefore to be ignored, or something closer to a prophet, and therefore worth attending to. The pathologist in Percy began to ponder a problem: Was it possible that the Gregor Samsas of literature were only extreme cases of a widespread cultural malady, cases in which one could more clearly read the "mechanism of the disease"?

Percy was in Smithwick's for about four months. At the end of December, a place came open at Trudeau, and he "moved up." Of necessity, life would be more sociable at the sanatorium—there were about two hundred patients and a large staff of doctors, nurses, and therapists. Arriving in a cab, Percy was immediately impressed by the physical beauty of the place. It seemed like a small college, an impression that he later put to use in his apprentice novel, *The Gramercy Winner*. In the novel, the narrator describes the arrival of the central character, William Grey, at the "famous Lodge":

> It was like a campus. Sturdy little cottages were dotted at random under the trees, like fraternity houses, and young men lolled about in front. In the middle of it all there rambled away a fine old spa-hotel of a building with far-flung wings and high screen porches. They passed the craft shop; from within came a sound of whirring and a high clamor of talk. A pair of nurses came toward them, students in black stockings, their sleeves rolled up, their arms folded identically into their starched waists. They stopped and looked back as the convertible passed. A young man and a girl strolled hand in hand, he with a blanket thrown serape-wise over his shoulder. The sanitorium lay on a gentle hillside. Below, they caught glimpses of a green valley with a winding river. Above there stretched away a high mountain meadow dotted with clumps of shimmering poplars.

The first week or so was spent in the large admitting building, which had the facilities of a small hospital in addition to several sleeping porches. During this time, the patient had his history taken, received a physical examination, underwent X-rays and a series of lab tests. At the end of the week, each new case was presented at a staff meeting. There it was determined whether the patient would be assigned to the infirmaries, Ludington or Childs, or if his case was not serious, to one of the many cottages dotting the green and rolling grounds of the sanatorium. Percy's being a relatively mild case, he was assigned to one of the bed-rest cottages with ten to twelve other patients.

The first stage of treatment was known as being "on trays." Patients took and recorded their own temperatures and were visited daily by the physicians. This was by far the strangest stage of the cure. Patients were handled like living mummies, swaddled in three or four blankets (one of them usually electric) and carted in and out of doors by the Saranac attendants. Patients were strictly forbidden to leave the supine position. X-rays were taken every six weeks or so, and if a patient showed improvement he received walking permission, beginning with five minutes twice a day and slowly working up to an hour.

Once a patient graduated beyond an hour, walking freedom was unrestricted, and the patient could receive passes to go into town to a movie or restaurant. Whether "down" or "up," however, all patients were required to observe a fairly rigid schedule, including two-hour rest periods in the morning and the afternoon. Typically, patients rose at 7:00 A.M., ate a hearty breakfast (all meals were brought to patients until they were up; once up, they could go to the dining hall), and spent two hours resting. Lunch was followed by another rest period and a long stretch of free time, during which the ambulatory could stroll into town if they wished. In the evenings after supper, there might be a film in the Recreation Building, and there were always card games, billiards, or the seven-thousand-book Mellon Memorial Library for those patients looking for something to do. Lights were out at 9:00 P.M., though many stayed up till ten o'clock to hear the news commentary of Elmer Davis.

The "passive" treatment was the established regimen of Trudeau, and most of its physicians eschewed such aggressive procedures as the pneumothorax operation (in which one of the lungs was collapsed to give it rest). A patient's weight was considered a significant indicator of health, and a loss or gain affected one's walking privileges as much as a good or bad X-ray. Patients were encouraged to eat heavily and to drink milk at all times, and most of them did.

The routines of the "San" had a way of beguiling time. Patients were always surprised at how quickly it passed—and truly, when all was said and done, how pleasantly. The routines were so agreeable, in fact, that many patients held to them—or at least to parts of them—long after they left the sanatorium. Percy was no exception. For the rest of his life, he faithfully took naps in the afternoon, and when he began to write in earnest, he did most of the difficult first-draft composing lying down, stretched out upon a bed or sofa or reclining chair. Some of the dietary habits stuck as well. Though always a picky eater, he would faithfully drink his milk every day.

But in one respect, at least, Percy was not the typical "San" patient. He never seemed to get caught up in the group spirit of the cure. He was viewed as something of a loner, and many of his fellow patients considered him downright morose—a dangerous thing for a TB sufferer to be. Yet Percy was not a complete isolate. He made a number of good friends, including Edwin L. Kendig, a young physician who had entered Trudeau very shortly after Percy did. A 1936 graduate of the University of Virginia medical school, he had come down with TB in 1939 while doing a residency at Bellevue. Having gone through a successful cure in Arizona, he had returned to his native Virginia, but in the fall of 1942, while establishing his practice in Richmond, he had been called up to active military duty. A routine X-ray revealed activity in his lungs—a dreaded "break." This time he went north rather than west, ending up with the twenty other doctor-patients then at Trudeau.

Not surprisingly, the recurrence of the disease had left Kendig in very low spirits. He liked medicine and was a gifted clinician in pediatrics. To be pulled out of his career for a second time was particularly disheartening, and his misery was obvious. In fact, what struck Percy most when he first saw Kendig was his fellow patient's gloomy countenance. They had been in the waiting room of the radiology office, but neither spoke. Clearly, though, each had evaluated the other with a clinical eye. A few days later they bumped into each other again, and Percy confessed to the stranger that he had never seen a gloomier-looking man. "That's funny," Kendig replied, "I thought you looked like the sourest person I'd ever seen." The two men laughed. With that unflattering mutual appraisal a friendship began to grow.

Kendig might have assumed at first that Percy was out of sorts for the same reason he was, but he soon discovered otherwise. Unlike himself, Kendig learned, Percy did not miss medicine, did not even appear to like it. Kendig considered it strange, too, that the specialties Percy contemplated entering, pathology and psychiatry, were so completely different: "The one was the height of scientific precision. The other was so scientifically imprecise." Kendig concluded that Percy "liked the idea of medicine but not the reality of it." For the most part, the two men talked about matters other than medicine. They were broadly philosophical topics, as Kendig recalls. "I couldn't tell you that I thought he would be a philosophical novelist one day, but I thought he had a philosophical bent. Not that our discussions were on a very high philosophical plane. We just talked about our lives and what was happening in the world."

Kendig, like so many others who came to know Percy, was impressed by his friend's wit and quickness, but there was something about Percy that disturbed him. "I have never seen someone who could be so cynical, so nihilistic. It was a little frightening." Kendig never learned where these reserves of darkness might have come from—Percy never spoke about his family background—but he suspected that something was wrong.

Not that Percy went around baring the dark side of his soul to all he met. To most patients, he seemed an agreeable but somewhat retiring person. With Larry Doyle, the second baseman of the New York Giants, Percy would quite contentedly discuss baseball statistics. With Béla Bartók, the Hungarian composer, he would sometimes talk about music. With Arthur Fortugno, a college boy from Jersey City, New Jersey, he would argue Catholic theology. With Paul Downey, an obstetrician from Buffalo, he would discuss everything from the weather to women.

The latter topic was a popular one among the young men. The atmosphere of the "San" was thick with romance, and short liaisons—some adulterous—were quite common. Pairing off with a mate, either for friendship or romance, was called "cousining," and the more adventurous of the romantically inclined couples would sneak into town and take rooms in the hotels, in defiance of municipal ordinances. While he was in the "down" stage, Percy viewed "cousining" as nothing more than a theoretical proposition, a topic for discussion and gossip. Besides, he was still pining for a girl back in Greenville, even while he realized that he might never see her again. A letter to Bunt Townsend at the end of December expressed his regrets and fears: "Thank you for your kind thoughts. It was my first Xmas away from home. I am in Trudeau Sanatorium. It is just like college. From your description, Greenville sounds like a glorified cathouse. I predict you will find a nice lieutenant. . . . My kid brother is in a PT boat in the Pacific. . . . Wish I could kiss you over New Year's Eve."

Percy could not have known that his kid brother went out on his first patrol the night after he wrote Bunt. Under the cover of darkness, Phin's squadron headed toward Tulagi, near Guadalcanal, in search of Japanese ships that were running the "Slot." Phin was second in command on that first run, an eventless patrol, as it turned out. But a few nights later, the boat encountered enemy ships and the captain froze upon seeing enemy gunfire. After that disastrous outing, the skipper was relieved and Phin took command.

Skippering another boat in the same squadron was Lieutenant (j.g.) John F. Kennedy—"a great guy, a card player, and profane as hell," as Phin Percy remembered him. In fact, eight months into his Pacific assignment, riding as a "guest" on another boat, Phin Percy witnessed the ramming of Kennedy's *PT-109* and tried unsuccessfully to convince the commanding officer to look for survivors. The skipper refused. He said that no one could have survived. Phin protested, but the skipper remained firm. Later, Phin's instincts were proved right, but it was small consolation.

At about the same time as Phin's first patrols, Percy's other brother went out to the Greenville Army Air Base and enlisted. Now in basic training, Roy hoped when he finished to be accepted into the cadet training program and earn his wings. It looked for a while as though family history were repeating itself. Like his father (who also had two sons when he enlisted), Roy had chosen the Army Air Corps, and like his father he proved to be so able a pilot that he was made a flight instructor. Unlike his father, though, Roy would not miss the action, even though it would come toward the end of the war.

The fact that his two brothers were involved in the war effort heightened Percy's sense of self-disgust. Each news broadcast reminded him of what he was missing. Yet, at the same time, as Foote had seen, Percy felt an odd sort of contentment in the world of the consumptive. It was a peculiar malady, more often leaving the sufferer in a limbo state between health and sickness than in abject physical distress. Percy later discussed the strange health-in-sickness of the consumptive in notes that he jotted down in the early 1950s, before he started writing *The Gramercy Winner:* "Saranac story. The monstrous health of TB patients. No sickness, no symptoms, nothing acute, an X-ray disease. The long grayness. No sweat, no love, no exercise, no injury. The amazing result of moderation. The sweat glands atrophy."

When he came to writing his "Saranac story," *The Gramercy Winner,* Percy would make the seductive limbo state of the tuberculosis sufferer the book's central metaphor. The main character of the novel, significantly named William Grey, is intelligent, charming, but in some fundamental way colorless, passionless. A product of wealth—his family lives near New York City's Gramercy Park—and a Princeton man, he had joined the Marines and was preparing to go to the Pacific when a "spot" was discovered and he was sent to cure. Grey describes himself as a "spectator," like so many of Percy's characters and, indeed, like Percy himself. Grey is self-effacing in the extreme, a man without qualities, and finds himself increasingly attracted to the undemanding world that his small lesion has brought him to, a world that grants him reprieve from decisions, choice, and will (for as his first name reminds us, will is as important a part of the story as grayness). One of the doctors Will befriends, a fallen Catholic named Scanlon, warns Will against the seductions of the place. He tells him to clear out once he gets his "half hour twice." Will wants to know why, and Scanlon cuts loose with a diatribe that is only half ironical:

> Willy, it's a symbiotic society in an advanced state of decay. It's an organism healthy and suntanned without and all corruption within. There is a Faustian pact between man and bacillus and each lives feeding on the other. There is a breakdown and liquefaction of all strata and structure. It's all purulence and fornication and whoredom.

Scanlon's tirade is interrupted by another doctor who shares the cure cottage with them, a cynical pathologist named Jack van Norden, but Scanlon continues unabashed:

> Willy, a strange thing happens to a man when he comes up here. He comes to think the old world had given him a fingering and he's going to finger it back. He feels a peculiar license—it is the reverse of the juridical process: he receives his sentence first, that is, he gets his tuberculosis, and he reserves to himself the privilege of crime later. The consumptive is a variety of fascist, Willy—he really feels himself a lot better than others. He is a man of privileges. This is a strange little place, Willy—not subject to the laws and levies of the United States. Haven't you heard, for example, that the marriage contract is invalid north of Utica?

A world where normal laws are suspended, where people are freed from the consequences of their actions and indeed from the necessity of action itself is clearly a metaphor for more than a personal state of mind: It is, in Percy's novel, a metaphor of what the Western world is coming to.

Percy had no way of knowing during the war that a grayer, passionless world would emerge after it was over. He wrote The Gramercy Winner in the early 1950s, when such an outcome was becoming more obvious. But even when he was in the sanatorium, Percy was beginning to think that grayness was a sign of a deeper cultural problem, a problem with history. And he was beginning to see as well that his own devastating cynicism might be related to the pathology of the modern world.

Such intimations came mainly from reading the writers to whom he was now addicted—Dostoyevsky, Mann, Tolstoy, and Kafka. But Percy also began to explore areas that he had never looked at before, notably theology and philosophy. According to his friend Kendig, the catalyst for this novel line of investigation was a young man named Arthur Fortugno, a Catholic from Jersey City, New Jersey, a likeable companion but a feisty debater well versed in Catholic apologetics. Like Percy, he was a skilled logic chopper, and the fact that he could better his opponent got under Percy's skin. The only way to combat Fortugno, Percy decided, was to read what Fortugno had read; so he began to scavenge the Mellon Library for Augustine and Aquinas and other church fathers.

Percy was surprised to find that much of what he perused was good, particularly Aquinas. The appeal is not surprising, considering Percy's old attraction to system building, logic, and theoretical elegance. Percy admired Aquinas's dialectical style, his way of setting forth a proposition and its antithesis, and arguing through both to a conclusion. The power of such reasoning was impressive, but the dialectical method taught Percy something else as well: that intellectual categories were slippery, and that reasoning does not lead ineluctably to truth or certainty. Aquinas's work taught Percy how to be wary of the intellect, and mindful of its limitations, without being anti-intellectual. While Percy was not yet ready to jump into Aquinas's camp, he was at least intrigued.

Did the debates with Fortugno lead Percy to his first encounter with Søren Kierkegaard, perhaps the greatest single intellectual influence in his life? Percy himself was inconsistent on this point. He often said that he did not begin to read the Danish religious philosopher until the early 1950s, after his encounter with the French and German existentialists. Yet he admitted that he had read one of Kierkegaard's more important essays, "The Difference between a Genius and an Apostle," well before his conversion to Catholicism. Indeed, he claimed that he read that essay at Saranac. It would have been possible, certainly, since an English translation of the essay had been published, along with two other essays, in a volume entitled *The Present Age and Two Minor Ethico-Religious Treatises*, in 1940.

It would have been likely as well. The essay deals with the crux of the argument between Percy and Fortugno: the difference between truth as revelation and truth as intellectual discovery. In the essay, Kierkegaard asserts the difference between the profundity of the genius (whether philosophical, artistic, or scientific) and the authority of the apostle. To reduce the apostle to a variety of genius, as many liberal theologians of his day did, to talk about St. Paul as though he were comparable to Plato or Shakespeare, was, in Kierkegaard's mind, to miss the point entirely. The importance of the apostle's words derived not from their content— their wit or cleverness or brilliance or poetry—but from the fact that the apostle had been called, and thus authorized, to say them.

That the "good news" of Christianity was of a wholly different order from the statements of geniuses in art or science would have come as something of a revelation to Percy. After all, he had been introduced to Christianity by the liberal minister of Birmingham's Independent Presbyterian Church, a minister who had cast Jesus as a kind of ethical genius, not as a living paradox. To Percy, Kierkegaard's words might have sounded, at first reading, like those of firebrand fundamentalists. But there was an undeniable psychological subtlety and brilliance to Kierkegaard's way of putting things—and something else: an irony so fine that it seemed to cancel itself, leaving the man behind it vulnerable to the terrible God he desperately sought. That Kierkegaard challenged the intellectual orthodoxy of his day was also appealing to Percy, but this was an aspect of the Dane's work to which he would later pay more heed. What his first brush with Kierkegaard did was to leave Percy with a new understanding of Christianity itself, an understanding of its essentially authoritarian character. It also alerted him to an intriguing paradox: that true individuality, and indeed a kind of authenticity of self (which Percy believed he was sorely lacking), might be attained only through submission to some higher authority.

Percy's introduction to theology and religious thinking did not immediately pull him into the Catholic church or, for that matter, into any other. His skepticism and scientism were still strong. But he was not as content or certain in them as he had been before. His secret vanity—his intellectual pride—had been challenged. With his sparring partner Fortugno, Percy attended services at the local Catholic church, St. Bernard's. Kendig also went along. "We went out of curiosity," Kendig remembered. "It was Walker's and my first time in a Catholic church."

In the spring of 1943, Percy moved into an "up" cottage. Officially called James but generally referred to as the "doctors' cottage," it was home to twelve physicians or medical students, most of whom were in sufficiently good health to assume limited medical responsibilities around the sanitorium. Typically, the doctors of James went on rounds, worked in the X-ray clinic, assisted with the occasional surgery, or even did clinical or research work in the laboratories. Percy's interest in pathology would have made him particularly valuable to the laboratory director, Dr. Leroy Gardner, because the pathologist, Dr. Arthur Vorwald, had been called up to military service.

James was considered a choice cottage. It was lively, on occasions even raucous. Talk was often medical—there were weekly discussion groups that focused on cases written up in *The New England Journal of Medicine*—but not exclusively. Like most doctors, the residents of James were a somewhat cynical lot, at least outwardly inured to suffering and illness, and eager for a drink or two when the evening came. Soon after Percy moved in, he was joined by Kendig, and the two friends became even closer. Kendig could now observe Percy in his cure chair, noting, among other things, that he was an avid bird-watcher who kept his two volumes of *Birds of New York* always within reach.

Percy and Kendig would occasionally join their fellow physicians for nights on the town. One of their favorite spots was a restaurant named Henessey's (renamed Shaughnessy's in *The Gramercy Winner*), known for serving the best steaks in town. Henessey's was also the site of a good deal of drinking and dancing—and even some romancing.

Percy himself, now that he was up and about, was developing a more-than-theoretical interest in the practice of "cousining." One medical student in particular struck his fancy, the same woman, Barbara O'Neil, who had accompanied Marcelle Dunning on her visit to Percy at Smithwick's. Intelligent and witty, she had been a third-year student at the Women's Medical College of Philadelphia when she came down with TB. An attractive brunette, she was often accompanied by her good friend Marcelle Dunning, one of the few female doctors recovering at the "San." Percy hit it off with both women, escorting them into town or on the occasional outing. During the summer, they and a few other patients would rent motorboats and take picnic lunches out to the islands on the lake. Occasionally, Percy would head off alone with O'Neil for walks around the grounds or into town for a movie.

Percy seems to have been very fond of O'Neil, but the friendship never developed much beyond mutual affection. As much as he enjoyed O'Neil's wit, he was also a little intimidated by it. As he confessed to his friend Robert Coles many years later, intellectual women made him uncomfortable. He feared that he could not be at ease with such women —that they demanded more than he could provide. So far, in fact, the only woman that he had been completely at ease with was Bunt Townsend, but he thought it was unfair to keep her dangling. At the end of 1943, he sent her a Christmas card with nothing more than a row of x's and his signature. He was certain she had found someone else by then.

And even if she hadn't, Percy was entering a crisis in his life, a crisis from which he was not sure he would emerge. He alluded very briefly to the problem in an October letter to his college friend Ned Boone, who was in the Navy and stationed in Alaska. Boone had recently written to remind Percy of the tenth anniversary of their first meeting at the Old Well at Chapel Hill. After remarking upon the "fantastic turns" their lives had taken since that meeting, Percy described his current condition: "My lesion, as they call it, appears to be healed. I am still at Trudeau—really, the prospects are good, my only handicap being a colossal disgust with myself." The causes of this disgust were several—professional, philosophical, and personal—and each was tangled up with the others. Percy knew by now that he was ill-suited for any kind of clinical work in medicine. He was not really comfortable with patients and suspected that he never would be (a discomfort that militated strongly against psychiatry as a career). Research or teaching, or some combination of the two, seemed to him a possibility. But even the prospect of research gave him pause. He saw, as he has Binx Bolling say in *The Moviegoer*, that he was not "one of those scientists in the movies who don't care about anything but the problem in their heads." Yet, like Binx, he was not particularly envious of the fellow with "a flair for research," for such a person was "no more aware of the mystery which surrounds him than a fish is aware of the water it swims in."

For several years, despite growing doubts, Percy had clung to his belief that science would ultimately provide the answer to his specific problem, his unhappiness as a human being. He no longer could. He now understood something about science and its relation to self-knowledge that he had never understood before. More than thirty years later he described how this discovery dawned upon him at Saranac: "I gradually began to realize that as a scientist—a doctor, a pathologist—I knew so very much *about* man, but had little idea what man *is*." The positive result of this realization was that it gave Percy an idea of what his true calling might be—not research, with the aid of an elegant method, but a search, with the aid of nothing more than his own wits and intuition. He also knew what the object of his search should be: the mystery that surrounds the individual life. But the difficult thing about his discovery, and what made it into such a burden, was that Percy saw no way of making his distantly perceived calling into a career. Furthermore, he had a strong fear of becoming like one of those odd great-uncles that he had read about in Uncle Will's memoirs—feckless, idle, and terminally melancholic.

To complicate matters, Percy began to see his physical disease as related to his spiritual condition. He had succumbed, despite his medical understanding, to what Thomas Mann had gently mocked as the "philosophic" approach to the disease. (Borrowing directly from Mann, Percy has a physician in *The Gramercy Winner* warn the protagonist Will Grey against the Adirondack Lodge [that is, Trudeau]: "They are too—ah—philosophic about it up there.") As scientific as Dr. Percy was, he couldn't completely escape the old belief that his consumption was only an outward and visible sign of an inward and invisible corruption, a disease of the soul. "I knew that I was getting better," he later recounted, "but I still thought, irrationally, that I was never going to recover."

Throughout his life, even after miracle drugs were developed, Percy remained dreadfully afraid that his tuberculosis was returning. Even in the terminal stages of cancer, his fear of TB was stronger than his fear of the disease that was killing him. To him, clearly, TB had come to represent something worse than physical death: death-in-life, or despair.

Toward the end of 1943, Walker learned that his friend Foote had received orders to go overseas. He was assigned to the Fifth Division, which was then headquartered near Birmingham, England, but shortly after arriving, Foote was sent with his artillery battery, Battery A, to train in Northern Ireland, about fifty miles south of Belfast. Foote was itching for war experience. His great-grandfather had been a Civil War general and a hero, and Foote wondered how well he would stand up to the test of battle.

He would never find out. The same insubordinate streak that had gotten him into trouble in high school proved to be his nemesis again. The trouble began when his battalion commander, a lieutenant colonel and West Pointer, upbraided an enlisted man in Foote's battery. Foote believed that the reprimand had been unnecessary and told the lieutenant colonel so. From then on, as Foote put it, "he was keeping books."

The colonel soon had his revenge. Foote had started to see a young woman in Belfast named Tess Lavery, and on the return trip from one of his weekend visits his train broke down and Foote got back to camp two hours after his pass had expired. The battalion commander put Foote under arrest, but not for long. As soon as the facts were established, Foote was released with his commander's reluctant apologies. Now, however, the lieutenant colonel began to look for the slightest technicality to bust Foote on. After several smaller incidents, he found what he needed. Foote had taken a jeep on personal leave, which was permitted for trips up to fifty miles away from the camp. Belfast was slightly beyond that limit, but the difference was usually winked at. Not in Foote's case, though. When he returned from Belfast, his commander charged him with falsifying government documents, and this time the charge stuck. Foote—much to his shame and disgrace—was handed a discharge "without honor" (not to be confused with the far worse dishonorable discharge). He returned to the United States, this time to New York, where, in August of 1944, he landed a job with the Associated Press.

Shortly after setting himself up in the city, Foote took a trip up to Saranac Lake to see Percy. He had much to tell his old friend, and not only about the rotten turn of events in Northern Ireland. They had a lot of catching up to do on the book front, and most of all there was a big piece of personal news: Foote was planning to marry Tess Lavery in the fall, and he wondered whether Percy would be well enough to be his best man. Percy thought he would be. He had plans to leave the sanatorium at the end of the month and to return to New York in the fall. He had hopes of returning to Columbia as an instructor in pathology in the winter if his health held up.

Before Foote returned to New York, he and his friend had a near encounter with one of the more famous literary figures of the day. The two men were out for a walk when, as Robert Taylor describes it, "on the opposite side of the street approached the unmistakable figure of W. Somerset Maugham, then at the zenith of his fame." Maugham, as Percy already knew, was in Saranac Lake visiting his lover, a tuberculosis patient. But a meeting that could have turned into one of those little encounters of literary history was missed. "Foote, aspiring young novelist, hesitated, caught between the shock of recognition and the awkwardness of intruding on the great man. Maugham drew abreast, and the moment passed." Whatever the meeting would have amounted to, neither Percy nor Foote greatly regretted the failed opportunity. The truth was, neither thought too highly of Maugham's work. All the same, Percy might have wondered how Maugham had managed to write his way out of a medical career.

In September of 1944, Percy seemed to be back on the road to his own medical career. He planned in the winter to take up an instructorship at Columbia and begin introducing second-year medical students to the mysteries of pathology, but instead of living on the campus, Percy accepted the invitation of Huger Jervey to move into the servants' quarters of his large apartment at 1150 Fifth Avenue. The decision to live with Jervey—or Hugger, as he was called—might have revealed more about Percy's state of mind than he realized. For one thing, it showed a definite reluctance to strike out on his own. At the same time, it showed an abiding need for mentors, elderly male father surrogates. Moving in with Jervey, Uncle Will's closest male friend, was the closest thing possible to remaining under Uncle Will's tutelage.

Of course, the arrangement was attractive in its own right. Jervey, a native of Charleston, South Carolina, was an intelligent, cultured, and well-connected man about town. Except during World War I, he had lived in New York since 1910, where he studied, practiced, and taught law, serving as dean of the Columbia Law School between 1924 and 1928 and as director of the Parker School of International Studies between 1931 and his death in 1949. Jervey's interests ranged far beyond the law. Before entering law school, he had taught classics at Sewanee for six years, and the imprint of the scholar-humanist never wore off. He was in addition a competent musician and an avid symphony-goer (who as a younger man had been Mr. Stanley Morgan's regular Thursday night guest at the symphony). Percy clearly enjoyed himself in the company of Jervey, a short, gray-haired man with pop eyes. One of Walker's Georgia cousins, Ann Freeman, spent a memorable evening in Jervey's apartment during the fall of 1944 and recalled above all the jollity of the occasion, the good-natured bantering between Percy and his avuncular friend. Roy Percy also found his brother to be in outwardly good spirits when he passed through New York City in late 1944. Roy was on his way to the European theater—to Dijon, France, where he would join the Thirty-fourth Squadron of the Seventeenth Bomb Group and pilot a B-26 on twenty missions over Germany before the Third Reich capitulated on May 7 of the following spring. (Their youngest brother, Phin, had briefly returned to the States to retrain for the submarine service; he was now serving as communications officer on a submarine that was routinely cruising Japanese waters.)

Percy's outward appearance of contentment was not all a mask. He was young and unattached and certainly more free to roam about the city than when he was a student or intern, and the atmosphere of the city was cautiously upbeat. Everywhere the feeling ran strong that the war was going the Allies' way, what with the successful Normandy invasion the previous summer and a string of Allied victories in the Pacific. Percy and Shelby had time to gallivant about town and take in the occasional film, particularly before Shelby got married in late October. Foote, as usual, took pleasure in discussing his friend's political bugbear, FDR, whose election to a fourth term in the upcoming November election looked almost assured.

But Foote was not all jokes and good humor. He wanted to get back into the war before it ended. And he began to have second thoughts about his marriage even before Tess Lavery arrived for the ceremony. He had found an apartment at Eighty-sixth and Park and started to revise his apprentice novel. Now he was not so sure he wanted to give up his bachelorhood, fearing that marriage might cut into his writing. Percy could tell that his friend was nervous. As they drove together to the small Protestant chapel where the ceremony was to be held, Foote unconsciously whistled the Cole Porter tune "Don't Fence Me In." Nevertheless, the service went on, Percy standing as best man while Foote took the lovely Belfast woman as his bride. The only other person in attendance was Percy's date, Hope Galloway, a Memphis native who was then living in New York and whom Percy occasionally took out.

After the wedding, Percy and Jervey saw less of Foote. He had taken a larger apartment in Washington Heights. Marriage and the late-night shifts at AP left him little time for socializing. And his resolution to get back into the war finally met with success. In January, just before Percy started teaching at Columbia, Foote reported for Marine boot camp.

Percy's second tour in New York gave him the opportunity to take stock of something that he had never had time to think about during his medical-school days: the intellectual life of the city. While studying medicine Percy had taken only the occasional glimpse at those journals containing the arguments that divided the intellectuals of the city into pro-Stalinists and anti-Stalinists. Percy found both parties unacceptable and their arguments uninteresting. After all, he considered Roosevelt too far to the left.

During the war a new group of European emigrés had come onto the New York scene, and thinkers like Hannah Arendt and Theodor Adorno began to recast the terms of intellectual debate in America, not abandoning politics, exactly, but giving politics a more philosophical grounding in fundamental questions about being, alienation, and the implications of living in a technological age. *Partisan Review* and other journals were beginning to introduce the ideas of philosophers like Karl Jaspers, Martin Heidegger, and Jean-Paul Sartre to an American audience, and these were ideas that chimed with Percy's interests.

Also writing in New York at that time was the Columbia professor of English Lionel Trilling. Trilling was a well-known literary scholar before the war, but now he was acquiring a reputation for broader cultural criticism. The essays that came from his pen during the 1940s (and that would appear, collected and revised, in *The Liberal Imagination* in 1950) proposed that a tough-minded liberalism, charged with a strong awareness of limits and of the perverse dark side of human nature, offered the best alternative to the exhausted ideologies of the left and right alike. Whether these essays were read by Percy during his New York days is impossible to say, but he was alert enough to intellectual currents to catch the drift of Trilling's arguments. Living with Jervey, moreover, provided Percy with a direct link to the intellectual life at Columbia. It would have been hard for anyone interested in literature and ideas not to hear Trilling's clarion call for the artist who would "probe curiously into the hidden furtive recesses of the contemporary soul."

Just as hard to ignore would have been the equally tough-minded preachments of Reinhold Niebuhr at Union Theological Seminary. Appearing the same year that Percy lived in New York was Niebuhr's *The Children of Light and the Children of Darkness*, which could best be described as a chastisement of well-meaning but naive idealists. Niebuhr argued that the people with the best intentions—the "children of light" —were prey to the myth of human perfectibility and innate goodness.

Such credulity had made them vulnerable to the machinations of the children of darkness, who played according to the rules of unrestrained self-interest. Niebuhr appealed to the children of light to arm themselves "with the wisdom of the children of darkness but remain free from their malice" so that they might "beguile, deflect, harness and restrain self-interest, individuality and collectivity, for the sake of community."

On various fronts, then, New York intellectual culture of the mid-1940s seemed to be moving toward a deeper psychological and spiritual concern with the human condition. The trauma of war, the near-success of fascism, and the barbarisms committed by the Nazis in their death camps (about whose existence Americans had finally become convinced) all pointed to an evil that could not be explained away by social and political analysis—a radical evil at the heart of mankind. This awareness called for new and radical forms of analysis. According to Trilling, the age demanded a diagnostic art to plumb the dark sides of human character; according to Niebuhr, it called for a theology mindful of evil; and in the view of the Europeans associated with the New School, what was needed most was a consideration of the causes of man's estrangement from himself and his world. Percy was deaf to none of these appeals.

But before he got down to the business of responding, Percy would have to experience another repetition. In May 1945, after a routine X-ray, Percy was informed that the TB bacilli in his system had once again become active. He accepted the return of his old familiar with a fatalistic shrug, but rather than returning to Saranac Lake (beds there usually came open only in the early fall), he considered several places in the West before settling on one that was much closer by—Gaylord Farm Sanatorium in Wallingford, Connecticut, not far from New Haven.

If the place was different, the routines were not. The director of the sanatorium, Dr. Russell Lyman, was himself a graduate of Trudeau, having both convalesced and studied there in the early part of the century, and he imposed on Gaylord the same inflexible cure schedule that he had witnessed and been through at Saranac Lake.

Percy arrived with boxes of books and a readiness to submit to the regimen. " 'Well here you are again,' I thought. They noted that I was interested in literature so they assigned me to the same bed Eugene O'Neill had occupied in 1912—a strange, strange feeling." O'Neill had considered Gaylord the place of his "second birth" and had said just that in a letter he wrote to Dr. Lyman shortly after leaving the sanatorium:

> I am looking forward to some fine spring day when I shall be able to
> pay the farm a visit . . . although I trust all the patients I knew are

halely and heartily bucking the world, I still hope to find, among those attached to the San, some familiar face to remind me of the time I should have been cast down by my fate—and wasn't. If, as they say, it is sweet to visit the place one was born in, then it will be doubly sweet for me to visit the place I was reborn in—for my second birth was the only one that has my full approval.

Gaylord would be the site of Percy's second birth as well. It was here, as he later attested, that the possibility of a new calling hit him for the first time. True, he had been reading widely before he came to Gaylord, but now his reading became more pointed, more directed. He read like a person who was trying to define his subject, searching among his favorite writers for clues. One book that he read, or reread, was Dostoyevsky's *Notes from Underground.* What particularly impressed him about this unusual narrative was Dostoyevsky's weaving of cultural criticism with his fictional characterization of a man in extremis. The story set the wheels in Percy's mind turning: Could one really write a story this way? It was exhilarating to think that one could. Percy made hurried notes in the margins of his copy of the book, one of them a reflection on the character of Dostoyevsky's tormented antihero: "He is worse off than Kafka's hero who did become an insect." And then, as though he were pondering the task before him: "If D were alive, who would he attack?"

8

Drift and Resolution

"You will be thirty years old. Don't you think a thirty year old man
ought to know what he wants to do with his life?"
"Yes."

— WALKER PERCY, *The Moviegoer*

In May of 1946, Walker Percy contemplated the approach of his thir-
tieth birthday with something close to panic. Having left Gaylord at the
end of 1945, he had returned to Greenville and taken up residence—
temporary, he assumed—in the garage apartment behind Roy and Sarah's house on Percy Street. But temporary was beginning to stretch on.
The time since his return had passed quickly, uneventfully, though not
unpleasantly. He still had no job, not even part-time work at the clinic.
The only medical future he had given any consideration to was a possible
position in a sanatorium out West, but it was a thought that he tried on
one day and discarded the next. He realized that he didn't want to be a
doctor. He even had a gold-plated excuse for abandoning the profession,
the physicians at Gaylord having told him that he was likely to have
another break if he returned to medicine.

Besides, Percy by now knew what he wanted to do. He knew that he
wanted to write. But he faced the same problem that had once overwhelmed Uncle Will: what to write about? He suspected that his own
dreary self and his own dreary life were his only subjects, but he could
not say, at this point, what either amounted to, what kind of story they

would add up to. He had, he knew, some knack for hanging words together, but he lacked the instigating energy that the writer of stories needs, the energy that gives him the motivation to put words to paper and that transforms itself into plot. All Percy could say with certainty at this point was that he suffered from a profound moral listlessness and ambivalence, and both made him feel worse about himself. He was like one of those "superfluous men" in Russian literature that he had read about, an Oblomov who could barely lift himself from the divan of his lassitude.

For a time, at least, Percy's confusion blended quite inconspicuously with the postwar mood of the town that he had returned to. Having grown like Topsy during the war, thanks largely to the opening of the air base, Greenville was only now coming off its prolonged celebration. For most veterans—including Roy and Foote—it was time to return to business, whether that meant finishing school or settling into careers. Roy had two sons to take care of, and a third was on the way. Foote had his Irish bride, and though he was still determined to become the South's second Faulkner, he had taken a job writing ads at the local radio station to bring home a paycheck.

With everybody around him struggling to get back on track, Percy felt doubly derelict. He didn't even have the excuse of being a confused vet. All he had was too much time on his hands. To pass it, he took on odd projects. With Foote, he constructed a canoe in Roy and Sarah's back-yard, later launching it on Lake Ferguson. Percy even returned to one of his favorite boyhood pursuits. For two weeks he shut himself up in his apartment while he assembled a large balsa P-40 model airplane. It was a thing of beauty when he completed it, but few people had the chance to admire his handiwork. Roy's six-year-old son Billy found the plane and tossed it out of the second-floor window. The P-40 was completely destroyed.

Percy did not hold it against his nephew. In fact, Billy became his constant companion and sidekick. While all the grownups were busy at their jobs, Uncle Walker and Billy (and sometimes Billy's friends) played games or built models (smaller ones than the ambitious P-40). It was an odd sight to come across: the man and the boy sprawled on the living room floor of Roy and Sarah's house, shooting marbles while Brahms blared on the record player. In one respect at least, Percy was far more like Faulkner than his devoted admirer Foote was: Percy, like Faulkner, loved games and the company of children. He lost himself in both. He had fun. And children liked the way he could be on their level without condescending to them. He took their games and their talk seriously. Adults, and what they did, were the problem.

How great a problem would become clear only when he began to write his novels, but one thing he did during this time suggests how near he might have been to the brink of despair. For one dollar (and the promise that he would sell it back for the same amount), Percy bought from his nephew the German Luger that his father had brought back from Europe. To some extent, Percy's desire for the Luger bespoke an old fascination with things German. But it is hard to think that Percy purchased the gun without confused, and possibly quite desperate, motives, particularly considering the morbid thoughts a similar weapon stirs up in the protagonist of Percy's fifth novel, *The Second Coming.* The German weapon— cold, black, murderously efficient—was both an instrument and a talisman of death. In the desperate either/or straits in which Percy now found himself, the Luger represented one way out.

Percy did his best to stay ahead of despair. His social world was somewhat limited but busy. Most evenings were spent with Roy and Sarah, or with the Footes, or with his friends Kenneth and Josephine Haxton. A few years Percy's junior, Haxton ran a department store that he had inherited from his mother, but he and his wife were interested in books, music, theater, and ideas, and their house was a popular gathering spot for Percy's group. There they would gossip, play charades, listen to music (Haxton was a self-taught composer, among other things), and read aloud the plays of Shaw and Shakespeare. Josephine Haxton remembers that Percy's greatest literary enthusiasm of that period was Evelyn Waugh, but no one suspected that Percy might be slouching toward Rome. He still seemed to be the cynical scientist.

And something of a Lothario. As in the past, Walker had no trouble charming the ladies. The trouble was that the lady he most wanted to charm, Bunt Townsend, was no longer in town. Having worked at the clinic straight through the war, she had finally saved enough money to return to college in the fall of 1945—this time to Millsaps College in Jackson, Mississippi. "You picked a hell of a time to go to college," Percy joked in a letter. They arranged the occasional rendezvous, of course. Percy and she saw each other over Christmas vacation, and they hit it off as well as they had before the war. Yet Percy was clearly reluctant to impose his confusion on someone who seemed to be moving purposively forward in her life. Bunt Townsend had no shortage of suitors, and she wanted to finish her degree. As much as she was attracted to Percy— and she was attracted a great deal—she was also strong-willed and practical. She knew that she could ill afford the luxury of waiting for Percy to sort out his life.

Percy saw his dilemma clearly. So far, Bunt Townsend was the only woman he had ever been completely comfortable with. There was no woman he would rather be with. But he was afraid that if he did try to get closer to her in this time of indecision, he would end up trifling with her—in the way that he seemed compelled to trifle with other women.

Indeed, Percy's relations with other women during the spring and early summer of 1946 struck some who knew him as exceedingly strange. Superficially, his was the behavior of a Don Juan, a driven, insatiable seducer, but the object, in Percy's case, was not so much physical as psychological seduction. And even that does not quite describe what he was up to. On several women—in Greenville and in other Delta towns and even in Sewanee (where he continued to visit when the spirit moved him)—Percy pressed what seemed a most serious suit. The women, at least, were led to suspect that Percy's intentions were serious. Indeed, many thought he was on the verge of proposing marriage. But then, after a few nights of impassioned talk and vague intimations of betrothal to come, Percy would disappear, leave town, head up to Sewanee if the courtship had been going on in Greenville, or return to Greenville if the courtship had gone on elsewhere. Not surprisingly, his behavior ruffled feathers. More than a few women began to view him as a cad. It was becoming increasingly difficult for him to go anywhere without running into a woman whose feelings he had hurt.

What to make of this strange behavior, which in some ways seemed to mirror Kierkegaard's one famously tormented attempt at a romantic relationship? Percy was not a cruel man. Yet to say that he was confused sounds too much like a rationalization. Nevertheless, it is hard not to see Percy's relations with women as part of the problem that Janet Rioch had identified: a distrust of the maternal figure.

Percy's needs were complex in the extreme—and close to paradoxical. On one hand he craved intimacy, a closeness and all-enveloping warmth with another person. On the other, he needed great distance from whomever he was closest to, a distance that would protect him from exacting scrutiny of what he considered his "decrepit" self. This might be described as a need for the impossible: not only unconditional but unexamined acceptance and love. And satisfying such a need was not even the first part of the problem. The first part was understanding it.

Percy's romantic flailings during this period might be understood, then, as an attempt to understand what he needed in a relationship with a woman. Not knowing (although he had had a strong intimation that it might be what he experienced with Bunt Townsend), he decided to try out several possibilities. And trying out meant, in many cases, going right to the brink of marriage.

In many cases, but not all. Sometimes he reached conclusions almost summarily. Late in the spring, for example, he, Foote, and their friend

Ben Wasson went up to Memphis to see *Madama Butterfly*. Before the performance began, a beautiful woman came into the theater and took a seat not far from the Greenville men. Percy was immediately mesmerized. He said to Foote, "Have you ever seen somebody who you knew was just right for you, the woman you should marry, but you know you'll never see her again? There she is."

Foote was astonished by Percy's conviction. "Well if that's what you think, man, then you should go right up and introduce yourself."

"I can't do that," Percy replied, now knotted up in his own shyness. It was, he told Foote, a lost possibility.

The gods of perversity must have been listening that night. After the opera, the three men went to a Memphis country club to meet David Cohn, who had organized a little party for his friends. Arriving, Percy discovered that he had been fixed up with a dinner date, a Memphis woman named Elizabeth Farnsworth—the very woman, of course, he had earlier seen at the opera house. It was too good to be true.

Foote could hardly wait to find out what Percy and the woman of his dreams had talked about during dinner. But the outcome couldn't have been more anticlimactic.

"Well, what was she like?" Shelby asked when they were back on the road.

"I didn't like her," Percy replied. "She went to one of those Seven Sister colleges—Vassar, I think—and was full of false values."

Erratic as Percy's behavior was, Foote had little room to feel superior. He had learned something about love's perverse ways on his own. His marriage to Tess Lavery, shaky to begin with, had begun to founder when the two reunited in Greenville after the war. Things quickly went from bad to worse, and by March, Shelby was a single man again, chastened by the experience but at least free to spend more time with his best friend and to work on his writing.

Foote was now even contemplating selling some of his work, and he had Ben Wasson to help him. Wasson knew what he was doing, even though his days as a literary representative in New York (where he served as his friend Bill Faulkner's first agent) and on the West Coast were for the most part a thing of the past. He had returned to his native Greenville and taken a comfortable job as the *Delta Democrat-Times*'s literary editor. But for a friend like Foote, Wasson was willing to call on some of his old connections—and Foote now had something to sell. It was not actually new work but a twenty-two-page short story that Foote had managed to extract from the novel that Knopf had politely turned down before the war. Wasson sent the story to the fiction editor of *The Satur-*

day Evening Post, and within a few weeks Foote heard that it had been accepted. He couldn't quite believe it was true until a check for $750 arrived in the mail. Unable to contain himself, he rushed over to Percy's apartment to show off his trophy—validation that he was now truly a writer. Percy joined in the celebration. If he was envious—and he had good reason to be—he did a good job of hiding it.

Even before Percy turned thirty on May 28, the oppressive Delta heat arrived. It was more than Percy, now spoiled by cool summers in the Adirondacks and rural Connecticut, could handle, and he began to make more trips up to Sewanee, "stirring up a lot of commotion in the dovecotes," as Caroline Gordon later described his doings on the mountain. (Although Percy knew Gordon and her husband Allen Tate only slightly, he had met them at least once with Uncle Will on one of his Brinkwood vacations.) Some of the more proper Episcopalians were scandalized by the distress that Percy caused certain young women, but rumors of his misbehavior were greatly exaggerated. For the most part, Percy did what he usually did—he read and he visited with his good friends from earlier days. Robert Daniel, now teaching at Kenyon College, visited Sewanee during the summer to be with his aunt and guardian, Charlotte Gailor. Percy and he had always had a strong friendship, built largely around their love of books and their shared rueful cynicism. Another good friend who was there in the early part of the summer was Rosamond Myers, the daughter of a professor at the seminary. She was soon to marry an Englishman whom she had met while working for the Red Cross in Italy during the war, but she saw Percy on at least one of his trips up. Like most of Percy's Sewanee friends, she thought that he seemed confused. "We assumed it was because of his tuberculosis. We felt very sorry for him and worried about what was going to become of him."

Percy's own doubts about his future were making him restless. He decided that he would have to do something decisive—go somewhere, make a life. The West had always appealed to him. But where in the West? Finally, as Foote recalled, Percy came up with the idea of Santa Fe. He had been through the city at least once during his travels and had liked the cool, clear air. Besides, Santa Fe and nearby Taos had a certain literary allure. D. H. Lawrence had roamed around that part of the country, declaring it one of the magical spots of the world, and Percy and Foote were both beginning to like Lawrence.

The only problem was Bunt Townsend. Percy had continued to see her on occasional weekends, but now she was making plans that would take her in a different direction from Santa Fe. A doctor in New Orleans, an internist named St. Martin, had offered Bunt a job running his laboratory. Facing money problems again, she had accepted and was planning to be in New Orleans by July. As coincidence would have it, her former Greenville roommate and coworker Virginia (Jidge) Minyard was also moving to New Orleans the same month in order to start work on a graduate degree in biology at Sophie Newcomb. The two women decided that they would get an apartment together. Everything looked set. At least for Bunt.

Percy was torn. His experiments with other women had convinced him that Bunt Townsend was the only woman he wanted to be with. As he told her one day when he was driving her to Indianola to catch a bus back to Jackson, "If a man and a woman can drive alone in a car for two hundred miles, then there's a good chance they can be happily married." Now more than ever, though, he doubted his ability to make a stable life, even if his health held up. He saw Santa Fe as a big gamble, and how could he invite Bunt to take part in such an uncertain venture? Half-jokingly, he proposed that she accompany him to New Mexico, but he knew what her answer would be.

Percy put the same question to Foote, and Foote accepted. The two men got on the road in early July and drove hard and fast through the Southwest in Percy's green Packard convertible, taking turns driving and sleeping in the back seat. "I remember two things about that trip," Foote later recalled. "One was when I handed Walker a newly minted dime that had Franklin Roosevelt on it. 'Damn,' he said, 'now we'll never see the end of him.' The other was my spotting and identifying a scissor-tail flycatcher. That really threw Walker because I wasn't supposed to know anything about birds. He thought of himself as the bird-watcher, and I was poaching on his territory."

When they arrived in Santa Fe, a city of about twenty thousand in those days, they found a room in La Fonda Hotel, their base for the next ten days. During that time, they roamed the city and its environs, sightseeing and sometimes looking for a more permanent place for Percy. In addition to the Pueblo dwellings, they visited the naturalist writer Ernest Thompson Seton at his home in Seton Village and spent an afternoon talking to him. At night they would have drinks in La Fonda's open courtyard, talking and flirting with the single women. Here, one evening, quite out of the blue, Percy brought up the subject of his interest in Catholicism. Haltingly, somewhat nervously, he confessed that a religious commitment might be the only thing that would give his life any order, any meaning. "If you take the claims of Christianity seriously," Percy explained to his incredulous friend, "then it seems to me that Catholicism is where you have to end up."

Foote couldn't believe what he was hearing at first. Here was the high priest of scientific agnosticism, the southern Max Gottlieb, talking about Catholicism as though it were a serious option. When Foote realized that Percy was not putting him on, he unleashed his contempt. "Yours is a mind in full intellectual retreat," he declared. Foote did not realize until later that he had given their friendship one of its hardest tests when he said those words in Santa Fe.

Before Foote returned to Mississippi by plane, Percy found a room a few miles out of town at a ranch owned by a man named Jim Whittaker, a wealthy easterner and bachelor who had come out West for the good life. Whittaker's ranch—El Merced—was not a tourist or "dude" ranch but a real working ranch, with working cowboys living in the bunkhouse. Percy, however, had not signed on as a hand. He was planning to live in one of the guest rooms of the main house while he looked for work in or around Santa Fe.

That was the plan, anyway. But as the weeks stretched on, nothing happened. He made friends with some of Santa Fe "society," including two elderly women, Eleanor Brownell and Alice Howland, who ran something close to a literary salon in their large Spanish colonial home on a hill in the northern part of town. (Before coming to Santa Fe, Brownell and Howland had founded and run the Shipley School in Bryn Mawr, Pennsylvania.) But for the most part, Percy spent his days by himself, sometimes riding a strong and spirited quarterhorse named El Capitan, sometimes bird-watching, sometimes driving around the countryside in his car. He took at least one solitary drive to Alamogordo to see the site of the first atomic explosion, a trip that had reverberations not only in his memory but in his later writing, particularly *The Last Gentleman*. It seemed to him that he had come to the physical limit of Western civilization—ground zero (and not coincidentally, the first name he gave to *The Last Gentleman* was *Ground Zero*)—where some of the best scientific minds of the world had designed the atomic bomb.

Two questions come naturally to anyone who has read *The Last Gentleman*: Did Percy have his Luger with him on that trip to Alamogordo, and did he then, or at any other time in New Mexico, contemplate suicide? To the extent that the despairing physician Sutter Vaught represents Percy at this stage of his life, the possibility seems far from remote: for it was in New Mexico that Vaught shot out a chunk of his cheek while trying to kill himself.

But Percy's despair was of a lower order than Vaught's on most days, closer to Will Barrett's cosmic befuddlement at the sense of sheer possibility that the open expanses of New Mexico symbolized. Here was a place without the complications of family or history, a place that felt as remote from the entanglements of the South as the moon. Walking by fragrant piñon or through dried-up arroyos, Percy experienced the same sense of release that he has Barrett describe in the novel:

> Each passing second was packaged in cottony silence. It had no ante-cedents. Here was three o'clock but it was not like three o'clock in Mississippi. In Mississippi it is always Wednesday afternoon, or perhaps Thursday. The country there is peopled, a handful of soil strikes a pang to the heart, *deja vus* fly up like a shower of sparks. Even in the Southern wilderness there is ever the sense of someone close by, watch-ing from the woods. Here one was not watched. There was no one. The silence hushed everything up, the small trees were separated by a geometry of silence. The sky was empty, map space. Yonder at Albu-querque forty miles away a mountain reared like your hand in front of your face.
>
> This is the locus of pure possibility, he thought, his neck prickling. What a man can be the next minute bears no relation to what he is or what he was the minute before.

Wasn't this release from past entanglements precisely what Percy came West for? It would seem so. But now that he was living from second to isolated second in the rarefied atmosphere of pure possibility, he found that he was oddly dissatisfied, even a little fearful. His existence lacked gravity. If he could do anything, then what he *was*, everything that life had made him up to this point, was irrelevant. Percy had thought that he could give history the slip. Now he was doubtful. But if it were impossible to live amid the past and impossible to live beyond it, what was left? The option of the Luger loomed large.

So, mysteriously, did something else. It was something that occurred unexpectedly, like the flowers that pop up overnight after a rare desert rain. Despite the mess that he believed his life had become, Percy de-cided that he would have to accept it and live it. An odd thing to decide upon, some might think. After all, living a life would seem to be a given, something that we all of necessity do. Not Percy. He had long thought, starting shortly after his father's death, that he would have to understand Life—the whole buzzing mystery—before he could live his own. Now he realized that this gambit had been both misguided (science had not been able to answer the most important questions) and some-thing of a dodge. His pursuit of the perfectly objective scientific position, the Archimedean point, had, to some extent, been an attempt to escape from the difficulty and pain—and possible joy—of living a life.

Percy would later insist that there was nothing mystical about these discoveries. It was more a matter of coming to the end of a long line of thinking, and of waking up one morning in the early autumn on a ranch near Santa Fe and deciding, as he told a friend, "I've got to have a life. I'm going to be a writer. I am going to live in New Orleans. And I am going to marry Bunt." Bunt had been constantly on his mind, acutely so ever since he learned that her mother had died in July. Upon hearing the news, he had written her a long, heartfelt letter. The pain at the loss of a parent was something that he knew too well, and the shared experience made Percy feel even closer to Bunt.

Marriage to Bunt Townsend was not the only thing Percy was thinking about. He was brooding about another important decision—whether to take the message of Christianity seriously. Percy, who was now reading his Kierkegaard more carefully, believed that marriage signaled the passage from the aesthetic realm to the ethical, a passage that he was willing to attempt, however defective a moral being he thought he was. But the next Kierkegaardian stage, the passage to the spiritual, looked more daunting. It was a step for which he knew he was not yet ready.

As far as marrying Bunt, though, Percy began to act decisively. In the middle of September he wrote her a letter, stating his plans to move to New Orleans. "I have engaged a room on St. Charles starting October 1. Don't know whether I'll be there a week or a year." He also asked, a little less jokingly this time, if she would fly out and drive back with him. Knowing that she wouldn't, he took a plane, arriving in New Orleans and settling into his apartment on St. Charles in the middle of the Garden District. Townsend and Minyard lived not far away on Carondolet, in an old mansion that had been divided into several apartments. Percy called Townsend shortly after arriving to ask her out for a date. To his surprise, he was politely rebuffed. Townsend informed him that she already had a date, and she was not the kind of person to break a previous arrangement. Besides, much as she loved Percy, he had taken her on an emotional roller coaster for almost five years now. She had no reason to think that Percy had suddenly turned serious. All the same, she worried that he might not call back.

Percy did, of course, and they dated steadily throughout October, Jidge Minyard and her boyfriend Salvatore Milazzo sometimes joining them for a picnic at the park on Lake Pontchartrain. In Minyard's eyes, Percy seemed to be very "laid-back." She recalled that he dressed casually—khaki pants and a zip-front jacket were his usual attire, though he would put on a tie for an evening date. Minyard observed that Percy and Townsend had a completely relaxed and natural relationship. "Bunt was never a honey-dripping southern girl. She was blunt and straightforward, and she gave him stability, even when they were dating. He was smart enough to know that that was what he needed."

As set as Percy was in his own mind about marrying Bunt Townsend, he had a difficult time coming to the question. Being "laid-back," as Minyard described him, was not merely a matter of appearances. It was an expression of Percy's discomfort with formalities. Percy was no proto-hippie or beatnik, but he had a horror of giving in too much to the manners and conventions that he believed had overwhelmed his father. Not that Percy was ill-mannered or dismissive of all formalities. But he was wary of their power to take over a person's life. This wariness about social conventions was not a temporary concern for Percy. It was a life-or-death matter, and one that he struggled with throughout his life. It is hardly surprising, then, that the formal rituals of marriage—proposing and going through a ceremony—gave him particular unease.

When he finally made it, Percy's proposal came as a complete surprise to Bunt Townsend, maybe even to Percy himself. For one thing, Shelby Foote was in town, and the three of them were constantly together. Finally, Percy and Townsend did have a moment alone. They were sitting together on a bench while Foote went to the Jung Hotel to buy two plane tickets to Santa Fe. Percy had decided that he had to go back for his car and for his personal effects, and Foote had agreed to accompany him on the long drive. Percy was talking about the trip when Bunt realized that he was also making a proposal. "I am going by Greenville on the way back to get a ring"—it was, Townsend later learned, Percy's mother's ring—"and I want to marry you."

It was as simple and unexpected as that. Bunt Townsend said nothing. She didn't know what to think at first. Then she decided that anything could happen. Above all, she resolved, it would be unwise to get her hopes up. Percy was undaunted by her silence. At least he didn't take it as outright rejection.

As planned, the two men flew to Santa Fe, where they attended to some awkward business. Before he had decided to go to New Orleans to propose to Bunt Townsend, Percy had arranged to move into the house of Alice Howland and Eleanor Brownell. Now he was embarrassed about backing out of the arrangement. The two women were crazy about Percy, and he liked them. They were avid readers and treasured the idea of his company. So tortured was he about the whole thing that he cooked up a rather silly plot and called on Foote to help him execute it. With Foote, he went to their house and announced that he had had a "break" and was obliged to return East to a sanatorium. The women were terribly solicitous, and seemingly as much taken by Foote as they were by Percy. When Foote admired their complete New York edition of Henry James, they urged him to take the entire set. Both men felt ashamed when they left the ladies' house. It had been an awkward performance.

The men took the northern route back east, a long trip made even longer when Foote came down with the flu in Colorado. Nevertheless, Percy was back in New Orleans by the fifth of November, ring in hand and a bedraggled Foote in tow. While the two men traveled, Bunt Townsend had gone about organizing a wedding, even though she thought that it might not come off. "I wasn't sure we were getting married until right up to the end." It was a small group that gathered at the First Baptist Church on November 6. On Bunt's side, there was her father, her sister and brother-in-law Willie Ruth and Cliff Cowan (Willie Ruth was the bridesmaid), her cousin Randolph Johnson, her best friend Jidge Minyard, and Salvatore Milazzo. On Percy's side there was only the best man, Shelby Foote, still droopy from the flu. Roy and Sarah had not been able to make the wedding, because Sarah was then expecting her third child. Phin was stationed in Panama. Dr. St. Martin had been invited but had refused to come. He had disapproved of the marriage and told Bunt so. "Percy's not stable and it won't last," Dr. St. Martin warned. (Percy was furious when he learned what St. Martin had said. "He's just angry because he's losing you," Percy said to Bunt.)

The ceremony was performed by New Orleans' leading Baptist minister, Reverend J.D. Gray, a man with a polished public manner and a towering head of hair. All went without a hitch, except for a brief, difficult moment when the reverend said "May the love between you be as pure as the gold in the ring." Foote knew that the ring he was holding was platinum, but he dutifully bit his tongue to hold back the giggles.

The newlyweds spent their bridal night at the St. Charles Hotel, where Percy had to feel that a little bit of his history had come back to haunt him. The manager of the hotel, Captain Mike O'Leary, had got his start in life at the Birmingham Country Club, where he had been hired by the club president, LeRoy Percy.

"Sometimes I had the feeling that we could never be anywhere without Shelby being there, too," Bunt Percy once said of her years of off-again on-again courtship with Percy. She might have wondered whether marriage was to be any different. The day after the wedding, Percy and Bunt took the train to Chattanooga, Tennessee, and were met at the station by Foote, who had driven up with Percy's car. Before the couple headed up the mountain to Brinkwood, where they planned to stay at least for the winter, Percy bought a gift for Bunt—a black cocker spaniel puppy, which she promptly named Joey. Foote gave the couple perhaps the most practical of their wedding gifts: two pairs of wool ski pajamas. They would need them. Winters in the inadequately insulated mountain house could be bitterly cold and damp.

Setting up house in Sewanee was in some respects a strange decision, revealing a continued reluctance on Percy's part to establish a life on his own terms. The associations of Brinkwood with Will Percy and Huger Jervey (who visited at least once while the Percys lived there) was still powerful. In some ways, too, coming to Brinkwood was like returning to the otherworldly existence of the sanatorium, a resemblance that became all the more striking when a routine X-ray taken shortly after he arrived in Sewanee revealed activity in Percy's bad lung. Percy was once again the invalid. The routine of bed rest, milkshakes, and thermometer readings resumed.

If Percy was alarmed by the return of his old condition, he did not show it. He simply transformed the routines of the tubercular invalid into those of the apprentice writer. During the months at Brinkwood, Percy's main occupation was reading. Most of his mornings were spent in the living room in a large red leather armchair that once belonged to his father. In addition to making extensive annotations in the books he was reading, he jotted comments, observations, and ideas in little notebooks that he always kept with him; occasionally, he would take down longer things in the clunky, blue loose-leaf notebooks he had acquired in medical school (all of which were inscribed with his Bard Hall room number and address). His favored writing instrument, then as always, was a Scripto mechanical pencil. After a protein-rich lunch with a malted milkshake, Percy would go to bed for a couple of hours, to nap if possible but usually to read or to listen to the radio or to make more notes in his notebooks. In the afternoons, he and Bunt might go for a walk or play cards, battleship, or some other game.

Though Walker held rigidly to his schedule and Bunt supported him in doing so, the Percys' life was anything but reclusive at Brinkwood. Before his break, and later, when his health began to return in the spring, Percy and Bunt would go to tea or cocktails at the houses of Sewanee "society." "I remember," Bunt Percy recalls, "getting a card from Miss Eliot shortly after arriving up there inviting us to tea." Percy found such occasions trying—the atmosphere of the inevitably Episcopalian salon was a little stultifying—but he put on a good face, just as Bunt obligingly put on white gloves. Percy and his wife occasionally attended Episcopal church services, but as Bunt later explained, neither felt truly at home among the Episcopalians.

In addition to social calls, friends and relatives were always coming by, often staying for several days—or longer. In the spring, Phin Percy became a permanent member of the ménage, having resigned from the Navy and enrolled as a student at Sewanee while he figured out what to do next. Bunt's brother, Pascol Townsend, visited, and Roy and Sarah and the boys came up often, particularly when the weather got better.

In the summer, Robert Daniel and his wife Mary were reliable company, but by far the most regular visitor was Shelby Foote.

As well as being his friend, Foote was now, in Percy's eyes, a model of the successful writer. His career had moved forward, though not without a snag. He had sold another story to *The Saturday Evening Post* —this one, twice as long as the first, for fifteen hundred dollars—but a third and even longer story was rejected, apparently because of its undertones of incest. Foote was considering a new tack—actually, returning to an older one. He was making plans for a novel, this one about the battle of Shiloh in the Civil War, and the planning stage of a narrative was for Foote crucial. He was a writer who had to know where he was going and what effects he was trying to achieve before he sat down to the business of composing. Foote's example was a prod and challenge to Percy, but while he admired what Foote wrote, Percy already suspected that Foote's preoccupations with form and structure—with the artifices of art—were beyond both his own ability and his interest. The important thing for Percy was the motive, the all-important pretext. And so far he was having trouble finding one.

Whatever writing Percy himself was doing at this time was sketchy, highly provisional, and certainly, in his opinion, unfit for others' consumption. There is, in fact, great uncertainty about whether he produced any sustained writing during the Sewanee months. Bunt Percy insists that his writing then consisted only of random and discontinuous jottings in his notebooks. Percy's own recollections about the work of this period were inconsistent. Sometimes he would claim that he began work on his first unpublished novel, *The Charterhouse*, while in Brinkwood; at others, he would say he had started on it a year or so later.

Perhaps the strongest reason for concluding that the novel was started later was the book's decidedly Catholic argument, a quality that was noted and celebrated by the manuscript's closest and most enthusiastic reader, Caroline Gordon. While this point of view could have been worked into the novel later, it is highly unlikely that Percy would have been writing from so firm a position at Sewanee. At Brinkwood, Percy was still outside the church, even though he felt a powerful attraction to it, as he had already admitted to Shelby Foote.

To some extent, Percy's move toward Roman Catholicism might be viewed as part of a widespread cultural phenomenon. As one of Caroline Gordon's biographers, Ann Waldron, puts it, "there was a boomlet in Catholicism after World War II." Waldron points to the publishing efforts of Francis Sheed, to the string of well-known and glamorous figures—including Heywood Broun, Henry Ford II, and Clare Boothe Luce—who were personally instructed by the radio (and then television)

celebrity Bishop Fulton J. Sheen, and to the attraction of the Catholic
Worker movement to people with strong social-service convictions. "It
seemed easy, almost chic, to be a Catholic," Waldron concludes. Percy
listened to Bishop Sheen on the radio and even wrote him a letter asking
if he could receive instruction from him. (Sheen replied with the suggestion that he contact the Fathers of the Divine Word in Bay St. Louis,
Mississippi.)

But Percy had been inclining toward Rome well before it became
fashionable, perhaps ever since he locked horns with Art Fortugno at
Trudeau. His conversion seems different even from those of the literary
intellectuals who constituted a miniature American Oxford Movement
both before and after World War II. Robert Lowell, Jean Stafford, Caroline Gordon, and Allen Tate were among those writers who had converted to Roman Catholicism from Episcopalianism and other Protestant
denominations. These converts shared with their predecessors in the
original Oxford Movement of the 1840s a dissatisfaction with the doctrinal fuzziness of Protestant creeds and with Protestantism's suppression
of the ritual and even supernatural dimensions of faith. They admired
the scholastic rigor of Catholic theology, and they respected the church's
insistence upon obedience. Celebrating the lost unity of the medieval
world, they also saw Catholicism as the best hope for restoring an organ-
ically connected society. Anglicanism, which in its higher forms came
close to Catholicism, fell short of what was necessary. It was still in the
throes of a five-century-old identity crisis, uncertain where to locate
ultimate doctrinal authority. Catholicism, by contrast, represented a
higher order of purpose and resolve. To the literary converts, it was the
true path to both personal salvation and a restored community of the
faithful.

Percy was not ignorant of such arguments, and to some extent he
went along with them. He definitely saw that his arrival at the brink of
conversion came as the result of an intellectual process as well as grace.
He shared with the literary converts a certain disdain for the wishy-
washiness of Protestantism. And he might even have been attracted to
the idea of Catholicism as the foundation for a renewed human community, though Percy's concern for the social dimensions of his faith
seems to have come somewhat later.

Nevertheless, Percy's journey to Rome described an even more idiosyncratic and peculiar path than that of the literary converts. First,
Percy's intellectual journey took him by way of science and scientism
and involved a dialectical movement away from everything he once
believed toward its apparent antithesis—but only apparent. As Percy
would insist, science properly understood was not a contradiction of

faith. Percy never turned a hostile eye toward science and technology, as most of the literary converts did. But he would use his understanding of science to resist the view that science could account for everything, including everything about the human creature.

Percy's labors in science had brought him to the firm conclusion that the only things science could say about man were those generalizations that held for the entire species. But while science could generalize about the human creature, it could not put its finger on that creature's unique endowment, his individuality. Claiming that science could explain everything was not only scientific hubris but the root of much mischief and confusion in the modern world. And the supreme instance of that mischief, Percy came to believe, was its attempt to relegate that which it could not speak about, the individual's existence (much less his soul), to insignificance, and thereby to demote mankind to its generalizable qualities. Man thus conceived was no more than a beast.

If science could say nothing about the most important facet of the human creature—the joyous, suffering, and perverse self—what or who could? If man was free, and not simply an overdetermined animal, he was free to make choices. That created a problem, of course. For on what basis would one determine the right or wrong course of action, in the smallest matters as well as the largest? By what principles should one live a life? The perils of moral relativism were evident to Percy in his own disabling drift and lassitude, and the assorted postreligious solutions —the Kantian categorical imperative, utilitarian notions of the greatest good for the greatest number, and even the Nietzschean will to power— seemed to him inadequate. The first two led back to a dependence on the methods of science (ethics as decision science) and the third, potentially, to barbarism (for even though Nietzsche had intended his Superman to be everything Hitler was not, it was hard for Percy, who had himself experienced the attractions of Hitlerian fascism, to see how the degradation of Nietzsche's ideas into a justification of Nazism was avoidable).

The one nonreligious alternative to moral relativism that was closest to Percy was the Stoicism that had been so nobly represented by Uncle Will. But as beautiful and noble as this ethic was, Percy felt that it would never work for him—and wouldn't for the simple yet decisive reason that he lacked the strength of character, the *virtù*, that was necessary for the upholding of such an ethic. Percy's great feelings of self-disgust and unworthiness made the Stoic option seem beyond his reach.

Percy came to Christianity precisely out of this powerful sense of his own unworthiness. Indeed, it seemed to him the principal brilliance of the Christian "anthropology" (a word that he liked to use in its radical, nonacademic sense) was that it put human corruption and inadequacy at the center of its picture of man, and furthermore, that it taught that recognition of this inadequacy was the first step in hearing the Christian message.

Percy, at Brinkwood, was in a state of ready reception. For the first time since he was a boy in Reverend Edmonds's congregation, he began reading the Bible. From his reading of Kierkegaard, he came to the conclusion that there were people authorized to tell others what constituted the good life and that these people derived their authority not from themselves, not from their genius or wisdom or power, but from the authority of God. These people were apostles. But to fully receive the message of Christ and his apostles something else was needed—the mystery and gift of grace.

It is curious, perhaps, that a reader of Kierkegaard, a Danish Lutheran, should have come to believe that entry into the Roman Catholic church was the best means of receiving the gift of grace (though perhaps not so curious as it at first seems: Karl Barth, for example, argued that Kierkegaard, had he lived beyond his forty-two years, would have been compelled by his own reasoning to enter the Catholic church). Much as he admired Kierkegaard, though, Percy rejected the Dane's notion of the "leap of faith." *Credo quia absurdum est* seemed to Percy in itself nothing more than absurd. Faith was not absurd, in Percy's eyes, but wholly compatible with reason. Percy had come readily to the Thomist view that faith was a form of knowledge.

By the summer of 1947, Percy was prepared to take steps to enter the Catholic church. Following Bishop Sheen's advice, he wrote to the Fathers of the Divine Word, only to learn that they ministered exclusively to blacks. They suggested that he go to the Jesuits at Loyola University in New Orleans. The suggestion was well timed. The Percys by then had decided that they could not survive another winter in Brinkwood. The raw cold was a little too austere, even for someone with Adirondack cure porches in his past. The two places the Percys were then considering were New Orleans and Santa Fe. In the balance, New Orleans seemed a better gamble to Percy, a compromise between pure possibility and historical entanglements, or as Percy would later describe it, "both intimately related to the South, and yet in a real sense adrift not only from the South but from the rest of Louisiana, somewhat like Mont Saint-Michel awash at high tide." To Percy, so delicately attuned to the shaping power of an environment, New Orleans seemed to be a place where he could live without being overwhelmed.

Shortly after arriving in New Orleans in September, however, Percy found reason to suspect that even in the Crescent City the reach of the past was more extensive than he had imagined. Rising early in the morning to track down rentals that were advertised in the paper, Bunt Percy located a small house on Calhoun Street less than a block from Audubon Park. The owners of the house, Julius and Elise Friend, liked the sound of Bunt Percy over the phone, but when they learned who her husband was they were even more eager for her to take the house. Julius Friend was, in the true sense of the word, a man of letters. As well as a philosopher and coauthor (with a Tulane professor named James Feibleman) of two books on the philosophy of science, Julius Friend had been an editor of *The Double-Dealer*, a literary journal to which Will Percy had on occasion contributed work. Percy was a name that the Friends knew and respected.

Apart from the strange coincidence involved in its finding, the house could not have been better suited to the young couple's needs. For one thing, it had a library stocked with just the kind of books that Percy read: literature and philosophy. The house was in the heart of the "Uptown" district, and everything important to the Percys was within easy striking distance. They could walk and bird-watch in the nearby park; they were only a few blocks from the streetcar on St. Charles; and they had an easy stroll to Loyola.

Loyola was the focal point of the Percys' lives for their first three months in New Orleans. It was there that Walker and Bunt received instruction for entry into the church, instruction that Walker took with utmost gravity. (Bunt took the business of conversion somewhat more casually, though her commitment to Catholicism grew steadily after she entered the church.) For Percy, this instruction was not primarily an intellectual matter. He did not feel that he needed to hear any compelling arguments to bring him the last few steps into the church. He was ready intellectually. He did, however, want to know everything about doctrine and dogma. And above all, he wanted to be able to perform the duties of a good Catholic. Considering his needs, he was fortunate in the priest who was assigned to instruct him. Father J. J. McCarthy, though a Jesuit, was no intellectual. To the contrary, he was a meat-and-potatoes parish priest, more comfortable with pastoral responsibilities than with recondite questions of theology. Percy could not have been happier. Father McCarthy was just the sort of practical teacher he was looking for.

Walker, Bunt, and their friend Jidge Minyard (who was by now engaged to Sal Milazzo) started their instruction together in early September. At four o'clock on Tuesday and Thursday they came to a small room on the ground floor of the rectory and listened to Father McCarthy as he explained the church's teachings and what it expected of its members. Percy was the dutiful student, taking careful note of every word his catechist said. Father McCarthy, no doubt discerning that Percy was a man with intellectual tendencies, kept asking if he had any questions about where the church stood on the issues of the day. Truthfully, Percy did not, but he felt he should come up with something. Finally, he asked Father McCarthy what the church's stand on evolution was. "I am not sure," said Father McCarthy, "but I'll find out for you." Father McCarthy brought a copy of the 1930 edition of the *Catholic Encyclopedia* to the next class and gave it to Percy. "It was hopelessly outmoded and made no sense at all," Percy later explained, "but I couldn't have cared less."

Frequently, after class, Sal Milazzo would pick up the Percys and Jidge and drive them back to Calhoun Street, where quite often he and Jidge would stay on for drinks and a chat. Percy was very fond of Jidge's fiancé. He was a shy, somewhat self-effacing man, but quietly self-confident, a rock of sturdiness and good character. No doubt he brought back to Percy memories of another Italian-American, Art Fortugno, who had first prompted Percy to consider the arguments of Catholicism seriously. Milazzo, like Fortugno, was a New Jersey native. He was also a Navy veteran, a baseball player with professional potential, and now a student of engineering at Tulane. Percy, as well as liking Milazzo, saw him as a kind of test case of the "cradle Catholic," and with typical convert's zeal, he would pepper Milazzo with questions about the church. If Milazzo was somewhat amused by Percy's intensity, he nevertheless obliged, answering questions while they sat on the back porch and watched the autumn dusk close around them.

The truth was, this was one of the happier times of Percy's life. His marriage with Bunt had turned out, if anything, even better than he had hoped. She not only accepted his way of living—his need for rest and long stretches of solitude—but she supported it as both his nurse and his devoted mate. While Walker and Bunt could not have been more different personalities, their differences seemed to solidify rather than divide—indeed, to create a complementary whole. To anyone who met them, it was obvious that Bunt was as optimistic and outgoing as Walker was brooding and introspective. And while Bunt was no intellectual—and never pretended to be—she saw the world and other people with hardheaded clarity and intelligence. Percy valued her candor and judgment, and he trusted her intuition as much as he trusted her. Percy knew he was fortunate. A person who lives largely alone in his head is not the easiest person to live with, but Bunt had the inner strength to tolerate his remoteness while at the same time satisfying his need for intimacy. Not many women could have satisfied such contradictory needs—or been happy in doing so.

Not that Bunt considered herself a martyr to her husband's happiness.

She was as delighted with the man she had married as he was with her. Despite his erratic behavior before their marriage, Bunt now believed in Percy. She trusted in his ambition, even though she knew, as Percy himself did, that his apprenticeship would be long and hard and that the outcome was anything but certain. Bunt treasured those qualities that she had noticed in him when she first met him at Gamble Brothers Clinic—his gentleness, his tenderness, his concern. Far from least, she had fun with him. When he was in a good mood, his sense of play and humor were infectious and irresistible. "He always had a genius for organizing an outing—some place that we would go for a picnic, a drive, or just a walk."

While Walker and Bunt were perfectly content off to themselves, they took pleasure in their small circle of friends. There were of course more visits from Foote. In fact, when he came down in early September, he announced to his two friends that he was planning to remarry later the same month, this time to a Memphis woman named Marguerite Dessommes. When Jidge and Sal were married in March, the Percys held the reception in the Calhoun Street house. In addition to the Milazzos, the Percys also spent a fair amount of time with their landlords, Julius and Elise Friend, who had moved only a few streets away into the house of Julius Friend's ailing mother. The elderly couple took the Percys under their wing, inviting them to dinner or dropping by their house for drinks. Percy found in Friend a challenging intellectual companion. Thanks to Friend's casual tutelage—and his library—Percy's intuitive but somewhat inchoate dissatisfactions with science as a worldview began to take sharper definition.

It would be impossible to understand Percy's contentment at this time without describing the paramount importance of his newly found faith. The closer he came to his first confession, the more certain he grew that he had taken the right path, and that new certitude left him feeling profoundly grateful. At the end of one of the sessions with Father McCarthy, Percy tried to express his indebtedness: "I'm getting so much from the church, but I feel like I'm not giving anything back. What can I do for the church?"

"Don't worry about that, Walker," Father McCarthy assured him. "The church will see to that later."

One thing the church would get from Percy—although this was truly another gift from the church to him—was his increasing support for the civil rights effort. Not that the church was immediately at the vanguard of the movement. But at Loyola in the fall of 1947, just when Percy was receiving instructions at Thomas Hall, one of the more successful Catholic civil-rights activists of the 1950s and 1960s, Father Louis Twomey, was founding his Institute of Industrial Relations less than one hundred yards away. As well as Twomey, who first was more interested in labor than in racial issues, there were other Jesuits, including Father J. H. Fichter, who were urging the church and churchmen to take a more active role in pressing for social and racial justice. Percy, the old segregationist, rather assured in his social views, began to hear the message. His thinking on such issues would never be the same.

The last few weeks of instruction were private, one-on-one meetings, and Percy was brimming with eagerness. On Saturday, December 13, St. Lucy's Day, Bunt, Jidge, and Percy were provisionally baptized at Holy Name Church, Percy taking the name John as his baptismal name. The same day, the three new Catholics made their first confession, an experience that Bunt and Jidge approached with considerable apprehension: Confession seemed to them the most daunting requirement of their new church. Not to Percy. He seemed elated. "This is one of the main reasons I've become a Catholic," he told them. Jidge Minyard's response revealed her unease about the practice: "If you think it's so great, then why don't you go first?"

Later, in the spring, the three adults were confirmed along with about three hundred schoolchildren. Sal Milazzo had agreed to be Percy's sponsor, but he balked when Walker urged that they march in procession with the twelve-year-olds. Percy insisted. Everything had to be by the book. And it seemed right to him that, for this final step, he should be led into the church by children. Milazzo reluctantly gave in: The convert's enthusiasm was implacable.

If there was one blot on the Percys' early marital happiness, it was that Bunt had not yet become pregnant. In March of 1948, Shelby and his wife Marguerite (or Peggy, as she was called) had their first child, Margaret, and while Bunt and Percy were pleased to hear the news it could not help adding to their frustration. More than a year had gone by without Bunt's becoming pregnant, and Percy feared that years of routine X-rays had left him sterile. Increasingly doubtful about their own reproductive prospects, Bunt and Walker turned to a New Orleans adoption agency, expecting that it would take months, possibly a year, for an infant to be found.

At roughly the same time, Walker and Bunt decided to look for another house. The place at 1450 Calhoun had been perfect for their extended sojourn, but now they wanted to own a house, preferably something a little larger and with a little more property. The prospects of finding what they wanted in New Orleans, they quickly discovered, were very limited, and so on weekends they began to explore the outlying areas. Consulting the real-estate advertisements in the paper, they learned about a house with several acres of land near a little town on the northern shore of Lake Pontchartrain, a town called Covington.

Located in the western part of St. Tammany Parish a few miles north of the shorefront town of Mandeville, Covington had long enjoyed a reputation for its salubrious climate—supposedly the result of the ozone given off by the long-leaf pines that grew thickly throughout the parish and indeed throughout an area stretching about 150 miles east and 50 miles west of Covington. Others attributed Covington's therapeutic properties to its waters. Whatever the cause, Covington did seem to be a magical spot—and not without reason. The 1890 census revealed that it had the lowest death rate of any community in the United States. The figure is all the more surprising when one considers that physicians in New Orleans had been sending their consumptive patients to cottages and hotels in Covington ever since Reconstruction. Some even thought the ozone made the area germproof. Whenever epidemics hit the city (as yellow fever did in 1878 and 1897), people flocked to Covington, arriving either by train or by shallow-bottom steamers that crossed the lake and came up the twisting, tea-brown waters of the Bogue Falaya (Long River in Choctaw) to the Covington dock. Many who came to recover or escape disease liked the area so much that they built second homes there. Covington, like Mandeville and other northern shore communities, became a place the wealthy could escape to.

In 1948, Covington still retained the character of a remote resort town. The town proper had a village feel, with small stores and businesses, a hotel, a courthouse square, a train station, a dozen odd streets, many curiously named after New England cities and states (Boston was the town's main thoroughfare). The population of Covington stood somewhere around six thousand, and the main industry, apart from tending to the part-timers, was the nursery business.

Taking what was then the fastest route, the Percys came around the eastern rim of the lake, crossing the Five Mile Bridge between New Orleans and Slidell and then driving the twenty-six miles from Slidell to Covington, a journey that took a little over an hour. "When I first saw Covington . . ." Percy later wrote, "I took one look around, sniffed the ozone, and exclaimed unlike Brigham Young: 'This is the nonplace for me!' " The house itself was located about four miles east of the center of town on Military Road, and when the Percys came upon it they knew that they had found what they were looking for. The house—a two-story wood frame structure—was not grand, but it suited their needs. As well as bedrooms upstairs and down, it had a large living room with an exposed cathedral ceiling. Just off the living room was a little room that

Walker could make into a study. It felt liveable, manageable, and the grounds were, if anything, even more seductive—several acres of gently rolling land dotted with pines and live oaks and dogwoods. About 150 yards behind the house wound a small tributary of the Bogue Falaya, the "Little Bogue," as it was called, with a pleasant sandy beach where a person could cool his heels on a summer day. Almost halfway between the bogue and the house stood a small caretaker's cottage where a couple named Mr. and Mrs. Boyle lived until shortly after the Percys moved in.

Percy and his wife were ready to take the house immediately, but knowing that Roy and Sarah were coming down the next weekend, they decided to wait for their opinion. Before returning to New Orleans, the Percys stopped off at a little bar on Boston Street in town—Tugy's Bar, it was called, after its owner Julius Tugenhaft. While they were sipping their drinks, Tugy struck up a conversation with Percy, whom he quickly fell into calling "Doc." Learning that the "Doc" was interested in the Woodward place out on Military Road, he asked how much it was being sold for. Percy told him thirty thousand dollars. Tugy shook his head: "That's too much, Doc. You can get it for eighteen thousand dollars." Percy tucked away the tip, and after Roy and Sarah saw and approved the place the following weekend, Percy offered just what Tugy suggested. The sellers promptly accepted.

Percy, feeling every bit the proud owner, sent a couple of sketches of the house to Foote, one showing the house as it looked and one with projected changes. Foote wrote back saying his first reaction to the drawings was shock: "I recognized Brinkwood immediately, but 'Dear God,' I thought, 'they've moved the chimney!'" As to the proposed modifications, Foote wagered that the house would "sit there in all its pristine objectionableness—including gingerbread trim—until old age collapses it, with you and Bunt inside warming your aged toes by the fire and turning the pages of an album containing pictures of the fifteen or twenty children you will have had by then."

When they moved into the house in early June, Walker and Bunt did not come alone. The agency in New Orleans had located a child more quickly than anyone had thought possible. In May, the Percys adopted a ten-month-old girl (born July 25, 1947), whom they had baptized Mary Pratt. Jidge Milazzo thought she looked like Bunt, and the parents were as proud and doting as new parents could be.

While the Percys' move to the northern shore of Pontchartrain was prompted largely by financial considerations, it also reflected Percy's ideas about what he needed to do to get on with the vocation he had chosen. Much as he had liked New Orleans—and he had liked it very much—he still feared that it had too strong a character for him. "The occupational hazard of the writer in New Orleans," he later explained, "is a variety of the French flu, which might also be called the Vieux Carre syndrome. One is apt to turn fey, potter about a patio, and write feuilletons and vignettes or catty romans a clef, a pleasant enough life but for me too seductive." Percy cited the example of Faulkner, who, "charmed to a standstill" by New Orleans, never really got going "until he returned to Mississippi and invented his county."

One must take these words with more than a grain of salt. They were written thirty-two years after the fact. But Percy wasn't completely improvising when he described Covington's original charm as its "lack of identity, lack of placeness, even lack of history"; nor can we completely dismiss his claim to have been delighted by the fact that in Covington "I didn't know anybody, had no kin." Percy had set a task for himself— a task at which he knew he might fail. He wanted no major distractions from what he had set out to do, and perhaps just as important, he wanted as few people aware of what he was doing as was possible. A proud man, he had a horror of seeming to be the feckless potterer with literary pretensions. He was putting his self-respect on the line, but he preferred not to have a large audience if he failed. In fact, Percy never admitted to his fellow townsmen that he was a writer, and most had no idea until he won national acclaim. If people knew anything about Percy at all, they knew that he was a doctor who had had health problems and retired to a life of modest gentility: not an unusual case in Covington history.

In the two years since Percy had reached the self-described low point of his life—his personal "ground zero"—he had traveled a considerable distance. One would be tempted to call the beginning of this journey, particularly the moment when he came to himself in New Mexico, a second birth. But Percy himself was so profoundly skeptical of the twice-born phenomenon that one might more wisely honor Percy's own terms for what had happened.

While not discounting the mysterious power of grace, Percy believed that *coming to himself* placed on him the great burden of freedom. He was obliged to choose in order to live. Faced with two possible courses of action—a life of pure possibility and a life of commitments—he had opted for the latter. The chosen quality cannot be overstated. Voluntarism was at the heart of the Catholic faith he had embraced, and it was the center of what can only be described as his moral system, embryonic as it then was. A mechanistic universe, his study of science had taught him, was one in which everything was determined, but Percy no longer believed that man's unique and defining character was subject to mechanistic laws. He had rejected positivism largely because his own experience and observations led him to conclude that people did not behave like maximizers of pleasure or self-interest but instead often acted perversely. Even the most sophisticated positivism of Freud, which accounted for human perversity as a treatable dysfunction, seemed to him wrong. One cannot overestimate Percy's debt to Dostoyevsky's *Notes from Underground* for setting forth, in compelling dramatic form, the connection between human perversity and human freedom. Percy heard the message well. The acceptance of human perversity as index of human freedom was the beginning of Percy's career as a moralist.

For a moralist is what Percy became when he came to himself in New Mexico. A moralist puts himself forward as a test of his own freedom. He does so not only by choosing principles by which to live but by examining the consequences of those choices. If Uncle Will had himself been a powerful example of the career of a moralist, Percy had other models in mind, notably Kierkegaard and Pascal. All were individuals who rejected, or at least stood against, the orthodoxies of their day in order to arrive at their own understanding of the good life—and, then, to live according to that understanding. A moralist, above all, is someone who takes himself as a living test of the principles by which he has chosen to live. To some extent, of course, we are all moralists, but the moralist's distinction is, precisely, the self-consciousness he brings to understanding and articulating the consequences of living by certain principles.

Percy had decided what those principles would be: those of the Christian faith as embodied in the teachings and practices of the Roman Catholic church. To some extent, marriage had been the first step toward those higher commitments, a Kierkegaardian ascent from the aesthetic to the ethical mode of life. Movement toward the highest stage, the religious, would be harder, for Percy believed that conversion did not assure salvation. Grace could be gained, but it could also be lost. The journey to this point of resolution, and the consequences of the resolution, constituted a story, a story of pilgrimage. Percy now understood what it was his business to write about.

9

A Second
Apprenticeship

———◆———

As for what you say about Catholicism being implicit in the action (without ever being mentioned)—maybe so. In this novel [The Charterhouse] you are really treating of conversion—or lack of conversion, though, aren't you? That is, you are dramatizing the plight of a person like you or me who has a hell of a time getting into the Church.

—CAROLINE GORDON TO
WALKER PERCY, 1952

When *The Moviegoer* won the National Book Award in 1962, the vast majority of the reading public could only conclude that its author was some rare flash in the pan. Here, after all, was a thwarted, middle-aged M.D. who had somehow managed to produce a remarkable first novel from his home in the swamps of Louisiana. A smattering of that public knew that Dr. Percy had been contributing essays to high-brow journals from as early as 1954, but only Percy's family and close friends had any idea how long and difficult an apprenticeship he had put himself through in order to arrive at the mastery displayed in his first published novel. That he began this apprenticeship at an age when most people are coming to the end of theirs made the accomplishment all the more surprising.

Percy came late to the learning of his craft, but at least he came with certain advantages. For one thing, he had his inheritance from Uncle Will, though such security could have been a curse as much as a blessing. The annals of unfulfilled lives are littered with people who inherited what Edmund Wilson once described as "a small but adequate income."

But Percy possessed effective antidotes to such gradual demoralization—ambition, will, and considerable powers of concentration. Then, too, the Percy urge to excel, as well as a good dose of the Phinizy work ethic, ran strong in him.

Perhaps more important than financial security, Percy could count on his wife, Bunt, to provide domestic order and emotional support as well as a shield from the outside world. Having a child gave even more direction to her considerable energy, and though she employed a black woman named Roberta Nero to help around the house, she was constantly on the move, finding playmates for Mary Pratt and involving herself in church and other community activities. It was Bunt, not surprisingly, who initiated contacts with other people in town, but if people quickly came to know who the Percys were, she carefully guarded her husband from excessive exposure to the round of small-town social obligations that she knew would quickly exhaust him. Bunt quickly proved to be a skilled social diplomat, able to fend off without offending. Percy was grateful. Associating this period with one of his favorite childhood books, he remembered those early years in Covington as his "Swiss Family Robinson" era—a time when he was able to work hard and enjoy his small family in wooded seclusion from the rest of the world.

What Percy carried in his head was his greatest literary asset. To begin with, he possessed a complicated but rich family history, and while that may have been a psychological burden, it was also a writer's trove. Training in science and medicine gave Percy something any writer would envy: a grounding in a profession, with its own forms of knowledge and its own rich vocabulary. Percy's literary background—both his formal and his informal introduction to literature—was itself extensive. Uncle Will had continued what Walker's father began, regularly exposing his young charges to what he thought were the world's best books, and Percy's literary training in school and college—in German as well as English and American classics—was far from negligible. Not that Percy ever needed to be pushed toward a book or a magazine. He had always read more urgently than he ate.

However much he had going for him, Percy still faced formidable obstacles, not the least of which was the craft of fiction itself. Percy came to the task as a competent prose stylist. But it is a long way from writing strong discursive prose to writing fiction, and Percy knew it. Creating characters, building scenes, and inventing action were things Percy had never done before, and they did not come easy. In fact, there was something downright unsouthern in Percy's discomfort with narrative. ("You can be sure," he once told an interviewer, "that I didn't learn to write by sitting at the feet of old men on the front porch listening to them tell stories.") Unlike his friend Shelby Foote and most other southern writers, he was not a natural storyteller. Dialectic and argument—those most unsouthern modes of discourse—were his strengths, and accommodating them to fiction would be his greatest challenge. Considering the effort this would require, it is hardly surprising that in 1954 he would turn, with considerable relief, to the writing of reviews and philosophical essays, and that for the rest of his career he would alternate between fiction and nonfiction. But those first six years of apprenticeship were devoted exclusively and arduously to the craft of fiction.

As well as strenuous, Percy's apprenticeship was largely solitary. He did not live in a community of writers, among fellow toilers. He never had even a limited sojourn in literary bohemia. But he was not entirely on his own. From the beginning, he had Shelby Foote as a sounding board and mentor, roles that Foote was happy to assume. Foote did so not only because he wanted his friend to succeed but because he was literally indebted to Percy. Between book advances, Foote ran perilously low on cash, and Percy was always quick to help in tight times. Finally, Foote had a strong pedagogical streak, a strong urge to instruct, and the fact that his work was being published gave authority to his instructions.

Foote had made impressive progress ever since withdrawing from the magazine market. He had completed a second novel, Shiloh, in late 1947, and this time did not have to call on his friend Ben Wasson to help him sell it. On the strength of his published stories, several New York agents asked to represent him. Deciding on Jacques Chambrun, Foote waited several months before learning in June that Dial Press was interested in his book. The editors there, Bert Hoffman and George Joel, invited Foote to come up to New York to talk things over. Delighted at what he heard at first, Foote soon began to fear that he was receiving the same treatment that Knopf had given him with his first novel. The editors liked the book but feared it wouldn't sell. Did he have anything else he was working on?

He did. In fact, Foote was working on his third novel, what would eventually be Follow Me Down, but instead of talking about a work that was still in the embryonic stage, he summarized the plot of his first novel, Tournament. The two editors, liking what they heard, offered Foote a modest advance and asked how long he thought it would take him to finish the novel. About six months, he assured them. As things turned out, it took only three. Revising assiduously from July through September, Foote removed "nearly all the Joyce, most of the Wolfe, and some of the Faulkner" and sent it in to Dial. The editors were delighted and the book was set for publication the following year. It had been a circuitous journey, but Foote was pleased, as he later wrote, that "my first written novel was to be my first-published after all."

Even before his book was accepted by Dial, though, Foote began to proffer advice to his friend in Covington. Much of it was indirect, contained in his discussion of his own work and that of other writers, but some of it was delivered in direct, tutorial manner:

> If you are serious about wanting to write fiction you had better get to work. I honestly dont think it can be done without a background of four or five years of apprenticeship (probably more). Sit down with pen and paper and describe anything at all: do it again and again—either an object or an action—until you satisfy yourself. Then try telling a story that has a beginning, middle, and end. Then tear it up and do it over, and over, and over. Then try another one, and another one, and another one. Finally you may begin to feel like tackling something with strength to it (I hope you wont have felt up to any such thing before this, for if you have, youll have made a botch of it) . . . So much for the execution. I cant even begin to speak of conception—it comes from God.

How much of this or other advice Percy took to heart is hard to say, but he certainly did not have to be told where the conception came from. He already had firm ideas about that. The whole impetus behind Percy's attempt to write fiction was to express something quite mysterious: the journey that led to his accepting a transcendent order and purpose. This motive was central to the conception not only of his first extended narrative but of all his work. But, as Percy realized, he could not simply rewrite *Pilgrim's Progress* or Dostoyevsky. He had to write out of his own place and time in order to create characters who appear to be struggling within believable, recognizable situations. He had to come to terms with the literary moment, or else produce a curious anachronism cut off from the literary conversation of his period.

How well Percy succeeded in his first apprentice work, *The Charterhouse,* is hard to say. Unfortunately, Percy eventually decided to destroy the manuscript (a fate that the second unpublished novel, *The Gramercy Winner,* was happily spared). Yet despite Percy's efforts to consign his first novel to oblivion, we do have some evidence, anecdotal and epistolary, of what Percy attempted.

The first person to take a look at *The Charterhouse* was Percy's brother Phin. After a year of study at Sewanee, Phin had gone on a tour of Europe with several friends from the "Mountain." Returning to the States around Christmas, he came to his oldest brother for advice. He wanted to know what Walker thought about his idea of going to Columbia, earning a degree in English, and then taking up writing. Percy could not have been more discouraging: "First of all, if you want to write, write. Don't go to Columbia. And second, don't do it. It's the loneliest, most depressing work you can do."

Phin got more than advice. His brother handed him a huge typescript, asking him to read it and render an opinion. Carrying *The Charterhouse* under his arm, Phin trudged off to the guest cottage (the former caretaker's house) to carry out his assignment. An impossible task, as it turned out: Phin could read no more than fifty pages or so before giving up. "It wasn't badly written," Phin Percy decided, "but it just didn't go anywhere. It was boring as hell." Phin returned the manuscript with the unhappy verdict. Whether it was his brother's advice or the prospect of producing an equally unpromising elephant, Phin decided not to pursue a literary career. He applied to the University of Virginia Law School and was accepted in the class of 1952.

If Phin's evaluation had been discouraging, it did not weaken his brother's resolve. Percy kept at his book, revising and adding to it. After breakfast every day, he would repair to his little study off the living room, plop down on a day bed, and pull up his hospital writing stand. Then, in his big blue ring-binder notebooks from medical school days, he would write steadily until noon, usually with classical music playing quietly on his radio. He held to the same schedule that he had established in Sewanee and maintained in New Orleans: work in the morning, lunch and a nap, then more work before breaking for a walk, perhaps some bird-watching and in warmer weather, a splash in the bogue. Occasionally, he and Bunt would see one or another of the few couples they had befriended, particularly, in the first years, Jack and Edith Harrington, who lived not far away on Military Road. Jack Harrington was a fellow tubercular who had lost a lung to the disease. Having retired from a job with the United Fruit Company, he now busied himself with raising chickens and selling eggs to selected buyers in New Orleans. Though not robust, Jack Harrington was an outdoorsman, an avid hunter and fisher, and Percy took to him. He was one of those people Percy both liked and liked to study.

To a remarkable degree, though, Percy was able to live and work in relative isolation and anonymity. Unquestionably, the intensity of his faith at this time made his cloistered existence not only tolerable but even desirable. Jidge Milazzo recalled that he was still riding a beneficent "high" that had come with his entry into the church. As well as being a faithful and generous parishioner of St. Peter's Church in Covington, Percy had discovered a nearby Benedictine abbey—St. Joseph's—and went there occasionally for mass. The solemnity and purpose of the monks at the abbey struck a deep chord; their commitment represented an ideal of single-minded devotion and sacrifice that Percy hoped to emulate in his own work and life. And the monastic life had a powerful aesthetic appeal as well. On one of their visits to the Percys before leaving New Orleans in 1951, Jidge and Sal Milazzo were surprised to see an unusually ebullient Percy come bounding from the house as they pulled into the driveway. "Wait till you see the surprise I have for you," Percy erupted. The surprise, they learned the next day, was high mass, complete with Gregorian chanting, at the abbey church.

Faith was not merely Percy's source of strength. It was the subject of his work-in-progress. The novel that Phin had attempted to read dealt with a young southerner of good family named Ben Cleburne, a troubled young man who, as the novel begins, is completing a stay in a fancy mental institution, the "Retreat," located in a mountain town unmistakably patterned after Sewanee. Cleburne has been in the care of a psychiatrist named Dr. Betty Jane (patterned, one imagines, after Janet Rioch), who judges Ben's relationship with his father "unsatisfactory." Ben knows that there is some truth to this, but the diagnosis seems in some deeper way to miss the point.

In a somewhat cryptic but revealing remark included among the notes that he wrote in 1951–52, Percy suggested what the real point was: "The only way Ben can avoid killing his father and killing himself with guilt is to become a Christian. Then he may still disagree with his father, leave, but still honor him." Ben, still at loose ends, returns to his family's home in Birmingham ("Vulcan over the doomed city," Percy observed in his notes), has unsatisfactory talks with his father, and runs into his childhood friend, Ignatz (Ignatius), who has recently dropped out of a Catholic seminary. The two friends hang out at the country club, the eponymous Charterhouse, a name that invites ironic comparison of the values of a secularized suburban world with those of a true Carthusian monastery. Dedicated to denying the consequences of the Fall, the country club, as Percy well knew from living around such institutions in his early years, offers itself as a new Eden, membership in which is determined by class and worldly attainments. It is the corrupted human community writ large, and all the worse for not knowing so. Playing golf at Charterhouse, Ben meets a young woman named Abby, to whom he immediately and somewhat inexplicably proposes. The action of the rest of the novel deals with the consequences of Ben's reunion with Ignatz and his impulsive proposal.

According to those who read it, the novel suffered from the usual deficiency of first novels: a lack of dramatic tautness. It consisted largely of scenes in which characters rather ponderously discuss Big Questions. There are a number of religiously symbolic dreams, and Ben, without quite understanding his own ascetic yearnings, fantasizes about opening a service station in a desert in the Far West. While it is a little hard to reconstruct what happens at the end, it seems that Ben's father dies, Ignatz rededicates himself to a religious career, and Ben and Abby marry. Ben's progress toward a religious understanding of his life is apparently incomplete at the novel's end. He still has not grasped the significance of what Ignatz and his own unconscious have been trying to tell him. But he seems to be on to something.

Readers of Percy's published fiction will find many of the elements and motifs of *The Charterhouse* familiar. The confused young protagonist, the search for meaning beyond despair, the possibility of an ethical life through marriage, the movement toward religious conversion—all are found in *The Moviegoer* or *The Last Gentleman,* or both. Their presence in *The Charterhouse* shows that Percy clearly knew from the start what his subject was. But how well did he bring it off? Again, we must rely on others' testimony.

Fairly early on, perhaps as early as the autumn of 1949, Percy began sending Shelby Foote parts of his work-in-progress. In one side of a rich correspondence that began in the late 1940s (Percy's side, up to 1970, is lost), a correspondence full of personal news, hesitant requests for loans, discussions of books and music, Foote would not only counsel Percy on the general principles of the craft of fiction but would respond to specific aspects of Percy's work. It is quite clear, from the earliest letters on, that Foote was troubled by the religious tenor of his friend's work. Foote believed that a writer could serve only one master, his art, and that allegiance to anything other than aesthetic ideals produced second-rate work. Quoting his beloved Proust—"One should never be afraid to go too far, for the truth is beyond"—Foote worried that Percy's religion would prevent him from taking the risks that were essential to great art:

> And that is what I find most regrettable about your going into the Church—you wouldnt dare go beyond. There is something terribly cowardly (at least spiritually) about the risks to which you wont expose your soul. Pushed, youll admit that doubt is a healthy thing, closely connected with faith; but you wont follow it. I believe that truth lies beyond and I'm willing to step into the mire of "The Almond Tree" and "Follow Me Down" because I know Ill find what I'm after, on the other side—beyond. You draw back. . . . I seriously think that no good practicing Catholic can ever be a great artist; art is by definition a product of doubt; it has to be pursued. Dostoevsky had it to a degree beyond any I know: it seems even to have led him to tamper with little

girls; it certainly led him to the conception of Ivan Karamazov and the
Grand Inquisitor.

Some of this tirade was motivated by irritation. Percy had described
certain parts of his friend's second novel, *Follow Me Down*, as pornographic and therefore destructive of the novel's unity, and Foote had
been stung by the criticism. That Percy had couched his criticism in
Thomistic categories—he had been reading Maritain's *Art and Scholasticism*—made it no less stinging, perhaps even more so. Foote smelled
Sunday School moralizing and struck back.

Foote could praise as well as censure. In a letter written almost a year
after the attack, Foote confessed to being pleasantly surprised by how
well Percy's novel was shaping up. "I was most surprised to see that you
kept your sense of humor; I hadnt thought you could." More specifically,
based on the chapter that he had read, he thought that Percy had forged
a style that "crossed Wolfe with Kafka," quickly adding that he meant
that as praise, not as a reproach. Foote cited other successful hybrids:
"Faulkner crossed Conrad with Sherwood Anderson. Dostoevsky crossed
Gogol with Dickens. Etc." Taking his examination even closer, Foote
corrected individual sentences:

> p229: "What was he doing in this forlorn street in Ohio?" Here's a
> little lesson in style: too many "in's". Make it, "What was he doing in
> this forlorn Ohio street?"

To show how Percy might sharpen his effects, Foote even rewrote an
entire paragraph (one that describes Ben Cleburne violently throwing
up after a night of too much drinking). Freely as he gave his advice,
however, Foote concluded by urging his friend not to pay it too much
heed. "Go on and write it. Then when you have finished you can look
back. Right now, it's best to keep going."

Foote's letters in the fall and winter of 1950 offered equally helpful
and encouraging suggestions. He talked about the importance of effective prose rhythm, and he urged Percy to make his scenes more dramatic.
At the end of one of his letters, Foote told Percy that he was sending
him a copy of Flaubert's *Sentimental Education*: "It's Flaubert's handling
of your theme: a young man in search of his soul—and he doesnt find it,
either."

Foote balanced realism with encouragement, even cautioning Percy
that he probably would not succeed in getting *The Charterhouse* published. If Foote's honesty sometimes verged on the harsh, it was an
honesty that he turned on himself as well as others. For instance, much

as he warned Percy against didacticism, Foote admitted that he was more prone to the weakness than Percy was: "It's strange, in a way. I'm opposed to preaching in fiction; you sort of favor it. Yet when it comes to the actual work, I preach ten sermons to your one."

Foote sometimes took his role as taskmaster to rather Prussian extremes. In early 1951, Foote scolded Percy for his indolence and his lack of seriousness. Not only had Percy failed to write a word in more than a month but he was planning to go on a trip to Cuba with Bunt, Roy, Sarah, and Phin: "You said you havent written a line in over a month —in the middle of a novel, too!—and then you reward yourself with an ocean voyage." Foote urged Percy to be more strict with himself and "to organize a system of rewards and punishments, self-judged and self-rewarded." If he didn't, Foote warned, he would never amount to anything as a writer. "There is something immoral about piddling around with writing," Foote concluded, proving that he could sermonize in life as well as in fiction.

The lecture did not shame Percy out of taking the trip to Cuba. In fact, though the trip turned into something of a fiasco, Percy had a good time. The group first found themselves in an outrageously expensive hotel; so they moved to another, which proved to be close to a fleabag. Phin lost his luggage somewhere in transit, and then Roy and Sarah had to return home early when they heard about an ice storm back in Greenville and grew worried about their children. But Percy liked the Havana atmosphere. He even saw "Papa" Hemingway at La Floridita. No great encounter took place, however. Percy was too shy to intrude upon the writer.

Much as Percy would complain about travel in his later years, he had been an eager tourist for most of his life. As well as taking almost annual trips and vacations with his brothers and friends, Percy would often quite spontaneously pack up his small family and head toward the Gulf Coast or the mountains for a day trip or a weekend.

Travel was not a waste of time for the writer that Percy was becoming. For one thing, Percy worked diligently wherever he went. His self-discipline and powers of concentration made it possible for him to do so. But he also needed to work. No matter where he was, no matter how many other people happened to be around, Percy would always retreat to some quiet area and write.

More significantly, though, travel fed Percy's imagination. It gave him the opportunity to look around, to take the measure of the times, to conduct his own informal sociology of the American scene. His notes from the early 1950s show how he used his travels to explore his fellow creatures:

The "foreign" phenomenon (cf The "French Flu"). A tourist in the Spanish street will attach much more weight and significance to the stray remark overheard in the steet than to a comparable phrase in USA. The lust for the foreign and the dislike of our old familiar.

The great American trait. A common decency. The great decency of all Americans. A good humor. Sentimental. Ever-ready to help. From charity. From boredom.

Ever the pathologist, he was looking for telltale signs of the underlying condition. He wondered, for example, why he felt curiously at home in a place so impersonal and antiseptic as a motel room. The nonplaceness of such settings was not only oddly congenial but a powerful stimulus to his writing. Howard Johnson's seemed to do for him what Le Dome and La Coupole did for Hemingway. They were not only good places to write but provided clues to the larger predicament.

Yet curiously Percy's powers as a cultural diagnostician seem to have been put to only limited use in his first fictional efforts. Writers take time to discover their strengths, and Percy was no exception in this respect. This was not only a matter of Percy's development. The temper of the times was still somewhat inchoate. Except for growing jitters about the communist threat, heightened by the outbreak of war in Korea in the summer of 1950, the national character was still hard to define. Most veterans—at least those who had not been called back into the military —had completed their schooling on the GI Bill and were starting careers and families. Those things that came to be viewed as the hallmarks of the Eisenhower era—the conformism and complacency, the corporate culture and the suburban domestic ideal—were the very things young Americans were striving for. The gentle satire to which Percy would subject 1950s America in *The Moviegoer* would have been quite difficult, if not impossible, to bring off in his earlier efforts, although at least one reader of *The Charterhouse,* the poet Allen Tate, praised Percy's satirical portrait of the southern businessman. Still, one suspects this owed more to Percy's reading of Sinclair Lewis than to an acute reading of his own culture. Both apprentice novels, judged from fragments of the first and the manuscript of the second, read more like prewar than postwar products.

As Percy grew more confident in what he was doing, he began to hunger for a wider audience. Foote had been an honest and demanding critic, but he was still a friend. His judgment could not help being influenced by familiarity. So in the fall of 1951, Percy screwed up his courage and wrote Caroline Gordon, who was then living in Princeton, temporarily reconciled with her husband, Allen Tate. Gordon and Tate's rocky marriage would soon come to a final end, but at this point they were preparing to move together to teaching jobs in Minnesota. The peaceful interlude was made somewhat more so by the fact that Gordon had just completed a novel, *The Strange Children.*

Percy was fortunate to have made contact with Gordon at such a moment. An outstanding critic and teacher as well as a novelist, Gordon received more than her share of manuscripts by aspiring writers. (In fact, at just about the same time she received Percy's request, she received word from her friend Robert Fitzgerald about a first novel by a writer he much admired and whose work he wanted Gordon to see, Flannery O'Connor.) The amount of time and care she gave to the novices who came to her, particularly those with real talent, was something quite remarkable. It is hard to see how she had any time left over for her own work, much less for her busy life. She may have seen her services as repayment of the debt she owed Ford Madox Ford, who had paid similar attention to her early work and to that of many other fledgling writers. Whatever the reason, Caroline Gordon gave her students a full and rigorous course in the craft of fiction. Her standards were derived from Aristotle's *Poetics* and the examples of the best Modernist writers: Flaubert, Joyce, Conrad, James, and Ford. Control, objectivity, a sustained point of view, exactness of detail, and concern with presenting things and people so that they were *seen*—these were the principles that she insisted on. She also expected her charges to read and understand Aristotle's reflections on the primacy of plot.

Percy had personal as well as professional reasons for coming to Gordon. He had most likely met her in the summer of 1937, when she and Tate had spent a long working vacation at the cabin of their friend Andrew Lytle in Monteagle, Tennessee, not far from Uncle Will's mountain house. Uncle Will had long had sporadic dealings with Lytle, the Tates, and other writers associated with the Agrarian movement. He had been very much in sympathy with the social ideals set forth in their 1930 manifesto *I'll Take My Stand,* even though he didn't appreciate the Modernist modes of literary expression favored by most Agrarians. He would certainly have spoken very favorably of Allen Tate and Caroline Gordon to his adopted son, and Walker always respected his opinion. Something else drew Percy to Gordon. She too had entered the Catholic church—indeed, less than a month before he did. If anybody would be sympathetic to what he was trying to do, Percy thought, it would be Gordon.

When Gordon got Percy's request in the mail, she wrote back immediately, saying that she was pleased that he had entered the church and that she would gladly read his novel. (She charged him one hundred dollars for her labor, money that she said she would use for a "Catholic project.") Gordon indicated that she was encouraged by a conversation she had had with Percy many years before, for "in that conversation you revealed the fact that you already realized that techniques were involved in the writing of novels. A Catholic novelist who relies more on his technique than his piety is what is badly needed right now."

Gordon's ideas about religion and art were quite complicated. She disliked the work of obvious proselytizers or writers whose piety stood out—Bernanos, for example, she considered a bad novelist. Yet she believed that all good writers, whether they knew so or not, drew on the Christian myths for their plots. Ever since her conversion, moreover, she had come to believe that Catholic writers were more closely attuned to those myths than agnostics or Protestants. The Catholics' advantage came from their constant exposure to the lives of the saints. "The saints, the mystics are the proper companions of the fiction writer," Gordon wrote, "for as Jacques Maritain points out in *Art and Scholasticism,* 'they alone know what is in the human heart.' "

When she received Percy's novel, she felt that all her beliefs had been confirmed. "It's no accident," she wrote Brainerd Cheney, a friend from earlier years in Nashville, "that in the last two months the two best novels I've ever read have been by Catholic writers. The Protestant *mystique* has worn out, but people would have gone on forever writing those curiously dry novels (like Lionel Trilling or . . . Truman Capote) . . . if something new hadn't come along. And Walker's novel and Flannery's novel are IT. They are both so damned good."

Gordon's remarks to Percy in her letter of December 11, 1951, were just as enthusiastic. "Your novel is the way they will be talking next year and the year after that. It is the first novel of that kind that has come my way." Gordon was also perhaps the only reader of the novel to say that it had compelling action—"You know what your action is, all right. No trouble there." She did, however, find that the novel suffered from two major technical faults. First, it lacked what she called "composition of scene." The action, she complained, took place in a kind of vacuum; objects and people lacked substantial reality. "It is not enough to say a dog is large or small to make him come to life. That won't do it. As a rule, it takes three strokes—three activated sensuous details to bring anything to life in fiction." The same applied to his settings: "The Retreat, (and how I love the idea of making Sewanee, that stronghold of Episcopalianism, a caste-ridden mental nursing home!) figures very importantly in your action but you do not give us enough data to enable us to visualize it all. You show us a man thinking in a bed but the man and the bed seem to be floating in space."

The second major weakness, according to Gordon, was pacing. "You go too fast. You don't give us time to take in what is happening. Your scenes lack the pace of life." Gordon quoted the words of a black minister who had a formula for the perfect sermon: "First I tells 'em I'm going to tell 'em. Then I tell 'em. Then I tell 'em I done told 'em." Percy, she said, also tended to "muff" some of his most dramatic effects by "not leaving enough white space around them."

After devoting eight single-spaced pages to general weaknesses, Gordon gave another twelve to identifying and correcting particular problems, examples of what she considered faulty technique. Her remarks were not all scolding. Quite often, she would interrupt her criticism to congratulate Percy on what he was trying to do.

> The fact that he [Ben Cleburne] is thinking of opening a filling station in the desert is very important in the action. The human life is an analogue of the Divine Life. The desert figures in the life of anybody who makes any progress from the human towards the Divine. It was no whim but the same kind of necessity that is governing your hero that drove the early fathers out into the desert, that drove Mary Magdalen to wander in the desert for thirty years. (I think that here we ought to stop and say a few prayers of thanksgiving for the fact that you are a Catholic and therefore have some notion of what it's all about.)

Percy quite clearly had been right in thinking that Gordon would appreciate his larger design. As sensitive a reader as Foote had been, he had not discerned the possibility of hope that lay before the struggling Ben Cleburne. Gordon had. She had seen it in the novel's particulars— in Ben's attraction to the desert, for example—and also in the underlying *mythos* of the novel. This was why she thought Percy and her other Catholic writer, O'Connor, represented hope for the future. Writing that came out of what Gordon called the "Protestant mystique" was exhausted, she believed, because authors in this tradition (and she counted communist authors as secularized Protestants) always took on "the responsibility of setting up a new heaven and a new earth" as they went along. They tried to improvise the terms of a personal salvation, and in that they belonged to the doomed project of Romanticism. The impossibility of creating a new heaven and earth inevitably left the Romantic hero wallowing in wounded sensibility. "But a Catholic," Gordon wrote, "knows that God has already created the universe and that his job is to find his proper place in it."

Gordon liked Percy's novel so much that she got her husband to read it—something that Tate very rarely did. On New Year's Day, 1952, he wrote Percy detailing his own reactions. In later years, Percy somewhat misrepresented these remarks, making them sound far more negative than in fact they were. Tate did complain about the lack of strong, dramatic action, particularly in the first sixty pages (the very pages that Phin Percy had found impossible to read), but his remarks were generally favorable. He concluded his letter by saying that Percy's "great intelligence and power" would make him a "valuable novelist."

As well as providing further testimony to Percy's potential as a novelist, Tate's letter sheds revealing light on Percy's evolving attitude toward the South. We learn, specifically, that The Charterhouse contained what might have been Percy's first critique of the Roman-Stoic code of the southern upper class, a critique that he would later develop in one of his more important essays, "Stoicism in the South," as well as in The Moviegoer. Percy's first airing of these views clearly made an impression on Tate. "You are right," Tate wrote, "that the Roman myth still hangs on in the South, and that the South is not really Christian; it is merely reactionary without being traditional." The failure of Agrarians like Andrew Lytle and, to some extent, himself, Tate went on to confess, was their failure to see that the South had no tradition without the church—and specifically the Catholic church.

As the year 1952 began, Percy had good reason to pat himself on the back. Two outstanding writer-critics had heaped praise on his first literary effort, pronouncing him one of the bright new lights of American fiction. With such plaudits in mind, Percy set to work revising, which in most cases, according to Gordon's instructions, meant expanding scenes and developing characters. An already large manuscript of some five hundred tightly typed pages daily grew stouter.

While Percy's future seemed to take a promising turn at the beginning of the year, his friend Foote's took an unexpected turn for the worse. Indeed, Foote's entire life seemed suddenly to be in shambles. It was a strange turn of events, because the preceding year had been exceptionally good, perhaps the single best year in his career. It had begun with Faulkner's congratulating him on his novel Follow Me Down. (Shelby related his idol's words in a letter to Percy: " 'It's good,' he said and then looked at me rather piercingly and added, 'Do better next time.' ") In April, he had sent his publisher his third novel, Love in a Dry Season, and received the by now familiar words of praise. Wasting no time, he had immediately begun revising Shiloh, the first novel that he had shown Dial, and by the middle of May, he was ecstatic about how well the book was shaping up: "I am doing the final draft of SHILOH. I'll swear thats a good piece of work: it's a miracle to me how I did it." Foote told Percy that he was dedicating the novel to him—"For one thing, you financed me through it."

In July, Foote not only completed his revisions of *Shiloh* but started sketching what he believed would be his "big" novel, *Two Gates to the City*. All his other books up to this one, he said, were "student books," prepatory to the great task before him. His projected opus was to be constructed in five parts (alternating between the past and present) and to have five major characters who "rush about in a sort of Dostoevskian furor." It was to be the story of the region he had been born and raised in: "I am going to get the Delta into it as the Delta has never been got before."

Foote had visited Percy several times during the year, sometimes with Peggy and Margaret, sometimes alone (but to Shelby's great regret, never with his bulldog Bo: Percy was afraid that it would tear his little dog Joey to shreds). Typically, the two friends would drink and talk until Walker grew tired or exasperated; he then would retreat to his study, while Foote chatted with Bunt or made himself busy with some chore. (He was, it seems, forever organizing Percy's books or records.) Inevitably on those visits, conversation would come around to the oft-revisited subject: religion and art. Foote would grudingly allow his respect for Catholicism but steadfastly maintain that Catholicism had produced no great art since Dante.

Few people ever sounded more certain of their certainties than did Foote during the course of his *annus mirabilis*. The first reports on the progress of his big book (one-third of a first draft written by early December) seemed to confirm his seemingly boundless self-confidence. On New Year's Eve, just after reading page proofs of *Shiloh*, he wrote Percy from the top of his optimism: "Life is a wonderful thing, believe me: a God-given wonderful thing." The next sentence proved all too prophetic, though: "Or so I say now. Next month I'll be tearing my hair, messing up reams of paper with unsightly inkblots and cursing God for having put me on this clod of a planet."

Probably the first sign that something was going wrong was the overly exuberant, almost manic tone of Foote's letters. Percy knew something was up. Only one week into the new year, Percy's suspicions were confirmed. Foote confessed to Percy that he'd been on a "two-week holiday" of drinking and staying up late—and, most important, that he'd fallen in love. "To tell you the truth, I feel like hell and I'm confused and God knows what will come of all this." The only thing Foote said he remained sure of was the writing—"The writing is all right; the writing is fine."

It wasn't true. The writing was going badly. But so much of the rest of his life was spinning out of control—he was in love with a married woman, his own marriage was heading for the rocks, and he was having premonitions of death—that he had to think that the writing was going forward. But in fact he could barely sit still. He was traveling all the time: in Greenville one day, in Memphis the next. There were trips to New York and even one to Harrisburg, Pennsylvania. Relations with Peggy had been strained for some time. She was something of a Memphis society debutante who seemed to have no clear place in Greenville or in Foote's somewhat monastically organized existence. Now that Foote had fallen in love with someone else, the marriage looked doomed. In early March, Foote wrote to say that the divorce had gone through.

Foote's misery was so great that he wouldn't even let Percy bask in the momentary satisfaction of the Tates' praise. Instead, he lashed out against the Tates for trying to prune Percy into their kind of writer:

> No one—NO one—should ever monkey with a writer's manuscript. All it does is short-circuit the line of his talent, and absolutely no good can come of it. These articulate people who can put their finger on the trouble, and tell why, are archfiends incarnate. My perversity and unkindness toward the Tates, however, is based on something in ad- dition. I think they are to be avoided as you would avoid something contagious, for the simple reason that they have smothered their talent the very way I'm warning against. They know this very well and (at least in their subconscious) they are busy as bees trying to see that it happens to others.

Foote seemed to ignore that he had done quite a bit of "monkeying" himself, but he thought that what the Tates were doing was trying to interfere with his friend's way of seeing, his view of the world. "If you let anyone fiddle with your way of seeing—fiddle deliberately, I mean: not by example but by pointing out—youll nick this instrument beyond repair; youll wind up with nothing but regrets." Of course, Percy had been close to the Tates' "way of seeing" to begin with, and that may have been what irked Foote most: He saw his best friend being drawn into the other camp, the camp of "Sunday-school tract" writers. At bottom, of course, his pride was hurt and he felt abandoned in his darkest hour.

Things seemed to grow only worse. In March, he admitted that he wasn't writing: "I can't work till I get squared away, and getting squared away is not in my hands now." It wasn't because the woman he loved was married. "I am truly in love for the first time in my life and I am being kept from the woman I love." Foote knew that he was working himself into an "anxiety neurosis," but he couldn't pull himself out of his desolation. "I havent written one line in more than a month, and for all I know, I'm utterly through, both as a person and a writer. Suicide is much on my mind and I may come to it yet." Percy saw that the situation was grave and urged Shelby to "Live alone and at peace." Foote flung the counsel back at his friend. "Youve been a pretty coldblooded sort of fellow all your life. . . . 'Alone' and 'at peace' dont go together where I'm concerned, not now." Foote scattered even more insults among his lamentations: "You go on, do what you think is best about your work. I'm no one to advise. For all I know, you might do your best work writing a novel according to an outline someone sent you. It probably wouldnt be worth a damn but if it would be the best you could do, then thats the main thing."

Foote came down to Covington to see his friend toward the end of May, and they spent most of the time discussing Foote's woes. Foote apologized that they never got around to discussing *The Charterhouse*, which Percy was now revising. In fact, Percy felt that the writing on his book was going very well, although he feared that he didn't work diligently enough. Foote counseled that he adopt a fixed schedule and stick to it every day (except for Sundays and one short bimonthly vacation).

Percy was far more diligent than he gave himself credit for being. He had a schedule and stuck to it on most days. But he could never produce on the quota system in the way that Foote could—or at least in better days could. Percy wrote more like D. H. Lawrence (a writer he and Foote were reading a great deal of in the early 1950s), finding his way forward in the act of writing and never quite knowing where he was heading. Foote wrote a detailed outline and rarely swerved from it, and once he produced his daily quota of approximately six hundred to one thousand words, he would almost never go back and revise. Percy, by contrast, revised constantly.

But though he believed he was doing the right thing, these were hard years for Percy. As of yet he had no proof that his labors amounted to anything. Encouraging words were fine, of course, but Percy had enough of his grandmother Phinizy's practicality to be dissatisfied with a lack of concrete results. His brothers seemed to be moving purposefully forward in their lives. Phin had graduated that June from the University of Virginia Law School and was hired the following fall by the Central Intelligence Agency. Roy's various enterprises—including a fertilizer company and a cotton compress plant as well as Trail Lake farm—were all doing well. He and Sarah now had four children (the fourth, a girl, had been born in 1950) and had built a new house outside of town. By comparison with his brothers' accomplishments—not to mention their impressive war records—Percy had to feel that his life was small potatoes.

By early November (despite a trip to Mexico in September), Percy had completed his revision of the novel and packed it off—all eight pounds and 942 pages of it—to Caroline Gordon in Minnesota. On November 25, Gordon wrote to say that she was halfway through the book and was mightily impressed: "This is a real book. You've done even better than I'd hoped. . . . In all the years that I have been trying to help writers I have never had one who so richly repaid my efforts." She congratulated Percy on having preserved everything that was good about the first draft, including the spontaneity, while mending the weaknesses. All the characters were now "done in the round." She liked the way the novel opened from Dr. Betty Jane's perspective, though she thought the name had to be changed to do justice to what the psychiatrist represented: "She represents a formidable force that is working in modern life, a force that is swayed now towards God, now towards the Devil. She may even represent an idolatry. Some people are idolaters about psycho-analysis. Betty Jane is too homely, too condescending a name for such a mighty force."

Gordon offered to send the box directly to her friend and editor Jack Wheelock at Scribner's, and Percy readily accepted. Shortly thereafter, Gordon received a note from Wheelock telling her that he had received the manuscript and that he would be reading it forthwith, but Gordon warned Percy that " 'forthwith' for Jack doesn't mean right off the bat."

Despite Foote's charges against Gordon's meddling, her help during the last year had been invaluable. She was, to be sure, a fellow believer, but her principles of what constituted a good work of fiction were almost identical to Foote's. She emphasized craft. She even believed that some Christian writers such as Mauriac and Bernanos were such bad craftsmen that they were "less Christian" than such avowed agnostics as Joyce. "There is a Manichean contempt for their craft, for, in fact, the whole natural order, that is fatal to a novelist." But she differed very strongly with Foote in her conviction that art and faith were profoundly compatible, indeed essential to each other. And she assured Percy that by being true to one he was also being true to the other.

This assurance was contrary to Foote's credo. He repeatedly warned Percy that his faith would prevent him from coming to grips with his experience, with those "formative events" of his life that are the artist's greatest birthright:

> I do know, from my own life, what will be the formative events of
> yours. I blame my father enormously for going into business; it took

him to Mobile, Alabama, where he had a date with a strep germ that took him off; he left me to fight this world alone. It must be far worse in your case, whose father left voluntarily and mysteriously—after which you were uprooted in a manner I never knew (mother and I came home, where I was born) and then lost her in a brutal way that could make a man hate God. As if this wasn't enough, as soon as youd found how to live with all this, or anyhow exist, then came TB—and with TB, conversion. The Church, doubtless, can give you highly satisfactory answers to all this, as far as they go. But the real answers, the answers that will bring you not peace but understanding, can only be found in art. . . . It will only be after a lifetime of work, transforming those shocks into something that will pulse with life long after you are gone, that youll have come to terms with it.

Foote's warning could not have proved more ironic. For while Percy did go on to investigate the formative events of his life quite directly in his mature fiction, Foote never did the same in his own. Indeed, Foote's discomfort with the autobiographical impulse gave his fiction a somewhat icy, impersonal quality. This was not merely artistic objectivity, in the Flaubertian sense that Foote so valued. Flaubert strove for the illusion of objectivity, but he infused his creations with his own passions ("Madame Bovary, c'est moi!"), something that Foote appeared to be hesitant about doing. For Foote, art was a refuge from the messiness and confusion of personal life, a hoped-for transcendence. But even art had let him down in 1952. The day after Christmas, he wrote Percy that "1952 was pure nightmare, and here comes 1953. Peace be with us."

Percy experienced very little peace during the first months of the new year. The waiting game was on, and Percy felt uncomfortable playing it. Caroline Gordon wrote him a reassuring note in the middle of January. "Every day I expect to get a letter from Jack Wheelock about your novel. It *must* come soon. Their keeping it this long is a good sign." In the gentlest ways, she even tried to prepare him for the jolt of rejection, assuring him there were other houses that would be interested.

Gordon had slightly more discouraging news in the letter she wrote at the end of the month. "I had a note from Jack Wheelock the other day, saying that he thought 'The Charterhouse' showed 'flashes of great talent' as well as 'serious weaknesses' and asking me to 'tell him something about the author.' I thought and Allen thought, too, that that meant that he wanted me to tell him what to think about the ms, so I told him as best as I could." Gordon sensed that worse was coming—and she was right. In early February she received a letter from Wheelock and sent it immediately on to Percy, along with her own acerbic commentary. "It is

absurd for him to go on about the novel's faults. Of course it has faults
—obvious faults. But what about the amateurish work of Jim Jones? It is
not the novel's faults but its theme that makes it unacceptable to Scribner's. They just don't get it." Wheelock tried to be as tactful as possible,
noting that there was "some exceedingly good work in these 942 pages."
He did, however, appear to be be somewhat obtuse about what Percy
was up to:

> It does not seem to us here that the novel as a whole is successful,
> or that its main theme is convincingly realized. Where the story deals
> with Ben and Abby, more especially in the early pages and against the
> background of a familiar locale, it not only comes to life but has great
> distinction. But the whole thing seems formless. Ben, by reason of his
> neurotic predicament, goes off into one erratic episode after another,
> and good as the telling of some of these episodes is—there's some
> wonderful writing in that part about Kitty and Ben—it doesn't seem
> to relate to what has gone before and gives somewhat the effect of a
> railroad flat, with one room stretching on after another instead of being
> built around a central core. To us, at least, a great deal of the material
> dealing with Ignatz is pretty unreal, and that's unfortunate because he
> is a very important character in the book. When the novel ends with
> Ben and Abby married, the theme of the book emerges almost for the
> first time, explicitly stated by the author—the wasteful tragedy of Ben's
> suffering which he had written off without understanding it or resolv-
> ing it. It's a fine theme, but shouldn't it have been implicit in the
> course of the story as it goes along?

At the bottom of this paragraph, Gordon penned in her own irritated
reaction: "It *is*, but the dope doesn't get it." This would not be the last
time a novel by Percy would be interpreted as a portrait of neurosis. Early
reviewers of *The Moviegoer* and *The Last Gentleman* would say similar
things, imposing a rigidly psychological interpretation on what were
more profoundly philosophical and religious themes. "I might extend to
you my sympathy about this initial experience," Gordon closed, "if I
didn't realize that much worse trials are in store for you."

Gordon suggested two possible courses of action. One was to send the
manuscript to Henry Regnery in Chicago, a firm that was publishing
Allen Tate's most recent collection of essays and that had decidedly
Catholic leanings. The other suggestion, which actually came from
Tate, was to send it to their friend Denver Lindley at Harcourt Brace.
Percy decided on the latter, and Gordon asked Wheelock to send the
manuscript to Lindley.

Gordon rendered a further service by putting Percy in touch with a woman named Susan Jenkins, an old friend of hers who operated as a kind of literary secretary and go-between in New York City. In March, Jenkins wrote Percy to describe what she might do for him. She proposed to serve not as his agent but as an assistant on the scene. In addition to helping him find an "established" literary agent, she would conduct "the necessary correspondences, phone calls, interviews, etc. to speed action" and do any manuscript typing that was necessary. Percy signed up with Jenkins—she charged $2.50 an hour—but it turned out to be a fairly short-lived relationship. (It did, however, have one lasting consequence. Through Jenkins he came into contact with the agent Elizabeth Otis, whose firm, McIntosh and Otis, soon took on Percy and would represent him for the rest of his career.)

Painfully aware of his novel's shortcomings, Percy was becoming more ambivalent about seeing it in print. His doubts grew when, toward the end of March, the manuscript returned from Harcourt with Lindley's reluctant letter of rejection. Despite the discouragement and his failing confidence, Percy allowed Jenkins to send it to Viking. Again, it was rejected. He decided he would give it one more try and asked Jenkins to mail it to Regnery. This time, to his surprise, there was a spark of interest. Regnery was tempted, the editors reported, but they wondered if Percy could cut and compress the novel. If he did so, they would seriously consider publishing it. Percy decided not to. Having spent almost a year adding to the book, he had trouble seeing how cuts would improve it. He may have concluded by then that the novel was simply not worth publishing, but it is just as possible that his thoughts were turned to other matters, specifically another novel.

That novel was the one that he and Foote had talked about for years —his "Magic Mountain" novel—and though we cannot say when Percy began to work on it, it is clear that it was well under way by the summer of 1953. (In a letter she wrote in April, Gordon congratulated Percy for starting a new novel.)

The challenge of such a book was great, not least because Thomas Mann's book lay before the undertaking like a stern "no trespassing" sign. Few works of Western literature are as finely realized as Mann's story of Hans Castorp's stay in Sanatorium Berghof, a novel whose power had startled even its creator. Mann had originally intended something quite modest, a "humorous companion-piece to *Death in Venice*," but the novel seemed to have a will of its own. It was perhaps the most elaborately composed statement of Mann's tragic understanding of life. "What Castorp comes to understand," Mann explained in his own commentary on the novel, "is that one must go through the deep experience of sickness and death to arrive at a higher sanity and health. . . . It is this notion of disease and death as a necessary route to knowledge, health, and life that makes *The Magic Mountain* a novel of *initiation.*"

Percy set out from the start to write a novel of initiation, but if he wrote with Mann's book in mind, indeed to the point of making clear parallels between his characters and those of *The Magic Mountain*, he intended a very different kind of initiation, an initation into a Christian-comic vision of truth rather than a tragic one. Set in an Adirondack town in the middle of World War II, *The Gramercy Winner* was ultimately a novel about baptism, and though Percy would handle the same theme far more adroitly in *The Last Gentleman*, the novel has interest as an early attempt to impose form on what Percy considered the most significant event of his life.

Will Grey, a well-off young man who was stricken by tuberculosis during Marine boot camp, is to some extent the prototype of the searchers who figure as the protagonists of the first two published novels, Binx Bolling and Will Barrett, but he is in even worse shape than they are. He has only the dimmest idea that he should hope for anything more than the "grayness" that defines his gentlemanly upper-class life. ("The progress of the neurotic toward a dreadful grey neutrality from which he cannot escape," Percy wrote in his notes from 1952.) In fact, Will Grey is so insubstantial that he poses a formal threat to the novel. Allen Tate had warned Percy against the fallacy of imitative form in *The Charterhouse*: "Because your character [Ben Cleburne] by nature can't act (but only move) your novel lacks action and substitutes a movement of episodes all of which are repetitions of the same quality of the hero." Similarly, Will's grayness threatens to cancel any interest we may have in him from the outset.

The problem stems partly from a curious authorial decision. For some reason, Percy made his central character a northerner, a New Yorker from, as the title suggests, Gramercy Park. Percy's knowledge of this social milieu was far too skimpy for him to be able to provide his character with convincingly real or textured background. Apart from a slight interest in science (Grey arrives at the first cure cottage with a huge physics book, *Subatomic Particles*, that he thinks will explain everything), Grey comes across as little more than the "type" that Percy intended him only partly to be: "He belonged to a type that is found so often in the Northeast, where great wealth and good schools have conspired to produce a happy new breed, a generation of great attractiveness and simplicity."

There are interesting parallels between the protagonists of *The Gramercy Winner* and *The Last Gentleman*. In addition to sharing the same first name (a name that gives some clue to their problem), Will Grey and Will Barrett resemble each other in other important ways: "He [Grey] was the perfect spectator, content always to be in the stands when his school played, content at his college club (he had been a Princeton sophomore) to stay smilingly among his friends while someone else shone." But while Will Barrett's reasons for being a spectator are partly tied to the family history that he reluctantly but ultimately confronts, Will Grey's reasons for being one seem nebulous: "His nonparticipation was not a case of laziness or ineptitude but rather another element of his good taste, a prescience that excelling, winning, would be almost as gross a lapse as failing." One hears the faint echoes of a Jamesian predicament in this characterization (and Percy had been reading a great deal of Henry James in the early 1950s), but in Grey's case it doesn't make for very interesting drama. Will Barrett's search for a way out of his despair is necessary and urgent. Will Grey's spiritual journey seems to have little to do with his will; he is pulled out of self-satisfaction by illness and other people around him.

These other people, as characters, are perhaps the greatest strength of the novel, and their points of resemblance to (and difference from) parallel characters in Mann's *Magic Mountain* have been painstakingly drawn by the critic Gary M. Ciuba. A vital and exuberant southerner named Laverne Sutter—an aviator before he was stricken by the disease —joins Grey in the first cure cottage, Mrs. McLeod's. Just as Mann's Mynheer Peeperkorn enchants the staid young naval architect from Hamburg, so Sutter, Ciuba notes, "can captivate William by the sheer charisma of his commanding and reckless personality." But the bond of brotherly affection that grows between the two men is threatened by Sutter's wife, Allison, a beautiful, intelligent, but somewhat confused woman whose affection for Will seems alternately innocent and seductive. Allison is Percy's Clavdia Chauchat, the character who in Mann's novel introduces the protagonist to the insistence of erotic drives. Yet Allison is different from Chauchat: Allison offers the possibility of a more profound spiritual love, a possibility that Will ultimately misses.

Moving from one cure cottage to another, Grey falls under the influence of two brilliant and jestingly antagonistic physician-patients, Dr. Van Norden and Dr. Scanlon. To some extent, the running argument between the skeptical materialist Van Norden and the fallen Catholic Scanlon duplicates the quarrel between Mann's Herr Settembrini, the supreme rationalist, and Herr Naptha, the Jesuit and communist. Van Norden first exerts the stronger pull, drawing Will to him with his agile, scientific mind (he is a pathologist), his love of music, and his witty if sometimes frightening cynicism. Will laughs at Van Norden's dismissal of Scanlon's views as medieval humbuggery—"His view of disease is still chivalric and anthropomorphic. He still conceives of the evil bacillus attacking the good human."

Will is so charmed by Van Norden that he not only embraces his crude scientific positivism but goes beyond it to a kind of callous nihilism, as we see in a scene depicting an autopsy. At the end of the autopsy that Van Norden has invited Grey to witness, Will discovers that the body is that of his friend Laverne Sutter, but rather than saddening him, the discovery leaves him feeling empty. Not even the medical details that interest Van Norden—the mechanism of the disease as evidenced in the tissue—interest Will. The spectacle of the dead body before him only confirms what he says he had been sure of all his life, that "there is nothing."

Will makes this confession of his nihilism to Scanlon after his health has taken a sudden and unexpected turn for the worse, indeed after entering the first stages of terminal tubercular meningitis. Somewhat drunk on barbiturates, he begins to badger Scanlon. "Scanlon, I see you sitting there like a damn buddha. Like you know something. What do you know, Scanlon?" Scanlon, the fallen Catholic, asks his friend what denomination he is, and Will tells him that he is a Unitarian, an answer that sets up the all-important scene to come.

Will's bravado begins to dissolve when he thinks Scanlon is going to leave the room. He begs him not to and Scanlon assures him that he won't. Then Will seems to lose all self-possession:

> "What's the matter, Willy?"
> "I don't know, Scanlon. I'm homesick."
> "How long have you been homesick?"
> "All my life."

After this most heartfelt of confessions, Will dreams of his childhood friend George Boetjeman, who had been shot and killed by a sniper in the Pacific campaign. The dream takes Will back to the time when he and Boetjeman were teenagers setting out to roam through New York City on their own, a dream that unfolds in an image of beatitude as the two friends head up the stairs of Penn Station to the Eighth Avenue exit: "They went up the last steps, George going first to use the electric eye, through the concourse and out into the city."

The epilogue of the novel presents both the dry scientific description of Will's demise and the somewhat maudlin reactions of his friends and family. But between both we learn of Scanlon's "scandalous" behavior. Before lapsing into his final coma, Grey repeatedly summoned Scanlon to his side, and the two men, according to the Night Supervisor, would "converse by the hour—Dr. Scanlon mostly, his voice low and em-phatic, discursive—as if he were imparting information, data, of great value and usefulness." Stranger yet, they sometimes "spoke in tones of unmistakable levity and even laughed out loud." But the great scandal was what the nurse saw two nights before Will's death: "Dr. Scanlon bending over William, *baptising* him with water." No one seems more ashamed of this impropriety than Scanlon himself, who, the narrator explains, shortly thereafter left the Lodge.

Percy's second apprentice novel ends even more triumphantly than the first, with its protagonist winning grace—the great mercy cryptically announced in the novel's title. But whether it was because the novel had so strong and clear a religious message, or because Percy was dissat-isfied with its technical weaknesses (his training at Gordon's feet would have made him painfully mindful of how undeveloped certain scenes were), Percy made little if any effort to get this novel published. It seems that he was reluctant to show it even to his small audience of readers.

Shelby Foote, who had moved to Memphis in early December and was now living in an apartment on the bluffs overlooking the Mississippi, did learn in early 1954 that his friend was well along in his second novel. By February, Foote was writing to congratulate Percy on completing it: "I dont know how you feel about it but if youre willing I'd like to read the recent novel." Percy, apparently, was not willing. Having devoted six years to fiction, he seemed suddenly to grow tired of the business of making up stories, even somewhat disgusted with it.

To an extent, Foote had been correct in charging that Percy did not take art seriously enough. At times, Percy exhibited an almost puritani-cal contempt for the artifice of art, and in that state of mind he would crave a more direct medium for expressing what he had to say. Such an idea was heresy to Foote, who believed that, for the artist, the medium was inseparable from the message. In the same letter in which he asked to see Percy's new manuscript, Foote almost uncannily addressed the question that was now vexing his friend:

> Philosophy is the coré of the arts; without it, none of them is any-thing. But to my mind it must be so much a part of the man that he uses it only as an expression of his being. Therefore, for a writer, his study of philosophy will avail him nothing until he has assimilated it into his being—until it literally affects profoundly (I would add, un-consciously) his way of viewing the world.

Percy could appreciate the truth of Foote's remarks—they were, at bottom, a recapitulation of the High Modernist creed of writers like

Joyce and James—but he feared that going the way Foote urged would lead only to aestheticism, an idolatry of the art object. For Percy, the most important thing about art remained its end, its object—specifically, to depict man as a creature in desperate need of "Good News." Achieving this end without heavy-handed didacticism, without pamphleteering, was the challenge, and in The Gramercy Winner Percy feared that he had fallen short of success. And possibly, he now thought, literary fiction might not be the appropriate medium for communicating what he had to say.

Other matters were also weighing on Percy as 1954 began. He was thirty-eight years old, the father of one child, and soon to be the father of a second. (Despite all their earlier fears of Percy's sterility, Bunt had become pregnant and was expecting in July.) His first child, Mary Pratt, was now enrolled in the first grade of St. Peter's parochial school, and like all little children of her age she was beginning to wonder about the ways her family differed from other families. It was nice that her father was home all day. He played with her when he came out of his little room, and he told her wonderful stories, mostly about a little creature called Mooch who lived in a curious habitation called a "cawl." But now that she was entering the wider world, she wondered why her daddy didn't go away during the daytime like other daddies did. One day she came home with an assignment from her teacher: She was supposed to find out what her father did for a living. "Daddy looked a little perplexed," Mary Pratt recalled. "Then he said that I could tell my teacher that he was a philosopher." The word being a little more than the six-year-old girl could handle, Mary Pratt ended up telling her classmates that her daddy was a "silosopher."

The "silosopher" was beginning to be more of a known person in Covington. In addition to his Military Road friends, the Harringtons and Charlie and M'Adele Read, a couple named Lawrence (Chink) and Betty Baldwin became regular friends of the Percys starting in the early 1950s. Chink Baldwin remembers the night he first met Percy, an experience that seemed to typify the strange and unpredictable driftings of the man he came to know and love. Chink Baldwin was about as close to being a native of the town as one could be. His parents had moved there from New Orleans in 1935, and after the war and college, Baldwin had, in 1950, opened a car dealership on the eastern edge of town. One night while he was working late, he looked up from his desk to see a tall figure staring in the showroom window at one of the cars. Baldwin walked out and introduced himself to the shy, somewhat self-conscious man. Percy said that he was interested in one of the cars—a black four-door Lincoln sedan. Baldwin said he could buy it for twenty-seven hundred dollars, a price that struck Percy as reasonable.

Soon thereafter, the Baldwins and the Percys began to take more notice of each other. They all went to the same church, and two of the Baldwin children, John and Elizabeth, were close to Mary Pratt's age. In those days, social life in Covington consisted of a great deal of informal "dropping in," and it was not unusual for either family to come by the other's house in the late afternoon for an impromptu visit, sometimes a game of badminton, and not infrequently, these visits would spill over into meal time—in those days most families in the Percys' crowd had "help" who could cook and clean up. Ida Mae Griffin had become the Percys' cook and housecleaner in 1950, and she was used to preparing meals, lunch as well as dinner, for the droppers-by. The Baldwins' house, where the Percys dropped in just as often, was an active social hub in Covington. The Baldwins knew everybody, and by entering their world the Percys began to know everybody as well. This was not altogether comforting to the man who cherished his anonymity. "It was clear to me from the first time I met him," said Baldwin, "that Walker was a quiet, reserved man who stayed away from crowds. He told me about his health background, and I just assumed that he lived on a private income."

Percy clearly would have preferred remaining in relative solitude, but with Mary Pratt going to school and another child on the way, and with small towns being what they inevitably are, it was impossible for him to remain completely on the sidelines of Covington society. Circumstances were forcing him to be part of the larger community. Percy's loss was literature's gain. The characters who would stock his later novels were drawn from the wide assortment of types that simmered in the St. Tammany Parish melting pot—the coon-ass Cajuns and the tub-thumping Baptists, the Italians and the Jews, the blacks and the rednecks, and the slightly displaced New Orleans gentility and the even more displaced Yankee professionals. These were the people Percy was now beginning to know.

But contact with this wider social world was something Percy always partly resisted. He was prepared to go only so far with congeniality. Beyond a certain point, the pressure of socializing would make him not only taciturn but sometimes rude. People talking to him would suddenly realize that he was not listening to a word they were saying. He would fade out, become lost in reverie; and sometimes, he would appear visibly uncomfortable, almost panic-sticken, like a cornered animal. On some social occasions he and Bunt would suddenly disappear, leaving a party or gathering that was in full sway. Not surprisingly, there were those who took offense at Percy's ways, and for many years Bunt did her best to soothe hurt feelings, but those closest to the man would simply say, "That's Walker."

Phin Percy remembers his brother's acute discomfort during this period. "There was just not much he could point to. He knew he was a writer, but he hadn't published anything. So it just made him real jumpy when people asked him what he did." Phin could sympathize. He was going through something of a career crisis himself. His brief tour in the CIA had not worked out. After several months of training, he had been offered three possible stations abroad—Taiwan, Saigon, and the Middle East—but none of them appealed to him and he had resigned. The first year after his graduation from law school would have been a complete bust had it not been for one thing. In the fall of 1952, he had traveled to New York City to see a World Series game and while there met a young lady whom Shelby Foote had put him in touch with. She caught Phin's fancy. Her name was Jaye Dobbs, the stepdaughter of Alan Rinehart, a cofounder with Henry Luce of *Time* magazine. The fancy proved durable, and the next summer—on August 13, 1953—Phin and Jaye were married. After a long honeymoon, Phin and Jaye came down to Covington and spent the month of December in the guest cottage while they figured out what to do next. Phin was there just as his brother was winding up his second apprentice novel and beginning to wonder whether his efforts would ever come to anything. For Percy, it must have been both comforting and embarrassing to have his brother there at that time. Having so often been the one to give advice, he seemed the one now in need of it. By the end of the month, Phin and Jaye had made a decision. They would move to New Orleans, find a house, and Phin would study the Napoleonic Code at Tulane Law School.

Percy was on the brink of a decision, too. It was not one that would change any of the outward appearances of his life, but it would prove to be as consequential as any he had made during the last eight years.

10

The Consolations
of Philosophy

―――――•―――――

I have tried to bridge this huge gap between the scientist's view of man and the
novelist-existentialist's view of man, both of which I thought were valid. And the
only way to do it—it came over me as a kind of revelation—was through language.

—WALKER PERCY

If Walker Percy's literary apprenticeship took place in relative isolation, his training in philosophy was even more a labor of solitude. Even
his closest friend, Shelby Foote, had no idea about Percy's interest until he saw him reading a book by Jacques Maritain on one of Foote's
early visits to the house on Military Road. It was a pursuit from which
Foote felt completely—and, truth be known, quite happily—excluded.
He had no more patience for abstract argument than Percy had for
Proust.

Maritain's works—particulary *Art and Scholasticism* and *The Dream of*
Descartes—were staples of Percy's reading at this time, but he had been
studying Maritain and other philosophers well before he moved to Covington. His informal introduction to the field began at Trudeau, under
the influence of the genially combative Art Fortugno. There, in addition
to Scholastic and neo-Scholastic thinkers, he seems to have taken his
first dip into some of the shorter and more accessible essays of Kierkegaard. Later, in New Mexico and Sewanee, he returned to the Danish
thinker, for it was Kierkegaard, Percy claimed, who moved him the last
few steps toward conversion. The important texts of these early encoun-

ters were "The Present Age," "The Difference between a Genius and an Apostle," and parts of *Either/Or*, particularly the section entitled "Diary of a Seducer."

This introduction to Kierkegaard was just the beginning of a long and often trying relationship. In the early 1950s Percy again took up Kierkegaard but was quickly discouraged. Apart from the "Diary of a Seducer," he found most of *Either/Or* impenetrable. He then tried *Sickness Unto Death* and *Repetition* and found them equally opaque. On the verge of giving up, he skipped to *Concluding Unscientific Postscript*, a later book in which Kierkegaard not only spoke directly to the reader but also summarized many of his crucial ideas, including his notion of the "stages" on life's way. Using *Postscript* as his touchstone, Percy slowly worked his way through the other books, a process that went on for several years and to some extent never ended.

Percy's debt to Kierkegaard was so obvious in his first published novel, *The Moviegoer*, that many of his early admirers overlooked the breadth of his philosophical borrowings. Prominent as his ideas are in Percy's work, Kierkegaard was only one figure at one *pole* of Percy's philosophical investigations, the existential pole. An invaluable trot for his readings in this area was James Collins's *The Existentialists* (1952), a thoughtful survey of existentialist thought by a Thomist thinker and a book that Percy filled with notes. But Percy also went to many of the original sources as soon as they were available in English translations. Percy began in the early 1950s to read the first translations of important French authors, including those parts of Sartre's *Being and Nothingness* that appeared in the 1953 translation of *Existential Psychoanalysis*, and he also read some of Sartre's plays, which had been translated even earlier. Percy's enthusiasm for Sartre may seem strange. After all, Sartre's militant atheism could not have been more different from Percy's convinced fideism. But Percy found the difference a tonic and a challenge. Certainly, a more congenial influence was Camus, two of whose books, *The Stranger* and *The Plague*, had appeared in English versions in 1946 and 1948, respectively. Camus was a writer who got under Percy's skin, stylistically even more than philosophically. As Percy himself admitted, he was drawn to "the sparseness, the laconic brevity, and precision" of Camus' sentences and sought to emulate that style in his own prose.

Philosophically, however, Percy's closest *semblable* among the French existentialists was the Catholic Gabriel Marcel, whose *Being and Having* and *Mystery of Being* both appeared in English translations in 1951. Even biographically, the parallels between the two men were uncanny, Marcel being a convert who had lost his parents when he was young. Marcel's emphasis upon intersubjectivity, his critique of technological and consumer society, and his image of man as wayfarer all became central to Percy's work.

The French were not the only existentialist sources that Percy borrowed from. His knowledge of German had given him early access to Karl Jaspers, Edmund Husserl, and perhaps the most profound and difficult of the existence philosophers, Martin Heidegger. Heidegger's association with the Nazis has cast a problematic shadow over his work, but it is hard to deny the importance or influence of his ideas. That Percy, a reader of German, could go to the Heideggerian source gave him a leg up on those Anglo-American readers who came to existentialism strictly through French sources. Heidegger's approach to the being question through his critique of language and thinking—and particularly his claim that language had lost its originary, poetic, and nominative force by its having been reduced either to an instrument for manipulating the world or to a medium for idle, "inauthentic" chatter (evacuated of meaning, as Percy would often say)—struck home in Percy. Finally, Heidegger's philosophical romanticism, his conviction that being was inseparable from nonbeing, from its potential for annihilation and death, corresponded both with Percy's inherited romantic views (acquired largely from Uncle Will) and his own experience of a life-threatening illness. Percy could appreciate Heidegger's argument that only a full awareness of death makes one able to appreciate the mystery and fullness of being.

Though Percy read heavily among the Thomists and existentialists, he did not turn his back on other traditions of philosophical inquiry, specifically those that dealt with epistemology—the study of how we know what we know—and the philosophy of science. Percy had received a fortunate boost in these studies through his friendship with his New Orleans landlord, Julius Friend. In his own writing and in books that he wrote with the Tulane professor of philosophy, James Feibleman, Friend had attempted to define what modern empirical science was (and what it was not) and to show its limitations as a basis for knowledge. In some respects, Friend was a secular Thomist who tried to reinstitute a faith in rationality as the only solid foundation of knowledge, including that which proceeds by the methods of empirical science. His ambition, set forth most explicitly in his *Science and the Spirit of Man* (1933), was to reconcile "the truths expressed by old philosophies," specifically those of Platonic realism (the Idea is real; the concrete particular, illusory) and nominalism (the particular is real; the Idea is only a name for particulars that possess similar qualities).

"The fallacy of Platonic realism," Friend wrote in a passage pregnant with meaning for Percy's future philosophical forays, consists in its setting up universals as ultimate, and thus assigning a secondary reality to particulars, which we have shown to be not of a different nature but simply of a different category of value. The fallacy of nominalism, conversely, consists in assigning primary reality to particulars, throwing a doubt on universals and consequently on reason. The first may be described as a too rigid intellectualism; the second as an unbridled irrationalism. Reason deals with a world susceptible to reason, because the mode of perception (which is rational) breaks up basic unity into discrete unities or particularities; and therefore these discrete unities, or particulars, are rational. In other words, discrete unity is itself the basic concept, and a particular only becomes a particular because of reason (that is, only becomes known through the application to it of universals).

By reinstating reason and rationality as the foundation of knowledge, Friend hoped to bring down both scientism and idealism. Reason, according to Friend, not only breaks up the discrete unity of reality into the "world of experience" but then tries to piece together and integrate "by more and more inclusive meanings the world of experience, toward an approximation of this basic unity." Approximation is the key word. The unity can never be fully recovered. And the means of approximation, Friend proposed, are "symbolic, fictional." Suggestive words, those last two, particularly to Percy. But how exactly did reason break up and then attempt to recover the primordial unity of reality?

As a man trained in science, Percy remained respectful of the elegance of the scientific method—and its efficacy. Within its properly circumscribed realm, science worked, producing marvels of medicine and technology, among other things. What was troubling about science was its way of creeping beyond its proper realm, of becoming, often without people realizing it, the foundation of an all-embracing view of the world, the basis of knowledge and of ethics. This was troubling to Percy because he believed that science could speak about man only in general terms, that is, in those ways an individual resembled all other humans. The distinction of man, Percy believed, was precisely his individual existence: It was in the individual that the human mystery resided. Behavioristic science tended to dispose of this mystery in order to vindicate its claim of all-explaining truth.

But, Percy wondered, did that mean there could not be a proper science of man, a science that would comprehend the understanding of the best existentialist thinkers as well as that of the behavioral scientists, thus bridging the gap between the two? Friend's work suggested that a new appreciation of human reason might provide the clue to such a new science. But how, again, would one discuss the operations of human reason?

Percy's attempt to find answers to this question led him not only through dense philosophical thickets, through readings of Alfred North Whitehead, Ernst Cassirer, Bertrand Russell, Rudolf Carnap and assorted idealists, logical positivists, semanticists, and symbolic logicians, but also through the works of linguists and anthropologists. Giving order and purpose to these eclectic readings was an underlying conviction, born of his earlier confrontations with Aquinas, Maritain, and Friend, that a true understanding of man and existence required the reestablishment of what Friend called "the primacy of the essential religious impulse." Percy knew that it was hopeless to talk about such matters in the manner of the medieval schoolmen. Even using the vocabulary of philosophical realism would turn most contemporaries away. Nevertheless, Percy's attraction to speculative thought was no different, at bottom, from Aquinas's: He hoped to show not only the compatibility of faith and knowledge but their interconnection. The problem was finding the right key in which to make this demonstration.

The key was handed to him in a book that could not have been more appropriately titled: *Philosophy in a New Key*. The book's author, Susanne Langer, was a Radcliffe-educated philosopher, the daughter of German emigrés, and a close reader of the idealist Ernst Cassirer, whose most famous book was *The Philosophy of Symbolic Forms*. Langer, however, counted herself no idealist, believing that her arguments proceeded from a "naturalistic" basis. Nevertheless, she followed Cassirer in focusing on the trait that she believed distinguished humans from all other natural creatures—the capacity for symbol making. Langer proposed that attention to symbolization, already in wide evidence in the early twentieth century, would enable Western philosophy to move beyond the strictures of naive empiricism—namely, the belief that there could be no real knowledge beyond that discovered by empirical fact-finding through the methods of science.

Percy read with keen attention Langer's critique of the epistemological confusion of modern science. The positivists were naive, she explained, in thinking they could dismiss as unimportant all approaches to knowledge that did not employ the experimental methods of science. Even from the onset of the scientific revolution, scientists depended more heavily than they would admit upon a purely rational (or symbolic) helpmate: mathematics. "No one observed, amid the first passion of empirical fact-finding, that the ancient science of mathematics still went its undisturbed way of pure reason," Langer wrote. Some empiricists who did notice this discrepancy tried to resolve it by finding a factual basis for mathematics. They notoriously failed. Furthermore, as science evolved and became more complex, scientists depended less on empirical observation of data and more on the symbolic procedures of *calculation*.

Nowhere was this more obvious than in the frontier science of physics, where it was increasingly evident that the sense data were, as Langer put it, *"primarily symbols."* The positivists' dream of transcending the "philosophical stage of learning" was a vain hope, as all who looked honestly at the procedures of modern science could see. Suddenly, Langer observed, "the edifice of human knowledge stands before us, not as a vast collection of sense reports, but as a structure of *facts that are symbols* and *laws that are their meanings.* A new philosophical theme has been set forth to a coming age: an epistemological theme, the comprehension of science. The power of symbolism is its cue, as the finality of sense-data was a cue of a former epoch."

To support her contention that symbolization was the cue to the new theme of philosophy, Langer pointed not only to numerous works of philosophy proper but to developments in modern psychology and logic. The widespread attention being paid to symbolization indicated two things to her: first, that symbolization promised a superior epistemology; and, second, that symbolization offered a better means of understanding man himself.

Langer's critique of the limitations of the scientific method was music to Percy's ears. So was her appeal for an alternative philosophical approach, one that would "illumine questions of life and consciousness, instead of obscuring them as traditional 'scientific methods' have done."

But Percy differed with Langer on several points, and it was his desire to elaborate these differences that led to his first published philosophical essay—a review essay dealing ostensibly with Langer's second book, *Feeling and Form* (published in 1953) but in fact going after what he believed was an errant premise in her earlier book. "I thought she had gotten hold of something and then turned around and let it get away from her," he later explained. So at some point in the spring or early summer of 1954, shortly after he completed *The Gramercy Winner,* Percy sat down to write an article "saying what was right and what was wrong with her book."

The great power of *Philosophy in a New Key,* Percy held, was its effectiveness in pressing home the point that symbols did not merely signal basic biological needs or announce objects but instead made knowledge possible. What baffled Percy was that Langer could be so persuasive in saying what the symbol was *not,* yet so confused in saying what it was. That she disagreed with her intellectual mentor, Ernst Cassirer, was not the problem. Her rejection of the idealist view that symbols constitute meanings made sense to Percy. After all, such idealism perpetuated Cartesian solipsism, the belief in the reflecting ego as the sole source of meaning. But if symbolization was neither "a refinement of an animal function nor an idealist *logos* which constitutes the world," then what was it? Langer proposed that it was a new basic "need" —an "elementary need" that had emerged with the development of the cerebral cortex and that could not be explained by "conventional biological concepts." Percy, the scientist, rightly smelled a rat. The word "need," he saw, was being distorted to the point of meaninglessness:

> Everyone agrees that in the genetic or naturalist schema the responses of an organism to the environment are adaptive and are specified by the needs of the organism. These needs are variously characterized as sex, hunger, defense, etc, but are all reducible to the service of two basic biological requirements: maintenance of the internal milieu and parturition. . . . Now how can the *basic human need of symbolization* be subsumed under these valid biological categories?

To Percy, obviously, it could not. And that, to him, was Langer's crucial mistake. More the pity, too, Percy believed, because she could have opened up the mystery of symbolization if she had talked about the symbolic transformation in general as she had about the art symbol in specific—that is, as a means of knowing and not as some inchoate "need." Had she done so, Percy argued, she would have shown that symbolic transformation arrives at knowledge not, as the empiricists would argue, through the accumulation of sense data but rather through the identification of the knower with the object known, through an agreement between percept and object. In other words, she would have shown how words, the language symbols, transform sensory content into the stuff of our ideas.

Percy also believed that Langer missed the boat by inadequately attending to the social character of symbolizing. This aspect of language would become central to his subsequent philosophical writings—as central as it was to the later Wittgenstein (whom Percy approvingly read) —but he alluded to it only briefly in three short sentences of the review. "When I am told as a child that this flower is a lupin, when you name something for me and I confirm it by saying it too—what I know now is not only that the flower *is* something but that it is something for you and me. Our common existence is validated. It is the foundation of what Marcel calls the metaphysics of *we are* instead of *I think*."

Within the compass of a short, nine-page review essay, then, Percy had done far more than point out the virtues and shortcomings of Langer's book. Announcing that the way to a radical science of man, a true anthropology, was by way of the human symbolizing function, specifi-

cally language, he had set his own agenda for future philosophical investigations.

Having written the article, Percy decided that he should do something
with it. It was appropriate, he knew, for a "serious" journal, but he also
knew that the essay had an underlying argument that might be taken
seriously only by editors tolerant of a religious perspective. So he decided
to send it to *Thought*, a quarterly published by Fordham University in
New York City. To his delight, the article was accepted and slated for
the autumn 1954 issue. "I got no money," Percy later related, "but they
sent me a whole stack of reprints. . . . Anyway, I thought, 'Gee, this is
great. I can write something and publish it.' "

The acceptance of his essay was a liberating moment for Percy. After the
struggle of trying to find a publisher for his first novel and after consign-
ing his second effort to the dark of his drawer, it gave Percy hope that
he might find an audience for what he had to say. It also suggested that
his medium might be the discursive philosophical essay and not the
novel. In any case, the essay was not the only piece of philosophical
writing he attempted that year. Toward the end of the summer, Percy
sent a long, exploratory essay to the living philosopher he most admired,
Jacques Maritain, who was then residing in Princeton, New Jersey. Maritain's response was at least as encouraging as *Thought*'s acceptance of his
other essay: "Many thanks," Maritain wrote, "for sending me your paper
Symbol and Magic Cognition. I read it with extreme interest and am
very pleased by the way in which you make the idea I proposed of magic
sign as a 'state' of human mentality bear new and remarkable fruit."

Strangely enough, the essay that elicited such high praise from Maritain did not find its way into print. Instead, it became part of a larger
project, a lengthy manuscript that Percy would work on for several years.
This manuscript, entitled *Symbol and Existence*, would itself never be
published, but it would provide ideas and arguments for the essays that
Percy contributed to journals during the next twenty years, many of
which would eventually be collected in the 1975 volume *The Message in
the Bottle*. But whether his work was published or praised, Percy believed
he was on to something, and for the time being at least, his philosophical
passion eclipsed any interest he had in writing novels. It seemed indeed
that he was becoming what his daughter called a "silosopher."

As Percy's literary career took a new direction, so, by strange coincidence, did his friend Shelby Foote's. At the end of 1953, Foote had
moved from Greenville to Memphis, where he rented half a duplex on
the bluffs overlooking the Mississippi River. (This mostly black neigh-

borhood, soon to go bohemian, would be put to use more than twenty years later in his novel *September September*.)

The move was not the only change. A few months later, just as his collection of stories *Jordan County* was coming out, Foote traveled to New York to talk with Bennett Cerf at Random House. A fan of the novel *Shiloh*, Cerf was interested in Foote's writing a short narrative history of the Civil War. Foote liked the idea, and since it seemed to require only a short detour from his big novel (which, in any case, was not going well), he accepted. When Foote sat down that summer to block out the history, he realized that it would be hard to keep the story short. So he made a counterproposal to Random House: Instead of writing a short history, he would produce a three-volume narrative history. Random House agreed, promising a five-thousand-dollar advance for each volume.

It has the makings of one of those neat parallels in literary history: Percy putting aside fiction to take up philosophy just as Foote turned from fiction to write history. In fact, though, these seeming breaks in their respective careers were not so much discontinuities as continuations by other means. Underlying Foote's first four novels and his short stories was a concern for history, the power of the past over the present. Much of the technical virtuosity displayed in his early fiction focused on temporal shiftings and layerings, jumps forward and backward rather than simple chronological progression, a virtuosity that attested to Foote's belief in the active hold of the past upon the actions and characters of people in the present. And for the people he wrote about, few historical events had a more decisive influence on the present—on the myths and realities of everyday life—than the Civil War. Furthermore, Foote saw his history as a deliberately literary undertaking—a "narrative" descended in the great epic tradition from the *Iliad*.

Percy's turn to philosophy, similarly, was not a departure from his original concerns but an adaptation of rhetorical modes: a turn toward directness, argument, and analysis. Percy's great theme was human sadness—specifically, as he once put it, the question of why man feels so sad in the twentieth century—and this it remained, only now Percy was coming at the question by radically questioning his culture's dominant form of knowledge, the scientific world view, and the theory of man implicit in this world view. His ambition to find a science of man, an anthropology, free from the positivistic presuppositions of scientism, was ultimately an effort to restore a lost philosophical connection between spiritual categories and phenomenological ones. The impulse here is that of a religious moralist, the same impulse that drove him in the writing of fiction.

.   .   .

In Percy's case there is a further coincidence, an almost fateful synchronism of his inner and outer lives. On July 11, 1954, his and Bunt's second child, Ann Boyd, was born. The new parents were delighted that their earlier fears of sterility had been proved wrong, and as the weeks progressed they were even happier to see that they had a robust girl. For several months, in fact, Percy and Bunt had no reason to believe that their daughter was anything other than completely healthy. But then in the autumn, in early November, their confidence was rudely shattered.

Following their usual practice on warm afternoons, Percy, Bunt, and Mary Pratt set off for the bayou, Bunt carrying their three-month-old child and Percy toting a shotgun just in case they came upon a snake that sometimes menaced the trail. As the group approached the bluff overlooking the bogue, Percy spotted the snake. Ordering Bunt to back away, he took aim and fired. The snake flopped over dead. Looking back at Bunt, Percy could see that she was upset, but it was neither the snake nor the gunshot that had alarmed her. What troubled her was her baby's indifference to the gun's loud report. Ann had not cried or even turned her head. Bunt was worried something was wrong with Ann's hearing. Percy tried to reassure his wife. After all, he explained, a lack of reaction to loud noises was not that unusual among infants. But Bunt insisted on taking Ann immediately to see their pediatrician in New Orleans. The results of the examination were not reassuring, and the doctor urged the Percys to see a hearing specialist right away. The specialist confirmed Bunt's fears: Ann had, at best, only minimal hearing.

The news was devastating, but the Percys refused to be discouraged. Bunt responded by researching everything there was to know about the condition, the various diagnostic procedures and the different approaches to treatment. Percy and Bunt were still not sure of the extent of Ann's problem, but since they were given reason to hope that she had some minimal hearing, they began to investigate both mechanical aids and learning strategies. The big question was whether to put Ann in a special institution or to give her supplemental education and training in a normal setting. In February of 1955, they went to St. Louis and Chicago to look at special schools, but neither Bunt nor Percy was wholly comfortable with the idea of turning Ann over to an institution. Furthermore, Ann seemed to be more advanced, more responsive to language cues, than most other children in the special school. Driving back to Covington, Percy put the question to Bunt and Mary Pratt: "What are we going to do as a family? Are we going to send Ann off, or are we going to stay together?"

There seems to have been little doubt what the answer would be. As Bunt told her friend Jidge Milazzo, "I was afraid we would lose her if we sent her to a special school." Shortly after they returned from St. Louis, Percy received a letter from Foote containing the name and address of a teacher who had developed her own special method of teaching the deaf. She had been recommended by a Memphis physician, Dr. John Shea, who, as Foote put it, "thinks she hung the moon."

Percy took the tip and wrote to the teacher, Miss Dorris Mirrielees, at her home in Pompano Beach, Florida, asking her if she would come to see their daughter. The Percys were fortunate, because Miss Mirrielees happened to have an open spot in her busy schedule that spring.

When Miss Mirrielees arrived—and nobody ever called her anything but *Miss* Mirrielees—life on Military Road was radically transformed. From the moment she walked into the house, it was clear that she was no mere teacher but a woman with a mission, a miracle worker every bit as determined as Helen Keller's teacher, Annie Sullivan. Even her looks commanded attention. Tall, thin, her gray hair rolled tightly in a bun, she never wore anything but simple, practical clothes, tennis shoes, and white socks that always seemed to be falling down about her ankles. Her severe expression was as fixed and determined as her will. There was also an air of sadness about her. Born and raised in the Midwest and educated at the Chicago Normal School, Miss Mirrielees had been jilted in the one great love affair of her life.

Her early professional career had not been much happier. Working with deaf students, Miss Mirrielees had quickly determined that the existing methods of instruction were not merely deficient but damaging. Typically, deaf children were taught too little, too late. According to the established methods, a child might learn no more than a word or two a week, simple words for simple objects; he or she would be given no idea of how words link to form statements or questions. The deaf were treated almost as though they were mentally retarded, and their education as much as guaranteed that they would become so. Seeing the obvious, Miss Mirrielees began to develop her own techniques for teaching the deaf. Such independence inevitably produced friction between her and the school administrators.

Fired from her job, Miss Mirrielees became an itinerant teacher, hiring on with individual families for whatever they could afford to pay. In most cases, she would stay with a family for several weeks a year, returning as many years as was necessary, and working as intensively with parents and other family members as much as she did with the hearing-impaired child. That, in fact, was the first principle of the Mirrielees Method: The whole family had to be involved in teaching the deaf child.

The second principle was that the teaching process should begin as early as possible in the infant's life so that he or she would not fall behind other children. One of her star pupils, the newspaperman and

critic Henry Kisor, describes the core of Mirrielees's method in his remarkable memoir, *What's That Pig Outdoors?*:

> The catching-up process should begin immediately, Miss Mirrielees
> maintained, with parents placing their faces in the baby's line of vision,
> so that the child could associate the movements of their lips with
> objects and actions and begin learning the rudiments of lipreading. But
> Miss Mirrielees knew that lipreading was too exhausting a method of
> taking in large amounts of information over long periods of time. The
> answer, instead, lay in the printed symbol of the spoken word.
>
> In short, she believed in teaching deaf children to read almost as
> soon as they could focus their eyes. And not just in single words but in
> entire phrases and sentences with the full rhythm and content of spo-
> ken English, in the same way hearing children learned language. The
> difference was that deaf children would "hear" with their eyes, not
> their ears—and would do so *before* they learned to speak.
>
> Miss Mirrielees believed that deaf children could become familiar
> with words, and their proper order, by actually handling them—by
> choosing them from among other words and placing them in sentence
> form. . . .
>
> Chart Work began with Miss Mirrielees creating an event in the
> child's life, such as taking the youngster to a farm. She'd make sure
> that the child not only saw a cow, for instance, but also saw that it ate
> hay and produced milk, which was collected in a bucket. When they
> returned home, she would draw a picture on a blackboard of the cow,
> the hay, and the bucket of milk. As she drew the objects and acted
> out their relationship, she would also say their names, making sure the
> child watched her lips. Then she would write the name of each object
> under its picture, saying the name as she did so.
>
> But she did not stop there. This was not merely "cow," "hay," and
> "milk." "The cow," she would say slowly, "eats hay and gives milk,"
> acting out the verbs as she wrote them along with their nouns on the
> blackboard. She would repeat the words, pointing to their pictorial
> and written representations on the blackboard, until the child had
> made the connections among the three kinds of symbols—pictorial,
> written, and spoken. . . .
>
> The goal was for the child to learn not merely what the shapes—
> drawn, printed, and spoken—stood for but also their proper arrange-
> ment. As time went on, the child learned to place each cardboard
> rectangle containing a word on the table in correct order, mimicking
> that on the chart. This was how Miss Mirrielees taught English syntax.
> The meaning and order of concrete nouns and verbs were easy, but the
> abstract parts of speech—articles and conjunctions—took longer to
> learn. This, however, is exactly the way hearing children experience
> language. Only in this case the form of the symbols was different.

It was, to say the least, a demanding approach, but to Dr. Percy it seemed both pragmatically and philosophically sound. Miss Mirrielees's method was, in fact, an almost perfect pedagogical analogue to his theories about the differences between the signaling and symbolizing functions of language. While the traditional method reduced the deaf child to rudimentary signaling, using words as signals to satisfy needs, the Mirrielees method brought the full symbolic power of language to deaf children. It taught them to use words as a means of knowing the world and themselves.

Ann made impressive progress. By eleven months, she was already lipreading, perhaps aided by some residual hearing. Even before Miss Mirrielees arrived, Ann was fitted with a hearing aid at Tulane, the first of several rather cumbersome devices that she later claimed did nothing for her. Bunt, however, remained certain that Ann could detect some sounds for the first few years of her life, at least until she suffered a series of violent earaches.

Whatever the case, Ann would have made little progress without the absolute dedication of her family, and that was what she got. The kitchen became the main classroom, where the charts were assembled and put on the stands. There most of the formal teaching took place. When Miss Mirrielees was not visiting, Bunt was the constant tutor, taking Ann through hours of drills each day. Percy and Mary Pratt took their parts as well. Typically, Percy would take Ann on outings to the drugstore or the train station or the local dairy where she would see firsthand the things and processes that would later be represented on the charts. Mary Pratt attended the classes on Saturday mornings during the school year and every day during the summers so that she would be able to work with Ann when her parents could not.

If anything suffered during these first years of Ann's life, it was Percy's work. Two years would pass between the publication of his first article and the publication of his second—a long stretch by anyone's standard. Not that Percy gave up writing. He faithfully went to his study most mornings and afternoons, at least when the family was not on the road, but the only thing he seems to have done during this time was to add to his philosophical manuscript.

Percy's work was further hampered by the recurrence of tuberculosis toward the end of 1955. It is not surprising that he had a "break." Percy's health was delicate even in the best of times, and with a new baby in the house the chronic insomniac found it even more difficult to get sufficient rest. The strain of a more demanding life brought down Percy's resistance, and the dreaded bacilli, which can lie dormant in scar tissue for years, began to multiply. If it was depressing to be confronted once

again by his old malady, Percy could at least take heart in the fact that
there were now effective medical cures for the disease. Put on a course
of isoniazid (INH), a miracle drug that had been in use since 1952, Percy
recovered so quickly that he stayed with his plan to take his family on a
Caribbean cruise to Caracas, Venezuela, in December.

Ann's hearing problem and his own delicate health were not the only
things that seemed to stand in the way of Percy's work during these
years. History itself seemed to distract him from his intellectual concerns. For all of his reclusiveness and worldly reticence, Percy was remarkably attuned to the temper of the times. He read the newspapers
and the newsmagazines faithfully. He subscribed to a number of opinion
journals, from the liberal Catholic *Commonweal* to the conservative
National Review. And he constantly monitored the news on the radio
and the television.

In the early 1950s, as later, Percy was reluctant to label himself politically. Despite his aversion to FDR, he maintained that he always voted
for Democrats in presidential elections, but he was never particularly
partisan in his political thinking. To him, the categories of liberal and
conservative were almost meaningless, and he believed that they became
even more so during the last two decades of his life. During the 1950s
and 1960s, however, he did seem to to find a position on the political
continuum—that of a moderate liberal, concerned domestically with
civil rights and greater social justice, and internationally with the con-
tainment of communism.

The interest in civil rights and social justice was something relatively
new for Percy. To put it more accurately, the concern was not new, but
the form it took was. He had always been a compassionate man, fully
aware that the lot of blacks in America was a bad one, but he had viewed
political or legal solutions to their problems as bootless. Like most white
southerners of his class, he had believed that segregation was a necessary
part of the southern way of life. Like many white southerners, he saw
Reconstruction as compelling proof that such solutions wouldn't work.
The problem was rooted in attitudes, in beliefs, in people's hearts—and
those would change slowly, with time.

But in the early 1950s, Percy's understanding of the problem began to
change. Circumstances forced him to examine those sentimental and
cultural presuppositions that Uncle Will had passed on to him. Preliminary signs of this reconsideration appeared in his criticism of southern
Stoic values in his first apprentice novel, *The Charterhouse*, an attack
that Allen Tate had been quick to pick up and praise. Where this change
in Percy's outlook came from is impossible to say with any exactness.

Shelby Foote claimed some credit, and this may well be true. But, as Foote himself readily admitted, Percy's religion played a more decisive role. Beginning soon after his conversion and entry into the church, Percy began to take the social message of the Gospels seriously. Percy's reading and his contacts with Caroline Gordon had made him aware of the activist movement within Catholicism—not only the Catholic Worker movement of Dorothy Day but also the labor and civil rights activities of Father Louis Twomey and others. (Since 1948, he had been an avid reader of "Christian Conscience," a little news sheet produced by Father Fichter and others at Loyola. "My sincere thanks for sending me copies of 'Christian Conscience,' " he wrote Father Fichter in the fall of 1948. "It is wonderful to see such a publication in the Deep South.") Percy was not about to become an activist himself—in fact, he was always somewhat wary of Catholic activism—but the words and actions of committed Catholic reformers forced him to question and revise his older assumptions about what needed to be done.

Percy was hardly a lone struggler with the race question. National events were forcing all Americans to take clearer stands. Two months before Ann was born, on May 17, 1954, the Supreme Court issued its landmark ruling in *Brown* v. *Board of Education,* outlawing "separate but equal" facilities in public school systems. The dismantling of Jim Crow segregation, which to some extent had begun with the integration of the military during the Korean War, was now becoming a fact of national concern and urgency. Three years after the decision, even the great compromiser, Dwight D. Eisenhower, would reluctantly take a stand in Little Rock, Arkansas, sending in airborne troops to enforce school desegregation.

Well before that, though, Percy saw his own brother, Roy, become directly involved in the fight in Mississippi. Shortly after the *Brown* decision, reactionaries throughout Missippippi (and in other southern states) began to form Citizens' Councils to combat desegregation policies. In the spring of 1955, a number of Greenvillians interested in starting such a council in their own community invited prominent town leaders, including Roy Percy, his father-in-law, Mr. Farish, and Judge Emmet Hardy, to discuss ways of "protecting our way of life." Percy, Farish, and Hardy immediately knew what the organizers were up to. Percy denounced them for trying to start an "uptown Ku Klux Klan." Shortly after the meeting, Hodding Carter weighed in with a scathing editorial denouncing the Citizens' Councils. As a result of this early resistance, the Council never gained a very strong foothold in Greenville.

But the struggle was far from over, even in Greenville. After hearing a report from his hometown, Foote wrote to Percy describing the challenge that faced Roy: "He is doing a fine job (I hear) of counteracting the Citizens' Council: not by open warfare, but by using his influence with friends of his who otherwise would be taken in. It's a serious thing down there, no easy thing to meet effectively, and I for one am proud of the way he has met it. . . . Senator Percy's fight against the Ku Klux was a small skirmish compared with what Roy has before him, I'm afraid. It's worse than you may know down there." As successful as Percy and his allies were in fighting the Citizens' Council, they would not win all of the battles. In fact, they probably lost the biggest one. Unable to stem the "white flight" to segregated academies, they saw the town's public schools, once the pride of Greenville, go steadily downhill, losing both their demographic and their economic base.

The same sorts of things were occurring in Louisiana, of course, and Percy saw them as proof that the old mixture of paternalism and well-intentioned gradualism was not enough. The more he read about resistance to school desegregation, the more troubled he grew. One early witness of Percy's struggle with the civil-rights issue was a psychiatrist named Bill Sorum, a big, forceful man with passionately held views and a history of involvement with the American Communist party. When Sorum met Percy in early 1955, he was working at the Southeastern Louisiana Hospital in Mandeville, having not long before completed training in psychiatry at Tulane University. Many years before, as an undergraduate at the University of Alabama, Sorum had developed a sense of outrage about the situation of blacks in the South. Looking for answers, he had joined the Communist party, thinking it was the only serious way to combat the injustices of segregation. By the end of the Korean War, however, he was largely disillusioned with both the party and Marxism.

In fact, when Sorum met Percy, he was in emotional and intellectual turmoil, desperately casting about for something to believe in. Having met Percy through a mutual friend, Mrs. Olga Hess, who worked at the Tulane Law School, Sorum became even more curious about the shy, retired doctor when someone showed him a copy of the Thought essay. "I realized this was somebody you could discuss ideas with, and I was desperate for intellectual companionship in those days." Sorum began to drop by Percy's house in the late afternoons, and the two men would launch into animated, sometimes heated, discussions of everything from psychiatry to civil rights. (It was through Sorum that Percy first learned of the work of the Tulane neuropsychiatrist Dr. Robert Heath, whose controversial work with electrical implants in human brains might have provided the original inspiration for Dr. Tom More and his obsession with perfecting the soul-healing lapsometer.)

To Sorum's nihilism and views about human perfidy, Percy opposed his faith and his vision of a more forgiving Christian outlook. "He would refuse to grant me any of my more extreme positions," Sorum recalled. "I would rail about the southern racists, and he would say that the racists had to be looked at fairly, too. He would always talk about the Baptist minister Will Campbell, who stood up for blacks but also stood up for Klansmen. He would mention the gallantry of the South, and I would sarcastically talk about the gallantry of the Nazi soldiers at Stalingrad. He practically threw me out of the house sometimes—I remember standing up in his living room and shouting something about the inanity of the virgin birth—but he was always the gentleman, something I was not. I think he put up with me because he could see how much I needed him. He was a rudder for me at a time when my beliefs about Marxism were lost. I turned to him, and without him I don't think I would have survived."

The fiery iconoclast certainly softened under Percy's influence. Before long, Sorum was attending mass with his friend, and though he never quite made it to Rome, he did become an Episcopalian. Sorum was not the only one to profit from the relationship. His criticism of what was wrong with the nation and the South was extreme, but Percy heard it— and the stronger points registered. Where, after all, had the Christian churchgoers been all these years, and why weren't they more actively involved in combating the South's greatest moral outrage? Percy would defend his religion and his region when they were criticized, but he harbored secret disappointments with both.

Percy's arguments with Sorum spurred him not only to think about contemporary issues but also to articulate in writing something close to a public philosophy. Percy came to social criticism somewhat uneasily, doubtful as he was about his own moral authority. But extraordinary times required extraordinary measures, and politics in his home state were becoming nasty. Louisiana courts and lawmakers were continuing to throw up obstacles to school desegregation, a situation that became so egregious that on February 15, 1956, a federal court in New Orleans had to ban all Louisiana statutes that opposed *Brown* v. *Board of Education*. It was an ignoble moment, and Percy took it hard that the white leadership in his state, as in much of the rest of the South, had done so little to work for what was so obviously a just cause—and worse, had often stood in the way of that cause. Adding to his anger was the behavior of many of his fellow churchmen in response to the pastoral letter of February 19 written by the archbishop of New Orleans, a letter declaring segregation sinful. For his efforts, Archbishop Joseph Rummel had been subjected not only to the old Klan treatment—a burning cross in his yard—but to the grumbling of his own flock.

Percy was sufficiently embittered to take to pen, and the product of his indignation, an essay entitled "Stoicism in the South," appeared in the July 6 issue of *Commonweal*. Yet if this was *public* philosophy, Percy could not have developed it in a more personal way. Underlying his criticism of the moral failure of the southern leadership was a family quarrel, a respectful but nevertheless firm disagreement with the ethos of Uncle Will.

The opening proposition was straightforward. Percy asserted that until recent times the "champion of Negro rights in the South, and of fair-mindedness and toleration in general, was the upper-class white South-erner." This he was no more. Indeed, Percy observed, "With a few courageous exceptions, he is either silent or he is leading the Citizens' Councils." Percy also dismissed the justification put forward by the typi-cal upper-class southerner in 1956, "that it is not he who has changed but the Supreme Court, that he is still fighting to preserve the same way of life he defended when he opposed the Klan thirty years ago."

Percy's main point, echoing what he earlier wrote in *The Charterhouse*, was that "neither the ethos nor the traditional world-view of the upper-class white Southerner" was any longer adequate to the situation in the South. That ethos was an amalgam of Roman-Stoic virtues and Chris-tianity, with a decided emphasis on the former. "The Southern gentle-man did live in a Christian edifice," Percy wrote, "but he lived there in the strange fashion Chesterton spoke of, that of a man who will neither go inside nor put it entirely behind him but stands forever grumbling on the porch." Percy admitted that this stronger commitment to the values of the porch—the *Stoa*—had provided a workable formula for decent human relations in the hierarchical agrarian society of the nineteenth-century South. The "stern inner summons to man's full estate, to duty, to honor, to generosity toward his fellowmen and above all to his infe-riors" conduced to a benign paternalism—"*noblesse oblige* on one side and an extraordinary native courtesy and dignity on the other." The reason for the Stoic's benevolence was important to bear in mind, though. His concern for fairness came not from the belief that other people were made in the image of God but from the conviction that doing others an injustice was a breach of personal honor and a defilement of "the inner fortress, which was oneself."

When the old hierarchical social order dissolved, the Stoic could only feel defeated, his values imperiled by the rise of the masses, including blacks, who seemed no longer grateful for paternal concern. Stoicism under the new dispensation became little more than an attitude of tight-lipped pessimism, "which took a grim satisfaction in the dissolution of its values—because social decay confirmed one in his original choice of the wintry kingdom of self."

This would not do, Percy argued. The South could no longer afford to maintain "the Stoa beside the Christian edifice." Now it was time for nominal Christians to become Christians in heart and deed. If the Stoics turned their back on the "mob," Christians were obliged to accept and help it. "What the Stoic sees as the insolence of his former charge—and this is what he can't tolerate, the Negro's demanding his rights instead of being thankful for the squire's generosity—is in the Christian scheme the sacred right which must be accorded the individual, whether deemed insolent or not."

It would be easy to read into Percy's essay an unequivocal rejection of everything Will Percy had stood for. It was not. Will was far too valuable and beloved an intellectual adversary to banish in any summary manner. In fact, the essay was only the beginning of a sustained dialogue between Walker and Will's ghost, an effort on the part of the former to tease out of his elder's creed its best and truest points, and equally, to show where and why Uncle Will went wrong.

The essay also marked Percy's entrance into the public life of his time. Because of his private nature, he would never become more than a half-hearted public man, reluctantly serving on civil-rights committees, working for Head Start, making public testimonies against the use of the Confederate flag in Louisiana public schools, but Percy nevertheless served, and usually with good effect. His involvement influenced those who knew him and, in growing numbers, those who read him. His pronouncements upon public issues were always made with reticence and an honest acknowledgment of his own shortcomings. As he said in "Stoicism in the South," no white southerner "can write a j'accuse without making a mea culpa." Percy found it hard to feel superior to his segregationist friends, having been one himself. He tried to persuade not by hectoring or shaming but by explaining the moral and intellectual process that had brought him to where he stood.

"Stoicism in the South" was not Percy's only publication in 1956. In June, a journal published out of the University of Buffalo, Philosophy and Phenomenological Research, ran Percy's second consideration of the problem of the symbol. It is not one of Percy's stronger pieces. "Symbol as Hermeneutic in Existentialism" makes a number of interesting assertions about the "intersubjective" character of symbol using, but the points are insufficiently argued and, perhaps worse, their ramifications are inadequately developed. The essay leaves the reader both tantalized and confused.

Reading this essay, one can easily share the befuddlement that was felt by some of Percy's friends when they were given copies of his work. Chink Baldwin received galley proofs of several of Percy's early philo-

sophical essays and dutifully attempted to make sense of them. "God, I'd
think, what goes on in his mind?" For the sake of their friendship,
Baldwin was glad that Percy never pushed him for a reaction.

Shelby Foote was less reticent about his bafflement. Visiting Percy in
May of 1956, he got a preview of "Symbol as Hermeneutic." Once back
in Memphis, he wrote to Percy to explain why the essay left him perplexed:

> I wish there were some way I could follow what youre doing; but I
> cant. The best I can do is sense how right it is—the basic position, I
> mean, in its challenge of what has gone before. I know a man is more
> than the sum of his parts, more than top creature on the animal totem
> pole; it even interests me; but I cant follow until you proceed to the
> specific—the psychological, I guess I mean. There I see it and applaud.
> Otherwise I'm lost in a welter of vague spinnings. Philosophy—Lord!

Such expressions of incomprehension did not prevent Percy from continuing to explore the philosophical questions he had raised, but they
hurt his vanity. He wanted a wide audience, and not just the academic
crowd, even though reaching the academic crowd would have been
difficult enough.

Percy, in fact, was in a very peculiar position in American intellectual
culture. He was an amateur writing in a field that had become not only
professionalized but balkanized into a number of mutually hostile (or at
least indifferent) camps. He was close to the continental existentialists
and phenomenologists, but he was also respectful of the Anglo-American thinkers and even saw himself as trying to build a bridge between
the two. That he was also interested in linguistics, semantics, anthropology, and theology placed him well beyond most established philosophical pales. An intellectual renegade, he was vain enough to think
that he might reach not only some academic readers but also the (perhaps mythical) common reader. Consequently, the silence of friends, or
their frank admission of perplexity, was troubling.

By contrast, Percy's first attempt at public philosophy, his "Stoicism
in the South" essay, seemed to find a wider readership, and while not all
of it was pleased by what Percy said, they at least understood what he
was saying. Because it was one of those articles that readers tended to
save or circulate among their friends, the essay enjoyed a half-life that
most ephemeral magazine pieces never experience. In fact, it created a
minor stir, all the more remarkable for its having appeared in a relatively
small-circulation magazine. Shelby Foote's response was in many ways
typical. He liked it so much that he lent the copy to Faulkner, who

never returned it. And *Commonweal* was sufficiently pleased by the response to pester the author for further contributions.

Percy was happy to see that the article created interest, but not even this satisfaction could overcome his reluctance to editorialize on public issues. Opinion mongering seemed to leave out too much of the truth, too much of the ambiguity, and though he would write more social criticism when the occasions demanded, he would do so with considerable uneasiness. Then, too, Percy believed that he had larger fish to fry and that these essays were little more than exercises preparatory to the larger undertaking. Percy was still a writer in search of a form that would best contain all of his writerly virtues—the moral passion and combativeness of his social criticism, the intellectual rigor and metaphysical questioning of his philosophical essays, and the feel for character and place that he demonstrated in his apprentice fiction.

Percy would draw closer to what he was looking for in the third of the essays that he got published in 1956. This essay, entitled "The Man on the Train: Three Existential Modes," appeared in the fall issue of *Partisan Review*, a journal that still enjoyed the reputation of being one of the nation's foremost intellectual reviews. This renown rested largely on its vigorous anti-Stalinist leftism and its alertness to the literary, philosophical, and artistic avant-garde. What attracted Percy to *PR*, though, and what made him proud to be published on its pages, was the fact that it was one of the earlier importers of European existential thought to American shores.

What was distinctive about Percy's article was its playful approach to serious philosophical issues, its ability to make the existential categories of alienation, rotation, and repetition clear and accessible through the central conceit of a middle-class train commuter and scores of other wittily drawn examples (many of which were drawn from pop-cultural sources). The essay is not, by any stretch, original philosophy, but it is not quite popularization, either. It is more a kind of playing with ideas, embodying them in concrete moments, experiences, and characters.

The central point of the essay is neither difficult nor obscure: The most alienated individual, Percy asserts, is the one who is least aware of the fact of his alienation. He then proceeds to show how the hypothetical commuter may wittingly or unwittingly stumble out of his alienated state. One involves the commuter taking consciousness of his alienation. As Percy says in the third sentence of the essay, "There is a great deal of difference between an alienated commuter riding a train and this same commuter reading a book about an alienated commuter riding a train." Another way involves the commuter's escaping from the conditions of his alienation, a stepping across "zones" such as might occur if the train breaks down somewhere in the middle of New Jersey and the commuter gets off, strolls down the right-of-way, and is suddenly addressed by the man who lives in a house, "a yellow cottage with a certain lobular stain on the wall," that the commuter sees, but doesn't really see, every working day of his life. In this moment, the commuter steps, philosophically, from the insularly contained world of his own subjectivity into the resistant world of other objects. The shock of the zone-crossing—which Percy calls, after Kierkegaard, a rotation—brings the commuter into the realm of possibility, where anything may be dared and anything may happen. It is a profound aesthetic pleasure.

The other release from the everydayness of our alienated condition is what Percy calls, again after Kierkegaard, repetition, the Return. Repetition occurs when the train rider returns home with a deliberate mission, voyaging "into his own past in the search for himself." Actually, there are two kinds of repetitions, according to Percy, one aesthetic and the other existential. The former is mainly a savoring of the interesting, an "occasion for the connoisseur sampling of a rare emotion," while the latter is a quest for a clue to the enigma of one's own self. Percy cites as a fine example of the latter Vittorini's novel In Sicily, in which the narrator leaves the everydayness of his present life in Milan and returns, at the behest of his father, to his native Sicily. Percy elaborates upon other examples of repetitions, their virtues, and their shortcomings.

Charming as this essay is, the reader may at times wonder why Percy so painstakingly explains these assorted escapes from everydayness. Percy's point is so casually made that we may easily miss it: namely, that the escapes are ultimately unavailing. Novelty, pure possibility, amnesia, going home again—all, whether experienced directly or vicariously, fail to lift man out of his alienated condition. And to the extent such rotations and repetitions beguile people out of recognizing their alienation, they aggravate the condition of alienation. The moviegoer or the reader of the novel who attempts to imitate (or even fantasizes about imitating) the fictional hero's perfectly realized rotation is at peril. He will fail miserably and look the fool. Or just as bad, he will become some horrible simulacrum of his hero, while at the center of his being remains a howling emptiness. Repetitions are just as dangerous in their own way. They all tend to boil down to a great banality: "By returning to his roots, X found what he had been looking for—himself."

If disenchantment, bad faith, or banality seem to be the ultimate consequences of rotation and repetition, Percy would seem to be drawing a bleak, perhaps hopeless, picture of the human condition. But this is not quite so. Near the end of the essay he returns to the point he made at the beginning: The man who is aware of his alienation is better off than the one who isn't. "To say the least of it, then," Percy unemphatically observes (he will never announce his main points emphatically):

> whatever the ultimate metaphysical issues may be, the alienated man has in literature, as reader or writer, three alternatives. He may simply affirm alienation for what it is and as the supreme intersubjective achievement of art set forth the truth of it: how it stands with both of us. Such is Joseph K.: Kafkas's pointing at and naming alienation has already reversed it, healing the very wound it re-presents. For an intersubjective discovery of alienation is already its opposite.

This alternative is clearly the best to Percy. He has already shown how the other two, rotation and repetition, are inadequate, except as temporary (and perhaps instructive) releases from everydayness. True wisdom, then, consists in accepting alienation as the inescapable fact of life, as the condition of being, although what one then does with this condition depends on how one resolves those "metaphysical issues" that Percy only alludes to. This essay—like so much of the fiction that he would later write—is concerned with establishing the inescapable terms of our being, in the hope that presenting these terms clearly will impel the reader to make those all-important metaphysical (Percy will not say religious, not in *Partisan Review*) decisions.

The astonishing thing about this essay is how thoroughly it anticipates Percy's future work in fiction, particularly his first two published novels, *The Moviegoer* and *The Last Gentleman*. We see this not only in the ideas that are discussed but in the ways they are dramatized, concretely and wittily, in the examples. The mechanism by which the aesthetic consumer of rotations grows disillusioned with the rotation—one of the main themes of *The Moviegoer* and *The Last Gentleman*—is set forth in a matter of sentences in "The Man on the Train":

> The young man in a Robert Nathan novel or in a Huxleyan novel of the Days after the Bomb may rest assured that if he lies under his bush in Central Park, sooner or later *she* will trip over him. But what of the reader? He falls prey to his desperately unauthentic art by transposing the perfect aesthetic rotation to the existential: He will lie in his green shade until doomsday and no fugitive Pier Angeli will ever trip over him. He must seek an introduction; his speech will be halting, his gestures will not come off, and having once committed himself to the ritual criterion of his art and falling short of it, he can only be— nothing. . . . His alienated art of rotation instead of healing him catches him up in a spiral of despair whose only term is suicide or total self-loss.

Binx Bolling and Will Barrett will both explore the possibilities of rotation (and repetition) before discovering that neither can save them from
despair. Both protagonists must find other ways of coming to terms with
their alienation.

As important as the broad themes and the presentation of the various
existential categories is the tone that Percy sometimes assumes in the
essay, a tone that would appear in his novels and that he would one day
describe as "flip-savage satirical." The tone is never quite savage in "The
Man on the Train," but it comes close in a number of places. On the
subject of the anxiety supposedly inspired by the fear of the Bomb, for
example, Percy casts a very cold and unsentimental eye: "The contin-
gency 'what if the Bomb should fall?' is not only not a cause of anxiety
in the alienated man but is one of his few remaining refuges from it.
When everything else fails, we may always turn to our good friend just
back from Washington or Moscow, who obliges us with his sober second
thought—'I can tell you this much, I am profoundly disturbed . . .'—
and each of us has what he came for, the old authentic thrill of the
Bomb and the Coming of the Last Days. Like Ortega's romantic, the
heart's desire of the alienated man is to see vines sprouting through the
masonry." We can recognize a hint of flip-savagery in these lines, as well
as the adumbration of one of Percy's favorite themes: the secret yearning
for apocalyptic times.

"The Man on the Train," and indeed much of the work that Percy
accomplished in 1956, marked something of a breakthrough. While not
abandoning his more arcane concerns with the symbol and the philosophy of language, Percy had extended his reach to subjects that would
more readily concern the general reader.

Percy received strong encouragement from those closest to him—his
wife and his friends included—to keep working the more popular vein.
Foote had been much impressed with the Stoicism essay (even though
he thought Percy exaggerated the virtues of the old southern gentry),
but his enthusiasm for "The Man on the Train" was at least as strong: "I
don't know when Ive enjoyed anything more than I enjoyed your Partisan Review article. What encouraged me most about it was your seeing
an answer in art (openly expressed) as well as in Jesus (only implied, and
hardly that)."

Percy, in fact, began to hear more from Foote again, largely because
the latter's life had settled down considerably since the earlier upheavals.
Being in Memphis close to his daughter Margaret helped, and in the fall
he had married again, this time to a twenty-six-year-old divorcee, Gwyn
Shea (the former wife of the doctor who had recommended Miss Mirrie-

lees). Most calming, though, was the work. Foote believed increasingly that he had found his subject, and though he knew the task before him was huge, he approached it each day with the enthusiasm for writing that he earlier feared he had lost. That others deemed his work important—he had received the first of three consecutive Guggenheim grants in 1955—helped him believe he was on the right track. Back on his feet, Foote was glad to see that his friend who had stood by him in hard times was making such promising strides in his own writing. If there was any envy or jealousy, it was very well hidden. Foote, after all, was encouraging Percy to move in the direction that would garner him even wider recognition.

And Foote was not the only friend to do so. In July of 1956, Percy had taken his family to Point Clear on Alabama's Mobile Bay and met his old Sewanee companion, Robert Daniel. Percy always enjoyed his time with Daniel, but he was particularly happy on this occasion to hear Daniel's good words about the essays. From a greater distance, Caroline Gordon congratulated Percy on each of his publications, often requesting more copies for her and her friends. If anything, her hopes for her former student were higher than ever.

Apart from his friends, Percy had no idea of whom he reached with his essays. He would claim many years later that writing for philosophical journals "was like dropping a message into the void," but whether he believed this was true about his more popularly aimed essays is hard to say. Certainly, the mail did not come pouring in. We do, however, know something about one of his early readers, because that reader would eventually become one of Percy's foremost fans and explainers, Dr. Robert Coles. While doing an internship in Chicago, Coles audited a course given by the theologian Paul Tillich. Tillich had come across Percy's article in *Partisan Review* and recommended it strongly to his class. Coles, then in considerable turmoil about what he was going to do with his career, read the article and was strongly impressed: This, he thought, was a writer who went to the bottom of his own confusion. He didn't remember the name of the author, but the article remained fixed in his memory. Only many years later, when he came to know Percy's fiction and then Percy himself, did he realize that the author of *The Moviegoer* and the author of "The Man on the Train" were one and the same.

Dangerous though it is to generalize from single cases, it is hard to imagine there were not many readers who reacted to the essay like Tillich and Coles. Percy had tapped into a widespread uneasiness, the gray-flannel malaise of the 1950s, but he talked about it in a way that was not simply or snidely dismissive of the "bourgeois" way of life. In fact, alert readers could see that Percy was strongly sympathetic to those suffering from the malaise, and was so because he saw beyond its merely sociological aspect. He eschewed the spurious scientific objectivity of the "expert" commenting on a problem that the less enlightened suffer from. Percy knew that he was a man of the suburbs (increasingly so, in fact, ever since the causeway connecting New Orleans and Mandeville had been completed in 1954), sharing many of the disaffections that plagued his fellow suburbanites. Much of Percy's uniqueness as a writer came from his refusal to assume the old romantic posture of the artist-as-outsider. Partly because of his own modesty, partly out of the Catholic spirit of sodality, partly because of what Uncle Will said about the artist enjoying no special dispensation from civil behavior, Percy remained close to the plight of the average sensual man, and this proximity would give his work an almost Chaucerian sociability (this, paradoxically, de-spite the fact that Percy's fictional protagonists are painfully aware of their alienation from their kind). Like Chaucer, Percy wrote from *within* his society, as a fellow commuter, a fellow pilgrim on the train. And it is this placement of his authorial self that is one of the more striking achievements of the *Partisan Review* essay.

By 1957, Percy was confident that he had something important to say, but he was increasingly doubtful about the prospects of finding an audi-ence through his essays alone. "Nobody reads these things," he said to Bunt. "I need to put some of the things I'm saying into a novel so that people will read them." At the same time, Percy had strong doubts about his ability to succeed as a novelist. Percy did not abandon his essay writing. To the contrary, in 1957 he would place seven pieces in four different magazines, a record number of publications in one year for Percy.

But there is good reason to think that Percy started working on some-thing in addition to essays in early 1957, a novel that he never quite brought to a finish. We are on very shaky ground here, because Percy himself was consistently vague, even evasive, about whether he at-tempted another novel between *The Gramercy Winner* and *The Movie-goer*. He might have been genuinely confused. A surviving fragment entitled "Confessions of a Movie-goer (from the Diary of the Last Ro-mantic)" could have originally been intended as the opening chapter of a novel that he had casually mentioned to Shelby Foote, a novel that was to be set, as is the fragment, in New York City. Then again, it might have been nothing more than a preliminary sketch for *The Moviegoer*.

It is easy to see how it could have been the latter. The titles are obviously close cousins, and the central character of the fragment, a solitary, overly self-conscious young man who goes to the movies a great deal—and thinks about movies even more—reminds us both of the future Binx Bolling and, even more, of the future Will Barrett. Although he is a very shadowy figure, a barely embodied consciousness, the details of his life and personality draw on Percy's autobiography and on Percy family history—all discreetly scrambled and rearranged, of course. This character, the protagonist and narrator of the fragment, is a Princeton graduate; his claim to undergraduate fame is a college yearbook picture showing him in a line "at the local movie house (the armpit)"; his father is a doctor in Spartanburg, South Carolina, a lover of romantic music who listens to Wagner and Brahms on his Capehart, a student of things German who spent his *Wanderjahre* walking "down the Mosel, up the Rhine, and into the Schwarzwald"; the protagonist himself is spending his *Wanderjahre* in New York City, living in the West Side Y, supposedly contemplating a career in scientific research while he attends concerts but in fact going to movies in different theaters throughout New York's far-flung boroughs; he has a precise formula for what makes the perfect movie ("The things to look for, in the first moments and later, are the Man, the Escape, the Encounter, and the Ordeal"); this formula involves the Kierkegaardian strategies of escape from everydayness, particularly rotations and repetitions.

Such is the character and the nature of his obsessions. In fact, the bulk of the fragment details this character's minute analysis of the romantic promise offered by the perfect movie, an analysis that reminds us, even in specific examples, of "The Man on the Train." Percy, it seems, was trying to bring wholesale into fiction his deft analysis of "three existential" modes. The result is not altogether bad. To be sure, it lacks drama. The analysis goes on too long, and the main character is too much a mouthpiece and too little a person. Yet despite such shortcomings, the fiction has magnetic power. We are drawn toward the character and are intrigued by his predicament. We wonder why he has such an addiction to the movies, and we share his disappointment that life always fails to work out the way that movies do. Most of all we are amused by the self-described plight of this alienated young man who seeks release in aesthetic experiences that ultimately return him to himself and the world feeling even more lonely, cut off, desolate, and empty than he was before he sought release. The humor, the lightly self-mocking irony, is the real accomplishment of the piece. Take, for example, the narrator's account of why the romantic formula of the movies never seems to work in life:

> Here, too, in the Encounter, he [the movie hero] has the advantage of me. For he has the assurance that when at first she shows her suspicions of his carnal intentions and when in a righteous rage he

turns and flings out—he has reason to expect that she will call him back. We don't fear that she will let him leave; we may be quite certain that he will get no further than the hall before she cries "Wait!" He knows this—even as he walks away, he can feel her eyes between his shoulder blades. Moreover, since it is the rule of the movies that every gesture is efficacious and none is wasted, he may also be assured that when his old war wound bothers him and a spasm of pain flits across his face, she will not miss it. I have no such assurance. There is a good chance that when I leave resolutely, for one reason or another she might *not* call me back, or that when my wound hurts, she might not notice it. What then?

The Encounter never even comes to the moviegoer, because his studied indifference prevents him from approaching the woman of his desire. The catastrophe that always breaks the ice in the movies never occurs in real life, at least not at the right moment. "I know exactly what to do, what to say to this girl, if the hydrogen bomb should fall," the last romantic explains. "*But what if it does not?*" Painting the absurd terms of the moviegoer's aesthetic entrapment, Percy works the same vein of self-lacerating humor that Dostoyevsky works in *Notes from Underground*: "It would appear that the girls I have seen have interpreted my indifference on its face value—as indifference! The only response which my sparse and chivalric posture has provoked so far has been polite inquiries from the homosexuals at the Y."

The twenty-one-page fragment remains a tantalizing specimen of Percy's effort to move from the essay-argument to fictional form. Whether there was more of it, we shall probably never know. But even with the little evidence we have, we can see clearly that the distance from "Confessions of a Movie-goer" to *The Moviegoer* was not far. Indeed, the distance between the two fictions was little more than just that: a matter of distance, geography, place. Percy's hero—his moviegoer—would have to find his proper stomping ground before all the parts of a more satisfying fiction would begin to fall in place. Percy the author would soon discover what that ground should be.

Before he did, though, there would be other business to tend to. The essays that Percy placed in 1957 (some of which were completed in late 1956) covered both old ground and new. The old consisted of two further reflections on language and symbolization. "Semiotic and a Theory of Knowledge," appearing in *The Modern Schoolman*, not only developed Percy's idea about the necessarily social character of symbol using. It also attempted to lay the foundation for a radically anti-Cartesian epistemology. Knowledge of *what is*, he argues, comes not from the isolated reflections of the cogito but from the social activity of naming.

Naming is the breakthrough into knowledge, Percy asserts, using as his example the story of Helen Keller in the water house. When Helen feels water flowing over one hand and Miss Sullivan spelling out the word on the other and for the first time puts the two together, she suddenly understands that water *is*, a discovery that not only fills her with joy but arouses her desire "to know what everything else *is*." (This will not be the last time that Percy invokes the "Helen Keller phenomenon" to make his point.)

What is true for Keller is true for every person who experiences naming for the first time. "It is *only* if you say what the object *is* that you can know anything about it at all." We assert, therefore we know, Percy suggests. Knowledge is a social activity. Percy would not deny that we reason about the things we know in solitude, but those things we reason about have been provided through the gregarious activity of naming.

Gregarious and, one might add, mysterious. The latter quality would be the subject of the second philosophical essay of 1957. It appeared in the summer issue of *Forum*, a journal published by the University of Houston and edited by Donald Barthelme, an imaginative journalist-critic who would later be known for the absurdist fictional confections that he contributed for almost two decades to the The New Yorker. "The Act of Naming" (changed to "The Mystery of Language" in *The Message in the Bottle*) summarized in a relaxed way almost everything Percy had written to date about the peculiar nature of the symbol and symbol using. But the summarizing leads to an important point: The act of naming is an event unlike any other in the physical-biological world, an event so strange that man has not yet been able to sort out its strangeness (partly because he is required to use language to think about language). Indeed, Percy argued, philosophers, scientists, and other thinkers have devoted so much energy to showing how naming is like other human and animal behavior that they find any suggestion that it may be qualitatively different a "scandal." Percy's use of that word "scandal" was important. In private conversations and in his writing, Percy would frequently describe Christianity as a "scandal" to the unbeliever; it was a word that he savored, just as Pascal and Kierkegaard had, for its shocking rightness.

Percy's reason for using the word becomes clear as the essay moves toward its conclusion. The notion that naming might not be explained by physical laws was a scandal to minds bound by the scientific world view because it implied that there might be something equally unique about the namer, the human being, something that removed him from a strictly naturalistic explanation. As Percy notes, "An awareness of the nature of language must have the greatest possible consequences for our minimal concept of man." Just in case his point is missed, he makes clear what his concept is, using the terminology of one of his favorite philosophers, Martin Heidegger. "Man is not merely a higher organism responding to and controlling his environment. He is, in Heidegger's words, that being in the world whose calling it is to find a name for Being, to give testimony to it, and to provide for it a clearing." Percy could not have come much closer to an explicit statement of the meta-physical and even religious direction of his language philosophy.

Among the many remarkable things about Percy's philosophical pur-suit was its solitary character. Intellectually, Percy was very much alone in what he was doing. Even within the professionalized academic milieu, where one is assured at least a few readers and auditors, the pursuit of philosophy is lonely. It was all the more so for Percy. Clearly, he could not have undertaken something so difficult had it not been a matter of ultimate importance. And so it was. Percy's philosophy, with its empha-sis on man as the symbolizing creature, was an effort to overcome solip-sism, the fatal entrapment in the "citadel of the self" that Percy believed led to moral, metaphysical, spiritual, and possibly even literal death. Percy's hope was that by establishing the truly incommensurable and mysterious character of language and by putting language first (as the sine qua non of knowledge and even of consciousness itself) he could demonstrate that the real end of knowledge is the establishment of commonality with our fellow creatures and an awareness of our depen-dence upon the divine. His argument was both paradoxical and Chris-tian: that we find ourselves only through attentiveness to others and to God. To say this is what Percy believed is too easy; it is what he wanted to believe. Percy knew that faith was not assured. He had to fight for it. He was, in Kierkegaard's wonderful phrase, a "knight of faith," locked in perpetual combat with other, darker, more solitary voices.

Even as Percy elaborated the theoretical foundations of his language philosophy and what was clearly now an ambitious epistemology, he also headed into new areas of cultural criticism. In fact, the first essay that appeared (in two parts) in 1957 was devoted to psychiatry, a subject that had been much on his mind, thanks partly to his stormy afternoon symposia with Bill Sorum. In two January issues of the Jesuit weekly America, Percy forecast what he called "The Coming Crisis of Psychia-try." Not surprisingly, we find in it the by-now familiar argument against the behavioristic reduction. Adopted by the psychotherapeutic profes-sions, Percy argued, this reduction was not only misconceived but harm-ful. "The question, then, is no longer whether the social sciences, given sufficient time (as they like to say), may succeed in applying the biolog-ical method to man, but whether the very attempt to do so has not in fact worsened man's predicament in the world."

The danger, Percy proceeded to argue, was that most psychotherapeutic approaches treat as diseases those qualities that most truly define people as people—their anxiety, their guilt, their sense of homelessness in the world. Proposing that normality is a state in which all needs— from sexual to status needs—are met, psychiatry succeeds in making people only more alienated from their essential nature. Percy did not claim to be the first to see this dangerous therapeutic logic. He credited Erich Fromm for exposing the "pathology of normalcy," although Percy wondered why Fromm linked his diagnosis with a Marxian analysis and not with the insights of existentialist thinkers. (Percy's reluctance to look at any of the historical dimensions of the therapeutic culture revealed his own limitation as a culture critic and even as a philosopher. This limitation would remain a weakness of his theoretical and critical writing, and was tied, one suspects, to his own difficulty in confronting the past except through the indirect means of fiction.)

The great failing of psychiatry, Percy elaborated in the second part of his essay, is that it refuses to take seriously mankind's super-biological longings, its urge to surpass itself (in Nietzsche's words), its desire for transcendence. Percy acknowledged that one existential viewpoint describes this longing as a "useless passion" (Sartre), but even if it is, the failure of psychiatry to take account of it indicates a fatal and even unscientific dogmatism. ("It does not seem to be asking too much to require social science to be 'open' in its theoretical commitments, or as Christopher Dawson would say, to be more empirical and less religious.") At the very least, the good doctor concluded, psychiatry should not try to reduce the longing for transcendence to a neurosis treatable by fine tuning the biological organism.

Perhaps there is not enough that can be said against the dangers of the therapeutic culture, and Percy's critique was both convincing and prescient (or relatively so). That said, Percy created something of a straw man out of "psychiatry," implying far more theoretical homogeneity within the therapeutic profession than was the case even in the 1950s. Moreover, it is hard to say whether even Freud was as much a biological reductivist as Percy made him out to be. It would be harder yet to say that all of his intellectual progeny were. At the very least, many of them were agnostic about the final ends of mankind. At what point the suspension of teleological considerations becomes a dismissal of them is a point worthy of discussion, but Percy here (and in later swipes against "psychiatry") preferred broad strokes to fine lines. Percy's attraction to polemics sometimes got the better of his concern for truth. That it did so when he wrote about psychiatry was particularly unfortunate, because what he had to say about the problematic moral stance of the therapist in relation to his patient was terribly important. Percy was right in seeing that too many psychiatrists and other psychotherapists failed to view their own lives in the same terms that they often cast their patients'. Percy was also aware that much of the spurious authority of the therapist derived precisely from this unacknowledged double standard. But these were matters so nuanced that perhaps only fiction could get at them adequately.

In some ways the most self-revealing writing that Percy did this year was a brief essay on the Civil War—"The American War," it was enti-tled—which appeared in the March 27 issue of *Commonweal*. The essay was a meditation on what Percy believed was a new attitude toward the Civil War, an attitude that he described as dispassionate, nonideologi-cal, even nonpartisan. He praised works such as Bruce Catton's *This Hallowed Ground* and Shelby Foote's *Shiloh* for being so evenhanded that readers would be hard pressed to tell whether the authors came from the North or the South. What Percy valued above all else about the most recent reconsiderations of the war was that they had made it possible to look at the fight itself—and, as Percy enthusiastically noted, "What a fight it was!"

The amazing thing about the war, to Percy, was the almost suicidal abandon with which soldiers on both sides fought it. And it was this fascination with the selfless intensity of the soldiers that was so self-revealing about the essay: It showed the extent to which Percy still thought of life in Uncle Will's terms. "Yet with all the horror," Percy wrote, "or perhaps because of it, there was always the feeling then, and even now as we read about it, that the things a man lived through were somehow twice as real, twice as memorable as the peace that followed." The line could have come straight from *Lanterns on the Levee*.

The complexity of Percy's ties to his adoptive father were expressed even more directly in a letter he wrote to his cousin Phinizy Spalding only two months after his Civil War essay appeared. Spalding, then a graduate student at the University of Georgia, was writing a master's thesis about Will Percy's philosophy as expressed in his poetry. Spalding had solicited his cousin's thoughts on Will, and he got in return a surprisingly frank confession:

> I might even say that everything I am interested in writing about is a result of the impact of Uncle's Will's world-view upon me and what has germinated as a result of the ferment which followed (a fouled-up metaphor if I ever made one). I could write pages on it; but it would be only another reaction.

Percy would soon write very many pages on it. And it would be quite some reaction.

11

Carnival in Gentilly

If the future of the novel is not close to your heart, it should please you to see a philosopher writing one. Whenever philosophers insinuate themselves into letters, it is to exploit their confusion or to perpetuate their collapse.

—E. M. CIORAN, *The Temptation to Exist*

Dostoievski's way of creating characters from his own complexity. The Brothers. He is all three. Priest, atheist, worldling.

—WALKER PERCY, notebook, 1951

Number 1820 Milan Street—where the Percys would take up part-time residence in the fall of 1957—is in the "Uptown" district of New Orleans, about three blocks northeast of the intersection of St. Charles and Napoleon. Residents of the city pronounce the street's name with a long "i" and accent the first syllable, so that the word rhymes with highland, minus the terminal "d." The strangeness of the pronunciation is altogether consistent with the general eccentricity of New Orleans: yet another of the thousand-and-one little oddnesses that make the visitor scratch his head in bemused wonder.

No American city is more redolent of eccentricity, alluring vice, and local color than New Orleans. Sunbelt standardization—with its uniform march of highrises, malls, and suburban subdevelopments—had already started coming New Orleans's way in the 1950s, but the city retained its distinctive character. This could be read not only in the architecture of the quainter sections of the city, in the French Quarter and the Garden District above all, but also in the rich human gumbo that makes up the city's population. As a port town, New Orleans absorbs everything that the river brings to it from the north and much that comes bubbling up from the Latin-Caribbean world to the south. New Orleans is America's Marseilles, a Latin city, and what makes it so lastingly different from other American cities is its Creole culture. Catholic in both the religious and secular senses, it is a culture tolerant of diversity and forgiving of excess. Sin, penance, and forgiveness are woven into the ritual patterns of daily and yearly life—so much so that even Bible-thumping fundamentalists fall under its dispensation when they come to the Big Easy. License and corruption are both condoned and contained, indulged and forgiven, transformed into collective spectacle, a perpetual carnival that peaks on Mardi Gras but never fully subsides.

It can be tiring, of course, all this color and atmosphere. How could it not be? The citizens of New Orleans are always in danger of becoming prematurely worn-out veterans of their city's too-colorful life. They tend to become eccentric, their lives given over too exclusively to the business of being "characters." All in all, it is not the best place for the ambitious to live, particularly if they are writers, as Percy learned during his earlier sojourn in the city. Those who manage to write at all tend to become local colorists, explaining the quaintness of the city to outsiders. "The sheer differentness of the scene," as one critic has noted, "has tended to block writers from probing very deeply into the human condition and producing major fiction." The same critic cites Lafcadio Hearn, George W. Cable, Grace King, and Lyle Saxon as honorable literary casualties of New Orleans's atmospheric excess.

If New Orleans was so dangerously seductive to writers, why did Percy choose to return to it in 1957? The easy answer is that he did so for the good of his family. Even before Miss Mirrielees came for her first stay in the spring of 1955, Bunt Percy began taking Ann to doctors and therapists in New Orleans, and she continued to do so when Miss Mirrielees was not in Covington. In addition to visits to Tulane, Ann began to have regular sessions with a therapist named Mrs. Joseph, an audiologist who worked out of her apartment in the city. These trips to and from the city were not short. Even after the twenty-four-mile Lake Pontchartrain Causeway was completed in 1954, it was still close to an hour each way. Sometimes Percy would do the driving, allowing his wife to do exercises with Ann in the back seat during the long commute, but more often than not, the burden fell to Bunt, who would drive while the maid, Ida Mae Griffin, held Ann.

In addition to being something of an ordeal, the drive could be dangerous, as Bunt learned during the summer of 1956. Driving back from the city, she was almost halfway across the causeway—a frightening point even on the best of days, with land invisible in both directions—when a violent storm broke loose, raining down hail as large as golf balls. Though Bunt slowed the car to a crawl, the hail soon shattered the windshield, forcing her to come to a full stop. For several long and harrowing minutes, the storm raged on, Bunt fearing that at any moment a car approaching from either direction might plow into them. Luckily nothing happened, and Bunt and her passengers were rescued, but the experience left her rattled.

What Bunt now saw as something of an ordeal became even more onerous as the fall of 1957 approached. Ann was now at a point when she would need even more time with Mrs. Joseph, daily lessons if possible. The choice facing the Percys was either to drive her every day or to find a place in New Orleans and live there for at least part of the week. (That the latter was an option says something about how well Percy had been managing his inheritance.) When the family returned from a vacation on Sea Island, Georgia, in August, Percy decided on the latter course of action. Selling his Polaroid stock, he purchased a small house—a one-story, two-bedroom "Louisiana cottage"—on Milan Street, not far from Mrs. Joseph's apartment. For much of the next two years, the Percys would spend school days in the city and weekends and vacations in Covington. Mary Pratt, now in the fifth grade, would attend Sacred Heart School, while Ann and her mother would spend a few hours each day with Mrs. Joseph and work at home for the rest of the day. (Ann also attended a pre-kindergarten school on Coliseum Street.) As for Percy, he would set up shop in a little sunroom at the back of the house and write.

For Ann's sake, then: That is the easy answer to why the Percys moved to New Orleans. But Percy was a clever man and surely could have come up with other solutions to the problem if he had needed to stay put on Military Road. That he did not gives us room to speculate about another possible reason for his arranging the little house in New Orleans: namely, that he needed the move, needed the change in setting, needed even the danger that came from living in so seductive an environment—and needed them in order to bring forth the seed of an idea that had been germinating for several years.

For the planting of that idea, Shelby Foote deserves some credit. In the spring of 1951, as Percy was revising *The Charterhouse* and wondering what he might attempt next, Foote sent him a letter full of suggestions and advice. Urging Percy to try something more tightly plotted and controlled for his next novel, Foote almost offhandedly added: "New Orleans is right in your backyard and it has everything: intellectuals, whores, priests, merchant seamen: you could make it boil and bubble. . . . But the main thing is for you to plot it carefully from beginning to end, making it fit a rigid time-scheme: Mardi Gras, for instance, with its climax the following holy day."

Percy ignored what Foote called "the main thing." Despite his best friend's urgings, Percy could never plot anything in advance. It was simply not his way of writing fiction. He had to grope forward blindly, discovering what was right (or wrong) only after he wrote it. But the incidentals of Foote's advice—the locale and the time frame—were suggestions that lodged themselves in Percy's memory, and with time they began to germinate. They even gave impetus to the fiction that Percy had first attempted to write in "Confessions of a Movie-goer." Percy later described *The Moviegoer* as a breakthrough achieved only after the writing of "two bad novels"—and possibly an attempt at a third.

Percy often acknowledged the novels of Sartre and Camus as inspirations for what he attempted to bring off in *The Moviegoer*, and these inspirations were undoubtedly crucial. (Echoes of *The Stranger* are particularly clear in *The Moviegoer*.) But what seemed to move Percy from the level of his apprentice work to that of his attained work was a kind of imaginative surrender: "One begins to write not as one thinks he is supposed to write, and not even to write like the great models one admires, but rather to write as if he were the first man on earth ever to set pencil to paper." Yet for that surrender to work, Percy later explained, he still needed some minimal foundation on which to build:

> When I sat down to write *The Moviegoer*, I was very much aware of discarding the conventional notions of a plot and a set of characters, discarded because the traditional concept of plot-and-character itself reflects a view of reality which has been called into question. Rather would I begin with a man who finds himself in a world, a very concrete man who is located in a very concrete place and time. Such a man might be represented as coming to himself in somewhat the same sense as Robinson Crusoe came to himself on his island after his shipwreck, with the same wonder and curiosity.

What Percy left out of his explanation was the third ingredient: the idea, the philosophical argument, the working out of which would give the novel much of its structure and movement. Some elements of that argument were present in the "Confessions of a Movie-goer," borrowed from Kierkegaard by way of Percy's own "Man on the Train" essay. But the other two elements, the central character and the concrete place and time, were not strong enough to carry the intellectual freight. They were the wrong vehicles. The narrator-protagonist of the story was too young, too green, for the kind of intellectual search that the philosophical material called for. (The protagonist of the story is, in fact, a more telling precursor of the younger, more innocent Will Barrett of *The Last Gentleman* than of the cynical, somewhat jaded war veteran Binx Bolling.) In addition to the character's inappropriateness, the place and time —New York City in what seems to be the 1940s—did nothing to move the story forward. Possibly from the experience of writing *The Charterhouse*, much of which was set in Birmingham, Percy had learned the danger of setting his fiction too close to home. But in *The Gramercy Winner* and "Confessions of a Movie-goer," Percy tried to build on terrain that was too distant from the familial and social complications of his native ground. Percy would later learn to make better use of both New York City and Birmingham (as settings through which Will Barrett passes in the course of his peregrinations), but for the kind of novel that *The Moviegoer* would be, Percy needed one place that would be both strange and close to the central character, both free from and complicated by historical associations, in the South but not completely of it. New Orleans was an ideal setting—for reasons that Shelby Foote could never have guessed when he made his suggestion six years earlier, and for reasons that Percy himself might only have dimly intuited.

New Orleans worked for Percy, both as an imaginary landscape and as a place to write and live. Perhaps this was because he never got caught up in city life, never became drawn into any part of New Orleans society. The Percys, in fact, did very little socializing in the city. They were friendly with their neighbors, had drinks or the occasional meal with some of them, and Percy made a few new friends, including another Jesuit at Loyola, a musicologist and well-rounded man of letters named Father C. J. McNaspy. (A few years later, while working at the Jesuit weekly, *America*, McNaspy would bring Percy's novel *The Moviegoer* to the attention of the editor, Harold Gardiner.) But the pace of life during the week was demanding. Working with Ann was a full-time occupation for Bunt, and Percy and Mary Pratt continued to do their part as well. Percy did not even see that much of his brother Phin, though he and his family lived not far away on First Street. Putting in six- and seven-day weeks at his law firm, Phin was as busy with his career as Walker was with his writing. If the brothers and their wives got together only rarely —to watch the Mardi Gras processions at Phin's house or to take in the occasional movie—their children saw a great deal of one another. Phin and Jaye Percy's two daughters and son were all close contemporaries of

Ann, and their son, Will, who was only two months Ann's senior, would occasionally go with his cousin to her lessons at Mrs. Joseph's apartment.

For the most part, Percy stayed to himself and wrote. The condition of semitransiency, the weekly shuttling between Covington and New Orleans, seemed only to throw him more upon himself. Withdrawing to the sunroom in the morning with his radio, he would write until midday, break for lunch and a short rest, then write and read for a few more hours in the afternoon. Slowly, the blue medical-school notebooks filled with pages of indecipherable scrawl (which at intervals Percy would type up into readable drafts). For recreation and exercise, Percy liked to go on walks around his neighborhood, sometimes by himself and sometimes with Bunt. Occasionally, the two of them would end up at a seafood restaurant on Napoleon called Manale's, where they would have drinks or a meal. Thought to have one of the better oyster bars in New Orleans, Manale's drew a range of New Orleans types. It was a good place for an observer to observe.

One of the few extramural involvements Percy allowed himself during his New Orleans months was a loose affiliation with a group of men who met from time to time to discuss civil-rights issues. The guiding figure of this group was Father Louis Twomey, a Jesuit priest who in 1947 founded the Institute of Industrial Relations at Loyola to promote the cause of unionism and workers' rights. During the 1950s and 1960s, Father Twomey and his institute (renamed the Institute of Human Relations) took up race relations, and a number of professionals in New Orleans— most but not all Catholic laymen—began to hold informal meetings to discuss everything from the ethics to the tactics of desegregation. They also hosted gatherings to meet and mingle with prominent black leaders. Among the members of this group were Bill Sorum, two brothers named Ivor and Winter Trapolin, and a lawyer named Jack Nelson. "We were a bunch of white liberals worrying about the situation, trying to think of things to do to improve it," Bill Sorum explained. Percy came irregularly to these gatherings and played host to the group at his house on at least one occasion. Typically, he sat quietly on the sidelines and listened while others, particularly the voluble Father Twomey, talked. But the meetings clearly made an impression on him. Percy began to think long and hard about the realities of integration, particularly school integration, and in the fall of 1957, he began to work up an essay on the subject for *Commonweal*. Entitled "The Southern Moderate," it was an appeal for understanding on all sides—between blacks and whites, northerners and southerners.

In fact, it was a little too balanced and temporizing. Less generously, one could describe it as fence straddling. To his credit, though, Percy did at least ask the delicate question: Why was it that school integration in particular so horrified white southerners? Percy's answer was equally direct, though shaky in some of its contentions. Public schools in the South, he claimed, were as much social as educational institutions, and were so to a degree that made them qualitatively different from schools in the North. The reason for this high degree of intimate sociability in southern schools, Percy explained, was the "homogeneous character of the non-Negro population"—that is, its white, Anglo-Saxon, Protestant character. Allowing blacks to enter white schools was particularly frightening to whites because it meant opening an intimate social zone —one that was personal and even sexual—to the people they feared most. The only solution to the problem, Percy suggested, was for white southerners to see the "public school for what it is, a public place, as public as a post office or a department store elevator." How this change in perceptions was to be achieved Percy did not say, although he seemed to suggest that it would accompany the continuing modernization and urbanization of the South, a process that inevitably shrank the zones of sociability to one's immediate domicile.

While this essay, which appeared in December 1957, could be seen as proof of a retreat to older gradualist views not too unlike Uncle Will's, Percy in fact had quite prescient reasons for his appeal to moderation and the toning down of confrontational rhetoric. What he feared more than anything was a hardening of attitudes on both sides of the divide. The integrationists' stridency and threatening rhetoric, he warned, might drive white southerners to abandon public schools altogether, a possibility that was already becoming a reality in many parts of the South (as Percy knew from his brother in Greenville). "The entire U.S. Army could not enforce school integration in the South; the South would only close the schools," Percy wrote. Prescient as Percy's argument might have been, it is hard to imagine how school integration would have been achieved without the aggressive pushing of activists. There was a tragic logic at work in black-white relations, one that seemed to spell bad consequences for both parties, and Percy grew increasingly resigned (and sometimes even cynical) about the inexorability of that logic. It was yet another way in which history would disappoint him.

While the move to New Orleans was borne well by all members of the Percy family, and in fact seemed to be good for them, the winter of 1957–58 proved to be hard on Ann, the person for whom the move had been arranged. The problem was ear infections, and Bunt was concerned that they might jeopardize what little hearing her daughter had. Increasingly, the Percys began to fear that the sharp barometric fluctuations of the soggy New Orleans winters were contributing to Ann's ear problems, and while they rode out the worst months, they wondered whether it would be advisable to do so again.

Considering the unsettled quality of domestic life, it is astonishing that Percy accomplished as much as he did during the winter and spring of 1958. Among the essays he wrote during this period was a brilliant rumination on the nature of metaphors, "Metaphor as Mistake," which he submitted to Andrew Lytle (one of the last steadfast Agrarians) at *The Sewanee Review.* The essay was another attempt to show the connection between symbolization and knowledge, but Percy approached the subject by way of those colorful mistakes of speech—misnamings, misunderstandings, and misrememberings—that call forth the truth of things more tellingly than their correct names. Part of the charm of this essay is Percy's recollections from his own childhood of such metaphor-mistakes: Seeburg jukeboxes, which Mississippi blacks called seabirds; a wonderful bird that an Alabama hunting guide called a blue-dollar hawk (and that was, in less colorful fact, a blue darter hawk). The way in which such felicitous misnamings give us the world is, to Percy, not merely quaint but the very key to the mystery of knowledge. "This 'wrongness' of metaphor is seen to be not a vagary of poets," Percy says, "but a special case of that mysterious 'error' which is the very condition of our knowing anything at all."

Not all of Percy's essays were so gracefully written. At their worst, Percy's philosophical essays were prolix, almost tedious, in their development of ideas. In some, it seemed as though the author were more concerned with keeping himself convinced of a position than with pressing his ideas forward or even winning over his reader to a new or clearer understanding of the case. One senses this in the two essays that directly followed "Metaphor as Mistake," "Symbol, Consciousness, and Intersubjectivity" (which appeared in July in *Journal of Philosophy*) and "Culture: Antinomy of the Scientific Method" (which appeared in October in *New Scholasticism*), essays whose titles alone seem forebodingly dense.

However one evaluates Percy's philosophical essays, they more than justify themselves as springboards to his other writing. Percy would have been unable to conceive the novels that were to come had he not been engaged in a search for a philosophy that would shore up his Christian convictions. His semiotic theory and his existential psychology gave intellectual form to his novels and were crucial to the shaping of his fictional characters. To be sure, the philosophical character of his novels would not be applauded by all of Percy's readers; in fact, many would take it as their cardinal defect. But the novels would not have come into being without the philosophical motive behind them.

Percy was never more pregnant with his philosophical obsession than he was in the spring of 1958. He seemed to need a variety of formal outlets. Sandwiched between his semiotics essays he wrote another essay for *Commonweal*, "The Decline of the Western," lamenting the flattening of the western hero since Owen Wister's novel *The Virginian*.

Percy's speculations about popular culture were not restricted to this piece. During the same spring, he began to work on a novel that used films in much the same way the story fragment "Confessions of a Moviegoer" had. "I remember him starting to work on it right there on that back porch," Bunt Percy recalled. "Nothing could stop him once he started on it." But if Binx Bolling was conceived on the sunporch at 1820 Milan Street, his gestation, at least a good part of it, took place on the road. Percy's life was soon to enter one of its more transient phases.

In the spring, as planned, the Percys moved back across Lake Pontchartrain and stayed put on Military Road for most of the summer. Toward the end of June, they made a short trip to Greenville to visit Roy and Sarah's family, and while there Percy read a copy of his cousin Phinizy Spalding's thesis on Will Percy. Spalding's explication of the philosophy underlying Will Percy's poetry was then of considerable interest to Walker, not surprisingly, since Uncle Will was on his way to becoming a major character in Percy's novel (though discreetly disguised as someone of the opposite sex). Once back from Greenville, Percy wrote to Spalding to congratulate him on a perceptive job, adding, "We are spending a quiet summer in Covington where I hope to get a little work done between bouts of hay fever." The hay fever was no small impediment; as in past summers, oak pollen reduced him to paroxysms of weeping and sneezing.

As private an activity as novel writing is, it never takes place in a historical vacuum, and it was the fate of *The Moviegoer* to be written at the beginning of what the Chinese would call an "interesting" time. For better and for worse, Americans were growing dissatisfied with the benign somnolence of the Eisenhower era. The Beatniks, the new cult of rebels without a cause, and the anarchic defiance of rock and roll were only dots on the cultural canvas, but they signaled an underlying discontent with lockstep conformism and hinted at stronger rebellions to come. Even staid Americans wondered if the nation were not in need of a shakeup. Warnings about second-rate schools, for example, seemed less idle after the Soviets launched Sputnik in 1957, and in other areas America seemed to be falling behind its major competitor in the Cold War.

Real problems loomed on the domestic front as well. Race relations were tense, and many saw Eisenhower's fence straddling as no help.

Worst of all to the average American, the economy was turning sour. In the winter of 1958 the nation entered a serious recession, with unemployment reaching as high as 7.7 percent of the labor force. No wonder political analysts predicted big gains for the Democrats in the fall congressional elections, a prediction that proved to be accurate. In response to real and imagined national setbacks, Americans even began to have doubts about their much beloved president. To many of them, Ike appeared to be in premature retirement, more active on the golf links than in the Oval Office. Restless and increasingly cynical, the electorate began to cast about for someone who would give the nation new direction and vigor.

Percy was attuned to this change in the national mood. Indeed, what one critic wrote about F. Scott Fitzgerald could be said with equal justice of Percy, beginning with *The Moviegoer:* "He was afflicted, as it were, by an acute case of culture, taking on chameleonlike the subtlest colorations of its unspoken ideas and assumptions and giving them utterance in his work." In *The Moviegoer,* as one of Percy's more astute readers, Richard Ford, once noted, "we can watch the rough traverse from the Fifties to the Sixties, from desperate reliance on everything institutional, to a generation's attempt to negate institutions through a preoccupation with personality, glibness, and the glut of culture itself." There is a cheeky irreverence to the book, as well as a sly contempt for complacency, fifties-style Babbitry, and the insufficiently examined life. Yet the novel is not simply iconoclastic. At once rebellious and profoundly conservative, cynical and idealistic, ironic and earnest, the novel embodies some of the same paradoxical qualities of the man whose presidential ambitions would soon become known to the nation, a man whom Percy would admire beyond any other politician of his generation. That man, of course, was John F. Kennedy.

Why *The Moviegoer* was so accurately attuned to the *Zeitgeist* while his earlier apprentice novels were not must have had something to do with the imaginative surrender that Percy described many years after writing *The Moviegoer.* Instead of relying on the techniques of the carefully plotted "well-made" novel, he began (to repeat his words of explanation quoted earlier) with the idea of "a *man* who finds himself in a *world,* a very concrete man who is located in a very concrete place and time. Such a man might be represented as coming to himself in somewhat the same sense as Robinson Crusoe came to himself on his island after his shipwreck, with the same wonder and curiosity" (emphasis added).

The novel that Percy started on the sunporch on Milan Street was a novel of *voice*—or, more accurately, of voices. Even though Binx is the dominant consciousness of the novel, he, like Walt Whitman, contains

multitudes. A generation of criticism emphasizing the philosophical furnishings of the novel has to some extent dulled our awareness of the
novel's internal dissonance. As the critic Michael Kobre has cautioned,
"when we stress the philosophical content of Percy's fiction to the exclu-
sion of other factors, we risk describing his novels in terms that render
them overly schematic." Kobre believes that we do greater justice to the
imaginative force of Percy's novels if we consider their "dialogic" character. That is, instead of taking the novels to be single-voiced articulation of a certain philosophical position, we should take the philosophical
argument to be only one of several contending voices or languages within
the novel. This suggestion seems not only eminently sound but useful.
It allows us to see how the quality that Percy deemed his central defect
—his lack of a firm sense of self—became an invaluable imaginative
resource and, indeed, a literary method. Binx Bolling, to begin with, is
a dramatic illustration of the protean character that Percy himself was.
As Kobre notes, Binx spends much of his time not only "reading" but
mimicking the languages that surround him, sometimes adopting the
elegiac tone of Aunt Emily's aristocratic pessimism, sometimes sounding
like the objective researcher theorizing about the world, sometimes assuming the jocular voice of the sensual hedonist. Binx's forging of his
own distinctive voice from among the medley of contending voices out
of his past and present may even be what *The Moviegoer* is all about, as
Kobre suggests: "Ultimately, each of Percy's characters must find his own
voice within this echo chamber of other voices; he must learn to speak
for himself, to make the words that he will use to define himself ring
with his own inflections and intentions."

Kobre's suggestion for a more open way of reading Percy (a suggestion
that draws directly from the ideas of the Russian literary theorist Mikhail
Bakhtin) helps to illuminate the breakthrough that the author experienced when he began writing *The Moviegoer*. Percy's real work in fiction
began when he gave free rein to those daemonic voices raging within
him, when he allowed his lack of a central or integrated self to become
his real subject. To be sure, we are all many selves, but Percy was aware
of his internal fragmentation to a painful, almost crippling, degree. (We
may even speculate that this awareness was closely related to Percy's
melancholia, the disintegration of self being one of the very mechanisms
of depression.) At the same time, this awareness, when he learned how
to channel it into literary form, produced work of an overpowering
psychological intensity. Percy's imagination is most impressive in its
power to show how we are quite literally constructed by our social and
cultural ideolects. This awareness can lead to a psychological version of
nihilism, a frightening conviction that we are nothing more than the

sum of those discourses that constitute our consciousness. Percy himself had been long plagued by such nihilism, and even with the assurances of his faith he could never completely overcome it. The crucial thing about Percy's faith, though, was that it gave him hope that among the medley of discourses there was one that carried truth and authority. (That cluster of closely related words—author, authority, authorization—was terribly important to Percy.) Discerning this language, finding and heeding the "news" from across the seas, was the one thing that could rescue the individual from the internal Babel—a hope that Percy made explicit in an essay that he was working on toward the end of 1958, "The Message in the Bottle." Though more subtly expressed, that faith was also the undergirding of the novel he was struggling to write.

The family returned to Milan Street in the autumn, and Percy wrote with no serious interruptions through the New Year. Writing fiction was never easy for him; wrestling with the internal voices exhausted him. It also made him feel more cut off from his immediate life. Yet he remained an attentive father and husband. He told stories to the girls, played games with them, helped Ann with her lipreading and Mary Pratt with her homework. Mary Pratt remembers in particular how her father would engage her in serious discussions about what she believed. "He would propose these hypothetical situations. What would I say if the Communists took over the nation and made me defend my faith. How would I answer their arguments? Very serious questions, which of course I couldn't begin to answer. But he made me think about what the nuns were telling me to believe at school." Percy was still something of a master of ceremonies for the family, planning trips and outings, though fewer than usual during the fall of 1958. Percy saw his friends on occasion, including Sorum and the various Catholic laymen involved in integration efforts. He also made the acquaintance of a priest, Father Tom Clancy, an Arkansas-born Jesuit, who was in town visiting a friend. Despite what Clancy described as Percy's "typical convert's reverence for priests," Percy took to the shrewd and gregarious Jesuit, and when Clancy joined the Loyola faculty a year later, the friendship grew.

As winter came on, Ann's ear infections returned with a vengeance. This time they were so bad that doctors had to lance her ears to drain the infection. Audiograms showed that she still retained some trace of hearing, but Bunt Percy was certain she would lose even that if nothing were done to bring an end to the infections. Desperately seeking solutions, she and her husband decided Ann needed a drier climate, and in February Percy took his wife and Ann to Arizona, to a little resort outside Tucson called the Forty-Niner Ranch. After helping them settle in, Percy returned to New Orleans to take care of Mary Pratt. The resort, a miniature cowboy town, had its droll charms, but the move seemed to do no good for Ann. After two weeks and no improvement, she and her mother returned to New Orleans. Now, however, the Percys resolved not to spend another winter in New Orleans.

Despite the uncertainty and anxieties caused by Ann's condition, Percy finished his novel in early spring, had it typed, and sent it to Elizabeth Otis of McIntosh and Otis, the agent he had met through Susan Jenkins. One look at the manuscript, then titled, like the earlier story, *Confessions of a Moviegoer*, convinced Miss Otis that it was a promising piece of work, but she could see that it needed revision. She returned it to Percy with encouraging words and suggestions. Percy set immediately to work, and by June the novel was back in Miss Otis's hands. Though still not fully satisfied with its shape, Miss Otis sent the novel to an editor at Knopf who had recently called on her, a man named Stanley Kauffmann.

The forty-three-year-old Kauffmann was a man of many talents. Before coming to Knopf, he had worked as editor-in-chief at Ballantine Books and associate editor at Bantam. He was the author of seven novels and some forty plays, a former member of the Washington Square Players, and a film critic. Kauffmann later speculated that Miss Otis might have sent *Confessions of a Moviegoer* to him "because I was, had been for a year, the film critic of *The New Republic.*"

For all his attainments, Kauffmann was not very happy in his career in 1959. He had joined Knopf with a strong sense of foreboding, and his first few weeks in the office convinced him that everything he had heard about Mr. Knopf's bizarre management style—his peremptory literary judgments and his tyrannical rudeness with his staff—was true. (Mrs. Knopf's eccentricities, including the carefully maintained pretense that she read "everything," even though she was nearly blind, added to the atmosphere of unreality there.) Although Kauffmann had been hired specifically to strengthen Knopf's American fiction list, he had little experience in acquisition and even less taste for it. All in all, it seemed to him that he had made a terrible mistake by coming to Knopf.

The arrival of Percy's manuscript toward the end of June briefly lifted Kauffmann out of the doldrums. In her cover letter, Miss Otis warned him that the novel had some problems, but she promised that Percy's was "a strong new voice." As Kauffmann began reading, he saw that she was right, but his early high hopes were dashed when he reached the middle of the novel. Everything seemed to fall apart. As Kauffmann explained in a disappointed letter of rejection to Miss Otis, what began as a "novel of wit, pathos, and a Candide-like bland-savage satire" became a mechanical and overly contrived exercise: "It's not that its structure falters here [in the middle], because it never had a strong structure; it begins to assume a structure, a purpose, almost an obligation to have a more conventional plan and resolution." Kauffmann found that everything about Binx's "conversion to a sense of purpose and responsibility" in the second part of the novel was beneath the high level of insight that had been established for the character in the first part. Particularly weak, Kauffmann believed, was the use of a death (that of Binx's uncle, Jules Cutrer) and a conversation with a priest as the immediate causes of Binx's reengagement with the world. "At present," Kauffmann noted, "it is as if someone had suddenly switched on a lot of rosy lights."

A rejection, then, but not pure and simple. Kauffmann made it more than clear how regretful he was that he couldn't take the novel. (One wonders if he would have done so had he been on more certain ground at Knopf.) "A further paradox of this situation," Kauffmann wrote, "is that if the author were less unusual, if the book were one at a more predictable and mechanical level, it might be possible to discuss a contract at this point." Certainly, Miss Otis could see that he would not have made such careful suggestions for improving the novel if he had not harbored the hope that Percy would take them and resubmit the novel to Knopf. Kauffmann even included a carbon copy of his letter in the hope that Miss Otis would send it on to Percy. Not that he was confident he would hear from the author. As Kauffmann recounted in his memoir of his days at Knopf, he knew the novel was good enough that another publisher might take it, "risking loss, just to get the author."

Percy, naturally, was disappointed. He saw the justice of Kauffmann's remarks, but he also knew that it would take a great deal of effort to remedy the problems, and he was not sure he would satisfy Kauffmann even if he tried. The rejection added to his own career crisis, his uncertainty about whether to devote himself exclusively to philosophy or to continue trying his hand at fiction. So much rode on this book, in fact, that Percy had not even mentioned its existence (much less that he had sent it to a publisher) to his friend Shelby Foote when he and his wife visited New Orleans at the end of May. A week later, Percy sent Foote a copy of an essay that he had written for *Commonweal*, "The Culture Critics," but he continued to say nothing about the novel. Foote, who had completed the first volume of his history the previous summer, was impressed by the essay, even though it took contemporary critics to task for ignoring the religious dimensions of the modern malaise. ("How in God's name," Foote asked, "can Faith, no matter how desirable, be possible in this day?")

Foote had earlier suggested that Percy bring together some of his essays in a book, and when the rejection from Knopf arrived in late June Percy began to wonder whether this might not be a better way to go than to fiddle with a novel. In early July, the Footes came to Covington for a five-day visit, and the two friends discussed their favorite subjects—Mozart, Vermeer (Foote brought a book of the artist's reproductions), literature, and Greenville gossip—but Percy still said nothing about his novel. He had not reached a decision about what to do with it. A couple of days after the Footes left, Percy called Miss Otis to tell her he was thinking about Kauffmann's suggestions. Miss Otis passed the word on to Kauffmann, who was so delighted that he wrote Percy to assure him of his enthusiasm for his talent. Finally, on July 20, Percy sent off a short letter to Kauffmann thanking him for his thoughtful reactions to the book and, in the most cautious terms, intimating that he might attempt the repairs:

> I am going to have another go at it, at least another hard look-and-think, because your acute criticism (and Miss Otis's which has been much the same as yours all along) only confirms my own misgivings. I mean to say that all I can hope to do is please myself, so if you should see it again you need not worry that I have tried to fix it up to pass Knopf—much as I would like to do that. Right now I'm not even sure the thing *can* be finished satisfactorily.

Percy had more than a look-and-think. Having made plans to take his family to Deerfield Beach, Florida, at the end of November, he knew he had three months of uninterrupted time before him. By mid-October, he had completely reworked the second half of the book and sent it on to Miss Otis and Knopf. Kauffmann was delighted by what he saw, but he still found weaknesses in it. To ask for more changes from Percy, though, he knew that he would have to make some sort of good-faith offer. Having learned that Percy was related to another Knopf-published author, Kauffmann went to Mr. Knopf, explained who his author was and what he had written, and asked if he could offer Percy two hundred dollars against a thousand-dollar advance, the remainder to be paid upon successful revisions of the manuscript. Mr. Knopf was huffy, his color visibly rising, convinced once again that one of his staff was trying to put him into financial ruin. Kauffmann described the tense moment:

> "I think it's in order," I said. "After what he's done already. It's a gesture, of course, a token. Nothing to do with subsidizing him. In fact, I've heard that he is a man of independent means."

"Oh," said Mr. Knopf, his flush subsiding. "In that case, give him two-fifty."

Pleased if bewildered by his encounter with Knopf, Kauffmann wrote a four-page letter to Miss Otis, listing suggestions and the details of an agreement. Kauffmann's most substantial request was that Percy develop more thoroughly and explicitly the theme of the search. "The theme is a kind of spine for the book, and at present that spine is a little limp."

Percy's reaction was mysteriously cautious. He was afraid to be too hopeful until the manuscript was completely satisfactory to Kauffmann. In fact, he had great uncertainty about signing the contract, first telling Miss Otis that he would sign it, then telling Kauffmann that he would not. Percy wondered if it would not be wiser to resubmit the book after he worked on it at his own pace. Among other things, he was worried that he might not be able to make the deadline:

> It may take a couple of weeks or it may take a couple of months. And I don't want to be worrying about a delivery date. I have a hunch that the last thirty pages are going to take some figuring. Moreover, I have some obligations and distractions coming up in the next few weeks.

The letter perplexed Kauffmann. He wrote back to assure Percy that the due date could be changed to suit his needs. This seemed to be enough to allay Percy's concerns, and on November 18, Miss Otis mailed Kauffmann a signed contract, with the deadline set for February 4, 1960.

Percy's concern about his pending obligations was not feigned. At the end of November, he packed up his family and drove them to Deerfield Beach, Florida, thinking he would have no difficulty locating an apartment. He was wrong. Most apartment managers, wary about losing their elderly tenants, refused to rent to people with children. (It didn't help that the Percys had brought their dog, a chihuahua named Pedro.) Finally, though, the Percys found a place that was tolerant enough to take both pets and children, the exotically named "House of Blue Lights." Here, in rather cramped quarters, the Percys set up home for several weeks until they found a slightly more roomy residence, a little yellow cottage called the "Purich House."

The Percys had obviously come to Florida in the hope that the mild winter climate would prevent Ann's ear infections, but they had chosen the unlikely town of Deerfield Beach because it was close to Miss Mirrielees, who lived in Pompano Beach. The town also had a decent school, Pinecrest Beach School, where Mary Pratt, who had been bounced around from school to school for the past two years, was enrolled for the winter months.

The somewhat chaotic conditions of life would seem to have been less than ideal for the demanding work that Percy now faced, but as in the past, he seemed to flourish in the most inappropriate circumstances. Both in the "House of Blue Lights" and in "Purich House," Percy got most of his work done out of doors, sprawled upon a lawn chair with a glass of iced tea and Pedro at his side. Percy, in fact, was delighted to be in this unfashionable little nonplace, basking in the flat winter sunlight, surrounded by elderly Yankee retirees, while he figured out how to make Binx Bolling's search a more substantial part of the narrative. Bunt Percy thought that he had never seemed happier. Even interruptions within interruptions—a short Christmas vacation on Sanibel Island off the western coast of Florida and a brief visit by Phin and Jaye—did not slow him. In the middle of January, he sent the second revised version of *Confessions of a Moviegoer* to Kauffmann. For the moment, the world looked good.

But only for the moment. The letter he received from Kauffmann in early February was a rude shock. The first two lines were enough to bring on despair: "The revised manuscript of *Confessions of a Moviegoer* has now been read by several editors here and discussed at great length. I'm sorry to report the consensus is that it is not yet—in our opinion—in publishable form, and I hasten to underscore the words 'not yet' in the hope that this will prevent discouragement on your part." Kauffmann was in a nightmare of a situation himself. A work that he had carefully nursed along and that he had earlier indicated was close to being ready had obviously failed to pass muster with other editors in the house. The best he could do was request further changes and hope that Percy would bear with him. The requests were numerous and substantial, ranging from character and scene changes to changes in thematic emphasis. The most distressing thing about the letter was that Kauffmann seemed to contradict his very first criticism of the manuscript. He was asking that the whole novel be more tightly plotted and developed, more, that is, like a traditional well-made novel:

> What all this comes to essentially, is that instead of a collection of brilliant and moving scenes rather arbitrarily bound together . . . we would like to see a more organic, better composed work in which the author had all his thematic and plot elements well in hand from the start and is moving them towards a conclusion. . . .
>
> There is no blinking the fact that what we are asking for amounts to a major re-writing of the book. It means that you would have to

consider this a first draft: a very extensively articulated first draft from
which you would draw a great deal of material (I would hate to lose
much of what is there now) to be fitted into a clear and effective
design. It means, figuratively, that you would have to stand off, take a
deep breath and plunge in again.

Percy clearly thought that enough was enough. Trying to restrain
himself, he wrote to explain his objections. To be sure, he agreed, the
manuscript suffered from "lapses and gaucheries here and there," but
such problems, in his opinion, called only for "tinkering and polishing,"
not the sort of major overhaul Kauffmann seemed to be requesting. Percy
then made an eloquent defense of the kind of novel he had written:

> It is not that I disagree with you that a complete re-write, from a
> higher level of consciousness so to speak, would make a better book.
> The trouble is that the endpoint which I would approach in that case
> appears to be different, to judge from your letter, from the endpoint
> you have in mind. Your calling attention to dropped characters and
> interrupted story-strands is certainly valid novelistic criticism, but it
> does not seem applicable here—at least it does not strike a chord with
> me. *Passage to India* is a much better constructed novel than *Nausea*,
> but *Nausea* would be wrecked by a revision along these lines. I suppose
> I am trying to say that the fragmented alienated consciousness, which
> is Mr. Binx Bolling, cannot be done up in a *novel* in the usual sense of
> the word. At least I would not have the stomach for the job. Also, I
> am working on something else.
>
> This is not to defend the book, of course, since it either stands or
> falls with the reading, only to explain my position.

Percy said that he would ask Miss Otis to return the manuscript so
that he could give it a quick reconsideration, but he also expressed
doubts about the wisdom of resubmitting it to Knopf, "for even if you
decided then to accept it, I hardly see how you all could take it on with
the enthusiasm and unanimity without which I'd rather you didn't take
it on at all." Thinking that that was perhaps too harsh a note to close
on, Percy praised Knopf for publishing "the greatest book of our time,
Camus' *The Stranger*," and politely inquired whether Kauffmann was the
"astute critic and inveterate moviegoer of the *New Republic*." But even
the friendly touches seemed a polite farewell. (And the former may even
have been something other than a compliment: a sly dig at Knopf for
publishing an innovative novel by a Frenchman but spurning one by an
American.)

Kauffmann did not lose faith. He wrote back expressing his "obstinate hopes for future association." Percy, for his part, did not rush to do anything with the manuscript. In fact, he was busy with something else —an essay called "Naming and Being," which was to appear in the spring issue of the *Personalist*. In addition, Percy had sent a version of chapter two of *Confessions of a Moviegoer* to Donald Barthelme in Houston. It would appear in the summer issue of *Forum* under the title "Carnival in Gentilly," a title that Percy liked so much that he decided to rename his novel *Carnival in Gentilly, Confessions of a Moviegoer*. Adding further to Percy's preoccupations was the move back to Covington at Easter. It was hard for him to think about revisions, but the link with Knopf was not completely broken. In early May, he approved a change in the contract, moving the deadline from February 4 to October 1. But no one—not Miss Otis, not Stanley Kauffmann, and not even Percy himself—knew whether he would return the manuscript to Kauffmann.

Also in early May Percy finally sent Foote the first dozen or so pages of his novel, and Foote was impressed. "It has a fine tone and carries right along; I wished hard for more." Percy also mentioned some of the difficulties he was having with Knopf. Foote gave vent to his undying distrust of editorial tampering: "In fact I'm somewhat alarmed at the notion of rewriting. Dont ever accept an editor's judgment on anything that has to do with literary matters. Believe me, they know less than anyone along those lines." There were times when there was nothing sweeter to Percy's ears than Foote's cocky irreverence.

Percy proceeded to do what he had told Kauffmann he would do, a light revision. After working on it for a few weeks, he showed it to Bunt, whose gut-level responses he had come to depend on, and she told him right away that it was a good novel. Emboldened, he sent the whole manuscript to Foote around the end of July, and Foote read it straight through in an afternoon and an evening. There had been and would be rough patches in the two writers' friendship, but on this occasion Foote felt nothing but pride in what his friend had accomplished. And in that level, somewhat understated way of his, he told Percy just what he needed to hear: "It's a real good book. . . . I take it as the best of all possible signs; a sort of breakthrough of the spirit. The genesis I guess was in the Man on a Train piece. But whenever it came it came just fine." Foote noted some weaknesses, particularly a change of tone in the last third of the novel, but he thought nothing diminished the overall power of the book. "I enjoyed it from start to finish and always with a sense of wonder." Percy was not unhappy to hear that Foote had detected Uncle Will in Aunt Emily.

Percy still had more than a month before the manuscript was due, but he sent it on. After a few days, on September 1, Miss Otis called Percy to say that Knopf had accepted it. Percy finally was ready to rejoice. There was only one problem. He and his wife had had a disagreement earlier in the day, and she was in the backyard laying bricks for a patio and letting off steam. Unable to contain himself, Percy called out to her, "They've accepted it!" Bunt jumped up and cheered. The spat was forgotten.

It is a long and somewhat tedious haul from the acceptance of a book to its publication, as Percy was now to learn. To begin with, there would be further negotiations over the manuscript. Kauffmann asked if they could jettison *Carnival in Gentilly* and title the book, simply, *The Moviegoer*. It was a good suggestion, like most that Kauffmann made, and Percy went along with it. In addition to other fixes, there were still clean copies of the text to be made, questionnaires to be filled out, legal problems to be resolved. ("Is it libellous," Percy asked, "to say 'as extinguished in her soul as Eva Marie Saint,' when I have no idea whether Miss Saint is extinguished in her soul or not—it is the personality she projects in her acting which concerns us, of course.") By the end of the month, though, Kauffmann had most of what he needed: two revised typescripts, a completed author's questionnaire, and a glossy photo. Percy asked Kauffmann if he would mind being recognized, along with Miss Otis, in an acknowledgment at the beginning of the book. Kauffmann modestly demurred. Finally, in early October, Kauffmann passed on a suggestion from one of his fellow editors that Percy include "a brief epigraph—possibly from Kierkegaard." Percy obliged with a line from *The Sickness Unto Death*: "the specific character of despair is precisely this: it is unaware of being despair."

In the middle of October, Percy rewarded himself for his labors by taking a weekend trip with Bunt to Vicksburg; they met the Footes there, and Shelby showed them around the battlefields. The timing was perfect. Foote was just coming to the Vicksburg campaign in his history, having recently "put the ax to Stonewall Jackson" in Chancellorsville, and so was steeped in battle lore. On Sunday, the Footes returned to Covington with the Percys for a few more days of lazy bumming about. Percy had good reason to let down his hair—what little he had left. His wide, noble brow was growing wider by the year.

Perhaps the greatest surprise of the month was a letter from Kauffmann announcing his departure from Knopf. Kauffmann had known that his relations with Mr. Knopf were uneasy, but he was surprised (and, truth be known, relieved) by the suddenness of his dismissal. Kauffmann meant what he said to Percy, though: "Let me say, with exact truth, that a chief pleasure in my work here has been my association with you and your novel."

2

LEFT: Thomas G. Percy (1786–1841), great-great-grandfather of the novelist, son of Charles Percy, the first American Percy.
RIGHT: William Alexander Percy (1834–1888), the "Grey Eagle of the Delta," was the great-grandfather of the novelist.

LEFT: Senator LeRoy Percy (1861–1929), one of the three sons of William Alexander, was the great uncle of the novelist.
RIGHT: Walker Percy (1864–1917), the grandfather of the novelist.

Walker Percy's mother,
Martha Susan Phinizy Percy,
was beautiful and well liked,
but somewhat distant from her
own sons.

LeRoy Pratt Percy (1889–
1929) poses in his Army Air
Corps uniform with his son
Roy on his right knee and
Walker on his left. To his keen
disappointment, he never flew
in combat during
World War I.

At the beach in the early
1920s, Walker Percy rubs
the stomach of his youngest
brother, Phin.

*Walker Percy at age 11, sitting for a school picture
at the Birmingham University (now Altamont) School.*

William Alexander Percy—lawyer, planter, poet, and war hero—
adopted the three Percy boys after the death of their mother.

The Percy house in Greenville before and after renovation in the 1920s.

Taking the prize for poetry, Percy, a senior (third from right, second row), helped his high school newspaper, The Pica, walk away with most of the awards given by the Mississippi High School Press Association in 1933. Also in the picture are Donald Wetherbee (center, first row), who would be Percy's roommate for one year at Chapel Hill, and Margaret Kirk (to Wetherbee's left), Percy's standing date in high school and college.

13

Camille Sarason, one year ahead of Percy at Greenville High School, was Percy's first editor and recruited him to write the gossip column for the newspaper. Percy had a secret crush on her.

14

A trio of undergraduates lounging on the lawn behind Uncle Will's house: left to right, LeRoy Percy, Shelby Foote, and Walker Percy.

15

The freshman moviegoer: Walker Percy, left leg thrust forward, waits in line for the 3:30 show at the Carolina Theater in Chapel Hill.

Percy sets off for a walk in the Black Forest during his summer of travel and study in Germany in 1934.

16

17

Walker Percy with Uncle Will at Brinkwood, probably during the summer of 1938.

18

Walker Percy at Trudeau Sanatorium with two fellow patients and friends, Marcelle Dunning (to Percy's right) and Barbara O'Neil.

19

Percy with the quarterhorse El Capitan at Rancho El Merced outside Santa Fe, New Mexico, in the fall of 1946.

Walker and Bunt Percy at Brinkwood shortly after their marriage in the fall of 1946. The black cocker spaniel, Joey, was Percy's gift to his new bride.

21

20

Walker and Bunt Percy in Havana in 1951. Percy saw Ernest Hemingway at "La Floridita" bar but was too shy to approach him.

22

Miss Doris Mirrielees, an itinerant teacher of the deaf who developed her own method of instruction, began working with the Percys' daughter Ann shortly after they discovered that the child had little, if any, hearing.

The Percy family on a Caribbean cruise in December, 1955. Mary Pratt is standing; Bunt Percy is holding Ann Boyd. Percy, suffering from a recurrence of TB, was taking medicine on the cruise.

Allen Tate and Caroline Gordon in New York not long before Gordon took Percy on as her student. Percy rewrote his apprentice novel, The Charterhouse, under her close instruction.

Percy receives the 1962 National Book Award for Fiction for The Moviegoer. To his right is Lewis Mumford, nonfiction winner, and to his left, Alan Dugan, winner of the poetry prize.

The three Percy brothers— Roy, Phin, and Walker—in front of the novelist's house in Covington in the early 1970s.

Thomas Merton at Gethsemani Abbey in the mid-1960s, around the time he and Percy began to correspond. Although they met in person only once, the connection was very important to Percy.

In addition to Walker Percy (first row, second from right), attendees at a 1989 meeting of the Fellowship of Southern Writers included C. Vann Woodward, Shelby Foote (front row, third and fourth from left), and William Styron (back row, fourth from left).

29

Robert Coles and Walker Percy met when Coles profiled Percy for The New Yorker. They remained friends.

30

Eudora Welty and Percy first met on the train to New York City in the spring of 1972. Both were on the way to receive honors from the American Academy of Arts and Letters and the National Institute of Arts and Letters.

Percy shaking hands with Pope John Paul II in January 1988.
Percy had come to the Vatican to participate in a meeting of the
Pontifical Council for Culture.

to catch something she was saying. But they passed without seeing
me. The reason for my embarrassment sounds trivial. What is wrong
with standing in line to see a movie, alone or otherwise? It is
a very small thing but the first thought that came to my mind when
I caught sight of Coates and Lucey was the memory of a picture of
me that had appeared in the Princeton annual. I did not have a
very distinguished career in college and the only picture of me,
besides the regular class picture, was a candid shot of students
queued up at the local movie house (the armpit). And now for some
reason or other I felt it to be a distinct disadvantage to be seen
doing the same thing, regardless of the nature of the thing. It
was the the repetition I wanted to avoid. Yet there was an unspoken
canon in college against going to the flicks alone. Two or three
or four might decide to go, but not one alone.

The line moved along and at last we turned the corner into Sixth
Avenue. It was a cloudy day, yet glary enough to hurt the eyes.
There were air hammers going in the street. But soon I had bought
my ticket and was inside. More or less absently I followed the
girl down an aisle and took the seat beside her. The stage show
was just ending. Tiny figures went scurrying for the wings. The
curtains parted and the great white screen flickered into life,
a bigger and more meaningful life than the minute scurrying; the
sound track came on, a new and greater dimension of sound. A change
came over the audience. Where before there had been a hum of conversation and a good-humored but careless attention toward the
dancing and juggling, now all was silence and expectation. The
girl beside me lifted herself clear of the seat, smoothed out the
raincoat beneath her. I felt the old happiness. It was a picture

32

*A manuscript page from the unpublished story "Confessions of a
Moviegoer (from the Diary of the Last Romantic)." The story was Percy's
first attempt to blend the discursive approach of his philosophical essays
with fiction, a fusion that he would more successfully realize in his first
published novel,* The Moviegoer. *From the Walker Percy Papers,
Southern Historical Collection, the Library of the University of
North Carolina at Chapel Hill.*

Bunt and Walker Percy on the porch of their house in Covington.

An editor named Angus Cameron took over the handling of *The Moviegoer*, but as conscientious as Cameron proved to be, it was a bad break for Percy. Apart from Kauffmann, there had been little enthusiasm for *The Moviegoer* among the editors, beginning most conspicuously with Alfred A. Knopf himself, and without the enthusiastic backing of an editor, a book tends to fall through the cracks, receiving at best only dutiful attention from the promotion and advertising departments. Happily for his peace of mind, Percy was ignorant of the publishing business —years later he would say that his distance from the publishing scene allowed him to view the whole process as magical—but he was sad to see Kauffmann go. Percy knew how much his book had been improved by Kauffmann's close reading and suggestions. "I have no idea how this book will go," Percy wrote Kauffmann, "but I know very well how little I could have dispensed with your help."

If Percy had any worries about what would happen with his book, he was soon distracted from them. The presidential election was fast approaching, and the two candidates, Richard Nixon and John Kennedy, were still in a dead heat. A good showing in the televised debates in September had given Kennedy a boost, but no one knew whether it would be enough to overcome the political stigma of his Catholicism. Of course, Percy was completely behind Kennedy. He knew that the man had flaws, Phin Percy having told him about some of Kennedy's all-too-human sides. (In fact, Phin, a staunch Republican, had politely declined the offer to head Kennedy's campaign in Louisiana.) But, in Percy's mind, there was no other American who combined, as Kennedy did, intelligence and wit with patriotism and political vision. On the night of the election, Percy and his wife went to Bill Sorum's to watch the returns on televison. Present also were the Trapolin brothers, Father Clancy (now teaching political science at Loyola), Father Twomey, and an English lecturer (and former communist), Douglas Hyde. It was an exciting evening, with a great deal of shouting, cheering, and drinking, but the tension became almost unbearable when the Illinois returns began to come in. Bill Sorum was so agitated that he began lifting weights in front of the television set. Douglas Hyde viewed these very American proceedings with an amused eye. But despite the circus intensity of the occasion, the spectators had to go home without knowing the outcome. They would not find out until the next morning that their man had won.

Elated as he was by what seemed a happy turn in both national and personal matters, Percy by December was beginning to suffer from the postpartum blues and a gnawing anxiety about what to do next. He seems to have tinkered briefly with what he described to Shelby Foote as a science-fiction fantasy, perhaps a premature cast in the direction of

Love in the Ruins. Some of his time was taken up with doing the last work on an article that he had submitted to *Psychiatry* magazine in 1959 and that was scheduled for publication in February of 1961.

Appearing in *Psychiatry* was important to Percy because the journal was associated with Harry Stack Sullivan and his interpersonal approach, an approach to which Percy felt intellectually indebted. Percy, believed that his ideas about language could contribute to Sullivanian theory. Perhaps the most interesting aspect of the essay was Percy's dissection of the therapeutic situation, particularly of the ways in which a misplaced faith in scientific authority and objectivity shaped the relationship between the analyst and the patient, sometimes to the detriment of the latter. Percy's thoughts about the "seductions of theory" were not only illuminating. They had practical application to a clinical study of schizophrenia in which he would later participate.

On April 7, 1961, Angus Cameron informed Miss Otis that copies of *The Moviegoer* were being sent out. (Knopf had printed fifteen hundred copies for the first edition.) He also let her know that he had prepared promotional copy for Mr. Knopf's *Quarterly* pointing out the connection between Walker and Will Percy. "I tried to tie this book up, and not in any way that's invidiously comparative, either, with the two outlooks of two generations of Southerners which Alfred A. Knopf has had the pleasure of publishing." Perhaps the most encouraging news Cameron had to report was that an old friend of Knopf's in New Orleans had been sent an early copy of the book and had raved about it. "This friend pointed out that it was in his opinion 'the first American novel which can be called Existentialist which hasn't one word of philosophy in it.' " The elderly New Orleans gentleman clearly did not know his Kierkegaard, but Cameron took it as a good sign that an intelligent reader had found the philosophy unobtrusive.

The early reviews were favorable—not gushes exactly but respectful appreciations of the author's intelligence and his literary skill. One of the first and most admiring reviews appeared in the May 19 issue of *Time:* "[H]e writes about New Orleans and the surrounding countryside as though he had created it, but that is almost the least of his virtues. The main fact is that his theme—the despair that attacks numberless people in their inmost minds—is handled with just the right degree of seriousness and humor, of rancor and indifference. . . . Percy has a rare talent for making his people, Negro, Jew, or Southern aristocrat, look and sound as though they were being seen and heard for the first time by anyone."

Not implausibly, Cameron hoped that more such reviews would stir up sufficient reader interest to justify Knopf's putting more money into promoting it. *The New York Times Book Review* chimed in with another favorable, if brief, evaluation on May 28, but as one Knopf staff member noted, the "sales response is light." It remained so. And not all reviews were laudatory. *The New Yorker* gave the book a brief notice and complained, rather archly, that Percy's prose "needs oil and a good checkup."

Taking their cue from the Kierkegaard epigraph, most critics concluded that the novel was a study of existential anguish. Only a few caught on to the fact that Percy was pointing the way beyond despair. One of them, Edwin Kennebeck, writing in *Commonweal*, understood exactly what movies meant to the central character. Binx Bolling, he wrote, "can bestow his extravagant appreciation on the images of John Wayne or Gregory Peck without being deceived about their quality. . . . His gift of appreciation derives from an honest, personal, helpless evaluation of his life, his city, the popular culture of his nation, and the wide gray sickness that lies over the land." Even more perceptively, Kennebeck saw that Bolling's most unsentimental decision to marry Kate Cutrer (his aunt's stepdaughter) was a signal of "his search ended and his ordeal begun"—one signal among many that Bolling, without ever saying as much, has by the novel's end moved beyond the self-conscious pursuit of diversion to commitment.

Another relatively early review that gave Percy great pleasure was written by a friend of Caroline Gordon's, a Nashville writer named Brainerd Cheney, for the autumn issue of *The Sewanee Review*. As well as identifying the novel's religious argument, he located the book in a line of literary argument challenging the grandiose claims of humanism, a line leading from Dostoyevsky's *Notes from Underground* through Camus' *The Fall* to *The Moviegoer*:

> The formal similarity of these three novels is marked and, I think, significant. Each presents a narrator-hero who reveals himself to be a villain—or, more exactly, a damned man seeking salvation. They report on humanism, however, at different points in history. In *Notes from Underground* scientific humanism is first *exposed*. In *The Fall* it is recognized for what it is, but through pride that apes humility, still clung to. In the world of *The Moviegoer*, however, it has already been abandoned and our hero stumbles amid shards and glimmering confusion toward a clear but distant candle.

Cheney's review was as flattering as it was perceptive, but in some ways Percy was fortunate that it would be several more years before critics began to unravel the book's philosophical and theological strands. An overawareness of the intellectual content would have stood in the way of a direct encounter with the novel, and it was precisely in those fresh, unmediated encounters that readers felt *The Moviegoer*'s power and mystery. The less paraphrasable aspects of the novel, including the play of voices and the uncanny evocation of the times, were what seduced readers into seeing so much of themselves and their own predicaments in the novel.

The subtle, understated quality of the novel is only one aspect of the book's artistic achievement. *The New Yorker* notwithstanding, most readers found *The Moviegoer* exquisitely written. Though shorn of the rhetorical excesses of a Faulkner or a Wolfe, Percy's sentences had the vividness and force of a new kind of southern prose-poetry. This style came partly by way of Camus, Hopkins, and Agee—writers whose use of language Percy greatly admired. But it had its own distinctive stamp. Consider, for example, the description of the New Orleans suburbs as seen by Binx from the train, a model of precision and metaphorical surprise:

> We glide through the cottages of Carrollton cutting off back yards in odd trapezoids, then through the country clubs and cemeteries of Metairie. In the gathering dusk the cemeteries look at first like cities, with their rows of white vaults, some two- and three-storied and forming flats and tenements, and the tiny streets and corners and curbs and even plots of lawn, all of such a proportion that in the very instant of being mistaken and from the eye's own necessity, they set themselves off into the distance like a city seen from far away. Now in the suburbs we ride at a witch's level above the gravelly roofs.

Just as unmistakable was the novel's fine edge of irony and humor, an edge that often revealed more than a hint of nastiness. Percy had an eye as malicious as it was fine, and he could, through the eyes of Binx Bolling, be as unsentimentally ruthless about the old family servant Mercer as he could about Kate Cutrer's earnest and shallow fiancé Walter Wade. Binx Bolling is a snob who has raised snobbery to an almost dialectic art: His decision to live in the decidedly déclassé Gentilly is a deft put-down of Garden District dwellers like his aunt (whose house is modeled closely after the famous Toby-Westvelt house, which stands at the corner of Prytania and First and was built around 1832).

Percy had accomplished a remarkable feat in *The Moviegoer*. He had learned how to transform autobiography, his own and his family's history, into fiction. But neither *The Moviegoer* nor the novels to come were ever autobiographical in any obvious or literal way. They couldn't be, because the drama of his life was less a story of events than an internal struggle—psychological but ultimately spiritual—to find a ground of certainty and security, a struggle to find among his many selves an essential self, a soul. Percy had finally learned how to project this internal quest upon a believable fictive world.

While it is tempting to locate the authorial consciousness exclusively in Binx Bolling, Percy is strongly present in many of his characters. In certain ways, there is more of Percy in the character of Kate Cutrer than there is in Binx Bolling. Kate, who has lost her mother and one fiancé to death and who cannot find her footing in the world, certainly speaks for Percy's profoundest longing when she says, "What I want is to believe in someone completely and then do what he wants me to do. If God were to tell me: Kate, here is what I want you to do; you get off this train right now and go over there to that corner . . . and stand there for the rest of your life and speak kindly to people—you think I would not do it? You think I would not be the happiest girl in Jackson, Mississippi? I would." Her marriage to Binx, who she says is not only "not religious" but "the most self-centered person alive," makes sense only in terms of her own search. Like Percy, she sees the world and other people like a dialectician, sensing that Binx's ruthless self-centeredness will ultimately lead him beyond himself.

Percy shows up grandly in the minor characters as well. The young romantic whom Binx Bolling sees on the bus reading *The Charterhouse of Parma*, for example, is that vulnerable, agonized side of Percy that will occupy center stage in *The Last Gentleman*:

> Now he closes his book and stares hard at it as if he would, by dint of staring alone, tear from it its soul in a word. "It's—very good," he says at last and blushes. The poor fellow. He has just begun to suffer from it, this miserable trick the romantic plays upon himself: of setting just beyond his reach the very thing he prizes. For he prizes just such a meeting, the chance meeting with a chance friend on a chance bus, a friend he can talk to, unburden himself of some of his terrible longings. Now having encountered such a one, me, the rare bus friend, of course he strikes himself dumb. It is a case for direct questioning.

Percy's fiction is never more charged than in those scenes where his contending selves meet—or when versions of himself meet with those powerful voices from his past, with his brilliant but lost father or with his idealistic and demanding Uncle Will. At such moments Percy's prose comes closest to poetic.

• • •

As remarkable a work as *The Moviegoer* was, it seemed to create only a ripple of interest among the reading public. Its admirers were avid but few. Percy did not take this badly. He had never expected that he would write a best-seller. Besides, the publication of the novel had given him what he needed most: a sense of concrete accomplishment, certification of his writerly credentials, and even a clearer sense of direction. Now it seemed less frivolous to write fiction as well as philosophical essays. Indeed, by the summer of 1961 he was writing both in tandem, a novel in the morning and a book of philosophy in the afternoon.

The summer kept him busy with more mundane matters as well. The year before, not long after bringing his family back from Florida, Percy began to be concerned about the dangers of Military Road. It was a narrow, heavily traveled highway with a number of treacherous curves, and the stretch between town and Percy's house had been the scene of many accidents, including one that had taken the life of a neighbor. The prospect of Bunt's negotiating the road several round trips a day— taking Mary Pratt and Ann to St. Peter's, among other trips—was not a happy one. Percy began looking for something closer to town. His timing could not have been better, because a widow living on Old Landing Road only a mile or so from the heart of town had decided to sell her place and the several acres of land it sat on. Mrs. Clarissa Grima's house was a distinguished-looking brick chateau with a small pond and well-tended shrubs in the front and a wide bend of the Bogue Falaya about thirty yards from the back door. Best of all, the house was only a few blocks from the girls' schools. Concerned about the price, Percy thought it would be wiser to buy the house but not all of the surrounding property, but his friend Chink Baldwin convinced him to extend himself and buy the whole package, advice that Percy would come later to appreciate.

The move to the new house was put off until the summer of 1961 to give Percy time to finish the book and to sell the house on Military Road. (The man who bought it, George Cross, an executive and engineer with Bethlehem Steel, soon became one of Percy's close friends.) Percy left the old place with a pang of sentimental regret. It was where he and Bunt had built a life and started a family. And it was where he had begun his serious work. Unlike the new house, which was grand of aspect and would take some getting used to, the old house had seemed to be a natural fit, modest but commodious. One thing Percy gave up in the move was his own workroom. The new house had one large central room with two bedrooms at one end and another bedroom and the kitchen at the other. In addition, there was a large screened porch off the central room and an unfinished attic. But though the rooms were themselves quite capacious, with high ceilings and tall windows, there were few of them. Lacking an office, Percy set up shop in the bedroom, writing on the bed and typing at a small table he installed next to the large secretary he had inherited from Uncle Will. It seemed strange, amid all this grandness, not to have his own room to work in, but Percy adapted in the same way he always did.

As fall came, he was well into something that he tentatively called *The Fall Out,* an early version of *The Last Gentleman,* but when his friend Foote was in New Orleans in late October to give a speech, Percy let him know that he was not very pleased with it. Once again, he was groping his way forward and not at all confident that he had the makings of a good book. All the same, in January of 1962, Percy let his editor know that he had two books in the works. "What I would like to do is reach a point in one or the other where I can see through to the end, or at least over the hump—then send you what I've got. Would value your opinion." Angus Cameron wrote Percy to tell him he was eager to see either of the works in progress, but before Cameron's note got to him, Percy heard something more encouraging from Knopf. His novel—along with J. D. Salinger's *Franny and Zooey,* Joseph Heller's *Catch-22,* and eight other novels—had been nominated for the National Book Award for fiction.

The serendipity by which *The Moviegoer* came to be nominated and then awarded the National Book Award has entered American publishing legend. That the book was considered at all was a stroke of good fortune. Most books considered for the awards came to the panels by way of publishers' recommendations, and Knopf had not even nominated *The Moviegoer.* Rumor had it that Mr. Knopf had been "baffled and somewhat irritated" by the novel, a disposition that poor sales only reinforced. He certainly did not consider it prize-worthy.

Unlikely as it sounds, *The Moviegoer* won the National Book Award in large part because of writer A. J. Liebling's interest in Earl Long and Louisiana politics. Having finished a book on the colorful and corrupt governor, Liebling happened to read a review of *The Moviegoer* that mentioned the book's New Orleans setting. Liebling bought a copy of the novel, read it, and was so impressed that he recommended it to his wife, Jean Stafford, who was then serving on the NBA fiction panel, along with Herbert Gold and Lewis Gannett. Stafford was equally taken by the novel and thought it far better than anything she had so far read. She asked the National Book Foundation to send copies of the books to the other two judges. When the three judges met in early March, they came swiftly and unanimously to the choice: *The Moviegoer.* (Because of the reporting of *New York Times* correspondent Gay Talese, it became part of the legend that Jean Stafford had convinced the other two judges to pick *The Moviegoer,* but in fact they came to the decision on their own, as A. J. Liebling made clear in a letter that appeared in the August 1962 issue of *Show* magazine.)

On March 8, five days before the award ceremony, Percy received a telegram from Harding Lemay of the National Book Foundation: "Congratulations," it began, "you have won Fiction NBA. Please call me immediately collect at Spring 76679 NYC after 5:30." Though asked to keep the news a secret, Percy naturally told his family and Shelby Foote. The day before the awards, Percy flew to New York alone, his wife having decided to remain at home with Ann. Once in the city, Percy was eager to make contact with the man he felt most grateful to, his former editor, Stanley Kauffmann. The two had actually met face-to-face the summer before while Percy was briefly in town on business. To show his gratitude, Percy had taken Kauffmann to the Plaza for lunch, but the meeting quickly turned lugubrious. Kauffmann had tried rather too strenuously to reassure Percy that *The Moviegoer* was a book to be proud of despite disappointing sales. "After about a half hour of trying to cheer him up," said Kauffmann, "I knew that he was feeling more sorry for me than he would ever possibly feel for himself. We parted, and sadly I thought that was that."

It wasn't, of course. Just before the ceremony on Tuesday, March 13, Kauffmann received a phone call: " 'Stanley,' a voice said, and I knew right away who it was. 'Walker,' I said. Then we both started laughing, and we laughed for two minutes solid. Those might have been the two happiest minutes I have spent in my life outside of my marriage."

The afternoon luncheon ceremony at the Astor Hotel proved to be somewhat less delightful. Percy's publishers, Alfred and Blanche Knopf, practically shunned their author. As A. J. Liebling observed, "When Percy . . . showed up to receive the award, his publishers treated him like an erring daughter with child at breast." Following the two other prize-winners—Alan Dugan for poetry and Lewis Mumford for nonfiction—Percy collected himself for the acceptance speech. Aiming for the light touch, he began his acceptance by admonishing the jury for giving him the award and thereby robbing him of the main source of the southern writer's creative energy: his "well-nourished rancor against Yankees." (Joke though it was, it was odd that Percy called attention to his southernness, an identification he was usually eager to shed.) Among his acknowledgments, Percy gave special thanks to Elizabeth Otis and to Stanley Kauffmann, "who contributed far beyond the call of duty and ten percent—in fact, I'd just as soon not say how much they did help me," and to "the house of Knopf, for their usual beautiful job of book-making, and my wife, for reasons known to her." Alluding to his days as a pathologist at Bellevue, Percy then ventured a few thoughts on the similarities between the career he almost had and the one he had ended up in:

> Now, I'm not recommending that novelists of the future serve their apprenticeships in the Bellevue morgue, and I'm not saying that our culture is dying and all that remains is to cut out the organs and see at last what was wrong. . . .
>
> But since it seems appropriate to say a word about *The Moviegoer*, it is perhaps not too farfetched to compare it in one respect with the science of pathology. Its posture is the posture of the pathologist with his suspicion that something is wrong. There is time for me to say only this: that the pathology in this case had to do with the loss of individuality and the loss of identity at the very time when words like the "dignity of the individual" and "self-realization" are being heard more frequently than ever. Yet the patient is not mortally ill. On the contrary, it speaks well for the national health that pathologists of one sort and another are tolerated and even encouraged.
>
> In short, the book attempts a modest restatement of the Judeo-Christian notion that man is more than an organism in an environment, more than an integrated personality, more even than a mature and creative individual, as the phrase goes. He is a wayfarer and a pilgrim.
>
> I doubt that I succeeded, but I thank you for what you have done.

Percy's stomach never held up well under tension; anxiety triggered a chronic affliction, diverticulosis. In the various pictures of Percy posed with the two other award recipients, he looked distinctly uneasy, pained, and even more stooped than usual.

At the reception immediately following the ceremony, Percy was surprised to find that Shelby and Gwyn Foote had come up to be present at his moment of glory. That took some of the edge off the occasion, but then Percy had to gird himself for another ordeal later in the evening. It was customary for Knopf prize-winners to be invited to Mrs. Knopf's apartment for a post-award celebration. At these crowded affairs, Mrs. Knopf would at some point ask the honored guest to autograph a copy of his or her book for her personal library. This was an established ritual, and Percy dutifully appeared. As the evening wore on, however, it became increasingly obvious that Mrs. Knopf was not going to ask the author to sign his book. Percy, fearing that she had forgotten, approached the formidable Blanche and asked if she would like him to sign her copy of the novel. "Oh, no," Mrs. Knopf replied, "that won't be necessary. I only get the signatures of our foreign authors." Percy was not the only person present who knew he had been snubbed. One of them, Robert Giroux, an editor at what was then known as Farrar,

Straus & Company, was delighted to make Percy's acquaintance. Possessed of a discerning literary eye, Giroux had an impressive list of authors writing for him, including a number of Catholic writers, Thomas Merton among them. Given the Knopfs' performance, Giroux had good reason to think that Percy might one day come looking for a new publisher.

Percy's obligations continued into the next day. He rose early in the morning to appear on *The Today Show,* an occasion for which his wife had bought him his first and only pair of over-the-calf socks. (Henceforth he would beg off TV appearances by pleading that he didn't have the right kind of socks.) The exchange between the *Today* host and Percy was memorable for two things: the host's confusion over Percy's name (he repeatedly called him Doctor Walker), and Percy's response to the question of why the South produced such good literature ("Because we lost the war"). Percy met the Footes after the show and was assured that his performance had been fine, but Percy had found the experience as disagreeable as he had feared it would be. To soothe his nerves, he drank, the bourbon bringing the desired peace of mind but aggravating his stomach problem. By the next day, his last in New York, Percy was feeling so out of sorts that he canceled a breakfast with Stanley and Laura Kauffmann. He was happy to board the plane and head back to Covington.

Percy found it hard to make sense of the experience he had just been through. Having written so perceptively about the mechanisms of the American culture "machine," he had now been subjected to its workings —awarded, feted, written about, televised, and launched into the world as a "celebrity." As a prize-winning author of a serious first novel, Percy would hardly qualify as a major celebrity; to most Americans he was still an unknown figure. But however modest his elevation in the world, he now had a public identity, and in myriad ways, both large and small, he would have to come to terms with the consequences. This was no small challenge to a private man who had lived in relative anonymity for forty-five years. Not that he abhorred his sudden recognition. He had wanted it more than he would like to admit. He had worked hard to accomplish distinction and would have been disappointed, perhaps even embittered, if he had failed. But success introduced new challenges to the delicate psychic and personal arrangements that had given order and direction to his life ever since he married Bunt in 1946. People now looked at him differently, even those Covingtonians who were his friends before the NBA. Old friends would claim that he was "just Walker," but he was not only "just Walker," even to friends and relatives. He had entered the hyperreality of the celebrity. To a man already terribly self-conscious about his place in the world, a man astute at reading authenticity or falseness behind every word or gesture, it was exquisite punishment to see himself performing on the stage of his small fame. Moreover, as a man who had made a serious spiritual commitment, he knew that the world was now a more dangerous place, its snares and temptations all the more powerful.

Back in Covington, Percy packed up his family and took them to the Gulf Coast for a weekend, a trip that seems to have returned some of his equilibrium. The following Monday Percy wrote letters to Stanley Kauffmann and Jean Stafford, apologizing to the former for missing their breakfast. His words to Stafford were just as heartfelt: "Only this morning did I receive a clipping of Gay Talese's story in the Thursday Times about your and Mr. Liebling's remarks at the Columbia seminar. This is the first inkling I've had of what happened." Now understanding the circumstances of the prize a little more clearly, Percy wanted Stafford to know how grateful he was both to her and to her husband:

> Knowing that you have already forgiven my obtuseness, I will ask you to pass on to Mr. Liebling the gratitude which I am only just now making out the dimensions of. . . . If I understand it correctly, had it not been for Mr. Liebling (and his recent interest in Louisiana), the Moviegoer might never, would never have been considered. To think then, that if it hadn't been for old Earl—etc. For the first time I feel kindly toward the old Longs.

Percy would soon have even more reason for thinking kindly of the Longs. Sales of his books in hardback began to pick up, and Popular Library bought paperback rights and was printing around two hundred thousand copies for its first run. Having more money was an unalloyed pleasure, allowing Percy to take his family West for part of the next summer—a trip that would include a short session for Ann at the Hear Foundation in Los Angeles and the ritual visit to Disneyland. Equally pleasing were the unexpected notes and letters from admirers of *The Moviegoer*. Perhaps none was more gratifying than the one that came from a fellow graduate of the Caroline Gordon school of writing, Flannery O'Connor, dated March 29:

> Dear Mr. Percy,
> I'm glad we lost the War and you won the Nat'l Book Award. I didn't think the judges would have that much sense but they surprized me.

Percy could feel confident that Flannery O'Connor was one reader who "got" his book, but he felt increasingly uncertain about how many other readers did. Even the second round of reviews that came out after the prize seemed to reduce Binx's problem to a psychological one. The reviewer for *The New Leader* went so far as to suggest that Binx might have profited from a little time on the psychoanalytic couch. John Crosby, writing for the *New York Herald Tribune*, suggested that Binx was an "anti-hero," not unlike the protagonist of John Updike's *Rabbit, Run.*

Such reviews perplexed—and to some extent troubled—the moralist in Percy. While committed to the integrity of the work of art, Percy still did not believe that art existed as its own justification. The end of art was knowledge, which to Percy was knowledge of the Christian message. But how was he to make clear this message without debasing the art? A letter of praise from Caroline Gordon prompted Percy to reflect upon his quandary, and his response to her is perhaps the most explicit statement he ever made about the dilemma facing the Christian artist:

> Your letter has the effect of encouraging me to expectorate a chronic bone-in-the-throat. It has to do with my main problem as a fiction writer. Actually I do not consider myself a novelist but a moralist or a propagandist. My spiritual father is Pascal (and/or Kierkegaard). And if I also kneel before the altar of Lawrence and Joyce and Flaubert, it is not because I wish to do what they did, even if I could. What I really want to do is to tell people *what they must do and what they must believe if they want to live.*

This desire would seem to be a recipe for artistic disaster, no matter how sympathetic one might be to Percy's moral and religious position. Percy seems to have realized this as well. He knew what Gordon's position was —that one should not strain to deliver the Christian message but "do what Augustine said: love God and do as you please." Percy nevertheless wondered if this strategy were adequate when his novel's "most enthusiastic admirers were precisely those people who misunderstood it worst." Somewhat melodramatically, he concluded that his novel was unsuccessful, "since it apparently failed of its primary purpose: that it was meant to be a novel of hope in the midst of pagan despair." Percy went on to suggest two reasons for the failure. The first was the difficulty of "suggesting a bridge or a religious yea-saying" once he had established the "flip-savage satirical tone," a problem that Shelby Foote had pointed out as one of the book's weaknesses (though he saw this as a structural problem rather than a theological one). The other had to do with what Percy described as "threadbareness of religious words," beginning with the word God:

When the holy has disappeared, how in blazes can a novelist expect to make use of it? Holderlin said that God had left us and I think that one can give this a Catholic reading that though he has not left us, his name is used in vain so often that there remains only one way to speak of him: in silence. Perhaps the craft of the religious novelist nowadays consists mainly in learning how to shout in silence. That plus what Jack Bolling called learning how to place a good kick in the ass. As far as I'm concerned, the latter comprises 90% of my vocation and my next novel shall be mainly given to ass-kicking for Jesus' sake.

Percy's declaration of his intentions is more than a literary statement. It suggests an almost hieratic ambition to preach the word, to spread the Good News, an ambition that would seem to be at odds with his frequent and modest disavowals of any authority to preach. Percy usually maintained, after Kierkegaard, that only those with apostolic authority could tell people what "they must do and what they must believe if they want to live." As he told one interviewer, "A novelist least of all has the authority to edify anyone or tell them good news, to pronounce Christ King." Yet here, in his letter to Gordon, Percy expressed a desire to move beyond the category of the artist (the "genius," in Kierkegaard's terminology) and to become an apostle—or at least to engage in the activity that he at other times claimed was reserved for the apostle. This striking inconsistency on what was clearly for Percy an important theological point can only raise questions. One cannot help seeing a certain spiritual hubris in Percy's stated ambition. At the very least, his becoming spiritual modesty was at odds with a more authoritarian urge to tell people what they must do.

Percy had come up against a challenge that he would face for the rest of life: How was he to be a moralist without moralizing? In fact, he had met this challenge brilliantly in *The Moviegoer*, granting his characters (and also his readers) the freedom to come of their own accord to the vision of truth that is offered at the novel's end. Thanks to his generosity toward his characters, we are not even certain how fully or "sincerely" the central characters, Binx and Kate, have come to this truth. Binx, as one critic has noted with dismay, is "deficient in charity" even at the novel's end. But this is a flaw neither of the novel nor of the religious vision that underlies it. Percy's point, quite clearly, is that Binx is still free within his faith, free even to lose it. Faith certainly does not guarantee a nicer person. Nothing is guaranteed. Nor is there any way for mere mortals to judge the spiritual conditions of others. What Binx says about a black man whom he observes entering and leaving a fashionable church on Ash Wednesday is true of what Percy, at his most clear-sighted moments, thinks of all mankind:

I watch him closely in the rear-view mirror. It is impossible to say why he is here. Is it part and parcel of the complex business of coming up in the world? Or is it because he believes that God himself is present here at the corner of Elysian Fields and Bons Enfants? Or is he here for both reasons: through some dim dazzling trick of grace, coming for the one and receiving the other as God's own importunate bonus?

It is impossible to say.

The question is why Percy could not remain content with this modest vision of what can be said and done about the spiritual lives of other people. Why did he feel bad about the open-endedness of his novel, an open-endedness that richly captures the ambiguities and possibilities of life as most of us know it? Perhaps what we hear in Percy's letter to Gordon is one of the important struggles within the man: the philosopher voicing discontent with the novelist (and the Puritan Calvinist with the more accepting Catholic). Percy the philosopher hovered slightly above life, supporting through logic and science the moral order he had come to believe in. The philosopher craved clarity, certainty, the purity of abstract formulation. But Percy the novelist had to be vulnerable to the murkiness and ambiguity of life, to the complications of memory, and to the inchoate whisperings of the heart. It was precisely this tension between artist and philosopher that made Percy into such an interesting moralist. But it was not easy living suspended between the two poles.

12

Peregrinations

———◆———

The falcon cannot hear the falconer.

—W. B. YEATS

In the spring of 1962, Percy found himself with a case of second-novel jitters. To some extent, this was nothing more than the generic affliction of the American writer. However many times it has been disproved, the bleak adage that there are no second acts in American literature has given anguish to even our more confident writers. That Percy saw himself as a certain kind of novelist—that is, as a moralist—made his predicament seem all the more precarious. Dissatisfied as he was with the misreadings of his first novel, he had good reason to wonder whether he could make his case any more artfully than he had in *The Moviegoer*. The garland of the National Book Award certified his attainment, at least in the world's eyes. Yet Percy had his reasons for pressing on. Pride was one. He wanted to prove that he could do it again. As he confessed to Jean Stafford many years later, "Maybe the main reason I tried hard on two more novels was to prove you were not batty."

Percy had made a somewhat sluggish start on a second novel even before winning the NBA, but the award challenged him to silence the doubters, including, most pointedly, his own publisher. There was a formal challenge as well. Having proved his hand at first-person narrative and the small canvas, he wondered if he could master the more difficult third person and a wider panorama. ("I am going to need all the help I can get for the novel I am working on now," he told Caroline Gordon in April, "since I am shifting from the colloquial 'I' narrator to the omniscient and so am discarding much of the armor you spoke of.") Finally, too, we must not discount his own professed dissatisfaction with *The Moviegoer*, specifically his concern that his point had been insufficiently clear. Getting a thing right was always one of Percy's main concerns, in fiction as well as in philosophy.

Clearly, though, it still worried Percy that he might be repeating himself, and he let Stanley Kauffmann know as much when he sent him a copy of the first 148 pages of the work-in-progress, then titled *Ground Zero*. Kauffmann responded with encouraging words, advising Percy to carry "a loaded automatic at all times to shoot at once and without mercy anyone who tells you that this book is merely a continuation of, or reminiscent of, THE MOVIEGOER." Among its virtues, Kauffmann believed that the new novel showed a greater degree of formal control than the first one had, although Percy's former editor did register one concern:

> Generally: In a novel of this kind ("of this kind," indeed!) there is a risk, a kind of worry in the experienced reader, that the author's ingenuity will give out before the end. The book seems a sequence of adventures, a kind of *internal* picaresque novel, rather than a tightly constructed plot, or even a fairly tightly constructed one whose general dynamics are clear by this point. . . . You can sustain the book in two ways (and forgive me if I sound magisterial). First, by having at this point a clear idea of where the action is going. Second, more important, by having the thematic action, the rationale, the purpose of the book clearly in mind. . . . This may seem a rather dull bit of advice but it is easy to overlook when you're sort of exploring life *with* a character, as you are, sort of discovering what's going to happen *as* it happens. That's fine, as long as you know more about the cosmos of the book than Bill Barrett does, and are, for this novel, the god descended to earth in man-form to make the journey alongside but with a knowledge of what's past the horizon.

With his usual perceptiveness, Kauffmann had discerned the direction and shape of the novel to come. Yet he underestimated Percy's clarity about his intentions. Percy knew very well where his novel was heading. He knew he was writing about the wanderings of a lost southern romantic, a spiritual as well as physical odyssey that would lead the troubled protagonist to a vision of possible salvation in the act of baptism (not the protagonist's baptism, as in *The Gramercy Winner*, but the baptism of another of the novel's characters). To some extent, Percy's model was Dostoyevsky's *Idiot*, although Percy envisioned a character even worse off than the epileptic holy fool, Prince Myshkin. Myshkin at least lives in a time when religion is still a recognizable force; he sees that the purpose of his life is a spiritual one. Will Barrett, living in a thoroughly secularized world, only dimly perceives that his life may have some meaning beyond this world.

We have seen prefigurations of the confused seeker in earlier works by Percy. He is the central character of the story fragment "Confessions of a Movie-goer," the fellow bus traveler in *The Moviegoer*, and possibly even the protagonist of the *The Charterhouse*, Ben Cleburne. This is a much softer and more vulnerable character than the cynical Binx Bolling (or the doctor-protagonist of *Love in the Ruins* and *The Thanatos Syndrome* or the embittered lawyer, Lance Lamar, in *Lancelot*). Williston Bibb Barrett may well be the person Percy might have become had he not made the commitments he made, a character who is always "setting beyond his reach the very thing he prizes." Like Percy, Barrett is the son of a suicidal father (not merely a fatal romantic, like Binx Bolling's father, who died over Crete in World War II while serving as a volunteer in the Royal Canadian Air Force). Barrett is a victim of excessive sensibility and awareness. A Princeton dropout who has signed on as a humidification engineer at Macy's while he undergoes psychotherapy, he is plagued by an assortment of nervous afflictions (amnesia, fugue states, strange muscular spasms), and suffers, as one of his many nicknames suggests, from a crippled will. His distance and detachment from life, and his self-assigned role as spectator and seeker after signs and portents, are established in the opening scene of the novel, as Will Barrett sets up his telescope in New York's Central Park hoping to see a peregrine falcon but instead seeing a woman with whom he instantly falls in love and with whose family his own fate will soon become entwined.

Kauffmann was right in concluding that *Ground Zero* was a kind of picaresque, but it is the oddest sort of picaresque, one in which the picaro, more *ingénu* than rogue, journeys in tandem with a family. Perhaps this was the only way a true southern picaresque could be written, with a family at its center, since it is almost impossible to disentangle southerners from the complex web of kin and relations. Will Barrett's thoughts certainly never stray far from familial matters. Not only does he ruminate upon his biological family as he journeys from New York to the South and then to the West; he also tries to comprehend the strange dynamics of the surrogate family, the Vaughts, to whose members he becomes variously attached. And one of the crucial questions of the

novel is whether—and how—he will marry one of the Vaught daughters, the lovely if somewhat vacuous Kitty.

Why, though, did Percy set out to write a picaresque novel? What
was he trying to establish through this strange tale of journey and adven-
ture? Quite clearly, the physical journal serves as analogue and frame for
a spiritual journey, the pilgrim's progress. The theme of search is as
central in the second novel as it was in the first, and it is grounded even
more obviously in the action. But there is also a slightly more mundane
purpose to the travel. By contriving a journey through an assortment of
American landscapes, Percy makes it possible for the reader to see Barrett and his afflictions within a larger cultural context. This, in turn,
obliges the reader to question whether Barrett's condition is merely a
peculiar malady, a strange psychoneurological disorder, or a condition
that is in various ways connected with a disorder in society itself. This
uncertainty is another aspect of the novel that links it with Dostoyevsky's *Idiot.*

Percy's attraction to the story of the wanderings of an alienated soul
clearly came out of his own experience. The years preceding his marriage
and conversion were years of peregrination, geographical, intellectual,
and spiritual. Living in New York City during medical school and between stays in Trudeau and Gaylord sanatoria, returning to Mississippi
and traveling about the state and nearby Tennnessee, setting out for the
West and a new life in New Mexico—all of these experiences form the
biographical palimpsest of the fictional wanderings that will take final
shape in *The Last Gentleman.* Place clearly matters a great deal in this
novel. It is crucial to the protagonist's effort to come to terms with
himself. Yet one of the novel's ironic truths is that place—geographical
and cultural—does not ultimately matter. Place is of ultimate importance only to those lost souls who hope that they can escape themselves,
a vanity to which Will Barrett, like Percy at an earlier age, is in varying
degrees attached. Yet to discover this truth one must first test the power
of place, and that in large measure is what Will Barrett does throughout
the novel. This testing begins with his marginal, anomic existence in
New York, continues with his passage through the hauntingly familiar
South, and concludes with his journey into the "pure possibility" of the
West.

Percy was grateful for Kauffmann's clear appraisal of the emerging
novel. He worked hard on the new novel for most of the summer,
breaking away only in July, when he took his family out to Los Angeles
so Ann could be fitted for a new hearing aid at the Hear Foundation.
Back in Covington by August, Percy returned to his novel. But *The
Moviegoer* was not quite ready to leave Percy alone. In September, he

learned that a Louisiana-born architect named Randy Cox was interested in turning the novel into a movie. By the strangest of coincidences, Cox, who lived and worked in New York, had asked Stanley Kauffmann to write the treatment, not knowing that Kauffmann had edited the novel. In fact, Cox had approached Kauffmann because he admired the latter's film criticism in *The New Republic*. Of course, when Cox learned about Kauffmann's involvement with the novel, he was delighted—and even more delighted when Kauffmann agreed to work with him. Kauffmann's connection with the movie project made it seem all the more attractive to Percy, who gave his former editor carte blanche to change whatever was necessary and even invited him and Cox to stay at the Bogue Falaya house when they came down in November. Kauffmann had strong ideas about how the book would work as a film and even about who would play the leading roles (Christopher Plummer as Binx; Jane Fonda as Kate). Unfortunately, all the efforts of Kauffmann and Cox came to nothing. Like many subsequent attempts to turn *The Moviegoer* and other Percy novels into films, this one foundered on the rocks of finance.

November was noteworthy for one other meeting, although it too proved to be something of a disappointment. Toward the end of the month, Flannery O'Connor came to Loyola University in New Orleans to deliver a short talk. Percy and Bunt were invited to a reception that was to follow. By all rights, it should have been a lively encounter. Fellow Catholics, fellow artists, fellow graduates of the Caroline Gordon School of Fiction, Percy and O'Connor had a great deal to talk about. In the annals of frustrating encounters, however, this one ranks regrettably high. To begin with, Percy and O'Connor were both bad at the quick and public encounter. They were the kind of people who need a little time and privacy to get a conversation going, and the occasion denied the possibility of either. In fact, they met in a crowded second-floor apartment shortly after O'Connor finished giving her reading. Although O'Connor took away fond memories of the talk—to her friend John Hawkes she described the Loyola audience as "superior"—it is hard to imagine that she thought much of the reception. The second-floor setting was in itself a piece of bad planning. O'Connor's lupus, then in an advanced stage, had left her all but crippled, certainly in no condition to take on a steep set of exterior stairs. Two people had a hard struggle bearing her up to the second floor. Once inside the room, a very tired O'Connor barely had time for more than a few friendly words with Percy, but they hit it off immediately, as Percy later related to his cousin Phinizy Spalding: "Went in a couple months ago to hear Flannery O'Connor. We had a drink with her after her lecture. When I said I had kinfolks in

Atlanta, she said, do you mean Phin Spalding? She is great. But I was
thrown at first by her deep Georgia accent."

"I liked her a lot," Percy later recalled, "but it was as though we never
had the chance to develop the friendship." O'Connor died a little over
a year and a half later, in August of 1964, but though Percy and she
never met again, Percy's admiration for her grew with the passing of
years. He thought of her as a model of personal courage and fierce faith,
as well as an uncompromising artist.

Apart from usual interruptions of daily life, Percy, now forty-six years
old, settled into one of his longest unbroken bouts of writing. Beginning
in the fall of 1962 and lasting through the summer of the next year, this
period of relative tranquility could not have come at a better time for
the sake of the book that he was working on, a book that posed more
artistic challenges than any other novel that Percy would write. It was,
for one thing, a tremendous challenge to Percy's inventive powers. A
journey narrative calls for adventures, and Percy always had trouble
thinking up dramatic vignettes. The strain of such invention led to some
peculiar gambits, perhaps the strangest of which is an episode involving
the "pseudo-Negro," a photojournalist with whom Will Barrett briefly
travels on his way to Birmingham. For this episode, Percy blatantly lifted
from John Howard Griffin's autobiographical account of his pigmenta-
tional masquerade as a black man in the South, Black Like Me. Percy did
so for satirical reasons. He wanted to poke fun at the bizarre extremes to
which well-meaning white liberals would go to establish their solidarity
with blacks, extremes which tended to be as artificial as Forney Aiken's
skin tone. The entire episode with Aiken and his collaborator, a Mail-
eresque writer named Mort Prince, is a pretty rough sendup of what
southerners often derisively refer to as "northern liberals." The effect is
to make these crusaders for racial justice seem as risible as a group of
vowel-twanging midwesterners whom Percy spoofs earlier in the novel.
(A true southern chauvinist, Percy cannot help depicting Americans
from other regions as one-dimensional, or very close to it.)

Percy was treading on delicate ground. It would be easy for an un-
generous reader to see the hand of a nasty reactionary at work in the
"pseudo-Negro" episode. In fact, though, the rather cynical view of
Yankee liberals does not signal any change in Percy's thinking about
civil rights and integration. It was wholly consistent with most of the
essays he wrote on the civil-rights issue for Commonweal. Percy's pro-
integration stand was firm. He had been horrified by the beating of
freedom riders in Birmingham in the spring of 1961 (which he took as
yet another reason for disliking his native city). But while Percy believed

that something had to be done to bring about integration, and that whites must play an active role in supporting these efforts, he had a lively horror of moral posturing and the inauthentic gesture.

Even though the mordantly drawn absurdities of northeastern radical chic are often quite funny, Percy was wise not to stretch many other parts of the novel to such satirical extremes. Had he done so, he would have damaged the dominant tone of the novel, the pathos that grows out of Will's predicament and the reverberations of his family's tragic history. Managing a long narrative with such potentially discordant tonalities was perhaps the greatest artistic challenge and achievement of this novel.

One reason Percy's satirical tendencies did not dominate the novel is that Percy, at least in the first years of the book's writing, was more at peace with his society than he had ever been—or, for that matter, ever would be again. Percy's faith in the country and the direction it seemed to be heading came from his unprecedented confidence in its leader. Even though Kennedy's presidency had started roughly with the disastrous Bay of Pigs invasion and a sluggish response to several civil-rights crises, he seemed to gain his footing in his second year of office. Rapid progress in the manned space program, the aura of renewed national purpose created by such programs as the Peace Corps, success in dismantling a number of remaining Jim Crow institutions and practices, and the confident handling of the Cuban missile crisis all redounded to the president's credit. Percy would later say of this brief idyll that it was the one time when he knew where he stood politically. Across the nation, there seemed reason to think that Kennedy's blend of realism and idealism, his tough-minded liberalism, would succeed, and Percy, as much as Shelby Foote, was caught up in Camelot fever.

Whether it was the propitiousness of the times or his own inner fire— or, possibly, both—Percy made great strides with his work-in-progress. Also helpful was the trip Percy took out West in the summer of 1963. In early July, Percy packed up his family in the blue Rambler and headed off on a trip that reminded him not only of his western expeditions with Foote but also of those trips he took in high school and at the end of medical school. The ultimate destination was White Grass Ranch in Jackson Hole, Wyoming, where Percy planned to meet his brother Roy and Roy's family, but there were many stops planned in both directions. The journey had its comic moments. On the way out, the family camped in Palo Duro Canyon, just outside Amarillo, Texas, Bunt and Ann bedding down in the car, while Walker and Mary Pratt slept in a tent. In the middle of the night, the Rambler's horn went off. Running to the locked car, Percy discovered that Ann's foot was pressing down on the horn, but he could wake neither her nor Bunt (who, hard of hearing in one ear, was sleeping on her "good" side). Only after a great deal of rocking and pounding did Percy pull Bunt out of sleep and restore peace and quiet to the canyon.

The trip also included a pass through Santa Fe, Percy pointing out the places he had stayed in 1946. When they finally reached White Grass Ranch, Percy had the chance to show off his riding skill. Marveling at how "natural" her father looked in the saddle, Mary Pratt thought that he seemed like a perfect cowboy. It is easy to understand how Mary Pratt thought this. The slouched posture, the laconic speech, the vigilant eyes, the coiled intensity behind the low-key manner all suggested the style of a cowboy as played by Clint Walker or Montgomery Clift. Percy the avid Western fan knew the role well, and played it magnificently. He even plucked cowboy songs—"Little Joe the Wrangler" and "Streets of Laredo"—on a guitar that he had bought for Mary Pratt in Los Angeles the year before. The trip, besides being fun, had practical value, providing Percy with a fresh stock of imagery that he could use in the western scenes of *The Last Gentleman.*

Percy allowed himself to do very little other writing while he was working on his second novel, although in the early winter of 1963, he wrote a short article for *Commonweal* about the reissue of Bruce Barton's best-seller of 1925, *The Man Nobody Knows.* By the summer he reported to Shelby Foote that he was pleased by what he had written on his novel, even though he was a little dismayed by the irregularity of his output. Foote sent reassurance and encouragement:

> Delighted to hear youre hard at it. How many hours you work a day is nothing; what matters is that youre at it. I always assume whatever we do is right for us, and I know for a fact that some of the best things Ive done have been the result of delays—happy things that came to me because I waited: not because I wanted time to think or anything like that, but just because I waited for no reason at all except apparent laziness. I always remember Keats: "Poetry has to work out its own salvation in a man," and that if it didnt come as naturally as the leaves on a tree it had better not come at all.

Ever faithful to the religion of art, Foote was at something of an intersection in his own career. Having completed the second volume of his trilogy in the spring, Foote, along with his wife and their one-and-a-half-year-old son, Huger, would be going in the fall to Washington, D.C., on a Ford Foundation fellowship. The grant would support him as playwright-in-residence at the Arena Stage while he dramatized parts of *Jordan County.* Foote was eager to get out of Memphis, and in fact had been contemplating moving permanently to Gulf Shores on the Alabama coast. "I feel death in the air in Memphis," he complained to Percy, "and I'm beginning to hate the one thing I ever really loved—the South. No, thats wrong: not hate—despise. Mostly I despise the leaders, the pussy-faced politicians, soft talking instruments of real evil. . . . I want to go live by the Gulf."

Percy shared Foote's disgust with the George Wallaces and the Ross Barnetts, but he was cautious to avoid introducing too much about the politics of race into his novel. While the race question is never far from the action in *The Last Gentleman,* whether it comes out in the complex relationships between white employers and black servants or in a violent scuffle in a bar in Barrett's hometown of Ithaca, one point of the novel is, precisely, that race cannot be reduced to an "issue."

A subject somewhat more peripheral to the central concerns of *The Last Gentleman* is psychiatry, though it is lightly satirized at the beginning of the novel through the character of Will's doctor, Dr. Gamow, and the character Sutter Vaught is himself a "failed" psychiatrist whose unorthodox (yet successful) methods of treating patients had led to the revocation of his medical insurance and his change to pathology. Given Percy's skepticism about the presuppositions and practices of psychiatry, expressed among other places in the two-part esssay he wrote for *America,* it may seem surprising that he allowed himself, beginning in the summer of 1963, to be drawn into a psychiatric research project. Toward the end of August, he received a letter from the chief of clinical studies at the National Institute of Mental Health, Dr. Gentry Harris, asking Percy if he would be interested in serving as a consultant in a "study of the therapy of schizophrenic patients." The teasing part of the offer was Dr. Harris's stated reason for coming to Percy: "I have been interested for some time in your work on symbolic structure, particularly the implications of your 'tetradic model,' " Harris announced in the first line of his August 23 letter. Harris was referring to the essay that Percy had published in the February 1961 issue of *Psychiatry,* "The Symbolic Structure of Interpersonal Process," and it clearly intrigued and flattered Percy that a practicing medical researcher had taken an interest in his ideas. That Harris was interested in exploring the "Helen Keller effect" in relation to schizophrenics further piqued Percy's curiosity. Couching his response in a number of modest disclaimers ("I am not a psychiatrist or even a physician. I am a novelist by trade and a theorist of behavior only by avocation") and qualifications ("I hardly see the feasibility of running back and forth to Washington"), Percy wrote back to say that he would be willing to review "tapes, histories, papers, etc.," and in any other way "contribute to the discussion at long range."

A long-range contribution proved to be perfectly acceptable to Dr. Harris, who was not bothered by the fact that Percy was a novelist. As it came out in the psychiatrist's next letter, Harris's intellectual interests and background were in many ways similar to Percy's. Born in 1920, Harris had studied literature at the University of North Carolina, taken his medical degree at the Medical College of South Carolina, and done psychiatric research "mainly with David Rioch, some of it under combat conditions during the Korean War and under garrison conditions in Japan." Another point of sympathy was Harris's "growing dissatisfaction with the limitations of the classical scientific approach to human problems." To get beyond these limitations, Harris delved into ethology, communications theory, and even (as it came out later) the semiotics of Charles Sanders Peirce, a philosopher whose ideas would figure increasingly in Percy's own language theory.

In early October Harris wrote again with an outline of what he hoped Percy would do:

> The gist of my present proposal is that you could become acquainted with the background of one to three families one member in each of which carries the label of "schizophrenia," and that thereafter at intervals of two months, you could furnish an analysis of the symbolic structure and functioning of each family with particular attention to changes in the patients' symbolic structure.

The rather formidable phrase "symbolic structure" meant, quite simply, the unstated (and partly unconscious) rules governing the use of language—both the language of the individual patient and the linguistic "world" that comes into being when a patient encounters a professional therapist in a scientific setting. In other words, Percy's job was to read and decode the linguistic performance of various members of a special "intersubjective" community. The object was to reveal not only how this particular language game worked but to determine how it affected the various players, the professionals as well as the schizophrenic patients and accompanying family members. Percy found the proposal to his liking. "I should be very glad to receive whatever material you might wish to send me on your 'families,' " he told Harris, reminding him again that he could only work part-time on the project. Harris let Percy know that he would send the first tapes in January.

Well before he received his first tapes from Gentry Harris, though, Percy would live through a national trauma that would have a decisive effect on his life and work. On Friday, November 22, Percy joined his brother

Phin for a weekend retreat at Manresa monastery in Convent, Louisiana. Just as the retreat was getting under way, a priest announced the news of John Kennedy's assassination in Dallas, Texas. Percy, like everyone else on the retreat (and, for that matter, in the country), was stunned. He and Phin decided to return to their homes immediately. The priest, however, urged all the men to remain at Manresa to reflect on the enormity of the event. Most of the men, including Percy and his brother, agreed to stay.

Whatever reflecting Percy did that weekend was not enough to dissipate the anger he felt at the loss of the one president he had ever believed in. "A man," Percy later explained, "has to have some sort of passion, either a dislike of something or a like for something—love or malice—to have enough energy to write about it." Yet, Percy continued, "there has to be a fine balance because if he is too consumed with his like or dislikes, then his art will be overwhelmed by his own predilections." The experience that taught him this lesson was his reaction to the Kennedy assassination:

> The assassination affected me so strongly it caused me to lose a year of work. It changed the whole direction of the book. I got off on the wrong track, wrote a long thing about Kennedy, brought Kennedy into the book, and I actually wasted a year. It was no good. I had to back up. And it took me a year. It really threw me. I ended up with about four lines referring to Kennedy in the book. He was mentioned once. And that was the residue of about three hundred pages.

Percy, in fact, wrote about eight lines about Kennedy. They are presented as the thoughts of Sutter Vaught, the cynical, burned-out physician who believes only in science, pornography, and the quick thrill of the one-night stand. Will Barrett finds these thoughts in Sutter's room in Rancho la Merced outside Santa Fe. They are scrawled around the edges of a Winston ad that has been torn out of a year-old copy of *Life* magazine. Hoping that the scrawled words will be a message to him, Barrett reads them:

> Kennedy. With all the hogwash, no one has said what he was. The reason he was a great man was that his derisiveness kept pace with his brilliance and his beauty and his love of country. He is the only public man I have ever believed. This is because no man now is believable unless he is derisive. In him I saw the old eagle beauty of the United States of America. I loved him. They, the ——— (unreadable: bourgeois? burghers? bastards?), wanted him dead. Very well, it will serve them right because now—

It is easy to see why the novel could not have borne much more than this. The sudden mention of a particular politician's name is oddly inconsistent with the presentation, or transmutation, of contemporary history in the rest of the novel. Even though the novel is written in the third person (though not in the omniscient third person, as Percy had wrongly indicated to Gordon), the narrative voice is filtered largely through Will Barrett's somewhat otherworldly perspective. The action thus takes place in a time that seems both in and out of actual history—a sort of hazy, generalized 1960s. The mere mention of Kennedy is a jarring intrusion of the too-real upon this highly subjectivized period atmosphere. Having the Kennedy reference inscribed on a page from a year-old issue of *Life* seems almost to have been Percy's way of trying to keep the reference at some temporal remove from the fictional present. But Barrett's reaction to Sutter's reflections on Kennedy is almost that of the reader. ("He frowned, feeling suddenly put off and out of sorts. This was not what he was looking for and did him no good at all.")

Percy was risking a great deal when he tampered with the spell of his art—that almost otherworldly atmosphere that comes as much out of what is not said as out of what is. Percy's art was so much a matter of indirection and apt reticences that he had to walk a very careful line, guarding constantly against saying too much. Perhaps no reader more keenly appreciated that dreamlike quality of Percy's fiction than a man who, by coincidence, initiated a correspondence with Percy at precisely the moment Percy most needed reminding of what was so magical about his work.

Thomas Merton, the Trappist monk and poet, had come to know of Percy's work in late 1963 or early 1964, when a fellow Trappist visiting Merton's monastery, Gethsemani, in Louisville, Kentucky, had fallen sick and written to Percy asking him to send him a copy of *The Moviegoer*. Percy had obliged. After finishing the novel, the monk gave his copy to Thomas Merton—or Father Louis, as he was called within the order. Merton's first reaction to the novel is recorded in the January 18 entry of his journal:

> The great impact of Walker Percy's novel, *The Moviegoer,* is that the whole book says in reality what the hero is not, and expresses his existential awareness of what he is not. His sense of alienation, his comparative refusal to be alienated as everybody else is (not successful), his comparative acceptance of this ambiguity and failure. This is a book full of emblems and patterns of light (the misty place where they fish, or rather, his mother fishes, is like a vague movie too).

This remarkable response to Percy's first novel, at once intellectual and deeply felt, goes on to celebrate Percy's "authentic expression," his gift for reaching beyond what we already know into the "surplus" of what "we do not yet know, and what will come to be known in our saying it to someone who will reply." What Merton admired in Percy's realized art was a quality that reflected both Percy's method (his way of discovering what he had to say as he said it) and his philosophical convictions.

Happily for Percy, Merton chose not to keep his high opinion of *The Moviegoer* secret. In an undated letter probably written in late January, Merton let Percy know how much he liked his novel. Laudatory and funny—"For a while," Merton wrote, "I was going around saying it was too bad guys like Hemingway were dead as if I really thought it"—the letter was an even more straightforward celebration of Percy's art of indirection and reticence than the journal entry:

> You are right all the time, not just sometimes. You are right all the time. You know just when to change and look at something else. Never too much of anyone. Just enough of Sharon. The reason the book is true is that you always stop at the point where more talk would have been false, untrue, confusing, irrelevant. It is not that what you say is true. It is neither true nor false, it points in the right direction, where there is something that has not been said and you know enough not to say it.

Merton told Percy he was "one of the most hopeful existentialists" he knew of and that he considered it inevitable that an American existentialist "would have a merry kind of nausea," which was, he added, "truer than the viscous kind." Merton showed himself to be an uncanny reader. He liked the fact that the characters were free from authorial control: "I think you started with the idea that Bolling would be a dope but he refused to be, and that is one of the best things about the book. Nice creative ambiguities in which the author and the character dialogue silently and wrestle for a kind of autonomy." Merton, without knowing Bakhtin, was one of the first readers to appreciate the dialogic character of Percy's fiction.

If there was anything troubling to Percy about Merton's remarks, it was his unequivocal dislike of Aunt Emily. "As for Southern aunts if they are like that you can keep them," Merton observed. Callow as this might have sounded to Percy, who could no more dismiss Aunt Emily than he could Uncle Will, it was at least a refreshing change from all those glowing reviews of Aunt Emily that he got from a certain kind of southern reactionary. Still, as Percy would come to see over the years,

Merton was a more doctrinaire liberal than he was. Besides, Merton, the product of a bohemian background, would have had no reason to know that there really were the occasional Stoics who stood firmly by what they purported to believe. Percy, having known one, knew there was far more substance to the Aunt Emilys than Merton could see.

Altogether, though, Percy would have had trouble seeing Merton's letter for anything other than what it was: a model of literary courtesy and appreciation. Merton begged to see anything else that Percy wrote and asked him if he would like anything of his in return—"I do artworks very abstract, maybe you'd like one. Let me know if you like abstract brush and calligraphies." He even volunteered to get in touch with his French publishers, Le Seuil, if Percy had not yet been published in France.

This unexpected correspondence from a man whom Percy greatly admired served as a partial antidote to the shock of the Kennedy assassination two months before. It might not have put Percy back on the right track immediately, but it reminded him what his best track was. Percy let Father Louis know how much his letter had meant to him: "I am a slow writer, easily discouraged, and depend on luck, grace, and a good word from others." He gratefully accepted the offer of a calligraphy and Merton's contact with Le Seuil. The calligraphy, when it arrived, was hung on the wall above Percy's desk next to the motto from Kafka, "Warte!" ("Wait!"), an injunction in whose wisdom Percy profoundly believed. Work, to him, was vigilant waiting.

The recognition of people whom Percy admired was flattering; so was the increasing number of requests from magazines and journals for his work. Percy was particularly pleased when one of the editors of the newly revived *Southern Review*, Donald Stafford, wrote to him in early January expressing his admiration and a desire to see any of his future work. Percy was honored to be approached by the journal, which, in its first incarnation under Cleanth Brooks and Robert Penn Warren, had published such prominent writers as T. S. Eliot, Allen Tate, R. P. Blackmur, and Wallace Stevens. (As important as Percy's connection with the revived journal was his growing friendship with its new editor, Lewis Simpson.) Even though Percy was busy with his novel, he took time to review Richard Hughes's novel, *The Fox in the Attic*, for Andrew Lytle at *Sewanee Review*. Percy's witty consideration of the first book in the English author's projected series of philosophical-historical novels is interesting mainly for its dissection of the differences between the English and the French novel—the metaphysical tendencies of the latter and the solidly plotted and realistically grounded qualities of the former: "So that while it is all in a day's reading to come across a Frenchman in a

novel sitting in a cafe and gazing at his own hand and deducing therefrom a metaphysic, try to imagine an Englishman sitting in a cafe in
Brighton doing the same thing!" What intrigued Percy was that Hughes,
though English, had attempted to write a rather French novel of ideas,
and though the result was lumpy, with Big Thoughts clumsily stirred in,
it was surprising to Percy that an Englishman had attempted such a book
at all.

Despite the growing attention of the wider world—and its increasing
demands—Percy remained close to the circle of friends that had sustained him and his family for what was now closing on sixteen years. In
the early 1960s, for example, Percy began taking lunch with a group of
men on most Wednesdays, a group that included George Cross (the steel
man who had bought his house on Military Road), an insurance salesman named Billy Gibert, Chink Baldwin, and his brother Phin, who
was now teaching at Tulane Law School. What Percy particularly valued
about the Wednesday group, which usually met at the Riverside Café
next to Baldwin Motors or at the Tchefunkte Country Club, was the
simple, unaffected camaraderie. While all the men were smart and accomplished in their respective fields, they were not, by any stretch,
intellectuals. Most of the men were Catholic, but religion was not the
bond. The gruff, hard-joking, and often heated conversation was what
drew them together every week—that and the sheer unbuttoned fun of
drinking and smoking cigarettes around a long, drawn-out meal. (Percy,
despite his history of lung disease, was a notorious and shameless "bum-
mer" of others' cigarettes.) They were all men with strong opinions on
the issues of the day, and they felt free to go at each other when they
disagreed. Percy's growing celebrity gave him no special status. In fact,
the men enjoyed taking the stuffing out of him, and Percy was glad that
they did. Percy, who attended the lunches only occasionally at first,
could sometimes grow impatient with his fellow luncheoners, and he
would quite often fade out in the middle of a conversation, particularly
when he was hard at work on a novel. But remaining close to the men
of this group was important to his life and his work. The world of the
professional man, the man in the middle, was the world that most
interested Percy, and one way he remained in touch with it was by
attending to the manners, jokes, and crotchets of each man in the group.
   The attention of the wider world was even less successful in pulling
Percy away from his family. If anything, Percy was now playing an even
more important role in Ann's education. When the news came on in
the evening, for example, Percy would sit next to the TV and mouth
the voiceover segments of the broadcast so Ann could follow what was

going on. He would engage in an even more strenuous exercise when he took her to the movies, sitting in the seat next to her with a small pen flashlight, which he would train upon his lips while he "translated" those parts of the film Ann that could not lipread. There was, as Bunt Percy observed, a special bond between father and daughter.

Percy and Bunt, in addition to bird-watching and fishing, began, in early 1964, to work together on the schizophrenia project. In January, as promised by Dr. Gentry Harris, Percy began to receive tapes of the sessions with the schizophrenics and their families. In the evening, after the children were put to bed, Percy and Bunt would listen to the tapes, taking notes and comparing their impressions when they finished each series. Bunt Percy could see that her husband took his assignment seriously, and she soon found that she was as interested in the cases as he was.

Dr. Harris received more than his money's worth for Percy's contribution to the project. After Percy and Bunt finished a group of tapes, Percy wrote out detailed analyses of the sessions. In addition to addressing theoretical questions such as how the scientific authority of the psychiatrist shapes (and in some ways limits) the therapeutic situation, Percy brought his novelist's eye to the particularities of each participant, suggesting how an individual's mannerisms and traits affect others in the group. Percy's decoding of these social settings reminds us of one of the finer comic aspects of his fictional art:

> Mrs. G. has a flat Midwestern schoolmarmish way of saying things, in sharp contrast to Mr. G's colloquial Southern style. Mr. G, I judged, sounded much the same in the first family session as he did in the 100th, with his rather trite anecdotal barbershop style, his conventional idiom, his conventional mores, his conventional noble sentiments and even conventional laugh, heh heh heh. All of which clearly irritates Dr. A. Mrs. G on the other hand is more responsive to the cues of the therapeutic game. She catches on so well that she often switches over to the therapeutic team. In fact, there are times when she sounds a great deal like Miss H. I couldn't help wondering whether this happens often: one of the "lay" people catching on to the style of the therapist and imitating him.

Percy did this not simply for the sake of vivid description. He had strong ideas about how these sessions might break free of the limiting bonds of therapeutic "appropriateness" and become more spontaneous, allowing the schizophrenic patient to see that others were beset by fears and anxieties as well as by the more usual confusions and uncertainties of everyday life. Percy insisted on seeing the patient, J., as a troubled pilgrim, a castaway, and a wayfarer—that is, as a person in a predicament that, while in degree worse than that of a "normal" person, could be understood in normal existential terms.

While the purpose of the project was to study the breakdown of communication in a schizophrenic's family, Percy was quick to show how certain barriers to communication were needlessly established in therapy, scientific artificialities that were unnecessary and perhaps obstacles to the schizophrenic's breakthrough into a more successful use of language. Percy concluded his first report with a strong suggestion:

> The set of the patient in this sort of symbolic structure is such that he is peculiarly open to exemplary suggestion. It has already been noted that there do in fact occur some obvious imitative behaviors—in speech characteristics, placements-in-the-world like "scientists," etc. Why should not such a group also provide opportunity for samples of behavior—"unscientific behavior"—illustrating more cogent and realistic attitudes in ordinary life-situations? The patient often learns to imitate the scientist as scientist. Why not imitate the scientist as man? Something of the sort seems to be happening here.

Dr. Harris was grateful for the report he received from the Louisiana novelist. He suggested that with a little expanding and editing it could be a paper in itself. Percy was glad that he had done a good job, but he confessed to Harris that he had ulterior motives for joining the study. As he put it, his main interest lay "in the direction of what you call a meta-system and a metalanguage, and what I call a semiotic: namely, a single organon with which to speak and think of the whole spectrum of symbol-communication." Percy also confessed to his conviction that what then passed for semiotics—behavioristics, mathematical logic, and semantics—was grossly incoherent, and incoherent, as he would later make clear, because it failed to take into account the behavior of those who theorize, those who use symbols to explain the symbol using of others. Percy, in other words, was on the way to attempting to build a science of man, a radical anthropology, as he would sometimes call it, that would take a hard look at the "objective" position of the scientist-observer.

At the same time, Percy thought that his philosophical ambitions had therapeutic consequences. He believed that much of what ailed people psychologically stemmed from their inability to use language authentically—to use it as creatures naming, and thus knowing, their world in concert with other creatures. What was most interesting about Percy's involvement with Dr. Harris and the schizophrenia project was that it gave Percy the chance to test his theory.

Percy was so intrigued by developments in Harris's project that he made a special effort to visit Washington during what would be a very busy summer. By the spring of 1964, Percy was approaching the end of the first draft of his manuscript, which now went under the title of *Centennial,* and he hoped to send a copy of it to Elizabeth Otis by the end of June. At the same time, he was anticipating a month-long stint at the Clarke School for the Deaf in Northampton, Massachusetts, where Percy and his wife planned to enroll in Clarke's Third Annual Summer Institute Program for Teachers of the Deaf during the month of July while Ann received speech lessons at the school. Writing to Dr. Harris in May, Percy asked whether he could stop by NIMH toward the end of June or in early August to observe one of the sessions. As things worked out, the days on which Percy would be in Washington—June 21, 22, and 23—were days when there would be no sessions, but Harris asked the Percys to have dinner at his house on the evening of the twenty-second and encouraged Percy to return to the institute at another time.

Things went a little less smoothly when the Percys arrived in Massachusetts. On the first day of class, the instructor, Miss Marjorie Magner, discovered that neither of the Percys was, strictly speaking, a teacher. Since the class was specifically intended for teachers seeking certification and was already, with fifty students, too crowded, Miss Magner was furious that two interlopers had enrolled. Marching down to the administration office, Miss Magner insisted that the Percys be ejected. Cooler heads prevailed, and the Percys were allowed to stay on, soon becoming close friends with Miss Magner. The Percys grew even closer to Magner when she agreed, after intitial reluctance, to tutor Ann. Magner was as impressed with the ten-year-old girl as she was by Ann's parents. "What amazed me," Magner remembered, "was that a man with that kind of mind, with that kind of ability, would have such unusual patience with a linguistically delayed child. He would go around in circles to make sure Ann understood. They even had their own private code they would use to discuss things. He was not satisfied with Ann's knowing what was going on; she had to understand the 'whys' behind it, the reasons, the causes."

Sticking to his schedule, Percy sent off his manuscript to Miss Otis in early July, and a few days later he flew down to Washington to observe a session with one of the families. Percy was thrilled by what he saw, as he indicated to Harris in his next letter:

I don't believe I conveyed to you my overall impression of that session: the sense that muddy waters are clearing a bit and that relationships are becoming more manifest. The G's were firing straight from the shoulder. Even J. with his stalling was quite aware of it as such. It was exciting to watch.

Percy found it heartening that his modest suggestions for "problematizing" the therapeutic situation were making it possible for the participants in the family sessions to break out of the dead language that had dominated the earlier meetings.

All in all, it proved to be a productive summer. By observing Miss Magner, Percy had learned to conduct audiotape speech drills, and for the next two years he would send her biweekly tapes of his sessions with Ann, which Magner would analyze and return. As for his literary labors, Percy received encouraging words from Miss Otis and another member of the agency, Patricia Schartle, who had gone through the manuscript with a hard critical eye. Miss Otis indicated that she agreed with most of Schartle's criticisms, including her belief that Jamie Vaught's death should be shown at the end of the novel rather than merely related by Sutter. Otis hoped that Percy could finish the revisions by November and urged him to start thinking about whether he wanted to stay with Knopf. "I think my own feeling has pretty well crystallized—" Otis added, "that we should make every effort to move to another publisher, but let me know what you think when you know yourself."

Schartle, as Percy learned, was an intelligent, painstaking, and extremely helpful editor. She suggested cutting about 15,000 words out of the 130,000-word manuscript (and marked the specific cuts), asked for the elimination of certain superfluous characters, pointed out confusing or inconsistent points, suggested ways in which certain devices (the telescope and the Travel-Aire camper) should be further exploited, and as Miss Otis indicated, called for the dramatic presentation of Jamie Vaught's death. Schartle also voted strongly against the use of the Kennedy material, for reasons that Percy quickly saw were sound: "I believe it would be more in keeping with the original and genuine tone of the book if that excellent tone is sustained and there are no excursions to other points of view which decidedly jolt the reader, replacing in the case of the Kennedy material and the Nov. 22 date, the ironic and individual with prose that, though beautiful, belongs elsewhere."

There were some tall demands in Schartle's letter, but Percy went along with most of them. Even some of her less forcefully made suggestions caused Percy to do some serious reconsidering. For example, she wondered about the ironic effectiveness of the Civil War centennial scenes, a concern that caused Percy to mute that theme and even to search for another title for the novel.

Percy set to work on the extensive job of revising when he got back to Covington in the middle of August, breaking away with Bunt for a short visit to Shelby Foote in early autumn. Foote and his wife had left Washington in the preceding spring but instead of returning to Memphis had rented a house in Gulf Shores while an architect drew up plans for a permanent home that they were hoping to build in the area. By the time Percy and Bunt visited, though, he could see that Foote was having some difficulty settling into the small Alabama community. Tension over race and integration had been running particularly high that summer throughout the South. The slaying of three civil-rights workers, whose bodies were discovered in an earthen dam outside Philadelphia, Mississippi, on August 4, brought home to everybody just how deadly serious the issue was. Foote was enraged and disappointed by what the racists were doing to the South, and to show his colors he affixed a Lyndon Johnson sticker on his car bumper, a gesture that marked him as an "agitator." He soon found himself embroiled in name-calling arguments with fiery-eyed racists wherever he went—at the gas station or in the local stores. The rumor was that the Klan took a dim view of this "liberal writer" from Memphis. Not surprisingly, the conversations during Percy's visit—the first of three during Foote's Gulf Shores sojourn— were devoted to the race situation, although developments in Southeast Asia, and particulary the Gulf of Tonkin Resolution of early August, were a matter of growing concern to the two old friends. (All was not storm and passion. The two gossiped, drank, and joked whenever they got together; and Bunt and Gwyn became close friends during these Gulf Shores visits.)

If Percy had wisely decided to deal with the race question only indirectly in his novel, he soon got the chance to deal with it head on. In the fall of 1964, the Mississippi writer Willie Morris, who was then working as associate editor of *Harper's*, called Percy to see if he would be interested in writing an essay on Mississippi for a book that he was putting together to mark the one-hundredth anniversary of Lee's surrender at Appomattox. Morris added that some of the essays would be run in a special issue of *Harper's* in the spring of 1965. The offer was too good to resist, even though Percy was busy with his revisions. It was something Percy felt he should write about. Then, too, he knew he could draw from many of the things that he had already written about the South for smaller magazines, including "Stoicism in the South" and "The Southern Moderate." The resulting essay, "Mississippi: the Fallen Paradise" (published first in the book *The South Today: 100 Years after Appomattox* and then in the April 1965 issue of *Harper's*), would be Percy's fullest, and most finished, statement on the question of race, civil rights, and the South.

The *Harper's* assignment was not the only other obligation. Several years before, through his friend Father Clancy, Percy had made the acquaintance of a feisty, crusading Baptist minister named Will Campbell. The son of a poor Mississippi farmer, Campbell had attended Wake Forest, Tulane, and Yale Divinity School after service in the South Pacific during World War II. Briefly working as a pastor in Taylor, Louisiana, Campbell became a troubleshooter for the National Council of Churches in the late 1950s. As well as being the only white man present when Martin Luther King, Jr., founded the Southern Christian Leadership Conference in 1957, he escorted black children to class in Little Rock, Arkansas, in the same year. Because of his growing preoccupation with racial matters, Campbell parted ways with the National Council of Churches in 1963 and helped launch the Committee of Southern Churchmen. As Campbell saw it, the main purpose of the committee was to tackle the race question head on: "You can't proclaim the Gospels in a vacuum," he would say. An effective armtwister, Campbell convinced Percy to serve on the editorial board of the committee's journal, Katallagete. "I think a big reason he joined was that Tom Merton was on the board, and he wanted to meet him," Campbell somewhat modestly explained. In fact, Percy joined because he was impressed by Campbell and by what he so vigorously stood for. Percy soon discovered that his position on the editorial board was not simply honorary. Campbell required work of his board members. Shortly after signing Percy up, Campbell asked him to write on the failure of southern Christians to advance the cause of racial justice. Although up to his neck in the essay for Harper's, Percy could think of no reason to refuse.

With all of his extrafictional activities—the work on the schizophrenia project also continued unabated through the fall—it would have been difficult for Percy to meet the November deadline optimistically set by Miss Otis. At least, though, he could give her some good news. In late August, Percy received a letter from an editor at Farrar, Straus & Giroux, Henry Robbins, reminding him that he had met Percy at the NBA proceedings when he was then working for Knopf. Robbins hoped that Percy would consider FSG if he was looking for a new publisher. Percy wrote back to say that he was very interested in the offer and that he would send a copy of Robbins's letter to Miss Otis. Although Percy had been entertaining thoughts of parting with Knopf for some time, this, it seems, was the first decisive step toward a new house—and one that Miss Otis heartily approved.

Percy had another deadline looming before him in the late spring of 1965. For years, he had been promising Bunt and his daughters that he would take them to Europe. Unfortunately, with all his obligations, this did not seem the best year to make good on his word, but Mary Pratt would be going off to college the following fall and Percy could imagine himself postponing the trip indefinitely. After all, he was always working on one thing or another.

Timing wasn't the only problem. Percy harbored secret misgivings about returning to Europe. Memories of his last trip across the Atlantic —that fateful journey of 1934—were tinted with regret and sadness, particularly in light of the nightmare that the Nazi experiment had become. However unpleasant such memories were, Percy made reservations for the *Queen Mary* and a Southdown bus tour of England and Scotland, and once he made his plans he stuck to them.

In early June, Percy cleaned up last-minute details at home. He sent one more lengthy report to Dr. Harris and told him that he would be leaving for England and would not be back until around July 30. Then he sent a copy of the novel to Farrar, Straus. Toward the middle of the month, Percy drove his family up to New Jersey to Jidge and Sal Milazzo's house. There they left their car, and the Milazzos drove them to New York City, where the Percys boarded the *Queen Mary*.

The voyage over proved uneventful but enjoyable—and certainly much more comfortable than the tramp steamer of his first Atlantic voyage. Percy even struck up a friendship with one of his fellow travelers. Robert Drake, a thirty-four-year-old writer and professor of English at the University of Tennessee, happened to check the passenger list on the first day out. The name Walker Percy struck him immediately. He had read *The Moviegoer* when it first came out but had not been terribly impressed. Shortly thereafter, though, while he was interviewing Flannery O'Connor in Milledgeville, Georgia, the subject of *The Moviegoer* came up and Drake confessed to his lack of enthusiasm. "You'd better read it again," O'Connor said in her simple but absolutely authoritative way. Drake did. And on the second reading, he saw that O'Connor was right.

Eager to meet the author of what he had come to believe was a remarkable work of literature, Drake wrote a note to propose a meeting. The two men—both writers and southerners—hit it off, and Drake spent a goodly part of the voyage with Percy and his family. What he remembered above all was Mary Pratt's remarkable string of good luck: She seemed to win every game of bingo that she played. He also found Percy to be a natural, completely unassuming man. There was almost no literary talk between them—nothing certainly that could be called an intellectual discussion—although Drake did give Percy a copy of his short-story collection, *Amazing Grace*. (Percy had one further rendezvous with Drake after leaving the boat: He and Drake were taken to lunch at the Garrick Club by one of Drake's friends, an associate editor of the London *Sunday Times.*)

The Southdown Tour of England and Scotland was something of a nine-day whirlwind, but Percy appeared to enjoy himself. He seemed to have a natural affinity for the Scots, finding their blend of understated humor and pessimism congenial. The girls were less delighted. The boredom of tourism lay heavily on their young shoulders, and Mary Pratt missed her friends back in Covington. She grew even more unhappy when the family flew to Lourdes, France, at the end of the Southdown Tour. Percy and Bunt wanted Ann to be immersed in the waters, but when Mary Pratt took one look at the human suffering and the less-than-salubrious-seeming waters, she wanted immediately to leave. Percy, however, seemed fascinated by Lourdes. For perhaps the first and last time in his life, he invoked his medical credentials so that he could visit the clinics. He even became a volunteer stretcher-bearer. Mary Pratt could not understand her father's strange fascination with this place of misery and desperate hope. Devout a Catholic as she was, she thought that her parents' determination to submerge Ann in the filthy-looking water was daft. Although Ann was more hopeful, even she had misgivings about being dunked in the waters. But they all got through it. Mary Pratt breathed a sigh of relief when the family returned to England and the *Queen Mary*.

Back in New York, Percy signed a contract with Farrar, Straus and then drove his family north to Nantucket, Miss Magner joining them for the week they were there. By now, despite their rocky introduction, the Percys and Miss Magner were fast friends. Between two daily speech tutorials with Ann, the group spent most of their time on the beach. Miss Magner recalled that Percy read constantly and voraciously, even under the sun's steady glare.

While in Nantucket, Percy received letters from Henry Robbins and Bob Giroux, both praising the novel but calling for a radical revision of what was then called the Epilogue. Both editors disliked the tacked-on quality of the ending, and Giroux urged that the important "colloquy" between Sutter and Will come before Jamie's death. Above all, Giroux wanted the ending of *The Last Gentleman* to be more in keeping with the manner of the rest of the book, "casual, unforced, with the kind of surprises you're so good at."

When Percy got back to Covington around August 20, he found his five-thousand-dollar advance from FSG and the Fourth Report on the schizophrenia project from Gentry Harris. Both seemed to be abrupt calls to work. Percy vented some of his frustration over what he feared had been an unproductive summer to Harris:

It was for me an exhausting summer. My three women all wanted to go to Europe and I didn't much. And of course there were 10 million Americans in Europe plus the prosperous new European proletariat, all taking vacations, and it like to have killed me—what with carrying all the female baggage.

In the same letter, Percy talked with surprising candor about one of the things he was trying to accomplish in his novel, an aspect of the book that he thought would interest Harris. It was odd that Percy did so, because Harris, though very interested in Percy's philosophical writing, evinced almost no curiosity about his consultant's literary endeavors. It is possible, of course, that Percy spoke so candidly precisely because he knew that Harris wasn't terribly interested in his fiction. Whatever the reason, Percy said more about his intentions and designs in this letter than in almost any other that he wrote:

> Have also been at work trying to beat a novel into shape against a deadline. It is (among other things) about a psychiatrist who quits a lucrative practice of psychiatry to become a pathologist, because he has fallen into the practice of putting "well" people (e.g. slightly neurotic) into the terminal ward where they tend to recover their sense of creatureness and of sovereignty, and to send terminal patients home, where as a consequence of the emancipating proximity of death, they are able to see the faces of their families and their own gardens. As a consequence he loses his medical insurance and has to quit. He takes up pathology because he too feels more alive among the dead. . . . He finally abandons pathology for pornography, because in his view the alienating forces of abstraction have become so powerful that the only mode of re-entry into the real is the sexual (cf., the genital orientation of popular culture). In the course of an ordeal, a suicide attempt, he recovers himself and experiences a conversion to a belief in God and His entry into space-time via Jews, Christ and the Church, the supreme scandal to the transcending posture of abstraction. There remains only the artistic problem of whether his suicide should succeed and he should die or whether he should return to psychiatry and "lead a useful and productive life."

Among other things, this letter shows how far Percy still was from resolving the conclusion of his novel. In the final version it is not at all clear that Sutter Vaught has been converted away from his nihilism.

However much work Percy had yet to do on the book, he wrote a reassuring letter to Henry Robbins on October 16, saying that he hoped the novel would be in FSG's hands by the end of the year. "That's wonderful news," Robbins replied, "that the manuscript will be ready before too long, even if with some problems unresolved." Robbins also requested a general statement of what the novel was about, for publicity and marketing purposes. Percy found the assigment vexing, as he indicated in a cover letter that accompanied the requested statement. "For some reason," he complained to Robbins, "I find myself almost at a total loss when it comes to saying something *about* this novel. This comes no doubt from being stuck with it for the past three years." But dutiful student that Percy always was, he had tried to fulfill his assigment. The novel, he explained in part of his 370-word statement, was, "among other things, an exploration of some of the qualities and possibilities of life in the post-modern age." This clearly wouldn't work as promotional or marketing material, as Robbins meekly admitted. The adjective "postmodern" would, he feared, make the book sound too futuristic.

Percy was still not happy with the final shape of the novel when he sent it off to Farrar, Straus in the middle of December. He had been so submerged in the book that he had not even seen much of his daughter Mary Pratt, a freshman at Trinity College in Washington, D.C., when she was home for Thanksgiving. Percy vented some of his frustration in a letter he wrote to her shortly after the vacation: "Finally got *The Last Gentleman* in the mail. It was not in the best of shape, but they wanted it by Dec. 1. Anyhow I had gone stale on it and couldn't see the woods for the trees." In the same letter, Percy ladled out some old-fashioned advice on the virtues of chastity, proof that his concern about the perils of the postmodern age was not merely literary.

Seeing Mary Pratt leave the nest had tugged on Percy's paternal heartstrings even more than he liked to admit. He felt tremendously content within his domestic world. Its snugness and security were something he had never experienced in his childhood. The first break in the tight family circle was, then, disturbing. He knew he was being overprotective toward Mary Pratt, but he couldn't help it: "Your old man loves you and must be forgiven for being a bore," he signed off reluctantly.

Shelby Foote shared none of his friend's misgivings about the new novel. Having received a copy in middle December, he had it read with growing pleasure—and with a sigh of relief for his friend. A few weeks before, Percy and Bunt had driven down to Gulf Shores to spend one night with Shelby and Gwyn, and during that short visit Percy had voiced his dissatisfaction and concern with the novel he had been laboring so hard on. (The evening had proved worrisome on another count: Foote's bull terrier, Rattler, had gotten into a fight with Percy's German shepherd, Lady, and Lady had bitten Foote on the hand when he separated them.) When Foote received the novel back in Memphis, he couldn't understand why his friend was worried. Foote wrote Percy in early January to assure him that it was a good novel. "As I said on the phone, God bless us all, it's very very good; much better I think than Moviegoer, especially the plotting and the writing itself." Foote's strongest objection was to the quotation from Guardini that Percy had used as one of his two epigraphs. It seemed to Foote "all too explicit in a work so utterly implicit." Foote's only other concern—echoing one of Patricia Schartle's criticisms—was the complete disappearance of the telescope. "It worried me he might have lost it—such an elegant thing as that in its leather case." In addition to praising such little touches as the "immortalization of Lije" (transformed into the Vaughts' servant, John Horton), Foote assured Percy that the novel held together, becoming tighter and more serious as it developed.

Henry Robbins and Bob Giroux were also pleased when they received the novel. They made no further requests for changes, and Robbins took over the business of shepherding it through to production. As for Percy, now fretting through the period between a book's completion and its appearance in print, it was time to take stock of what appeared to be an increasingly mad world, both near and far. The tempo of the war in Asia had picked up sharply—5,008 U.S. troops were killed in Vietnam that year alone—and the domestic scene, despite LBJ's heroic legislative accomplishments, was looking even more precarious. The riots in Watts the summer before had left Percy shaken, and he feared that the whole fabric of society was about to tear apart. "We live in unsettled revolutionary times," he wrote to Mary Pratt in late January of 1966. "A large segment of the Negro population is so alienated from the affluent society that they are verging on mass criminality." Percy did not blame the blacks for their anger. In fact, he often voiced his surprise that so many blacks had been able to check their rage and resentment for so long. Certainly, as he saw from up close, there was no shortage of provocation. So troubled was he by the Klan's burning of a black church in nearby Slidell that he bestirred himself from his bayou retreat and attended the trial. If racial strife had not yet erupted in Covington, Percy had little doubt that it soon would.

Now with free time on his hands, Percy had the chance to catch up with some of his distant friends, including his erstwhile tutor in the art of fiction, Caroline Gordon. From his cousin Jack Spalding in Atlanta —then the editor of the *Atlanta Constitution*—Percy learned that Gordon was teaching at Emory. "Hurray!" Percy rejoiced in a letter that he posted on February 11. "It must be one of the hottest spots and most exciting in the country, what with God being dead there, the Trappists praising a few miles away, Martin Luther King and the New South." Percy did not write just to celebrate her arrival in Atlanta. He enclosed a copy of the article he had just written for Will Campbell and warned her that she would soon be receiving galleys of *The Last Gentleman*. He also proposed that he fly over to Atlanta to visit her for a weekend. In his next letter he set forth a specific plan. He would fly to Atlanta on Friday, March 4, rent a car, and then drive Gordon out to the Trappist monastery in Conyers, where they would spend the weekend. As Percy later reported to Thomas Merton, "The monks didn't know quite how to house such a peculiar pair," but the weekend proved to be a success. Percy let Gordon take a look at his manuscript of *The Last Gentleman*, and Gordon made it clear that she liked what she read.

But Gordon's reaction to a novel was never quite so simple as that. When she returned home from Conyers, she found galleys of the novel waiting for her, and she read quickly to the end. Though her opinion remained high ("It is a *rich* book! Enough in it to make a dozen contemporary novels"), Gordon, the perpetual pedagogue, found technical problems, and she let Percy know immediately what they were. "Your novel starts more like *Crime and Punishment* than *The Idiot*. It takes genius to triumph over a start like that: *a young man alone, thinking!*" Gordon thought the opening scene showed inadequate concern for the reader and stayed too long with the solipsistic ruminations of Will Barrett.

Percy could have anticipated Gordon's criticism. He knew his teacher's principles all too well. Responding with a forthright mea culpa, he added that his faults were "incorrigible." Yet he begged her indulgence: "It is a deliberate sin and therefore all the more mortal, I reckon. I mean to say that, what with the times being what they are, one almost has to begin a book with a solitary young man. All my writings, for better or worse, take off from the solipsism which Allen described in his essay about Ode to the Confederate Dead. The best I can do is break him out of the solipsism." Percy could have added—but didn't—that he would never have become the writer he was had he scrupulously followed Gordon's recipe for the well-made novel. Percy felt genuine respect as well as compassion for Gordon. Her final break with Allen Tate had been terribly hard on her, a sad conclusion to a tempestuous marriage. Besides, Percy could tell that Gordon really did admire his novel. She meant what she said when she dubbed him "our white hope."

Not surprisingly, she had only good things to say about the book in a letter she wrote to Bob Giroux. "If I read it right," she wrote, providing what she hoped was appropriate blurb material, "this is the Odyssey of a Southern Prince Myshkin through regions as strange as Odysseus ever visited. The events which, at times, are almost incredible, take place on the Dostoyevskyan stage of the modern novel."

If Robbins and Giroux ever had any doubts about the literary excellence of *The Last Gentleman*, they were certainly dispelled by the comments of Gordon and other writers to whom they had sent galleys. Paul Horgan observed that "no one else has so delicately penetrated to the heart of the modern mystery of alienation." Hans Koningsberger hailed Percy as "a marvellous writer, I think, about the only one of the decade I *want* to read." And Peter Taylor, no profligate with praise, ranked *The Last Gentleman* as "one of only two new novels I have read in the past ten years that I thoroughly liked." Given his high opinion of *The Moviegoer*, it is not surprising that Thomas Merton waxed so enthusiastic over the new novel, although part of what he said might have been interpreted by Giroux and Robbins as a discouraging forecast for the book's popular and commercial prospects:

> This is in fact a haunting, disturbing, funny and fantastic anti-novel structured like a long dream and relentlessly insisting that most of reality is unconscious. It ends up by being one of the most intelligent and sophisticated statements about the South and about America, but one which too many people will probably find so baffling that they will not know what to make of it. Even then, if they persist in reading it, they cannot help being affected by the profoundly wacky wisdom of the book. Precisely because of the wackiness I would call it one of the sanest books I have read in a long time.

Farrar, Straus decided on a cautiously modest print run of ten thousand copies for the first edition, still a considerable improvement over the first edition of *The Moviegoer*. All in all, Percy felt as comfortable with his new publisher as his publisher did with him. If Henry Robbins was not as close and demanding an editor as Kauffmann, he was just as supportive.

The novel reached the bookstores early in June, following nicely upon a published excerpt of the novel in the May issue of *Harper's*. Reviews were not long in coming, most of them positive. *Time* weighed in quickly with strong kudos, declaring that *The Moviegoer* now had a "brilliant kid brother," one that was "sturdier in substance, more supple in style." Admiring the book's comedy of manners, the reviewer also appreciated the book's subtle religious intentions. Winning the National Book Award had at least one undeniable benefit: It assured prominent reviewers for second novels and prominent placement of their reviews. Benjamin DeMott in *The Washington Post Book World*, John Wain in *The New York Review of Books*, Granville Hicks in *Saturday Review*, Wilfrid Sheed in the *National Catholic Reporter*, Joyce Carol Oates in *The Nation*, and Peter Buitenhuis in *The New York Times* all penned thoughtful, balanced, and generally admiring reviews. Buitenhuis gave the most unqualified rave: "Resolving South and North, history and the new, conservatism and consumership, poetry and cliché, ultimately even death and life, is the task of Will. But where there's a will there's a way—by which I mean that a novelist who can find a hero who is adequate not only to the demands of his plot but also to the requirements of his complex civilization, of which the plot should be some kind of imitation, has found the way to write a distinguished work of art."

Even those critics who were hard on the novel were hard in the provocative way that makes the reader of the review curious to read the novel itself. Perhaps the most sharply dismissive evaluation came from Honor Tracy in *The New Republic:* "This is a curious, unfocused novel that rambles along with the wooden, almost arthritic gait so often found in the work of writers who begin in middle age." Moving beyond ad hominem, Tracy objected most to a certain insubstantiality of the characters: "Sutter, with his belief in lewdness and pornography as the Rock of our chaotic age, is a frame of mind, even if an interesting one. So is Val, who accepts the Catholic doctrine *in toto* but on whose angry heart the grace of God has never fallen. For all the perception that the author brings to Jamie, he remains just a dying youth rather than one particular boy."

Joyce Carol Oates, while also registering some strong complaints, understood more clearly why Percy fashioned characters of a certain type: "This novel is one no critic should want to snipe at, for it is rare to encounter a work so engaging in nearly every line; but Percy's strength simply does not extend to the naturalistic." This was a clear and perceptive judgment. Percy was a novelist who gave the deceptive appearance of working in the naturalistic mode but was really fashioning something far closer to a romance, an existential romance, to be sure, but still a tale of quest and spiritual testing. "Percy's writing," Oates continued, "is strangely similar to the highly gifted but rather hallucinatory pieces of Janet Frame: the more closely one looks at each sentence, each glimpse of a detail or image, the more hypnotic is the spell; but"—and here Oates seemed to ignore the wisdom of her earlier perception—"when one stands back for the larger view something has failed." That something is naturalistic reality, which of course was not Percy's literary goal.

While most of the critics wrote glowingly of Percy's art, many of them complained about some nagging lack or defect at the heart of the novel, usually having to do with tone or narrative point of view. Benjamin DeMott, for example, while for the most part laudatory, was troubled by the distant, ironic tone of the author toward his hero and his fictional world. "Put the negative case strongly and you say this writer's achieve-ment is to have taught the novel of violence and despair to behave as though it had taken an exceptionally potent tranquillizer—a pill trans-forming the familiar American terrors into comfortably endurable both-ers." One of the more thoughtful objections was registered by Frederick C. Crews in *Commentary*. He saw that Percy shared with Dostoyevsky a "predilection for seeing the decisions of his driven heroes as metaphysical imperatives." Yet Crews objected to the inadequately grounded—and inadequately dramatized—quality of these metaphysical concerns in Per-cy's characters. In Dostoyevsky, by contrast, "the suffering which pre-cedes those decisions is a primary reality that does not have to be established by symbolism and theory." Crews's conclusion raises a point that is well worth weighing: "If *The Last Gentleman*, despite its substan-tial virtues, finally fails to make a deep impression, the reason may be that Percy does not care either to inspect Will Barrett's conflicts at close range or to understand them much more clearly than Barrett does him-self."

Crews's criticism, and similar complaints from other reviewers, point to a problem in Percy's narrative art. One could describe it positively as artistic distance or negatively as evasion. However labeled or evaluated, it comes from something guarded or withheld in the author himself. Percy served many muses, but one of them was a severe, almost impos-sible, figure. This mysterious female "Other" might have been, at least in part, the internalized image of the distant mother he barely knew, the one he tried to approach but never reached in three years of psychoanal-ysis. For this cold taskmistress, Percy the artist fashioned stories about the vanities of the world, particularly the modern technocratic world that is constructed and run by men. Percy's central characters—Will Barrett even more dramatically than Binx Bolling—refuse to serve as cogs in this social mechanism. Their refusal may be ambivalent or equiv-ocal, as in Binx's case, or quite direct, as in Will's.

But Percy is subversive even of his characters' Grand Refusals. This subversion entails a rebellion against his first muse, for it mocks the almost invisible matriarchy—more visible in the South than in the North—that truly controls the so-called patriarchal order. It is the sub-tle power women exercise that can so often reduce men to sad half-creatures who play at life and become increasingly hollow in their social and professional roles. We see this quite clearly in *The Moviegoer*, where women manipulate men with the skill of professional puppeteers. Simi-larly, in *The Last Gentleman*, Percy hints at the canny ways the demure-seeming belles control their men (and he will suggest the same even more obviously, and indeed more chillingly, in later novels, particularly in *Lancelot*). The spectacle is frightening, which is why the attraction of the homophile alternative to the life of married desperation is so palpably present throughout the novel. This homophilia, philosophical rather than sexual, is dramatized through the relationships between Will and Sutter, a relationship that seems more highly charged than the one between Will and Kitty, and of course its distant models can be found in Percy's own relationships with male mentors, Will Percy, Willie von Glahn, and even Huger Jervey.

Finally, though, Percy is even more subversive than these various subversions of the passively accepted life would suggest. For Percy, by means of his journey of faith, has come to see the assorted woes of this world—the woe that is in marriage, the routinization and alienation in the working world, the folly of addictive consumerism, the bigotries that divide the human community, and the inadequate humanist strategies to heal those schisms—as parts of the comedy of Fallen Man. All of the woes are real, Percy suggests, but there is no beginning of healing them until one sees the source of the problem in the perversity and sinfulness of the individual human creature. That sinfulness manifests itself most terribly in the ambition to be the Creator, the controller and manipulator of others. Percy's fiction suggests that the human community is fallen almost beyond hope when most of its members seek through various agencies (power, money, knowledge) to manipulate other members of the community to further their own desire for absolute authority. From this satanic ambition stem all other depredations of the human spirit— the alienation, despair, and assorted sicknesses unto death. Percy's art— at least that which is written for his highest muse, the Mother Church —implies that the only way out of this deathtrap is the mysterious workings of grace, the apprehension of which may come only with a heightened awareness of mortality, one's own or that of someone close. And that implication is clearly bound up with the central action of his first two novels.

It is hard not to think that those who were most put off by Percy's second novel were objecting, at least in part, to the radically religious perspective of the novel. A critic such as Crews almost reflexively thinks that the real conflicts of life are rooted in the psychological realm of human existence, or in the economic and social particularities of history. But while Percy certainly appreciated the power of the psychological, he would not grant it sovereignty over the spiritual. (As Percy told Dr. Gentry Harris, "In my own experience the most valuable lesson of psychoanalysis was learning what it could not do.") His fiction, in fact, is a sustained argument against assorted notions of "psychological man."

It is fairer to say that Percy was less confident in his understanding of the relationship of the spiritual to the historical. Above all, he had profound difficulty understanding why the avowedly Christian citizens of the most God-fearing country in the world were capable of such moral enormities in dealing with their fellows. The inequities of his nation, and particularly his South, were undeniable facts, which so far he had shied away from addressing directly in his fiction. But Percy's puzzlement at the failure of the Christian message in this world would concern him directly in the works and days to come.

13

Apocalyptic Mirth

———

Is it that God has at last removed his blessing from the U.S.A. . . . ?
—WALKER PERCY, *Love in the Ruins*

Percy was looking forward to taking his family to Pawley's Island, South Carolina, for several weeks during the summer after *The Last Gentleman* was published. Bunt had located a huge, rambling house on the beach, a place that had once been used as the dormitory of a boys' summer camp. The room was necessary. Among other visitors, Roy and Sarah and two of their children were planning to come. Percy looked forward to the rest—and to seeing his old friend Robert Daniel, who had made plans to be on the island from mid-July through early August. Earlier in the year, before *The Last Gentleman* came out, Percy had sent galleys of his book to Daniel, and Daniel gave it the kind of sharp-eyed professorial reading that it needed. This labor of love saved Percy from a number of embarrassing gaffes. But it was not only out of gratitude that Percy hoped to see his old friend from Sewanee days. Daniel had a fine dry wit, and Percy enjoyed bantering with him, particularly when Percy was in one of his more jovial and puckish moods.

The Percys spent most of July and early August at Pawley's Island. Percy did what he always did—read, wrote some, and enjoyed his family. Robert Daniel would visit most days, terrifying everybody by flicking his lit cigarettes into the tall sea grass below the porch. (Fire was a big danger on an island where there was no fire department, and one of the Percys would always run down off the porch to find and stub out Daniel's smoldering butts.) Percy enjoyed catching up with his Sewanee friend, joking as they always did but also discussing the ominous events of the summer. The shooting and wounding of James Meredith on June 6 as he marched alone from Memphis, Tennessee, to Jackson, Mississippi, to encourage blacks to register to vote had spurred a mass march at the end of that month. The climax of this march was a debate between Martin Luther King, Jr., and Stokely Carmichael, the advocates, respectively, of nonviolence and violent confrontation. Forceful orator as King always was, Percy feared that Carmichael was the voice of things to come. Just as difficult to ignore that summer were the antiwar protests that seemed to grow in direct proportion with the mounting U.S. presence in South Vietnam. Percy, the anticommunist hawk, stood steadfastly by Lyndon Johnson's decision to prosecute the undeclared war, but he saw that the issue was dividing the nation into two intransigent camps, each unwilling to consider the arguments of the other. In Percy's eyes, the level of political discourse seemed to be declining daily, along with the clarity of fundamental political labels—conservative, liberal, and moderate. All in all, the state of the nation was enough to inspire despair—or, in Percy's case, satire.

The first recorded mention of work on *Love in the Ruins* does not appear until a January 1967 letter to Shelby Foote, but that same letter makes it clear that Percy had been long at work on the novel. The events of the summer of 1966 were its likely catalyst. Percy had little other writing to distract him from the new book during the following fall and winter. In late autumn he wrote a short but revealing piece for *The Washington Post Book World,* "From Facts to Fiction," telling "how it came to pass that a physician turned writer and became a novelist." The article set forth, in compact form, the standard literary autobiography that he would use for the next two decades whenever scholars or journalists showed up at his house for an interview.

Percy soon discovered that his *Post* essay had put a first-rate scholar onto his trail. Shortly after reading it, a thirty-five-year-old assistant professor at the University of Maryland, Lewis Lawson, wrote Percy to tell him of his interest in relating his nonfiction essays to his fiction. Lawson listed all of the essays he had been able to find and asked if there were any more. Percy replied, noting two essays that Lawson had missed. Emboldened, Lawson wrote again, this time asking if he might come down to Covington and read the two unpublished novels, a request to which Percy responded with mock horror. "As for the two earlier novels:

it would be over my dead body that you would see them. In fact, you put me in mind of it: since it might very well be over my dead body that somebody sees them, I aim to get up to the attic today and throw them both in the bayou."

Lawson was horrified that he might have "cost literary culture part of its riches," but his investigation of Percy's essays led to the first thoughtful unraveling of the theological and philosophical strands in Percy's first two novels, and particularly the Kierkegaardian influence. Before the end of the summer, Lawson sent Percy an early version of "Walker Percy's Indirect Communications" (which was not published until 1969), and Percy was greatly impressed, calling it "unprecedented in its scope, thoroughness and in its grasp of both the fiction and articles and the discovery of some basic themes appertaining." Percy's only minor cavil was that Lawson gave "a too strictly Kierkegaardian" reading of the theology of the first two novels. Percy suggested that Aquinas' notion of the "intuition of being" might have more to do with some of his characters' preoccupations and breakthroughs (their concern for "signs," for example) than anything Kierkegaard wrote. Though it would not be until near the end of his life that Percy would meet the soft-spoken, unassuming scholar, he was repeatedly gratified by Lawson's close explications of his novels, and their twenty-five-year correspondence was marked by frankness, humor, and growing mutual affection.

If the ominous character of contemporary events gave Percy a strong reason for writing a novel about a "Bad Catholic near the End of Time," his reasons for making his "Bad Catholic" a psychiatrist are just as clear. Most recently, of course, there had been Percy's involvement with Gentry Harris and the schizophrenia project. Although the project had come prematurely to an end in August 1966, when Harris's incipient emphysema forced him to seek a less polluted environment (first in Fort Worth, Texas, and then in San Francisco), the experience of eavesdropping on a professional at his job gave Percy an entry into the working world, a world that he had conspicuously scanted in his first two novels. Not that Percy modeled Tom More on Gentry Harris, or even More's daily work on Harris's work. Harris's style and manner of thinking were only a general inspiration.

Percy had a number of other models, including his friend Bill Sorum. But perhaps the single greatest inspiration for the character of Thomas More was a psychiatrist Percy knew only indirectly: Dr. Robert Heath. A neuropsychiatrist at Tulane, Heath was an indefatigable researcher who had written widely on the effects of surgery, electrical stimulation,

and drugs on some of the more intractable of mental disorders, particularly schizophrenia. His reading and alteration of the brain activity of
schizophrenics by means of deep electrical implants gained national attention during the 1950s; later, in the 1960s, his work on electrical
stimulation and the pleasure response (including the orgasm) made him
the object of considerable notoriety. What most interested Percy about
Heath's work was his focus on the nexus between the physical and the
psychological, soma and psyche, and his use of medical technology,
particularly electrodes and electroencephalograms. Both the focus and
the technology would be central to Thomas More's medical preoccupations. (More's Qualitative Quantitative Ontological Lapsometer is an
encephalograph without wires—a tele-encephalograph—used to measure electrical activity in different parts of the brain, which activity More
hopes to correlate "with the manifold woes of the Western world, its
terrors and rages and murderous impulses.")

To be sure, the most important model for the character of Dr. Tom
More was Percy himself. In this respect at least, *Love in the Ruins* was
not unlike the two preceding novels. Percy hoped to explore the problem
of a time out of joint, signaled most dramatically by the state of race
relations, but it was a matter of faith with Percy that the disjointedness
of the times owed to a sickness in souls, including his own. Strong
advocate of civil rights that he had become, Percy had long been irritated by the liberal pieties about the "conditions" in the South. As he
had noted the year before in an omnibus review of books about Mississippi and racial politics, there was little more that could be said analyti-
cally or prescriptively about the situation. "There is little to do but
document it."

A few weeks into the new year, he received a cheerful letter from
Shelby Foote, who talked about the twenty lectures on literature ("from
Chaucer through T.S. Eliot") that he was giving at Memphis State
University. The upbeat letter might have given Percy reason to regret
his refusal the spring before to teach a course at Kenyon College. Percy
confessed his writing blues to Foote. As well as doing "very little," Percy
wondered whether he might have taken on more than he could handle:

> I have in mind a futuristic novel dealing with the decline and fall of
> the U.S., the country rent almost hopelessly between the rural knot-
> headed right and the godless and alienated left, worse than the Civil
> War. Of that and the goodness of God, and of the merriness of living
> quite anonymously in the suburbs, drinking well, cooking out, attend-
> ing Mass at the usual silo-and-barn, the goodness of Brunswick bowling
> alleys (the good white maple and plastic balls), coming home of an

evening, with the twin rubies of the TV transmitter in the evening sky, having 4 drinks of good sourmash and assaulting one's wife in an armchair, etc. What we Catholics call the Sacramental Life.

But it won't go, it doesn't swing, I am hung up, alas, oh hopelessly hung; sitting in front of my paper at 9:05 and growing sleepier by the minute. . . .

Hope you do better. At least you are speaking to the young, for whom you have both a liking and a hope.

Winning a second National Book Award would have temporarily lifted Percy out of the doldrums, but it was not to be. Although *The Last Gentleman* was one of the finalists, the fiction jury decided on *The Fixer* by Bernard Malamud, a book that was as much out of step with the black-humor absurdist fashion of the mid-1960s as *The Last Gentleman* was. Henry Robbins let Percy know the outcome on February 24. That meant, of course, that Percy would not be coming to New York for the award proceedings, but he would come to the city later in the spring. He and Bunt were invited to the annual gathering of the National Institute of Arts and Letters on May 24, as well as to a dinner afterward at the townhouse of Roger and Dorothea Straus. The latter, happily for Percy, could not have been more different from the evening he experienced five years before in Blanche Knopf's apartment. Straus and his wife were fond of Percy, and proud that he was on FSG's list. One other meeting of moment took place on this trip. Through Henry Robbins's good offices, Percy arranged to see Wilfrid Sheed the day after the Institute gathering. Impressed by Sheed's review of *The Last Gentleman*, Percy had long wanted to meet the critic in the flesh. The meeting proved to be the beginning of one of many distant-yet-close friendships that Percy formed with fellow writers. From then on, Sheed's main line of communication with Percy would be the reviews he wrote of Percy's novels; Percy's, apart from a review of one of Sheed's novels, would largely consist of all-but-illegible letters. It was a friendship in which differences as well as commonalities were aired. When Sheed tried to enlist Percy to sign a peace letter against the Vietnam War, Percy wrote back, Sheed recalled, "to say that if I had heard L.B.J. called a 'nigger-lover' as much as he had, you really couldn't turn your back on him." Sheed also remembered the postscript: "You know, a Southerner never saw a war he didn't like!"

The year 1967 would be one in which Percy would initiate a number of important literary friendships, although to label them "literary" is perhaps too restrictive. In June, for example, Percy reviewed a book by a little-known Harvard psychiatrist, Dr. Robert Coles. The book, *Chil-*

dren of Crisis, was one that Percy could have been very hard on. A northern liberal's pronouncements on the race situation in the South was just the sort of thing Percy was sick and tired of. But when Percy began reading Coles's book, he realized it was the very kind of book he had called for in his omnibus review of race books two years before: a work of documentation, and a masterful work, at that. What impressed Percy was that Dr. Coles had not come South to preach or cluck. He had come to listen and learn. "Dr. Coles does not fit the mold, the people he interviews don't fit the mold, and their individual tragedies and triumphs and cowardices have nothing to do with the old ideological quarrels," Percy wrote. He also praised Coles's method: "He treads a narrow path between theorizing and novelizing and emerges as what in fact he is: physician, and a wise and gentle one. He is doctor to the worst of our ills."

Coles could not have been more thrilled by the review. An early fan of Percy, he had in fact been impressed by "The Man on the Train" in 1956, long before Percy's name meant anything to even well-informed readers. Many years later, after spending two years running the psychiatric unit at Keesler Air Force Base, in Biloxi, Mississippi, Coles took up residence in New Orleans. There, while receiving psychoanalytic training, he had his first encounter with Percy the novelist. After the thirty-two-year-old physician bought a copy of *The Moviegoer* at the Doubleday Book Store on Canal Street, he became so obsessed with Binx Bolling that his analyst began to wonder if his student-analysand weren't "shadowing" the fictional character. In the years that followed, as Coles researched and explored the social terrain that would become the subject of his later books, Percy's fiction remained a faithful companion and source of wisdom. In a letter of thanks that he wrote shortly after the review appeared, Coles attempted to explain his complicated debt to Percy:

> I can't tell you what it meant to me to read your review of my book in the *Times*. What I never could say in that book has to do with the years I spent in New Orleans having my head examined by a psychoanalyst and getting to know the city. When you write of the Gentilly section of the city in *The Moviegoer,* and indeed when you write as you did in that novel, I can only feel distantly close to you. For several years I wandered about in New Orleans, and I owe the South much more than any book can ever convey. I help teach a course here at Harvard—as a sort of assistant to Erik Erikson. In addition to his writings and those of Freud we are allowed to go off on our own and work with novels and poems. For the three years that I've been back in the North I've used *The Moviegoer* and this year *The Last Gentleman.*

Coles closed by asking if he could drop by one day when he was in New Orleans. Percy replied with a short note, encouraging Coles to drop by any time. But despite their eagerness to meet, it would be several years before their first face-to-face encounter.

One epistolary friendship was consummated in the flesh that summer, however. On the first Saturday in July, Percy flew up to Louisville, Kentucky, to attend an editorial board meeting of *Katallagete* at Gethsemani Abbey. Will Campbell, the magazine's publisher, later speculated that Percy came so he could meet Thomas Merton. Certainly, Percy was curious to meet the poet-monk who had written so eloquently about his own spiritual journey in *Seven Storey Mountain,* and not only because Merton had written so appreciatively about Percy's own work. "I'd heard the strangest things about Merton," Percy later told an interviewer. "One that he was schizophrenic and another was that he had left the Church or he had broken his vows or he was living with a couple of women." When the board members reached the abbey, they proceeded directly to Merton's cinder-block cottage, the "hermitage," about a half mile from the main building. Percy encountered a "pretty tough-looking guy" wearing jeans and a tee-shirt. Merton offered drinks to the group, and Percy took a bourbon and water. There was, as Percy recollected, "very little serious talk," mainly a lot of banter and kidding around. At one point, for about thirty minutes, Percy and Merton were left alone on the porch of the house, but they both turned awkward and shy. Percy wanted to ask Merton what was going on in his relationship with the abbot, but he was afraid of appearing presumptuous. In fact, he addressed Merton rather formally as Father Louis the whole time. Finally, Percy asked Merton what he thought about the future of monasticism, and Merton speculated that the day of the big abbey was over. In the future, Father Louis conjectured, there would be small communities of men living in cities, an opinion that Percy judged (silently) a "rather standard" 1960s view. As meetings go, it was not quite as disappointing as Percy's brief encounter with Flannery O'Connor, but it was not a great deal better.

It did not seem to leave the two men thinking any less of each other, however. Percy even made light of the anticlimactic encounter in his next letter to Merton. "I must admit I felt somewhat diffident, putting myself in your shoes and imagining how it would have put me out having that somewhat diverse crew straggling about your hillside." During their brief colloquy, Percy had alluded to the book he was working on, and Merton had mentioned a book on Bantu metaphysics that he thought might be of some use. Percy now thought so too, and he inquired after the title: "It suddenly fits into a novel I am trying to conceive. It concerns, as I think I told you, the decline and fall of the USA as a consequence of its failure with the Negroes. It takes place in a pleasant all-white 100% Christian exurb named Paradise." As Percy went on to explain, Bantu metaphysics would figure into that part of the novel that comes after the country has fallen apart and blacks have taken over Paradise, abandoning their former Christianity and adopting native African religion. Merton was forthcoming with more than a few suggestions for books and articles on the subject. The more Merton thought about Percy's book, the more he liked it—both its serious and its humorous sides. Near the end of the summer, he provided another title and a number of anecdotes about African religious eclecticism that could be put to comic use. "There is by the way an African Castor Oil Dead Church in which new life is acquired by laxatives." Merton even proposed a character: "There could of course be visits from fashionable Bantu prophets sent from Africa, one called T.S. Eliot who comes preaching toilet Zen." As for the serious side of what Percy was addressing, Merton sent his essay, "The Long Hot Summer of Sixty-Seven."

Percy was grateful for the suggestions and for Merton's encouragement. The essay, however, gave him some pause. Percy agreed with Merton's analysis of the dire racial situation. This, after all, had been the summer of several race riots, including the worst one in U.S. history: five days of violence in Detroit, Michigan, had left forty-three people dead and $200 million worth of damage. What Percy objected to was Merton's "uniting race and Vietnam under one rubric, since I regard one as the clearest kind of moral issue and the other as murderously complex and baffling." This difference might eventually have opened into a wider political rift between the two men, but Merton had little more time in this world. Father Louis accidentally electrocuted himself while traveling in Burma a year later.

Perhaps inspired by the example of Shelby Foote, perhaps simply fed up with the solitary business of arranging words on the page, Percy agreed to teach a course at Loyola University in the fall of 1967. Focused generally on existential themes in modern literature, English 395 was to be a small seminar of eight students meeting for three hours one evening a week. Seven of the eight students were Loyola undergraduates, selected by the English department chairman (and novelist) Bill Corrington. The eighth member of the class was a woman named Carol Livaudais, a graduate of Bennington and a former student of Francis Fergusson. Corrington hoped that she would keep things moving and, if necessary, serve as a buffer between possibly callow students and their inexperienced instructor. As it turned out no buffer was needed. "We all knew what a fine writer Walker was," Livaudais recounted, "and we knew how fortunate we were to be in his class."

All the same, the class was a little surprised to see how shy and uneasy their teacher was. The only other course he had ever taught was pathology as an assistant instructor at Columbia. As well as being diffident by nature, Percy always believed that he had gaping holes in his literary background (he had written to Lewis Lawson the preceding spring to ask for suggestions for his reading list), and he knew almost no critical jargon. Percy's only method was Socratic: "In this business," he declared at the first meeting, "everybody is right." Whatever the novel of the week was—Dostoyevsky's *Notes from Underground,* Camus' *The Stranger,* O'Connor's *Wise Blood,* Ellison's *Invisible Man*—Percy asked the same leading questions: What was the protagonist's problem? Why was he so alienated from the rest of society? How did each novel work as a diagnostic and cognitive tool? If the students left each class a little more puzzled than they were the week before, they nonetheless seemed to enjoy the course, even though they were unsuccessful in getting Percy to discuss his own work. When one student proposed that the class read *The Moviegoer,* Percy replied, "Well you won't need me for that."

As little preparation as the course required, Percy was a dutiful teacher, and by the end of each class (concluded with refreshments and informal talk), he would go back across the lake completely exhausted. After the semester at Loyola, Percy could never understand how people could write and teach at the same time.

Percy's friend Foote was already well aware of the incompatibility of the two activities, but in order to pay for his daughter Margaret's tuition, he had agreed to teach for a semester at Hollins College beginning in January 1968. In March, though, his academic idyll was shattered when he learned that his mother, Lillian Rosenstock Foote, had cancer. Lillian Foote's devotion to her son was close to legendary in Greenville, and Foote himself had often marveled at how steadfastly she had supported him: "It's a strange thing, being in close touch with a Saint," he wrote to Percy. Foote was just as moved by the way his wife Gwyn looked after his mother in Memphis while he was gone during the week: "Gwyn is by far the best practical help; Mother sees her as she saw herself forty years ago when my father's mother was dying the same way and none of her children had half the concern for her that Mother did."

These were matters that the stoical Foote could discuss only with Percy. It was remarkable, in fact, that despite the normal pressures and distractions of their lives—not to mention the added potential of professional rivalry—their friendship remained strong and in some ways grew stronger. They corresponded almost as frequently as they had back in the early 1950s. Foote did not lecture quite so strenuously in these letters, but he remained the steadfast champion of art for art's sake and would tweak Percy's Catholicism whenever he got the chance. Their differences over the ends of art remained essentially the same.

Percy was less inclined to discuss the objectives of his art with Foote and more inclined to discuss the conditions of its making. This was not, however, the case in interviews that Percy granted to visiting scholars during these years. In two fairly extensive interviews—the first with Ashley Brown in 1967 and the second with Carlton Cremeens in 1968 —Percy mixed elements of his now-standard autobiography with thoughts about his writing and his books. As well as discussing intellectual debts, favorite contemporary authors (mainly such Jewish authors as Bellow, Heller, Singer, and Malamud), Percy in the Cremeens interview seemed quite eager to talk about contemporary events and in particular to make clear—at least as clear as possible—his place in the current political confusion. His main point was that the liberal center was dead. The right, he argued, had turned rabid, abandoned true conservatism for reactionary radicalism, corrupted such words as "conservative" and "constitutional," and taken to attacking President Johnson for his domestic policy and his reluctance to use all available force to destroy the enemy in Vietnam. But the liberal intelligentsia had become just as mindlessly dogmatic, Percy insisted, and "almost as uniform and conformist—and irrational—in their hatred of President Johnson as the Southern right wingers." Percy generalized his own dismay with the political situation as the predicament of the "southern writer":

> Twenty years ago my natural sympathies would have been with the liberal tradition in the North. . . . But the recent changes are complicated by how close the wild-eyed have come to the high-browed. The Southern writer now finds himself in the middle of somewhere and not quite knowing where. He's caught between the right in the South and this intellectual herd in the North who profess to be free creative spirits, and yet, all conforming to the same lines, the same hatred and abuse of the things they oppose. So where does the Southern writer stand? It may be an advantage—living in the South. I don't know. Most writers in the North seem to be caught up in this intellectual community, while most Southern writers, who are any good, simply won't have anything to do with this hatred and abuse.

Though Cremeens could not have known it, Percy was sketching the predicament that he was then dramatizing in his work-in-progress—the predicament, it would seem, of the disillusioned liberal. In fact, though,

Percy had never been that charmed by the American liberal tradition, not even the agonized liberalism of Lionel Trilling, the liberalism of what Arthur Schlesinger called the "vital center." Percy's deepest political instincts were conservative, more conservative even than Uncle Will's. (For all his cultural conservatism, Uncle Will was—like his father before him—in most respects a typical progressive Democrat of his era.)

Percy had come to a rather fragile truce with liberalism during the 1950s out of disenchantment with the southern conservative tradition, particularly its failure to lead the way in addressing the South's racial inequities. Percy's conversion to Catholicism, and his involvement with Father Twomey and other Catholic activists, had brought him to the position that the treatment of blacks in the United States was something like America's Original Sin. Percy made peace with liberals, and liberalism, because doing so seemed the only way to work for a political solution to the problem. The charismatic figure of John F. Kennedy—Catholic, youthful cold warrior, and born-again champion of civil rights—made this alliance of necessity with liberalism not only bearable but attractive. Percy clearly saw Kennedy as a kind of political alter ego: a patrician, of sorts, who was doing the right thing out of Christian conviction, and doing it with the style and attitude of a noble personage. The death of Kennedy might not have broken Percy's fragile ties to liberalism, but it symbolically marked the beginning of their unraveling. Things would never again be quite so clear.

In the resulting murk, made worse by the divisiveness of the Vietnam War, Percy's deeper, more conservative tendencies began to resurface. Not that Percy abandoned his commitment to civil rights; in some ways, it became stronger and more personal. But Percy did betray a growing disenchantment with liberalism both for its confidence in social engineering and for its excessive faith in the democratic dogma. Percy advanced his views not so much by proselytizing for the conservative values of stability and hierarchy or championing moral absolutes as by pointing out, mainly through satire, the unfortunate consequences of a social order without such qualities. Percy's thoughts about the age, and about the novelist's role, were summed up in an article he wrote for *Katallagete* at the end of 1967, "Novel-Writing in an Apocalyptic Time":

> In such a time as this, a time of pollution and corruption of meaning, it is no wonder that the posture the novelist often finds natural is that of derision, mockery, subversion, and assault—to mock and subvert the words and symbols of the day in order that new words come into being or that old words be freshly minted—to assault the benumbed

sensibility of the poor media consumer, because anything other than
assault and satire can only be understood as a confirmation of the
current corrupted meanings of such honorable old words as love, truth,
beauty, brotherhood of man, life, and so on. There may be times when
the greatest service a novelist can do his fellow man is to follow General Patton's injunction: Attack, attack, attack. Attack the fake in the
name of the real.

Some readers of Percy have judged this turn toward mockery and derision
as a reversion to his elitist outlook, his "planter heritage." The critic
John F. Zeugner, for example, makes a strong case that this side of Percy
was present even in his first two novels. After The Last Gentleman (and
Kennedy's assassination), however, the snob and social ranker in Percy
began to crowd out the Christian existentialist: "What engages Percy's
interest," Zeugner writes, "what moves his heart and sends life though
his marvellously pellucid prose is not Roman ritual, though there is
plenty cited, not existential agony, though allusions to it abound, but
good old-fashioned Southern manners. The really written parts of Love
in the Ruins, as versus the merely recited parts, all concern the clash of
manners."

Zeugner holds that Percy's ultimate loyalty to the aristocratic outlook
also explains why, around 1965, he began to assert that the South had
something to teach the rest of the United States, that it might even, as
Percy wrote in his first essay for Katallagete, "save the country from the
Berkeley-Cambridge axis." Zeugner sees Percy's newly discovered faith
in the South's special mission as inseparable from the author's fondness
for the old hierarchical order.

There is some truth to Zeugner's claim. Percy never completely repudiated the old social arrangement, however much he wanted its Stoic
ethos to be modified by true Christian principles. But Zeugner overstates
his case by ignoring Percy's own agonized view of the failings of southern
society—and of the elite who guided it. Even if Percy believed, with
growing conviction, that the South had something of value in its old
social arrangement, he was just as convinced that this example would be
of no use if white southerners did not acknowledge and correct their
violation of the Christian injunction to love others as themselves. In
Percy's eyes, this great and all-important condition constituted a moral
challenge both to his region and to individuals, including himself.

Percy's efforts to address America's "Original Sin" had taken a number
of forms since the early 1950s. As well as his own writing, he had
supported and taken part in some of the activities of Father Twomey's
Institute of Human Relations. Yet Percy had never seen himself as an

activist, and he never would. Activism and movements were contrary to his nature. But after the summer of 1967, Percy felt compelled to devote more time, energy, and money to healing the social wound.

In early 1968 about twenty Covington citizens, black and white, came together to form the Community Relations Council of Greater Covington. A diverse group professionally, they ranged from psychologists at the Delta Primate Center to cabinet-makers and contractors, and they also counted among their ranks clergymen, a lawyer, several teachers from the public schools, housewives, and a novelist. Inspired in part by the Kerner Commission report on racial violence that came out in late February, the council hoped to open channels of communication between the black and white communities—a task that took on particular urgency after the assassination of Martin Luther King, Jr., on April 4. More than anything else, this tragedy, which triggered urban riots throughout the country, signaled the precariousness of a nonviolent solution to the racial divide. The council was particularly concerned with such issues as employment, housing, and school integration (which was only now beginning to be effectively enforced in Covington), and its members formed committees to address each of these concerns.

Percy sat on the education committee and took as his main responsibility the organizing and launching of a local Head Start Program and day-care center. The task, he quickly discovered, would not be easy. St. Tammany Parish school officials had long refused to provide facilities for such a program. Percy's hopes were lifted, though, when the Novitiate of the Eucharistic Sisters of St. Dominic offered some of their extra space. Still needing an established backer, Percy wrote to Father Twomey asking if Loyola University would agree to sponsor the council's application to the Office of Economic Opportunity. Twomey secured the university president's permission, and the program was soon off the ground. There were further complications—including finding and paying for buses and drivers—but Percy found solutions, often by contributing his own money and time. (As a substitute driver, Percy returned home one day to discover a napping child on one of the seats, a child who, when he was awakened, was none too sure about where he lived.)

Education was not Percy's only interest. Struck by the difficulty blacks faced in obtaining loans for business starts or home buying, Percy came up with the idea of founding a credit union under the aegis of the Community Relations Council. Emily Diamond, a teacher and friend, remembers Percy's beguiling way of recruiting her to serve as an officer of the credit union. Calling her one evening in the spring of 1969, Percy came right to the point: "Emily, how would you like to lend your integrity and be treasurer of the credit union?" With equal measures of charm

and persistence, Percy recruited officers, located backers, and brought in
a federal examiner from the national credit union administration. In
November of 1969 the Community Relations Council of Greater Covington Federal Credit Union was officially opened in space made available by Percy's long-time friend and neighbor, Nikky Barranger. The
annual rent for the space was one long-stemmed rose, which Percy
promptly delivered to the attorney every Easter.

Needless to say, there were those in Covington and environs who
considered the council members troublemakers and meddlers. Discreet
as their operations were—the council published no membership list, for
example, and it changed its venue each week—the council members
became known and many were subjected to threats and the usual Klan-
nish harassment. Curt Thomsen, a psychologist from the Delta Primate
Center, found a cross burning on his lawn, and other members found
that some of their old friends were not speaking to them. A number of
the council's projects, notably the Ramsey Park Development Corporation, which was started in an attempt to buy and sell land to blacks who
wanted to build single-family homes, were effectively killed by the parish's police jury (the Louisiana equivalent of a county board). Despite
the predictable resistance, the council had its triumphs, and that Covington experienced none of the major racial incidents that occurred in
many nearby towns and communities was at least in part a tribute to the
council's mediating role.

Percy was proud of the works of the council and would remain a
member and supporter of its many offshoots for the rest of his life. But
even when he was most actively involved in the late 1960s and early
1970s, Percy maintained a low profile. Never one to speak in meetings,
he preferred to lobby quietly for his ideas. And his financial contributions to various projects were always made under the strict condition of
anonymity. This was not so much a becoming modesty as a desire to
avoid being labeled a do-gooder or a member of a particular camp. Some
of Percy's best friends were people none too enthusiastic about the council's activities, and Percy did not want to present himself, or be presented, as their enemy or their better. He did not want to set himself
against any part of the community he had become a part of. If Percy the
novelist knew how important it was to be able to move among all camps
within Covington, Percy the Christian knew that it was not his place to
cast stones. He recognized the racist in himself all too well. As he often
told his friend Nikki Barranger, he believed that all people were racist
and never fully overcame their racism. Percy was not above using the
word "nigger" in his letters to Shelby Foote and other friends, and
though there was always some irony or self-mockery intended, he had to

know that there was almost no way of using the word without violating the principles that he was quietly working for in other ways.

For all Percy's quietness, however, those who knew what he accomplished were appreciative. Mrs. Helen Frick, a teacher and leading figure in the black community, summed up his contribution succinctly: "He was a fine man who did a lot for the community. You couldn't find a man who did more." Zeugner may be right in seeing the persistence of the old aristocratic outlook in Percy, complete with its snobberies. But if Percy was motivated as much by noblesse oblige as by Christian principle, his sense of oblige was almost as strong as Uncle Will's.

Racial conflict, escalating political divisiveness and discontent, the intolerance of radicals of all stripes, the tyranny of scientific expertise, the decay of language—these were among the public issues that quickened Percy's satirical impulses in the novel he was working on. But Percy was also concerned with matters closer to the individual human heart—love and sex as well as the soul's salvation—as the novel's title clearly suggests. While the world falls apart and Dr. Tom More seeks to perfect his lapsometer, the alcoholic doctor is also trying to navigate his way across the sea of love, triangulating among three very different women.

Love and sex are not new concerns in Percy's fiction. They figure just as importantly in Percy's first two novels. For Binx Bolling, the two have become disastrously unlinked, although, by novel's end, the discovery of faith and the commitment of marriage hold forth the possibility of their reunion. For Will Barrett, sex and love are even more problematic. He is incapable of anything more than desperate lunges at both.

For Tom More, abandoned husband turned suburban Don Juan, sex is just too much, a horn of plenty whose fruits, and their tasting, can never be exhausted. Although he knows that fornication is a sin precisely because it can become its own adequate and self-delighting end, the problem, as he explains to his colleague and psychiatrist Max Gottlieb, is that he no longer feels guilty about committing it. (Gottlieb, the good neobehaviorist, cannot understand why More feels bad about *not* feeling guilty about something so *natural* as sex with a consenting adult partner.)

To say that sex enjoyed a central place in the culture of the sixties (really the decade that extends from 1965 to 1975) is to state the obvious in two ways. Sex plays a central part in the culture of any age, since cultures are greatly concerned with the organization of biological drives, sex being prominent among them. But in America in the sixties, sex enjoyed a unique preeminence in American culture, a prominence that made the libidinal loosening-up of the twenties seem modest by comparison. Sex was brought out in the open, desublimated, and celebrated.

Percy, an astute consumer and critic of culture, was well aware of what the culture was saying. Yet he also wanted to understand why. To some extent, he saw the obsession with sexuality as a further consequence of the seventeenth-century separation of the self from its world, a separation that began, intellectually, with Descartes' positing of a *res cogitans*, a thinking thing, as different and distinct from *res extensa*, the physico-material world of extension (including, of course, one's own physical body). The Cartesian revolution produced, in Percy's opinion, a baleful anthropology, reducing the human self to a ghost in a machine. To the intellectual in particular, Percy wrote in 1969, "genital sexuality is the most urgent symptom" of abstracted "angelism"; it is an endless "reaching out for the flesh which has been shucked." The creature that has tried to become pure mind can reenter his body only in the act of sex. Sex thus becomes, in Percy's view, a debased sacrament, uniting material and spiritual worlds but failing to point toward that which makes both possible. Semiotically speaking, sex as its own end is a failed sign; it is a biochemical event, an energy exchange, pleasurable but not enriching (though the guilt that it may occasion lends it some faint spiritual piquancy).

This, of course, is what Percy depicts as Dr. Tom More's problem. Sex has ceased to be a meaningful sign, a part of a truly sacramental life. It once was such in his marriage to Doris. But things went wrong. Abandoned by his wife, More now has three girlfriends, little if any guilt about fornication, and an obsession with perfecting a device that will not only diagnose but repair man's riven nature, uniting his angelic and bestial sides. (One does not have to look too hard to see self-parody in this quest to perfect a Descartes-reverser.)

Dead end that it may ultimately be, then, "genital sexuality" and its grip on contemporary man and woman was a subject that Percy, as social diagnostician, could not ignore. But how was the novelist to handle it? Percy had deep misgivings about the depiction of the erotic in fiction. This was not merely prudishness. Almost two decades earlier, he had objected, on aesthetic grounds, to Shelby Foote's inclusion of an explicitly sexual scene in his novel *Follow Me Down*, arguing that it broke the spell of art, violating the work's all-important unity. Foote had come around to Percy's position somewhat, but not completely, and now again the two writers found themselves worrying the same bone, no doubt because Percy was wrestling directly with the question in his book. In the summer of 1968, Foote had strongly recommended John Updike's *Couples* as "better than any novel I've read in a long time." The "sex stuff," he assured Percy, was just "trappings," somewhat obscuring the fact that the novel was concerned with the "biggest problems of all, and profoundly moral—depicting a life in which Duty and Work have been replaced by Truth and Play, as goals or precepts." Foote felt sure that Percy would appreciate the novel if he could get past "the shocks and shudders that kind of thing arouses in that basically puritan soul of yours."

Percy had a long and lively interest in Updike's work. Back when Knopf was preparing *The Moviegoer* for publication, Percy had asked his editor for a copy of *Rabbit, Run*. Since then, he had followed Updike's career closely. Among other things, Percy knew of Updike's interest in Kierkegaard and other religious thinkers. Percy wondered, though, what these theological interests amounted to. Were they just "trappings" and sex the real thing, or vice versa? In any case, Percy needed no encouragement to read *Couples*. He was already reading it when Foote made the recommendation. We know this because in June he received a letter from Lewis Lawson asking whether he knew of any other American writers who were directly influenced by Kierkegaard. Percy promptly replied:

> Casting about for an answer to your question, the only candidate which comes to mind is Updike's *Couples* and I'm not even sure about that. I mention it because (1) Updike has written on SK and (2) *Couples* is evidently open to an obvious Kierkegaardian explication: e.g. fucking elevated to a kind of religion, SK's sphere of esthetic-damnation, and then transcended and discarded—for the ethical? for the religious? Even so, I couldn't swear that Updike had SK in mind when he wrote it. But he probably did.

As much as Percy admired Updike as a thinker and prose stylist, he was puzzled by his treatment of sex—his elevation of coitus to a kind of ultimate epistemology, and his minute depiction of the act itself. Percy could not help feeling that the effect was, despite all intentions, pornographic. High pornography, to be sure, but still pornography.

Percy and Foote's discussion of the role of sex in art continued intensively through the writing of *Love in the Ruins*. In the spring of the following year, Shelby and Gwyn came to Mary Pratt's wedding. She and Byrne Robert Lobdell, a Covington native and the son of friends of the Percys, were married at St. Peter's Church on May 31, just three days after Percy's fifty-third birthday. In the swirl of dinner, ceremonies, and receptions, Foote and Percy managed to have the beginning of one of their old-style literary discussions. "You must come up here before too long and give us a chance to get down to talking about books and writing," Foote wrote the week after the wedding. "We got started again once between drinks at your house but there was no time."

The depiction of sex was not the only literary matter the two writers grappled with. In October, shortly after Percy gave him a copy of Flannery O'Connor's collected essays, *Mystery and Manners,* Foote responded to the gift with a rambling disquisition on O'Connor's place in American letters. Judging her a "minor-minor writer" who had possessed the talent but not had time or experience to become a major one, Foote took the occasion to get in a few jabs at Catholic writers. Surprisingly, though, Foote told Percy not to take offense, because he did not consider him true to type: "I dont consider you a Catholic writer at all, except in your spare time out of hope of heaven." It was an odd exemption, yet in some ways Percy went along with it. (Many months later, Percy would even admit that Foote had been right "about me not being a Catholic writer as Flannery was.")

By late autumn, Percy had completed a first draft of the novel and was working with revisions and additions. He confessed to Foote how tempting it was to go on tinkering indefinitely, but Foote cautioned that "reading it over and looking back youll always see how much more you could have made of it—so you go back and do. Knowing when to turn loose and move on is one of the big problems; 'a general mess of imprecision,' Eliot said, and truly. A sad trade."

Despite the warning, Percy slid through the New Year and the winter revising compulsively. Unlike Foote, who would not leave a day's work until it was polished beyond possible further revision, Percy went repeatedly over his manuscripts. In early spring, he took some time away from his book to respond to the queries of another scholar, Martin Luschei, an assistant professor at California Polytechnic State University, who was hard at work transforming his dissertation on Percy—what he called an intellectual biography—into a book. Percy gave full answers to questions about the value of his scientific background, his preferred schools of psychiatry, the role of the modern novelist, and the character of the new era. Percy was reluctant to say much about the novel he was working on, except to divulge its current title: *How to Make Love in the Ruins, or: The Adventures of a Bad Catholic at a Time Near the End of the World.* Percy also indicated that his novel would not follow, "except very loosely, the article in *Katallagete,* being at once less solemn, less literal and more contemporary." Noting that Luschei was covering ground similar to that treated by Lewis Lawson, Percy also recommended that Luschei look at Lawson's forthcoming essay, "Walker Percy's Southern Stoic."

In late spring, the southern Stoic found himself involved in a local controversy, one that recalls, in some ways, the controversies that earlier generations of Percys found themselves caught up in. This one was a legal controversy that developed indirectly out of recent federal court efforts to integrate Louisiana's public schools. Specifically, black students at the St. Tammany's high school had objected to the presence of the Confederate flag in the principal's office, and their objection had finally made its way before the U.S. District Court in New Orleans. Percy had been called to appear on May 11 as an "expert witness (an observer of the culture)," as he told Foote, to support the blacks' contention that the flag was an offense and a provocation. Despite the effort of the opposing attorney to discredit the witness's "expertise" on something so broad as southern culture, Percy was allowed to make his presentation. His point, in brief, was that the flag had once meant something honorable, connoting the valor and patriotism of those who fought under it, but that during the past fifteen years or so, since the Supreme Court decision of 1954, it had come "to stand specifically as a symbol of segregation, a symbol of opposition to desegregation of the public schools," and that no one in the contemporary South could fail to see it as anything other than a representation of "segregation, white supremacy, and racism." Percy's contribution to the winning side earned him a a bomb threat from the local Klan, and for two weeks he and his family slept upstairs in the attic. Percy annoyed others in Covington when he accused the local Catholic school of "running a seg school with holy water thrown on it." As he told Foote, "Now the Catholics (most) are mad at me. And I do believe they're more unpleasant than the Klan."

Giving offense and going on the attack had become, it seems, more than a literary strategy. Nor did Percy restrict himself to the race issue. Later in the summer, he wrote a letter to *Commonweal* protesting the burning of draft board records by Daniel and Philip Berrigan, among others. Percy dismissed as specious their justification that they were opposing an immoral U.S. foreign policy. "No society could long endure if many people resorted to the same violent, not to say illegal, means of translating belief into action," Percy warned, and he likened the Berrigans' lawlessness to that of the Klan:

> As it happens, I stand a good deal closer to the Berrigans than to the Klan. The point is, however: God save us all from the moral zealot who places himself above the law and who is willing to burn my house down, and yours, providing he feels he is sufficiently right and I sufficiently wrong.

The novel that he was writing could contain much of Percy's anger about the current age but not all of it; and by August, he no longer had the novel as an outlet for his spleen. "Yes," he told Foote on August 4, "I'm shut of this son of a bitch at last, just got back from town and mailing off two copies to agent." Within a month, Henry Robbins reported that everything about the book looked good except the epilogue. It needed "tightening," and Percy agreed. Also, though he didn't say so to Robbins, Percy was still unhappy about the title. *How to Make Love in the Ruins* was supposed to suggest a self-improvement manual, but it sounded clunky. Percy was also considering another possibility, *The Center Did Not Hold,* but Foote said it was no good. In fact, Foote didn't think much of either possibility and proposed another alternative, *The Fall Out,* a title that Percy had once considered using for the book that became *The Last Gentleman.*

Except for the necessary work on the epilogue, Percy wanted to think no more about fiction. He had decided that his next project would be a theory of language. Apart from that, the only other thing that he wanted to think about was golf, which he had resumed playing after a thirty-year hiatus. He was surprised to discover that he shot what he had around 1941—around 90—but he was even more surprised that he had returned to the game at all. He had never been an avid golfer, although it held for him a certain aesthetic charm and a certain mystery. The trouble was, the mystery was not particularly agreeable, consisting as it did of troubling associations with his Birmingham childhood, the house on the golf course, and his brooding, unhappy father. Perhaps that explains the somewhat idiosyncratic way in which Percy played the game. For him there would be very few high-betting, eighteen-hole foursomes with the "boys." That was the way his father had played. Percy preferred to play at dusk with Bunt, never more than nine holes, and always on foot. It was more like walking than golfing. But it was still golf, and one cannot help seeing Percy's return to it as an involuntary return to an old, unresolved hurt. In certain ways, Percy seemed to be feeling more out of sorts than usual these days, more depressed and angry, and the shift was something that he could not attribute exclusively to the age or even to the finishing of a book. It also had to with his own age, his fifty-four years, and with changes in himself that he could not quite make sense of.

By February of 1971, Percy had finished work on the novel and settled definitely on the title. *How to Make* was removed from *Love in the Ruins* to make it sound less "Masters and Johnson," and the subtitle, *The Adventures of a Bad Catholic at a Time Near the End of the World,* was retained, over the protest of the sales department at Farrar, Straus & Giroux. "After all," as he observed to Caroline Gordon, "a *bad* Catholic ought to be attractive." Gordon, now in her upper seventies, had just completed a novel herself, *The Glory of Hera,* and was hoping that Percy would meet her at the abbey in Conyers for another reunion. Percy begged off, saying that he had to tutor his daughter every evening. He had another reason for not wanting to travel: a prior obligation to appear in New York in early March.

Percy faced two command performances in the city, both of which were flattering but also somewhat nervousness-making. The first, on the evening of March 2, was a dinner that Roger Straus and FSG were giving in his honor at the Four Seasons, a sizable affair to which many of New York's literati (and a few from beyond New York) were invited. The second was a short address—a few remarks about his forthcoming novel —that he had been invited to deliver at the Publishers' Publicity Association of the 1971 NBA.

The pressure of the events gave Percy a worse-than-usual case of what he later described to his publicist at Farrar, Straus as his New York Syndrome—a mix of amnesia, disorientation, and wild mood swings. Although he been determined to be on his best behavior at the Four Seasons, he felt afterward that he had performed abysmally, as he later confessed to Jean Stafford: "It's just as well you didn't come to the party, though I'd love to have seen you, because I found myself sitting at the table with Elizabeth Hardwick and the wife of that poet from Greensboro, NC [Randall Jarrell] but without quite knowing who either were, though both were very nice, but I was even more disoriented than usual."

The day after the Four Seasons dinner Percy spoke at the NBA ceremony about a subject that he admitted at the outset made him uneasy: his own work. It made him uneasy, he explained, because whatever he said about the novel would be misleading. If he said the novel was set in the future, for example, he would make it sound as though it were a futuristic novel. Similarly, if he said the novel satirized the right and left extremes in American political life, he would be giving the impression that the novel was a political satire, like Orwell's 1984, which it decidedly was not. "Actually," Percy explained, "the novel is only incidentally about politics. It is really about the pursuit of happiness."

For all his avowals of uneasiness, Percy proved to be an effective rhetorician. By repeatedly saying what the book was not, he gave a pretty good idea of what it was—or what he wanted his audience to think it was. He closed his remarks by calling attention to two things about himself. The first was that he was a doctor by training and that, as a result, his literary concerns were "perhaps more diagnostic and therapeutic than they otherwise would be." This, he hoped, would not make his novel too moralizing or heavy-handed. The second thing he called attention to was that he came from the Deep South at a time when the South had finally ceased being the most morally tainted region of the Union.

"It's not that the South has got rid of its ancient stigma and is out of trouble," he noted. "It is rather that the rest of the country is now also stigmatized and is in even deeper trouble." Percy used his "mission of the South" theme as the dramatic finale to his book-launching speech, a decision that may reveal more of what Percy thought about (and hoped of) his novel than anything else in the speech. "So if the novel has any messages," he perorated, "one might be this: Don't give up, New York, California, Chicago, Philadelphia! Louisiana is with you. Georgia is on your side."

The speech went down so smoothly that most of the audience might not have noticed how radical Percy's words were—radical, not in any partisan political sense, but in their implicit criticism of the dominant American ideology of progressive optimism. Percy made the point almost in passing, and not very clearly, in the middle of his speech, when he said that he wanted his novel to call a bluff: "For it has often seemed to me that much of the violence and alienation of today can be traced to a secret and paradoxical conviction that America is immovable and indestructible." What Percy was suggesting—and here one must interpolate —is that Americans have too long believed in their exceptional role in history, have thought too long that they were the chosen people occupying the "city on the hill." This notion, originally arising out of Puritanism, had of course long lost its religious underpinnings. Under the influence of Emerson and other American transcendentalists, the American became the New Man, a creature who believed that if he recognized his originality and cultivated his talents, he could become master of all he surveyed. Thus was born the true American ideology, the boundless faith in individual autonomy (the perfectible self) and progress.

Percy, however, believed that America was now facing the rebuttal of its core ideology. The center was not holding. Liberalism, stripped of its Puritan sense of sin, promised all but required nothing in return, assured rights but exacted no responsibilities. Failing to acknowledge the perversity of human beings, the liberal faith was beginning to break down. Yet Americans were still having trouble facing failure, or even limits, and that, Percy believed, was why Americans had something to learn from the South. For the South, despite all its changes, still had a tragic sense. Having experienced defeat, southerners understood limits. The South also had this advantage: Its culture was still strongly imbued with a theological sense of man. On this point Percy could have quoted Flannery O'Connor's view that "while the South was hardly Christ-centered, it is most certainly Christ-haunted." The South, in other words, could remind the rest of the Union that humans were fallen creatures, imperfectible, and doomed to despair to the extent they thought otherwise.

. . .

Percy had thought—hoping as much as fearing—that his book would offend everyone, but when Shelby Foote (to whom Percy dedicated the novel) read the manuscript the summer before it came out, he predicted, for the most part correctly, that such notions were groundless:

> Dont worry for a minute about various groups taking offense. You know any bookreading Panthers or Kluxers? And most liberals dont consider themselves liberals of this type. They feel about other liberals the ways Jews feel about Kikes, and are happy to see them taken down. Conservatives, stolid creatures that they are, will think you are approving of their position—they see it expressed so seldom in hard covers. As for your fellow Catholics, I guess you just have to settle for being considered immoral, like the rest of us modern writers.

The early reviews, most emanating from the dens of northeastern liberalism, were largely favorable, some almost embarrassingly so. Martha Duffy of *Time* declared the novel an "abrupt departure from the past" but made it abundantly clear that the change was all to the good. Peter Prescott of *Newsweek* couldn't praise it enough: "Have I said how much I like this book?" he asked (unnecessarily) at the conclusion of his review. " 'Love in the Ruins' is Percy's best novel, his least elusive and least mannered novel, his gentlest, his funniest novel. Charming: there is no other word for it." The daily reviews in *The Washington Post*, the *Chicago Sun-Times*, and *The New York Times* could only add to the publisher's pleasure. Percy felt a little uneasy. Of course, he appreciated praise and he wanted his book to sell, but he had a healthy skepticism about nice words of any kind.

The second wave of reviews, those written in the weekend book supplements and the intellectual journals, cast a more critical eye on the literary weaknesses of the novel. The novelist Thomas McGuane in *The New York Times Book Review* found that characterization in the novel was often "replaced by a kind of friendly sociology of distinctions that may seem trifling in a novel that is about the detachment of the soul. . . . At one point the Georgia Presbyterians, Tyler Texans, West Virginia tomboys or rounded Shenandoah Valley girls rain upon the reader's eye like ciphers." He also argued, less convincingly, that Percy's efforts to fictionalize "Catholic ontology" were unsuccessful, that "Aquinas never does look right alongside lawnmowers or golf clubs." Despite both his legitimate and his peevish complaints, McGuane expressed the fellow craftsman's awe at a novelist who could write at such an "extraordinary level of physical perceptions." McGuane also acknowledged one of the more remarkable things about Percy the artist—that he was "capable, moment by moment, of being better than one can quickly see."

In *The New York Review of Books*, V. S. Pritchett called Percy "a spirited and inventive writer" with a "charred hell-fire edge to his observations." But in that completely modest, nonchalant way of going right to the heart of the matter, Pritchett put his finger on the novelist's greatest weakness: "I am afraid that in the eye of this hurricane of laughing anger, there is a sentimentalist. Still, a very clever one, full of ideas." This was not at all a condescending English put-down of a Yank novelist. It was simply true. Pritchett did not name the brand of Percy's sentimentalism, but the life Percy has Tom More and his wife Ellen living after the revolution that has put the Bantus in Paradise is very close to the preindustrial, collard-hoeing, close-to-the-earth ideal of the Agrarians, revivified by a strong dose of Catholic sacramentalism—and by a complete reversal of the old social hierarchy, with the bottom rail now definitely on top. (It is interesting that shortly before *Love in the Ruins* appeared, Percy wrote Lewis Simpson to praise his article, "The Southern Writer and the Great Literary Secession," for formulating so well what Percy described as his "own vague speculations on the absence of the tradition of literary alienation in the South and both the value and the odd fecklessness of Agrarianism." Percy must have been at least partially aware that his novel proposed an Agrarian ideal shorn of its more feckless features. If the price of this fancy was sentimentality, Percy had apparently been willing to pay it—at least this time.)

Though Percy had done his best to agitate his fellow Catholics, liberals and conservatives alike, Catholic reviewers certainly showed no signs of unhappiness. In the novel, for example, Percy has the former priest Kev Kevin reading *Commonweal* while he sits at the console of the vaginal indicators at the Love Clinic, but *Commonweal*'s review of *Love in the Ruins* rose nowhere close to the bait. "*Love in the Ruins* is a remarkable anatomy of our times, and one that may offer a possibility, if not quite a promise, of deliverance," concluded Mark Taylor.

The most explicitly Catholic reading of the novel was offered by Wilfrid Sheed, in a followup essay that appeared in the July 4 issue of *The New York Times Book Review*. It was anything but hostile. Sheed marveled that Percy had gotten away with writing a "blatantly theological novel" at a time when nobody, "not even a clergyman over 40, would buy a theological novel if you called it that." Sheed concluded that he had done so because most readers ignored the book's religious themes and motifs. Yet this, he insisted, ultimately did the book an injustice. For "while Percy's wit and style have been properly noted, there is a danger his book may seem frothy and aimlessly crotchety if the heavy religious motif is overlooked." As well as unpacking some of the Catholic theology in the novel, Sheed also discussed the possible offensiveness of Percy's southernness and his "sly conservatism." Sheed pointed to a passage in which Percy tells a Bantu revolutionary, "I don't think you [people] can make it," which some readers took as proof of Percy's true reactionary colors, as in fact a far more inclusive statement of Percy's notion of human fallibility: "The Bantus may not make it," Sheed observed, "but then, nobody else has made it either."

One reader who saw nothing but froth and crotchetiness in the novel was L. E. Sissman in *The New Yorker*, but Sissman did not so much ignore the book's theological vision as disallow it as a legitimate excuse for spleen. Sissman ticked off a list of technical failings. The tone, "controlled, sardonic, flat, flip, smart-ass," was incongruent with the bright, unstable narrator-protagonist Tom More. The futuristic landscape failed to be anything more than a heap of "shallow, warmed-over clichés of the American sixties." The symbolism and "mythico-naturalistic doings" of More were too "obvious and crypto-obvious." The novelist did not take his own characters seriously enough. And all of these failings were bound up with Percy's theological commitments. "There is a suspicious sourness in all this . . ." Sissman declared, "which almost makes me wonder whether Walker Percy has given up on man as a fit subject for rehabilitation, and whether, in 'Love in the Ruins,' he is baiting and mocking man, in an affirmation of faith, to the greater glory of God." Percy must have found it some consolation that he had managed to rile at least one humanist. (Percy, moreover, was learning that he could count on *The New Yorker* either to attack or to ignore him. After the snide short review of *The Moviegoer*, it had not even deigned to review *The Last Gentleman*.)

The range of readers who liked *Love in the Ruins* was both pleasing and baffling to Percy. On one hand, all of Percy's friends from college and medical school as well as those in Covington and New Orleans thought the novel was the best thing he had written. His SAE brother from Chapel Hill, Charles Poe, now a lawyer in Raleigh, North Carolina, had thought Percy's first couple of novels "too apathetic," but *Love in the Ruins* seemed to him an unmitigated success. Another friend from Chapel Hill days, Ned Boone, wrote to say that he was "shocked at" Sissman's review. "I don't know what Sissman means by 'mythico-naturalistic' and I doubt that he does," Boone snorted. Percy was touched by the show of solidarity, but he assured Boone that he was so sick of his novel that he was as "fed up with 'good' reviews as with bad." He also could not resist passing on Bunt's reaction to Sissman's review: "My wife says Sissman is right—I *am* a smart-ass."

The favorable reactions of his old-boy network were far less surprising than the reaction of another bloc of readers: "The book is taking off in

California," he told Foote. "Don't know whether it's the hippies who are reading the truth about themselves or the Knotheads who think they are." Then of course there were the unclassifiable admirers, among them Robert Coles. Talking like a fellow physician, Coles let Percy know that the book was taking over both him and his wife. "My hypothalamus, with its 'laughing center' and its 'sadness' (the ones that always stain purple) has been particularly affected."

Despite the encouraging words from expected and unexpected corners, Percy harbored a private, nagging feeling that the book had finally not come off. In truth, he had thought that the novel would have been more of a sensation—at least as much of one as Bellow's *Mr. Sammler's Planet*, which he had read around the time his own book came out and had admired tremendously. In some ways, Percy had more vanity attached to *Ruins* than he had had to the previous two novels. He saw it as his big statement, his big novel. Now, he had serious doubts, about both the book and his expectations for it. In early autumn, Percy made an unusual confession to his editor Henry Robbins: "To tell you the truth —though I haven't admitted it to anybody else—I'm disappointed *Love in the Ruins* didn't do better." He was talking mainly about the commercial performance of the book, of course, but there was an undertone of larger dissatisfaction, a hint of disappointment with his art. (The sales of the book had not been bad, and paperback sales would be excellent. Furthermore, the book came within a vote of winning the National Book Award the following year, the deciding vote having been withheld by Christopher Lehmann-Haupt, who objected to Percy's winning the award a second time.) So many reviewers had praised him as a writer of "charm" that he might have wondered if he had turned soft at the center, and Pritchett's words about the "sentimentalist" at the eye of the storm might have stung far more smartly than Sissman's charge of "smart-ass." Percy had to wonder if in being nice, in being charming, he had betrayed the very object of his fiction: the difficult truth.

14

The Third Half
of Life

———◆———

This is a strange business.

—WALKER PERCY TO SHELBY
FOOTE, February 3, 1971

Although his tone was jesting, Percy meant it when he told Shelby
Foote in the summer of 1970 that he was going to turn his attention to
a major work of philosophy. Percy believed that the project he had in
mind might even stand as his major intellectual accomplishment, a work
of more permanent worth than any of his novels. It was no small ambition, and Percy would, in fact, accomplish some part of it—if not the
grand edifice he originally envisioned, at least a block or two of the
projected structure. What would turn him aside from this enterprise
would be the itch to make up another story. Most surprising to Percy
was how quickly it came on. By February of 1971, only six months after
his grand declaration of intent, and four months before *Love in the Ruins*
even appeared in the bookstores, he was already feeling the urge to tell
another story. The itch was not the only thing that made him think that
he was caught up in a "strange business," as he explained to Foote:

> Believe it or not, I am thinking about writing a proper planned-out
> Footean architechtonic novel. It's about a man who finds himself am-
> nesic in a hospital for the criminally insane. What he does not know,

and has made himself forget, and pieces together later, is that he has killed his wife and infant son. . . . The attraction of amnesia: with it one can explore the psychology of things, even the best of things, getting old and used up, and the reverse phenomenon of the amnesiac's being born again into a new world.

With the exception of one detail—the infant son—Percy had accurately adumbrated the novel that he would work on, fitfully and uncomfortably, for the next six years. "Uncomfortably" is actually an understatement, for the writing of this novel was a profoundly unsettling experience. Percy went through a kind of personal hell to create *Lancelot* —appropriately, to some extent, because *Lancelot* would be Percy's darkest, most infernal novel.

The connection between Percy's life and his work during the years he wrote *Lancelot* may well be one of the greater mysteries of his biography. Put rather simply, the mystery boils down to this: Did Percy write an infernal novel because he was going through a hellish time in his life, or did he compel himself to go through hell in order to write an infernal novel?

Of course, there is no reason to suppose that an imaginative writer must experience what he writes about. One need only recall Tolstoy's remark that a woman novelist peering into a military barracks for five minutes will learn all she needs to know to write about soldiering. But Percy was something of a special case. Though not in any literal way an autobiographical writer, he drew on his life in very decisive ways. His novels grew out of states of mind—psychological, moral, and spiritual predicaments—through which he himself had passed.

Percy, furthermore, had something to prove when he began writing *Lancelot,* something he feared that he had failed to make convincing in *Love in the Ruins,* and something he had barely dealt with in his first two novels: the reality and presence of evil. Evil has its place in *Love in the Ruins,* notably in Tom More's concern that he no longer feels guilt over his sins and in the appearance of the devil himself, Art Immelmann. But perhaps out of formal necessity—it was, after all, a comic novel as well as a satire—evil appears to be a rather light matter. More's moral numbness seems to be a temporary dysfunction that he will surely overcome, and Immelmann, like most devils in literature, arouses more curiosity than horror.

Percy's comic outlook was nothing he was ashamed of. In fact, he frequently alluded to Kierkegaard's belief in the proximity of the comic to the religious mode. A comic outlook, however, is something that must be earned. Without a sense of evil or tragedy or hopelessness—

those things over which comedy must triumph—the comic vision may seem shallow and sentimental. Dante, in order to make a complete *commedia*, had first to create his inferno. Percy knew that he would have to do the same. (And in fact, Percy had Dante very much in mind while writing *Lancelot*. At one point he would tell Foote—only half in jest—that he was going to appropriate the famous first lines of the *Inferno* for the opening of his novel: "Now in the middle of this journey of our life, I came to myself in a dark wood.")

When *Lancelot* appeared in 1977, reviewers and critics would say many things about it, many of them unfavorable, many of them silly, but no critic would suggest, as V. S. Pritchett had of *Love in the Ruins*, that behind the storm and fury of the novel there lurked a sentimentalist. Indeed, many people would wonder how the man who had written this novel had also written his previous three. Seeing the apocalyptic mirth of *Love in the Ruins* replaced by apocalyptic fury in *Lancelot*, critics, friends, and even family would wonder if something had gone terribly wrong, if hope and grace had been lost and despair come rushing in. The novel itself provided the best response to this widespread concern, but the point was so subtly made that many people ignored it. Percy had been in hell. But he had made it through.

On one level, *Lancelot* might be seen as Percy's struggle with his greatest moral weakness, his pride, his *superbia*. Pride was the sin he had fought against all his life, even before he knew that it was a sin. Percy's pride took the form of indignation at the imposition of life itself; it was an attitude, or disposition, bound up with an almost innate sense that he should not be burdened by the pettiness and complications of existence or by the offensive humanity of other people. Shyness is the earliest expression of this pride: an instinctive withdrawal before the superfluity of the world and others. Shyness may be an endearing quality in the young, and it was in Percy, but with the passing of years, it inevitably becomes something far less appealing. Then the superior, self-contained soul emerges as the snob he is.

To be sure, this vanity can take many complicated and deceptive forms. It may even tame itself into a civilized affectation of concern for one's "lessers." Percy understood very well the strategies of noblesse oblige, having learned them at the feet of a master. The artful exercise of such noblesse was indeed the main form that Percy's sense of superiority took, even after his conversion to Christianity made him see such noblesse for what it truly was. But he was capable of assuming other forms of superiority as well. We find their literary reflections, for example, in Sutter Vaught (the icy, cynical intellectual snob that Percy

sometimes was) or in Binx Bolling (the "smart-assed" flaneur and dilet-
tantish clown who Percy, in his lighter moods, sometimes became).

Snobbery and art have a special and dangerous affinity as well. An
attitude of superiority may not be indispensable to the artist, but aesthetic distance and snobbish disdain have something in common, and
the former certainly may reinforce the latter. Percy, good Kierkegaardian
that he was, fully appreciated the temptations and dangers of the aesthetic posture, and he did everything in his power not to succumb to it.
He did so not only because religious principles obliged him to recognize
his radical kinship with his fellow man but also because he saw the
subsumption of the self under the aspect of the artist as a form of bad
faith, a capitulation to one of the dominant myths of modern life (that
is, the myth of the artist as superior being). Talent was mysterious, but
Percy recognized it as what it was—a gift—and not as a sign of individual superiority.

Of course, knowing something and living by it are two different
things, and many artists who have understood the danger of succumbing
to the aesthetic role have nevertheless done so. It is hard not to. Even in
a post-romantic age, the artist is granted an exalted status, and if others
insist on seeing the writer or painter as special or different, it is hard for
the artist to disabuse them of their awe. Then, too, it is much easier to
live in the realm of aesthetic detachment and to imagine, for as long
as one can, that one is truly above the human predicament. After all,
the artist *is* to a great extent detached; it is the attitude he must
assume when he works. All the more tempting, then, to cultivate that
attitude even when he isn't (even though doing so may eventually kill
his art).

Percy certainly knew the temptation—and felt it never more keenly
than during the years after *Love in the Ruins* appeared. These were years
of great honors and accolades, years when scholars, journalists, and other
admirers would come unstintingly to his door, years when it would have
been all too easy to accept an exalted idea of himself. Yet he resisted the
temptation, even as he turned it, the alluring vanity of it all, to use in
the book he was writing. Percy resisted because he knew that he and his
art would be lost if he gave in. Still, it was not easy remaining a man in
his own skin, a husband and father in his family, a citizen in his community.

Above all else, Percy's family remained his strongest anchor; his home,
his sanctuary and source of strength. There is something characteristi-
cally southern about this attachment, of course, but in Percy's case there
was something even more powerful than culture at work. As a child,

Percy had seen his family disintegrate before his eyes, and even when both his parents were alive, family life was neither reassuring nor joyful. Recall Roy Percy's words: "It was not a happy family." Percy's ambivalence toward marriage and family appears in his first two novels, reflecting the doubt and vacillation he went through in the years preceding his marriage to Bunt Townsend. Marriage to him was fraught with dangers, including the possible repetition of the fateful Percy pattern. But running from marriage and family seem to point to an equally desolate end: the freedom of pure possibility and solitude. Marriage was part of the larger gamble that Percy decided to make when he reached his lowest point, his ground zero, in New Mexico. In marrying Bunt, Percy gambled upon finding what he had never experienced in childhood, and the gamble succeeded. Bunt and he had made a strong and happy family, and it, in return, had sustained him for more than twenty years.

Yet even his family was changing during these years. Mary Pratt had already left the nest and married. (Percy found some compensation for this loss when Mary Pratt had her first son, John Walker, in the spring of 1970, and her second, Robert, a year later.) Percy's other daughter, Ann, was also moving closer to independence. Finishing her junior year at Saint Scholastica in the same spring that *Love in the Ruins* appeared, she did so well in her courses that she was allowed to enter a special program for seniors at Southeastern Louisiana in Hammond. Percy was proud of his daughter's achievement but at the same time sad to see her already pulling away from home. He and his second daughter had, as Bunt often observed, a "special bond" that came partly from natural affinity and partly from years of working together to overcome her handicap.

Friends of the girls who often came to the house thought of the Percys as the most tight-knit of families, a family held together by its daily, weekly, and annual rituals. Over the years, the Percys' circle of friends had come to count on these ritual occasions—a big midday Easter-egg hunt on Easter, for example, or a festive party on Christmas Eve. The family, including in-laws and grandchildren in the later years, could count on a big sit-down meal at noon every Saturday.

There was always a great deal of fun at the Percys' house. In the warmer months, the family and friends would take to the bogue, swimming or boating or playing around the dock. When the weather turned bad, the games and other activities would move indoors. Percy was unperturbed, even pleased by all the activity around him. Ann and Mary Pratt's friends remembered him as a quiet, friendly presence, occasionally coming out of his bedroom office to see what was happening, stalking around the yard with his hands stuck in his pockets, or sitting on the dock watching ducks, egrets, and other waterfowl pass in quiet procession. But Percy was not, in any sense, distant. He would often throw himself right into whatever the children were doing. Betsy O'Brien, one of Ann's oldest friends, remembers his love of games. "He'd play Monopoly or charades with us—charades with great gusto—or whatever else we were playing." Ann's friends had some slight sense of what Percy did, but only slight. They saw a man who was always at home, pensive, very serious, yet also capable of cutting up and being funny, a man who would park cars at the Saint Scholastica prom. Percy the writer was something of a mystery to them. In fact, when he finished the last revisions of *Love in the Ruins*, one of Ann's friends made him a cake to celebrate the novel's acceptance. She had no idea, as a writer for *Time* magazine once put it, that most New York publishers by now would swim across Lake Pontchartrain to get a novel by Walker Percy.

Some of the young who came by the Percy house did have more of an inkling of what the writer was up to. Walter Isaacson, the future journalist and author, was a bright teenager from New Orleans when he first started coming to Covington to visit a cousin who lived around a bend of the Bogue Falaya from the Percy house. Through Percy's nephew (Bunt's sister's son) Tom Cowan, he met the Percy family, and when he entered the upper grades of Newman School in New Orleans he began to read Percy's novels. Isaacson was affected both by the man and by his work: "At Harvard I switched from political science to history and literature because of him. A lot of what I ended up doing in life, studying philosophy [at Oxford as a Rhodes Scholar], writing, being interested in ethical and moral dilemmas came from his influence." In Percy's eyes, Isaacson went from being one of the boys who dropped by the house to a young man with a serious interest in ideas and books, and when Isaacson came by on his vacations from college, Percy would take time to talk to him about both.

And what Percy did with Isaacson he did with scores of other people, children, friends in Covington, aspiring writers from all over: He made himself available. This was perhaps his greatest victory over the pride that he saw as his constant adversary. It would have been easier not to bother with the endless needs and requirements of others. It would have been far easier to burrow into his hole and indulge his misanthropy, the depths of which were obvious to anyone who had known him for any time (or, for that matter, to anyone who had read his novels carefully). The strain often showed. His limited tolerance for social occasions upset some of his oldest friends in Covington. (His failures to show up at parties and his early fade-outs seemed to increase during the 1970s.) The old excuse, "That's just Walker," wore thin, and Bunt began to refuse the role of social buffer. This intolerance, however, was something Percy struggled against and, in his own way, tried to make amends for. Particularly to those people whom he saw as fellow struggling souls, Percy made an effort to make himself available.

The novelist and native Mississippian Berry Morgan was just one of the many people to be startled by how generous Percy could be with his time. Living in New Orleans when she read *The Moviegoer*, she was so impressed that she immediately wrote Percy a fan letter. Percy responded with a friendly note. A few years later, in 1966, when she finished her first book, she sent the manuscript to Percy, who not only read it and marked it up—"He would write NO in big bold letters in the margin next to a part that he thought didn't work," Morgan recalled—but invited her to stop by the house to discuss it. Morgan, who was about Percy's age, could not have been more delighted. Percy spoke candidly of the book's strengths and flaws, but what pleased her most was when he said, "This book might make it." Percy's encouragement was decisive, the book made it, and Morgan became and remained a friend.

But it was not only with writers or intellectuals that Percy cultivated ties. Although he would sometimes exasperate them, Percy considered it important to keep up with all of his Covington friends. He would rarely miss his Wednesday lunch with Baldwin, Cross, Gibert, and his brother Phin. In the the early 1970s, moreover, Percy and Bunt joined a book club that included, among others friends, their neighbor Nikky Barranger, Father James Boulware (the president of the college at St. Joseph's Abbey), Ed Ballard (the head of the Tulane philosophy department) and his wife, Lucy, Judge Steve Ellis, Dick and Nicole Spangenburg, and an Episcopalian priest named William Barnwell. The club started by reading the "Great Books" series but after a few years turned mainly to short stories. Sometimes, the group would read something Percy had written, usually an essay, but Percy would absent himself on those occasions. "He was always curious about what other people thought about what they read," James Boulware recalled. "It was as though he was using us as a spectrum of literary taste."

Boulware (who, to Percy's sorrow, left the priesthood in 1979) had a privileged view of Percy during the years he knew him. Associated with St. Joseph's Abbey since the middle 1950s, he had come to know Percy well through his work on the Community Relations Council of Greater Covington, and Percy took a strong liking to him. Father James frequently said mass at the chapel at St. Paul's School, where Percy and Bunt liked to come for evening services during the week. It was only a few minutes' walk from the school to the Percys' house, and Father James would often drop by after mass for a drink and conversation. One of the things the two men would talk about was the church. Father James quickly found that Percy's devotion to his adopted faith was great, but he also saw that Percy was deeply troubled by what the church stood for. Particularly during the early 1970s, Father James heard Percy lament the lack of pastoral concern for the poor and for social problems in general. "It was clear to me," Boulware remembered, "that he wanted the church to keep the world from going down the tubes." But it was also clear to Boulware that the church was Percy's anchor. "He heard from me a much more liberal—and cynical—interpretation of the church than perhaps he was always comfortable with. I talked about the inner machinations of the hierarchy, and I would say that the American hierarchy needed to face the issues of the day. He agreed in part, but he still wouldn't go all the way. He was reluctant to take the valuable and throw out the rest. He didn't do that with his life; so he couldn't do it with his faith."

Boulware was also perceptive about Percy's profound ambivalence toward other people: "He exhibited in his life an openness and a timidity. He wanted to discuss the most important things with you and, at the same time, remain private. He could be personable and warm at one moment, and then you would turn around and he'd be gone. As close as we were, our friendship had a formality about it. It was based on issues of life and death."

What Boulware saw was, in fact, Percy's great problem with other people. He could not take them in a light, superficial way. It was far easier for him to be with other people when something serious or purposeful was at issue. But Percy was wise enough to see that this was an impossible demand to put on others. As he well knew, the mere dailiness of living occupies most people most of the time, and Percy wanted to remain in touch with that wider world, boring, petty, and irritating though it often was. He wanted to make an art that reflected his involvement with such a world. That was the very serious point of what he jokingly referred to as the Sacramental Life—and, indeed, of Sacramental Art. That was why he rejected the aloof persona of the intellectual or the precious manner of the artist. That was why he was wary of literary cliques and literary havens. As fed up as he could sometimes feel with his chosen town, he knew that it sustained him and his work. If Percy was remote and aloof by nature, he did everything in his power to resist his inclination. Yet as rooted as Percy was, he quickly found the 1970s a disorienting decade, a time when he lost his footing and seemed almost to lose his bearings. But again: Did the work-in-progress necessitate the confusion, or did the confusion engender the book?

. . .

Percy was certainly no newcomer to fame, but in the early 1970s he began to feel more subject than ever to the scrutinizing eyes of the public. Even before *Love in the Ruins* was published, for example, Alfred Kazin came down to Covington to interview Percy for a major essay that he was writing for *Harper's*. This was heady indeed. The attention of Kazin, author of *On Native Ground*, was something very close to literary canonization.

Kazin came in early November and stayed for several days, quickly finding himself a part of a busy household. Doing his share, he even helped Ann write an essay for her English class (and might have been chagrined to learn that the paper received only a C plus). Percy and Kazin hit it off. Sipping bourbon, they sat on the screened veranda overlooking the bogue while Kazin questioned Percy about his background. Perhaps the biggest surprise was the discovery that both of them had been psychoanalyzed by Janet Rioch. As his piece in *Harper's* would show when it appeared the following summer, Kazin's main interests were the formative influences in Percy's life and the factors behind his emergence as a writer. Fascinated by Percy's Greenville days and the romantic figure of Will Percy, Kazin traveled to Greenville after Covington to interview Roy Percy and to survey the ancestral stomping ground. The critic's southern journey ended in Memphis, with an afternoon interview with Shelby Foote, who reported the encounter to Percy:

> Kazin was by here last Tuesday. A nice, likeable man, very Jewish New York; much taken with you, incidentally, and with Roy. . . . I told him what I could about the South and Art: both of which, it seemed to me, were something of a mystery to him. Maybe, though, he was just in a baffled state from a week of exposure to you-alls and Louisiana food. I envy New Yorkers' year-round exposure to music and all the new movies, but thats about it. The rest is muggings and intellectualism.

Foote's view of the New York scene was close to Percy's own, but it did not bother Percy that New York intellectuals were paying attention to his work. He was flattered.

And the attention, from New York and elsewhere, only increased with the publication of *Love in the Ruins*. In addition to the usual newspaper profiles (including a funny insider's sketch by Hodding Carter's son Philip in *The Washington Post*), there were at least two major interviews during the summer of 1971, one with Charles Bunting for *Notes on Mississippi Writers* and the other with John C. Carr for *The Georgia Review*. Later in the year, on December 23, Percy finally met the man who was writing the first book-length appraisal of his work, Martin Luschei.

Luschei arrived in the morning looking rumpled and worn out, having just gotten off the plane from Los Angeles. The first draft of his book all but finished, Luschei had had misgivings about coming, fearing that he would find "the man behind the books I admired a disappointment." The forty-two-year-old assistant professor was quickly relieved to discover that Percy was "the same man who wrote the books," modest, accessible, and eager to put his interviewer at ease. The interview began in the living room and was interrupted after a couple of hours by drinks and lunch. After the meal, Percy showed off a model railroad that he had set up for his grandson in the living room (Bunt hinting broadly that the train was really more for Percy's benefit than for his grandson's), and then the interview resumed outside. Though Percy did not grill Luschei as extensively as he did some interviewers (particularly in later years, when he grew sick and tired of talking about himself), he managed to find out that Luschei was a Nebraskan "Huguenot" with some interest in writing fiction himself. Late in the afternoon, Percy and Bunt drove Luschei back to New Orleans. Crossing the causeway, Percy nodded toward the lake and said, "That's the swamp," meaning, Luschei realized, the swamp that figures so prominently in *Love in the Ruins*. Though it was a short visit, Luschei returned to California happy with what he had seen and learned. Percy's candor had been particularly helpful in clearing up some of Luschei's misconceptions about *Love in the Ruins*. In early January, Luschei sent Percy a draft of the first chapter of *The Sovereign Wayfarer*, which impressed Percy both by its generosity and by its thorough explication of the intellectual substructure of his fiction. Almost a year later, when Percy read the finished book, he was even more effusive in his praise of his assiduous critic:

> I want to thank you again and express my gratitude for the job well done if overly generous. But perhaps I am most grateful for its affirmatory properties—that perhaps the "act of naming" did not go altogether unheard. It might even serve to lift me out of a congenital depression and encourage me to "make up another story," as Flannery would say.
>
> The section on *Love in the Ruins* was perhaps most valuable to me, serving as it did to show me what a mishmash it is—too much! It was a letting go, or rather a letting fly in all directions, as you noticed. I have it in mind to do a much simpler thing with less horseplay.

Percy's postscript was both impish and heartfelt: "A final political observation: if a Huguenot Yankee can deal so kindly with a Southern Roman Catholic, the U.S. is not yet up the creek."

It was a strange and flattering thing, being explained so well and at such length. In some ways, though, as Percy was beginning to realize, it made the business of writing more difficult. An artist needs *not* to see or understand his work too clearly. Too much self-consciousness can lead to artistic narcissism or to blockage; the writer either repeats himself too lovingly, or, out of fear of repeating himself (which he must do to some extent), finds that he cannot write at all. Critics always remark with some astonishment on how much writers forget of their own work, little appreciating how important it is for the writer to do so. Percy's problem was that he was not being allowed to forget. His past achievements were too much with him.

The attention was hard to resist, particularly when it came from people he respected and admired. Only three months after Luschei sent him the draft of his book, Percy received a letter from Robert Coles, asking if he could come down for a visit in late spring or early summer:

> Months ago I asked the editor of The New Yorker whether I could do a profile of you, if you were willing; and he said yes. I've held off asking you, because I wanted to go through the three novels (again!) carefully, and also read a number of your articles, going back to the fifties. Now, somewhat nervously, I write to ask whether I could come and talk with you. I can only say that I would try to write something understandable and sensible—and hopefully at least somewhat responsive to what I believe you are trying to do and say.
>
> What do you think? Could we at least have a little bourbon and discuss all this?

Percy responded immediately and with no apparent hesitation: "I'd be delighted and honored to see you any time—whether the profile works out or not." As a token of his receptiveness, he offered not only to put Coles up but to ferry him to and from the airport. He did, however, warn Coles that the only other person he knew who had been on the cover of *Time* had, shortly after his appearance in the magazine, "developed a manic-depressive psychosis and run off to South America with a young English girl." Not immediately fearing for his mental health, Coles proposed a date in early May, but since May was crowded with honors of other sorts for Percy, they finally settled on June 14 and 15.

The two men were both a little nervous about the meeting. Percy was one of Coles's intellectual and moral heroes, and Percy was genuinely impressed by what Coles had written and done. Percy's uneasiness was not quickly allayed when Coles arrived. Not that they didn't hit it off. They did. As well as being temperamentally at ease with each other, they had much to talk about and much in common, including Columbia's College of Physicians and Surgeons, an interest in psychiatry, the

South, religion, and books. What made Percy uneasy was his uncertainty about what Coles was hoping to learn. He also wondered when Coles would begin the interview. The first night together stretched long into the wee hours, the bourbon flowing freely as it did, but at no point did Coles get down to business. Percy chalked it up to ice-breaking. The next day, though, things continued in the same way. Coles just sort of hung around, asked a question now and then but never really settled into anything structured. Even Bunt grew a little concerned. She could tell that her husband didn't know whether he should go about his business, do a little work, or continue making himself available. It was all a little awkward. The Percys had no way of knowing that this *was* Coles's way of "interviewing": unstructured, impressionistic. After a couple of days of friendly but dilatory back-and-forth, Coles got back into his rental car and returned to New Orleans.

If the meeting itself was strange, what followed was just as mysterious. Writing to thank Percy for the hospitality, Coles explained that he would soon be heading off to New Mexico. Then, almost as an after-thought, he added in the postscript:

> Walker, especially after meeting you, I feel annoyed and frustrated that I have these three lectures to prepare for the University of Virginia; I promised to do them a couple of years ago (!) and they have to be delivered this winter. But, by the end of the year I'll be done with them, and free to start pulling together some thoughts on your thoughts and novels, and a little bit, your life. So I'll look forward to seeing you between Christmas and Easter!

Coles did make his way back South the next year to do further research for his profile, but others he interviewed found, as had Percy, that the doctor's ways were both charming and mysterious. In a letter to Percy, dated March 13, Shelby Foote sounded the common theme:

> Robert Coles was here on Tuesday; had been in Greenville the day before, with Roy and Sarah—a wonderfully likeable man, but some-what puzzling in that I couldnt tell what he had come for, what he was after; mainly I guess because he doesnt take notes or press you for information. I approve of that, but scarcely know what to make of it. He will be back though, and I reckon he'll know what he wants by then if he doesnt already. I did like him, very much, and so did Gwyn.

At some point after his second southern swing and further conversations by phone with Percy, Coles started writing the profile and soon turned it in to *The New Yorker*. But that did not bring an end to the mysteries. The piece didn't appear. By 1975, when Percy's collection of essays, *The Message in the Bottle*, was about to come out, Robert Giroux at FSG wrote Coles to see if there was any chance that the profile would be appearing soon. Coles replied on May 3: "They keep telling me (1) how wonderful it is (2) that it is long and will be published 'soon'!" But "soon" at *The New Yorker*, whose bank of backlogged essays is legendary, can mean something quite different from what it means to the rest of the world. In March of 1977, the month *Lancelot* was published, Roger Straus wrote William Shawn to ask whether the profile would come out before the summer. It would not. In fact, the first part of the two-part profile would not appear until October 2, 1978, and then only because Coles had followed the advice of a friend and found a book publisher, Little, Brown. *The New Yorker*, not wanting to lose its place in line, finally relented and ran the pieces shortly before they were published in book form under the title *Walker Percy: An American Search*.

Byzantine as the whole episode turned out to be, the writing of the profile forged a strong and lasting friendship between Coles and Percy. The flow of letters remained constant and affectionate, and the two men would always take special pleasure in seeing each other whenever the opportunity allowed. Yet Percy always remained somewhat mystified by Coles, baffled, in particular, by what Coles had *not* gone into in his interviews or in the profile that eventually appeared. Percy wondered why Coles, a psychiatrist, had never asked him about his childhood years in Birmingham, never questioned him about his father or mother, never even touched on the suicides in his family. Percy had no way of knowing that Coles's reluctance to touch on these matters was tied up with his own deep ambivalence about the legitimacy of psychiatric explanations. Coles would sometimes bristle when people suggested that he had written an *intellectual* biography of Percy. He believed that the intellectual and moral concerns of the man *were* Percy's life story, far more so than any account of Percy's childhood difficulties and of the problems arising therefrom. Coles, in short, had not wanted to psychoanalyze his subject and indeed questioned the validity of doing so.

Percy, of course, had similar misgivings about the tyranny of the psychological. Having devoted much of his early adulthood to a psychoanalytical exploration of his "problems," he had come away from the experience highly skeptical. A number of his essays elaborated his doubts, notably his two-part essay for *America*, "The Coming Crisis of Psychiatry." All the more curious, then, that Percy was bothered, even somewhat offended, by Coles's rather dogged refusal to pursue any psychological line of questioning. And Percy was bothered. Coles could see so. In one of their follow-up phone conversations, Coles recalled, Percy himself brought up the matter of his father's suicide, clearly concerned that Coles at least know about it. But beyond tersely mentioning the fact in the profile, Coles never explored the subject. Indeed, Coles gave only an overview of Percy's life—intelligent, perceptive, but rather distant. Most of his attention was devoted to a close and sympathetic reading of Percy's works, from his earliest essays through his (then) most recent novel, *Lancelot.*

Someone less skeptical of psychological explanations would have had a hard time not concluding that what went on between Percy and Coles was itself a fairly intense psychodrama. In this drama, one sees Percy, the desperate analysand, trying urgently to open up in front of an analyst who refuses to analyze. It is a complicated story. Why does a man skeptical of psychoanalysis invest this reluctant practitioner of the craft with special power and authority? It is not simply that Coles is likeable, gifted, and famous—though he is all of these, and all count for something. But what makes Coles so seductive to Percy is precisely that he is a psychiatrist who repudiates psychiatry, and repudiates it on many of the same moral and philosophical grounds that Percy does. Yet there is still some aura of the psychiatrist—the ur-psychiatrist—about Coles, and Percy wants to know what this paradoxical figure will do with his "material." Vanity and narcissism: Percy knows the game well but cannot help wanting to play it, cannot help wanting to tell his deepest story. But the analyst refuses to hear it. For after all, Percy is one of the psychiatrist's idols, one of the figures whose books have helped him to transcend, while still remaining within, the profession that he reluctantly entered in the first place. (As a literature student at Harvard, Coles had contemplated a career teaching literature until William Carlos Williams, the subject of his senior thesis, urged him to study medicine, advice that, with considerable misgivings and emotional struggle, he followed.)

As much as the two men liked each other, as hard as they laughed at each other's jokes, as generously as they celebrated each other's work, both felt that a final connection had been missed. "He tried to make me over in his own image," Percy once explained, "to make me the generous, concerned, liberal soul that he was. He didn't want to recognize my nasty, conservative, mean side." In saying that, of course, Percy revealed his blindness to the "other" side of Coles, who was anything but a doctrinaire liberal. Coles later acknowledged that Percy might have been asking for more than he had been prepared or willing to give. Their friendship was an elaborate waltz of approaches and avoidances, yet in some ways probably all the stronger for being so.

· · ·

Along with Luschei's book, various articles, and profiles came an assortment of equally head-turning honors and awards. In the spring of 1972 alone, there were three honorary doctorates, one from Loyola in New Orleans, one from Saint Scholastica in Duluth, Minnesota, and one from his alma mater, the University of North Carolina. Gratifying as they were, the wearisome traveling from campus to campus prompted Percy to formulate a policy of accepting no further honorary degrees, a policy that he only rarely violated in the years to follow. More gratifying than the degrees, though, was Percy's induction that same busy spring into the American Academy of Arts and Letters and the National Institute of Arts and Letters. The recognition of his peers in the arts meant more than Percy was usually willing to acknowledge; and as he would confide to the novelist Elizabeth Spencer a dozen years later, he found the annual event "a pleasant alcoholic way to meet other writers—some whom you'd like to punch ordinarily are under the circumstances *very nice.*"

Even the overnight train trip up to New York proved to be rewarding. Rising early in the morning, Bunt went to the dining car to have coffee. There she met Eudora Welty, and the two Mississippians had a pleasant chat. When she returned to the roomette, Percy couldn't believe who she had been with—or that Welty had told Bunt that she would like to meet her husband. "He thought I was half-teasing," Bunt Percy later related, "but finally decided to take a chance and knock on her roomette door. They sat knee to knee and rejoiced that they were heading to the same event." Welty, they learned, would be receiving the Academy's Gold Medal for the Novel at the May 17 ceremony, and the Percys were even more delighted when they discovered that they would all be staying at the Algonquin Hotel together. For the Percys and Welty, it was the beginning of a friendship.

Percy and Welty would meet again even sooner than they imagined. Though both writers had an aversion to appearing on television, William F. Buckley, working through a personal friend of both writers, a Greenvillian named Clark Reed, enticed them onto *Firing Line* a few months later. At first it seemed that Percy would not accept. "We planned to proceed with Miss Welty," Buckley recalled. "At the last minute, Dr. Percy called Clark Reed who called the producer to say that he had decided to come along, on the grounds 'that it wouldn't be right to let Miss Welty bear the whole of the burden.'" Taped on December 12, 1972, at WMAA in Jackson, the show included Buckley, his two guests, and an assortment of scholars from various Mississippi colleges. Buckley set the theme of the show in his opening remarks: "What exactly is the Southern imagination? What does it come from and why? Does it have anything distinctive to say? What are its particular attributes?" The problem with such a reso-

lutely set agenda was that it produced few, if any, surprises. Buckley did
his best, pressed hard, but when, for example, he asked why the Pacific
Northwest or the Rocky Mountain states had no literary tradition comparable to the South's, Welty couldn't help evincing a little fatigue with the
question:

> Miss Welty: Well, I don't know. I think this probably has been said a
> thousand times because all sorts of things have been said.
>
> Mr. Buckley: Well, it could be true then, if it was said a thousand
> times.
>
> Miss Welty [not wanting to be a complete wet blanket]: Yes. But I
> think the Southerner is a talker by nature, but not only a talker—we
> are used to an audience. We are used to a listener and that does
> something to our narrative style, I think. I think you could talk in the
> Rocky Mountains. You wouldn't get anything back but an echo.
> (laughter)
>
> Mr. Buckley: Well, does that mean that because you're talkers by
> nature you develop the art?
>
> Miss Welty: Yes, we like to entertain and please, and we also rejoice
> in response, and I think that helps the narrative style.

Percy's contribution to the discussion was essentially an elaboration of
what he had said on the *Today Show* thirteen years before when he was
asked why the South produced such fine literature: "Because we lost the
War." To expand upon this explanation—to say, for example, whether
the defeat was a tragedy or a "fortunate fall"—is perhaps worthwhile in
a kind of dutiful academic way, but it destroys the epigrammatic beauty
of those five adequate words. Some of the exchanges between Buckley
and Percy did come alive, however, particularly when the host asked
why the southern literary flowering came so long after the South's actual
defeat:

> Mr. Buckley: And why did that [tragic sense of life] not, during the
> 19th century, result in interesting novels? You said because it was over-
> defensive?
>
> Mr. Percy: I think it was defensive. It was either romantic or defensive
> and there was too much hurt and too much anger. I think it took a
> while to be digested and I think it happened along about 1920 or '30.
>
> Mr. Buckley: Would you say that Japan and Germany will need them-
> selves also to pass a couple of generations before their writers can write
> interestingly?
>
> Mr. Percy: Well, they got help from the United States in their recon-
> struction. (laughter)

Running as a sort of subtext throughout the show was the question of whether the South would continue to be the same culture that had given rise to a distinctive literary imagination or would go the way of the rest of the nation, headlong into mass commercial culture. Percy, echoing his earlier address to the NBA, held on to the hope that the South might have a humanizing mission, that having finally overcome its defensiveness and its preoccupation with preserving segregation, it might become a leader in American political as well as cultural life. Welty's attitude toward the same subject brought out a striking difference between the two writers. She found it difficult to speak in terms of national trends or sweeping cultural developments. Her imagination and intelligence were so bound up with the particularities of people and place that she was all but incapable of "committing" sociology. Yet she made it clear that she still found in Jackson at least a sufficient minimum of what she considered most nurturing about the South: a closeness to other people and an awareness of their life stories. "You know what happened to So-and-So clear through his life," Welty quietly explained. "You get a narrative sense of your next door neighbor instead of someone you just meet in the supermarket which you do today, or you just see people in flashes." Percy and Welty valued the same things about the South, but the way in which Welty expressed her appreciation was truer to the things valued than Percy's somewhat theoretical manner.

Percy's fondness for Welty was as great as his respect for her art, and he tipped his hat her way during the show by describing her as "about the best we've got," meaning, of course, the South's best living writer. Yet Percy believed that Welty represented the last as well as the best of a tradition of southern storytelling, a tradition that he was not always above describing as "white ladies' fiction." That tradition was built upon the yarn-spinning style that one learned by sitting on the porch as a child and attending carefully to the talk of one's "elders and betters," and Percy often confessed that he had a limited tolerance for the fiction it produced, however finely wrought it was. To his taste, it lacked some critical bite into the hard, alienated reality of postmodern life, and as he told one interviewer in 1971, "Whatever impetus I had toward writing owes nothing to sitting on a porch listening to anybody tell stories about the South, believe me."

His roots, as he always pointed out (though not altogether truthfully, considering his years in Greenville), were in the New South, the world of suburbs and country clubs. Yet Percy, despite his disparaging remarks about a "phased-out genre," owed the old storytelling tradition a great deal, perhaps more than he was willing to admit. The novel that he was now working on would draw quite clearly on the narrative strategy of Camus' novel *The Fall*, but in both its rhetoric and its focus on the story of a family's decline it owed just as much to the dying southern storytelling tradition. As one critic shrewdly noted, *Lancelot* "both repudiates old southern stories as calcified and commodified *and* acknowledges their lingering and compelling power." Whether he knew so or not, Percy was effecting a curious marriage of the European novel of alienation and the southern gothic, and revitalizing both by doing so.

But how much did Percy understand about what he was doing? His way of writing a novel always involved a little more method and calculation than he was prepared to admit, even though he wrote gropingly, inventing as he went on, discovering what gambits and formal strategies worked as he read and revised. In the case of *Lancelot*, though, Percy claimed that he had "a proper planned-out" novel in mind. And, in fact, he seems to have written more preliminary notes and outlines for this novel than he had for his previous three (or at least more such jottings survive among his manuscripts of *Lancelot* than do among those of *The Moviegoer, The Last Gentleman,* and *Love in the Ruins*). For all his preliminary plotting, however, Percy felt frustrated by his successive efforts to write the novel. He would have a go at it for a while, then read it, find it unsatisfactory, and reject large parts of it. It was maddening; and Percy felt that the problem was tied up with a growing confusion about his own life.

The most starkly revealing statement of this problem appears in a pair of letters that he wrote to Shelby Foote in the autumn of 1972:

> I have come to the damndest watershed in my life—done what I wanted to do in the novel, with linguistics, children gone [Ann had just enrolled at LSU], sitting down here with my old lady in the Louisiana autumn. Everything quiet. What now? It would be a good time to die, but on the other hand I'd as soon not. It's all very spooky. Life is much stranger than art—and often more geometrical. My life breaks exactly in half: 1st half = growing up Southern and medical; 2nd half = imposing art on 1st half. 3rd half? Sitting on bayou and repeating over and over again like old Buddenbrooks: *Kurios!*
>
> Actually I know what I want to do for # 4. It's a good idea but I must wait for the winds to pick me up out of these 56 yr old horse latitudes.

It had been some wait already. Percy had first mentioned his idea for the novel in February of 1971. More than a year and a half had passed. Not that he had been idle during this time. As well as receiving a steady stream of interviewers and traipsing around the country to accept degrees and other honors, he had written and seen published the first installment of the "Peirce-Percy theory of meaning." "Toward a Triadic Theory of

Meaning," which came out in *Psychiatry* in February of 1972, was Percy's first full-bore effort to apply Charles Peirce's concepts to the fundamental distinction between signaling behavior and the mystery of symbol using. The essay was a formally elegant presentation of some of his oldest ideas about the uniqueness of the language, made somewhat specific by show-ing the application of the "triadic" theory of language to the practice of psychiatry (and here, of course, the influence of his years of work with Dr. Gentry Harris is evident).

Apart from this essay and a long review of two books about the black American experience (by two black authors) for *Tulane Law Review*, Percy's only other attempts at writing had been unsuccessful swipes at the novel. In fact, his lack of success on that front had prompted him in the summer of 1972 to start another language essay, "more arcane and opaque" than the last one, he warned Foote. (More than a year later, he would pitch this essay to Lewis Simpson at the *Southern Review* as "quite condensed, unreadable and probably the most important piece I'll ever write.") But why did Percy keep finding himself thwarted by the novel he wanted to write? Percy hoped to discuss the problem with Foote up in Sewanee on the weekend of October 13 and 14, when he was to take part in the dedication of the James Agee Memorial Library at St. An-drew's School, but Foote reported that he couldn't make it. He was bearing down hard on the last part of the third volume of his history and was coming out of his burrow only for the occasional speech. ("The three volumes will total 1,523,500 words," he had crowed to Percy earlier in the year. "Thats a bit longer than Proust; the same length, sweet Christ, as Gibbon's Decline & Fall—which, incidentally, also took twenty years to write.") Unable to talk it out with his old friend, Percy tried to explain the cause of his literary frustrations in a letter dated October 6, 1972. Once again, he drew on the familiar maritime metaphor:

> Right now I'm in the horse latitudes, caught between thinking (lin-guistics) and imagining (literature), a bad place to be. A rock and a hard place. So I'll wait around. It's amazing how little one learns from this craft. All I know now I didn't know before is not to write the first sentence until the tone of voice is right. I can see you sneering.

For Percy, the heart of fictional art was voice, and if the voice didn't work, the novel wouldn't go. Percy never explained why he had such trouble with the voice in the early stages of writing *Lancelot*, but we can make some reasonable inferences from remarks he made about both his life and his book.

About his life, first of all, Percy seemed increasingly despondent. The departure of Ann for college in the autumn of 1972 had broken the daily routines of family life, which for so long had been centered on her. For the first time since 1948, Percy and Bunt found themselves facing each other alone in their own house. It was a little strange and a little unsettling, getting to know each other again, but they set about it in the ways they always had—by doing things, going on bird-watching expeditions, attending symphonies in New Orleans, taking trips to Gulf Shores or the mountains or to places closer by. (One such day trip through the plantation district on River Road in early 1973 had a decisive influence on *Lancelot*, though not quite the generative one that Percy attributed to it in an interview with Herbert Mitgang of *The New York Times* several years later: "The young guides [in the antebellum houses] weren't much interested in General Beauregard and the Confederacy. They only came alive when talking about the last time a Hollywood company rented the homes for local color. Where Olivia de Havilland stood in 'Hush . . . Hush, Sweet Charlotte' had become the new reality. That viewpoint became the genesis for the novel, which shows the life of the River Road gentry and Hollywood.")

For all Percy and Bunt's activities together, and for all their separate involvements (Bunt was involved in more charitable and service activities than most people could keep up with), Percy still felt profoundly disengaged and superfluous—as though he were in the "third half" of his life. To his constant foe, pride, he now added sloth, the profound moral sloth of the soul, which he frequently referred to by its Latin name, *accedie*. He recognized worrisome signs in his behavior. He was, for one, more self-absorbed, morbidly picking away at the weaknesses of his character, just as he had done in his student days. Not since he was undergoing psychoanalysis, in fact, had Percy been so interested in his own psyche (which explains in part why his vanity had been hurt the summer before when Dr. Coles showed so little interest in that part of him). To some extent, of course, this was the return of the old Percy melancholia, compounded by a gradual increase in his consumption of alcohol.

Alcohol and the writer, a relationship shrouded in romantic vapors, is a topic of endless fascination and speculation, and much has already been conjectured about Percy's relationship to the bottle (conjecture largely encouraged by Percy's own writing). Quite simply, Percy liked to drink, bourbon mostly but other spirits as well, depending on the occasion. Though not above taking a snort when his imagination would not fire, he usually drank socially and, by relaxed southern Louisiana standards, moderately: two, maybe three strong drinks at a time. If Percy exceeded his moderate dose—and he rarely did—he tended to suffer intestinal consequences, the main reason, as he explained in his famous

Esquire essay, "Bourbon," why he was not an alcoholic. All the same, Percy's fondness for the bosky bite of bourbon neat fell just short of idolatry. He waxed somewhat ironic in the *Esquire* essay when he described the complex satisfactions of bourbon, but only somewhat. A man with such an affection could only be grateful for the moderating effects of what he described as "a bad GI tract, diverticulosis, neurotic colon, and a mild recurring nausea."

Even so, Percy began in the horse latitude period of the third half of his life to drink more than he should; and when he did, the geniality that usually accompanied a moderate dose of alcohol would give way to a peevish sharpness, even to meanness. ("I am told I am a mean low-down drunk, many sneers and insults to waiters etc.," he once confessed to Foote.)

Conditions in the winter and spring of 1973 were a little more conducive to drink than usual, partly because of trips that Percy made to New York to serve as a judge on the fiction panel of the National Book Award. Meeting first in late February, the panel—Evan Connell, Leslie Fiedler, William Gass, Jonathan Yardley, and Percy—gathered briefly in the offices of the National Book Committee at 1 Park Avenue before deciding on a more congenial venue, a nearby bar. After lunch and libations loosened them up, the group discovered, in Yardley's words, "that we got along famously—and agreed about almost nothing." Five divergent literary sensibilities compromised on a dozen books as finalists. On April 9, the group reconvened, this time in the Rose Room of the Algonquin Hotel. As well as a hefty dinner bill (thanks to drinks and four bottles of expensive French wine), Yardley remembered the boisterous proceedings:

> We got right down to business; Percy and I voted for Eudora Welty's "The Optimist's Daughter," Connell for John Williams's "Augustus," Fiedler and Gass for John Barth's "Chimera." In very little time it became clear that no single book could get five votes; so we decided, for better or worse, to divide the award. Percy and I, less determined in defense of our candidate than were our fellow judges, ended up the losers: The 1973 National Book Award for Fiction went to "Augustus" and "Chimera."

When the split decision was announced on April 11, *The New York Times* described it as "an unprecedented display of public disagreement" and reported that "the meetings of the five fiction judges had been noisy and argumentative." Noisy they might have been, but according to Yardley, the noise owed not to acrimony but to high spirits—and to the

generous flow of wine. After the awards were handed out at the April 12
ceremony, the panel took the two winners out for drinks. "Percy and I
agreed that we liked the men better than their books," Yardley recalled,
"and with characteristic courtesy Percy worried that the passing furor
over the divided award might somehow diminish the pleasure that both
Barth and Williams clearly took in it." The revelry did not end with
that round of drinks. Percy later joined Willie Morris (a panelist on the
history jury), James Jones, and William Styron at the bar of the Black-
stone Hotel. About the bibulous late-night convention of coregionalists,
Percy reported only this to Shelby Foote: "Southron Writers!" And that
said it all.

Percy's sullen side did not come out when he drank on his trips away
from home. The distractions of the city kept his spirits high—dangerously so, in fact. Returning home would invariably involve a difficult
reentry, the perils of which he would describe so precisely in *Lost in the
Cosmos.* Back in Covington, drinking would sometimes assume a more
desperate character, and the solitary snorts would increase in frequency.
His daughter Mary Pratt remembers being confronted by her father after
a Sunday lunch during this dark period. He confessed that he had not
been in the best state of mind and that he was drinking in order to
remain euphoric. Then, to her astonishment, he asked her what she
could do about it.

"Nothing," Mary Pratt replied. "You'll just have to crawl out of that
bottle on your own."

It would be a gross exaggeration to suggest that Percy suddenly turned
into a morose, drink-sodden monster. His friends saw no sudden change
in him. Judge Steve Ellis, who became closer to the Percys at this time
(and who would soon become one of their steadier friends), never saw
Percy take more than two drinks at a time. "Walker didn't drink like a
boozer," Ellis later explained, "he drank like a college sophomore who
thought it was a little naughty, and he talked about it that way." Most
of the time, Percy was his usual equable self, though somewhat more
remote. But those in his own family could tell that he was going through
a particularly hard patch. His lows, when they came, seemed to dip a
little lower, and to last a little longer, than they usually did. He could
be short with Bunt, or worse, inattentive to her. Mary Pratt saw this,
and so did Ann when she came home for holidays and vacations. Raised
to be forthright, Ann in particular never hesitated to tell her father that
he was being unkind, and Percy knew that she was right. Her words
stung.

Percy's daughters could also see what few others saw: that Percy was
going through a difficult period with his faith. This came out in a variety

of ways, including an increasing reluctance to receive the host at mass. At lunch one Saturday, Mary Pratt could not help observing that her father had failed to say grace. "I will say the damn grace if I feel like it," Percy exploded. Later, when he was calmer, Mary Pratt tried to bring up what she knew was a painful subject. She had not gone through a rigorous catechism at her father's knees for nothing. "You can't turn your back on the church," she said to Percy. "It's just too much a part of your life." Percy sat silent and grim-faced on the couch. He could not reply because he had no response. He felt empty.

Yet, once again, it is hard to say whether the unhappiness was making it difficult to write the novel—or making it possible. Consciously or not, Percy seemed to be trying to reach the state of mind out of which the right voice would come. His inability to attain that state pushed him deeper into despair, even as it forced him to attempt other literary gambits, none of which worked. But one of those gambits, at least for a time, seemed to. Instead of beginning inside the head of the central character (Lancelot Lamar Andrews), Percy decided to open with the priest-psychiatrist Percival. It seemed to be a promising opening move. He explained it to Foote in the same July 4 letter in which he had jokingly talked about appropriating the opening lines of Dante's *Inferno*. In a postscript that ran longer than the letter itself, Percy described what he called the "alternative" beginning:

> P.S. An alternative beginning (the novel opens with a 45-yr-old priest who has gone sour, is about to chuck the whole thing and take off with a 20-yr-old Bobby McGee type):
> The morning after All Soul's Day I stood looking down at my mother's grave in the Felicity Street Cemetery in old New Orleans and I came to myself in the middle of my life and I knew that I knew nothing and cared for nothing but following her. She was singing,
>
> > Freedom ain't nothing, Lord, but nothing left to lose
> > Freedom was all she left to me
> > Loving her was easy, Lord, when Bobby sang the blues
> > Loving her was good enough for me
> > Good enough for me and Bobby McGee.
>
> It's a menopausal novel. The priest is not the main character, who is a noble murderer like Ulysses. *Ulysses*, a good title—has it been used? Shall probably have to settle for *Lancelot* or *Lancelot in Hell*. Which sounds better?

More for this novel than for any other, Percy used Foote as a literary midwife, trying out ideas on him, talking to him about books, describing to him his growing sense of moral rottenness. Percy's eagerness to see Foote had never been quite so strong. Beginning as early as January of 1973, for example, Percy urged that they get together at Gulf Shores during the summer, a request that he repeated many times. Foote finally agreed tentatively on a rendezvous in July. He was closing on Appomattox Courthouse and Lincoln's "Good Friday appointment with Booth's derringer," and he hoped to be finished with the trilogy by summer. Considering how absorbed he was in the crucial closing stages of his narrative history, Foote played the midwife role with surprising generosity. As well as pressing books on Percy—he strongly recommended Thomas G. Bergin's translation of *The Divine Comedy* as well as Bergin's general introduction to the poem—he urged his friend to reach for his big novel, "a big three-main-character work." Such talk about the "big novel" frightened Percy, but he welcomed the more practical suggestions, including the Dante selections. Above all, though, he was grateful for the steady flow of supportive words that he knew he could count on from Foote. When all else was appearing fragile, this oldest friendship served Percy well.

Though Foote was a little vague about when he would make it down to the beach in July, Percy and Bunt went ahead with their plans, reserving two different cottages in Gulf Shores for most of June and July. Percy was hoping that the sea would cure his "Louisiana swamp rot." He planned "to get a small boat and anchor out on the reef and fish & schnorkel." And, as he promised Foote, "Since I'm not working, I'd be happy to correct proofs."

Percy was not quite so indolent as he made out. In the spring, as well as working on his book, he reviewed for *America* magazine a novel by his friend Wilfrid Sheed, *People Will Always Be Kind.* It was something of a tricky assignment, because Percy liked Sheed and was grateful for the trenchant reviews that Sheed had written of his own novels. Yet Percy feared that what was often said about Sheed—that he was a brilliant critic but a somewhat dutiful novelist—was true. Addressing that perception head on in his opening paragraphs, Percy proceeded to argue that Sheed had written a better-than-dutiful novel, in fact quite a good one, but one whose merits, notably its underlying religious argument, might be missed because of Sheed's overly subtle ways.

If the review of Sheed's novel was something of a labor of love, and difficult for being so, another assignment Percy took on in the spring of 1973 was even more of both. Charles East, director of the Louisiana State University Press, approached Percy in May with the request that he write an introduction to *Lanterns on the Levee,* paperback rights to which LSU had just acquired. The press was planning to run the book as part of its Library of Southern Civilization Series, whose chief editor was Lewis Simpson. For two reasons, then—his growing fondness for Simpson and his profound debt to Uncle Will—Percy accepted. The writing of the piece proved as difficult as he feared, first, because it was hard to do full justice to a complex man and, second, because Percy wanted to challenge the interpretations of two very different kinds of readers of *Lanterns:* those who embraced it is as an almost sacred testament to what was true, good, and beautiful about the Old South; and those who wanted to discredit it as reactionary apologetics for racism and social inequality. Percy succeeded on both counts. With strictest economy, the essay brings Will Percy, both his physical presence and his moral complexity, clearly before the reader's eye.

Percy continued to work on the essay about Uncle Will at his Gulf Shores vacation cottage. Doing his best to dry out his "Louisiana rot," he spent most of his days sailing and fishing with Bunt, sometimes accompanied by their nephew Tom Cowan. There was the usual vacation commotion: Ann was visited by a young man from Kentucky whom she had met the summer before; Mary Pratt, her husband Byrne, and their two sons came down for two long weekends; Phin and Jaye visited; and Roy and Sarah had a place nearby on Mobile Bay. In addition to family distractions, Percy soon found himself drawn to the coverage of the national political drama, the Watergate affair. In fact, just seven days shy of the first anniversary of the June 17 burglary of the Democratic party headquarters, Percy was watching Jeb Stuart Magruder, deputy director of the Committee for the Re-Election of the President (CREEP), testify before the Senate Select Committee on Presidential Campaign Activities. "Jeb Magruder on the tube now," Percy reported to Foote. "He's no Jeb Stuart."

On July 16, the plot would become even thicker, when a former White House aide, Alexander Butterfield, revealed the existence of taped Oval Room conversations. Percy watched the drama unfold all summer, feeling worse each day that he allowed it to take up so much of his attention. ("Let's don't speak of Watergate," he wrote Martin Luschei on September 1. "I watched that soap opera all summer instead of doing any work—and am still in a state of foul bemusement.") Yet even those lost months spent following the saga of presidential dirty tricks had their literary uses: They would enrich the vein of spleen and outrage that would spill out in the vituperation of Lancelot Andrews Lamar.

Shelby and Gwyn Foote made it down for only a few days, from July 17 to July 20. The last part of the third volume was going slower than Foote had anticipated, and he wanted to get back to Memphis fast before losing the thread. Foote's best intentions were thwarted when he returned, though. Besieged by a vicious head cold, he spent two weeks watching Watergate. He gave his estimate of the whole White House crew to Percy in a letter dated August 16:

> Sorry bunch of coves. Nixon's the one; the coviest of them all. Heard him on the tube last night. Not even pitiful: just clonk. He *deserves* paralysis. Which is what weve got for the next three years or more. . . . One thing, though, We dont want Congress running the country. We had that once, during Reconstruction, and believe me we dont need any more of that. Rum go.

Autumn brought at least some good developments Percy's way. He finally finished his introduction to *Lanterns* and was pleased with it. And Lewis Simpson wrote to say that he was interested in seeing Percy's "Theory of Language" essay for possible inclusion in *The Southern Review*. "I certainly will send you this here essay when I finish it," Percy wrote back on October 14. "Not that I think you can use it but (1) I'd be glad to have you look at it and (2) it gives me a reason to finish it." Percy had many reasons for liking Simpson. One was his unassuming, unpretentious manner. Bluff scholarly know-it-alls gave Percy the hives, but the soft-spoken Texas native put on no airs. What attracted Percy most to Simpson, though, was his depth. Simpson was a first-rate intellectual historian as well as a literary critic. Over the years of their acquaintance, Percy would frequently write to praise Simpson for essays or books that he had written—works that almost invariably shed light on subjects of interest to Percy, whether they treated broad themes (*The Man of Letters in New England and the South*), or individual writers ("Faulkner and the Legend of the Artist") or thinkers ("Voegelin and the Story of the Clerks"). The measure of Percy's regard for Simpson was his eagerness to publish what he believed would be his most important essay on the philosophy of language in the review that Lewis Simpson edited. Percy knew it was not the sort of article *The Southern Review* tended to run. Yet he suspected that Simpson was the kind of person to take a risk on something that was a little off the path. He was pleased that his suspicion proved true.

A number of things drew Percy toward Baton Rouge and LSU during these years. In addition to Simpson, there was, of course, Ann, who was entering her second year at the university and doing well, despite some remarkably insensitive professors who required her to sit in her alphabetically assigned seat instead of the front row where she could more easily read their lips. Yet another attraction to LSU was a discussion group that Percy attended every week. Meeting on Thurday afternoons from three to four under the loose guidance of a German-born psychologist named Susanne Jensen, the group of twelve faculty and staff members (plus the outsider Percy) would talk about almost anything, individual problems, the issues of the day, their students. Percy had become interested in the group the previous winter, during Mardi Gras, when he ran into Susanne Jensen, who, along with her husband, an entomologist at LSU, also lived in Covington. Jensen mentioned the group, and Percy asked if he might join. Jensen said that she would ask the other participants, and they all approved. For three years Percy attended these meetings with some regularity, never asserting his presence, talking sometimes, but mainly quietly listening. "He seemed to be looking for something," Jensen recalled, "a philosophy that would help him integrate himself and also help him make sense of the times. He wanted to understand what was happening in a time that he thought, like Romano Guardino, was a transitional time." Percy's philosophical interests became apparent to the group. He would talk about the lack of any coherent theory of man. He would make the case that man should be thought of not as Homo sapiens but as Homo loquens. He would joke about being a bad Catholic. "I don't think he believed that psychology, any kind of psychology, would provide a substitute for religion," said Jensen, "but he believed that it might help him understand what was going on in himself and in the times." Jensen also felt that Percy was in need of a community, and the group, at least for a time, satisfied part of that need. While Percy would rarely talk about his fiction, Jensen distinctly remembered his announcing in one session (she doesn't remember when), "I have been working for months on one sentence, and I have finally got it: 'Come into my cell.' " It was the first sentence of the voice he had been looking for.

Percy had not lost his faith—at least not completely—but he did feel cut off from the community of his fellow believers. In fact, he was feeling more than ever like the morose, isolated Protestant who he believed still lurked beneath the Catholic veneer, as he admitted to Shelby Foote in the middle of October:

Re Catholicism: I think that culturally speaking I am still a gloomy Georgia Presbyterian. It is impossible to escape one's origins completely. I believe in the One Holy Catholic and Apostolic Church etc but it is intellectual and I often don't feel a part of the feast like merry Louisianians. Also, the conviction is growing that an end is at hand, whether the end of the U.S. or the West or the world I don't know yet; maybe all three. But as the Mass said this morning: Christ died,

Christ is risen, Christ will come again. Don't doubt it: the Great Beast of Bethlehem is coming back.

At that moment, though, it was the Rough Beast at the center of his novel that was giving Percy the greatest difficulty: "I think what's got me down is that the novel is attempting the impossible: to write about the great traditional themes, sin, god, death, etc., when in fact these themes are no longer with us, we've left them, even death, or they've left us. I've been in a long spell of accidie, anomie and aridity, in which, unlike the saints who writhe under the assaults of devils, I simply get sleepy and doze off."

15

The Knight, Death, and the Devil

Come into my cell.

—WALKER PERCY, *Lancelot*

Percy had little hope for a revival of his spirits with the coming of the New Year. At least in this expectation he was not disappointed. "Holidays lousy as usual," he reported to Foote. "I have to go to *parties* to talk to people about Watergate etc." The holidays had not really been that bad. Just before Christmas, Walter Isaacson had brought one of his professors from Harvard, Daniel Aaron, out to meet Percy, and a late-afternoon chat around drinks and hogshead cheese had spun out late and agreeably into the evening. And Percy always liked seeing his children and grandchildren gathered for the festivities. Nevertheless, the strain of the season seemed to be greater than usual this year.

Foote, responding to his friend's doldrums, wrote to cheer him up. He told Percy how much he liked the essay on Uncle Will, adding that the full introduction in the book was even better than the cut version that had appeared in the *Saturday Review* the previous November. Then, in that uncanny way of his, he suggested that Percy consider assembling his philosophical essays in a book. "I think it would make a likely volume; something to take off from." The suggestion was well timed and in fact came close to an idea Percy had entertained during the summer of 1972, when he had written to Henry Robbins and Elizabeth Otis to see what they thought about publishing the language essays he was then working on. It would be a short book, he said, and he even proposed a title: *Sentences.* The idea had not gone much beyond that, partly because Percy was having such a hard time writing the essays. But Foote's suggestion that he bring together all of his philosophically oriented essays dating from 1954 planted a new seed. Percy began to give it some thought.

In fact, he now began to work on a piece that he thought would serve as the introduction to just such a collection. In early February, he wrote to Ann, now living in the Chi Omega sorority house at LSU, telling her that he was sorry that he had been unable to accompany Bunt to LSU on her recent visit:

> I'm sorry I didn't see you; but I had to work—or at least try, which was fortunate because I had a good morning, wrote something I'd been stuck on for weeks (an Introduction to my old essays written over the past 20 years, which I'll probably collect & publish.)
>
> I've not felt much like writing for the past year (as you know) a certain loss of motivation—OK I wrote for the past 15 years, did what I wanted to do, succeeded—so what? There doesn't seem to be a great deal of point. Middle-age depression no doubt, plus a Percyean disposition toward melancholia. Yet I have the feeling that patience & time cures most things and that eventually I'll feel like taking the trouble to write seriously. Like today: a good morning. A happy paragraph or two.

It was a rather strong dose of woe to unload on his daughter, as Percy himself seemed to realize. To offset the gloom, he brought up some of the things that made life worth living, namely the round of golf that he and Bunt played most days. Working to sustain the upbeat note, Percy concluded his letter with a list of favorite Goldwynisms (Sam Goldwyn had died that day), including the MGM magnate's response to someone who told him that there weren't enough Indians for a scene in one of his movies: "There are plenty of Indians at the reservoir!" To Percy, Goldwyn had been a walking anthology of "metaphors as mistakes."

In another letter to Ann later that month, Percy announced that he had given up on the novel altogether, that it was "killing him." Fortunately, this was not quite the truth. But he was mired. To Caroline Gordon, who was now teaching creative writing at the University of Dallas, he described his predicament a little more precisely: "I'm hopelessly stuck with [my novel], hopeless because I can't get it right and I can't let it go. . . . For the present, all I have is a title, *The Knight, Death, and the Devil.* (Remember the Dürer engraving?)" Percy's flirtation with a different title, inspired by one of his favorite pieces of art, was revealing. It sounded—perhaps too blatantly for his final comfort—the major themes of the novel: the chivalric ideal gone awry, physical and spiritual death, and evil. The sheer introspective gloom of Durer's northern European imagination comported well with Percy's despairing mood, but Percy would eventually return to the more ambiguous title, *Lancelot.*

Percy saw so little progress in his novel that by April he was willing to entertain an offer to teach at LSU the following fall. On April 3, he wrote to Simpson saying that he was eager to talk with him and Dr. Otis Wheeler, the chairman of the English department, on April 18 about a possible teaching job at the university for the following year. "The truth is, Lewis, I'd like very much to work out something at LSU and your department." At the meeting two weeks later, it was agreed that Percy would teach a literature course in the fall and a creative writing seminar in the spring. At least he would be doing something useful, Percy thought.

Even before the meeting, Percy sent Simpson the first draft of "A Theory of Language." Simpson had had some quiet misgivings about the essay ever since Percy's October 14 letter described it as part of his "extra-literary pursuits." Simpson was beginning to fear that it might be too technical. Seeming to anticipate Simpson's concerns, Percy, in the cover letter accompanying the article, gave Simpson a respectable way of getting out of his obligation to publish the piece: "I send it mainly to support my conviction that I don't see how the SR could use it, since it is mainly an attack on three schools of linguistic theory, mostly contra Chomsky, and this ain't exactly what your subscribers is paying their money for." But Percy would not make things too easy for Simpson: For the second time, he declared it the most important thing he had written, "but it will be twenty years before anybody realizes it." Simpson took heart when he read the essay's subtitle: *A Martian View of Linguistic Theory, Plus the Discovery That an Explanatory Theory Does Not Presently Exist, Plus the Offering of a Crude Explanatory Model on the Theory That Something Is Better than Nothing.* For a moment Simpson was hopeful, thinking that Percy had written "an erudite spoof that would be thoroughly available and entertaining to any reasonably sophisticated reader." His hopes were quickly deflated. "I soon realized that what I had before me—a manuscript cluttered with linguistic equations and diagrams—was not, as Walker had warned me, what our subscribers paid to see." Simpson felt he was too far in to back out now. He let Percy know that he was looking forward to the final draft, which Percy had mentioned he would soon be sending on.

Pleased by Simpson's acceptance of the essay—and unaware of the discomfort he had caused—Percy set about doing the final revision of "A Theory of Language," breaking off only briefly on May 10, when he and Bunt journeyed up to Memphis to join in celebrating the completion of Foote's history. The Footes had organized a big dinner for that Friday evening, and Foote had made it clear that no excuse would suffice for Percy's missing it. Percy needed no threats. For more than a year now he had been looking forward to this celebration, and only a family tragedy could have prevented him from coming. The party was a great success, and afterward Percy wrote to compliment Foote both on the wine ("I wasn't even hung over") and on his friends, "rich though they may be." Percy told his friend that he had followed his advice and pulled together his essays "plus an introduction, plus a long unreadable article (but most important I'll ever write) called 'A Theory of Language' which will also be published in Southern Review." He also reported that he was reading Joseph Blotner's biography of Faulkner and enjoying the details that the "reviewers deplored"; indeed, he regretted that discretion had compelled Blotner to remain silent about some of the more sensitive matters in Faulkner's life: "F's relation to Estelle, how come Jill hated life at home. . . ."

A few weeks later, Percy received galleys of most of the third volume of Foote's trilogy and read them with growing awe at his friend's accomplishment. His only quibble was that the last part focused too heavily on Jefferson Davis. Percy was afraid that the emphasis on "Lucifer" gave too southern a bias to a book that was otherwise remarkably evenhanded. "O.K., I'm not picking—otherwise it is The Iliad." Percy found the last chapter, when it arrived in early July, just as good as Foote hoped he would, though he still questioned the prominence of Davis.

By the end of July, it was becoming clear to Percy that his physical condition, a low-grade fever in particular, might have something to do with his low spirits. He felt so weak that he was unable to work, and he began to worry that his old nemesis, TB, had returned. Finally Percy decided to check into Ochsner Hospital in New Orleans and submitted to a battery of tests. The results revealed that Percy had hepatitis, a discovery that would have brought him some consolation had it not been for the necessity of abandoning all alcohol. Even though he would not admit it, this was probably the happiest necessity ever imposed on Percy. The alcohol had been driving him dangerously deep into depression.

Not that the temporary parting of ways with drink made his spirits suddenly soar. When Caroline Gordon wrote toward the end of August asking if Percy would meet with a friend of hers, Bob Sordello, Percy wrote back to say that he would, adding that he wouldn't argue with Sordello (or her) about Jung or the principles of fiction writing. The mysterious allusion to Jung seemed to prompt a confession, perhaps the most thorough analysis of his demoralization that he would ever offer (and all the more interesting for what it showed about Percy's awareness of a possible link between his mental state and the book he was trying to write):

> Truth is, the older I get, the less I know. Time was, however, when Jung would irritate me with his patronizing approval of religion—e.g. the cult of the Virgin not because it was true but because it conformed to his "anima" archetype. I preferred Freud's old-fashioned atheism. Now, however, don't ask me.
>
> My hepatitis and depression are better. Maybe one caused the other. Truthfully I don't know whether I've been overtaken by a virus or male menopause or the devil—who I am quite willing to believe does indeed roam about the world seeking whom he may devour. Anyhow it takes the form in my case of disinterest, accidie, little or no use for the things of God and the old virtues. I'd rather chase women (not that I do, but how strange to have come to this pass). I think it has something to do with laziness or the inability to give birth to a 2-year-old fetus of a novel. I don't like it at all and keep tearing it up. I feel like a Borgia Pope, I still believe the whole thing, but oh you Italian girls!
>
> I'll get over it—it might even help the novel. Your friend, William Faulkner, said many foolish things but he said one true thing: if a writer doesn't write, he is sure to commit moral outrages.

Percy was feeling well enough by September to be able to tell Foote that he was back to his "*normal* depression"; well enough, also, to be able to teach his course at LSU. His convalescence had not been completely idle. While on his back, Percy had managed to complete yet another revision of his "Theory of Language." The first he had sent in on May 20, along with another cover letter expressing his gratitude to Simpson for taking what Percy knew was a difficult piece. Poking fun at the Tom More side of his personality, Percy admitted that one reason he was so eager to see it in print as soon as possible was that he was "sufficiently seduced by the angelism-bestialism of the scientist to want to get it in the public domain before being scooped. The vanity of theorists!" Simpson politely replied that he planned to run the essay in the January 1975 number of *Southern Review*. On September 20 Simpson received yet another letter from Percy listing eleven more changes but assuring him that they could go over them on Wednesday or Thursday, the days Percy came to Baton Rouge for his discussion group and his class. But the biggest surprise of the letter was Percy's offer of an entirely different article. Since "A Theory of Language" would appear in a collection that Farrar, Straus was bringing out in the spring, Percy explained, it would be quite all right if Simpson decided not to run it at all. Instead, he might consider something "even queerer," a piece entitled "The Delta Factor." Unpacking the manuscript envelope, Lewis found the new essay. As Simpson put it, "I joyfully discovered that I really was off the hook with an essay that, anticipating the style and method of *Lost in the Cosmos*, was—in contrast to the 'scientific' statement in 'A Theory of Language'—a mostly nontechnical presentation of the story of Helen Keller and altogether an intriguing and challenging literary statement, a dramatization of the essential core of Percy's prophetic theory of language." Needless to say, Simpson went with the second essay, and in October Percy informed his editor, Robert Giroux, that "The Delta Factor" would appear in *Southern Review.*

One of the many pleasures of publishing with Farrar, Straus, Percy had learned over the years, was receiving copies of their newly published books. Percy usually found a few titles on each season's list that strongly grabbed his attention, but one book on the fall 1974 list, a collection of two novellas and a memoir by the Austrian writer Peter Handke, so greatly impressed him that he wrote a note of praise to Giroux: "The book by Peter Handke is a joy." Percy liked all three pieces, "The Goalie's Anxiety at the Penalty Kick," "Short Letter, Long Farewell," and "A Sorrow Beyond Dreams," but the last in particular, which deals with the suicide of Handke's mother, deeply affected Percy. Percy's interest in Handke apparently got around the Farrar, Straus office, and one of the editors there sent Handke a copy of Percy's novel, *The Moviegoer.* The attraction proved reciprocal; later, Handke would translate both *The Moviegoer* and *The Last Gentleman* for Suhrkamp Verlag, an experience that he would describe as a "voyage towards the center of my (our) existence, a voyage of images, spaces, inner situations. And it was good that I never reached the center, always felt it near, nearer and nearer, a warm thing." Handke's reaction to Percy's work was in many respects similar to Thomas Merton's. To both of these close readers, the most powerful aspect of Percy's fiction was the spell it wove, its atmosphere of enchantment. "No warmer and more secret books than these two," Handke continued about the two novels he translated. "And the secret is not made, cooked—it is not cheap mystery, it is felt and developed with writing, work."

Lewis Simpson once speculated that Percy's experience at LSU during the 1974–75 academic year had a decisive influence on the writing of

Lancelot. The hunch seems sound, vague as Simpson remained about the precise nature of the influence. One fact about Percy's year at Baton Rouge is obvious: It took him out of his usual world and exposed him to two subcultures with which he usually had only limited or distant dealings—American youth and American academia. Moreover, this exposure came at a time when both subcultures were entering the last phase of that cultural period loosely called the sixties. Hippiedom, drugs, radical politics, disaffection with mainstream America—all aspects of the truly inchoate counterculture—were losing both their attraction and their following. Developments in American political and economic life hastened their demise: the resignation of Nixon in the summer of 1974, the winding down of the Vietnam War (starting with the signing of the peace agreement on January 22, 1973), and a sliding economy that would be further weakened by an oil embargo and rising oil prices. The Age of Aquarius was not dead at LSU, but it was certainly moribund. At the same time, of course, a new age was aborning, one whose forms and preoccupations were still undefined.

Percy was teaching at LSU at this pivotal moment. And looking both ways—sniffing the winds from each direction—he did not particularly like what he saw or smelled. It seemed to be a sad, dispirited, selfish time following on the heels of an irresponsible, infantile time. Yet despite his ultimate disappointment with the sixties, Percy had been, in certain ways, strongly sympathetic to the spirit of the counterculture. Foote often accused Percy of being far more indulgent of hippies than he, a work-ethic man to the core, could ever be. This was a fair charge. Percy would have found it impossible not to sympathize with people who were seekers, although he was troubled by the irrationalism and, even more, the fecklessness of most counterculturalists. He thought they were not serious enough—or that their seriousness was misplaced.

By all appearances, Percy had a pleasant and rewarding year at LSU. He liked the teaching, he worked with responsive students, and he enjoyed the company and respect of intelligent professors in both the English and philosophy departments. Yet, ironically, the sum of all this agreeableness made him even more confused and sour. The deeper, darker mood of despair would erupt in strange ways. Susanne Jensen would see signs of it in the group discussions on Thursday afternoon, in his strenuous intellectual effort to make sense of inner and outer chaos. "He was trying to hold everything together—his view of the world, his place in his family, his religious faith." His wife and children saw it in his brooding despondency and outbursts of temper. Perhaps the least expected witness to Percy's darkness was one of the students in his seminar. Almost without exception, Percy was friendly, relaxed, but never intimate with the young men and women in English 292, as his course in existential literature was listed. The students felt that it was an exciting class, that Percy was engaged with the authors they were reading, but as with the Loyola class several years before, he would never talk about himself or his work. One afternoon, though, one of his students, Wyatt Prunty (who later became a poet and critic), was walking by the English department when he happened to see Percy sitting alone in an office, apparently doing nothing. In his usual casual attire, khaki pants, plaid shirt, and wallabee shoes, Percy, as Prunty recalls, looked as though he had stepped out of an L. L. Bean catalogue. His arms crossed and his gaze fixed in the middle distance, he had his feet propped up on another chair and on one of them had rested his canvas pork-pie hat. Hearing Prunty, Percy turned and called him into the room. "Well, hello, Wyatt," Percy said, and almost without pausing a beat, added, "I guess the central mystery of my life will always be why my father killed himself. Come here, have a seat."

Strangely abrupt as it was, Percy's announcement had a peculiar logic to it. In one of the classes, Prunty had talked about his brother-in-law, a former military doctor in Vietnam, who had committed suicide after returning to the States. That had grabbed Percy's attention. In fact, a number of things Prunty had said had stayed with Percy. During a discussion of Meursault in *The Stranger*, Prunty had suggested that Meursault did what he did because he was an "absolutist." That description struck a chord in Percy. But despite all these quite reasonable "reasons" for Percy's bringing up a private topic in front of a student whom he liked, there was still something strangely gratuitous and self-dramatizing about it. It did not conform to Percy's usual manner, his usual reticent persona. The directness of the voice was different; it was the voice of a man in desperate straits, a man looking for someone to hear his confession. But there is something else quite interesting about this confession: If we attend carefully to the last words of Percy's invitation to Prunty—"Come here, have a seat"—we hear something very close to the first lines of *Lancelot*. Percy had not yet found those lines, but he was drawing closer.

The opening lines would not come to him until the spring of the next year. With considerable elation, he announced to the members of his discussion group that he had been working for weeks—years would have been closer to the truth—on the first line of his novel and that it had finally come to him: "Come into my cell. Make yourself at home."

First, though, with the arrival of winter would come another setback, this one physical. As far as his health went at least, Percy had started to feel better by late autumn. He was out of the worst stages of hepatitis, still not allowed to drink, but feeling quite a bit better. His essays wrapped up, he had sent Foote pages from the first part of his forthcoming book, reciprocating for the early copy of volume three that Foote had sent him. In an accompanying letter Percy noted the coincidence that he had worked on his philosophical writing for as long as Foote had worked on his history—from 1954 to 1974. "Strange parallel, nicht? You fighting in war, me laying into old Homo himself (I'm afraid I didn't win this war either)." Shelby was astonished by the coincidence—and by the sheer longevity of their labors. "Twenty years. Holy Mother! . . . Thank God for my narrower scope; I'll take Mars Robert every time." In a follow-up letter praising "The Delta Factor" Foote confessed that he was finally beginning to understand Percy's point about language. "I think youre right about the importance of language and the difference even a vestige of it makes; I think youre right too about the thing it grows from—symbolism." To overcome Foote's aversion to the abstract was a signal accomplishment, and one in which Percy took considerable pride. It gave him hope that his essays might even have some appeal to the intelligent general reader.

But even as such small triumphs were bolstering his spirits against the onslaught of the holidays, Percy began to have intestinal pains, and in the third week of December he underwent surgery to repair a bilateral hernia. The operation went well but left him "sore and tottery," as he explained to Lewis Simpson. Nevertheless, by mid-January he was strong enough to return to teaching at LSU. His class this term was fiction writing, and it included seven graduate students. Having read samples of the students' work in December, Percy came to the class with low expectations, but this did not prevent him from investing a great deal of time and energy in the class. As a number of his colleagues noted, Percy seemed in some ways more comfortable during the second semester than he had during the first. Panthea Reid Broughton, a professor in the English department who later edited a volume of scholarly essays on Percy's work, thought it had something to do with the location of his office: "[F]or one semester he had an office that had once been Cleanth Brooks's; for the second semester he had an office in a new building occupied principally by mathematicians and philosophers. He seemed accessible in the first but, I think, happier in the second." Broughton, who had come to know Percy quite well during the first semester, had impressed him with her drive and ambition; some thought that she might even have been a partial inspiration for the character of Margot, Lance Lamar's wife in Lancelot. The figure of the forceful, ambitious, and even somewhat domineering woman was both fascinating and frightening to Percy.

And as things turned out, he would come to know another such woman that spring. In early 1975, Bunt Percy had become president of the St. Tammany Art Association, a community group that supported and exhibited the works of local artists. The association owned two fine old buildings on the edge of town, one a Victorian house converted into offices and exhibition space, and the other, a sort of narrow barn of a building, converted into four artists' studios. One of the studios happened to be unused and Bunt suggested that Walker take a look at it. She had often heard him talk about keeping an office in town, and she thought that his having a place to go every day might help bring him out of the doldrums. Percy visited the studio and liked it. It was a fourteen-by-twelve corner room with a small kitchenette and a bathroom and windows on the front and side. Deciding to rent it, Percy furnished it simply with a makeshift daybed (a mattress on a sheet of wood supported by sawhorses), his writing stand, a typing table, and a radio.

Working next door to Percy was an artist named Lyn Hill. He had met her the previous fall after Bunt had seen some of her work—a series of ink resists inspired by the 139th Psalm—and recommended that Percy look at them. Percy, too, had been impressed and tried to buy one, but Hill had told him that she was making them for friends. Now working as neighbors, Percy and Hill became fast friends, dropping by each other's office almost daily to talk about their work and anything else on their minds. Hill, then twenty-eight, had just lost a very close friend in a fire and was not in the best of spirits herself; to some extent, Percy and Hill were partners in despondency as well as art. As Percy quickly learned, Hill had strong opinions and intuitions, something of a mystical streak, and an interest in Jung. (Percy and Bunt had not long before become involved in a Jungian discussion group, and Percy's interest in Jung's theories of the unconscious had never been stronger.) Soon, a friend of Hill's, a young man named Bob Milling, started coming by their studios. He was an intelligent, engaging man, though clearly at loose ends. A Princeton graduate and a former naval officer, he had vague ambitions to write but was having trouble finding focus. The three decided to formalize their meetings by gathering for lunch each Thursday at a restaurant on Lake Pontchartrain called Bechacs. They dubbed themselves the "Sons and Daughters of the Apocalypse," and were soon joined by several other young artists and writers in the area. At first the discussions were devoted to Jung, but they quickly decided that such heavy fare called for a more private setting. So another group, this one including Hill, Milling, Percy, and Charles Bigger (a professor of philosophy at LSU), began to meet at Milling's house once or twice a month to discuss Jung. The Bechacs Thursday group became and remained a less structured gathering, dropping or adding new members over the years until it finally wound down in the mid-1980s. In addition to Milling, Percy, and Hill, the group in the early days included a sculptor named Bill Binnings, a journalist named David Chandler, the owner of the Maple Street Bookstore in New Orleans, Rhoda Faust, and various others. Bechacs itself was an old, well-seasoned restaurant with high ceilings and broad windows that faced the lake. The tone of the place was largely set by a pair of wizened black waiters. Far from "step-and-fetchits," they were both distant, somewhat aloof men who moved at their own pace, made no special effort to please anyone, and thus ended up commanding the loyalty and respect of the restaurant's regular patrons.

The Bechacs lunch group, the Jung circles, the class at LSU, Jensen's discussion group, not to mention the Wednesday lunch bunch, the book club, his church, and the daily round of golf with Bunt—Percy had so many daily and weekly commitments that it is surprising he managed to write at all. Percy did of course keep his mornings to himself. Even when nothing came—and that was most days during this fallow period—he knew he had to be behind his writing stand each morning, staring at the ruled white pages in his blue medical school notebooks. Percy continued to follow Kafka's dictum: *Warte!* But the emptiness that tended to fill these hours of waiting made him eager for companionship, and that he clearly found in his busy round of activities. Even after he made his big breakthrough in the middle of the spring semester and found the right opening sentences for his book, the writing came slowly. And the prospect of his book of essays coming out in June gave him a mild case of jitters. He knew that his *Message in the Bottle* would reach far fewer readers than his novels had, but he didn't want his intellectual passion of the past twenty years to seem like a complete self-indulgence.

Winding up his class in early May, Percy proposed to take Bunt and his daughters up to New York City later in the month for some shopping and gadding about. It was an attempt to make up for his recent beastliness, inadequate, he knew, but a gesture. "We're all going to be in NYC, the Plaza, May 29–June 4," Percy wrote to Foote. "For no reason. Except the ladies want to get at Bergdorfs and Bonwits." Percy, in the same letter, expressed his disappointment and regret that Foote's history had not won the NBA. *The Civil War: A Narrative* had received rave reviews in the months after it came out, but almost unaccountably it won none of the prizes that it should handily have taken—not the NBA, not the Pulitzer, not the Parkman, not the Bancroft. More than anything else, this neglect was a tribute to the narrow professionalism of the age and to the inability of most prize judges (usually specialists themselves) to appreciate a work that transcended its genre. By writing a history that went beyond history, by writing in effect a historical epic, Foote eluded both the strict *littérateurs* and the even stricter professional historians. Foote bore this slight with Stoic composure, but it hurt. "I really thought I had it sewed up—the Pulitzer at least. Shows you how stupid I can get, to think that I could crack through that academic screen."

The Message in the Bottle came out in the middle of June, and the reviews that followed shortly thereafter were mostly sympathetic and intelligent, if not as prominently placed as reviews for Percy's novels tended to be. James Boatwright in *The New Republic* gave what might be called the typical intelligent generalist's assessment of the book: "His theory of man for a new age grows out of an intellectual tradition which seems not to have much affected our scientific-humanist consciousness: Percy's teachers are Aquinas and Kierkegaard, Heidegger and Marcel, Cassirer and Peirce—and with their help he mounts a frontal assault on how we fail to handle the predicament of our being human, on the ways in which we misconceive ourselves, and our great, mysterious, unique gift, language."

A stricter and far less admiring philosophical appraisal of the book came in the September 18 issue of *The New York Review of Books*. Thomas Nagel slapped Percy's wrists for not knowing sufficiently whereof he spoke. Nagel correctly identified the ethical and even religious intent behind Percy's view of language but failed to understand how the establishment of man as the languaged creature necessarily supported the ethical or religious claims. "Percy is right to wish for an expanded understanding of language, but what is required is a view of how language is used by those who use it: a view from within the community of speakers and not a spiritualizing of the subject." Nagel felt that Percy's theory of language was trying to have things two ways: On one hand, like Wittgenstein's view of language games, it argued the necessarily communal or "intersubjective" character of language; yet it also attempted to explain language from an external perspective (that of Percy's figurative Martian) and to posit a kind of mysterious mechanism, the coupler, which unites word and object in the act of asserting. The proposal of such a coupler, which Percy said may or may not be "an 'I,' a 'self,' or some neurophysiological correlate thereof," was, in Nagel's astute judgment, a case of positivist hubris, though somewhat shrouded in mystery. Nagel reminded Percy that this was precisely Tom More's problem: "This calls to mind the fantasy of a neuroanatomical key to universal happiness and the salvation of society in *Love in the Ruins*. Unable to comprehend language by conventional physiology, Percy can get no farther than to invent a mythical physiology instead."

Shrewd as this appraisal was, it was a bit like saying that Einstein had never contributed anything of value to physics because he failed to bring off his Grand Unified Theory. Percy had failed to bring off his Grand Unified Theory of language, but that did not vitiate all aspects of his inquiry. Nagel seemed almost to resent Percy's presumption and ambition for attempting so much, for trying to consider all aspects of language —behavioral, syntactic, semantic—and to arrive at some sense of what they added up to as the defining quality of human beings. If this is hubris, Nagel might have acknowledged, intellectual life needed such hubris. Percy himself was not blind to the folly of his reach. After all, he had created the character of Tom More, among other reasons, to satirize himself. Percy recognized the trap of positivism, but he also knew there was no way completely around it at this point in our intellectual history (a necessity that other intelligent critics of Percy's language philosophy seem to ignore).

Perhaps the most knowing and appreciative of appraisals came from Hugh Kenner in the September 12 issue of the *National Review.* Kenner, the quirky and original polymath, suggested that Percy had "probably made a breakthrough."

> If he has—such is the importance of its subject—*The Message in the Bottle* may one day rank with *De Revolutionibis Orbium Coelestium,* and 2475 be marked by semi-millennial celebrations.
>
> This analogy isn't random. Mr. Percy's tone of congenital depression is strongly reminiscent of Copernicus' furtiveness about his own theory. Moreover, Copernicus had a lot of the facts wrong, and most of the details. What we honor him for is having drawn a picture with the main essential correct: the sun at the center. Mr. Percy doesn't pretend to have done more than that, and what he puts at the center is as simple and blinding as the sun: the Naming Faculty.

Even before the earliest reviews came in, though, Percy had begun to sink into another depression. He could drink again, his liver having recovered from the hepatitis, but he was not drinking heavily, and drink was not causing his unhappiness. His melancholia seemed rather to come from a profound sense of stagnation in his life. Some of the members of the Bechacs group interpreted this as unhappiness with his conventional life. Some thought that he was overly burdened by guilt and even by an excessive consciousness of his future reputation. "He was almost afraid of having too much fun, of being too much at ease," Lyn Hill explained. "You could see that even in the way he acted at the lunches. At bottom, he didn't believe he deserved happiness. He would often say that man was not put in this world to be happy."

Lyn Hill was a woman of strong views and perceptions—one reason Percy was so interested in her—but she, like the other members of the Bechacs group, tended to simplify the causes of Percy's unhappiness. Percy, to be sure, was strongly attracted and attached to the youthful crowd that gathered every Thursday. In some ways, he even romanticized this group as the first real community he had ever belonged to. A poem that he gave to Lyn Hill, entitled "Community," described his feelings about the Bechacs crowd. But as the last five lines of the poem show, the poem makes an argument that was flatly untrue to the facts of Percy's life, particularly to the other forms of community that had been sustaining in previous years:

> But what a surprise!
> Twenty years of solitariness and success at solitariness,
> Solitary with his family like the Swiss family on their island,
> Then all at once community.
> Community? What friends out there in the world?
> Yes.

What was so special about the Bechacs circle was precisely its self-consciousness about being an authentic "community," a select circle of like-minded souls. And clearly one part of Percy hearkened to this somewhat charged ideal of authentic community.

Yet as much as Percy fantasized about freedom and a new life (as he made more than clear in his letters to Foote), and as much as he envied his young friends' footloose ways, he knew that their ways finally were not his. Percy believed that the conflict he was caught up in was not merely an overdue midlife crisis. He believed that it was bound up with a struggle between good and evil and indeed with the fate of his immortal soul. He had not been jesting in his letter to Caroline Gordon when he talked about the devil stalking the world in search of vulnerable souls. This may not make sense to a psychological age, but it made ultimate sense to Percy. There was something else the Bechacs circle might not have been able to fathom, and that was the depth of Percy's love for his wife—and of his need for her sustaining love.

The torment of Percy's internal struggle grew unbearable that summer. Almost too appropriately, he had finally gotten around to reading Bergin's translation of *The Divine Comedy*. As he made his way through the *Inferno*, he felt a kind of rage and impotent fury building up in himself. In early August, unable to stand it, he impulsively boarded a plane for

Las Vegas, holed up for a couple of nights in the Holiday Inn on the downtown strip, then rented a car and a tent and went up into the Sierra Nevadas for a few days. Once again, the West—the locus of pure possibility—served Percy well. If he was going to wrestle with his demons, he needed the absolute and arid emptiness of the desert to do it properly.

The surprising outcome of this desert retreat is that, to some extent, it worked. It did not end his depression, but he experienced a kind of purging that allowed him to write—and to write furiously. The voice that he had discovered the spring before now seemed to carry him along. Percy's anger with the world and himself fueled the flow of the narrative and the unholy spleen of the central character. Using the narrative strategy of Camus' novel *The Fall*—one man confessing his story to another—Percy has the character of Lancelot tell his friend Percival the whole murderous tale. Embarked on a quest to uncover the mechanism of evil in his wife's adultery—and, thereby, at least some possibility of a spiritual order in the cosmos—Lancelot uncovers a more profound evil in himself, an emptiness that allows him to commit the sin of murder with an almost chillingly scientific indifference. This discovery does not lead Lancelot to faith, however, but to an even stronger contempt for his age and a desire to start a new order built upon Nietzschean "Superman" values and southern chivalry. Yet even though the story is told by Lance, its point does not rest upon Lance's vision. In the figure of the all but mute priest, Percival, glimmers the faint hope of an alternative to Lance's solution. It is astonishing that so much can depend on a character whose presence in the novel is so marginal, so liminal. In earlier versions, Percival dominated the opening section of the novel, but by the final version he is presented only indirectly, almost exclusively through Lance's words. Yet paradoxically this shadowiness only increases his power. The weight of the entire novel comes to rest on Percival's laconic but affirmative "Yes" to his friend's final challenge, "Very well. I've finished. Is there anything you wish to tell me before I leave?"

Percy was in fact writing a kind of Jungian drama between a self and a counterself, the self, one might say, and its shadow. Both figures bear biographical resemblances, superficial and deep, to Percy (and to various ancestral Percys). Lance, like Percy, has worked for civil-rights causes, drinks more than is good for him, feels increasingly contemptuous of the modern age and increasingly purposeless in his own life. Percival is linked most obviously to Percy by his name. He is even given the same college nickname, "Pussy," that some of Percy's SAE brothers had given him; born in a house named Northumberland, he is a "bad Catholic" struggling with his faith. But these biographical links between the characters and their creator are relatively trivial. The salient connection

between them and Percy is their dramatization of his own internal conflict between despair and hope, selfishness and selflessness, contempt
for the world and charity. Percy once explained that he could not give
these opposing voices equal time in the way that Dostoyevsky had;
the age would not tolerate such preaching. But he could transform the
dialogue into a monologue, allow the side of darkness to talk itself
out in one long-winded rant, and by subtlest hints imply a response.
The strategy required much of the reader—more, perhaps, than Percy
had reason to expect, and more than many early readers were willing to
give.

Once Percy had settled firmly into the narrative line, the writing went
fairly quickly. There were the usual interruptions to contend with, but
none seemed to put him off stride. In early September, Marcus Smith, a
professor of English at Loyola, came out to Covington to interview Percy
for the *New Orleans Review*. Smith, who had only recently joined the
Loyola faculty, had met Percy at a book signing at Rhoda Faust's Maple
Street Bookstore earlier in the summer and shortly thereafter asked if he
could interview Percy on his language theory. Percy agreed. Perhaps
because it was so tightly focused, the interview proved to be one of the
more revealing that Percy ever cooperated in. Smith in fact brought up
a fairly significant flaw in Percy's use of the "Helen Keller phenomenon"
as a model for the breakthrough into language:

> Smith: In *The Message in the Bottle* you put a great deal of emphasis, an
> almost crucial emphasis, upon the case of Helen Keller. It sent me
> back to her biography. I found there that she was nineteen months old
> before she lost her hearing and vision. You yourself state that it's the
> first two years of life that is crucial in language acquisition. Helen
> Keller had the bulk of those two years. Also, in the biography she
> describes that remarkable moment with Miss Sullivan, the water on
> one hand, the word on the other, as a recollection. Doesn't this reopen
> the behaviorism door?
>
> Percy: Yes, that's a very legitimate criticism, so much so as almost to
> disqualify that example, except for the fact that the same experience is
> reported in other cases, such as those of wild or feral boys. And more
> importantly, in the acquisition of speech by the normal child, you do
> have this extraordinary thing which Roger Brown and other psycho-
> linguists talk about, of the child doing what Helen Keller does, not in
> the space of fifteen minutes, but stretched out over say three or four
> months. The child goes into the naming stage, and he seems to be
> interested in almost nothing else but going around naming everything,
> or asking its name, and being fascinated by this extraordinary connec-
> tion between name and thing. So, if it all depended on the single case

of Helen Keller, I think your criticism would be devastating. What was important to me was that the well-house episode distilled the essential elements of the normal naming experience.

Despite this chastening reminder of the facts of Helen Keller's case, Percy continued to use it as a key example of his theory.

In October, Percy flew up to Virginia to attend a two-day symposium on American fiction at Washington-Lee College. The other panelists were Donald Barthelme, Grace Paley, and William Gass, the last, like Percy, a philosopher and novelist. The discussion almost rose above the usual panel fare when Percy and Gass disagreed over whether art was a form of knowledge. Ultimately, though, neither man really seemed to come to terms with the arguments of the other. Gass maintained that a work of art was not a form of knowledge because it could not be reduced to a statement that could then be tested and verified; Percy, flabbergasted by what he took to be rank positivism, said that he would have no reason to write unless he thought he was approaching the truth. Much as Percy admired Gass's fiction, both *Omensetter's Luck* and *In the Heart of the Heart of the Country,* he found his nonreferential formalism an austere and unnourishing aesthetic. The "angelistic" intellectuality of the symposium panel was compensated for by the "bestialism" of the evening activities. Percy, according to a number of Washington-Lee faculty members, drank heavily and behaved in something less than a manner befitting a gentleman. (One can only wonder whether it was partly from shame at his performance on the Shenandoah Valley campus that Percy decided to make the Shenandoah Valley the site of Lance's proposed "Third Revolution," a revolution led by men who still know what is right and proper.)

Percy was in something of a savage state these days, perhaps because he was so deeply sunk into the character of Lancelot. When Foote announced to Percy in early October that he had been up to something a little strange, reading Shelley five hours a day, Percy responded with a rare burst of coarseness:

> What kind of fellow are you? Are you telling me that you can sit there in your castle in Memphis happily reading Shelley 5 hours a day? You are certainly a happier man than I, but I'm not really sure I envy you. Shelley five hours per day?
>
> Don't you ever want to (1) shoot your wife (2) burn your house (3) run off with 2 26-year-old lovely Foote-admiring graduate N.C. students (incidentally, congrats on your U.N.C. honor—Louis Rubin

told me last year) (3) shoot your mother-in-law (4) move to
Greece . . . ?

Christ, you sound like Ralph Waldo Emerson. Please forward the
secret of your maturity to a demoralized Catholic.

Everything seemed to be disorienting to Percy in this period of life,
perhaps nothing more than the November 29 wedding of his daughter
Ann. Percy liked her bridegroom, John David Moores. He was a quiet,
serious business major who had dated Ann ever since they were freshmen
at LSU. Nevertheless, Percy could not help feeling some ambivalence
toward the event that would bring a definitive end to the old family
arrangement.

Despite all the distractions of the autumn, Percy worked hard, managing not only to knock out his "Bourbon" essay in time for the December issue of Esquire but also to finish a first draft of his novel in early
January. In a letter dated January 10, Percy wrote to praise Lewis Simpson for his article, "Faulkner and the Legend of the Artist." Percy noted
that it formulated a major theme of Lancelot: "i.e., the incapacity of the
post-modern consciousness to deal with sexuality." Less than a month
later, in another letter to Simpson, Percy reported even more explicitly
on the state of his book: "Yes, I've finished a draft of the novel, but can't
even bring myself to read it." Percy did soon manage to sneak some looks
and scribble in changes, and by March he had hired Betty Ellis, the wife
of his friend Steve, to retype a marked-up copy of the manuscript.

Percy didn't sit idle while Betty Ellis typed. In early April, he flew up
to Washington, D.C., to deliver the Frieda Fromm-Reichmann Memorial Lectures at the National Institute for Health auditorium. Percy was
unhappy with the lecture, which dealt broadly with popular culture, and
he refused to let Psychiatry publish it, but he was at least happy to have
affirmed his old tie with the Sullivanians of the Washington School for
Psychiatry, the sponsors of the lecture. One disappointment to Percy
was that he didn't meet Lewis Lawson, who had been in the crowd but
had been too shy to introduce himself after the lecture. "I met some of
your students and was hoping to meet you," Percy wrote Lawson shortly
after returning to Covington.

On April 19 Percy informed Robert Giroux that he should be receiving a copy of the novel in a "week to 10 days." This was the first time
that Percy would work directly with Giroux on a manuscript. Henry
Robbins, who had done the line editing of The Last Gentleman and Love
in the Ruins, had moved to Simon and Schuster in 1973 (and would
move on to E. P. Dutton before his death, by heart attack, in 1979).
But Percy was pleased to discover that his working relationship with

Giroux was as smooth and helpful as the relationship with Robbins had been. (Ever since Stanley Kauffmann—and in truth ever since Camille Sarason in high school and Joe Sugarman in college—Percy had been blessed by good editors.) Giroux's suggestions were generally light ones, for example, urging Percy to make clearer in the opening scene the nature of Percival's relationship to Lance. (Percy fixed this by having Lance admit in the second chapter that he had only been pretending that he didn't know Percival the first time he beckoned him into his "cell.")

In the summer of 1976, Percy and Bunt went to Highlands, North Carolina, with their friends Betty and Steve Ellis. Ellis, a shrewd, conservative judge in the district court of appeals, was respected by lawyers as tough, fair, and wise. He was a perceptive man, a quick and sure appraiser of character, and although he could appear forbiddingly cool, he had a sly, joking way with friends and considerable warmth beneath his stern façade. Percy liked everything about the man—his character, his sense of humor, his curiosity. Among other things, Ellis was interested in local history, and Percy found his tales about the region's past fascinating. Ellis's wife was known about town as a difficult woman, smart but also very sarcastic and cutting; nevertheless, Percy and Bunt got along with her as well as they did with her husband, and soon the two couples were spending time together, sailing on Lake Pontchartrain, traveling to the Yucatan in the winter of 1976, taking vacations down on the Gulf or up in the mountains of North Carolina. Highlands in particular would be a favorite place in the coming years, and the Percys and Ellises would often rent a cottage called Brown House that was located beside a quiet lake. The foursome enjoyed hiking on the nearby trails, swimming in the lake, and playing the occasional round of golf. Percy liked the cool tranquility of the mountains. Spreading out on the porch, he would read, write, and listen to the radio.

During the summer of 1976, he had a fair amount of obligatory reading to finish. He had agreed to teach another writing seminar at Loyola during the fall of 1976, and the class was to be formed on the basis of manuscript submissions. Fliers and radio announcements encouraged writers throughout the New Orleans area to submit samples of their work. Percy ended up with 150 manuscripts, from which he chose twelve writers. Not all of the students he selected were strangers to Percy: They included Carol Livaudais, Walter Isaacson (who, having returned from two years at Oxford, was a reporter on the staff of the Times-Picayune), Kenneth Holditch (a professor at the University of New Orleans whom Percy had known for more than ten years). As well as English teachers and housewives and a secretary, there was a young novelist named Valerie Martin who had already published a novel, *Set in Motion*, based on her experiences as a social worker.

Beginning in September, the class met every Thursday at five-thirty, usually for two to three hours, depending on how long it took for two or three students to read aloud from their work and receive criticism from the group. Percy also consulted individually with students during his office hours on Thursday afternoon, elaborating on the cryptic and usually indecipherable remarks that he had scribbled in the margins of the students' manuscripts. Percy told the group at the first meeting that they had been selected because each was "trying something different, experimenting in a particular way." Ken Holditch observed quite a few more similarities than differences among the students' work. He thought it noteworthy that all the manuscripts "were being written in the first person, that all except one had New Orleans settings, that all had a certain jaundiced, cynical, notes-from-underground quality with heroes and heroines (a bit like Percy characters Binx Bolling or Will Barrett, in a couple of cases) who are alienated in one way or another."

Percy pretty much held to his dictum that creative writing could not be taught, but he managed to communicate a few of his writerly prejudices and preoccupations. He often dwelt upon the importance of the first sentence and the first paragraph, and would read examples of what he thought were particularly good opening lines (including those from *A Farewell to Arms*, *Moby Dick*, and *The Stranger*). He insisted that underwriting was a lesser sin than overwriting, that novels should not end with a meaningless defeat, and that the writer should tend to the needs of the reader. (Caroline Gordon's instruction had not been completely lost on him.) The convivial atmosphere of the seminars was helped along by wine, brought by a different student each week. One evening, Percy even broke with his usual practice and read the first two chapters of *Lancelot*. Most of the students liked what they heard, but one of them, a woman, objected strongly to what she called the misogynist tone of the book.

One surprising consequence of Percy's teaching at Loyola was a literary discovery—in fact a fairly major one. One Thursday afternoon in the middle of November, a very determined elderly woman bearing a cardboard box showed up at the English department offices looking for Dr. Walker Percy. Marcus Smith, who happened to be in his office at the time, told her that Percy would be in a little later. Unperturbed, the woman announced that she would wait, and Smith fixed her a cup of tea. As Smith was leaving the office around four o'clock, he ran into Percy and warned him that there was a "formidable woman waiting for you and she has her dead son's novel in a box." Percy already had some idea who Thelma Toole was. She had called him several times on the phone asking if he would read her son's manuscript. "Why would I want to do that?" Percy had asked her. "Because it is a great novel," was her ready reply.

Now faced by this implacable woman, the box clutched in her hands, Percy realized that he was trapped, that there was no way out of doing the decent thing. Percy held out only one hope for himself: "that I could read a few pages and that they would be bad enough for me, in good conscience, to read no farther. . . . My only fear was that this one might not be bad enough, or might be just good enough, so that I would have to keep reading." Percy was particularly concerned when he saw the condition of the manuscript, "a badly smeared, scarcely readable carbon." His concern mounted as he began to read, for in this case, as he put it, "I read on. And on. First with the sinking feeling that it was not bad enough to quit, then with a prickle of interest, then a growing excitement, and finally an incredulity: surely it was not possible that it was so good."

What Percy had before him was the story of Ignatius Reilly, the protagonist of A Confederacy of Dunces, a figure whom Percy later described as a "slob extraordinary, a mad Oliver Hardy, a fat Don Quixote, a perverse Thomas Aquinas rolled into one." Percy was bowled over by everything about the book, its comic energy, its invention, its use of New Orleans, and even its underlying sadness—a sadness heightened by Percy's knowledge that its author had taken his own life. What Percy could not understand was why the book had not been published. (He had no way of knowing then how tantalizingly close it had come to making its way into print: For several years in the mid-1960s, John Kennedy Toole and Robert Gottlieb, then an editor at Simon and Schuster, had gone back and forth over the manuscript, Gottlieb admiring it tremendously but judging it deficient in so many particulars that he couldn't bring himself to publish it, despite repeated revisions by Toole.) Wondering if his judgment was sound, Percy read parts of the manuscript to his class and parts of it to the Bechacs lunch group. Nobody seemed to be as delighted by the book as he was; some even suspected that he had written it on a lark. Percy finally gave it to the person whose intuitive judgment he most trusted. Without a word of promotion, he handed it to Bunt: "Here, would you read this and tell me what you think?" To Percy's relief, Bunt thought it was good—even more than good. She saw the weaknesses that others had pointed out, but she thought it had life and originality.

Convinced that his first impressions had been sound, Percy wrote a letter to Thelma Toole, telling her that it was "an astonishingly original

and talented novel." Percy explained that the book had weaknesses—
"too much dialogue here, not enough action there"—and that publishers
might not be interested in it in its present form, but he wondered if he
could pass it on to Marcus Smith to consider for excerption in the *New
Orleans Review*. Mrs. Toole approved. Smith, when he read it, was also
impressed. Although he didn't think the whole thing worked well as a
novel—"it lacks sufficient movement or development," he told Percy—
he did think there was "an excisable section" that could be run in the
New Orleans Review.

Percy, now more hopeful about this orphan manuscript, would soon
make even stronger efforts to see it published, but for the moment he
had to tend to his own affairs. His own novel was moving smartly toward
publication, and that meant proofreading galleys and making corrections. As usual, Percy sent a set of galleys to Foote. Well along in the
writing of his own novel *September September*, Foote responded with the
usual encouraging words: "It's a good book, sharp incisive, mean as a
booger; an excellent warmup for thickening the texture of the big novel
that follows your LAST GENTLEMAN to where he was about to take
you." The news from Percy's publisher had been even more encouraging.
In early November he learned from Giroux that the Book-of-the-Month
Club had decided on *Lancelot* as one of its main selections for the following March. Percy agreed to attend a BOMC lunch and submit to interviews when he came up to New York the second week of November to
sit on a prize panel of the National Institute of Arts and Letters. He
even agreed to come up again in February to receive a bound copy of the
book from the Book-of-the-Month Club. If Percy was unusually accommodating, it was largely because he needed the money. He and Bunt
had launched Ann on her own business enterprise the summer before—
a book and antique store in town—and Percy was counting on a boost
in his earnings. Working further toward that end, Percy had also agreed
to deliver the Chekhov Lecture at Cornell University on February 3,
two days after the annual National Institute gathering.

The Chekhov talk, "Novelist as Diagnostician of the Modern Malaise," was not too difficult for Percy to prepare. It was largely a compen-
dium of many of his earlier talks and essays, particularly those dealing
with the diagnostic and cognitive power of fiction. In many ways it was
typical of the lectures that Percy would give for the next ten years or so:
a well-cobbled reworking of the central philosophical and literary themes
developed in his earlier essays. The freshest part of the lecture was the
opening remarks about Chekhov as "the literary clinician, the pathologist of the strange spiritual malady of the modern age." For all their
differences—Chekhov was as great a skeptic as Percy was a believer—
Percy felt a strong affinity for his fellow physician-writer, and he found

himself turning to his stories more and more during the last years of his life. Apart from sparking a growing interest in Chekhov, what impressed Percy most about the festival was the brightness of the Cornell students. "Hate to admit it," he wrote to Foote after returning home, "but the Yankee boys and girls are keener than ours, at least ours here in Louisiana." And Percy did hate to admit it. It angered him that the nefariousness of Louisiana politicians had for years been responsible for the steadily declining quality of the state's public schools, even that of the university that Huey Long had once so richly built up.

By the time Percy was back from his New York trip, his *Lancelot* was well launched upon the world. Because his novel was a Book-of-the-Month Club selection, Percy was encouraged to think that it might earn him as much as $250,000 in the first year alone. When the reviews began to come in toward the end of February and in early March, he started to have doubts. To begin with, he received bad notices both from the daily *New York Times* and the Sunday *New York Times Book Review*. The latter particularly hurt, considering the wide circulation of the *Times Book Review* among booksellers and other readers beyond the New York City area, not to mention among the hefty New York readership itself. To make matters worse, the review, written by the novelist John Gardner, opened on the first page. (Balancing it on the other side of the page was the beginning of a profile of Percy by Herbert Mitgang, included, one suspects, to take some sting out of what the editors must have seen as a quite venomous review.) Even in his opening words about the quality of Percy's earlier novels, Gardner managed to be cutting. "Though he cares about plot and character, making fictions that easily translate into movies, he is a serious even moderately philosophical novelist not at all ashamed of his seriousness." (The film rights of *The Moviegoer* were now in the hands of the third would-be producers, Karen Black and Kit Carson; yet neither it nor any other novel by Percy would be made into a film during the author's lifetime. While Percy's novels may yet make good movies, no one so far has found them easy to translate into film.) From this less than accurate observation, Gardner quickly moved on to the real business of demolition, charging Percy with everything from errors of "scientific and mythic fact" to a lack of literary seriousness: "Also, as I've said, the 'confession' sounds written, not spoken—a bad fault, since it shows that the writer is not serious about creating a fictional illusion but is after only a moderately successful 'vehicle,' like the occasions of Chairman Mao's verse." What bothered Gardner most was Percy's failure to present a convincing response to Lancelot's ranting denunciation of the modern world. There was more than a touch of self-congratulation in this remark, for Gardner's own *Sunlight Dialogues* offered just the sort of point-counterpoint philosophical dialogue that Gardner found lacking in Percy's monologue (and which Percy feared would sound overly tendentious). Refusing to grant the legitimacy of a different formal strategy, Gardner concluded that Percy was not even serious about ideas. *Lancelot,* he pronounced, "for all its dramatic philosophical intensity, is bad art, and what's worse, typical bad art. Like Tom Stoppard's plays, it fools around with philosophy, only in this case not for laughs but for fashionable groans. Art, it seems to me, should be a little less pompous, a lot more serious. It should stop sniveling and go for answers or else shut up."

There were, as Percy once noted, "good bad" reviews and "bad bad" reviews, and he had received his share of both in his time. This, however, was by far the worst "bad bad" review he had ever received, and perhaps the only one that ever truly angered him. Robert Giroux, who had seen an early copy of the *Times,* let Percy know what he thought of the broadside: "I thought John Gardner went bananas." Percy did not quite agree; he felt there had been far more calculation and bad faith than craziness in the review. The members of the Bechacs crowd never heard Percy sound more bitter than when he mentioned John Gardner.

The reviews that followed were a mixed lot, some favorable and some unfavorable, but none of the latter stooped to Gardner-style cheap shots. Joyce Carol Oates thought that Lance's ravings were "uncomfortably close to ideas Percy has expressed elsewhere with less vehemence and more art." She found the tone confused and felt that Percival should have been "allowed into the story." Reynolds Price in *The Washington Post* also voiced some disappointment at not hearing more of Percival's side of the story, but there was a world of difference between Price's way of making the point and Gardner's:

> The fury with which he has transcribed Lance's wail (binding the comic-awful plot with sheer hot fury) and the daring with which he has left us at the end to imagine the priest's calm answer to the wail— and left us with a gradually implied complete outline for the priest's reply—are the measures of his skill and urgency.
>
> Yet he also leaves me wishing that he'd written the reply. I say that he left us with an outline, but how many contemporary readers of fiction are equipped or even prone to provide a sufficient counter statement?—a full intellectual and emotional Defense of the Faith, and in the implicitly fascinating voice of this particular friend and priest.

Some of the negative reviews were extremely astute. Even though he considered it arcane game playing, Robert Towers in *The New York*

Review of Books picked up the authorial self splitting at work in the two main characters. He also noted—again disapprovingly—Percy's blending of different literary modes and levels of reality: "documentary, Gothic, satiric, symbolic." While Towers maintained that these elements were insufficiently resolved, it would not take much ingeniousness to argue that these were precisely among the signal artistic accomplishments of the novel, the very factors that made it a dramatic polyphony of contending voices, outlooks, and values. The novel may have suffered from an apparent lack of resolution, but Percy was not writing a nineteenth-century novel. He did not have the authority to resolve. He could only present.

There were some unqualified raves, including those from the reliable Percy supporters, *Time* and *Newsweek*. Andre Dubus in *Harper's* made perhaps the most laudatory appraisal by arguing that Percy's fictions were not repetitions but successive and artistically varying struggles with the same theme and the same fundamental question: "What is one to do on an ordinary afternoon? Therefore, what is time for? What is a human being for?" Dubus recognized that Percy was arguing throughout his novels for the possibility of a moral life. "In *Lancelot*, Percy is again confronting the forces which make it so difficult for us to make moral choices and live by them. And his hero, Lancelot Lamar, is angry. Because of this, the novel goes further, more deeply, than the three before." Richard Todd in *The Atlantic* heard the quieter appeal sounding from the corners of the novel: "Despite the antic nihilism of *Lancelot*, despite the devout respect [Percy] pays doubt, it seems plain that he means to call attention to the possibility of faith."

A number of reviews, including those in *The New Yorker* and in *America*, noted the coincidence of Percy's *Lancelot* and John Cheever's *Falconer* both being set in prisons (or at least, in *Lancelot*'s case, a prisonlike mental institution), but it was a coincidence that could not be milked for much.

Except for the Gardner review, the wave of criticism left Percy in a benumbed state. The writing of the book had exacted such a large toll that he had even less desire than usual to think further about it. Joyce Carol Oates was right about how close Percy's ideas were to those of Lancelot. And not just his ideas. Lancelot, in all his fury and anger against the modern world, was both temperamentally and intellectually what Percy would have been were it not for one all-important difference: his faith. And in writing this hellish novel, Percy had come perilously close to losing that. No wonder it had exhausted him. Apart from the money he was hoping it would bring in—not as much, he soon discovered, as he had expected—he wanted the novel behind him.

16

Second Sightings

———◆———

This is all going to end badly. I'm going to end up old, broke and a flasher.

—WALKER PERCY TO SHELBY
FOOTE, November 28, 1977

At a point when Percy might have found it very easy to sit back and enjoy the fruits of his labor, he found himself, with some irritation, scrambling to stay ahead of debts. His high expections for *Lancelot* were partly responsible for the problem. Hoping for the best, he had begun to live and spend a little more extravagantly than was his wont. Bunt and he had made plans to go to Europe in July, and their ambitious itinerary included a week in a farmhouse near Aix-en-Provence with Phin and Jaye, a Mediterranean cruise with their friends Ed and Lucy Ballard, and a week in Venice at the end of the cruise. (Percy and Bunt counted their time in Venice as one of their happier memories.)

During the same summer, in what he thought would be a smart investment, Percy bought an antebellum cottage in the lakefront town of Mandeville. But the price of fixing up the cottage had quickly gotten out of hand, and by the end of November Percy feared that he would have to sell the place at a loss. How, he wondered, could he have been so off in his calculations? And why hadn't his book done better? A year after *Lancelot* came out, Percy offered a possible explanation to his publisher, Roger Straus: "I'll tell you why *Lancelot* didn't do better, if you're interested. The same reason Camus' *The Fall* didn't sell better. It is an uncongenial form, the dramatic monologue. People like a once-upon-a-time narrative better. Me too. Well, better luck next time."

The string of lectures to which Percy had committed himself helped to compensate for the book's lackluster earnings. In addition to the talk at the Chekhov festival in February, he delivered the Hopwood Lecture at the University of Michigan the following month. "The State of the Novel: Dying Art or New Science," as the latter was entitled, had been gathering dust in Percy's drawer for some time. As far back as 1975 Lewis Simpson had heard about it and asked if he might take a look at it for publication in *The Southern Review*. Percy had declined, saying that he was going to "work it up to a standard lecture which might be repeated at widely separated places with all the appearances of novelty." Not surprisingly, many of the main points of the Chekhov Lecture looked as though they had wandered in from "The State of the Novel," but if Percy was not above recycling his thoughts, he at least went to the trouble of rewording them.

As far as more serious work was concerned, Percy did have to consider, more urgently than he would have hoped, the inevitable question of what next. In early 1977, he had discussed a number of options with Foote, including a "semiotic experiment" and two possible novels. One would be a "dreamlike novel exploring all the fuckups, options and delights of the new consciousness," a novel that would be "Kierkegaard translated into Huck Finn, H.C. Earwicker transposed to Louisiana." The other would be a "Gulliver's Travels sort of fable-satire . . . a modern version of Body Snatchers." If Percy made headway with either of these books, no evidence survives. Instead, what Percy wrote was the very sort of book he told Foote he would not write:

> The only thing I'm sure of is that I can't do what you suggested, write a novel-type novel, the doings of Will Barrett after he leaves Santa Fe. I think what you were saying was that is what you can do. We are hoeing different rows, you know.

Percy had no idea that he would indeed return to Will Barrett in his next novel. But the genesis of *The Second Coming* had nothing to do with Will Barrett or *The Last Gentleman*. In fact, it had far more to do with the strange and unexpected visit of a college fraternity brother, Ansley Cope, a few years before, in March of 1972. Cope had been a senior at Chapel Hill when Percy was a freshman, but though the two were separated by several classes, they had developed a fond and jesting relationship. In later years, while Cope worked as a steel executive in Pittsburgh, he had followed Percy's literary successes and written him

short, congratulatory notes, to which Percy always replied. That was all
Percy knew of Cope until he heard someone knocking at the front door
one spring afternoon. To his surprise, Percy found before him a man
who looked disheveled, distraught, and vaguely familiar. Cope introduced himself, and the two men went out behind the house to talk.
Cope, with nonstop urgency, told Percy the story of his life, an account
that Percy recalled almost verbatim:

> After graduation, I married and went up North. Soon my wife and I
> were doing well and we joined all kinds of organizations where we
> made lots of friends. My business was doing more than thriving when
> I began to get restless—I felt there was more out there than either of
> us knew about.
>
> So I retired early. We pulled up stakes and moved to the mountains
> of North Carolina. We found the perfect lot with a great view and
> decided to build on it. When the house was finished, we moved into
> it, found just the right place for everything, including the piano and
> the art we had collected, and sat back to relax after all our hard work.
> Things were fine—for a while. And then it slowly came to me that
> something was wrong. I had missed it. I didn't know how to explain
> this strange restlessness to my wife, especially after she had to leave all
> our friends to move to North Carolina.
>
> On Sunday, I told her I was going out for some cigarettes. I found
> myself instead at the bus station and hopped on the bus that was going
> the farthest—the one to New Orleans. On my way down here, I
> remembered, Walker, that you lived not far from here—and here I
> am. I don't know where else to go now, or really what to do. Do you
> have any idea about this boredom and restlessness?

Percy talked with Cope for several hours and determined that he was
suffering not only from despair but also from acute clinical depression.
As Cope later recalled, "Walker told me very calmly what I should do.
He said he would take me to the airport and put me on a plane back to
North Carolina. Then he would locate the best psychiatrist in the area
for me to see. And that's just what he did."
Percy's friendly but firm counsel helped pull Cope out of his downward
spiral, but the encounter had almost as great an effect on Percy as it did
on his distraught friend. During the years that he was writing *Lancelot*,
and particularly in the worst moments of doubt and despair, Cope's
plaintive appeal came back to haunt him. Even now that he had finished
that book, he did not feel completely out of the Dantean "dark wood."
Exhausted and a bit unstrung, Percy did the only thing he knew to do.
He began writing a novel about a successful retiree living in the moun-

tains of North Carolina slowly sinking into suicidal despair. By November Percy had written enough to know that he didn't like it. So he tore it up and started again. This time, about one hundred pages into the novel, he made a surprising discovery. His main character was Will Barrett, or at least, Percy realized, he should be. The discovery posed problems—sorting out chronology, deciding what had happened between Santa Fe and retirement both to Barrett and to others from the earlier novel—but Percy felt there was no way around what his imagination had led him to. He would have to write a "novel-type novel."

At this point, though, Percy wasn't free to devote all his attention to the further adventures of Will Barrett. He had agreed to undertake another assignment in the fall, a self-interview for *Esquire*. He had not wanted to do it, he told Lyn Hill (whose portrait of Percy not only accompanies the article but is analyzed in it), but he needed the money. However onerous he found the writing, the self-interview proved to be one of Percy's more successful literary gambits, a self-portrait of the artist that is every bit as ironic and unsettling as Kierkegaard's *Point of View for My Work as an Author*. What Percy revealed in this piece was something that no interviewer had ever managed to reach, the persona of the artist, a much less sweet and agreeable figure than the usual interview subject, fiercer, more smart-ass, far more troubling, and, in certain ways, more honest. The tone of the "interview" ("Questions They Never Asked Me So He Asked Them Himself") is set in the first exchange:

Question: Will you consent to an interview?

Answer: No.

Q: Why not?

A: Interviewers always ask the same questions, such as: What time of day do you write? Do you type or write longhand? What do you think of the South? What do you think of the New South? What do you think of southern writers? Who are your favorite writers? What do you think of Jimmy Carter?

Percy sustains this flippant, cynical tone throughout most of the piece, voicing his fatigue with the questions that he is repeatedly asked about the New South, Kierkegaard, Catholicism, his writing habits, his opinion of other writers. Occasionally, though, Percy talks around, or through, the voice of the ironist to reveal an even more complicated man (and possibly a more hopeful one). When he asks himself how he became a writer, for example, he feints and jabs through several answers before coming to a truthful confession: He did so, he relates, because he

had the knack, "a little trick one gets into." This knack, moreover, has
something magical about it, possessing "theological, demonic and sexual
components." Percy insists that the knack can never be reduced to a
mechanism, can never be explained away as the sublimation of sexual
drives, for example, but must ultimately remain what it is: a mystery
compounded of several mysteries, each involving different parts of the
artist.

Another obligation Percy undertook in the fall was to find a publisher
for A Confederacy of Dunces, a book for which he still harbored strong
hopes, despite the mixed reviews of others to whom he had shown it.
Percy believed in the novel so much that he did something he had never
done before and would never do again: He sent it to Robert Giroux.
Percy was not completely surprised when Giroux rejected it. It was,
Giroux admitted, "an extraordinary book in many ways, or rather he is
an extraordinary writer, and the book grows in one's mind. But it is also
seriously flawed, much too long, and when you add it all up self-defeating." Like others, he thought that it might work well published in "short
pieces." (And in fact parts of it did appear in the New Orleans Review.)
Giroux added another reservation over the phone, one that mildly annoyed Percy. He said that the book would have only local appeal. The
rejection made Percy only more determined, and he decided to send it
to Les Phillabaum, Martha Hall, and Dawson Gaillard at LSU Press.
Percy had known Gaillard when she taught at Loyola, and Percy was
aware LSU was starting a fiction series, then an unusual move for a
university press. With Percy's strong recommendation, the editors at
LSU decided that they would publish the novel, even though they expected that it would lose money. Percy was delighted. The novel would
not come out until 1980, but placing the book made him feel as though
he had discharged an important trust.

Percy's obligations seemed only to ramify with the coming of 1978, a
year that got off on a sad note with the death of his and Bunt's friend
Betty Ellis on January 12. There were more requests than Percy could
handle, much as he needed the money. He turned down an offer to
appear on Dick Cavett's talk show, apologizing to the host that though
he liked the show he "didn't do a good job" on television. One of Percy's
major obligations was an upcoming lecture in Georgia, the Ferdinand
Phinizy lecture, on February 17. The lecture represented a homecoming
of sorts, not only because it was named after his ancestor, the first
American Phinizy, but also because it was to be delivered in Athens,
Georgia, where Percy had spent the first year after his father's suicide.

Although going back to his old haunts always stirred up ambivalent
feelings, Percy was eager to see his Georgia cousins, particularly the

Spalding brothers, Hughes (an attorney in Atlanta), Jack (editor of the *Atlanta Constitution*), and Phinizy (a professor of history at the University of Georgia). Some 170 other Phinizy kin and relations showed up at the lecture. One Georgia student in attendance at the Fine Arts Auditorium was so impressed by the prosperous appearance of this extended clan that he observed to a reporter, "This is certainly evidence that literature is elitist."

At one of the many receptions and parties surrounding the lecture, Percy ran into a woman with whom he had corresponded for years, Louise Abbot, the wife of a small-town Georgia attorney and a friend of Flannery O'Connor. Abbot recalled the encounter. "He was working on *The Second Coming,* and someone was asking questions he probably wished they wouldn't. Nevertheless, I stepped in and inquired about Sutter's fate in the new book. He looked astounded. 'Sutter!' he said, 'Sutter. I had forgotten all about Sutter! I'm so glad you mentioned him.' "

The lecture itself, "Going Back to Georgia," began with personal reminiscences of his year in Athens and then moved into a discussion of how and in what channels "Southern energies" might be directed now that the obsession with race and segregation was in the past. "Will Southerners have a distinctive contribution to make—say, in politics or literature?" Percy asked. "Or will they simply meld into the great American flux?" Percy's tentative response to his questions was guardedly hopeful. He admitted that the economic boom of the South might well lead to the region's becoming "a quaint corner of the teeming prosperous Southern Rim" whose supreme cultural achievement will be "the year Alabama ranked number one, the Falcons won the Super Bowl, and another Bobby Jones made it a grand slam at Augusta." But he held out hope that something else could happen in the old Southeast, "something besides the building of new Hyatts and Hiltons and the preserving of old buildings, something comparable to the astonishing burst of creative energy in Virginia two hundred years ago." Even as he voiced such sentiments, though, Percy was writing a novel that painted a far bleaker picture of the chances of a southern cultural awakening.

Neither Percy nor Shelby Foote ever missed an opportunity to tweak the other's vanity. "Dear Phinizy Lecturer" Foote saluted Percy in a letter he sent on March 1. Foote enclosed a newspaper photograph, taken at the lecture, which he declared made Percy look like Barry Goldwater. Foote also reported that his novel, *September September,* had been selling decently ever since it came out in February but that he was expecting it to take off at any time. Percy had read the novel in typescript the summer before and praised it strongly (particularly its depiction of a black middle-class family), but he warned Foote against setting his hopes too high. The disappointment of *Lancelot* was still fresh in his mind. And, in fact, sales of *September September* did soon peak at about fifteen thousand copies, a figure that left Foote mildly disappointed.

The Percys and the Footes got together in the middle of March for a meal at the Pontchartrain Hotel, and the two friends briefly explored their plans for the summer. Percy hoped to stay put and finish the novel he was struggling with; Foote thought he would burrow in and return to his long-deferred epic of the Delta, *Two Gates to the City*, the novel on which he had become blocked before turning to the Civil War history. As the following months unfolded, Percy stuck fairly steadfastly to his plan, taking only short trips to the mountains and to the beach, including a few days at the end of July with Roy and Sarah Percy at their cottage in Point Clear, Alabama. The reunions with his brothers became, if anything, even more important during Percy's later years, and it was a rare six months that they didn't get together at one home or another or at some vacation spot on the coast or in the mountains. And of course Percy saw his brother Phin nearly every week at the Wednesday lunches. If there was one happy consequence of their early family tragedies, it was the resilience of their fraternal bond.

By sticking close to his office at the Art Association, Percy accomplished most of a first draft during the summer. In the middle of September, he issued a progress report to Foote:

> I'm reaching the end of first draft of this thing—which seems as always such a mess and this time might be sure enough, though I see a few glimmers of virtue. I realize now I've been suspending everything until I can get through it—I haven't swept my office room for two years—so I'll have to rake it.

In October, the profile that Robert Coles had started working on six years earlier finally appeared in two consecutive issues of *The New Yorker*. Shortly thereafter, Coles's book, *Walker Percy: An American Search*, came out. Percy was flattered and let Coles know how much he appreciated his work. Foote, too, liked the profile, and wrote Coles in early January to tell him so. He was surprised to receive a gloomy note in reply, some of whose contents he passed on to Percy: "I get depressed more often than I have any excuse for—" Coles wrote, "and wonder what the point of it all is. There may not be any real point, but it's nice to know that a bit of one's intentions get across, sometimes." Coles's lament stirred up something in Percy. He was profoundly grateful to Coles, of course, for writing such a thorough and understanding profile, and he admitted to Coles in several letters that the article had given him a swollen head. At the same time, though, as he tried to explain to Foote, Percy felt that the article slightly misrepresented him:

Sorry Bob Coles sounded depressed. I hope he wasn't depressed about my response to the book. I am of course very grateful to him for what he did, in fact overwhelmed that he should even undertake such a task—and I have written him so. And he has succeeded in plowing through the articles unlike almost anybody else, and—unlike almost anybody else, actually making sense of and understanding them. Yet I am somewhat embarrassed by the profiles and book. I do not altogether recognize myself. I think it is because he is projecting a good deal of himself, a kind of good-hearted Colesian decency which may apply to him but not exactly to me. I feel a good deal more malevolent, oblique, phony, ironical and, I hope, more entertaining. His WP is both a good deal more worthy and admirable but also, I hope, less dull. Then again I am having the uncomfortable feeling of having at last been stuck in my slot—as a "Christian existentialist." I hear the sighs of relief all over: now that they know what I am, they don't have to worry about me. It is like being kicked upstairs from coach to Athletic Director or maybe being made professor emeritus—a good deal of admiration but at the same time I've been slipped out of gear. This is not Coles' fault. It's the nature of "existentialism," a word I was never sure I understood in the first place and which now means nothing at all. So I may have to write a mean nasty novel to break out of this mold.

Then again, I am as usual somewhat guilty just at the spectacle of Bob Coles' industry, decency, and out-goingness . . . none of which virtues I have. What little I accomplish seems to get accomplished through a peculiar dialectic of laziness, malice and self-centeredness. I've tried to explain this to Bob (actually the Esquire self-interview comes closer to the derisive tone I find natural rather than Coles' edifying tone) and I think he understands but he still tends to give me more credit than is warranted. You, for example, know exactly what I am talking about because you are a writer and because we have known each other forever—and because we are Southern?

Percy knew that the novel he had just finished—he announced the completion of the first draft in the same letter to Foote—would not be the one to break the mold in which he feared Coles's profile had set him. There would be considerable anguish and anger and railing against the world in The Second Coming, but the novel would be far more a romantic fairy tale than a jeremiad. Indeed, Percy would eventually describe it as "the first unalienated novel since War and Peace."

The completion of the first draft of the novel in the autumn of 1978

allowed Percy to sit down to a task that he feared would be difficult: a
review of a collection of Kierkegaard's letters and documents for *The
New York Times.* To Foote, Percy described the assignment as "a larger
job than I wanted, entails going back to SK whom I hadn't visited for
years—but it's a valuable thing to do." Valuable, one suspects, because
Percy saw it as the discharging of a large intellectual debt—and all the
more difficult for being so. Percy's review turned out to be a modest piece
of writing, pleasant to read but not particularly revealing about Percy's
relationship to Kierkegaard's thought. Percy reported a few small surprises, such as the fact that the morose Dane was regarded by his school
principal as "good-natured," "wholly devoid of seriousness," and
"merry." Of the letters in general, Percy warned that the nonspecialist
would have trouble making sense of them unless he held a copy of
Kierkegaard's *Journals* in the other hand. The letters were often as cryptic
as the "indirect" pseudonymous writings, "remarkable," Percy wrote,
"less for what they reveal than for what they conceal."

Undoubtedly one of the brightest spots in Percy's life in these years was
the gradual reconstitution of the family circle, this time largely around
grandsons rather than daughters. With the birth of Ann's second son
the preceding December, Percy in early 1979 found himself with four
grandsons: the nine-year-old John Walker Lobdell, the eight-year-old
Robert Lobdell, the one-and-a-half-year-old David Moores, and the
freshly minted John Moores. Percy enjoyed the role of paterfamilias. His
attachment to the boys was fierce, and he delighted in having them
around, playing games with them and reading to them. (The grandsons
called Percy "Gega," a name that came from the toddler John Walker's
association of his grandfather with the crucified figure of Jesus that hung
in his bedroom.)

In one difficult respect, family history seemed to repeat itself. Shortly
after Ann's first son, David, was born, it was discovered that he had a
serious hearing impairment, a discovery that plunged Ann into despondency and a crisis of faith. It was not a heartwarming experience to be
told that her infant son would be better off spending time with someone
whose speaking and hearing abilities were normal so that he would
receive the "proper" influences. Nor was it encouraging to think that
her next child might be afflicted with the same problem. (By the time
she learned that David had a hearing problem, she was already pregnant
with her second son, Jack.) It was a difficult trial for Ann, who had
always been a figure of strength in the family. Percy was particularly
concerned about her religious doubts. Even though he had recently gone
through a struggle with his own faith, Percy counseled Ann not to

abandon hers. "You can always count on the church," he would tell her. "Don't turn your back on the church. It's what saved me at the worst time of my life." Ann listened to her father, but for several years she stopped going to mass. Her way of combating despondency was to work harder in her business. And, in fact, her business, the Kumquat, was going so well that in early 1979 she and her husband started building a new store across the street from their shop on Lee Lane and were planning to move in during the summer. (Percy had arranged to rent the attic room in the building for his new office.) But work could not take care of all of Ann's unhappiness. As close and supportive as her family was, she had to face some struggles on her own.

Just about the time Percy was beginning to work his way out of his own doldrums, something happened that both troubled and confused him. For some time, his friendship with Lyn Hill had been the subject of village gossip: Predictably, some of the rumors suggested that the friendship was more than a friendship. It wasn't. Ever since their first meeting in Hill's studio, Percy and she had been close friends. They found they had many things in common and many things over which they heatedly disagreed. Above all, Percy was both envious and skeptical of Hill's mystical, almost Blakean sense of the world. Part of him, the hard-headed rationalist, dismissed such mysticism as sentimental nonsense, but another side wondered if there were not something in himself that he had long denied. To some extent, too, Percy's friendship with Hill was closely tied to his exploration of Jungian ideas, for which, as he had earlier confessed to Caroline Gordon, he found a new respect. The effect of all this was quite obvious in Percy's writing, as one can see in the lively play of Jungian notions throughout *The Second Coming*. (One reviewer suggested that the novel contained "enough archetypal symbolism and mythopoetic incident to employ a busy Jungian researcher for a decade.") Will Barrett's descent into the cave, for instance, is a very carefully contrived encounter between the self and its "shadow"; his relationship with Allie dramatizes the relationship between the self and its female side, its "anima." Although it would be unwise to reduce the novel to a Jungian allegory, it can be read on one level as just that. Percy even went so far as to tell one scholar that he intended "Jungian individuation" to be an essential theme of his novel.

Hill, then, like his other friends in the Bechacs group, had an effect on Percy's thought and imagination, an effect that made itself clear in his fiction. For that stimulation, as well as for the sheer pleasure of companionship, Percy was deeply grateful. Gossip, however, can be a vicious thing, and its ubiquitous reach is one of the hazards of small-town life. To some extent, Percy and Hill could laugh it off, even when they discovered one of the town snoops hiding behind a tree beside the Art Association studios, clearly checking on Percy's and Hill's comings and goings. But it was not amusing when these rumors made their way to Bunt—or when Percy began to hear from other people that Bunt was bound to be upset. Perhaps the greatest shock came when one of Percy's oldest friends told him bluntly that he was making a fool of himself as well as causing Bunt great pain. There was no malice in his friend's words; in fact, there was nothing but good intent. Nevertheless, they left Percy perplexed. He knew that his relationship with Hill was innocent, but he did not want to cause Bunt pain or discomfort.

In some ways, the unhappy situation took care of itself. Percy's move into the upstairs of the new Kumquat Bookstore in the summer of 1979 put some distance between Hill and Percy, although they continued to meet and talk whenever they wanted to. But even without the move, irreparable damage had been done to their friendship. The taint of scandal hung about it, and the awareness of this taint affected both Percy and Hill. Gradually, imperceptibly at first, there was a parting of ways. Percy would remain Hill's close friend until his death; he was, among other things, her daughter's godfather. But a former easiness and spontaneity had been lost. Percy and Hill's relationship was no longer innocent. As their mutual friend Bob Milling observed, "The whole business was an unfortunate triumph of public opinion and small-mindedness." The episode left Percy sad but not disillusioned. He had had no illusions about the fallen world and the sadnesses attendant on it. In a way, the outcome was confirmation of what his darker, more Calvinist self expected of life. Perfectly happy endings were the stuff of fairy tales.

Which raises the question of why Percy, in *The Second Coming*, had written just that: a kind of fairy tale. Was *The Second Coming* a working out of what Percy believed was impossible in his own life? To some extent, certainly. It would be hard not to see the novel as an elaborate wish-fulfillment dream, a highly coded fantasy in which the protagonist is both Percy and not Percy—or, alternatively, a version of what Percy might have become had he not made the commitments and decisions that he had made. As with most Percy protagonists, autobiographical references abound. The young Will Barrett's unacted-upon infatuation with his high school classmate Ethel Rosenblum recapitulates Percy's own unrequited longing for Camille Sarason. Will's near fatal hunting trip with his father in Georgia draws on that terrifying trip that Percy and his brother Roy took with their father when he was in one of his dark moods. The father's suicide itself (here more vividly evoked than it was in *The Last Gentleman*) is a frightening recreation of the scene in the Birmingham attic. The Luger that Will Barrett toys with as the instrument of his contemplated suicide is the Luger that Percy bought from his nephew back in 1946. Even the Linwood setting is a blend of familiar Percy haunts, partly Highlands and partly Sewanee (the cove and the cave in the novel are the ones Percy used to explore near Brinkwood).

All of these elements identify Percy strongly, almost inextricably, with his protagonist. Yet Percy also includes a significant detail of difference: Will Barrett's religion. Barrett's rather lukewarm Episcopalianism encodes a world of difference between him and his creator. It is hard to overstate the importance of this difference, even though it is one of many in a novel that overflows with signifiers of similarity and difference. Episcopalianism is the religion closest to Catholicism—so close that the points that distinguish it from the older sect make it stand out all the more boldly from its fellow Protestant sects. Put positively, Episcopalianism is Catholicism without absolutism; put negatively, it is Catholicism without a spine, invertebrate Catholicism. Yet here enters the complexity of Percy as a novelist: He does not judge Barrett's religion as a lesser thing. In fact, Percy's novel seems generously to imply that the fuzzy accommodationism of the Episcopal communion may have something more to recommend it than the principled dogmatism of his own church. Not that Percy believes this. (Percy, one might say, is to Will Barrett what Catholicism is to Episcopalianism.) But as a novelist, Percy cuts against his own grain, against the bias of his own belief, in order to play with possibilities beyond his knowing. This constitutes the dialectical, or dialogic, aspect of his fiction, and it is one reason why his novels are sometimes accused of being unresolved. They are unresolved, disturbingly so, perhaps none more than *The Second Coming*, even though it appears to be the most firmly resolved of all his novels. The questions raised by *The Second Coming* impel the reader to think beyond the immediate text and to consider its relationship to the other fictional works created by Percy. What does it mean, for instance, that the Episcopalian Barrett gets what he wants in this world while, in other novels, assorted Catholic protagonists seem to settle for something less? Is Percy suggesting something about the deceptiveness of happiness in this world? It is hard to conclude that he is not. Percy was finally very close to the outlook of two Catholic writers he greatly admired, John Henry Newman and Gerard Manley Hopkins, an outlook summed up in the former's dictum, "we succeed by failing." To think that defeat in this world is the best preparation for happiness in the next is Stoicism with a Christian reward attached to it. It is easy to see why Newman's Catholicism appealed to the adoptive son of Will Percy.

Percy's faith was, if anything, becoming stronger during the writing of

The Second Coming. It was a time when he again began attending mass
every day at the small chapel at St. Paul's School; it was also a time
when his concern with last things became more pronounced than ever.
In April, for example, he sent Foote *The Habit of Being,* the collected
letters of Flannery O'Connor. "Am sending you this," he added in a
note, "because otherwise you might not see it. I attach great importance
to it—a truly remarkable lady, laconic, funny, tough, smart, hard-
headed, no-nonsense, the very best of US, South, and Catholicism."
Then, in what at first appeared to be a non sequitur, Percy brought up
the fact that he had just finished reading Troyat's biography of Tolstoy.
But his point—and his concern—slowly emerged:

> Do you think I do not understand completely how Tolstoy could have
> been so great and so phony and in the end ludicrous? What a way to
> go. It just occurs to me to compare his going out with Flannery's—
> with all her sacraments which he would have had only contempt for—
> and to be so sure she had the better of it—let alone which was right.
> [One can only wonder here whether the syntax was intentionally
> snarled.] Just when I'm thinking what an inflated ego Tolstoy was, I
> read *The Death of Ivan Ilich* (last night) and am astounded by how good
> it is. Pore damn writers—we're lucky to die with any dignity at all.

Percy's growing confidence in matters of faith was accompanied by
growing uncertainty about how one communicated one's vision of the
truth in a work of art, particularly a novel. "I'm convinced," he wrote
later in the spring as he struggled with revisions of *The Second Coming,*
"that times were never worse for novelists in the sense that somehow
the straight narrative form is in default and so one must resort to all
manner of tricks, cons, blandishments, obfuscations, curses, lies, jokes,
animadversions. It is a matter of semiotic breakdown."

To some extent, this sounds as though Percy had just discovered the
challenge of Modernist art, but his complaint was related to something
more complicated—to what Percy perceived as the breakdown in the
communicative circuitry between the writer and the reader. While Percy
had something of the sly Modernist about him, he did not share the
elitism of the Modernists or their fondness for the esoteric. His fiction is
cunning and richly allusive, but he did not see his art as a test of cultural
literacy. Percy's artistic impulse was more democratic, even populist. He
wanted to entertain and involve his reader, all the better to beguile him
into confronting the book's more involved communications. Yet Percy
was finding the art of literary seduction harder and harder to accomplish.
The problem was that the dominant forms of communication, the electronic media, and particularly television, were shaping the way messages

were being transmitted and received. The linear, progressive, and logical modes of print were having a hard time competing with the imagistic, juxtapositional, impressionistic modes of the electronic visual media.

On one hand, Percy was both contemptuous and resentful of the tyranny of television. Like many dinosaurs of the book, he felt that it was creating an unlettered, barbarous populace. On the other, Percy was fascinated by the power of the medium, destructive though it seemed to him to be. Indeed, as Percy told Foote, he wanted to "spend a few years figuring out *how* TV rots the brain (nobody knows)." Percy himself was something of a TV junkie. For years, he and Foote faithfully watched the daytime soap opera *As the World Turns,* keeping each other abreast of the daily developments if one or the other missed a show. Percy tended to watch the television in an idiosyncratic, slant manner, usually leaving the volume off, checking in from time to time while reading a book, scribbling letters, revising manuscripts, or listening to music on the radio. He viewed this generally subliminal activity both as a means of remaining informed about the state of the world ("I keep it on so I'll know if the world suddenly comes to an end," he often joked) and as a way of keeping in touch with the national ideolect. Percy always knew the names of the current shows and their characters.

Percy learned a great deal about the medium by watching it in his peculiar way. He absorbed its techniques of cutting and montage and its relentless use of repetition. The power of the medium, Percy quickly perceived, was its hypnotic redundancy, its only slightly varying repetitions of the same message. What Percy learned from television was the art of simplification and repetition. The challenge was to give this rudimentary technique a subtle twist, to deepen it by giving each repetition shadings and ironic counterpoints: to start with something that looks as mindless as repeated television "bites" and end with something as complex as the variations in a fugue. Percy, from his first published novel on, not only showed an awareness of the formal strategies of film and television but increasingly incorporated them into his own way of composing a novel. (Martin Luschei was one of the first critics to comment on the use of film techniques, particularly the "dissolve," in *The Moviegoer;* he also pointed out how "enormously challenging" it would be to make a good film out of *The Moviegoer*—and would be, one might add, precisely because Percy stretched the film techniques beyond their usual semiotic capabilities, freighting them with greater irony and undertone than any visual image alone could carry.)

In no novel did Percy more fully exploit such devices as quick cutting and flashback than in *The Second Coming.* But it is the television technique of repetition that gives the novel its hypnotic force. We see it in the repetition of certain key words (such as "sign," which is introduced in the first sentence), certain epithets (the Shakespearean "old mole" for Will Barrett's father), or in certain images, visual, auditory, or olfactory. To be sure, one finds similar repetition in any carefully worked novel, but in *The Second Coming* the amount of repetition—and the emphasis given to it—is quantitatively and qualitatively different. The effect, depending largely on the reader, can be either seductive or suffocating. Whichever effect it produces, this is a novel that requires its reader to heed its manifold signs. The danger of so much repetition, as Percy well knew, is semiotic deadening: Through too much careless repetition, signs can become—again, in Percy's phrasing—"evacuated of meaning." Percy seemed to flirt quite intentionally with this danger as he wrote *The Second Coming,* as if to show how precariously signs can teeter between meaning and meaninglessness. Both in obvious ways, such as the "language game" established between Will and Allie, and in subtler ones, *The Second Coming* was a novel about communication, language, semiotics.

The formal complexity of *The Second Coming* is indebted not merely to film and television; it owes quite as much to musical composition. In certain respects—including the repeated *leitmotifs*—the novel seems to aspire to the formal purity of music. (To deaden a linguistic sign is also to transform it into a mere sound, a potential that Percy might also have been playing with in the writing of *The Second Coming.*) It was no mere coincidence that Percy and Foote engaged in some of their more extensive discussions of music during the writing of *The Second Coming.* To look at only one of Foote's letters from this period is to see how willingly Foote played the role of musicologist as he led Percy through discussions of Mozart, Bach, and in this case, Beethoven:

> Another cassette goes into this mail. I promise I wont bombard you with these things, but at least I wanted you to have these two monuments from the quartet literature, Beethoven's 14th and 15th. The latter (written first) is the one with the Heiliger Dankgesang for the middle of its five movements. The former, in C-sharp Minor, is the miracle of all chamber music, the most daring and, after a good many listenings, the most beautiful piece of music ever written. It is in seven movements, with no break between any of them, but it boils down to a true four-movement quartet with certain embellishments. Like so:
>
> 1. A long fugue introduction.
> 2. Actual first movement (ABA, "arch" form).
> 3. A bridge passage.
> 4. Actual second movement; theme and seven variations, plus coda.

5. Third movement: Scherzo.
6. Bridge-introduction to the finale.
7. Fourth movement—Finale. (Sonata form)

I dont know whether you have listened to much late-Beethoven these past few years, but if you havent, you will come back to it with a considerable pang of recognition—most obviously to the 15th's Adagio (the Dankgesang) but even more so to the whole 14th, beginning with the introductory fugue. It's a goddam miracle! In the variation movement, he throws away the first three or four variations, then finally gets down to work on the last three—and caps them with a coda that goes beyond anything ever dreamed in the first half of the movement.

These lessons had a profound effect on Percy, particularly as he entered the summer of 1979, the period when he worked most exhaustively on revising *The Second Coming*. In his next-to-final draft he even labeled one short section of the novel "intermezzo."

At the end of a summer of steady work—interrupted only by the move to his new office in the Kumquat, a one-day appearance at a National Endowment for the Humanities seminar at LSU, and a short trip to Gulf Shores, Percy reported with relief that he had finally brought the novel to an end. "All I know," Percy complained to Foote, "is that I don't want to write another novel now, maybe ever. A novel is an incredible ordeal, which gets worse and worse, requiring all manner of alternating despairs, piss-offs, deaths and rebirths, too much for an aging infirm novelist." In addition to showing it to Foote—who pointed out chronological inconsistencies with the *The Last Gentleman*—Percy let four other people read it, Bunt, Robert Daniel, Lyn Hill, and his agent. From all he got strong votes of confidence, but for some reason, perhaps fatigue, he was not eager to hand the novel over to his publisher, at least not immediately. By the end of the month, Percy was ready for his agent to give Giroux the novel. Giroux was very pleased by what he saw, though he thought certain structural changes were needed, particularly the breaking up of the long fifth chapter in part one and the addition of a new section about Allie. The latter suggestion proved felicitous. Percy added the scene in which Allie singlehandedly engineers the moving of a large stove into her greenhouse home, a scene that not only is a fine piece of descriptive writing but makes dramatically clear the independence and ingenuity of Allie. (In response to the charge that he never created competent, capable women, Percy could at least point to Allie.) By mid-January, Giroux reported that the manuscript, except for some minor changes, looked ready to print.

Percy was, of course, glad to hear that his publisher was pleased—they were even planning a first-edition print run of thirty thousand copies—but in many ways the novel was already behind him. Once again, he was contemplating the work that he still believed would be remembered as his major cultural contribution: a book that would prove the uniqueness of man through his capacity for language. In early March, Percy wrote Lewis Lawson to thank him for his perceptive essay "The Gnostic Vision in *Lancelot*." Lawson shrewdly deciphered Percy's debt to the Austrian emigré philosopher (and former LSU faculty member) Eric Voegelin, showing how Lance's denunciation of the modern world and his plan for a new order recapitulated the archetypal Gnostic effort to locate the end and meaning of history in this world rather than in the transcendent order of the divine. Percy appreciated Lawson's rescuing him from charges of abandoning his faith. ("Some thought I was simply perverse; one critic said I had ceased to be a Catholic novelist; maybe I had, in his book. God help us, maybe I had."). As well as thanking him for coming to the rescue, Percy told Lawson that he was indebted to the essay in another way:

> At any rate, let me report that what came as a piece of luck to me was your comment on the Voegelin quote (p. 54) about men turning to a consideration of the world as an immanence—e.g. scientism. This was exciting to read, because I've been contemplating a sort of sequel to *Message in the Bottle*, i.e., an amateur venture into semiotics, which assays a semiotic investigation of the *self*, the stranded consciousness, which is left over after a man (scientist or consumer) has fallen prey to the immanentism of science, that is to say: after he has acquiesced in the standard propositions that man (and he) has been dethroned from (1) the center of the universe (Copernicus) (2) the lordship of creation (Darwin) and (3) even the sovereignty over himself (Freud & behaviorists), what options are open to him? This would be a sort of phenomenology of the stranded self.

Pursuing his philosophical obsession, Percy also planned to take a course in semiotics the coming June. Bunt and he had arranged to travel to Toronto, where the semiotician Thomas Sebeok would be teaching a course at the University of Toronto. Percy was keen to study with Sebeok for many reasons, not least of which was Sebeok's interest in Charles Sanders Peirce. Percy particularly wanted to see how he applied Peirce's ideas to such things as animal communication.

The timing of the trip was good for another reason: It coincided with the publication of *The Second Coming* and the first round of reviews, two things Percy always preferred to deal with at as great a distance as possible. There was one set of reviews that Percy was happy to see before he left the country: those of *Confederacy of Dunces*. To Percy's delight, most were favorable. Lewis Simpson wrote Percy toward the end of the month to thank him, on behalf of LSU, for what he had done in bringing them a "remarkable" book that "might not have seen the light of day" without his efforts. Settled in Toronto, Percy sent word to Thelma Toole that he had read so many raves of her son's book that he knew she must be proud. "This should be a time of rejoicing for you—though I know it makes you sad to think of losing Ken—as it does me. But remember that you saved his book! and you should be glad of that."

The reviews of *The Second Coming* that started coming out toward the end of June and in early July gave Percy further reason to rejoice. Reviewers seemed to be surprised to see the fury of the former novels modulating into something so radically different, nothing less than a romance with a happy ending. "I wonder what, at this hour," Benjamin DeMott wrote at the end of his review for *The Atlantic*, "such a work could reasonably be called except an enchantment." The most consistent complaint against the novel was its excessiveness, its surfeit of themes, its formal risks, and its stretching of credulity to nearly unbearable limits. (Gene Lyons in *The Nation*, for example, found the relationship between Allie and Barrett unbearably forced, and Robert Towers in *The New York Review of Books* thought it had enough plot "for three ordinary novels, sufficient theme for a dozen.") But no reviewer gave a shrewder appraisal of the value of such excesses than Richard Gilman in *The New Republic*:

> I spoke before of Percy's vices being the costs of his virtues. What I came to see as I read his new book was that one had to be willing to grant him his excesses and even follies. The point isn't that he could somehow learn to give them up, to write more *acceptably*; he writes as he does and can, and if in order to emerge into the clear tonic air of revelation he had to go through much murk and absurdity, so it must be. Like any novelist he needs plot to frame and impel his sense of things, and because this sense is rarer and more elusive than that of most writers, an awareness of eternity mocked by the here and now yet sustaining it, a religious sense without explicit creed or dogma, his plots have to reach further than most and are subject to afflictions as they go.
>
> I'll therefore amend what I said before: that I simply endured the inferior elements for the sake of the good. What I did was take them up together, knowing I couldn't really separate them, grumbling, exasperated at times, but full, in the end, of praise.

Apart from his remark about Percy's being without "explicit creed or dogma"—based, perhaps, on Gilman's identification of Barrett with his creator—Gilman understood how important it was to Percy to stretch the limits of art and artfulness, even to violate them, in order to communicate the most profoundly difficult of understandings. This strategy was exactly what Percy had referred to when he talked about the novelist's need to resort to "all manner of tricks, cons, blandishments." The necessity was not merely literary; Percy needed to bring about peace inside himself, to calm his warring elements, a task that would require its share of blandishments and cons.

The relationship of the artist's life to his work, always a tricky business, is very tricky indeed in the case of Percy and *The Second Coming*. To the biographer, it is hard not to see this novel as a philosophical fairy tale that its author needed to write in order to tie up and resolve, at least in the realm of the imaginary, the chaos of feelings he had lived through for close to a decade. The desire to throw everything over, to start a new life—all this and to have God, too—was a desire for nothing less than Edenic perfection, hope raised to the highest power. And of course it was, as Percy knew, impossible. Such hopes can be fulfilled only within the worlds of "enchantment," to use DeMott's word, within the spell of literature.

This is not to denigrate the achievement of *The Second Coming*. Adults need fairy tales as much as children do. And yet, delightful as readers may find this spell, one feels that it is finally a work that falls short in terms of the moral order that Percy chose to live by himself. Something vital seems to be missing within the work, some fictional embodiment of the author's own otherness from the fantasy he created, some Prospero-like figure who bids farewell to the idyll that he himself has conjured. We need to hear from the Christian ironist before this novel ends; but we don't. Instead, we have Adam going off to join his Eve. What one distrusts most about this in some ways brilliant and beguiling novel is that it serves too therapeutic an end rather than the harder truth as Percy saw it. Ultimately, though, a therapy that is more willed than truthful may prove unsatisfactory, may be nothing more than a diversion, a repetition, to use the Kierkegaardian formula. And Percy was well aware of the dangers of repetition.

After returning from Canada, Percy remained a few days in Covington to attend book signings at two stores. One was at his friend Rhoda Faust's Maple Street Bookstore, where he was surprised to receive a bouquet of flowers from Thelma Toole. The second was at his daughter's bookstore, the Kumquat. Discharging his authorly duties, Percy went up to Highlands with Bunt, Steve Ellis, and Ellis's new wife, Haydee. These trips to the mountains, usually to Highlands, were becoming more an annual necessity to Percy, who found the summer heat increasingly unbearable.

In August Percy was surprised to receive a letter from someone he had not heard from since high school years, Camille Cohan (born Sarason), the model for Ethel Rosenblum. She told Percy that she had been reviewing his novels for years for various library groups (always announcing that she had given Percy his start in writing) and that she was looking forward to reading his newest novel. Percy promptly replied, acknowledging that she indeed had given him his start in literature by making him a gossip columnist. "See what you started. You must take some responsibility." Percy added that she might get a. "few vibes from Chap I of 2nd Coming." Camille Cohan got more than a few vibes when she read of Will Barrett's unrequited longing for Ethel Rosenblum, although she chided Percy for giving her kinky hair and slightly pocked skin. ("I forgive you the indignation of the 'kinky' and 'pocked' for the unadulterable delight of the 'satinity' and 'compaction.' " Then Camille confessed the most surprising truth: "You want to know something?! I had a crush on you for a while in my Senior year." Percy wrote back immediately:

Dear Ethel,
   Well I'll be damned. You should have said something. You see, that's what the book is about.
   Thanks so much for being so smart—as well as being cheerleader. The kinkiness and pocks were to mislead the reader.
   Well—I'll be seeing you Ethel—I think it probably worked out pretty well.

Will

Percy's half-jesting remark—"that's what the book is about"—is as interesting as it is ambiguous. Was Percy saying that his book was about the importance of not getting what one fantasizes about or the importance of getting it? If the latter, then certainly this book would be a repudiation of Percy's stern Kierkegaardian and Newmanian vision of the necessity of unhappiness as preparation for the soul's salvation. Romantic love is one of the more tempting of diversions from the purity of heart that Kierkegaard extolled. Had Percy tried to overcome his Kierkegaardian view in The Second Coming? One would have to conclude that some part of him had. But only part. Back up in Highlands for a week in September, Percy was interviewed by a reporter from the Times-Picayune, and at one point in their conversation Percy revealed how strongly he remained under the spell of his theological avatar, the somber Dane: "The trick is doing what you're doing without getting the itch. The itch usually doesn't work. You move on, and it's the same thing. Repetition is one of the six great themes in literature. Figuring out how you can live in the same place without being miserable. It takes a conscious cultivation of the ordinary." If one did not know better, one would not automatically assume that the speaker of these words was the author of *The Second Coming,* a novel that celebrates a rather exotic break with the ordinary. The question is whether this literary diversion would make it possible for its creator to return, with equanimity and calm, to the world as he once knew it.

To begin to answer this question, one does well to recall the words of James Boulware: "I think Walker tried to reconcile the irreconcilable in faith. He was reluctant to take the valuable and throw out the rest. He didn't do that with his life; so he couldn't do it with his faith." For Percy, there were no lukewarm positions. A liberal, latitudinarian approach to matters of faith was, to Percy, worse than no faith at all. As a young man writing his first apprentice novel, *Charterhouse,* he had explained to Caroline Gordon his deep aversion to that tepid, reasonable religiosity that he had seen in his father's generation: "When I look at my father's library comprising as it does, many religious works, but all of the liberal-scholarly-protestant variety which stemmed from 19th century German rationalism by way of English divines, it gives me the creeps. It is much more lethal to the Faith than, say, the violent atheism of a Spanish Mason."

That view remained essentially unchanged, although one could argue that *The Second Coming* revealed its author chafing at the bit of his absolutism. Nevertheless, after finishing *The Second Coming,* Percy would become even more resolute a churchman. Indeed, perhaps because he had come close to losing his faith during the 1970s, Percy's wholehearted return to the fold seemed to include an almost penitential commitment to serving and defending the faith. For Percy, this service would consist largely of vigorous affirmations of the authority, dogma, and magisterium of the church, and particularly of the Holy Father himself, all of which he thought were under attack both from without and within the church. While never one to agonize over such things as the abandonment of the Latin mass, Percy was deeply troubled by any attempts to dilute dogma or to challenge the position and authority of the pope, and during the last decade of his life, he would become a forceful defender of orthodoxy, one of the more articulate and forceful the church would have in late twentieth-century American culture.

To some extent, Percy had always been a polemicist for his faith both in his philosophical and literary work. Now, however, his polemicism became even more direct and pugnacious. This would become apparent in the work that he had decided to write after finishing *The Second*

Coming. Percy had begun work on the book, with the usual grunts and moans, in early September. He was not feeling at the top of his form, and in addition to giving up sleeping pills (his long-time ally in his constant struggle against insomnia) he was also considering giving up alcohol, which he feared was making him "liverish." On September 10, he wrote Foote to complain that he, too, was blocked on a book that he envisioned as "a sequel to Message in Bottle." He had a thoroughly mapped out plan for what he was then calling *Novum Organum:*

> The plan of the book is simple. Three parts. First part, list some of the familiar oddities and anomalies of modern times, e.g., the rise of boredom and suicide, the good life, the longing of people for UFOs and trivial magic, the eroticization of society, T.V. junkies, why people applaud frantically on the Carson show when their hometowns are mentioned, the frantic efforts of primatologists to teach chimps to talk, desire for bad news (doesn't everyone remember Pearl Harbor? why?), Darwin sitting alone at his fireside in Kent, a shrinking violet, and dismantling (as he saw it) Christendom.
>
> These apparently disparate and disconnected little antinomies are related with a straight face and in a way that everybody recognizes.
>
> Part II: a setting forth of the Novum Organum, which is semiotic theory. (My Helen Keller triangle and tetrad.)
>
> I can already see you making faces, but this part can be done without jargon and technicalities, in an understandable way.
>
> Part III: the disparate left-overs and oddities are now reprised and like members of a ballet, array themselves gracefully and in perfect order along the model, like a quadrille.
>
> As you can see, this is not an entirely serious book, and yet it is serious. What it is getting at is of course my old hobby-horse that science is extraordinarily stupid about people as people and the consequence of this stupidity (combined with an instinctual confidence in science) is going to do us all in if we don't do something about it.

Percy talked more about his intentions for the next book in an interview that he granted to a friend and scholar, Linda Hobson, in the early fall. He had met Hobson the year before, shortly after she had moved to New Orleans, a freshly minted Ph.D. from the University of Alabama. A native of Cleveland, Ohio, Hobson had studied at Denison and Duke before coming to Alabama, where she had written her dissertation on Percy. Teaching at the University of New Orleans, she had arranged to meet Percy at a Bechacs lunch on October 4, 1979. Somewhat stiffly, Percy asked, "Miss Hobson, where are you from?" Hobson replied "Well actually, Dr. Percy, I am a chicken-shit Ohioan." Courtliness having thus been quickly dispatched, they found that they had much to say to each other. Percy became a kind of mentor as well as friend to Hobson, and with her he was candid both about his life and his work. What struck her was his attentiveness. "Most men will only listen to women for so long, but he would really listen to what you had to say."

Percy certainly had no reluctance to submit to an interview when Hobson asked. He knew that it would be an intelligent discussion, and it proved to be just that. As well as questioning him about his last novel, Hobson managed to draw Percy out on what he was still calling his *Novum Organum*, his attempt to develop a theory of "what it is to be the organism which uses language."

As well as answering the big questions about life, Percy half-jokingly added, his semiotic approach would explain what happens to people's consciousness when they watch television: "Maybe it can't be done; I don't know. Of course, if I watch enough of *The Incredible Hulk*, either I'll get anesthetized or I'll have an idea."

Despite having such a firm sense of where he was going in his book, he was having a hard time finding the right style, a difficulty that boiled down to a choice between "being aphoristic (like Pascal or Wittgenstein) or play[ing] it dead cool and laid back like Machiavelli who gets his best effects through coolness." By mid-November, Percy seems to have come to a decision, settling on a cool, even parodic approach. In a letter to Roger Straus dated November 15, Percy hinted at what genre he would parody: The title of the book, he announced, would be *The Last Self-Help Book*. By the New Year, at latest, Percy was writing steadily, and by autumn he had finished the first draft. The speed with which he finished the book was remarkable, all the more so considering the activity around his home. Bunt and he had decided to give their house to David and Ann and build what they rather modestly called a "Cajun shack" less than fifty yards down the bogue for themselves. The design of the house followed the Cajun style, with a central "dog-trot" hallway leading from the front door to large room extending the width of the back of the house. At one end of the room was the kitchen; at the other, the living area. A wall of windows in this bright large room faced the Bogue Falaya, offering a generous view of a wide bend in the river and the sand bar on the opposite shore. Off the dog-trot hallway in the front of the "shack" were two other rooms, the bedroom and a library—what Percy boasted of to Foote as his first "working library."

House business anchored Percy to Covington for most of the summer, but he did travel to Jackson, Mississippi, in the middle of June to receive the Mississippi Medal for the Arts from Governor William Winter. A banquet was held in Percy's honor in the governor's mansion on the night of June 16, and Percy was delighted to find that Eudora Welty was his dinner partner. Willie Morris, who was also present, sat across the table from Percy and Welty. Impressed by the intensity of their conversation throughout the dinner, Morris approached Welty afterward to ask what she and Percy had been discussing so seriously.

"Oh," said Welty, "we were talking about *The Incredible Hulk.* Have you ever seen that show?"

By September, when everything but the books was moved from the old to the new house, Percy was ready to give copies of his manuscript to select readers. Robert Coles was coming down that month to deliver a lecture on *A Confederacy of Dunces* at the University of Southwestern Louisiana in Lafayette, and Percy asked him if they could meet somewhere and have "6 drinks and/or six dozen crawfish." Coles was only too happy to stop by, and the two had rather too good a time—far more drinks than crawfish—before Percy's nephews Phin and Will drove Coles over to Lafayette for his lecture. In addition to plying his visitor with bourbon, Percy gave Coles a copy of his manuscript, and in a few weeks Coles reported back that he and his wife Jane had read it and "loved it all." "You've done a sort of rotation on yourself—taking themes you always use and putting them to the reader in a different form." Like many admirers of Percy's early novels, Coles had been a little concerned by the increasingly angry tone in Percy's more recent work, but if he had any misgivings about *Lost in the Cosmos,* as it was now called (in mock tribute to Carl Sagan's successful PBS show, *Cosmos*), he did not voice them.

But not all readers of Percy's manuscript were so circumspect. One of them was a young psychologist named Patricia Mayknuth. A friend of Lyn Hill's, Mayknuth had been a graduate student in psychology at Emory when she began attending some of the Bechacs lunches and reading group meetings in the late 1970s. She was a hard-headed empiricist and an admirer of Susanne Langer, and she and Percy had locked horns on more than a few occasions even before he let her read the manuscript of his book.

One issue of contention was abortion, a matter about which Percy felt passionately. (Even during the 1970s, when his faith had been most sorely tried, Percy had been an ardent supporter of a national program to promote a natural method of birth control, a program organized and run by a Covington friend named Mercedes Wilson. His support for this effort stemmed in large measure from his abhorrence of those methods that, in effect, caused spontaneous abortions, notably the intrauterine device.) In April of 1981, he had written a long letter to Walter Isaacson, now at *Time* magazine, objecting to what he felt was the proabortion bias of a long article that he had written on the subject. "Once abortion is sanctioned," Percy cautioned, "for whatever good and humane reasons, I don't see why we can't get rid of the aged and useless and infirm for similar reasons." Percy added that he didn't believe such things because he was a Catholic, but that he was a Catholic because he believed such things. Percy was sufficiently exercised over the issue to submit an op-ed essay to *The New York Times* only a few weeks later. "A View of Abortion, with Something to Offend Everybody" appeared in the June 11, 1981, edition, and while it did take swipes at Moral Majoritarians, Jesse Helms, and other pro-lifers who seemed to show little regard for the already living, the brunt of the essay's criticism was directed at what Percy called the "juridical-journalistic establishment," guilty, he charged, of playing fast and loose with language. The "con" perpetrated by this establishment, Percy elaborated, was its claim of uncertainty about when life begins. Percy noted the irony that it was secularists who were trying to ignore an elementary fact of science—that life begins from the moment of the fertilization of a single cell—and he proposed a modern version of Galileo's trial in which a biology teacher is told by the court that "it is only his personal opinion that the fertilized human ovum is an individual human life" and ordered not to teach his private opinions in public school. "Like Galileo," Percy writes, "he caves in, submits, but in turning away is heard to murmur, 'But it's still alive!' "

To Mayknuth, Percy admitted to some of the misgivings he had about the abortion issue. He believed that it should be a matter of conscience, a decision reached between man or woman and God, and he admitted that if he were a woman faced by an "unwanted pregnancy," he did not know if he would finally have the courage of his convictions. But given that Americans had forced the issue into the legal and political arena, particularly with the *Roe* v. *Wade* decision in 1973, Percy could not remain neutral. And he certainly could not condone a position that in any way suggested that abortion was not the taking of life. To Mayknuth, also, Percy confessed his deepest fear (a fear that would soon become the generative idea of his last novel): that to condone abortion was to open the door to the most dangerous quality-of-life arguments put forward by advocates of eugenics and euthanasia:

> I heard Dr. Christiaan Barnard say that what mattered was quality of life and that therefore euthanasia could be defended. Dick Cavett asked him who made the decision about the quality of life. Said Doc Barnard: "Why, the doctors."

Now the time may come when this society does dispose of human life according to pragmatic principles, and come to look upon the "sacredness of life" as either an empty slogan or as an outworn religious dogma. But if that happens—as in fact it already is—we're in deep trouble. The main difference is that I am more pessimistic than you. I think we're much more like the Nazis and Dachau than we imagine. (Did you know that euthanasia was practiced first not by the Nazis but by the smart German doctors in the Weimar Republic?)

As fundamentally as Percy disagreed with Mayknuth, he liked her and found her a useful sparring partner—as useful, in a different way, as Lyn Hill was. "They're the best and brightest of their generation," Percy explained to Bob Milling, "albeit in totally different ways. One is 99% located in her left brain—to use a current metaphor—the other 99% in her right." Percy could see more than a little of his earlier, skeptical self in Mayknuth, and found it worth the effort to try to score points against her. But Mayknuth also scored a few of her own. After reading the manuscript of Lost in the Cosmos, she came down very hard on what she called the sexist and homophobic aspects of the book. Percy did not believe that he was being any more homophobic than heterophobic in discussing the rampant promiscuity that he believed had become one of the symptoms of the abstracted and "lost" self, but he cut some of the harsher scenes (some thirty or forty pages, according to Mayknuth) and some of those that Mayknuth claimed were nothing more than the working out of anger and frustration. Percy, in a letter dated November 1, thanked Mayknuth for her "cool reading" of the book and admitted to some of his own difficulties with it:

> I am not submitting the book for publication now. I think it is too rancorous and mean and smart-assed in parts. So I'm putting it aside for a spell. Also, the dirty words bother me. Leaving aside the prudes, I really don't want to offend decent conventional folk who will read it (looking for something edifying and uplifting from a "Catholic writer.") This bothers me, because the shock value of the French-Quarter "chicken-hawk" exchange is deliberately calculated and integral to my purpose. Oh me, what to do?

Percy did not take all the bite out of the book—a scene in which talk show host Phil Donahue presses a San Francisco homosexual to explain the "cruising" techniques he uses at Buena Vista Park remains firmly intact—but the final published version of the book is a much kinder, gentler polemic than it earlier had been.

Percy was telling nothing less than the truth when he said he was not rushing to have the book published. It would be about a year and a half before *Lost in the Cosmos* would appear in print. During that long hiatus, Percy tinkered with the manuscript, wrote some occasional pieces, and finished settling into his new house.

One of the major steps of the last project involved moving some five thousand books from the attic of the old house to the new one. Percy was quite proud of himself for a labor-saving system that he devised. From the attic to the back of his little blue Datsun pickup truck he stretched a long sheet of sturdy plastic. Down this improvised slide Percy slid his massive library, book by book, unloading them at the other house into A&P shopping carts. "I don't think I've ever seen him more proud of himself than when he devised that way of moving his books," Bunt recalled. Percy boasted that it all came from laziness. "I'll do anything to avoid pointless exercise."

Percy may have been somewhat lazy when it came to physical labor (although, according to Bunt, Percy would often take up some physical chore to work off extra energy), but he never stopped doing things for friends and fellow writers. In the summer he read the final manuscript of Steve Ellis's history of St. Tammany Parish, a book for which Percy had earlier written a generous introduction. Ellis's history would in fact have a very direct influence on Percy's own writing. The opening section of *The Thanatos Syndrome,* the tribute to the fictional Feliciana Parish, owes directly to the lore and history contained in Ellis's *St. Tammany Parish: L'Autre Côté du Lac.* Above all, Percy was delighted to learn about "a certain ornery independence of thought and action, an inexhaustible talent for dissent" that distinguished the parish's citizens from colonial times on. Percy's summary of this history of dissent in the introduction to Ellis's book reads very much like a trial run for the introduction to *The Thanatos Syndrome.*

As the new year broke, Percy was busy at work on another tribute to a friend, this one to Eudora Welty. Thanks largely to his brother Roy and to the First Mississippi Corporation, Millsaps College in Jackson was inaugurating the Eudora Welty Chair of Southern Studies, and Percy was invited to deliver the inaugural address on March 15. Percy, for several reasons, was happy to do so. First, it was a promising step toward what he had called for in his Phinizy Lecture: a conscious effort to cultivate southern cultural life. Second, it was an acknowledgment of a writer he greatly admired. Third, the first occupant of the chair would be Cleanth Brooks, whom Percy had admired and counted as a friend ever since he met him in the early 1960s at the New Orleans home of a lawyer and politician named Ben Toledano. And finally, Percy's nephew Roy was on the English faculty at Millsaps.

The lecture, "Novel-Writing in an Apocalyptic Time," was Percy's confession of befuddlement before the extraordinary contradictoriness of his time—a century of marvelous achievements and marvelous barbarities—and the seeming incomprehension or indifference with which most people take these contradictions. "And to tell you the truth," Percy observed, "I am still not sure which is right: whether it is the poet and novelist who, like the man in Allen Tate's definition, is a shaky man trying to reassure himself in a generally sane world, or whether it is the population at large which is slowly going mad and the poet who has the sensibility or vulnerability—thin skin—to notice it."

As Percy's lectures went, this one ranked among the better, perhaps because he had been working on it for some time. In fact, Percy had delivered a preliminary version of the lecture the year before, on April 25, 1981, at a conference on southern literature sponsored by the newly formed Fellowship of Southern Writers at the University of Tennessee at Chattanooga. Before delivering the final version at Millsaps, he gave the lecture to a new assistant editor at *The Southern Review*, Jo Marie Gulledge.

Gulledge, who had recently completed a master's thesis at Clemson on the women in Percy's novels, had come to LSU with the intention of editing a volume of William Alexander Percy's letters. She had written to Percy in early February to ask if she could meet him. Percy invited her to come to Bechacs for lunch, an offer that she readily accepted. At lunch, the two hit it off, and Percy invited her to dine at his house the next week. Percy enjoyed Gulledge's no-nonsense directness—in fact, he told her that she reminded him of his daughter Mary Pratt—and he respected her critical judgment. Shortly after the dinner, he sent her a copy of the Millsaps lecture, and Gulledge went over it, locating weak spots and tightening some of the language. For the next few years, Percy counted Gulledge one of his closer friends and one of his stricter readers. And strict she was. Finding little that was amusing in *Lost in the Cosmos*, she would be even harder on *The Thanatos Syndrome*, parts of which Percy read aloud to her. It was curious, this need Percy had of readers who he knew would be hard on him—Lyn Hill, Patricia Mayknuth, Linda Hobson, and now Jo Gulledge. It was as though he wanted to test himself against the very readers he knew would most resist his view.

For her part, Gulledge restricted her criticism to Percy's writing. She realized it was hopeless to try to get him to improve his lecturing style, which, as she saw at the Millsaps lecture, was incurably strange. As often as Percy found himself giving lectures during these years, his delivery never improved. A certain hesitation or borderline stutter became more pronounced when he spoke, and he swallowed his words. Worse, he seemed almost to read against the rhythms and cadences of his own written words, like a clumsy dancer tripping up his more graceful partner.

Having barely stepped down from one rostrum, Percy found himself mounting two others in the following month. The first was in Charlottesville, Virginia, site of the second annual PEN Faulkner awards. Percy was one of three writers (Wesley Brown and John Hawkes were the other two) to be honored by citations from the organization. It was, for the most part, a pleasant weekend event, which Percy managed to enjoy despite his misgivings about gatherings of writers. (It seemed to him that writers in groups were fatally prone to posturing for one another.) During part of the weekend, Percy and Bunt paired up with a young writer, Richard Bausch, and his wife, Karen. Bausch remembers Percy as being the master of the understated one-liner. Wandering through a bookstore in town, Percy came across some novels by Henry James. "I once had a student who discovered James," Percy remarked. "Never heard from her again." On Sunday the Percys and Bausches went hunting for a Catholic church on foot. Spotting an ecclesiastical structure in the distance, Percy shook his head and announced, "It doesn't look like one of ours. Too nice." It turned out to be an Episcopal church. When the group finally located one of "theirs," it confirmed all of their expectations of architectural immiserization. Making their way into their pew, Percy thought he saw disapproval in Karen Bausch's look. "I don't think she likes our architecture," Percy whispered to Bausch.

Returned from Charlottesville, Percy barely had time to finish a lecture that he was to deliver at the University of Southwestern Louisiana on April 21. For the third Flora Levy Lecture (the first had been delivered the year before by Isaac Bashevis Singer and the second by Robert Coles the previous September) Percy spoke on "How to Be a Novelist in Spite of Being Southern and Catholic." The speech contained a full statement of Percy's literary creed: that the artist's sense of alienation from the world was his greatest gift. (And the more the southern writer still felt cut off from mainstream America, Percy argued, the better off he was.) Above all, Percy insisted upon the essentially religious character of the artist's vocation, the artist's obligation to be open to the mystery of human character:

> By this openness and this mystery, I am speaking of a necessary sensitivity to the hidden dimensions and energies of his characters and of the presence of the mystery which may always erupt in their lives and which, for want of a better word, we may call grace. Neither he nor his characters may know why certain things happen as they do. But unless such things do happen and unless he, the novelist, is open

to them, he is forever doomed to a literary sociology and psychology, or to being politicized, and whether it is liberal or conservative politics, it doesn't matter: the writing is going to be bad.

For many reasons, this is a powerful statement of literary principle, a kind of manifesto, in fact. But it also tempts one to turn the statement on Percy himself: To what extent, for example, did he resist the politicization that he saw as the mark of the second-rate artist?

Throughout most of his life, even before he committed himself to a literary career, Percy tended to view politics as a secondary concern, a consequence, rather than a cause of more important considerations. As his friend Ben Toledano once said, "Walker is interested in politics— from a hundred miles away," and this was largely true.

All the same, Percy's political views were an indicator of his own internal struggles. Such was the case in his attitude toward FDR, which was tied up with his struggle to come out from under the powerful influence of Uncle Will. Later, Percy's attraction to John Kennedy reflected some of the social commitments that he had made as a result of his conversion to Catholicism, above all his commitment to civil rights. Indeed, it was largely because of Kennedy that Percy moved into the liberal camp in American politics.

But even though Percy continued to identify himself, with strong reservations, as a moderate Democrat until the end of his life, he was never truly a liberal. His instincts and deepest convictions were conservative. It is hard to imagine how they could have been otherwise. Liberal dogma was too thoroughly entwined with the secular, progressive scientism of the Enlightenment for Percy ever to be completely at home with it. A chastened liberalism that acknowledged limits on perfectibility and recognized the reality of evil was palatable to Percy, but like many other moderate Democrats, Percy felt that liberalism lost all sense of limits during the sixties. Consequently, while he tended to vote for Democrats in presidential elections out of lingering loyalty to what Kennedy and Johnson stood for, he often found himself strongly defending Republican leaders. And though Percy voted for Carter and thought the Georgian's heart was in the right place, he was disappointed by his lackluster leadership and by his ineptitude in choosing subordinates. Percy voted again for Carter in the 1980 election, but he was not greatly upset by Reagan's victory. As James Boulware observed, Percy wanted to believe in Reagan, but he could never quite convince himself that there was any real substance to the man. All the same, like many Americans, he liked the old actor.

As well as being attracted to the hard-nosed "realism" of the Republican leaders, Percy, particularly in the last decade of his life, found the GOP stand on certain issues closer to his own. On no issue was this more true than abortion, an issue that was of growing importance to him. Finally, however, what kept him within the Democratic fold was his conviction that, despite all their weaknesses and follies, despite even the pernicious effects of their ill-conceived welfare projects, the Democrats still had the interests of the poor at heart and the Republicans did not. And for that reason alone, Percy held his nose and remained a Democrat. But that did not mean Percy would remain silent on what he perceived as the wrong-minded sentimentality of liberalism. Indeed, the polemical force of his late writings would be largely devoted to exposing the evil consequences of unexamined liberal pieties. Percy's greatest fear was a "Weimar" America, and to combat such an eventuality he would risk even the integrity of his art.

Although Percy continued to revise *Lost in the Cosmos* in the summer and fall of 1982, he was already entering that passive stage of receptivity that preceded the formulation of an idea for a novel. One of the many short trips that he took during the summer included a visit to St. Francisville, where, for many generations, descendants of Charles Percy and his first wife have lived (and indeed, where one descendant, Lucy Percy Madox, continues to live, occupying the old Percy plantation, Ellerslie). It is impossible to say whether it was this trip to St. Francisville that got Percy moving in the direction of his last novel, *The Thanatos Syndrome*, but it is hard to imagine that it did not stir up thoughts about Don Carlos, the story of the warring wives, and his ignominious plunge into the creek with a sugar kettle tied around his neck—details of the Percy legend that would play mysteriously in the background of the novel's main action.

In September, Percy and Bunt met Shelby and Gwyn Foote in Chicago and boarded an Amtrak train, the Zephyr, for San Francisco. It promised to be an ideal vacation, scenic views of western landscape and conversation among best friends. But on the evening of the second day (September 19), near Ogden, Utah, at midnight all Amtrak employees went on strike. Percy, who had taken his sleeping pills and settled in for sleep, was roused by the conductor, who said that all passengers would have to leave the train and board buses for the rest of the journey to San Francisco. Amtrak's timing could not have been worse. Percy was in one of his more obdurate moods. Neither he nor his wife or friends would leave the train that night, he announced, and he added that in no case would they travel the rest of the distance to San Francisco by bus. The conductor warned that he would shut off the air-conditioner if Percy and his party did not comply with his request. This only made Percy more furious. "If you do," Percy warned, his voice now brimming with menace, "I will sue Amtrak." The conductor had no idea that Percy was a well-known writer; nor would he have cared if he had. What he did know was that he had before him a man who looked and sounded deadly serious. The air-conditioning remained on, and the next day the Percys and the Footes were shuttled by bus to nearby Salt Lake City, where they were put on a plane to San Francisco. The rest of the journey—a car trip down the coast to Los Angeles and flights back to Tennessee and Louisiana—proved relaxing and relatively uneventful.

Percy had always been a creature of principle, but with age he seemed to act more decisively (even dramatically) on his beliefs. In October, for example, he flew up to Washington to attend his first meeting as a member of the board of trustees of Gallaudet College, the national university founded expressly for the deaf. When Percy learned that the school approved only of sign languge, however, he promptly resigned from the board. While Percy had nothing against the use of sign language, he had a horror of those dogmatists who claimed that Sign (American Sign Language, or ASL) was the only legitimate language for the deaf. Too much of his and his family's life had been devoted to proving that other possibilities were just as good.

Just how ornery Percy was becoming the world would soon see. Percy had sent Farrar, Straus his much-worked-over revision of *Lost in the Cosmos* in November, and he received no requests for changes. His publisher did, however, ask that Percy come up to New York in early December to give the sales representatives a "handle" on the book. Percy combined the trip with a stop in Washington, where he served on a panel of the National Endowment for the Arts reviewing grants to literary quarterlies.

Farrar, Straus planned on bringing out *Lost in the Cosmos* in May, the book to be preceded by a first serial excerpt in the May issue of *Vanity Fair*. Robert Giroux and Roger Straus had far more confidence in the sales potential of this work of nonfiction than they had had for Percy's previous book of essays. The print run of the first edition was set for thirty-five thousand copies. (Their confidence was well placed: *Lost in the Cosmos* would eventually prove to be one of Percy's stronger-selling books.) Percy, at this point, knew better than to get his hopes up. He busied himself with other affairs, including a short lecture that he was expected to deliver in Washington on May 17.

The 1982–83 Frank Nelson Doubleday Lectures featured a kind of intellectual triple-header: Percy, Eudora Welty, and C. Vann Woodward speaking respectively on Melville, Hawthorne, and Parkman. It was an ingenious idea, having three southern writers comment on the works of three distinguished northern writers. In Percy's case particularly, it gave rise to one of the best lectures he ever wrote.

What most piqued Percy's interest in Melville was the mysterious way in which Melville had been overtaken by *Moby Dick* while he wrote it, overwhelmed not by its allegorical apparatus ("An allegory is a dreary business," Percy noted) but by the sheer force of the story itself:

> The happiness of Melville in *Moby Dick* is the happiness of the artist discovering, breaking through into the freedom of his art. Through no particular virtue of his own, he hits on a mother lode. The novel— the freedom of its form often paralyzing to the novelist—suddenly finds itself being shaped by a larger unity which cannot be violated. . . .
>
> The freedom and happiness of the artist is attested by his playfulness, his tricks, his malice, his underhandedness, his naughtiness, his hood-winking the reader. So happy is the metaphorical distance between the novelist and his narrative that he's free to cover his tracks at will. Not only do I not have to strive to mean such-and-such, he seems to say, but I deny that I mean it. I might mean the opposite, because with the *Pequod* under full sail through the night with its try-pots blazing I don't have to worry about a thing. . . .

Percy celebrates in Melville the mysterious autonomy of art. As the work compels itself toward the completion of its unity, the artist more or less becomes an amanuensis to his demonic voices.

But what of the author's ideas and beliefs? Percy says that these matter and indeed that "Melville impresses Southern writers for the same reason Dostoyevsky impresses Southerners. Neither was afraid to deal with ultimate questions." Of course, Percy must conclude that Melville, unlike Dostoyevsky, got it wrong, the latter seeing man's depravity as the occasion of his salvation, the former seeing it as proof of God's depravity. Percy, in concluding, shows how such a confused view could only lead to the "eminently readable science fiction of *Billy Budd*":

> In Melville, the only believable part of Judeo-Christianity (as Schopenhauer put it)—the innocence—comes not from human nature but from outer space. Billy Budd is man before the Fall, man exempted from the Fall, a creature dragged in from some loony planet invented by Melville and Rousseau, who neither understands evil nor needs salvation from it. Dostoyevsky would have laughed out loud. Billy Budd, in Dostoyevsky's hands, would have turned out to be a child molester.

> And therefore a good deal more believable. But Melville was not afraid to address such matters, and that's why he means so much to us.

As well as being a fine piece of literary criticism and cultural history, this talk reveals Percy's own conflict between his commitment to the mysterious autonomy of the artistic process and his equally powerful commitment to the idea of art as a vehicle of knowledge and truth. One acknowledges freedom as paramount; the other, necessity. What, if anything, mediates between these seemingly exclusive commitments Percy does not say. Yet he does seem to imply that freedom and necessity, art and truth, may at times coexist even in contradiction. But that coexistence will not necessarily endure. For Percy also suggests that artistic genius will produce deformities if it is not accompanied by a full or convincing conception of truth. A reader curious about Percy's aesthetic principles, his notions of beauty and truth, may do no better than to start with this surprisingly rich little speech.

The reviews of *Lost in the Cosmos* began coming in shortly after Percy returned from Washington. By the end of June, the tenor of critical opinion was fairly well established. The response was mixed. (The West Coast reviewers were far more favorable than those on the East Coast, a geographical trend confirmed by Percy's winning the *Los Angeles Times* Book Prize the following November.) Some reviewers sympathized with Percy's religious and philosophical intentions but deplored his technique (Francine du Plessix Gray in *The New York Times Book Review*), others delighted in his method and rejected his argument (Jack Beatty in *The New Republic*), while some few felt nothing but unilateral contempt. Thomas Disch in *The Washington Post* panned it with the fury of an angry former Catholic, concluding that it was "neither good philosophy nor a good read nor yet a book likely to help any Self I know of, including its author." *The New Yorker*, in its brief review, assumed an attitude of Olympian condescension: "A diverting restatement of the by now familiar notion that the loss of some kinds of certainty essential to emotional well-being—a loss common in modern societies—is due to the decay of formal or traditional religious faith."

Percy had little inclination, and less time, to dwell on the reviews. He had more than the usual number of appointments and obligations to meet, including, shortly after his return from Washington, an address to the graduating class at St. Joseph's College Seminary. Percy did not exaggerate when he told the college seminarians that he envied them their four years in the Benedictine community. Percy strongly fantasized about the monastic life; more realistically, he had once attempted to buy a house near the abbey so he could hear its bells and live according to its rhythms. The address, entitled "A 'Cranky Novelist' Reflects on the Church," surveyed the assorted challenges to the church from both within and without. Perhaps most interesting was his view of the Christian fundamentalists, "who ought," Percy said, "to be reckoned a friend and ally but in these peculiar times may not be." Percy feared that the influence of the fundamentalists was particularly invidious in the South, where they dominated the airwaves and uttered "the name of the Lord loudest and most often."

> In my opinion, they do a disservice by cheapening the vocabulary of Christianity and pandering to a crude emotionalism divorced from reason. I know that St. Paul said that the Gospel was a stumbling block to the wise, but it does not follow that in order to save the faith it is necessary to believe that the universe was created six thousand years ago. And it is not necessary, to save the integrity of man's soul and its likeness to God, to believe that God could not have created man's body through an evolution from lower species.

To his friend Foote, Percy reported that he was enjoying the summer "doing nothing by the pool." But Percy seldom was doing nothing. Among other projects, he moved offices in July. Percy had never felt completely comfortable in his workroom over the Kumquat. He found the place too distracting, what with the chatter of customers downstairs and of passers-by outside. So in July he rented a room at 5 Columbia Quarter, a group of small offices in a converted brick slaves' quarters on the other side of town from the Kumquat (and a little closer to the post office, where Percy walked every day to pick up his mail, using his three iron as his walking stick). The fourteen-by-twenty room had a fireplace and was on the ground floor facing a quiet courtyard. By July 14, the office was in good enough shape for Percy to be able to receive one of his first visitors. Jo Gulledge came for one of many talks that would lead to a long interview in *The Southern Review*, "The Reentry Option," focusing largely on Percy's semiotic theory.

Though he didn't want to talk about his next book for the interview, Percy clearly made a number of off-the-record remarks about what he was contemplating—a sort of "Invasion of the Bodysnatchers" science-fiction fantasy with a serious point, he told Gulledge. (Even before *Lost in the Cosmos* came out, Percy had outlined the general plot of *The Thanatos Syndrome* to his friend Haydee Ellis.) Toward the end of July, Gulledge wrote Percy a long, playful letter suggesting that he bring back Tom More, now fifteen years into his marriage with Ellen and director of a hospital. She offered other details: The marriage has begun to die, and More acts strangely, hiding under a desk at work to avoid colleagues and nurses. He begins to notice something: that people who leave his hospital act strangely, seem not to be "here" but live strangely in the future or the past. At this point, Gulledge suggested, he should bring in his "Bodysnatchers" idea.

But that was not all that Gulledge proposed. Having written about the women in Percy's novels (and having been told rather snootily by Panthea Reid Broughton at LSU that there "are no women" in Percy's fiction), Gulledge made a further suggestion:

> Dr. Tom then runs into a new staff member—for heavens sake, make her a solid person. She's late thirties, just beginning (this is her first *real* job after internship), she got a late start in school because she put her husband through (also a dr., psych, whatever) and he died six months ago—heart attack or something. . . . Dr. Tom and ———— (let me call her Charlotte for the time being) develop a comfortable friendship: she finds him intelligent, admires his work, and in general likes all things about him. She is new to the field and he wants to genuinely help her along, realizing her dedication to her work. . . . Together they know something is "wrong" at the hospital—seriously wrong, and they seem to be the only ones left that are "here." But before anything really develops between them, there are hints that she is losing More to whatever is happening to the Others, but she's not really sure. It's not until the end of the book that she realizes that he's been "on the other side" for quite a while and she's now alone. What to do when one is completely alone? Can she rescue him? What happens between them if she can? So you end up having the hero not a man but a woman, as you wanted, but it's a kick-twist that comes at the very end of the book. . . .

It is not the plot of *The Thanatos Syndrome*, but there is much in Gulledge's suggestion that found its way into Percy's next novel, including the resurrection of Tom More, the collapse of More's relationship with his wife, and the relationship between More and a female doctor who helps him discover why people are becoming so strangely bland. Percy thanked Gulledge for her ideas in a short postcard that he wrote at the end of July: "Plot interesting, especially Charlotte—but can't put Dr. More under desk—too much like Will B. falling down in bunkers and seeing clouds."

Gulledge's ideas were only one source feeding Percy's imagination. Ever since his trip there the previous year, Percy had felt the urge to return to St. Francisville, and before the end of the summer he did so, with Bunt and the Ellises. They spent the weekend at a place called the Cottage in St. Francisville and visited the Ellerslie Plantation. As Percy told Haydee Ellis, he wanted to see a fancy house that had gone downhill. For reasons that he could not fully understand, family history was forcing itself upon Percy, insisting on inclusion in the futuristic fantasy that he was playing with.

Another subject weighed on Percy's mind. He found himself frequently thinking about his experience in Germany in 1934. He talked to his friend Nikki Barranger about how difficult it was to understand how the good German burghers had gone along with the crime of the Holocaust. "You should write about it," Barranger would say. "No," came Percy's inevitable reply. "Everyone who has done so has come a cropper." Percy had in mind William Styron's *Sophie's Choice*, a novel that he felt had been terribly inadequate to the enormity of its subject.

"It doesn't matter," Barranger said. "You should try."

So many things seemed to be coming at Percy at once—so many things that he *should* write about. Was he simply repeating himself, he wondered, bringing back old characters, revisiting the same ideas, conjuring up his own past and the deeper history of his family? Or were all these "second comings" necessary—the only way of coming to terms with the hours and days that lay ahead? It was becoming too demanding, this business of making up stories. Percy wondered if he could do it yet again.

17

Thanatos— and After

One clue to the origin of *The Thanatos Syndrome* can be found in the letter Percy wrote to Shelby Foote in the winter of 1977 outlining the two kinds of novels he was then stuck between writing. The first he described as a "dreamlike novel . . . Kierkegaard translated into Huck Finn, H. C. Earwicker transposed to Louisiana"; the second, as "a Gulliver's Travel sort of fable-satire . . . a modern version of Body Snatchers." He wrote neither, of course. *The Second Coming* came instead. Yet those two hypothetical fictions were not forgotten. Even before *Lost in the Cosmos* came out, Percy began to talk about his next novel, and while those who heard him describe it could not have known so, it was very close to a hybrid of the two he had earlier contemplated: a dreamlike novel combined with a fable-satire. When it was completed on July 12, 1985, the novel would be far more fable-satire than Joycean exploration of the unconscious, but certain hallucinatory, dreamlike episodes as well as a pervasive dreamlike atmosphere would play subtly against the satire, deepening and often adding a mysteriously autobiographical dimension to the unfolding action.

No novel by Percy was more ambitiously conceived than *The Thanatos*

Syndrome. Yet it is hard to avoid the conclusion that Percy's reach exceeded his grasp. *The Thanatos Syndrome* is something less than successful, as Percy himself seemed to realize after finishing it. All the same, *The Thanatos Syndrome* is more interesting in its overweening failings than many tidily well-made novels are in their more modest successes. One cannot help marveling at its parts—at the moments of exactly crafted prose, at passages of great comic invention, at the weight of its ambitious moral argument, and at the strange and seductive atmosphere of mystery that infuses the whole—even as one feels that it is a novel pulling apart at the seams, a novel that finally will not cohere, despite the labors of its author. One problem is that those labors threaten to translate into an obvious laboriousness, even as they reveal Percy's urge to impose the order of art on the most chaotic of materials: mankind's fatal romance with death. His satirical portrait of what might be described as "Weimar" America is an attempt to fuse his vision of the folly of a dangerously sentimentalized, scientized, and desacralized world with his own personal struggle against the attractions of death, a struggle with deep ancestral antecedents. It would have been very hard, even for a younger artist at the top of his powers, to bring off such an ambitious novel, but Percy was no longer at the top of his powers.

Signs of slippage, evident in *The Second Coming,* abound in *The Thanatos Syndrome.* In *The Fiction of Walker Percy,* the meticulously close reader John Hardy details numerous errors and inconsistencies of chronology and geography which, by themselves, threaten to reduce the novel to incoherence (yet which also, one could argue, add to the dreamlike quality of the novel). Hardy points out, for example, the impossibility of Dr. More's claim (on page sixteen of *Thanatos*) to have served a residency under Harry Stack Sullivan. "In *Love in the Ruins,*" Hardy notes, "we are plainly told that Tom More is forty-five years old. Assuming, again, that the year of the main action of that novel is fictional 1983—and nobody, to my knowledge has suggested an *earlier* date—More would have been born in 1938. Since Harry Stack Sullivan died in January, 1949, Tom More, at the age of ten years or less, must have been one of the youngest medical residents on record." Hardy concludes that such muddles hardly have the look of "confusion by design," and one must sadly agree. At the same time, though, Hardy suggests that they may raise questions "of great interest to anyone proposing an investigation of the author psychology of Walker Percy." And so they do. Among other things, they show a compulsion on Percy's part to make Thomas More even more of an autobiographical projection than he was in *Love in the Ruins.* This compulsion reveals itself in More's acquisition of Percy's ancestral past (shared by Lucy Lipscombe, More's distant cousin, collaborator, and, briefly, lover). There is, in fact, a true eruption of the autobiographical in this novel, with certain details from Percy's life and family history generously, and sometimes almost gratuitously, distributed among the novel's characters. (Mickey LaFaye, the patient whose behavior tips Dr. More off to a growing strangeness among people around him, lives close by a new country club "next to number-six fairway"—no more fateful a fairway in Percy's memory; Father Smith's experiences in Germany during the 1930s duplicate some of Percy's own.)

Percy's inattention to consistencies between "real" and fictional time was not unique to his last novel. (In *The Moviegoer,* as Hardy points out, it is impossible to square Binx Bolling's age with his military service in the Korean War.) The recurrent difficulty stems largely from Percy's manner of literary composition, the passive, almost trancelike state of receptivity that he needed to enter in order to give play to the contending voices, selves, and demons within him. At the same time Percy had to bring this medley of voices under control, shape them according to a dominant voice, whose crucial tone and timbre, Percy believed, had to be established in the first sentence and sustained throughout. So much depended on maintaining the music of the prose that Percy's mind could often stray from the more rudimentary exigencies of plot, including chronological consistencies. Even though he often had a general idea of where he was heading, and sometimes sketched out rough outlines while writing, Percy tended to keep all of the details and threads of the novel in his head. But even the most concentrated of minds can lose their way, become distracted by certain details, head off on tangents, forget to return to questions that have been raised, fail to account for developments, even seem to contradict themselves—and Percy seems to have fallen prey to all of these dangers in *The Thanatos Syndrome.* (One thinks of the way in which the character of Lucy Lipscombe is dropped after she has performed her plot function, as though she were a minor walk-on character and not someone with whom More has developed a complicated relationship.) Percy wrote the novel like a man distracted, distracted not only by his life or even an observable weakening of his mental powers, but also by the moral argument that he wanted his novel to make. Between the moralist and the artist in Percy, there had always been a powerful but creative tension. Writing *Thanatos,* though, Percy seemed to lose his balance.

Hectic may be too strong a description of Percy's life during the writing of *The Thanatos Syndrome,* but it was certainly full of activity. In the fall of 1983, not long after the trip to St. Francisville, Percy and Bunt went up to Highlands with Steve and Haydee Ellis and another couple, Will and Nell Pape Waring, both physicians with practices in New Orleans. For a full week in early October, the six friends stayed in the Brown House, hiking, lounging on the porch, or driving through the countryside in the Warings' International Scout. (Percy always rode curled up in the far back with the backpacks and his Welsh corgi, Sweet Thing.) As he often did on his vacations, Percy mixed business with pleasure, reading through a stack of manuscripts that he was judging for the fiction panel of the National Endowment for the Arts. In fact, nightly readings from the manuscripts became one of the group's main pastimes—those and Ellis's somewhat painful apprentice solos on his violin. Everybody thought Percy was in top form, full of jokes, vigorous, sociable. His chronic insomnia would have him up in the middle of the night, listening to the radio and reading or writing, but he made light even of that: "I try not to lose any sleep over it," he quipped.

Less than a month after returning from the mountains, the Percys packed for another trip, this one to Los Angeles in November with Shelby and Gwyn Foote. The occasion was the *Los Angeles Times* Book Prize; *Lost in the Cosmos* was to receive the award for the best current interest book. But the prize was really only an excuse to take a trip. Surprisingly, considering their experience with Amtrak the year before, they decided to go by train. Boarding in New Orleans on November 16, celebrating Foote's sixty-seventh birthday the next day as the train rolled across Texas (Foote, six months younger than Percy, would hoot at him every May for being the year older), they arrived in Los Angeles on the morning of the eighteenth well in time for the ceremony that evening at the Times Mirror Building. Robert Giroux had also come West for the ceremony, meeting the Footes—whom he took to immediately—for the first time. The Percys and Footes stayed in Los Angeles for only one night, November 16. The next evening the foursome boarded the train East. Intending to make the return trip something of a sentimental journey, they got off in Albuquerque, rented a car, and drove to Santa Fe, where they stayed through Thanksgiving in a two-bedroom suite at the top of La Fonda Hotel. Percy and Foote showed their wives all the places they had visited and come to know in 1946, Seton Village, the Whittaker ranch, and the Brownell-Howland house where Percy had almost stayed. Sitting in the central courtyard of La Fonda, Percy no doubt recalled the time he and Foote sat there thirty-seven years before, Foote denouncing him for being a "mind in full intellectual retreat." Their friendship, both men realized, had endured that and many another hurled barb—hurled, to be sure, in both directions.

The trip West had no direct influence on the writing of *Thanatos*, but, like all his journeys West, it left Percy with a familiar metaphysical exhilaration that he described, in Kierkegaardian terms, as a sense of "pure possibility." It was in the West as a much younger man that Percy had first felt that exhilaration. It was what had drawn him to the idea of living there. But he quickly discovered that pure possibility did not solve the problem of his burdensome self; in some ways, it even made it worse.

Only a few months before his trip to California, Percy had read an essay by his friend Lewis Simpson that nearly took his breath away. "But the real savage eye-opener," Percy wrote to Simpson on August 1, "is the sentence on p. 58 of 'Home by Way of California': 'On the path to the realm of the Oversoul they had made a choice and effected a kill: they had murdered the self that is the creature of history and society." Percy saw a connection, a fatal link, between the urge for absolute autonomy and a certain "murderous" disregard for those things that restrain the self: society, others, history, even the awareness of one's own frailty, incompleteness, and physical mortality. In the modern age, of course, science had become the most powerful and seductive voice of immanentism. Science proposes that the self is a piece of behavioral technology, which, through the techniques of science, can be brought to perfection, self-sufficiency. An attractive doctrine, Percy acknowledged, embraced, more often than not unconsciously, by most people living in the modern world. But he also believed that it was a fatal doctrine that threatened to make ours the most innocently, even sentimentally, death-dealing of ages—an age that kills in the name of goodness.

Percy had read, many years before, Frederic Werham's book, *A Sign for Cain: An Exploration of Human Violence* (1966). Now one of the points of that book—that the decent, cultured doctors of Weimar Germany, not the Nazi physicians, had been the first to propose programs for the elimination of "defective," "inferior," or "unfit" members of the human species—preyed very much on his mind. It was not the first time that Percy had contemplated the link between German schemes for social engineering and what was going on in contemporary America, most dramatically, Percy believed, in the routinization of abortion. He had discussed such matters with like-minded friends such as Mercedes Wilson (for whose natural birth control program Percy continued to work, editing reports and speeches and even writing editorials in support of the method) as well as with friends who disagreed, including Walter Isaacson and Patricia Mayknuth. Percy had even taken a public stand on the issue in the op-ed piece he had written for *The New York Times* in 1981. Now, though, he wanted to understand how this phenomenon of legally sanctioned life-taking related to a larger cultural malaise—or syndrome. His goal, in writing *The Thanatos Syndrome*, was precisely to give this complex of cultural attitudes its proper name. For it was Percy's conviction that those implicated in the syndrome had no idea of what they were truly pursuing. Evil, to them, was simply a consequence of social imperfections, of those impediments to healthy self-fulfillment and a higher quality of life. Such a view of evil, Percy held, denied the true character of evil: the despair and emptiness that drive people toward the endless pursuit of happiness in the first place; the despair, moreover, which can be healed only by its acknowledgment, and by acknowledgment of its cause—man's radical alienation from his soul and his creator.

But tying together all of the elements of his diagnosis was proving to be every bit as difficult as Percy feared it might be. Even as he bore down on his book in the winter months of 1983–84, he felt as though it were overwhelming him. "I'm having trouble shifting gears from smart-alec nonfiction to making up a story," Percy complained to a friend, the writer Elizabeth Spencer, in January. Two months later, when he wrote to congratulate her on her latest book, *The Salt Line*, he could not report great progress: "Me, I'm having trouble as usual with a troublesome novel."

This was not merely talk. His wife and friends could see that the strain of this novel was great. Always somewhat absentminded, he seemed constantly preoccupied and at times frighteningly forgetful. He missed appointments, repeated himself, and at times seemed incapable of attending to a word anybody else said. His lunch partners in the Wednesday group had long humored his inattention, but even they couldn't help remarking upon how distant he seemed. Chink Baldwin said to him one day, "Walker, you haven't heard a single word we've said," and Percy was clearly embarrassed.

Percy also began to modify, even narrow, the range of his social life. To the Thursday Bechacs lunch, for example, he came less and less regularly. As much as he valued this gathering and his friendship with everybody who had taken part in it over the years (two of the more recent additions were the novelists Sheila Bosworth and Nancy Lemann), Percy felt a certain distance opening between himself and his younger friends. He saw himself becoming crankier and a bit less tolerant of their bright but sometimes callow irreverence. His lunch partners noticed his uneasiness. Bob Milling at one gathering said something slighting about the idea of miracles—nothing particularly irreverent but apparently enough to get under Percy's skin. A few days later Milling was surprised to receive a letter from Percy in which Percy acknowledged the validity of Milling's skepticism but at the same time urged him to consider what Pascal meant when he called the Christian story a "scandal" to the modern mind. Adverting to Pascal in this way, Percy seemed almost to be saying that faith could not be reasoned about—a view that was quite different from his usual litigious Thomism. With Sheila Bosworth, one of the group's many "cradle" Catholics, Percy would occasionally get into friendly disagreements about the church. "I would tell him that his church was not my church," Bosworth recalled, "because mine included mean nuns." As he had with Milling, Percy wrote Bosworth cautioning her not to be overly critical of the church. In order to live the life you want to lead, he told her, you must hold to certain convictions. "I won't settle for anything less than what the Catholic faith proposes." In some ways, Percy had simply tired of arguing for his more orthodox and conservative views. It was not insignificant that his attendance at the Wednesday lunches remained constant while his attendance at the Thursday affairs became increasingly occasional.

Percy stayed fairly close to home during the first half of 1984, but there were occasional trips and vacations. In February he flew up to Chicago to receive the Humanities Award from Loyola. In the spring there were more panels to sit on and conferences to attend. In May, he took another week in Highlands with the Ellises, and later in the summer he and Bunt went to Martinique with Phin and Jaye Percy. (Bunt grew a little concerned when, a few months after this trip, somebody mentioned the Martinique trip and Percy could not remember having been on it.) He even went on a couple of research expeditions closer to home. He and Bunt drove to Angola, the site of the state penitentiary, and ended up lost on a dirt road in the backwoods of western Louisiana.

Apart from a short piece about Uncle Will's house that he wrote for the October issue of *Architectural Digest*, Percy worked only on his novel during the summer. In June, Jo Gulledge asked him if he would write a short introduction to a selection of letters between Will Percy and various Fugitive poets that she was editing for *The Southern Review*. Gulledge would have been the only person to shake loose any commitments from Percy at this point. She had been serving as a kind of informal literary assistant for several months, commenting on his manuscript, helping out with assorted requests from magazines for photographs and information, and offering a sympathetic ear when Percy grew frustrated with the work in progress. As much as he was indebted to her, Percy insisted that he had to work on nothing but the novel at least until October. "Okay, " he wrote to her, "I'll take a look at those WAP letters, but I don't want to commit myself to anything until October, when I hope to have this novel under control and to be finished with the final meeting of the NEA (Oct. 6)."

On August 14, Percy made yet another progress report to Elizabeth

Spencer, this one the most painfully truthful of them all: "I am writing a preposterous novel which no-one could possibly write (or maybe read) if all his cerebral arteries were intact." For all his doubts, though, Percy persisted. He even occasionally allowed himself to sound guardedly optimistic. "I am working on a real mess of a novel," he told Roger Straus in November. "It's either going to do me in or—it might work." "Mess of a novel" had become Percy's standard description of the work in progress.

Percy, for all his absorption in *Thanatos*, made good on his promise to Jo Gulledge. On December 31, he sent her his introduction to her "William Alexander Percy and the Fugitives: A Literary Correspondence, 1921, 1923." Perhaps the most interesting touch in this further installment of Percy's literary filiopiety was his discussion of Will Percy's grudge against H. L. Mencken, the great mocker of southern cultural aridity:

> There is something doubly ironic about the issue between Percy and Mencken. First, it is ironic that at the very time Mencken was letting the South have it, there was already getting underway what would later be recognized as perhaps the major American literary revival of the twentieth century both in poetry and criticism, the Fugitive poets and later the New Criticism, both almost exclusively southern in provenance. And William Faulkner was beginning to write novels. The other irony is that Uncle Will, if the truth be known, had not a great deal of use for any of the Fugitive poets, not for the New Criticism, and not for William Faulkner. He'd have taken his stand with the Fugitives and the Agrarians on the common ground of gentility, honor, but he'd have staked out his territory of an unashamed lyricism and romanticism against what he might have called the Fugitives' modernist or even "ultramodern" experiments in both poetry and criticism.

As devoted as Percy continued to be to the memory of Uncle Will, he was nothing less than absolutely honest about his estimation of Will Percy's rather sentimental literary tastes. Still, Will remained the spur, the instigator, the one against whom Walker continued to define himself.

In January, Percy decided to abandon his office in town and try working in his library at home. It was something of a gamble, he realized, because the library doubled as a guest bedroom, and Bunt and he always seemed to have a relative dropping by for the night. Nevertheless, the risk was worth what he then considered the greater good: closeness with his family, and particularly with Bunt. Percy still felt bad about his behavior during the mid-1970s, when he had been distant and difficult.

Now there seemed not enough he could do to make amends for that earlier insensitivity. Percy had never been one to discuss his marriage or his wife, but even this reticence began to dissolve. The first time Sheila Bosworth attended a Bechacs lunch in November of 1983, Percy turned to her and made a completely unexpected confession: "When I was young I was very quiet and shy around girls. I thought women were these special, exotic creatures. Then I met Bunt and she became my best friend —and she still is."

In the second week of February Percy and his extended family went to Vail, Colorado, for a ten-day skiing vacation. Percy, however, took one look at the slopes and decided that he would sit it out. In fact, he came down with a cold that took almost no time turning into bronchitis. Laid up in his room, he rested, worked on his manuscript, and read, with keen interest, an extended study of his language philosophy by Patricia Lewis Poteat, *Walker Percy and the Old Modern Age*. What he read did not cheer him up, though he thought the book advanced an intelligent, closely reasoned thesis. Poteat argued that Percy's philosophical writings fell victim to the very Cartesian theoretical malady that they set out to diagnose; moreover, Poteat believed, Percy's fiction offered a better philosophical critique of the Cartesian affliction than did all of Percy's theoretical offerings. As Poteat put it:

> The "Enlightened earnestness" and extreme abstraction of "Theory" set side by side with the acuity, wit and concreteness of *Lancelot* and *The Second Coming* confirms the thesis that Percy's strengths and weaknesses as a critic of modern Western culture and its dominant philosophic tradition rooted in Descartes are logically of a piece with the inconsistencies and contradictions of that tradition; and that it is the novel, not the philosophic essay, which provides the conceptual tools most efficacious both for disclosing the incoherence of that tradition and for developing a radical alternative to it.

Percy was not completely unprepared for this line of criticism. Several years before, Poteat's husband, William Poteat, a professor of religion at Duke, had made a very similar argument in an essay that appeared in Panthea Reid Broughton's collection *The Art of Walker Percy: Stratagems for Being*. (In fact, Percy would refer to their ideas collectively as "the Poteat position.") That he never marshaled a reply to "the Poteat position," certainly the most thorough appraisal of his language philosophy to appear during his lifetime, is in itself significant. To Jo Gulledge, though, in a letter written shortly after he returned from Vail, he hinted at his irritation: "She thinks it is dehumanizing to try to figure out what's

going on in somebody's head when *she* names something or utters a
sentence. She is probably (1) partly right (2) partly a victim of the old
humanities-science split."

Through the spring, Percy continued to live and work in his rather
dazed condition. Having dinner with Haydee and Steve Ellis at a restaurant in town, Percy astonished Haydee by saying that he never remembered their trip to St. Francisville and Ellerslie Plantation. That Percy
used things that he had seen on that trip in his novel makes this lapse of
memory seem particularly mysterious. It was almost as though, in Percy's
mind, the real had merged indistinguishably with the imaginary, the
Ellerslie of fact becoming the Pantherburn of fiction, and vice versa.

On May 17, Percy and Bunt drove into New Orleans to hear Cleanth
Brooks speak at Tulane. Percy was not only fond of Brooks and his wife,
Tinkum, but had great respect for Brooks's low-keyed sagacity. He particularly wanted to hear what Brooks had to say about the new breed of
literary critics, the poststructuralists who were increasingly ruling the
roost in literature departments throughout the country. Although these
critics shared Percy's interest in semiotics and linguistics, Percy could
not understand their attraction to such French theorists as Derrida. He
saw the deconstructive enterprise as little more than rehashed Nietz-
scheanism, an attempt to get rid of God by first disposing of grammar.

Percy's irritation with the deconstructionists—his desire to get a fix
on them in order to attack them—was just one way in which Percy was
becoming a more aggressive intellectual defender of the faith. Percy, in
fact, seemed more and more comfortable with his identification as a
Catholic writer. If people wanted to explain him away or dismiss him on
those grounds, Percy as much as said, then let them do so. Percy also
knew that there were worlds and worlds within the Catholic church,
which was held together, only barely, by its bedrock of doctrine. ("If
you talk to three hundred Catholic priests," he once told his friend
Ansley Cope, "you'll end up with three hundred versions of Catholicism.") Percy relished the paradox of diversity within orthodoxy, of
freedom achieved through submission and obedience to authority, and
he was increasingly quick to stand up and defend his idea of the church.

In June, Percy was invited to receive another honor from his church,
the Compostela Award, given by St. James Cathedral Basilica in Brooklyn. Eudora Welty was also in New York at the time, and on the day of
the ceremony, June 7, she accompanied the Percys to the cathedral. The
cab journey proved to be a harrowing experience. Only moments after
pulling away from the Algonquin, the passengers realized that their
driver, a West Indian, was not in a fully responsible condition. He
swerved in and out of traffic and took corners at hair-raising speeds.

Several times, Welty and Bunt were nearly thrown from the seat, and the bone-jarring bumps were particularly hard on Welty's arthritis. "Listen, man," Percy said, barely containing his anger, "you must slow down." But the driver ignored Percy's repeated demands. Welty was not sure which frightened her more: the prospect of a wreck or Percy's mounting fury. When they arrived at the cathedral, miraculously intact, Percy paid the fare but refused to give the driver a tip. "You are in trouble," Percy told him. The driver, unfazed, turned his cab around and went barreling back to Manhattan.

The surprises did not end with the cab ride. Percy recounted what happened next in a letter to Robert Coles, written four days after the ceremony:

> Imagine my astonishment last Friday when Bunt and I were sitting with some nice folks in Brooklyn (!) with a couple of very nice priests in an old cathedral pavilion (like a K.C. hall in La.), listening to Margaret Whiting (!) whom I haven't heard since the Lucky Strike Hit Parade—when somebody starts reading a letter to *me*, far too gracious, then lo and behold, it was signed by YOU!—I have it framed.
>
> Anyhow it was a remarkable occasion—the Compostela Awards—and I felt totally unworthy sitting next to Mary Hale, a lovely lady who saves newborn addicted babies from heroin addicted mothers—by holding them and loving them for 6 weeks or so. No place for writers —a bad lot. And Dave Brubeck!—remember him—
>
> Anyhow you were very nice to do it and Father Hinchey, a nice guy, was very proud—as was Bunt. I was floored.

Within a month of his New York trip, Percy completed the first draft of *Thanatos,* but he knew it was far from finished. More so for *Thanatos* than for any novel since *The Moviegoer,* revision would be extensive and critical. As well as tying up loose ends, Percy would add some of the more important scenes in the novel, including Father Smith's confession, the long account of his travels in Germany in the early 1930s, and his discovery of the Weimar physicians and their schemes for culling out the less desirable.

In October, Percy gave his first public reading of a fragment from the unfinished novel. The occasion was the fiftieth anniversary celebration of *The Southern Review* at Baton Rouge, a gathering of the southern literary lions, or at least of those who had contributed to the journal over the years. In addition to the founding editors Robert Penn Warren and Cleanth Brooks, the speakers included Eudora Welty, Elizabeth Spencer, Louis Rubin, Houston Baker, Gloria Naylor, Walter Sullivan, Ernest Gaines, Percy, and many others. Though the celebration lasted from October 9 to October 11, Percy stayed only for the day of his reading. Much as he liked seeing all his friends—"I felt like the kid on the block with all those great old folks," he told Elizabeth Spencer—the large gathering had its usual unsettling effect on him, and he appeared to be restless.

One of the southern writers whom Percy didn't see at *The Southern Review* gathering was Shelby Foote, but even though he was absent (never having contributed to the journal), he was much on Percy's mind. A few months before the celebration, *The Southern Review* had in fact published a very flattering article about Foote, its author, James Cox, comparing Foote's history to the work of Thucydides. After reading the article, Percy let Simpson know that he thought Cox had done his good friend justice. "Thucydides, hmm—It will probably go to his head, as I told him, yet between you and me I think it is a fair comparison." So fair, in fact, that it made Percy even more regretful about his repeated failures to bring about Foote's election to the National Institute. Seeing Elizabeth Spencer at *The Southern Review* affair put an idea in Percy's head, though. Spencer had been elected to the Institute earlier in the year and was, Percy knew, an admirer and friend of Foote's. "I have a proposition for you," Percy wrote to Spencer in early December.

> If you're of a mind, fine. If not, okay too.
> It's about Shelby Foote. I think it is a scandal he is not in the Institute. *The Civil War: A Narrative* is emerging as one of the great American works of this century.
> I've nominated him in the past without success. Maybe my colleagues think I'm pushing a friend—log rolling—
> Anyhow, it's a suggestion.

Percy's one venture into literary-political scheming came a cropper. Despite his and Spencer's efforts, the Institute passed Foote over. ("Thanks for giving it a try for Shelby," he would write to her the following fall.)

Honors did not stop coming Percy's way. On February 2, at the Dana Center at Loyola University, the Catholic Book Club presented Percy the twentieth annual Campion Award. Percy valued the prize for several reasons, among them the historical significance of Thomas Campion, the poet-Jesuit who had remained a faithful defender of the Catholic church during the religious persecutions of Queen Elizabeth. (The general performance of the English Catholic church during the Reformation was a cause of deep ancestral shame to Percy—one reason he esteemed the exceptions, the Mores and the Campions, all the more highly.) Percy was also pleased to be recognized by the Jesuits, the order that had been instrumental in bringing him into the church. Beginning with Father J. J. McCarthy, who had instructed him and Bunt, a number of Jesuits at Loyola (and from elsewhere), Father Tom Clancy, Father Louis Twomey, and Father C. J. McNaspy had become trusted friends. Percy was not above poking fun at the Jesuits' intellectual pride and their sometimes questionable loyalty to the cause they were supposed to serve, but Percy saw their mission as not so unlike his own. If he found the modesty of the Benedictines more attractive, he knew he was, in temperament, closer to the Jesuits.

Presenting the prize that evening was a young Jesuit from New York City, Father Patrick Samway, the literary editor of *America* and a scholar of southern literature. A month before the ceremony, Samway had written to Percy asking permission to write his biography. Percy granted the request, although he insisted that Samway not subject him to interviews about "his past life, recollections of family, etc.," the mere thought of which, Percy said, bored him "stiff." (Percy was not as averse to biographical inquiries as he sometimes protested. Four years earlier he had been most encouraging when Lewis Lawson proposed a similar project, even offering to sit down and talk with him should Lawson desire; poor health, however, had made it impossible for Lawson to pursue the biography.)

Little distracted Percy during the next few months. Percy's revisions went as well as they could, although the book still struck him as an unsatisfactory mess. *Harper's* came begging for a contribution, but Percy, having no time to write anything new, gave them his Chekhov Lecture (which had been published in a limited edition by Rhoda Faust in 1985). The editors at *Harper's* shortened and revised it—as they had earlier done with the Phinizy Lecture—and the results appeared in the June issue under the title "The Diagnostic Novel." To readers who had been wondering what Percy was up to next, the author's identification at the beginning of the article provided the answer: "He currently is at work on his sixth novel, *The Thanatos Syndrome.*"

And quite far along, in fact. On May 19, Percy sent Robert Giroux what he described as the "first ribbon typescript" of the novel. The novel was passed around the office and read by many on the staff. At Percy's request, Helene Atwan, Farrar, Straus's publicist, gave it to her sister-in-law, Lisa Lewis, a computer specialist who also happened to have a degree in physical anthropology. Although Percy had been eager for Lewis to check for mistakes in his computer terminology, she found a problem with his gorilla Eve: Percy had made her far too large.

"Enjoyed Helene's sister-in-law's comments very much," Percy wrote to Giroux. "They're also valuable and reduce somewhat my chances of looking foolish. Too bad in a way, though: I did want Eve to weigh 350 lbs. and to rest high in an oak, so she could yank Dr. Van Dorn skyward."

By the end of July, Giroux reported that everyone "here seems to be enjoying *The Thanatos Syndrome*, a good omen." Among other things, the omen encouraged the publishers to contemplate a seventy-five-thousand-copy print run (later reduced to fifty-nine thousand), the largest first-edition run Percy had ever had. During the summer and fall Percy mailed in further changes, usually in response to comments from friends who had read it. At the end of the month, the brothers Percy and their families converged on Covington to celebrate Walker's seventieth birthday—an occasion that Percy regarded with rue and amazement. Male Percys didn't usually live so long. During this busy week, Percy drove over the causeway to Ochsner Hospital for his annual physical and was relieved to receive a clean bill of health.

If Percy was feeling a bit more civil, he was certainly in no mood to pick up honorary degrees, not even from Harvard—particularly not from Harvard. On June 4, he wrote to Robert Coles, begging him to defuse any efforts to award him a degree. (Coles had earlier warned him that such efforts were underway.) Much as he wanted to see Coles, Percy told him that it would have to be in March of 1987, when both were expected to speak at the National Convention of Catholic Educators in New Orleans.

While Percy had given copies of the novel to a number of readers after he turned in the typescript to Farrar, Straus, he was somewhat slower in getting copies to two readers whose opinions he particularly valued—Shelby Foote and Robert Coles. On July 15, after making further small corrections, Percy finally sent Coles a corrected copy of the novel, asking him to "point out the more egregious psychiatric blunders." Percy was concerned about far more than minor mistakes. He wanted to know what Coles made of the book's larger argument. The reason is obvious. Coles, and his career, were direct inspirations of the novel, as the book's dedication would make clear. After finishing the novel, Coles called Percy to tell him that he liked it; at the same time, however, he told him to expect the worst from the "secular humanists." "You'd better be ready to take some blows," he warned Percy, "because you're going right to the heart of the problem." Percy wrote to thank Coles for his candor:

> Am most deeply grateful for your taking the trouble to read that messy novel. And for your comments.
> It has caused me much distress—the distress of the subject matter—
> I find myself, like Fr. Smith, somewhat deranged and thinking about

being in Germany in 1934 and staying with a family in Bonn—and the distress of art: spoiling a novel by didacticism, shaking a finger at the "secular humanists." You can really mess up a novel doing this— as well as enrage most reviewers and at least half of women.

Well at least it's good to be rid of it and a source of derangement. My wife thinks I have Alzheimer's.

If Percy went to Coles for an ethical and philosophical reading of the novel, he went to Foote for an aesthetic judgment. He knew that if Foote sensed that the art had been debased for the sake of the message, he would say so. To Percy's surprise, Foote gave a generally encouraging response, tempered by strong reservations about Father Smith's speeches. Although Foote did not greatly object to the priest's confession in the firetower, he found everthing else Smith said heavy-handed and didactic. Percy was relieved that Foote had not objected to more:

> I deeply appreciate your taking time with that peculiar novel—and pinpointing what's wrong. Well, you're right. Every time Fr Smith opens his mouth, he, I, is in trouble. What I do is cut, cut, cut. Thanks to you, I'll probably cut again. You can't get away with a Fr Zossima these days—and probably shouldn't.
>
> My larger concern was with the tone and coherence of the book. Okay, I gather from you and Gwyn that the humor and irony came across. But I worried about the heaviness of the idea—the warning about the Nazi and the pre-Nazi "humanist" scientists. Since you did not object too much to Fr S's "Confession," I reckon you didn't mind. Some folks will—

Percy was clearly divided about his own book. He recognized the conflict it marked between his aesthetic and moral commitments. His lack of confidence is somewhat curious. After all, in that frank letter that he had written to Caroline Gordon after *The Moviegoer* won the National Book Award, he had confessed to being, above all, a "moralist." Yet obviously it was important for him not to seem too much the moralist. Percy's uneasiness over *Thanatos* reveals a concern neither strictly aesthetic nor moral but something of both. There was, as Percy himself realized, something different about this novel. Although all of his novels were animated by a palpable moral and religious sense, they created the illusion of freedom, possibility. Neither characters nor actions seemed predetermined. In *Thanatos*, however, as Percy sensed, the deck seems to have been stacked. He had wanted to make a strong statement; he believed in its truth. But the way in which he had gone about making that statement now seemed less than truthful—truthful, that is, according to the standards of literary truth established by his earlier novels.

Despite Percy's best efforts to short-circuit offers of honors from Harvard, they still came: not only the offer of an honorary degree but an invitation (engineered largely by Dr. William Alfred of the English department) to give the Emerson Lecture in 1987. Percy turned down both. In a letter that he wrote to Robert Coles at the end of September, Percy explained why he did not want to give the lecture: "I felt downright embarrassed about giving the Emerson lecture since, sad to say, I have read very little of Emerson. Like I told you, Bob, I am ill educated—what with pre-med and medical school. I'm still trying to catch up."

This was far from the whole truth. Percy had something close to an obsession with Emerson, Harvard, and the New England intellectual tradition that both represented. (Some of this was doubtless bound up with personal resentment, stemming from his rejection by the school in which both his biological and adoptive fathers had done their graduate work.) As a result of reading Lewis Simpson's essay, Percy had come even more to the view that Emerson's was the mind most singly responsible for legitimizing the abandonment of tradition, history, and even society in the name of the imperial Self and the pursuit of happiness. It was against the more fatal consequences of such thinking that Percy had so long argued. An occasion that would have brought the two thinkers into direct confrontation would have been even more revealing than Percy's confrontation with Melville. Percy's refusal was one of his few displays of intellectual timidity.

In fairness, though, he was not at the top of his powers when he received the invitation. He did not use the word lightly when he told Coles that the novel left him feeling "deranged." (Similarly, in mid-July, he had told Cleanth Brooks that the book had left him in a state of "depression and disorientation.") His mood during the time between his completion of the novel and its publication in March of 1987 vacillated between a kind of sentimental elation and bedrock despair. Writing to Robert Coles on Christmas night, for example, he confessed to grave misgivings about the state of the nation, particularly about the race situation and the rise of a permanent underclass. In the midst of his bleak litany, Percy abruptly shifted subjects, bringing up something that had taken him completely by surprise during Christmas mass:

> The mass was going on, the homily standard—that is, "true" but customary. A not-so-good choir of young rock musicians got going on "Joy to the World," the vocals not so good but enthusiastic. Then it

hit me: What if it should be the case that the entire *Cosmos* had a creator and what if he decided for reasons of his own to show up as a little baby, conceived and born under suspicious circumstances? Well, Bob, you can lay it to Alzheimer's or hang-over or whatever, but—it hit me—I had to pretend I had an allergy attack so I could take out my handkerchief.

For a man who, by his own admission, had never had anything close to a mystical experience, never even a twinge of pentecostal enthusiasm, it was a surprising moment. (He later complained to his friend Berry Morgan, who had moved to West Virginia in 1974, that he wouldn't mind growing old "if God weren't so close-mouthed.") All his life, Percy had been such an intellectually controlling man, such a creature of reason in most respects, that this completely unexpected experience of something beyond his rational ken was both gratifying and frightening.

Despite his many misgiving about *Thanatos*, Percy had strong hopes for its commercial success, even stronger than he had had for *Lancelot*. He knew that he had written a real story, even something of a thriller. The Robert Ludlumesque title conjured high suspense and intrigue. Percy thought it was quite possible that even those readers who objected to the underlying moral argument might be taken in by the yarn. At Roger Straus's request, Percy even agreed to go on a book-promotion tour in late April, something he had never before done. But as he made clear to Farrar, Straus's publicist, Helene Atwan, in a letter he wrote at the end of December, talking about the novel was one thing that he would not do, and particularly not on talk shows:

> I wouldn't mind, if I had written a cookbook or a travel book or a New Orleans historical novel, but *The Thanatos Syndrome* is a carefully wrought novel which was conceived as a whole and is delivered without comment—at least from me. It speaks for itself. There is no way, after all these years and what I have tried to accomplish, that I am going to get in line for "talk shows" with the likes of Jackie Collins and Stephen King.
>
> Try to imagine Faulkner being called on to explain The Sound and the Fury to his talk-show host: "Well, it starts off with this idiot Benjy, see, and—"
>
> Or Graham Greene being "questioned" about Scobie's suicide in the The Heart of the Matter: "Well, it's like this—"
>
> I'll leave it to Andrew Greeley to talk about sex and the love of God.
>
> When I finish "Walker Percy's Creole Cookbook," I'm your man.

Until then, I'm not talking—except for interviews I've already agreed to.

Nevertheless, Percy's willingness to "hawk a book, go to bookstores, read, act nice, sign," as he said to Foote, was itself a significant departure from his usual practice. It may sound melodramatic to assign too ominous a motive to this decision, but it is hard not to think that one reason was his intuition that this might be his last literary outing. The Presbyterian in Percy wanted to "provide," both for himself and for his family, just in case it was.

The book itself appeared in March, a month earlier than originally planned, and, as Percy and Farrar, Straus hoped, the prepublication announcements and early reviews and comments emphasized the "well-told-tale" quality of the novel. *Publishers Weekly*, for instance, said that Percy, without abandoning his serious interests, had "integrated his philosophizing into a fast-paced narrative with the suspense of a thriller." A highly sympathetic profile in *U.S. News & World Report* reported Roger Straus's confidence that *Thanatos* would be a "breakthrough book." The profile's author, Julia Reed, called the book "wildly entertaining, but also deadly serious." *The New York Times Magazine* ran a well crafted profile by Malcolm Jones in its March 22 edition. Jones brought together elements of Percy's life story, vignettes of Percy at and about home, and a few remarks about the novel that once again emphasized its taut, dramatic plot. *Time* magazine, unswervingly generous to Percy's books from *The Moviegoer* on, proved true to form: "The theme may be familiar," Paul Gray wrote, "but the variations decidedly are not. For one thing, this novel embodies Percy's most explicit attack on contemporary materialism and science. For another, the philosophical warfare has been artfully disguised as a thriller."

The eastern leg of Percy's five-day "reading tour" began on April 13, when he and Bunt flew to New York. The next day, Tuesday, included a Book-of-the-Month Club luncheon (*Thanatos* was a club "dual main selection") and afternoon and early evening "stop-in-and-signs" at four different bookstores. Wednesday opened with informal "stop-ins" at two stores. These were followed by lunch with Mitchel Levitas, editor of *The New York Times Book Review*, a visit to the Farrar, Straus offices to sign books for out-of-city stores and then one more informal "stop-in" and a short break before the night's activity. At seven-thirty, before a crowd that spilled out into the street, Percy read from several of his novels at Books & Co. The next day included a morning flight to Washington, a couple of afternoon stop-ins, and a formal signing at Kramer Books in the evening. At Kramer's, as at other stores, it was impossible for Percy to accommodate all who had lined up to have their books signed. He was tired, sleeping more poorly than usual at night, and his old intestinal troubles were beginning to flare up. Yet there were still two more stop-ins the next morning before the Percys boarded a plane to fly back to Louisiana. The plan was to rest for two weeks before embarking on the western leg of the tour, but the plan soon had to be scuttled. Percy's intestinal troubles had grown worse. Severe esophageal constrictions had led to something called a "Mallory-Weiss tear," which caused internal bleeding. Although Percy appeared to be on the mend, his internist, Dr. George Riser, cautioned against resuming the "reading tour." Riser's concern proved sound, for the constrictions returned in May, and on June 5 Percy had to enter the hospital for an esophageal endoscopy and dilation of his stricture.

While recuperating, Percy took perverse pleasure in reading one of the more intelligently dismissive reviews of *Thanatos* that was to appear. Terrence Rafferty in *The New Yorker* found Percy's latest offering, like all of his work since *Lancelot*, another windy denunciation of the modern world. Reading it, Rafferty complained, was like "tuning in, unawares, to the Christian Broadcasting Network, whose mixture of talk-shows, Bible-thumping oratory, commercials for Jesus, and 'Man from U.N.C.L.E.' reruns is so rivetingly weird." Rafferty granted that a "generous explanation" of the newest novel would acknowledge that Percy was "trying to get his message across in what he takes to be the authentic language of his times—the language of the tube," but Rafferty felt Percy's play with the idiom was inept, lacking irony, a bit like "an author on a talk show who finds himself talking about Vegas with the celebs." The real gravamen of his critique, though, was directed against what he called the "formal bad faith" apparent in Percy's effort to depict the decline of American civilization:

> His imperfect Southern knight, Tom More, is less a vehicle for genuine social satire than a prime-time fantasy avenger, an Equalizer who em-bodies the combined virtues of Kierkegaard, Harry Stack Sullivan, and Robert E. Lee. If his creator showed any awareness that the need for such figures is itself an expression of impotence—a product of the living room philosopher's frustration at his remoteness from the cul-ture's catastrophes—he'd be a lot more persuasive.

Rafferty's criticism was at once so fine and so wrong that Percy did not quite know how to square its contradiction. On one hand, Percy thought Rafferty was one of the few reviewers who was truly "on to" him, who saw the real anger and spleen in his denunciations of the contemporary world. ("This is one mad Irish ex-Catholic, I bet, and he sure smoked me out," Percy joked to one acquaintance.) But he also felt Rafferty somehow missed the crucial point: the comic hope behind the apocalyptic grimness. And Percy had intended that hope to come out precisely through his quite conscious construction of a character, an "imperfect Southern knight," who is the very embodiment of Percy's own impotence—impotence and emptiness and sickness unto death. More *is* remote from his culture's catastrophes. He tries to unravel the mystery of a pervasive strangeness, but his motive is curiosity, not the desire to avenge. The significance of what he discovers is revealed to him by Father Rinaldo Smith, the whiskey priest who descries a similarity between the lethal sentimentality of our good-hearted "qualitarians" and that of the good Weimar physicians. (One of the maddening paradoxes of this age, Father Smith declares in his brilliant, deranged homily at the novel's end, is that it is a time of "Believing thieves and decent unbelievers," when the greatest evils are committed "tenderly," in the name of the Good.)

More's highest function in this novel is to apprehend the meaning of the apocalyptic vision that is revealed to him by Father Smith. But—and this is what Rafferty seemed to miss—the apocalyptic imagination is not primarily concerned with what Rafferty described as "marking time until the end, the fiery climax." The apocalyptic narrative—and Percy's ultimate model was the Revelation of St. John—does reveal the tragic, self-destructive pattern of human history that issues, again and again, in fiery climaxes, but it presents this vision of the end in order to open the eyes of those who read or hear it. The apocalyptic vision allows man to see history somewhat as God does, not only to observe the workings of evil but also to be able to start life anew, now with greater understanding and with hope. The apocalyptic vision is profoundly hopeful, but Rafferty mistook it for mere jeremiad.

As Percy regained his strength, he took a few short trips, one, in late July, up to Sewanee, where he and Bunt visited Brinkwood and hiked on the trails that ran near it. To Foote, he later reported that he walked to the teahouse that the two of them had helped build almost fifty years before. "I seemed to recall an inscription," he told Foote. "Nothing visible. We began brushing away the dirt of the doorstep and here it is, more unmistakable than in the photo: July 4, 1938."

By September, Percy was willing to take on something even more strenuous. He had been invited to attend a White House dinner honoring the state visit of the Swedish prime minister, Ingvar Carlsson. On the surface, there would appear to have been little rhyme or reason to Percy's invitation, apart from his being one of those figures of accomplishment in the arts, or sports, or business who are routinely invited to White House affairs to give them an air of distinction. Yet, in fact, there might have been some slight significance to Percy's being invited— recognition, on the part of Reagan staffers, that Percy had written a novel quite congenial to Reagan's stand on an increasingly volatile social issue. It did not trouble Percy that he was suddenly becoming a darling of the Right, but he had strong doubts about accepting the invitation. Bunt, however, gave him just enough encouragement so that he could say he accepted for her sake. The truth was, he was flattered and curious. The dinner was on Wednesday, September 9, at seven-thirty, and it went by in a blur of formalities and stiff exchanges. At one point, though, he did have a few words with President Reagan about their respective bouts with skin cancer. It was obvious to Percy, but not in the least surprising, that President Reagan had no idea what Percy did. But like most of his countrymen, Percy found the president a genial, affable man.

In early October, Percy, Bunt, and the Ellises flew up to Maine and spent a week in quiet seclusion in Tenants Harbor. (Percy and Bunt had come up to the same place the previous October with Phin and Roy and their wives.) Percy was already thinking about another book—in fact, had been thinking about it since early summer—and was now reading the works of a rather obscure sixteenth-century scholastic, John of Ponsot, in preparation for what he thought might be his last major work of philosophy, something explicitly combining semiotics and theology. Percy hoped to begin his book by showing how completely inadequate the social sciences were in presenting a satisfactory theory of man. This would be the prolegomenon to his more explicitly religious argument.

Back in Covington, Percy wrote to a scholar with whom he had been corresponding for some time, Dr. Ken Ketner, a Peircean and a professor of philosophy at Texas Tech. "Here is my situation," Percy explained:

> I'm thinking about writing a book, perhaps entitled "Thirdness" (Can't call it The Delta Factor). The thesis is that CSP's [Charles Sanders Peirce's] Thirdness, triadicity, properly understood and properly applied, can go a long way in pointing some right directions in the current mess in which the social sciences find themselves. Or, as Thomas Kuhn puts it in his "Structure of Scientific Revolutions": the traditional scientific paradigm (Cartesian and Newtonian), which has been so extraordinarily successful in the physical, chemical and biological sciences—has proved quite as spectacularly unsuccessful in the so-called social sciences, i.e. the sciences of man *qua* man. . . .

> True enough. Of course, what Kuhn does not know (here at least) is that there may be a paradigm which could do the job, Peirce's triadic theory—applied correctly—and I mean quite as rigorously (if not deterministically) and scientifically as Newtonian mechanics.

What Percy particularly wanted from Ketner was help in finding books that documented and deplored the existing chaos in the social sciences. In this, however, Percy could find little satisfaction. As he soon discovered, there was almost no literature written either from within or without the social sciences that even acknowledged the sort of incoherence Percy saw. But this in no way lessened his desire to make the case himself; it only confirmed his intuition that there was need for the kind of book he was trying to write.

On Friday, October 23, Gwyn and Shelby Foote arrived in Covington to spend a few nights. Percy decided to take Bunt, Shelby, Gwyn, and a visiting researcher to Bechacs. It was a brilliant, crystal-clear day, perfect for looking out over Lake Pontchartrain, eating seafood, and drinking bourbon. Over drinks, the two old friends indulged in their usual banter, including a discussion of the regional variations on the meaning of the word "cock" (the peculiarity being that in some parts of the South it meant the penis, while in others it meant the vagina). Talk of organs prompted Percy to announce that his were soon to receive a thorough going over. His annual physical at Ochsner was coming up in early November. Foote, turning partially serious, urged Percy not to let the doctors cut if they discovered prostate problems. Foote spoke from experience: He had received successful radiation treatment for prostate cancer a few years before. "Just don't let them cut without considering other possibilities," he warned. Percy said it was not his prostate but his memory that worried him. "Yes," Foote added, "but try to remember what I just told you."

A few weeks later, Percy came home from Ochsner with a clean bill of health. Everything looked fine, according to the doctors. Continuing with his work, he read John of Ponsot and reread Peirce, making notes and writing preliminary arguments. On January 9, he sent Roger Straus a playful warning: "I'm working on a book on semiotics which will sell at the most 200 copies. But since FSG has gotten rich on *Presumed Innocent* and *Bonfire,* you can afford a tremendous advance."

Percy had also been working on a short address that he would deliver less than a week later before the Pontifical Council for Culture (PCC) in Rome. Percy's invitation to serve as a participant on the International Council of the PCC resulted from the good offices of Father C. J. McNaspy, who had been in Rome for six months the previous year working on the encyclopedia of Jesuit history. One of the council organizers, Father Herve Carrier, had asked McNaspy who would be a good representative from the South. "Walker Percy," was McNaspy's immediate reply. Father Carrier wrote, and Percy accepted. He would be one of fourteen lay contributors to the council at the January 14–17 sessions. Bunt came along, busying herself with sight-seeing while her husband put in long days at the Palazzo San Calisto at the Vatican. The first meeting began on Thursday morning at nine-thirty, lasted until twelve-thirty, and resumed in the midafternoon after lunch and a long break—a schedule that more or less held for the next three days. Apart from an audience with Pope John Paul and mass on Sunday, the group stayed at the table, heard reports on the activities of the PCC, and then listened to ideas for evangelization put forth by each of the participants. When Percy's time came—he spoke between a member of Britain's House of Lords and a Nigerian feminist—he read a fourteen-page paper that he had finished writing only the day before the meeting started.

In his address, Percy cited all the usual cultural suspects contributing to the spiritual decline of the nation: the deadening power of the mass media, consumerism, and the tyranny of scientific expertise and scien-tism. "To state the matter plainly: to the layman, the ordinary denizen of the modern technological society, it seems only natural that, in the face of the mysteries of life which confront him, the mysteries of nature, his own health, indeed of his very self and his existence, the secret of his being—nothing seems more natural than that *they* know the answers. *They* of course are scientists, the experts, the professors, the technolo-gists of whatever fields."

Percy then gave perhaps his clearest explanation of why he believed the Christian story was such a scandal to the modern mind: It is precisely the generalizing habit inculcated by the scientific worldview—a habit that "awards degrees of significance and value in direct proportion to the level of abstraction"—that is so offended and befuddled by a teaching that rests on a "single historical event." The modern mind tries to tame this scandal by generalizing it into what Percy called "an instance of such-and-such recurring human proclivity for attributing divine manifes-tations to particular historical events." To the extent it succeeds, it relegates Christianity to an ethical system based on a quaint "myth."

Percy, however, did not conclude that secularism would necessarily triumph. As he saw the matter, evangelization would have a better chance of succeeding in a "thoroughly secularized United States in the year 2000" than it would in a society "nominally and perhaps superfi-cially Christian, say that of Victorian England or 19th-century Austria."

The reason was dialectical: The promises of secularism will have thoroughly exhausted themselves in that none-too-distant future society, the anonymous consumer having by then "exhausted the roster of 'needs-satisfaction' . . . whether the latter be the consumption of the manifold goods of a sophisticated consumer society or the services of four hundred or so different schools of psychotherapy."

After this guardedly optimistic note, Percy discussed the possible uses of television for evangelization, possibilities fraught with danger because of the association of televangelists with hucksterism and fraudulent behavior. Nevertheless, Percy held that the radio and television broadcasts of Monsignor Fulton Sheen some thirty years in the past had been tremendously successful.

Most important, Percy concluded, was that the church not succumb to what he called the "dangers of over-acculturation." He reminded his fellow panelists of what had happened when mainline Protestant denominations paid too much attention to the opinion polls: "Instead of serving as the yeast which leavens the cultural lump, they tend to disappear into the culture." Percy offered his own vision of what the church should do:

> By remaining faithful to its original commission, by serving its people with love, especially the poor, the lonely and the dispossessed, and by not surrendering its doctrinal steadfastness, sometimes even the very contradiction of culture by which it serves as a sign, surely it serves culture best.

The rest of the panel received Percy's words graciously, though he sensed that some might have been put off by his conservatism. Most questions addressed to him concerned the uses of television, the character of televangelists in general—and of Jimmy Swaggart in particular.

Percy returned from Rome feeling tired and sickly. He and Bunt assumed it was the result of travel. In early February, Percy noticed that he was getting up frequently in the night to urinate. When he complained to Bunt, she suggested that he see Dr. James Roberts, a professor of urology at Tulane who also had a practice in Covington. Percy was not greatly concerned. He had received a good report from Ochsner only three months before. But, to be safe, he made an appointment.

Bunt Percy was trying to take a nap in the afternoon of Tuesday, February 9, when she heard her husband return from his check-up. She immediately sensed that something was wrong, sensed it in the tentative way that her husband opened the bedroom door.

"Bunt," Percy hesitated. "Dr. Roberts saw something he didn't like."

The problem was the prostate, and, fearing the worst, Dr. Roberts said that Percy would need to have an operation as soon as possible. The operation was tentatively set for early March. Roy and Sarah drove over from Greenville to be with Bunt, but Percy came down with a cold, and the operation was put off a few days. Finally, on, Thursday, March 10, in the St. Tammany Parish Hospital, Dr. Roberts performed the operation. Shortly after making an incision, Roberts saw that the situation was worse than he had suspected. Cancer had not only invaded the prostate but metastasized to surrounding tissue and the lymph nodes. If it had been five years earlier, Roberts later explained, he would have sewn Percy back up, but he knew there were new treatments that might give his patient a chance. Roberts performed a radical prostatectomy and a bilateral lymphadenectomy, removing as much of the malignant material as he could reach without risking further complications. After the operation, Roberts gave Bunt and Percy the full truth. He described the extent of the cancer and said that there was only a small hope of arresting its spread. Percy absorbed the news with a mixture of resignation and anger. Medicine, he knew, was a sloppy science, but it disappointed him that his physcians at Ochsner had missed the problem. (In fact, as George Riser later explained, it was quite easy to miss such a cancer in a routine examination.) To make matters worse, Percy's recovery from the operation was slow and painful. Four weeks after the first operation, on April 13, Percy was opened up again, this time for a radical orchiectomy, to lower his testosterone level. Once back on his feet, he was put on a new hormonal treatment ("They preferred this to radiation," he wrote to fraternity brother Charles Poe, who had recently written to describe his own bout with prostate cancer. "I hope they know what they're doing.") To most friends and acquaintances he presented as good a face as possible. But the doctor in Percy knew too well that his time was short.

Awareness of the prognosis did not seem to slow Percy down, at least not at first. He decided that he would keep doing what he had always done: write and stay close to his family. In May, he received a call from Lynne Cheney, the head of the National Endowment for the Humanities, asking him if he would accept the honor of delivering the Jefferson Lecture in 1989. After some hesitation, Percy accepted. He decided that he would use what he was then working on—Peircean semiotics as a basis for a new science of man—as the material for his speech. Although the lectureship was not officially announced until August, Lewis Simpson got wind of the appointment through Ellis Sandoz, a member of the LSU political science department and of the National Council on the Humanities, the body that selected the Jefferson Lecturer. On June 2,

Simpson wrote to congratulate Percy on being the fourth "literary person" to receive the "unique recognition" of the Lectureship (the other
three being Lionel Trilling, Robert Penn Warren, and Cleanth Brooks).

Recognition of Percy's accomplishments and his place in American letters came in many ways and from many directions. Percy's admiring
readers, always a devoted group, grew steadily in number, and Percy
made his best effort to remain accessible to those who tried to speak to
him. For most years of his writing life he kept a listed phone number and
would talk patiently with callers who sounded moderately sane. (Percy
spoke for more than an hour with one distraught woman caller, trying
to coax her out of her despondency. At the end of their conversation,
she thanked him effusively, adding that she wouldn't have bothered him
if she had been able to reach Norman Mailer first. Percy felt suitably
chastened.) Percy took even more time responding to the hundreds of
letters he received. It was, to him, almost a point of principle that he do
so. He saw his novels as the first gestures in the act of communication;
the responses and counter-responses completed the act. But there was
also something of that old sense of obligation that he had acquired from
Uncle Will: a willingness to hear the troubles of others, and to offer
advice and help when possible. Those who wrote asking for money—
and they were more than a few—often received what they asked for.

Sometimes coping with fans could be amusing. One weekday in the
summer of 1988, for example, Percy drove his truck to Wendy's to pick
up one of his favorite fast-food lunches, a bacon cheeseburger and iced
tea. While he was waiting in the drive-in line, an earnest college-age
boy—an Episcopalian minister's son from Baton Rouge, it turned out—
hopped into the front seat next to Percy and began talking quickly.
Having read that Wendy's was Percy's favorite restaurant, and also that
Percy drove a pickup, he had been loitering around the restaurant all
morning in the hope that Percy would drive up so that he could ask for
an interview. Percy was so astonished by the boy's determination that
he took him home and talked to him for an hour.

Percy's sense of obligation sometimes got the better of him. One
Friday in 1988—June 17, in fact—he received an early morning call
from the Louisiana governor, Buddy Roemer. The governor wanted to
know if Percy would serve on the LSU Board of Supervisors. Percy, a bit
flustered but feeling somewhere in his heart that he should do something
for his state, accepted. Attending his first meeting the following Friday,
Percy realized that he had made a bad mistake. He said very little during
the short, routine discussion of leases and scholarships, but he saw and
heard enough to realize that he had no business being there. The following week, he resigned, citing health reasons.

Health was no empty excuse, but if Percy was ailing, he put up a good front among his friends. In the middle of July, he and Bunt and their grandsons, Jack and David, joined the Ellises in Highlands, and Percy was strong enough to climb to the top of Mount Satulah. Percy, perhaps a little more than usual, did need his time off, and the Ellises accommodated by taking the grandson off for hikes. Percy was devoted to all his grandsons, and in David, something of a loner and a reader, he saw a great deal of himself.

On August 7, Percy wrote Simpson to say that he was just getting over surgery and a three-week vacation in the mountains. Above all, though, he wanted to thank Simpson and Sandoz for the part they had played in getting him the Jefferson Lectureship. "I'm really not much on such occasions, as you know, but this one I couldn't turn down (and Bunt wouldn't let me)." There had been one other offer Percy had been unable to refuse. In the spring, shortly after recovering from the operation, he had been notified by Thomas Fleming, editor of *Chronicles*, a conservative journal of cultural commentary published in Rockland, Illinois, that he had won the Ingersoll Foundation's T. S. Eliot Award. Since 1983, the first year of the award, all winners had been European and Latin American, Jorge Luis Borges and Octavio Paz among them. Percy was flattered by the honor and impressed by the fifteen-thousand-dollar honorarium. Even though it meant traveling to Chicago in November and giving a speech, Percy accepted.

By late summer, though, he was beginning to have doubts. In the middle of August he began to suffer from a low-grade fever—"pyrexia of unknown origin," as he explained to one correspondent—and in early September he went to the hospital for more tests. No explanation could be found, though, and by the end of the month Percy seemed resigned to living and writing with discomfort. "I have been tolerably well," he reported to Lewis Simpson, "but still annoyed by a low-grade fever, which they can't track down. I'm thinking of throwing away the thermometer (which, like Hans Castorp, I came to know as the 'trouble stick')." The allusion to Mann's famous tubercular was not whimsical: Percy had begun to fear that his old familiar, TB, had returned. Indeed, his physican, George Riser, was surprised to see that Percy often seemed more disturbed by the possible return of his old disease than he was by the cancer.

Percy continued to be the voracious reader that he always had been. In the autumn, as well as going through a collection of essays on Eric Voegelin edited by Ellis Sandoz and a biography of Caroline Gordon recently completed by Ann Waldron, he read Chekhov's short stories with renewed fondness. "I don't really care for the plays," he told Shelby Foote, "but I believe he has no equal in the short story." It was not

simply the artistry Percy admired, but the fine, subtle humor, which to
Percy seemed to suggest a religious sense of life despite Chekhov's
avowed atheism.

On November 3, Percy and Bunt made the trip to Chicago for the
Eliot Award. In the city that always reminded Percy of that dread summer when his father committed suicide, the Percys stayed in the Drake
Hotel. That night they had dinner with Thomas Fleming, and afterward
Percy invited the editor up to his hotel room to watch a football game
and share a bottle of bourbon. "Bunt kept a close eye on how many
drinks he had," Fleming later recalled. "It was clear she was concerned
about his health, but he gave no sign of being ill." The awards dinner
was held the next night in the Drake's turn-of-the century ballroom.
Fleming introduced Percy to Edward Shills, the recipient of the other
award that evening (the Richard M. Weaver Award for Scholarly
Letters) as well as to the other editors on the *Chronicles* staff. All of
them, like Fleming himself, had degrees from the University of North
Carolina.

"Good God, Tom," Percy remarked, "are you running some sort of
Tarheel conspiracy here?"

"Why do you think you are here?" Fleming replied.

For his speech, Percy gave yet another version of his novelist-as-
diagnostician theme, but if "Physician as Novelist" had the air of the
tried and true, it was at least succinct in formulation. "But what I wish
to propose to you is this," Percy announced near the beginning of his
talk:

> . . . that for a certain type of educated denizen of this age it is only
> through, first, the love of the scientific method and, second, through
> its elevation and exhaustion as the ultimate method of knowing that
> one becomes open to other forms of knowing—sciencing in the root
> sense of the word—and accordingly, at least I think so, to a new kind
> of revival of Western humanism and the Judeo-Christian tradition—if
> we survive.

Almost immediately upon returning from Chicago, Percy set to work
on his Jefferson Lecture, and by the end of December he had completed
a forty-one-page typescript, which he titled "Science, Religion and the
Tertium Quid." The tertium quid was what Percy elsewhere called
"thirdness," the application of Peirce's triadic model of human communication to that unbridgeable gap between the scientific and Judeo-
Christian explanations of man. Percy was not happy with the paper,
much of which he had pirated from an essay that he had written many

years before but never published, "Is a Theory of Man Possible?" Nevertheless, he sent the speech off to several people to read and settled in for
the ordeal of the holidays. After New Year's, Percy and Bunt drove down
to Perdido Key, Florida, for three days to join in celebrating Roy and
Sarah's fiftieth anniversary. "The old folks had a good time," Percy
reported to Foote.

Back in his study, Percy decided to cut the first twenty or so pages of
his lecture, a long section dealing with the differences between the
religious and scientific views of man. Instead, he decided he would con-
centrate almost exclusively on the radical incoherence within the sciences themselves, particularly when they tried to square their picture of
man as an organism with their understanding of mental phenomena. As
he would say in the final version, "Can anyone imagine how a psychology of the psyche, like Freud's or Jung's, however advanced, can ever
make contact with a Skinnerian psychology of neurones, however modified and elaborated it is, for example, by some such refinements as
Gestalt and 'cognitive' psychology?" The way through this impasse,
Percy would propose, was application of Peirce's triadic model to man's
unique capacity for asserting meanings through symbols, above all language.

By the middle of January the lecture had assumed a very different shape
and even a new title. As Percy told Lewis Lawson in a letter dated
January 17, "Present title: 'The Fateful Rift: The San Andreas Fault of
the Mind.' " (Percy had written Lawson mainly to thank him for *Following Percy*, a collection of the essays that the University of Maryland
scholar had been writing since the 1960s. Percy considered the book one
of the better critical studies of his work.)

Percy talked very little about his health. In a letter to Robert Coles,
he talked about his prostate operation but said that he was "doing all
right now." Though Percy did not complain, his friends could see that
he did not look strong.

Percy held up fairly well during the week of the Jefferson Lecture.
Arriving on May 1, he submitted to several interviews and meetings
both before and after the lecture, which was held Wednesday night, May
3, in the capacious Department of Commerce auditorium on Constitution Avenue. Percy did not look or sound his best that evening. The
auditorium was full, and the atmosphere was expectant. Lynne Cheney
and Robert Hollander, a professor of literature at Princeton, made introductory remarks, while Percy sat somewhat uneasily in his chair, trying
to make out his family in the front row. (Bunt, Roy, Sarah, Ann and
her two sons, and assorted Percy nephews, nieces, and cousins were in

attendance.) Percy had a hard time settling into his speech, but even if he had been in top form, it would have been difficult to delight the crowd with the rather abstract paper that he had written. The intellectual crusader in Percy had won out over the beguiling entertainer, at least for the Jefferson Lecture. But in a way it didn't matter. Most people in the audience were there because of the man and the body of work. The resounding applause at the end of the speech was more for the man and the body of his work than for the speech. Most of that audience made their way across the street for the reception at the American History Museum, and Percy dutifully shook hands with almost all of them. There was, however, one person in the crowd whose hand Percy was delighted to shake. Lewis Lawson, the man who had been following Percy so faithfully and intelligently for years, finally came face to face with his subject. Their exchange, though short, was like the resumption of a long dialogue. Lawson told Percy that he had read an 1865 speech by Peirce in which the Harvard philosopher noted that his triadic model had the same shape as the Trinity, Peirce quickly adding that he hoped that religious believers would not be offended by his pointing out the similarity. "I wish you had told me that before the lecture," Percy said. Lawson was struck by how frail and tired Percy looked. He feared that his first meeting with the man would also be the last.

Less than a week after returning home Percy began to feel abdominal and back pain. As he told Foote in a letter of June 8, he thought at first that it was his usual diverticulitis, but when weeks passed and it did not relent he went to the hospital for an examination. "Colon was normal," he reported, "but there were masses around the aorta and along spine. Don't yet know what it is, but presumably it's metastases from prostate carcinoma or pancreatic C A."

The cancer clearly was on the move again, and Percy, if he had given in to his wishes, would have done nothing about it. But he could tell that Bunt wanted him to fight. First he saw doctors at Johns Hopkins, but they had nothing to offer over what was being tried in Covington. In July, though, Percy learned of a new experimental treatment being administered at the Mayo Clinic in Minnesota. He dreaded the prospect of traveling back and forth, but it seemed worth one last effort. Percy wrote Foote on July 29, telling him that he was off to Mayo the next day —"on the strength of a new drug combo (something called interferon and 5-FW) said to be promising in some cancers." Percy's reservations about going through the ordeal were strong:

> The worst thing is the travelling and hospitals. Flying around the U.S. is awful and hospitals are no place for anyone, let alone a sick man.

I'll tell you what I've discovered. Dying, if that's what it comes to, is no big thing, since I'm ready for it, am prepared for it by the Catholic faith which I believe. What is a pain is not even the pain but the nuisance. It is a tremendous bother (and expense) to everyone. Worst of all is the indignity. Who wants to go to pot before strangers, be an object of head shaking for friends, a lot of trouble to kin? I know the answer to this of course: false pride—who are you to be too proud to go the way of all flesh—or as you would write on the chart at Bellevue: "—the patient went rapidly downhill and made his exitus."

Seriously, and now that I think of it, in this age of unbelief I am astounded at how few people facing certain indignity in chronic illness make an end to it. Few if any. I am not permitted to.

Given his preferences, as Percy went on to say, he would stay in Covington and work on what he was now calling *Contra Gentiles*, "a somewhat smart ass collection of occasional pieces, including one which should interest you—'Three New Signs, All More Important Than and Different From the 59,018 Signs of Charles Sanders Peirce.' "

What would have gone into this volume is unclear. Possibly a reworking of the Jefferson Lecture, probably a personal reverie entitled a "Lenten Diary," and possibly an essay that Clifton Fadiman had commissioned him to write on what he believed (and which would appear in the book *Living Philosophers: The Reflections of Some Eminent Men and Women of Our Time*). Percy had to chuckle somewhat at accepting Fadiman's commission because it reminded him too clearly of the "This I Believe" show that he had mocked in *The Moviegoer*. "If you live long enough," he told a friend, "you end up being the butt of the jokes you told when young." Percy used his discomfort as the introduction to his essay, "Why Are You a Catholic?":

> This assignment and the question above (which is sometimes asked in the same context) arouse in me, I'll admit, certain misgivings. One reason, the first that comes to mind, is that the prospect of giving one's "testament," saying it straight out, puts me in mind of an old radio program on which people, mostly show-business types as I recall, uttered their resounding credos, which ended with a sonorous Ed Murrow flourish: *This—I Believe.*

Despite his misgivings, the resulting essay was a wise and funny exploration of the near-tautology he enunciated at the beginning: "The reason I am a Catholic is that I believe that what the Catholic Church proposes is true." Reading this essay, one wishes all the more that Percy had not abandoned the more explicitly religious material that he had developed in the first draft of his Jefferson Lecture.

One of the interesting points of the essay was Percy's disquisition on the Jews. From *The Moviegoer* on, Percy's more perceptive readers had noticed his preoccupation with Jews, the alienated people par excellence, as the most reliable barometers of the spiritual state of the world. Although his remarks about the role of the Jews in history were somewhat cryptic, in this credo he made his view explicit. Apart from the sign of one's self, the Jews, Percy argued, were the "only other sign in the world which cannot be encompassed by theory." That, he explained, was why they were "hated by theorists like Hitler and Stalin. The Jews cannot be gotten around."

> Semitic? Semiotic? Jews and the science of signs? Yes, because in this age of the lost self, lost in the desert of theory and consumption, nothing of significance remains but signs. And only two signs are of significance in a world where all theoretical cats are gray. One is oneself and the other is the Jews. But for the self that finds itself lost in the desert of theory and consumption, there remains only one sign, the Jews. By "the Jews" I mean not only Israel, the exclusive people of God, but the worldwide *ecclesia* instituted by one of them, God-become-man, a Jew.

The "scandal" of the Jews, Percy argued, was their historical reality. They were not a myth; they were not generalizable. Their plight was specific, historical, real, and ultimately significant—and Percy's access to the truth of what the Jews signified was by way of what he called "that Jewish sect, Catholicism."

For a few months, the Mayo treatment seemed to work. It kept the disease from advancing further. But the treatment was itself exhausting and left Percy's bowels in disorder for days. Getting to and from Mayo was itself an ordeal, although Roy made it somewhat less so by flying Bunt and Percy on some of the trips. Percy continued to hold to most of his routines through the fall, attending the book club with Bunt and the Wednesday lunches with the men. He continued to read the dozens of manuscripts sent to him by publishers eager for comment and to help young writers whenever and however he could. The time he valued most, though, was the time alone with his family, the Saturday lunches in particular, when he sat down with Bunt, Mary Pratt, Ann, John, and his grandsons (or at least three of the four: Robert was off in the Navy).

It was very important to him at this time to make things clear to his daughters. Of the two, Percy was in some ways more worried about Ann. Mary Pratt had gone through hard times in her marriage with Byrne

Lobdell, but Percy was confident of her strength and particularly of her faith. Then, too, Percy had a special bond with Mary Pratt: They had both been orphaned. He often affectionately addressed her as Sissy, as though she were a kind of sibling in their shared experience.

Percy also had great confidence in Ann's character and determination. He was vastly proud of all that she had accomplished in school, in her work, and in her family. His one concern was that she might forever abandon the faith that he knew had saved his life. One afternoon, he talked to her about the importance of that faith. He told Ann about how he had almost lost his in the 1970s, when he turned to psychology and other supports, even though they had failed him earlier in his life. Percy confessed to her that turning away from the church at that time had been the worst mistake in his life. It had been hard, he admitted, to find his way back. Even harder to admit to—though he did—was the sadness he felt at how badly he had treated his family during that dark time. It made him all the more grateful for how closely they had stood by him, and he was particularly grateful for Ann's bravery and honesty in confronting him when he had been most neglectful. "I think sometimes," he said to Ann, "that God gave me such a wonderful family later in life to make up for the sadness that went on in my family when I was young." Percy urged her repeatedly not to turn away from the church. "It was what saved my life," he said. It and his family, he told her, were his strength.

By late November, Percy was finding it hard to write. The pain in his back and his stomach was returning. A visiting researcher who had come to look through Percy's library witnessed Percy writing what might have been one of his last commissioned works. *Condé Nast Traveler*, for a spread about the South, had asked a number of southern cultural figures to write on assorted regional topics. For some curious reason, they had asked Percy to write about Louisiana food. Percy growled to his guest that Condé Nast had made a bad mistake. He had little fondness for Louisiana food. (In fact, he had never cared much about any kind of food.) But if there was any kind of food he would praise, it would be the food he got at the Waffle House, his favorite eatery.

"Why don't you write about that?" his guest suggested.

"You think they would take it?" Percy asked.

"Of course they would."

Percy sat down in the living room and wrote for about ten minutes. Then he returned to the library and tried it on his guest.

I may not be the best person to ask about Louisiana food, and restaurants, but since you've asked, I'll tell you. I really can't stand

Cajun food, despite its high fashion nationwide. One look at K Paul's chef piling all that heavy cream sauce and messed-up shrimp on a perfectly good fish, and the gorge rises. The best restaurant in New Orleans is still Galatoire's: straightforward fish and undisguised lamb chops done to a turn without a mountain of stuff—which usually means they've got something to hide.

The best restaurant near Covington, where I live, is the Waffle House, a chain restaurant located just off the Interstates throughout the South. Not only is the standard waffle and sausages superb, the chicken is the best anywhere. The people are pleasant. There are truckers off the Interstate and Phoenix retirees headed for the Carolina mountains. There are regular locals—for example, a foursome of good old boys from their gun-racked pickups, thirtyish, mustachioed Tom Sellecks—wise, stoutish, baseball-capped. The booths are back-to-back, and one can't help overhearing. They talk about their wives: "And I told that woman, one more crack out of her and she's gone—or I'm gone." One bite of waffle drenched in butter and corn syrup, plus Tennessee sausage, plus a huge glass of sweet iced tea, the waitress calling you honey, the *Picayune* opened to the latest political skulduggery, the traffic on U.S. 190 booming along—it's not a bad life.

"You really think they'll take this craziness?" Percy asked, when he finished reading.

The researcher only laughed. But as he returned to his work in the library, the light quickly fading at the end of the autumn day, he had to wonder: Was it possible that he had just heard Percy's last valentine to the fallen world?

By January, it was clear that the treatment was no longer helping. Percy's condition was declining—not rapidly but steadily—and the pain in his back was growing sharper. He stopped going to Mayo but began to make trips to Ochsner for radiation treatments. The doctors hoped the radiation would provide some relief for the pain. For a time it did, though Percy dreaded the drive to and from the hospital. The only good thing about the trips was that they gave Percy another chance to visit his brother Phin. They would always meet below the levee near Ochsner for a picnic lunch that Bunt prepared. Bunt remembers Percy anxiously looking about as they waited for Phin, concerned that he might not arrive in time. When Walker saw Phin's car approaching, his face would immediately brighten. Bunt would excuse herself and go for a short walk on the levee so that the two brothers—always close, but never closer than now—could have a little time alone.

Sometimes, his Wednesday lunchmates, George Cross or Chink Baldwin, would drive him to and from Ochsner. Coming back from one trip, Percy turned to Baldwin and thanked him: "You know, our lunches together have been one of the most important things in my life. I wanted you to know that." It was not easy for Baldwin to talk during the rest of that long ride across the causeway.

Little things brought Percy great pleasure during these last months of his life. He seemed to gain in peace of mind. An article he read in *America* magazine by Andrew Greeley, "The Catholic Imagination of Bruce Springsteen," moved him to write Springsteen a letter. Already a fan of Springsteen's music, having been introduced to it by his nephew Will, he was curious to learn more about Springsteen's interest in Flannery O'Connor and any other details of what Percy called his "spiritual journey." Both being believing Catholics, Percy said, "it would appear that the two of us are rarities in our profession: you as a post-modern musician, I as a writer, a novelist and philosopher." To his mild disappointment, Percy never received a reply.

Percy had always been pleased by the work of his "close" readers, including Martin Luschei, Lewis Lawson, Robert Coles, Ralph Wood, and even "the Poteats," but he took special delight in a Harvard senior thesis sent to him in early March by a young woman named Julie Gantz. Entitled "The Two Will Barretts: Defeating 'Death-in-Life' in Walker Percy's *The Last Gentleman* and *The Second Coming*," the thesis struck him as a piece of fresh, original work, unencumbered by the existing scholarship. "What I like best about it," Percy wrote Gantz, "was the strong impression that this is indeed your *own* interpretation and that you were never awed by the 'experts.' This, plus the first-rate craftsmanship, makes it superior to most graduate theses and even published works."

By the end of March, Percy had had enough of the trips to Ochsner. They were now more painful than the little relief he got from the radiation. He was ready to die on his own terms, and he wanted, above all, to remain at home and be as little a nuisance as possible. He asked George Riser to prescribe strong pain killers, which he took liberally. (One day when he ran out of pills and the pharmacist would not refill his prescription, Percy called Riser and announced, a little huffily, "From now on, I'm taking charge of my own case.")

In April Percy stopped going out and began to spend most of his days in bed. Friends dropped by for short visits—George Cross, Steve and Haydee Ellis, Chink Baldwin—and as Ellis recalled, "He would usually make some smart-ass remark." Chink Baldwin had a long talk with Percy on Easter, as the Percys' annual egg hunt went on outside. "He didn't say anything sentimental. We just talked about the usual things," Baldwin recalled. But everyone could see that Percy was withdrawing into himself, preparing for the end that he equably accepted. "You okay?" Bunt would routinely ask when she checked on him during the day or at night when he lay unable to sleep in his bed. "*You* okay?" Percy would always reply. He knew it was hard on Bunt, but he asked her to be strong for the sake of the grandsons. Asking Bunt to be strong was perhaps the only unnecessary demand Percy had ever made on his wife.

Roy and Sarah dropped by the first weekend of April and spent the night. "He was still getting around the house," Roy remembered, "but I could see it was not long." Percy's condition rapidly declined after that visit, and the pain grew so sharp that he found it difficult to sleep at all. Mary Pratt came over to help out so that Bunt could get some sleep, but even she found things difficult. One night, after taking a new pain-killer and sedative combination, Percy rose from his bed in a delirious state. Unable to control him, Mary Pratt called John Moores, who came over, coaxed Percy back into bed, and then tied him in. It was one of those last bursts of abnormal strength that the dying sometimes show near the end.

Shortly thereafter, Dr. Riser arranged for a continuous infusion pump to be installed next to Percy's bed. Now Percy could administer his own morphine whenever the pain increased. Percy was eating nothing by the last week of April, and Riser, thinking his patient might die at any time, suggested to Bunt that she tell Roy the end was not far. Roy and Sarah immediately returned to Covington, and Phin and Jaye began coming over every day. Riser also arranged for an assistant nurse from Bogalusa, a fifty-one-year-old black woman named Liz Halton, to come care for Percy at night. "When I came in in the evening," Halton recalled, "he would always say, 'My fellow American has arrived.' " They would watch television or listen to the radio together, and sometimes Percy would ask her to read from the Bible. His favorite chapter, according to Halton, was John 13—the account of the Last Supper, when Jesus washes his disciples' feet and announces that one will betray him.

Percy received last rites from Father Maur Robira of St. Peter's Church on the afternoon of Friday, April 27. George Cross happened to come by with strawberries just as the priest was leaving. Bunt and he could only nod at each other as they passed in the hall. Bunt found it hardest to retain her composure when she saw Percy's friends. Cross continued into the kitchen, put the strawberries in the refrigerator, and departed quietly. He knew there was nothing left to say.

"Walker's spirit was ready," Shelby Foote later said, "but his body wouldn't let go." On the evening of the twenty-eighth, Foote called the house and got Roy, who was sitting next to his brother. Percy realized who Roy was talking to and asked for the phone.

"I've got an hour, maybe an hour and twenty minutes," he said in a voice that sounded removed, almost disembodied. "Goodbye."

Although he had been expecting the worst, Foote could not restrain himself: "My God, Walker, I'm an only child, and you're the closest thing to a brother I ever had."

But Percy would have none of that. Before handing the phone back to Roy, he said, simply, "Goodbye."

Roy told Foote that his brother might hold on for several more days. It was impossible to tell when he would go, he said. Foote tried to stay put in Memphis, but on Wednesday, May 2, he called down to say that he and Gwyn were coming the next day. They arrived on the afternoon of May 3, and Foote sat with his friend for a while. "Sad time, but a good time, too," Foote wrote in his diary. Like so many other people, Foote was both moved and impressed by how firmly his oldest friend controlled the terms of his dying. He too could feel what others in the house felt—a peace that went quite beyond this world.

For his part, Percy occasionally grew impatient. "It's embarrassing," he told Bunt, "everybody gathered here and I just won't die." By May 7, Percy had gone almost a full week without solid food. The only nourishment he would take was sweetened water, which Roy—whom Percy jokingly called "Cotton Man"—would squirt into his mouth. At night, unable to sleep, Percy would listen to Larry King or some other talk show. Both Bunt and Liz Halton would sometimes pray with him. One night near the end, he said to Halton, "Don't ask the Lord to keep me here. Ask Him to have mercy." It was now impossible for Percy to turn from one side to the other without Halton's help. Sometimes he would ask, and sometimes he didn't have to. Halton would see the grimace of pain on his face. Once Percy asked Halton if she would turn him over so he could see his wife. Halton did so and then asked if she should wake Bunt. "No," Percy said. "She understands."

On May 8, Percy began to drift in and out of consciousness. Everybody took turns sitting with him—Bunt, Roy, Phin, and Shelby, Mary Pratt, and Ann. John Moores and the grandsons would visit every day, and Percy would say a few words to each of them when he was awake. On one visit, John Moores, a Presbyterian, told his father-in-law that he had decided to receive Catholic instruction. Percy was pleased, but he urged John not to do it for his sake. John Moores assured him that it was something he wanted for himself.

On Thursday morning, May 10, Liz Halton bade farewell to Percy. "I'll see you tonight," she said, but Percy, who usually responded, said nothing this time. He only shook his head. Percy soon therafter drifted off and was unconcious for most of the day. In the middle of the afternoon, Phin took his turn, holding his brother's hand as he sat in a chair next to the bed. Sitting there quietly, watching the faint pulse of a vein in his brother's neck, Phin thought about what his brother had written at the end of his introduction to *Lanterns on the Levee*, his declaration that he owed Uncle Will a debt "which cannot be paid." It occurred to Phin—and he would say so in a letter that he would write to the *Times-Picayune* a few days later—that his brother had made good on his debt to Uncle Will, made good in full.

His eyes fixed on the vein in his brother's neck, Phin saw Percy's pulse grow slower, come almost to a standstill. Then it accelerated, racing forward in one last assertion of life. Bunt and Ann, who were standing on the porch and looking through the window, could see that Percy's breathing was rapid and shallow. They immediately came in to be by Percy's side as he breathed his last few breaths. The end had finally come. Knowing that his brother was dead, Phin went out on the porch to tell the others. It was 3:40 P.M., and almost eerily George Riser arrived just as Phin came out. Everybody went into the room to bid the first of the farewells. After paying his respects, Foote returned to the porch so the family could be alone—so he too could be alone. It was a beautiful spring afternoon, with a clear cerulean sky, and Foote remembered that May 10 was the day that Stonewall Jackson had died. He also remembered that of the many descriptions of Jackson's death that Percy had read, Percy had liked his description best of all. Somehow thinking this made Foote feel close to his oldest friend.

Walker Percy was buried two days later, on May 12, at St. Joseph's Abbey, a place that he dearly loved. Only a few years before, he had become a member of the Benedictines' lay confraternity just so that his body could one day be laid to rest on the abbey grounds.

The abbey church, a large Romanesque structure whose interior walls are adorned with the haunting frescoes of the Dutch monk Gregory Dewitt, was full long before the funeral mass began. Percy's family and kin filled several pews in the front, and friends from near and far filled the rest. Next to the church, on the grounds surrounding the abbey pond, a large group of Latinos were having a picnic, and the sounds of their festivities provided an ironic but somehow fitting counterpoint to the solemn occasion. At three o'clock, Steve Ellis, George Cross, Shelby Foote, Chink Baldwin, Billy Percy (Roy's oldest son), and Will Percy (Phin's oldest) bore the coffin into the church, and the services began. The retired and current archbishops of New Orleans were both present, and a dozen priests served as concelebrants of the mass. The archbishops offered their reminiscences, and Father Tom Clancy eulogized Percy as a writer and man of charm. Charm, Clancy reminded his listeners, was related to the Greek word *charis*, which in the New Testament is translated as "grace."

After the mass, the coffin was borne back outside and put in the hearse. The mourners followed it a few hundred yards to the abbey cemetery, passing picnickers at play. After the mourners had assembled around the grave, Monsignor Elmo L. Romagosa read the final prayers. Bunt, with her daughters and grandsons beside her, honored her husband's request. She remained strong the whole time. It had been gray and ominous all day, a swampy, humid, southern Louisiana day, but now the clouds massed even more threateningly in the sky. The wind picked up, and small birds skittered by. But the mourners—relatives, friends, and admirers—lingered at the cemetery, held by the charm that Father Clancy had earlier described. One of those reluctant to leave was a young man who had flown in from San Diego. He had never met Percy, but he had written him once and received a letter in reply. As he later explained, he just wanted to be there, to pay his respects in person, when Percy was buried. Remarkable though it might have seemed to some, the presence of this solitary wayfarer—his name was Steve Kanaga—should have struck no one who knew Percy as strange. It was to such people that Percy had always been speaking.

Epilogue

Walker Percy's work lies before us, almost complete. In years ahead, there will be additions to the published corpus, including assorted correspondence, the stray essay here or there, and possibly the surviving apprentice novel, *The Gramercy Winner*. But for the most part, what Percy wanted us to see—including six novels, two works of philosophical nonfiction, and his assorted (and posthumously published) essays—is available for readers to peruse and judge.

And how will readers judge this corpus? How in particular will those who establish the "canon" judge Dr. Percy's legacy? Will it be granted a place among the great works of American letters?

Not without considerable resistance, I suspect, and not securely, at least for some time. The reasons are not hard to find. Percy's conservatism, to begin with, makes him unpalatable to most schools of the "politically correct." But this is hardly surprising. Percy was a thinker and artist at odds with his time, both with the various and local zeitgeists of postwar America and, more generally, with the spirit and intellectual tenor of what might crudely be called modernity. Percy, moreover, was uncomfortable with the dominant ethos of his culture, occasionally even at war with it. The idolatry of the autonomous individual, the pursuit of happiness, and the boundless belief in those techniques (or experts) intended to help us achieve this happiness—Percy viewed all of these with a profoundly skeptical eye. Even more, he took it as his life's work to show how all of them drew from a tragic misconception of what the human being is. Put one way, his work was an effort to deconstruct the Enlightenment conception of man and his purposes, particularly as that conception was embodied in the values of the nation that he loved.

Obviously, Percy undertook this labor from a position of religious belief, from within what he often called the "scandal" of Christian faith. This does not mean that one must be of Percy's persuasion to like his work, any more than it means that those of Percy's party will necessarily be drawn to it. (Percy always took pleasure in earnest Catholic attacks on such Catholic writers as Waugh and O'Connor—and indeed himself. Such internal conflicts confirmed his faith in the comic confusion of this world.) At the same time, however, to view Percy's work as something significantly other from what he held to be ultimately true is, I believe, a mistake.

"*Non serviam*," declares James Joyce's young artist Stephen Dedalus, meaning that he shall serve no church of God but only the church of Art. His is a culminating statement of the Romantic and Modernist creeds. It expresses the belief in the religion of Art as the only acceptable alternative to the religions of "superstition," as so defined by that most pervasive of modern orthodoxies, the orthodoxy of science.

"*Serviam*," Percy's art as much as declares, and for that reason it may, for years to come, be devalued, rejected, or simply misunderstood.

One such misunderstanding was expressed by Percy's oldest and closest friend, Shelby Foote, an artist as much committed to upholding the absolutes of Modernism as Percy was to subverting them. Foote's misapprehension was nothing new. It was merely the last installment in his long-running quarrel with his Greenville boyhood friend. But it was beautifully and persuasively put.

The occasion was the memorial service held in Percy's honor at New York's St. Ignatius Church on October 24, 1990, one of several such services and in some ways the most powerful. Late on a gray afternoon, more than 1,200 people came to hear seven of Percy's friends commemorate the man whose absence was still felt, as one of those friends, Wilfrid Sheed, put it, like "a cold draft." Foote came next to last, after moving tributes by Robert Giroux, Eudora Welty, Sheed, Mary Lee Settle, and Stanley Kauffmann. Composed as the Stoic he had always been, choking only toward the end, when his emotions crested, Foote began steadily in his deep Delta tones:

The English essayist E. H. Carr said at the close of his early-thirties critical biography of Dostoyevsky: "A hundred years hence, when Dostoyevsky's psychology will seem as much of a historical curiosity as his theology seems to us now, the true proportions of his work will emerge; and posterity, removed from the controversies of the early twentieth century, will once more be able to regard it as an artistic whole."

Similarly, I would state my hope that Walker Percy will be seen in time for what he was in simple and solemn fact—a novelist, not merely an explicator of various philosophers and divines, existentialist or otherwise. He was no more indebted to them or even influenced by them, than was Proust (say) to or by Schopenhauer and Bergson. Proust absorbed them, and so did Walker absorb his preceptors. Like Flannery O'Connor, he found William Faulkner what Henry James called Maupassant, "a lion in the path." He solved this leonine problem much as Dante did on the outskirts of hell: he took a different path, around him. Their subject, his and Faulkner's—and all the rest of ours, for that matter—was the same: "the human heart in conflict with itself."

It is hard to disagree with a judgment so eloquently put, and in fact I would agree with much that Foote claims for his friend. Percy was no mere explicator of philosophical or theological notions, and his artistry and resources as a novelist were great. Few writers have been better observers of social manners, those of the South as well as of other American regions, and Percy used this gift for high comedic ends. His ear for American dialects was as sharp as Twain's, in some ways sharper, capturing undertones of speech even more deftly than have some of our best playwrights, including Tennessee Williams. Percy's ability to evoke a scene, whether a New Orleans suburb or an arroyo in New Mexico, is often breathtaking. Can we ever see such places again without partially knowing them through Percy's words?

And what about those words, the language itself? To be sure, his literary models were many and diverse, ranging from Camus to Hopkins, but Percy shaped a prose that was indelibly his own, a rhythmic, cadenced, and often periodic prose, surprising in its turns and sudden arrests. Percy's language sings, testimony as much to what he listened to in music and in companionable speech as to what he read.

Nor did Percy's work ever scant the central concern of literary art— "the human heart in conflict with itself." Percy dissected his own heart with a scrupulousness and precision that would have won admiring nods from all his teachers of pathology, medical and literary.

But where I must part ways with Foote is in his interpretation of the relation between Percy's art and the governing ideas and beliefs of his life. The latter were never merely the furnishings or adornments of his fiction. They were not even simply the subjects of discussion or reflection among his fictional characters, though they could sometimes also serve as such. Faith as a means of knowledge, as perhaps the highest form of knowledge, was the enabling condition of Percy's art. It was the substance of his artistic vision, and the final justification of his labor.

Art, Percy knew, is itself a form of knowledge, wonderful in its ways, but he also believed that it is a form insufficient unto itself—and insufficient because it can become, like the naturalistic sciences, its own hollow idol. What Modernism, in the words of such masters as Flaubert and Joyce, proposes as its own complete and self-justifying end is a knowledge as "objective" as that proposed by the modern sciences— knowledge, in Art's case, as the objectification of sensibility, of an affective exquisiteness. But it is precisely because of its claims to objectivity, and its elevation of sensibility above all else, that Art can only mistakenly be considered a fully adequate response to questions about the ethics and ends of human lives. Yet this mistake is the hallmark of Modernism, a creed which, however etiolated, still defines the regnant aesthetic principles of the Western world.

For Percy, such notions would not do. As he often said, he demanded more. And to demand more, to believe as Percy did, and to live the many ramifications of this belief is to make oneself a stranger in one's own land and one's own time. When and if Percy comes to seem less the stranger, his work may be more clearly recognized for what it greatly is.

Abbreviations Used in End Notes

Notes

1. MAGIC CITY

19 "building of a city": Ethel Armes, *The Story of Coal and Iron in Alabama*, p. 216.

19 English industrial city: L. R. Atkins, *The Valley and the Hills*, p. 49.

20 pre–Civil War Alabama: Justin Fuller, "Henry F. DeBardeleben, Industrialist of the New South," *The Alabama Review*, January 1986, pp. 3–5.

21 "company in Alabama": Ibid., p. 6.

23 "into Northern hands": Ibid., p. 15.

23 "city from tidewater": C. Vann Woodward, *Origins of the New South*, p. 300.

26 in the city: Int. Samuel H. Burr.

26 "admired Walker Percy": Sallie B. Comer Lathrop, *The Comer Family Grows Up*, pp. 38–39.

28 "may be suspended": Unpublished history of Birmingham Country Club, p. 5.

31 "on eating oatmeal": William Alexander Percy, *Lanterns on the Levee*, pp. 149–50.

32 few years before: Int. Jack Johnson Spalding.

33 "house on TV": Int. WP.

34 named Will Denson: Int. Robert McD. Smith; also Samuel H. Burr.

35 a "great speech": LeRoy P. Percy to Senator LeRoy Percy, March 11, 1922, Percy Family Papers, MDAH.

35 "they are not": Ibid.

36 "for five years": Ibid.

37 "along Highland Avenue": Ann Burkhardt, "Town Within a City: The Five Points South Neighborhood," *Journal of the Birmingham Historical Society*, November 1982, p. 52.

37 "religion, and nationality": Ibid., p. 53.

38 "way of baby-sitting": Ibid., p. ii.

38 working on weekends: Int. Tony Davis.

38 major theological controversy: B. Dwain Waldrep, "Henry Edmonds and His Controversy with the Southern Presbyterian Church," *Journal of the Birmingham Historical Society*, December 1985, pp. 41–48.

39 "she does right": *LITR*, p. 157.

39 an "infernal scoundrel": Int. WP; also Paschal Shook.

39 him a drink: Int. WP.

40 magazine never replied: Int. WP.

40 the "Rock House": Int. Mrs. Charles Allison.

40 windup portable victrola: Int. Jack Spalding.

42 Nell Johnson, recalled: Int. Nell Bolling Johnson.

42 his father insisted: Int. LeRoy Pratt Percy, Jr.

42 the Boston Club: John Griffin Jones int. of WP, *Conversations*, p. 250.

42 the most memorable: Int. LeRoy Pratt Percy, Jr.

42 "was a non-event": *TSC*, p. 52.

42 "is really forgotten": Ibid., p. 7.

43 "have, I have": Ibid., p. 62.

43 "loved me too": Ibid., pp. 125–26.

43 across the Pacific: Int. WP.

44 attempt at suicide: Int. Robert McDavid Smith.

44 officials shot themselves: Bertram Wyatt-Brown, "Walker, Will and Honor Dying: The Percys and Literary Creativity," in Winfred B. Moore, Jr., and Joseph F. Tripp, eds., *Looking South: Chapters in the Story of an American Region*, p. 232.

45 "was the best": Martha Susan Percy to Senator LeRoy Percy, undated, Percy Family Papers, MDAH.

45 "It's LeRoy": Int. Mrs. Charles Allison.

2. From New South to Old

46 rest of his life: Int. WP.

47 after LeRoy's funeral: Int. Mrs. Charles Allison.

47 Athens nieces remembered: Int. Nell Bolling Johnson.

48 almost terrible intensity: Int. B. Phinizy Percy.

48 end, "Catfish" Smith: Percy, "Going Back to Georgia," *Signposts*, p. 27.

49 "they were dead": Percy, "Uncle Will," *Signposts*, p. 53.

49 "shadowed by sadness": Ibid., p. 54.

49 "under it all death": *TSC*, p. 72.

50 Susanna as his stepmother: Lewis Baker, *The Percys of Mississippi*, p. 3.

51 "had his points": William Alexander Percy, *Lanterns on the Levee*, p. 40.

51 to northern Alabama: Mack Swearingen, *The Early Life of George Poindexter*, pp. 133–35.

52 "been doubly consoling": William Alexander Percy, *Lanterns on the Levee*, p. 8.

53 "the thousand-acre place": Ibid., p. 9.

53 "that cotton crop": Ibid., p. 10.

54 "a gallant fray": Lewis Baker, *The Percys of Mississippi*, p. 6.

54 "to a letterhead": C. Vann Woodward, *Origins of the New South*, p. 14.

55 "be brought in": Lewis Baker, *The Percys of Mississippi*, p. 9.

57 "the white counties": C. Vann Woodward, *Origins of the New South*, p. 79.

58 they were undemocratic: Lewis Baker, *The Percys of Mississippi*, p. 15.

58 "Lyon or Tours": William Alexander Percy, *Lanterns on the Levee*, p. 35.

58 "as an immutability": Ibid., p. 37.

59 "right thing to do": *TLG*, pp. 9–10.

63 "had once died": William Alexander Percy, *Lanterns on the Levee*, p. 152.

63 "since expected victory": Ibid., p. 151.

3. UNCLE WILL

64 "out of the house": Int. WP.

65 "could not explain": William Alexander Percy, *Lanterns on the Levee*, p. 27.

65 "would live, without": Ibid.

66 "would burn up": Ibid., p. 48.

66 "months of my childhood": Ibid., p. 49.

67 high school graduation: Bern Keating, *A History of Washington County, Mississippi*, p. 60.

67 "sort of Bergson bug": William Alexander Percy, *Lanterns on the Levee*, p. 84.

67 "their dissecting boards": *TMITB*, p. 60.

68 "and Confederate generals": Ibid., p. 93.

68 "my own self": Ibid., p. 95.

69 "faithful to me": Ibid., p. 112.

69 "palpitating speck, myself": Ibid., p. 114.

70 "Harvard Law School": Ibid., p. 115.

70 "Will remained alone": Lewis Baker, *The Percys of Mississippi*, p. 65.

71 lived through it: see Paul Fussell, *The Great War and Modern Memory*.

73 "isolated and lonely": Ibid., p. 223.

73 "happen to me": Int. WP.

75 "party will be you": William Alexander Percy, *Lanterns on the Levee*, p. 236.

76 "disguised as friends": Ibid., p. 237.

76 "numbers don't change": Ibid., p. 241.

76 "in Southern culture": Richard King, *A Southern Renaissance*, p. 8.

77 "eyes are full": quoted in Frederick R. Karl, *William Faulkner*, p. 155.

78 "the Negroes' welfare": William Alexander Percy, *Lanterns on the Levee*, p. 257.

78 "father had shown": Richard King, *A Southern Renaissance*, p. 94.

4. GREENVILLE DAYS

79 "the soul's America": Charles Bell, *Delta Democrat-Times*, April 25, 1982, pp. 3, 11.

79 travel by plane: Bern Keating, *A History of Washington County, Mississippi*, p. 72.

80 its Jewish community: Int. Josephine Haxton.

81 "itinerant harmonica players": WP, "Uncle Will," *Signposts*, p. 54.

82 "stuck on the other": WP, "Uncle Will's House," *Signposts*, pp. 63–64.

83 of kindred sympathy: Int. WP.

83 "a certain sadness": Int. SF.

83 "while they're here": John Griffin Jones, *Mississippi Writers Talking*, p. 44.

84 short by death: Int. SF.

84 and Raymond Kimble: Int. LeRoy P. Percy, Jr.

85   drove human history: Int. Charles Bell.
85   of aesthetic contemplation: Int. SF.
86   he read on: Int. WP.
87   of absolute gloom: Int. WP.
88   "Ford is mine": William Alexander Percy, *Lanterns on the Levee*, p. 287.
89   "soft as a feather": *TLG*, p. 160.
90   they took her: Int. B. Phinizy Percy.
90   year at G.H.S.: Int. WP; high school transcript, Greenville High School.
91   ahead of Walker: Int. Camille Sarason Cohan.
92   "for four years": *TSC*, p. 7.
92   "feet that year": Int. Camille Sarason Cohan.
93   "that so seriously": WP, *Pica*, November 25, 1931, p. 6.
93   "cold as an icicle": Int. SF.
94   "back the row": WP, "In a Cotton Field," *Pica*, March 17, 1932, p. 2.
94   "for the present day": WP, "Soup Kitchen Open to All," *Pica*, April 25, 1931, p. 2.
95   "remembers nor plans": William Alexander Percy, *Lanterns on the Levee*, p. 23.
95   "a garden plot": Jack Kirby, *Rural Worlds Lost*, pp. 137–38.
95   "and their insecurity": William Alexander Percy, *Lanterns on the Levee*, p. 280.
96   "laughing to theyselves": Ibid., p. 291.
96   Franklin Delano Roosevelt: Int. WP.
99   back to the house: Ints. B. Phinizy Percy, LeRoy P. Percy, Jr. See also the factually inaccurate account in *Democrat-Times*, April 2, 1932.
99   "my mother": Int. John Branton.
99   "family like Nemesis": George Waring Ball diary. William Alexander Percy Library, Greenville, Mississippi.
100   was quite successful: Int. B. Phinizy Percy.
100   also went along: Int. LeRoy P. Percy, Jr.
101   observant reporter recalled: WP, "Chinatown—The Orient and the Occident Meet," *Pica*, October 5, 1932, p. 2.
101   "notice him then": Int. Camille Sarason Cohan.
102   gave people hope: Int. WP.
103   "near perfect life": William Alexander Percy, *Pica*, December 21, 1932.
104   "someone, against someone": WP, "Herman Melville," *Signposts*, p. 200.
104   ode to Einstein: WP, "Einstein," *Pica*, December 21, 1932, p. 3.
104   "of many colors": WP, "Bitter, Lazy, Lordly River," *Pica*, January 24, 1933, p. 2.
106   photograph was of her: Int. Sarah Farish Percy.
108   *The Brothers Karamazov: Conversations*, p. 136.
108   and ethical man: For a full discussion of Percy's literary debt to Sinclair Lewis, see Lewis Lawson, "*Love in the Ruins*: Sequel to *Arrowsmith*," *Following Percy*, pp. 164–77.

5. Chapel Hill

109   "movies in the afternoon": Harriet Doar, "Former UNC Student Wins Novel Award," *The Charlotte Observer*, March 14, 1963, p. B12.
110   "church and in liberalism": J. H. Roper, *C. Vann Woodward, Southerner*, p. 87.
110   "racism everywhere else": Ibid.
110   his flummoxed opponents: Ibid., p. 88.
111   treatment of sharecroppers: William Alexander Percy, *Lanterns on the Levee*, pp. 278–79.

111 "being political either": WP to Edwin P. T. Boone, November 16, 1973.

111 Sunday, September 17: Int. Dr. Donald Wetherbee.

112 no college credits: Int. SF.

113 "weren't any answers": Int. Dr. Donald Wetherbee.

113 "Schopenhauer and Nietzsche": Int. Ansley Cope.

114 in Hitler's Germany: Int. WP.

115 "Tremendously impressed": Int. SF.

116 a luxury cruise: Int. Professor John Kendrick.

116 "different from me": Ibid.

116 "world of nature": Unpublished travel diary of Professor John Kendrick, July 1934.

117 "most formidable enemy": *Pica*, October, 1934.

117 "tremendous mystique there": Phil McCombs, "Century of Thanatos: Walker Percy and His 'Subversive Message,' " *Southern Review*, 24 (autumn 1988), p. 809.

118 "the German army": *TTS*, p. 239.

118 "ready to die": Ibid., p. 247.

118 "I left": Ibid., p. 248.

118 "from the infidel: Ibid.

119 "isolated and lonely": William Alexander Percy, *Lanterns on the Levee*, p. 223.

119 out for praise: *The Daily Tarheel*, January 13, 1935.

120 "aimless experimental narration": *Yackety Yack* (1935), p. 178.

120 "condescension to popular fiction": WP, "The Willard Huntington Wright Murder Case," *The Carolina Magazine*, January 1935, p. 5.

120 "fruits of his labor": Ibid., p. 4.

121 "as they were amusing": Ibid.

121 "regular intervals indefinitely": Ibid., p. 6.

121 "one of his characters": WP, "Reviewing the Books," *The Carolina Magazine*, February 1935, p. 28.

121 "philosophy of life": WP, "The Movie Magazine: A Low 'Slick,' " *The Carolina Magazine*, March 1935, p. 5.

122 "generous and sweet person": Ibid., p. 6.

122 "the movie stars": Ibid., p. 8.

122 "of Francis' character": WP, "Reviewing the Books," *The Carolina Magazine*, April 1935, p. 29.

123 Club in Harlem: WP to Stanley Kauffmann, April 1962.

124 Roy Percy recalled: Int. Leroy P. Percy, Jr.

126 "precocious graduate student": SF, *Tournament*, preface.

127 time and our own: Int. James Sprunt (1990).

127 on Sunday mornings: Int. WP.

128 not badly damaged: Int. SF.

128 "bastards all together": *TLG*, p. 146.

128 Percy once marveled: Int. Leroy P. Percy, Jr.

129 "would say that": Int. SF.

130 children of that era: Int. David Lee Scott.

131 "and Negro sappiness": *TLG*, p. 196.

131 "you, them, us": *TLG*, p. 198.

132 "in *The Moviegoer*": Scott Byrd, "Mysteries and Movies: Walker Percy's College Articles and *The Moviegoer*," *The Mississippi Quarterly*, xxv (spring 1972), p. 168.

6. THE HEALER'S ART

133   "the disordered city": Cited in Robert A. Stern, Gregory Gilmartin, and Thomas Mellins, *New York 1930*, p. 682.

134   "its functional honesty": Ibid., p. 113.

134   New York's Rockefeller Institute: Int. Dr. Charles Flood.

134   "on 183 Street": Herbert Mitgang int. of WP, *Conversations*, p. 148.

135   "stiff to work on": William Alexander Percy to Charlotte Gailor, September 22, 1937.

135   enjoyed their differences: Int. Dr. Frank Hardart.

135   upper front teeth: Int. WP.

136   Broadway for drinks: Int. Dr. Frank Hardart.

136   "get great grades": Int. Fred Dieterle.

137   "as a doctor does": Robert Coles, *Walker Percy: An American Search*, p. 64.

138   had ever seen: Int. Dr. Earl Witenberg.

138   had been impressed: Int. WP.

138   Percy later explained: Robert Coles, *Walker Percy: An American Search*, p. 63.

139   attention and affection: Int. Margaret Rioch.

139   "preeminently a clinician": Int. Dr. Earl Witenberg.

142   "a new insight": Janet MacKenzie Rioch, "The Transference Phenomenon in Psychoanalytic Therapy," *Psychiatry: Journal of the Biology and Pathology of Interpersonal Relations*, 1943, Vol. 6, p. 152.

143   "hire a whore": Int. LeRoy P. Percy, Jr.

143   "end of that": John Griffin Jones int. of LeRoy Pratt Percy, December 13, 1979, p. 10, MDAH.

144   "the middle twenties": Ibid.

144   "individual good life": Cited in Phinizy Spalding, "William Alexander Percy: His Philosophy of Life as Reflected in His Poetry." Master's Thesis. University of Georgia, 1957.

144   first of several: Int. SF.

145   "for a drive": Ben Wasson, *Count No 'Count: Flashbacks to Faulkner*, p. 63.

145   "be just fine": Ibid., p. 162.

145   entitled *Body Water*: Int. SF.

146   around the house: Int. David Scott.

147   miles per hour: Barrington Boardman, *Flappers, Bootleggers, "Typhoid Mary" & the Bomb: An Anecdotal History of the United States from 1923–1945*, p. 209.

148   "its altered physiology": Dr. Charles Flood, *P&S: The College of Physicians and Surgeons* (an unpublished history), p. 313.

148   "the disease process": WP, "From Facts to Fiction," *Signposts*, p. 187.

149   a deep impression: Int. Dr. Frank Hardart; also Dr. Charles Flood.

149   "not worth fighting": Cited in Lewis Baker, *The Percys of Mississippi*, p. 166.

150   so far away: Int. David Scott.

151   "psychiatrist, I'm sure": Int. B. Phinizy Percy.

151   "effect a transference": Int. SF.

152   if he left: Int. Dr. Robert Coles.

152   his first novel: SF, "Introduction," *Tournament*.

153   friendly and distant: Int. Eleanor MacKenzie Mudge.

153   "away from home": *TLG*, p. 22.

153   "back on it": Ibid., p. 18.

155   Will had created: Int. Dr. Frank Hardart.

156   "completely by surprise": Ibid.

156   "F.H. and C.B.": WP, "Notebook—1951," p. 23.

156   "Protestant's interior religion": Ibid.

156   "sure of themselves?": Int. Sarah Farish Percy.

157   impressed by Will: Int. Dr. Gilbert Mudge.

157   "out of here": John Griffin Jones int. of WP, *Conversations,* p. 264.

157   "something like that": Ibid.

158   were dating regularly: Int. Mary Bernice Percy.

158   his closest friend: Int. Sheila Bosworth.

158   two women fished: Int. Mary Bernice Percy.

159   "let's go shooting": Ibid.

7. THE SHADOW OF DEATH

160   to Bunt Townsend: WP to Mary Bernice Townsend, January 2, 1942.

161   "movies with you": Ibid.

161   "anchor was gone": John Griffin Jones int. of B. Phinizy Percy, MDAH.

162   into the Navy: WP to Mary Bernice Townsend, March 14, 1942.

162   "easier than surgery": WP to Mary Bernice Townsend, March 17, 1942.

162   and other interns: Int. Dr. Marcelle Dunning.

162   "the best-looking": WP, "Bourbon," *Signposts,* p. 106.

162   for gin fizzes: Ibid.

163   his right lung: WP to Mary Bernice Townsend, June 9, 1942.

163   "and quit medicine": James Atlas int. of WP, *Conversations,* p. 185.

163   said in one: WP to Mary Bernice Townsend, n.d. (probably July 1942)

164   "types of inflammations": Robert Taylor, *Saranac: America's Magic Mountain,* p. 46.

165   or optimistic man: Int. B. Phinizy Percy.

165   pass to come to: Int. WP.

165   "resort for the consumptive": Mark Caldwell, *The Last Crusade,* p. 43.

166   stocks and bonds: William Alexander Percy, "Last Will and Testament," July 17, 1941.

166   "with your soldiers": WP to Mary Bernice Townsend, August 31, 1942.

166   "of Lake Flower": Mark Caldwell, *The Last Crusade,* p. 136.

167   open at the "San": Int. Dr. Marcelle Dunning.

167   "don't need them": Int. SF.

167   "and very depressed": Robert Taylor, *Saranac,* p. 233.

168   "of shimmering poplars": WP, ms. *The Gramercy Winner,* p. 104, SHC.

169   twelve other patients: Int. WP.

170   then at Trudeau: Int. Dr. Edwin L. Kendig.

170   began to grow: Ibid.

171   weather to women: Int. Dr. Paul Downey.

171   "New Year's Eve": WP to Mary Bernice Townsend, December 30, 1942.

172   Phin took command: Int. B. Phinizy Percy.

172   "sweat glands atrophy": WP, "Notebook—1951," p. 29, private papers of WP.

173   "north of Utica?": WP, ms. *The Gramercy Winner,* p. 148.

174   in Catholic apologetics: Int. Dr. Edmund L. Kendig.

174   at least intrigued: Int. WP.

174   and German existentialists: Bradley Dewey int. of WP, *Conversations,* p. 107.

175   but not exclusively: Int. Dr. Marcelle Dunning.

176   steaks in town: Int. Dr. Paul Downey.

176   town for a movie: Int. Dr. Marcelle Dunning.

176 and his signature: WP to Mary Bernice Townsend, December 15, 1943, private papers of WP.

177 "disgust with myself": WP to Ned Boone, October 2, 1943, SHC.

177 "it swims in": *TM*, p. 52.

177 "what man *is*": Robert Coles, *Walker Percy*, p. 66.

177 "about it up there": WP, ms. *The Gramercy Winner*, p. 9.

177 "going to recover": Int. WP.

178 "was keeping books": Int. SF.

179 "the moment passed": Robert Taylor, *Saranac*, p. 237.

181 "the contemporary soul": Lionel Trilling, *The Liberal Imagination*, p. 8.

182 "sake of community": Reinhold Niebuhr, *The Children of Light and the Children of Darkness*, p. 41.

182 "strange, strange feeling": Robert Taylor, *Saranac*, p. 237.

183 "my full approval": Cited in Ruth Galwey et al., *The Spirit of Gaylord, A History* (Gaylord, 1983), pp. 4–5.

183 "would he attack?": Int. WP; WP's personal copy of *Notes from Underground*.

8. DRIFT AND RESOLUTION

184 returned to medicine: Int. WP.

185 on Lake Ferguson: Int. Kenneth Haxton.

185 was completely destroyed: Int. William Alexander Percy II.

185 the record player: WP to Mary Bernice Townsend, February 2, 1946, private papers of WP.

186 back from Europe: Int. William Alexander Percy II.

186 Shaw and Shakespeare: Int. Kenneth Haxton.

186 slouching toward Rome: Int. Josephine Haxton.

186 joked in a letter: WP to Mary Bernice Townsend, February 2, 1946.

186 sort out his life: Int. Mary Bernice Percy.

188 good to be true: Int. SF.

189 had been accepted: Int. SF.

189 doings on the mountain: Ann Waldron, *Close Connections*, p. 284.

189 "become of him": Int. Lady Thornton (born Rosamond Myers).

190 "be happily married": Int. Mary Bernice Percy.

190 "poaching on his territory": Int. SF.

190 "have to end up": Int. SF.

192 "the minute before": *TLG*, p. 356.

193 "to marry Bunt": Int. Nancy Lemann.

193 closer to Bunt: Int. Mary Bernice Percy.

193 "week or a year": WP to Mary Bernice Townsend, September 1946, private papers of WP.

193 not call back: Int. Mary Bernice Percy.

193 very "laid-back": Int. Virginia Milazzo.

194 "to marry you": Int. Mary Bernice Percy.

194 an awkward performance: Int. SF.

195 "up to the end": Int. Mary Bernice Percy.

195 said to Bunt: Int. Mary Bernice Percy.

195 president, LeRoy Percy: Int. WP.

197 undertones of incest: SF, *Tournament*, "Preface."

197 "after World War II": Ann Waldron, *Close Connections*, p. 257.

198 Waldron concludes: Ibid., pp. 257–58.

198	Bay St. Louis, Mississippi: Int. Virginia Milazzo.
200	more than absurd: WP to Jay Tolson, February 11, 1988.
200	University in New Orleans: Int. Virginia Milazzo.
200	"at high tide": WP, "New Orleans Mon Amour," *Signposts*, pp. 11–12.
201	was no intellectual: Int. Fr. Tom Clancy.
202	"have cared less": Int. WP.
203	"just a walk": Int. Mary Bernice Percy.
204	"you go first?": Int. Virginia Milazzo.
205	"nonplace for me!": WP, "Why I Live Where I Live," *Signposts*, pp. 6–7.
206	"had by then": SF to WP, May 1, 1948.
207	"invented his county": WP, "Why I Live Where I Live," *Signposts*, p. 9.
207	"had no kin": Ibid., p. 7.

9. A Second Apprenticeship

211	"them tell stories": John Jones int. of WP, *Mississippi Writers Talking II*, p. 35.
211	talk things over: Int. SF.
212	"first-published after all": SF, *Tournament*, "Preface."
212	"comes from God": SF to WP, May 1, 1948, SHC.
213	"work you can do": Int. B. Phinizy Percy.
213	into the church: Int. Virginia Milazzo.
214	"still honor him": WP, "Notebook—1951," p. 29.
216	"the Grand Inquisitor": SF to WP, November 19, 1949, SHC.
216	"thought you could": SF to WP, November 22, 1950, SHC.
216	"forlorn Ohio street?" SF to WP, November 22, 1950, SHC.
216	"to keep going": Ibid.
216	"find it, either": SF to WP, December 1, 1950, SHC.
217	"to your one": SF to WP, December 22, 1950, SHC.
217	in his fiction: SF to WP, January 20, 1950, SHC.
217	upon the writer: Int. WP.
218	"our old familiar": WP, "Notebook—1951," p. 21.
218	"From boredom": Ibid., p. 22.
219	see, Flannery O'Connor: Ann Waldron, *Close Connections*, pp. 284–86.
219	Will's mountain house: Int. Andrew Lytle.
220	"needed right now": Caroline Gordon to WP, n.d. (autumn 1951 likely), SHC.
220	for their plots: Ann Waldron, *Close Connections*, p. 259.
220	"the human heart": Caroline Gordon to WP, December 11, 1951, SHC.
220	"so damned good": Cited in Ann Waldron, *Close Connections*, pp. 285–86.
222	a "valuable novelist": Allen Tate to WP, January 1, 1952, SHC.
222	"better next time": SF to WP, January 1951, SHC.
223	"me through it": SF to WP, May 16, 1951, SHC.
223	"been got before": SF to WP, July 5, 1951, SHC.
223	"clod of a planet": SF to WP, December 31, 1951, SHC.
223	"writing is fine": SF to WP, January 5, 1951, SHC.
224	"happens to others": SF to WP, February 16, 1952, SHC.
224	"nothing but regrets": SF to WP, February 18, 1952, SHC.
224	"my hands now": SF to WP, n.d. (likely March 1952), SHC.
224	"woman I love": SF to WP, April 9, 1952, SHC.
225	"come to it yet": Ibid.
225	"thats the main thing": Ibid.

226   "such a mighty force": Caroline Gordon to WP, November 25, 1952, SHC.

226   "off the bat": Caroline Gordon to WP, December 1952, SHC.

226   "fatal to a novelist": Caroline Gordon to WP, November 25, 1952, SHC.

227   "terms with it": SF to WP, July 20, 1952, SHC.

227   "Peace be with us": SF to WP, December 26, 1952, SHC.

227   "a good sign": Caroline Gordon to WP, January 1953, SHC.

227   "as I could": Caroline Gordon to WP, January 31, 1953, SHC.

228   "don't get it": Caroline Gordon to WP, February 1953 (likely), SHC.

228   "it goes along?": Jack Wheelock, February 3, 1953, SHC.

229   that was necessary: Susan Jenkins to WP, March 17, 1953, SHC.

229   starting a new novel: Caroline Gordon to WP, April 27, 1953, SHC.

229   will of its own: Thomas Mann, "The Making of The Magic Mountain," The Magic Mountain, p. 722.

230   "novel of initiation": Ibid., p. 727.

230   notes from 1952: WP, "Notebook—1951," p. 35.

230   "quality of the hero": Allen Tate to WP, January 1, 1952, SHC.

230   "attractiveness and simplicity": WP, ms. of The Gramercy Winner, p. 2.

231   "someone else shone": Ibid., p. 3.

231   "lapse as failing": Ibid.

231   "and reckless personality": Gary M. Ciuba, "Walker Percy's Enchanted Mountain," in Jan Nordby Gretlund and Karl Heinz Westarp, eds., Walker Percy: Novelist and Philosopher, p. 15.

232   "the good human": WP, ms. of The Gramercy Winner, p. 194.

232   "you know, Scanlon?": Ibid., p. 333.

232   "All my life": Ibid., p. 334.

232   "into the city": Ibid., 336.

233   "laughed out loud": Ibid., p. 341.

233   "the recent novel": SF to WP, February 19, 1954, SHC.

233   "viewing the world": SF to WP, February 19, 1954, SHC.

234   was a "silosopher": Int. Mary Pratt Percy Lobdell.

235   Percy as reasonable: Int. Lawrence Baldwin.

235   "a private income": Ibid.

236   "what he did": Int. B. Phinizy Percy.

10. The Consolations of Philosophy

237   "was through language": Marcus Smith int. of WP, Conversations, p. 137.

238   filled with notes: int. WP.

238   his own prose: John Jones int. of WP, Conversations, p. 275.

240   "it of universals": James Feibleman and Julius Friend, Science and the Spirit of Man, pp. 123–24.

241   "essential religious impulse": Ibid., p. 123.

241   "reason," Langer wrote: Susanne Langer, Philosophy in a New Key, p. 27.

242   "a former epoch": Ibid., p. 29.

242   " 'scientific methods' have done": Ibid., p. 32.

242   he later explained: Barbara King int. of WP, Conversations, p. 93.

242   "with her book": Ibid.

243   "valid biological categories?": "Symbol as Need," TMITB, pp. 295–96.

243   "of I think": Ibid., p. 295.

244   "and publish it": Barbara King int. of WP, Conversations, p. 93.

244   "and remarkable fruit": Jacques Maritain to WP, August 21, 1954.

245   for each volume: Int. SF.

246 only minimal hearing: Int. Mary Bernice Percy.

246 "to stay together?": Ibid.

247 "hung the moon": SF to WP, Saturday, n.d. [early 1955?], SHC.

247 of her life: Ints. WP, Mary Pratt Percy Lobdell, Ann Boyd Percy Moores; see also Henry Kisor, *What's That Pig Outdoors?*

248 symbols was different: Henry Kisor, *What's That Pig Outdoors?*, pp. 27–29.

249 of violent earaches: Int. Mary Bernice Percy.

251 "the Deep South": WP to Father J. H. Fichter, November 13, 1948. Department of Special Collections and Archives of Loyola University Library.

251 "way of life": Int. LeRoy Pratt Percy, Jr.

252 "know down there": SF to WP, May 10, 1955, SHC.

252 American Communist party: Int. Dr. William Sorum.

252 "in those days": Ibid.

253 "would have survived": Ibid.

254 "thirty years ago": WP, "Stoicism in the South," *Signposts*, p. 83.

254 "grumbling on the porch": Ibid., p. 84.

254 "dignity on the other": Ibid., p. 85.

255 "insolent or not": Ibid., p. 86.

256 for a reaction: Int. Lawrence Baldwin.

256 "Philosophy—Lord!": SF to WP, May 24, 1956, SHC.

257 "riding a train": *TMITB*, p. 83.

258 day of his life: Ibid., p. 88.

258 "search for himself": Ibid., p. 95.

258 "a rare emotion": Ibid., p. 96.

259 "already its opposite": Ibid., pp. 96–97.

259 "or total self-loss": Ibid., pp. 94–95.

260 "flip-savage satirical": WP to Caroline Gordon, April 6, 1962, private collection of Ashley Brown.

260 "through the masonry": WP, "The Man on the Train," *TMITB*, p. 84.

260 "and hardly that": SF to WP, November 29, 1956, SHC.

261 "into the void": John Jones int. of WP, *Conversations*, p. 274.

261 one and the same: Int. Dr. Robert Coles.

262 "will read them": Int. Mary Bernice Percy.

263 "movie house (the armpit)": WP, ms., "Confessions of a Movie-goer," p. 2, SHC.

263 "into the Schwarzwald": Ibid., p. 4.

264 "What then?": Ibid., p. 19.

264 "*it does not?*": Ibid., p. 20.

264 "homosexuals at the Y": Ibid., p. 21.

265 "everything else *is*": WP, "Semiotic and a Theory of Knowledge," *TMITB*, p. 259.

265 "about it at all": Ibid., p. 263.

265 "concept of man": WP, "The Mystery of Language," *TMITB*, pp. 157–58.

266 "it a clearing": Ibid., p. 158.

266 "predicament in the world": WP, "The Coming Crisis of Psychiatry," *Signposts*, p. 252.

267 "and less religious": Ibid., p. 262.

268 "fight it was!": WP, "The American War," *Signposts*, p. 73.

268 "peace that followed": Ibid., pp. 74–75.

268 "only another reaction": WP to Phinizy Spalding, May 30, 1957, private papers of Phinizy Spalding.

11. CARNIVAL IN GENTILLY

270   "producing major fiction": Max Webb, "Binx Bolling's New Orleans," in Panthea Reid Broughton, ed., *The Art of Walker Percy: Stratagems for Being*, p. 13.

271   left her rattled: Int. Mary Bernice Percy.

272   "following holy day": SF to WP, May 1951, SHC.

272   "pencil to paper": *Signposts*, p. 190.

273   of one another: Int. B. Phinizy Percy.

274   Mrs. Joseph's apartment: Int. William Alexander Percy.

274   observer to observe: Int. WP.

275   "department store elevator": WP, "The Southern Moderate," *Signposts*, p. 100.

275   "schools," Percy wrote: Ibid., p. 95.

276   "anything at all": WP, "Metaphor as Mistake," *TMITB*, p. 83.

277   "of hay fever": WP to Phinizy Spalding, June 28, 1948, private papers of Phinizy Spalding.

278   "utterance in his work": John Paul Eakin, *Fictions in Autobiography*, p. 207.

278   "of culture itself": Richard Ford, "Not Just Whistling Dixie," *National Review*, May 13, 1977, p. 558.

278   "wonder and curiosity": WP, "From Facts to Fiction," *Signposts*, p. 190.

279   "them overly schematic": Michael Kobre, "The Consolations of Fiction: Walker Percy's Dialogic Art," *New Orleans Review*, Winter 1989, p. 46.

279   "inflections and intentions": Ibid., p. 49.

280   "believe at school": Int. Mary Pratt Percy Lobdell.

280   the friendship grew: Int. Father Tom Clancy.

281   named Stanley Kauffmann: Int. Stanley Kauffmann.

281   "of *The New Republic*": Stanley Kauffmann, "Album of the Knopfs," *The American Scholar*, Summer 1987, p. 377.

281   "strong new voice": Elizabeth Otis to Stanley Kauffmann, June 24, 1959, HRHRC.

282   "plan and resolution": Stanley Kauffmann to Elizabeth Otis, July 9, 1959, HRHRC.

282   "get the author": Stanley Kauffmann, "Album of the Knopfs," *The American Scholar*, Summer 1987, p. 377.

282   "possible in this day?": SF to WP, June 18, 1959, SHC.

283   "be finished satisfactorily": WP to Stanley Kauffmann, July 20, 1959, SHC.

284   " 'give him two-fifty' ": Stanley Kauffmann, "Album of the Knopfs," *The American Scholar*, Summer 1987, p. 377.

284   "a little limp": Stanley Kauffmann to Elizabeth Otis, October 21, 1959, HRHRC.

284   would sign it: WP to Elizabeth Otis, October 26, 1959, HRHRC.

284   "next few weeks": WP to Stanley Kauffmann, November 6, 1959, HRHRC.

284   the "Purich House": Int. Mary Pratt Percy Lobdell.

286   "plunge in again": Stanley Kauffmann to WP, February 5, 1960, HRHRC.

286   "explain my position": WP to Stanley Kauffmann, February 11, 1960, HRHRC.

287   "for future association": Stanley Kauffmann to WP, February 12, 1960, HRHRC.

287   "hard for more": SF to WP, May 15, 1960, SHC.

287   "along those lines": Ibid.

287   "came just fine": SF to WP, August 7, 1960, SHC.

288   "us, of course": WP to Stanley Kauffmann, September 3, 1960, HRHRC.

288   "possibly from Kierkegaard": Stanley Kauffmann to WP, October 4, 1960, HRHRC.

288   "and your novel": Stanley Kauffmann to WP, October 24, 1960, HRHRC.

289   "with your help": WP to Stanley Kauffmann, October 28, 1960, HRHRC.

289   man had won: Int. Dr. William Sorum.

289   science-fiction fantasy: SF to WP, December 12, 1960, SHC.

290   "pleasure of publishing": Angus Cameron to Elizabeth Otis, April 7, 1961, HRHRC.

290   "time by anyone": "Two True Sounds from Dixie," *Time,* May 19, 1961, p. 105.

291   "a good checkup": "Briefly Noted," *The New Yorker,* July 22, 1961, pp. 78–79.

291   "over the land": Edwin Kennebeck, "The Search," *Commonweal,* June 2, 1961, pp. 260–61.

291   "but distant candle": Brainerd Cheney, "To Restore a Fragmented Image," *Sewanee Review,* Autumn 1961, p. 691.

292   "the gravelly roofs": *TM,* p. 185.

293   "I would": Ibid., p. 197.

293   "for direct questioning": Ibid., p. 215.

294   later to appreciate: Int. Lawrence Baldwin.

295   "value your opinion": WP to Angus Cameron, January 31, 1962, HRHRC.

295   sales only reinforced: Gay Talese, "Critics Hear Tale of Novel's Prize," *The New York Times,* March 15, 1962.

296   "that was that": From Stanley Kauffmann's tribute to WP at Saint Ignatius Church in New York City, October 24, 1990 (published in chapbook form by Farrar Straus Giroux).

296   "of my marriage": Int. Stanley Kauffmann.

296   "child at breast": A. J. Liebling, "Letters," *Show,* August 1962.

297   "you have done": WP, "Accepting the National Book Award for *The Moviegoer,*" *Signposts,* p. 246.

297   "our foreign authors": Ints. WP, SF, Robert Giroux.

299   "had of what happened": WP to Stanley Kauffmann, March 19, 1962, private papers of Stanley Kauffmann.

299   "the old Longs": WP to Jean Stafford, March 19, 1962, U. Va.

299   "they surprised me": Flannery O'Connor to WP, March 29, 1962, *Flannery O'Connor: Collected Works,* p. 1159.

300   *"want to live":* WP to Caroline Gordon, April 6, 1962, private papers of Ashley Brown.

301   "for Jesus' sake": Ibid.

301   "pronounce Christ King": John Carr int. of WP, *Conversations,* p. 64.

301   the novel's end: John Edward Hardy, *The Fiction of Walker Percy,* p. 56.

302   "impossible to say": *TM,* p. 235.

12. PEREGRINATIONS

303   "were not batty": WP to Jean Stafford, October 17, 1971, U. Va.

304   "you spoke of": WP to Caroline Gordon, April 6, 1962, SHC.

304   "of, THE MOVIEGOER": Stanley Kauffmann to WP, June 8, 1962, private papers of Stanley Kauffmann.

304   "past the horizon": Ibid.

307   into a movie: Int. Stanley Kauffmann.

308 "deep Georgia accent": WP to Phinizy Spalding, March 1, 1963, private papers of Phinizy Spalding.

308 "develop the friendship": Int. WP.

310 to the canyon: Int. Mary Pratt Percy Lobdell.

310 "come at all": SF to WP, August 13, 1963, SHC.

311 "live by the Gulf": Ibid.

311 August 23 letter: Dr. Gentry Harris to WP, August 23, 1963, private papers of Dr. Gentry Harris.

311 "at long range": WP to Dr. Gentry Harris, September 8, 1963, Harris papers.

312 "to *human* problems": Dr. Gentry Harris to WP, September 19, 1963, Harris papers.

312 "patients' symbolic structure": Dr. Gentry Harris to WP, October 2, 1963, Harris papers.

312 on the project: WP to Gentry Harris, October 7, 1963, Harris papers.

313 agreed to stay: Int. WP.

313 "write about it": Carlton Cremeens int. of WP, *Conversations*, p. 19.

313 "his own predilections": Ibid.

313 "three hundred pages": Ibid.

313 "right because now—": *TLG*, p. 357.

314 "vague movie too": Thomas Merton, *A Vow of Conversation*, pp. 15–16.

315 "not to say it": Thomas Merton to WP, n.d. (probably January 1964), TMSC.

316 "word from others": WP to Thomas Merton, February 14, 1964, TMSC.

316 his future work: Donald Stafford to WP, January 15, 1964, *SR* files.

317 man in the group: Ints. WP, B. Phinizy Percy, Lawrence Baldwin, George Cross.

318 "and imitating him": WP to Dr. Gentry Harris, January 29, 1964, Harris papers.

319 "be happening here": Ibid.

319 "spectrum of symbol-communication": WP to Dr. Gentry Harris, March 2, 1964, Harris papers.

320 at another time: Int. Dr. Gentry Harris.

320 speaking, a teacher: Int. Marjorie Magner.

320 "reasons, the causes": Int. Marjorie Magner.

321 "exciting to watch": WP to Gentry Harris, July 15, 1964, Harris papers.

321 "you know yourself": Elizabeth Otis to WP, August 7, 1964, SHC.

321 "beautiful, belongs elsewhere": Patricia Schartle, August 6, 1964, SHC.

323 somewhat modestly explained: Int. Will Campbell.

323 reason to refuse: Ibid.

323 a new publisher: Henry Robbins to WP, August 28, 1964, FSG files.

324 stuck to them: Ints. Mary Bernice Percy, Mary Pratt Percy Lobdell, Ann Boyd Percy Moores.

324 first day out: Int. Robert Drake.

325 the *Queen Mary*: Int. Mary Pratt Percy Lobdell.

325 "so good at": Robert Giroux to WP, August 6, 1965, FSG files.

326 "all the female baggage": WP to Dr. Gentry Harris, August 21, 1965, Harris papers.

326 "and productive life": Ibid.

327 "some problems unresolved": Henry Robbins to WP, October 25, 1965, FSG files.

327 "past three years": WP to Henry Robbins, October 31, 1965, FSG files.

327 "woods for the trees": WP to Mary Pratt Percy, undated (early December 1965), Lobdell papers.

327 signed off reluctantly: Ibid.

328 "the writing itself": SF to WP, January 10, 1966, SHC.

328 "on mass criminality": WP to Mary Pratt Percy, January 28, 1966, Lobdell papers.

328 "the New South": WP to Caroline Gordon, February 11, 1966, FLPU.

329 *"man alone, thinking!"*: Caroline Gordon to WP, March 7, 1966, FLPU.

329 "out of the solipsism": WP to Caroline Gordon, March 1966, FLPU.

329 "the modern novel": Caroline Gordon to Robert Giroux, March 11, 1966, FLPU.

330 "mystery of alienation": Paul Horgan to Robert Giroux, April 26, 1966, FSG files.

330 *"want* to read": Hans Koningsberger to Henry Robbins, May 6, 1966, FSG files.

330 "I thoroughly liked": Peter Taylor to Robert Giroux, n.d., FSG files.

330 "in a long time": Thomas Merton to Robert Giroux, May 22, 1966, FSG files.

330 "supple in style": "Guidebook for Lost Pilgrims," *Time,* June 17, 1966, p. 104.

331 "work of art": Peter Buitenhuis, "A Watcher, a Listener, a Wanderer," *New York Times Book Review,* June 26, 1966, p. 5.

331 "one particular boy": Honor Tracy, "Humidification Engineer," *The New Republic,* June 18, 1966, pp. 27–28.

331 "something has failed": Joyce Carol Oates, "Gentleman Without a Past," *The Nation,* August 8, 1966, pp. 129–39.

332 "comfortably endurable bothers": Benjamin DeMott, "The Good and the True," *Washington Post Book World,* June 12, 1966, p. 9.

332 "Barrett does himself": Frederick Crews, "The Hero as Case," *Commentary,* September 1966, pp. 100–102.

333 "could not do": WP to Dr. Gentry Harris, June 9, 1965, Harris papers.

13. APOCALYPTIC MIRTH

335 a boy's summer camp: Int. Mary Bernice Percy.

336 arguments of the other: Int. WP.

337 "both in the bayou": WP to Lewis Lawson, May 16, 1967, Lawson papers.

337 "of its riches": Lewis Lawson, *Following Percy,* p. 2.

337 "basic themes appertaining": WP. to Lewis Lawson, July 9, 1967, Lawson papers.

338 "but document it": WP, "The Fire This Time," *New York Review of Books,* July 1, 1965, p. 5.

339 "liking and a hope": WP to SF, n.d. (late January 1967?), SHC.

339 writers in the trade: Int. Wilfrid Sheed.

339 "he didn't like!": From Wilfrid Sheed's tribute to WP, St. Ignatius Church, New York City, October 24, 1990 (published in chapbook form by FSG).

340 "quarrels," Percy wrote: WP, "The Doctor Listened," *New York Times Book Review,* June 6, 1967, p. 7.

340 "worst of our ills": Ibid.

340 thrilled by the review: Int. Dr. Robert Coles.

340 *"The Last Gentleman"*: Robert Coles to WP, June 22, 1967, Coles papers.

341 "a couple of women": Victor Kramer and Dewey Kramer int. of WP, *Conversations,* p. 311.

341 "standard" 1960s view: Ibid., p. 312.

342   "exurb named Paradise": WP to Thomas Merton, July 13, 1967, TMSC.

342   articles on the subject: Thomas Merton to WP, July 30, 1967, TMSC.

342   "preaching toilet Zen": Thomas Merton to WP, August 24, 1967, TMSC.

342   "complex and baffling": WP to Thomas Merton, August 27, 1967, TMSC.

343   "in his class": Int. Carol Livaudais.

343   "me for that": Int. Carol Livaudais.

343   "that Mother did": SF to WP, March 19, 1968, SHC.

344   "hatred and abuse": Carlton Cremeens int. of WP, *Conversations*, p. 23.

346   "name of the real": WP, "Novel-Writing in an Apocalyptic Time," *Signposts*, p. 161.

346   "clash of manners": John Zeugner, "Walker Percy and Gabriel Marcel: The Castaway and the Wayfarer," *Mississippi Quarterly*, Winter 1974–75, p. 51.

347   and a novelist: Ints. Emily Diamond, Helen Frick, Dr. Charles Hill.

347   of Economic Opportunity: WP to Father Louis Twomey, April 3, 1968, Special Collection and Archives of Loyola University Library.

347   where he lived: Int. Mary Bernice Percy.

348   attorney every Easter: Int. Emily Diamond.

350   "has been shucked": WP, "Eudora Welty in Jackson," *Signposts*, p. 223.

350   "a long time": SF to WP, May 23, 1968, SHC.

351   "he probably did": WP to Lewis Lawson, June 25, 1968, Lawson papers.

351   "was no time": SF to WP, June 8, 1969, SHC.

352   "hope of heaven": SF to WP, October 28, 1969, SHC.

352   "as Flannery was": WP to SF, August 4, 1970, SHC.

352   "A sad trade": SF to WP, November 17, 1969, SHC.

352   "and more contemporary": WP to Martin Luschei, April 19, 1979, Luschei papers.

353   he told Foote: WP to SF, June 12, 1970, SHC.

353   "supremacy, and racism": From transcript of WP testimony, U.S. District Court, Eastern District of Louisiana, New Orleans, Louisiana, May 11, 1970, Ben C. Toledano papers.

353   "than the Klan": WP to SF, June 12, 1970, SHC.

353   "I sufficiently wrong": WP, "The Discussion Continues," *Commonweal*, September 4, 1970, p. 431.

354   "copies to agent": WP to SF, August 4, 1970, SHC.

354   less "Masters and Johnson": WP to Lewis Simpson, March 19, 1971, SR files.

354   "ought to be attractive": WP to Caroline Gordon, February 6, 1971, FLPU.

355   wild mood swings: WP to Julie Coryn, March 14, 1971, FSG files.

355   "disoriented than usual": WP to Jean Stafford, Manuscripts Department, U. Va. Library.

355   "pursuit of happiness": WP, "Concerning *Love in the Ruins*," *Signposts*, p. 248.

356   "on your side": Ibid., p. 250.

356   "immovable and indestructible": Ibid., p. 249.

356   "certainly Christ-haunted": Flannery O'Connor, *Mystery and Manners*, p. 44.

357   "us modern writers": SF to WP, August 22, 1970, SHC.

357   all to the good: Martha Duffy, "Lapsometer Legend," *Time*, May 17, 1971, p. 74.

357   "word for it": Peter Prescott, *Newsweek*, May 17, 1971, p. 107.

357   "can quickly see": Thomas McGuane, *New York Times Book Review*, May 23, 1971, pp. 7, 37.

358   "full of ideas": V. S. Pritchett, "Clowns," *New York Review of Books*, July 1, 1971, p. 15.

358   *"fecklessness of Agrarianism"*: WP to Lewis Simpson, March 19, 1971, SR files.

358   concluded Mark Taylor: Mary Taylor, *Commonweal*, October 29, 1971, p. 119.

359   "made it either": Wilfrid Sheed, "The Good Word: Walker Percy Redivivus,
       New York Times Book Review, July 4, 1971, p. 2.

359   "glory of God": L. E. Sissman, "Inventions," *New Yorker*, September 11, 1971,
       pp. 121–24.

359   an unmitigated success: Int. Charles Poe.

359   Boone snorted: Ned Boone to WP, September 9, 1971, SHC.

359   "*am* a smart-ass": WP to Ned Boone: September 22, 1971, SHC.

360   "think they are": WP to SF, July 9, 1971, SHC.

360   "been particularly affected": Robert Coles to WP, May 21, 1971, Coles papers.

360   had admired tremendously: Charles Bunting int. of WP, *Conversations*, p. 50.

360   "didn't do better": WP to Henry Robbins, September 27, 1971, FSG files.

360   a second time: *Saturday Review*, April 1973, pp. 33–35.

14. THE THIRD HALF OF LIFE

361   any of his novels: WP to SF, July 25, 1970, SHC.

362   a new world: WP to SF, February 3, 1971, SHC.

363   "a dark wood": WP to SF, July 4, 1973, SHC.

366   "we were playing": Int. Betsy O'Brien.

366   "from his influence": Int. Walter Isaacson.

367   remained a friend: Int. Berry Morgan.

367   "of literary taste": Int. James Boulware.

368   "with his faith": Ibid.

369   a busy household: Ints. Alfred Kazin, Mary Pratt Percy Lobdell.

369   "muggings and intellectualism": SF to WP, November 23, 1970, SHC.

370   "admired a disappointment": Int. Martin Luschei.

370   "with less horseplay": WP to Martin Luschei, December 8, 1972, Luschei
       papers.

371   "discuss all this?": Dr. Robert Coles to Walker Percy, n.d. (late February
       1972?), Coles papers.

371   "works out or not": WP to Robert Coles, March 5, 1970, Coles papers.

372   "Christmas and Easter!": Dr. Robert Coles to WP, June 26, 1972, Coles papers.

372   "and so did Gwyn": SF to WP, March 17, 1973, SHC.

373   "be published 'soon'!": Dr. Robert Coles to WP, May 3, 1975, Coles papers.

373   before the summer: FSG files.

374   "conservative, mean side": Int. WP.

375   "circumstances *very nice*": WP to Elizabeth Spencer, July 12, 1984, National
       Library of Canada.

375   " 'whole of the burden' ": William F. Buckley, Jr., to J. T., February 24, 1993.

376   "the narrative style": "The Southern Imagination: An Interview with Eudora
       Welty and Walker Percy," transcript of William F. Buckley, Jr.'s *Firing Line*.
       Mississippi Quarterly, Fall 1973, p. 495.

376   "in their reconstruction": Ibid., pp. 515–16.

377   "South, believe me": John Carr int. of WP, *Conversations*, p. 69.

378   "and compelling power": Susan V. Donaldson, "Tradition in Amber: Walker
       Percy's *Lancelot* as Southern Metafiction," in Jan Nordby Gretlund and Karl
       Heinz Westarp, eds., *Walker Percy: Novelist and Philosopher*, p. 65.

378   "old horse latitudes": WP to SF, September 14, 1972, SHC.

379   "I'll ever write": WP to Lewis Simpson, October 4, 1973, *SR* files.

379   "years to write": SF to WP, February 3, 1972, SHC.

379   "see you sneering": WP to SF, October 6, 1972.

380   "gentry and Hollywood": Herbert Mitgang, "A Talk With Walker Percy," *New York Times Book Review,* February 20, 1977, p. 20.

381   confessed to Foote: WP to SF, July 9, 1971, SHC.

381   " 'Augustus' and 'Chimera' ": Jonathan Yardley, "The Verdict on Walker Percy," *The Washington Post,* May 14, 1990, p. B2.

382   flow of wine: Int. Jonathan Yardley.

382   "took in it": Jonathan Yardley, "The Verdict on Walker Percy," op. cit.

382   "on your own": Int. Mary Pratt Percy Lobdell.

382   "it that way": Judge Steve Ellis to Jay Tolson, September 27, 1991.

383   "Which sounds better?" WP to SF, July 4, 1973, SHC.

384   trilogy by summer: SF to WP, January 26, 1973, SHC.

384   "three-main-character work": SF to WP, March 17, 1973, SHC.

384   "Louisiana swamp rot": WP to SF, March 1, 1973, SHC.

385   "no Jeb Stuart": WP to SF, June 13, 1973, SHC.

385   "of foul bemusement": WP to Martin Luschei, September 1, 1973, Luschei papers.

386   "Rum go": SF to WP, August 16, 1973, SHC.

386   "to finish it": WP to Lewis Simpson, October 14, 1973, SR files.

387   "a transitional time": Int. Dr. Susanne Jensen.

388   "is coming back": WP to SF, October 19, 1973, SHC.

388   "and doze off": WP to SF, October 19, 1973.

15. THE KNIGHT, DEATH, AND THE DEVIL

389   "about Watergate etc.": WP to SF, January 3, 1974, SHC.

389   "take off from": SF to WP, January 22, 1974, SHC.

390   a title: *Sentences:* WP to Henry Robbins, July 14, 1972, FSG files.

390   "paragraph or two": WP to Ann Boyd Percy, February 2, 1974, Ann Percy Moores papers.

391   "the Durer engraving?": WP to Caroline Gordon, FLPU.

391   "and your department": WP to Lewis Simpson, April 3, 1974, SR files.

391   "their money for": WP to Lewis Simpson, April 11, 1974, SR files.

391   "paid to see": Lewis Simpson, "Walker Percy's Vision of the Modern World," Flora Levy Lecture in the Humanities, University of Southwestern Louisiana, Spring 1991.

392   "hated life at home": WP to SF, May 23, 1973, SHC.

392   "is *The Iliad*": WP to SF, June 12, 1974, SHC.

393   "commit moral outrages": WP to Caroline Gordon, August 30, 1974, FLPU.

393   his "*normal* depression": WP to SF, September 9, 1974, SHC.

393   "vanity of theorists!": WP to Lewis Simpson, May 20, 1974, SR files.

394   something "even queerer": WP to Lewis Simpson, September 20, 1974, SR files.

394   "theory of language": Lewis Simpson, "Walker Percy's Vision of the Modern World," Flora Levy Lecture, op. cit., p. 23.

394   "is a joy": WP to Robert Giroux, October 27, 1974, FSG files.

394   "with writing, work": Peter Handke to Jay Tolson, December 11, 1990.

395   could ever be: Int. SF.

395   "his religious faith": Int. Susanne Jensen.

396   "have a seat": Int. Wyatt Prunty.

396   in the spring: Int. Susanne Jensen.

397   "this war either": WP to SF, n.d., (November 1974?), SHC.

397   "Robert every time": SF to WP, November 7, 1974, SHC.

397   "grows from—symbolism": SF to WP, December 4, 1974, SHC.

397   "happier in the second": Panthea Reid Broughton, *The Art of Walker Percy: Stratagems for Being*, p. xiii.

399   "Bergdorfs and Bonwits": WP to SF, May 1, 1975, SHC.

400   "that academic screen": SF to WP, May 5, 1975, SHC.

400   "unique gift, language": James Boatwright, "Matters of Life," *The New Republic*, July 19, 1975, p. 28.

400   "mythical physiology instead": Thomas Nagel, "Sin and Significance," *New York Review of Books*, September 18, 1975, pp. 54–56.

401   "the Naming Faculty": Hugh Kenner, "On Man the Sad Talker," *National Review*, September 12, 1975, p. 1000.

402   "Yes": WP, "Community," Lyn Hill Hayward papers.

404   his language theory: Int. Marcus Smith.

405   "normal naming experience": Marcus Smith int. of WP, *Conversations*, pp. 131–32.

405   and unnourishing aesthetic: For text of discussion, see "A Symposium on Fiction: Donald Barthelme, William Gass, Grace Paley, Walker Percy," *Shenandoah*, Winter 1976, pp. 3–31.

406   "a demoralized Catholic": WP to SF, October 9, 1975, SHC.

406   "deal with sexuality": WP to Lewis Simpson, January 10, 1976, SR files.

406   "to read it": WP to Lewis Simpson, February 8, 1976, SR files.

406   returning to Covington: WP to Lewis Lawson, April 9, 1976, Lawson papers.

406   "to 10 days": WP to Robert Giroux, April 19, 1976, FSG files.

408   "way or another": Kenneth Holditch, "The Last Gentleman Grades Papers," *The Courier*, January 20–26, 1977, p. 9.

408   "in a box": Int. Marcus Smith.

409   her ready reply: WP, "Foreword to *A Confederacy of Dunces*," *Signposts*, p. 224.

409   "to keep reading": Ibid., pp. 224–25.

409   "was so good": Ibid., p. 225.

409   life and originality: Int. Mary Bernice Percy.

410   "and talented novel": WP to Thelma Toole, December 7, 1976, Tulane.

410   run in the *New Orleans Review*: Marcus Smith to WP, January 13, 1977, Loyola.

410   "to take you": SF to WP, November 17, 1976, SHC.

410   Arts and Letters: WP to Robert Giroux, November 4, 1976, FSG files.

411   "here in Louisiana": WP to SF, February 8, 1977, SHC.

411   "of his seriousness": John Gardner, *New York Times Book Review*, February 20, 1977, p. 1.

412   "else shut up": Ibid., p. 20.

412   "Gardner went bananas": Robert Giroux, February 20, 1977, FSG files.

412   "into the story": Joyce Carol Oates, *The New Republic*, February 5, 1977, pp. 32–33.

412   "friend and priest": Reynolds Price, "God and Man in Louisiana," *Washington Post Book World*, February 27, 1977, p. E-10.

413   "Gothic, satiric, symbolic": Robert Towers, "Southern Discomfort," *New York Review of Books*, March 31, 1977, p. 8.

413   "the three before": Andre Dubus, "Paths to Redemption," *Harper's*, April 1977, p. 87.

413   "possibility of faith": Richard Todd, "Lead Us into Temptation, Deliver Us Evil," *The Atlantic*, March 1977, p. 115.

16. Second Sightings

414   their happier memories: Int. Mary Bernice Percy.

415   "luck next time": WP to Roger Straus, February 21, 1978, FSG files.

415   "appearances of novelty": WP to Lewis Simpson, March 22, 1975, *SR* files.

415   "rows, you know": WP to SF, February 8, 1977, SHC.

416   "boredom and restlessness?": Cited in Linda Hobson, *Understanding Walker Percy*, p. 114.

416   "what he did": Int. Ansley Cope.

417   needed the money: Int. Lyn Hill Hayward.

417   *as an Author:* For discussion of the parallels, see Marion Montgomery. "Kierkegaard and Percy: By Word, *Away from* the Philosophical," in Jan Nordby Gretlund and Karl Heinz Westarp, eds., *Walker Percy: Novelist and Philosopher*, pp. 99–109.

418   "and sexual components": WP, "Questions They Never Asked Me . . . ," *Conversations*, p. 164.

418   "all up self-defeating": Robert Giroux to WP, September 13, 1977, FSG files.

418   only local appeal: Int. WP.

418   "job" on television: WP to SF, January 5, 1978, SHC.

419   "literature is elitist": Unidentified clip in Percy family album.

419   " 'you mentioned him' ": Related by Louise Abbot to Sally Fitzgerald; Sally Fitzgerald to Jay Tolson, April 26, 1991.

419   "slam at Augusta": WP, "Going Back to Georgia," *Signposts*, p. 37.

419   "two hundred years ago": Ibid.

419   at any time: SF to WP, March 1, 1978, SHC.

420   hopes too high: WP to SF, March 4, 1978, SHC.

420   "to rake it": WP to SF, September 18, 1978, SHC.

420   "get across, sometimes": Cited in SF to WP, January 25, 1979, SHC.

421   "we are Southern?": WP to SF, January 29, 1979, SHC.

421   "since *War and Peace*": Ben Forkner and J. Gerald Kennedy int. of WP, *Conversations*, p. 235.

422   "thing to do": WP to SF, January 29, 1979, SHC.

422   "what they conceal": WP, review of *Letters and Documents*, by Søren Kierkegaard, *New York Times Book Review*, p. 29.

423   "researcher for a decade": Robert Towers, "To the Greenhouse," *New York Review of Books*, August 14, 1980, p. 40.

423   theme of his novel: WP to Ted Spivey, October 29, 1979, cited in Ted R. Spivey, *The Writer as Shaman: The Pilgrimages of Conrad Aiken and Walker Percy*, p. 144.

424   comings and goings: Int. Lyn Hill Hayward.

424   "and small-mindedness": Int. Bob Milling.

426   "South, and Catholicism": WP to SF, April 18, 1979, SHC.

426   "dignity at all": Ibid.

426   "of semiotic breakdown": WP to SF, May 21, 1979, SHC.

427   "brain (nobody knows)": WP to SF, May 21, 1979, SHC.

427   out of *The Moviegoer*: Martin Luschei, "*The Moviegoer* as Dissolve," Panthea Reid Broughton, ed., *The Art of Walker Percy*, pp. 24–36.

429   "half of the movement": SF to WP, March 10, 1979, SHC.

429   "aging infirm novelist": WP to SF, August 29, 1979, SHC.

429   ready to print: Robert Giroux to WP, January 14, 1980, FSG files.

430   "maybe I had": WP to Lewis Lawson, March 4, 1980, Lawson papers.

430 "the stranded self": Ibid.

430 as animal communication: Int. WP.

431 without his efforts: Lewis Simpson to WP, May 21, 1980, SR files.

431 "glad of that": WP to Thelma Toole, June 12, 1990, Tulane.

431 "except an enchantment": Benjamin DeMott, "A Thinking Man's Kurt Vonnegut," *The Atlantic Monthly*, July 1980, p. 84.

431 "theme for a dozen": Robert Towers, "To the Greenhouse," *New York Review of Books*, August 14, 1980, p. 40.

431 "end, of praise": Richard Gilman, *The New Republic*, July 5–12, 1980, p. 31.

433 his newest novel: Camille S. Cohan to WP, July 24, 1980, Cohan papers.

433 "of *2nd Coming*": WP to Camille S. Cohan, August 3, 1980, Cohan papers.

433 "my Senior year": Camille S. Cohan to WP, August 8, 1980, Cohan papers.

433 "out pretty well": WP to Camille S. Cohan, August 13, 1980, Cohan papers.

434 "cultivation of the ordinary": Dannye Romine int. of WP, *Conversations*, p. 202.

434 "a Spanish Mason": Included in undated letter from Caroline Gordon to Robert Lowell (c. 1951), Houghton Library, Harvard University.

435 "something about it": WP to SF, September 10, 1980, SHC.

436 "had to say": Int. Linda Hobson.

436 "which uses language": Linda Hobson int. of WP, *Conversations*, p. 222.

436 "have an idea": Ibid., p. 225.

436 "effects through coolness": WP to SF, September 10, 1980, SHC.

436 first "working library": WP to SF, November 5, 1981, SHC.

437 "six dozen crawfish": WP to Robert Coles, September 8, 1981, Coles papers.

437 "a different form": Robert Coles to WP, October 18, 1981, SHC.

438 "for similar reasons": WP to Walter Isaacson, April 11, 1981, Percy papers.

438 "it's still alive!": WP, "A View of Abortion, With Something to Offend Everybody," *Signposts*, p. 342.

439 "the Weimar Republic?": WP to Patricia Mayknuth, n.d. (October 1981?), Mayknuth papers.

439 "in her right": WP to Bob Milling, November 11, 1981.

439 "what to do": WP to Patricia Mayknuth, November 1, 1981, Mayknuth papers.

440 "avoid pointless exercise": WP to Patricia Mayknuth, November 1, 1981, Mayknuth papers.

441 "to notice it": WP, "Novel-Writing in an Apocalyptic Time," *Signposts*, p. 157.

441 aloud to her: Int. Jo Marie Gulledge.

442 whispered to Bausch: Int. Richard Bausch.

443 "going to be bad": "How To Be an American Novelist in Spite of Being Southern and Catholic," *Signposts*, p. 179.

443 was largely true: Int. Ben C. Toledano.

444 remained a Democrat: Int. WP.

444 novel's main action: Int. Steve and Haydee Ellis.

445 and relatively uneventful: Int. Mary Bernice Percy.

445 on the book: WP to Jo Marie Gulledge, December 4, 1982, Gulledge papers.

446 "about a thing": WP, "Herman Melville," *Signposts*, p. 202.

446 "with ultimate questions": Ibid.

447 "much to us": Ibid., p. 203.

447 "including its author": Thomas Disch, "Walker Percy's Summa Semiotica," *Washington Post Book World*, June 19, 1983, p. 5.

447 "traditional religious faith": *New Yorker*, July 18, 1983, p. 97.

448 "may not be": WP, "A 'Cranky Novelist' Reflects on the Church," *Signposts*, p. 323.

448 "from lower species": Ibid., pp. 323–24.

448 "nothing by the pool": WP to SF, June 25, 1983, SHC.

448 he told Gulledge: Int. Jo Marie Gulledge.

449 "end of the book": Jo Marie Gulledge to WP, July 1983, Gulledge papers.

449 "and seeing clouds": WP to Jo Marie Gulledge, July 15, 1983, Gulledge papers.

450 "You should try": Int. Nikki Barranger.

17. Thanatos—and After

451 "of Body Snatchers": WP to SF, February 8, 1977.

452 "residents on record": John Edward Hardy, *The Fiction of Walker Percy*, p. 228.

452 "of Walker Percy": Ibid., p. 227.

454 Endowment for the Arts: Int. Judge Steve Ellis.

455 "history and society": WP to Lewis Simpson, August 1, 1983, SR files.

456 Spencer, in January: WP to Elizabeth Spencer, January 19, 1984, National Library of Canada.

456 "a troublesome novel": WP to Elizabeth Spencer, March 11, 1984, National Library of Canada.

456 was clearly embarrassed: Int. Lawrence Baldwin.

457 usual litigious Thomism: Int. Bob Milling.

457 "proposes," he added: Int. Sheila Bosworth.

457 "of the NEA (Oct. 6)": WP to Jo Marie Gulledge, June 27, 1984, Gulledge papers.

458 "arteries were intact": WP to Elizabeth Spencer, August 14, 1984, National Library of Canada.

458 "it might work": WP to Roger Straus, November 12, 1984, FSG files.

458 "poetry and criticism": WP introduction to "William Alexander Percy and the Fugitives: A Literary Correspondence, 1921, 1923," Jo Gulledge, ed., *Southern Review*, 21.2 (1985), p. 418.

459 "she still is": Int. Sheila Bosworth.

459 "alternative to it": Patricia Lewis Poteat, *Walker Percy and the Old Modern Age*, p. 139.

460 "humanities-science split": WP to Jo Marie Gulledge, February 1985, Gulledge papers.

460 a harrowing experience: Int. Eudora Welty.

461 "I was floored": WP to Robert Coles, June 11, 1985, Coles papers.

462 he told Elizabeth Spencer: WP to Elizabeth Spencer, December 5, 1985, National Library of Canada.

462 "a fair comparison": WP to Lewis Simpson, June 8, 1985, SR files.

462 "it's a suggestion": WP to Elizabeth Spencer, December 5, 1985, National Library of Canada.

462 the following fall: WP to Elizabeth Spencer, October 31, 1986, National Library of Canada.

463 "bored him stiff": WP to Father Patrick Samway, January 8, 1986.

463 "typescript" of the novel: WP to Robert Giroux, May 19, 1986, FSG files.

464 "Van Dorn skyward": WP to Robert Giroux, July 16, 1986, FSG files.

464 Educators in New Orleans: WP to Robert Coles, June 4, 1986, Coles papers.

464 "egregious psychiatric blunders": WP to Robert Coles, July 15, 1986, Coles papers.

464   "heart of the problem": Int. Robert Coles.

465   "I have Alzheimer's": WP to Robert Coles, August 19, 1986, Coles papers.

465   "Some folks will—": WP to SF, September 20, 1986, SHC.

466   "to catch up": WP to Robert Coles, September 27, 1987, Coles papers.

466   "depression and disorientation": WP to Cleanth Brooks, July 17, 1986, Beinecke Library.

467   "out my handkerchief": WP to Robert Coles, December 25, 1985, Coles papers.

467   "so close-mouthed": Int. Berry Morgan.

468   "already agreed to": WP to Helene Atwan, December 31, 1986, FSG files.

468   said to Foote: WP to SF, February 28, 1987, SHC.

468   "suspense of a thriller": *Publishers Weekly*, February 6, 1987.

468   "also deadly serious": Julia Reed, "The Last Southern Gentleman," *U.S. News & World Report*, March 16, 1987, p. 76.

468   "disguised as a thriller": Paul Gray, "Implications of Apocalypse," *Time*, March 30, 1987, p. 71.

469   "with the celebs": Terrence Rafferty, "The Last Fiction Show," *New Yorker*, June 15, 1987, p. 91.

469   "lot more persuasive": Ibid., p. 92.

470   to one acquaintance: Int. WP.

470   for mere jeremiad: For the definitive discussion of Percy's apocalyptic vision, see Gary M. Ciuba, *Walker Percy: Books of Revelations*.

470   "July 4, 1938": WP to SF, August 4, 1987, SHC.

472   "as Newtonian mechanics": WP to Ken Ketner, October 20, 1987.

472   "a tremendous advance": WP to Roger Straus, January 9, 1988, FSG files.

473   McNaspy's immediate reply: Int. Father C. J. McNaspy.

473   "of whatever fields": WP, "Culture, the Church, and Evangelization," *Signposts*, pp. 297–98.

474   "schools of psychotherapy": Ibid., p. 299.

474   "serves culture best": Ibid., p. 303.

474   Swaggart in particular: Int. WP.

475   "what they're doing": WP to Charles Poe, April 30, 1988, Poe papers.

476   and Cleanth Brooks: Lewis Simpson to WP, June 2, 1988, *SR* files.

477   "wouldn't let me": WP to Lewis Simpson, August 7, 1988, *SR* files.

477   to one correspondent: WP to Jay Tolson, August 11, 1988.

477   "the 'trouble stick' ": WP to Lewis Simpson, September 24, 1988, *SR* files.

477   "the short story": WP to SF, December 24, 1988, SHC.

478   "of being ill": Int. Thomas Fleming.

478   "if we survive": WP, "Physician as Novelist," *Signposts*, p. 192.

479   reported to Foote: WP to SF, January 8, 1989, SHC.

479   "and 'cognitive' psychology?": WP, "The Fateful Rift: The San Andreas Fault in the Modern Mind," *Signposts*, p. 276.

479   "all right now": WP to Robert Coles, January 10, 1989, Coles papers.

480   be the last: Int. Lewis Lawson.

480   "or pancreatic C A": WP to SF, June 8, 1989, SHC.

480   "in some cancers": WP to SF, July 29, 1989, SHC.

481   "not permitted to": Ibid.

481   *"This—I Believe"*: WP, "Why Are You a Catholic?" *Signposts*, p. 304.

482   "encompassed by theory": Ibid., p. 313.

482   "a Jew": Ibid., p. 314.

483   were his strength: Int. Ann Percy Moores.

484   little time alone: Int. Mary Bernice Percy.

485   across the causeway: Int. Lawrence Baldwin.

485   "novelist and philosopher": WP to Bruce Springsteen, February 23, 1990.

485   "even published works": WP to Julie Gantz, March 18, 1990.

486   "American has arrived": Int. Liz Halton.

487   said, simply, "Goodbye": Int. SF.

487   shook his head: Int. Liz Halton.

488   the abbey grounds: Int. Mary Bernice Percy.

Bibliography

Armes, Ethel. *The Story of Coal and Iron in Alabama.* Birmingham Chamber of Commerce, 1910.

Atkins, Leah Rawls. *The Valley and the Hills: An Illustrated History of Birmingham and Jefferson County.* Windsor Publications, 1981.

Baker, Lewis. *The Percys of Mississippi.* Louisiana State University Press, 1983.

Bartley, William Warren. *The Retreat to Commitment.* Open Court, 1984.

Boardman, Barrington. *Flappers, Bootleggers, "Typhoid Mary," & the Bomb: An Anecdotal History of the United States from 1923–1945.* Perennial Library, Harper & Row, 1988.

Brinkmeyer, Robert H., Jr. *Three Catholic Writers of the Modern South.* University Press of Mississippi, 1985.

Brooks, Cleanth. *The Language of the American South.* Mercer University Lamar Memorial Lecture No. 28. University of Georgia Press, 1985.

Broughton, Panthea Reid, ed. *The Art of Walker Percy: Stratagems for Being.* Louisiana State University Press, 1979.

Caldwell, Mark. *The Last Crusade: The War on Consumption, 1862–1954.* Atheneum, 1988.

Calhoun, F. Phinizy, Jr. *Grandmother Was a Phinizy: A Registry of Phinizy Descendants and Allied Families.* Darby Printing Company, 1991.

Carter, Hodding. *Where Main Street Meets the River.* Rinehart and Company, 1952.

Carter, William C., ed. *Conversations with Shelby Foote.* University Press of Mississippi, 1989.

Cash, W. J. *The Mind of the South*. Alfred A. Knopf, 1941.

Cheever, John. *The Journals of John Cheever*. Alfred A. Knopf, 1991.

Ciuba, Gary M. *Walker Percy: Books of Revelations*. University of Georgia Press, 1991.

Cohn, David. *Where I Was Born and Raised*. Houghton Mifflin Company, 1948.

Coles, Robert. *Walker Percy: An American Search*. Little, Brown and Company, 1978.

Donald, David Herbert. *Look Homeward: A Life of Thomas Wolfe*. Fawcett Columbine, Ballantine Books, 1987.

Douglas, Ellen, *Walker Percy's "The Last Gentleman": Introduction and Commentary*. Pamphlet. Seabury Press, 1969.

Eakin, John Paul. *Fictions in Autobiography*. Princeton University Press, 1985.

Ellis, Frederick S. *St. Tammany Parish: L'Autre Côte Du Lac*. Pelican Publishing Company, 1982.

Feibleman, James, and Julius Weis Friend. *Science and the Spirit of Man: A New Ordering Experience*. Allen & Unwin, 1933.

Foote, Shelby. *The Civil War: A Narrative*. Vol. 1: *Fort Sumter to Perryville*. Random House, 1958.

————. *The Civil War: A Narrative*. Vol. 2: *Fredericksburg to Meridian*. Random House, 1963.

————. *The Civil War: A Narrative*. Vol. 3: *Red River to Appomattox*. Random House, 1974.

————. *Follow Me Down*. Dial Press, 1950.

————. *Jordan County: A Landscape in Narrative*. Random House, 1954.

————. *Love in a Dry Season*. Dial Press, 1951.

————. *September September*. Random House, 1978.

————. *Tournament*. Dial Press, 1949.

Fussell, Paul. *The Great War and Modern Memory*. Oxford, 1975.

Gretlund, Jan Nordby, and Karl Heinz Westarp, eds. *Walker Percy: Novelist and Philosopher*. University Press of Mississippi, 1991.

Hardy, John Edward. *The Fiction of Walker Percy*. University of Illinois Press, 1987.

Hobson, Linda Whitney. *Understanding Walker Percy*. University of South Carolina Press, 1988.

————. *Walker Percy: A Comprehensive Descriptive Bibliography*. Faust Publishing Company, 1988.

Jones, John Griffith, ed. *Mississippi Writers Talking*. University Press of Mississippi, 1982.

————. *Mississippi Writers Talking II*. University Press of Mississippi, 1983.

Karl, Frederick R. *William Faulkner, American Writer: A Biography*. Weidenfeld & Nicholson, 1989.

Keating, Bern. *A History of Washington County, Mississippi*. The Greenville Junior Auxiliary, 1976.

King, Richard H. *A Southern Renaissance: The Cultural Awakening of the American South, 1930–1955*. Oxford, 1980.

Kirby, Jack Temple. *Rural Worlds Lost: The American South, 1920–1960*. Louisiana State University Press, 1987.

Kirwin, Albert D. *Revolt of the Rednecks: Mississippi Politics, 1876–1925*. University of Kentucky Press, 1951.

Kisor, Henry. *What's That Pig Outdoors?: A Memoir of Deafness*. Hill and Wang, 1990.

Konner, Melvin. *Becoming a Doctor: A Journey of Initiation in Medical School*. Viking, 1987.

Langer, Susanne. *Philosophy in a New Key: A Study in the Symbolism of Reason, Rite, and Art*. Harvard University Press, 1942; New American Library, 1951.

Lathrop, Sallie B. Comer. *The Comer Family Grows Up.* Birmingham Printing Co., 1945.

Lawson, Lewis A. *Following Percy: Essays on Walker Percy's Work.* The Whitston Publishing Company, 1988.

Lawson, Lewis A., and Victor Kramer, eds. *Conversations with Walker Percy.* University Press of Mississippi, 1985.

Luschei, Martin. *The Sovereign Wayfarer: Walker Percy's Diagnosis of the Malaise.* Louisiana State University Press, 1972.

Makowsky, Veronica A. *Caroline Gordon: A Biography.* Oxford University Press, 1989.

Mann, Thomas. *The Magic Mountain.* (trans. by H. T. Lowe-Potter). Alfred A. Knopf, 1965.

Merton, Thomas. *The Road to Joy: Letters to New and Old Friends.* Selected and edited by Robert E. Daggy. Farrar, Straus and Giroux, 1989.

———. *A Vow of Conversation: Journals 1964–1965.* Edited with a preface by Naomi Burton Stone. Farrar, Straus and Giroux, 1988.

Mott, Michael. *The Seven Mountains of Thomas Merton.* Houghton Mifflin Company, 1984.

Niebuhr, Reinhold. *The Children of Light and the Children of Darkness.* Scribner's, 1944.

O'Connor, Flannery. *Collected Works.* Library of America, 1988.

———. *Mystery and Manners: Occasional Prose.* Selected and edited by Sally and Robert Fitzgerald. Farrar, Straus and Giroux, 1969.

Percy, Walker. "The Gramercy Winner." The Walker Percy Papers. The Southern Historical Collection, University of North Carolina.

———. *Lancelot.* Farrar, Straus and Giroux, 1977.

———. *The Last Gentleman.* Farrar, Straus and Giroux, 1966.

———. *Lost in the Cosmos: The Last Self-Help Book.* Farrar, Straus and Giroux, 1983.

———. *Love in the Ruins: The Adventures of a Bad Catholic at a Time Near the End of the World.* Farrar, Straus and Giroux, 1971.

———. *The Message in the Bottle: How Queer Man Is, How Queer Language Is, and What One Has to Do with the Other.* Farrar, Straus and Giroux, 1975.

———. *The Moviegoer.* Alfred A. Knopf, 1961.

———. *The Second Coming.* Farrar, Straus and Giroux, 1980.

———. *Signposts in a Strange Land.* Edited and with an introduction by Patrick Samway, S.J., Farrar, Straus and Giroux, 1991.

———. *The Thanatos Syndrome.* Farrar, Straus and Giroux, 1987.

Percy, William Alexander. *Lanterns on the Levee: Recollections of a Planter's Son.* Alfred A. Knopf, 1941.

Perry, Helen Swick. *Psychiatrist of America: The Life of Harry Stack Sullivan.* Harvard University Press, 1982.

Poteat, Patricia Lewis. *Walker Percy and the Old Modern Age: Reflections on Language, Argument, and the Telling of Stories.* Louisiana State University Press, 1982.

Roberts, David, *Jean Stafford: A Biography.* Little, Brown and Company, 1988.

Ronda, Bruce A. *Intellect and Spirit: The Life and Work of Robert Coles.* Continuum, 1989.

Roper, John Herbert. *C. Vann Woodward, Southerner.* University of Georgia Press, 1987.

Spivey, Ted Ray. *The Writer as Shaman: The Pilgrimages of Conrad Aiken and Walker Percy.* Mercer University Press, 1986.

Steiner, George. *Martin Heidegger.* Viking, 1978.

Stern, Robert A., Gregory Gilmartin, and Thomas Mellins. *New York 1930.* Rizzoli, 1987.

Storr, Anthony. *Solitude: A Return to the Self.* Free Press, 1988.

Swearingen, Mack. *The Early Life of George Poindexter.* Tulane University Press, 1934.

Taylor, Robert. *Saranac: America's Magic Mountain.* Houghton Mifflin Company, 1986.

Thompson, Josiah. *Kierkegaard.* Alfred A. Knopf, 1973.

Trilling, Lionel. *The Liberal Imagination: Essays on Literature and Society.* Viking, 1950.

Waldron, Ann. *Close Connections: Caroline Gordon and the Southern Renaissance.* G. P. Putnam's Sons, 1987.

Wertham, Frederic. *A Sign for Cain: An Exploration of Human Violence.* Macmillan Company, 1966.

Wasson, Ben. *Count No 'Count: Flashbacks to Faulkner.* University Press of Mississippi, 1983.

Wood, Ralph C. *The Comedy of Redemption: Christian Faith and Comic Vision in Four American Novelists.* University of Notre Dame Press, 1988.

Woodward, C. Vann. *Origins of the New South, 1877–1913.* Volume 9 of *The History of the South,* edited by Ellis Merton Coulter and Wendell Holmes Stephenson. Louisiana State University Press, 1951.

Wyatt-Brown, Bertram. *Southern Honor: Ethics and Behavior in the Old South.* Oxford, 1982.

Acknowledgments

Life is short; debts are long. And those of a biographer are almost endless.

First, I want to thank Mary Bernice Percy, whose unstinting assistance during the most difficult of times went far beyond the call of duty. Her devotion to the truth, her courage and energy, and her magnanimity in tolerating an interpretation of her husband's life that on many points differs strongly from her own are cause for admiration and gratitude.

Others in the Percy clan have rendered invaluable aid. I must particularly thank the Percy's two daughters, Ann Boyd Percy Moores and Mary Pratt Percy Lobdell, for giving me a glimpse of the family life that mattered so much to their father. Percy's brothers, Roy and Phin, and their respective wives, Sarah and Jaye, were always forthcoming and kind, as were their many children, most of whom I spoke to over the years. Countless cousins from the Phinizy side of the family kept me mindful of the Georgia influence. Above all, I want to thank three Spalding brothers—Jack, Hughes, and Phinizy—and Nell Bolling Johnson.

Of Percy's many friends, colleagues, and acquaintances, none was

more valuable to me than Shelby Foote. Apart from his own considerable accomplishments as a novelist and historian, he is a great raconteur,
an interviewer's dream; he also gave an early draft of this book a close
and helpful reading. I owe a similar debt to another friend of the subject,
Robert Coles, who was valuable as both an informant and a critic.
Scholars who made generous contributions to my understanding of Percy
both in their work and in conversation include: Cleanth Brooks, Jo
Gulledge, Jan Nordby Gretland, Linda Hobson, Alfred Kazin, Lewis
Lawson, Martin Luschei, Lewis Simpson, Louis Rubin, Father Patrick
Samway, Marcus Smith, Ralph C. Wood, and Bertram Wyatt-Brown.

Among the scores of other people I interviewed, frequently borrowed
correspondence from, and imposed upon in other ways, I would like to
thank the following: William Alfred, Mrs. Charles Allison, Lawrence
and Mary Baldwin, Charles and Danny Bell, Nikki Barranger, Richard
Bausch, Sheila Bosworth, James Boulware, John Branton, Ashley
Brown, Samuel H. Burr, William Campbell, James Carr, Mrs. Hodding
Carter, Hodding Carter, Jr., Philip Carter, David Chandler, Father Tom
Clancy, Camille Sarason Cohan, Ansley Cope, George Core, Tom
Cowan, George and Eleanor Cross, Mrs. Robert Daniel, Tony and Dana
Davis, Emily Diamond, Fred Dieterle, Robert Drake, Marcelle Dunning,
Steve and Haydee Ellis, Rhoda Faust, Richard Faust, Sally Fitzgerald,
Charles Flood, Gwyn Foote, Mrs. Judson Freeman, Julie Gantz, Harris
Gentry, Robert Giroux, Liz Halton, Frank and Fran Hardart, Kenneth
Haxton, Josephine Haxton, Lyn Hill Hayward, Charles Hill, Kenneth
Holditch, Walter Isaacson, Susanne Jensen, Stanley Kauffmann, Ed-
win L. Kendig, John Kendrick, Henry Kisor, Jill Krementz, Nancy
Lemann, Nicholas Lemann, Carol Livaudais, Andrew Lytle, Marjorie
Magner, Patricia Mayknuth, Father C. J. McNaspy, Virginia and Sal-
vatore Milazzo, Bob Milling, John Moores, Willy Morris, Berry Mor-
gan, Gilbert Mudge, Betsy O'Brien, Charles Poe, Wyatt Prunty,
Margaret Rioch, George Riser, David Roberts III, John Sharp Roberts,
David Scott, James Schwartz, Wilfrid Sheed, Paschal Shook, Jr., Robert
McDavid Smith, William Sorum, Elizabeth Spencer, James Sprunt,
Roger Straus, Harry Stovall, Ben C. Toledano, Pascal Townsend, Mar-
garet Kirk Verdun, Eudora Welty, Donald Wetherbee, Eugene Winick,
Jonathan Yardley.

Several institutions were indispensable to the writing of this book,
including my workaday home, the Woodrow Wilson International Center for Scholars, whose directors, James Billington and his successor,
Charles Blitzer, granted me leave at crucial times. Particular thanks go
to Peter Braestrup, former editor of *The Wilson Quarterly*, who encouraged and supported my work at an early stage, Publishers Warren Syer

and Kathy Read also helped make it possible for me to take time away from the magazine. Most appreciated was the steady companionship of my colleagues and friends at the *Quarterly*, Steve Lagerfeld, Jim Carman, Jeff Paine, Bob Landers, Suzanne Turk, and Sara Lawrence. A fellowship from the National Endowment for the Humanities made it possible for me to devote close to a year to uninterrupted writing; I thank the selection panel and Lynne Cheney for their vote of confidence.

I am grateful to the directors and staffs of the following institutions for their gracious and prompt assistance: the Birmingham Public Library, the Southern Historical Collection at the University of North Carolina, the Mississippi Department of Archives and History, the Harry Ransom Humanities Research Center at the University of Texas, the Princeton University Library, the Adirondack Collection of the Saranac Free Library, Historic Saranac Lake Preservation Enterprises, Inc., the National Library of Canada, the University of Virginia Library, the Beinecke Library of Yale University, the William Alexander Percy Library in Greenville, Mississippi, the Loyola University Library, Tulane University Library, the Thomas Merton Studies Center, and the Archives Division of the College of Physicians and Surgeons at Columbia University.

My editors at Simon & Schuster, Alice Mayhew and George Hodgman, as well as Marcia Peterson in copyediting, gave me steady and patient guidance. I also thank Georges Borchardt, my agent and supportive counselor. Many friends and family members provided shelter, food, and companionship when I was on the road. I thank Nancy Goldring and Ubaldo Arregui, Ed and Laurel Strong, Larry Russell and Karen Williamson, Tom and Diana Ricketts, J. W. and Josephine Bradshaw, Mary and John Bradshaw, my brother David, my sister Kyn, and my brother-in-law, David Holahan. Closer to home, I owe thanks to more friends than I can name, but I would particularly like to mention Bill McPherson, who gave the book a thorough going-over and offered many invaluable suggestions. Several people gave a hand with research, including Roberta Miller, Julie Gantz, Sian Hunter, and Jennifer Mendelsohn. I thank them all.

Finally, my family has my deepest gratitude: my son, Ben, for cheerfully putting up with my absences and oddnesses; my wife, Mary, for keeping me mindful of what is important.

Photo Credits

Index